Mastering Quantum Computing with Qiskit

Master the Fundamentals, Explore Algorithms, and Build Scalable Quantum Applications Using IBM Qiskit to Solve Real-World Problems

Shalini Devendrababu
Sai Nandan Morapakula
Srinjoy Ganguly

www.orangeava.com

First Published: February 2025
Published By: Orange Education Pvt Ltd, AVA®
Address: 9, Daryaganj, Delhi, 110002, India

275 New North Road Islington Suite 1314 London,
N1 7AA, United Kingdom

ISBN (PBK): 978-93-48107-00-8
ISBN (E-BOOK): 978-93-48107-18-3

Scan the QR code to explore our entire catalogue

www.orangeava.com

Dedicated To

To my late mother, whose love and wisdom continue to guide me from beyond the stars; to my dear father, whose strength and support are my constant anchors; to my cherished fiancé, the heartbeat of my soul and the joy of my life; to my beloved sibling, my lifelong friend and confidant; to my dear niece, who represents the promise of our family's future, and to my other family members. This book is a tribute to each of you, the pillars of my life.

- Shalini Devendrababu

To my beloved friends, family and mentors

- Sai Nandan Morapakula

To my beloved family, mentors, students, and the omniscient power that guides me in my life

- Srinjoy Ganguly

About the Authors

Shalini Devendrababu holds a Master's in Quantum Technologies from CSIC-UIMP, Spain. She is currently the lead Quantum AI Researcher at Fractal Quantum AI Lab. She authored a bestselling and highly rated Udemy course on Qiskit and has published research works on quantum material science with Springer and IEEE. She also wrote the world's first book exclusively dedicated to Product Managers in the field of quantum computing. She was featured in Times Square, New York Billboard as a part of mentoring and providing career guidance on Topmate in Quantum Computing, also she is a seasoned speaker on quantum computing at academic institutions as well as a writer on Medium.

Sai Nandan Morapakula is pursuing his PhD in quantum computing at the University of Massachusetts, Boston. He worked as an ex-Research Software Engineer at Qkrishi, where he focused on quantum finance, particularly portfolio optimization problems for financial corporations. Additionally, he has worked as a research intern at Fractal Quantum AI lab focusing on protein-ligand interaction problems using variational quantum algorithms. He has actively published research on various applications of quantum computing, ranging from natural language processing to finance and quantum chemistry. He leads and manages the Quantum Open Source Foundation Mentorship program globally.

Srinjoy Ganguly is a PhD researcher in quantum technologies at University College London and an IBM Qiskit Advocate. Formerly, he was a Lead Quantum AI Research Scientist at Fractal Quantum AI lab, a Clinical Professor of Practice for Quantum Technologies at Woxsen University, and an Associate Supervisor at the University of Southern Queensland supervising a PhD student in quantum machine learning. An author of multiple quantum books and research papers across quantum chemistry, quantum machine learning, quantum NLP, and materials science. He holds triple master's degrees in Quantum Technologies, Quantum Computing Technology, and AI, along with a bachelor's in electronics and communications engineering. He has published two Udemy courses – Quantum Computing Ultimate Masterclass (14,000+ enrollments globally) and QNLP using the Lambeq Toolkit (3000+ enrollments globally). Srinjoy has delivered expert talks at IITs, IEEE SPS, and various platforms on QML, QNLP, and Quantum Computing. His QNLP talk at IIT Madras earned praise from Bob Coecke (QNLP Pioneer and Chief Scientist at Quantinuum) and Ilyas Khan (CEO of Quantinuum). Currently, he manages the global QOSF mentorship program, serves on program committees for international conferences, and is an editor of a De Gruyter quantum computing book.

About the Technical Reviewers

Adarsh Kumar has over 19 years of experience in research and academics, specializing in computer science and information technology. He currently serves as a professor at the University of Petroleum and Energy Studies, Dehradun, India. He has also worked as a postdoctoral researcher at the Software Research Institute (SRI) at Athlone Institute of Technology, Ireland, and Mohammed VI Polytechnic University, Morocco. During this time, he contributed to multi-million euro research projects funded by Enterprise Ireland, Science Foundation Ireland, and the European Union H2020, focusing on developing methods to detect and combat cybersecurity attacks. These projects involved collaboration with ten partners from eight European countries, including renowned institutions such as the Technical University of Darmstadt (Germany), the University of Oxford (UK), and the Polish Academy of Sciences. Additionally, he has served as an assistant professor in the Department of Computer Science and Information Technology at Jaypee Institute of Information Technology, Noida, India.

Alberto Maldonado-Romo is a PhD in Computer Science. He currently leads the Quantum Open Source Foundation (QOSF), a prominent organization dedicated to fostering quantum technology development. His leadership was instrumental in organizing the 2022 QOSF mentorship program. As a passionate advocate for quantum computing, Alberto has held key roles in various organizations. He is an ambassador for the Unitary Fund and a dedicated Qiskit user. His skills and expertise have been recognized with prestigious awards, including victories in QCHack 2021 and QHack 2022. His professional journey has been enriched through internships at renowned organizations such as Entropica Labs, qBraid, and IBM Quantum. He has also contributed to the quantum community by organizing hackathons and colloquiums, as well as volunteering at Quantum Universal Education.

Acknowledgments

We would like to extend our sincere gratitude to the professionals who developed the open-source IBM quantum challenges, global summer school notebooks, and the latest Qiskit YouTube videos, whose materials have been utilized for writing a few chapters of this book. We would like to specifically mention their names as follows:

- **Lab 1 IBM Quantum Challenge 2024:** Created by James Weaver and Maria Gragera Garces; advised by Junye Huang.
- **Lab 3 AI-Transpiler IBM Quantum Challenge 2024:** Created by Vishal Sharathchandra Bajpe and David Kremer; advised by Junye Huang and Juan Cruz Benito.
- **Lab 3 Circuit Knitting IBM Quantum Challenge 2024:** Created by Kifumi Numata; advised by Jennifer Glick, Junye Huang, Vishal Sharathchandra Bajpe, and Takashi Imamichi.
- **Lab 3 Code Assistant IBM Quantum Challenge 2024:** Created by Siddharth Golecha and Vishal Sharathchandra Bajpe; advised by Junye Huang, David Kremer, Juan Cruz Benito, and Brian Ingmason.
- **Lab 3 Serverless IBM Quantum Challenge 2024:** Created by Vishal Sharathchandra Bajpe; advised by Tushar Mittal, Sanket Panda, Junye Huang, Jessie Yu, and Jennifer Glick.
- **Lab 1 QGSS 2024 Utility Scale QFT:** Created by Sebastian Brandhofer and the Qiskit developers.
- **Lab 2 QGSS Utility Scale Experiment:** Created by Samantha Barron and Haimeng Zhang.

We are grateful to Luis Gerardo Ayala Bertel for his crucial support with quantum challenges and the summer school, which was instrumental in completing this book. We also thank Dr. Adarsh Kumar and Dr. Alberto Maldonado Romo for their meticulous technical reviews. Our appreciation goes to the AVA team for their patience and support, allowing us to present the book in its best form. Given the vast scope of quantum computing, covering all problem classes in a single volume was not feasible without making it excessively lengthy.

— Shalini Devendrababu, Sai Nandan Morapakula, and Srinjoy Ganguly

Preface

This book covers a broad spectrum of subjects related to quantum computing, ranging from basic ideas to sophisticated uses. It provides a thorough grasp of the area by covering key ideas, including quantum machine learning, variational algorithms, and quantum gates. The book demonstrates the potential of quantum computing in fields such as quantum chemistry, encryption, and optimization by exploring both theoretical and practical aspects. It provides readers with the tools needed to efficiently develop, simulate, and execute quantum algorithms through practical implementations with Qiskit. Additionally, the book highlights the significance of circuit transpilation, pulse-level control, and error mitigation strategies, ensuring a comprehensive understanding of practical issues in quantum computing. This book provides insightful analysis and useful knowledge to help navigate the quickly changing field of quantum technology, regardless of experience level.

This book is divided into 15 chapters, covering a wide range of topics from fundamental concepts in quantum mechanics to advanced quantum algorithms. It includes chapters on quantum gates, quantum error mitigation, variational quantum algorithms, and quantum machine learning. Real-world examples and hands-on implementations using Qiskit are provided to engage learners and deepen their understanding of quantum computing. The detailed chapter breakdown is as follows:

Chapter 1 covers the basic mathematical ideas that are necessary for quantum computing. It covers coordinate systems for 2D and 3D geometry, complex numbers and their operations, and the fundamentals of trigonometry, including identities and functions. It also covers abstract algebra ideas like rings, fields, and groups, as well as linear algebraic topics like vectors, matrices, and eigenvalues. Tensor products are also introduced.

Chapter 2 lays out the framework for comprehending quantum mechanics, which begins with basic ideas such as the Compton effect, photoelectric effect, and black-body radiation. It explores particles, spins, and angular momentum before going over the wave functions and expectation values that are fundamental to quantum mechanics. The chapter also discusses density matrices, quantum measurements, and qubits and their quantum versus classical nature. Lastly, it delves into practical uses in quantum sensing, semiconductor technology, and MRI.

Chapter 3 explores the foundations of computation, with a comparison between classical and quantum methods. It goes over the theoretical models, historical background, and fundamental ideas of classical computing, such as circuits and logic gates. The chapter explores computational complexity, emphasizing factors related to time and space, and offers useful insights through algorithm analysis. Lastly, it draws comparisons between classical and quantum computing, emphasizing parallelism, theoretical underpinnings, and the difficulties in each discipline.

Chapter 4 introduces qubits and covers fundamental concepts such as quantum superposition and entanglement. It encompasses advanced technologies, including quantum dots, spin qubits, and topological qubits, as well as a variety of physical implementations, such as photonic, neutral atom, trapped ion, superconducting, and NMR qubits. The chapter concludes with a comparison of different qubit modalities, highlighting their advantages and disadvantages in quantum computing.

Chapter 5 describes Qiskit along with its SDK, ecosystem, and more sophisticated capabilities like Serverless, Transpiler as a Service, and Qiskit Runtime. In addition to explaining the new primitives like Estimator and Sampler, it tackles key Qiskit patterns like map, optimize, execute, and post-process. Key features of Qiskit 1.0 are highlighted in this chapter, such as native support for OpenQASM, improved performance, and a stable release cycle.

Chapter 6 covers the single qubit quantum logic gates, which also examines their basic characteristics and uses. It explores a wide range of gates, including the Phase gate, Hadamard, S and S dagger, T and T dagger, Pauli (X, Y, Z), and rotation gates (Rx, Ry, Rz), offering a thorough grasp of their functions in quantum computing.

Chapter 7 explores multi-qubit quantum gates, beginning with two-qubit gates such as CNOT, CY, CZ, SWAP, and CRx. The discussion then moves on to three-qubit gates, such as the Fredkin and Toffoli gates, examining their functions and importance in intricate quantum algorithms.

Chapter 8 lays out the advanced quantum programming principles alongside the art of transpilation using optimization levels and AI techniques. It also covers dynamic circuits with the Repeat Until Success approach. The chapter concludes with techniques for measuring error rates in quantum circuits and discusses serverless features, circuit knitting, and Qiskit's Code Assistant.

Chapter 9 begins with an overview of both classical and quantum oracles, followed by an exploration of oracle-based quantum algorithms. It covers the principles, quantum circuit analysis, and mathematical derivations of the Deutsch, Deutsch-Jozsa, Bernstein-Vazirani, and Simon's algorithms. Each algorithm's real-world Qiskit implementations are included in this chapter.

Chapter 10 delves into the fundamentals of quantum algorithms, beginning with the Quantum Fourier Transform (QFT) and Quantum Phase Estimation (QPE), as well as how Qiskit implements them. Shor's algorithm is covered in detail, along with its protocol and applications. Grover's search method is then discussed, along with a comparison to conventional approaches, mathematical derivations, and pictorial intuition. Qiskit implementations for every algorithm are included in the chapter.

Chapter 11 provides in-depth protocols and Qiskit implementations for quantum teleportation and superdense coding as quantum communication protocols. It examines the fundamentals, benefits, and difficulties of quantum cryptography before moving on to discuss the uses and potential developments of quantum communication technology.

Chapter 12 dives into the design and application of variational quantum algorithms (VQAs), along with a discussion of their main elements, varieties, and benefits. It provides an in-depth examination of the VQE and QAOA algorithms, covering how they are implemented in Qiskit, variations, applications, and difficulties encountered in real-world use.

Chapter 13 moves on to Quantum Machine Learning (QML) and presents the classical machine learning ideas and techniques. It describes the process of converting conventional data into quantum states and investigates Qiskit methods, including Quantum Neural Networks (QNNs) for classification. The chapter covers obstacles and future possibilities in the field of QML and shows applications such as quantum-enhanced optimization and anomaly detection.

Chapter 14 presents the principles of quantum error mitigation and contrasts them with quantum error correction. It covers important methods, including Clifford Data Regression, Probabilistic Error Cancellation, and Zero-Noise Extrapolation. The chapter explores real-world Qiskit implementations, such as mthree and runtime-based techniques. Applications from optimization, machine learning, quantum chemistry, and other fields are included in the chapter's conclusion, emphasizing their contribution to the development of fault-tolerant quantum computing.

Chapter 15 introduces the circuit QED, where topics such as the LC oscillator and anharmonic oscillator are covered. It examines the purpose, characteristics, and uses of Qiskit Pulse. The chapter describes quantum gate pulse schedules for Hadamard, Pauli X, and CNOT gates. It also covers Qiskit Dynamics and dynamic decoupling calibration methods for CNOT and Pauli X gates.

Downloading the code bundles and colored images

You can find code bundles of our books on our official Github Repository. Please follow the links or scan the QR codes to download the **Code Bundles and Images** of the book:

https://github.com/ava-orange-education/Mastering-Quantum-Computing-with-Qiskit

The code bundles and images of the book are also hosted on

https://rebrand.ly/cd24ac

In case there's an update to the code, it will be updated on the existing GitHub repository.

Errata

We take immense pride in our work at **Orange Education Pvt Ltd**, and follow best practices to ensure the accuracy of our content to provide an indulging reading experience to our subscribers. Our readers are our mirrors, and we use their inputs to reflect and improve upon human errors, if any, that may have occurred during the publishing processes involved. To let us maintain the quality and help us reach out to any readers who might be having difficulties due to any unforeseen errors, please write to us at:
errata@orangeava.com
Your support, suggestions, and feedback are highly appreciated.

DID YOU KNOW

Did you know that Orange Education Pvt Ltd offers eBook versions of every book published, with PDF and ePub files available? You can upgrade to the eBook version at **www.orangeava.com** and as a print book customer, you are entitled to a discount on the eBook copy. Get in touch with us at: **info@orangeava.com** for more details.

At **www.orangeava.com**, you can also read a collection of free technical articles, sign up for a range of free newsletters, and receive exclusive discounts and offers on Print Books and eBooks.

PIRACY

If you come across any illegal copies of our works in any form on the internet, we would be grateful if you would provide us with the location address or website name. Please contact us at **info@orangeava.com** with a link to the material.

ARE YOU INTERESTED IN AUTHORING WITH US?

If there is a topic that you have expertise in, and you are interested in either writing or contributing to a book, please write to us at **business@orangeava.com**. We are on a journey to help developers and tech professionals to gain insights on the present technological advancements and innovations happening across the globe and build a community that believes knowledge is best acquired by sharing and learning with others. Please reach out to us to learn what our audience demands and how you can be part of this educational reform. We also welcome ideas from tech experts and help them build learning and development content for their domains.

REVIEWS

Please leave a review. Once you have read and used this book, why not leave a review on the site that you purchased it from? Potential readers can then see and use your unbiased opinion to make purchase decisions. We at Orange Education would love to know what you think about our products, and our authors can learn from your feedback. Thank you!

For more information about Orange Education, please visit **www.orangeava.com**.

Table of Contents

1. **Foundational Mathematics** 1
    - Introduction 1
    - Structure 2
    - 2D and 3D Geometry 3
        - *Coordinate Systems* 3
    - Basics of Trigonometry 7
        - *Trigonometric Functions* 8
        - *Radians versus Degrees* 9
        - *Trigonometric Identities* 9
        - *Phase and Amplitude* 10
    - Complex Numbers 11
        - *Introduction* 12
        - *Complex Number Operations* 13
    - Linear Algebra 15
        - *Vectors* 15
        - *Vector space* 18
        - *Hilbert space* 19
        - *Matrices* 21
        - *Trace* 24
        - *Determinants* 25
        - *Eigenvalues and Eigenvectors* 27
    - Tensor Products 30
        - *Basics of Tensor Products* 31
        - *Properties of Tensor Products* 32
    - Abstract Algebra 34
        - *Groups* 35
        - *Rings* 35
        - *Fields* 35

Conclusion 36

2. **Quantum Mechanics** **37**

Introduction 37

Structure 37

Foundations of Quantum Mechanics 38

Black-Body Radiation 39

Photoelectric Effect 40

Compton Effect 42

Particles, Spins and Angular Momentum 42

Particles in Quantum Mechanics 42

Spins 43

Angular Momentum 44

Postulates of Quantum Mechanics 44

Postulate 1 - The Wave Function Postulate 45

Postulate 2 - Experimental Observables 45

Postulate 3 - Individual Measurements 46

Postulate 4 - Expectation Values and Collapse of the Wavefunction 47

Postulate 5 - Time Evolution 47

Quantum Bits (Qubits) 48

Classical Bits vs. Qubits 48

Realization of Qubits 48

Quantum Measurements 49

Basic Principles of Quantum Measurements 50

Measurement Problem and Interpretations 51

Interpretations of Quantum Mechanics 52

Practical Implications and No-Cloning Theorem 53

Density Matrices for Mixed and Pure States 55

Density Matrices 55

Pure vs Mixed States 56

Applications of Quantum Mechanics 58

MRI and NMR Spectroscopy 58

Semiconductor Technologies 60

Quantum Sensing and Metrology 61

Conclusion 63

3. **Fundamentals of Computation** **65**

Introduction 65

Structure 66

Understanding Computation 67

Historical Context 67

Computation in Classical Computing 67

Computation in Quantum Computing 67

Theoretical Models of Computation 68

Basics of Classical Computing and Circuits 68

Logic Gates and Circuits 68

From Gates to Processors 69

Programming in Classical Computing 69

Practical Application: Building a Basic Circuit 70

Computational Complexity - Time and Space 70

Time Complexity 70

Polynomial vs. Exponential Complexity 71

Complexity Classes 71

Practical Example: Analyzing Algorithm Complexity 71

Classical Computing vs Quantum Computing 72

Theoretical Foundations and Computational Models 72

Parallelism and Entanglement 73

Practical and Technological Challenges 73

Conclusion 74

4. **Qubit Modalities** **75**

Introduction 75

Structure 76

Introduction to Qubits 76

Quantum Superposition 76

Quantum Entanglement 77

Physical Implementation of Qubits 78

Superconducting Qubits 78

Trapped Ion Qubits 81

Photonic Qubits 84

Neutral Atom-based Qubits 87

Nuclear Magnetic Resonance Qubits 90

Quantum Dots: Nanoscale Semiconductors for Quantum Computing ... 94
Semiconductor Spin Qubits: Advancing Quantum Computing with Spin States ... 97
Comparing Quantum Computing Modalities ... 100
Conclusion ... 101

5. **An Introduction to Qiskit** ... **103**
Introduction ... 103
Structure ... 104
Getting Started with Qiskit ... 104
The Qiskit Ecosystem ... 105
The Qiskit SDK ... 105
Qiskit Runtime ... 106
Qiskit Serverless ... 107
Qiskit Transpiler as a Service ... 108
Qiskit Patterns ... 109
Map ... 110
Optimize ... 111
Execute ... 113
Post-Process ... 114
Primitives ... 114
Estimator ... 115
Sampler ... 116
Features and Highlights of Qiskit 1.0 ... 117
High Performance SDK ... 117
New primitive designs ... 117
Memory usage ... 117
Speed ... 117
Native OpenQasm support ... 118
Stable release cycle ... 118
Prominent Qiskit changes ... 118
Conclusion ... 120
References ... 120

6. **Single Qubit Quantum Logic Gates** ... **123**
Introduction ... 123

Structure 124
Single Qubit Quantum Logic Gates 124
Properties of Quantum Gates 125
Pauli X Gate 128
Pauli Y Gate 134
Pauli Z Gate 136
Hadamard Gate 138
S Gate 141
$S^{\dagger}$ *Gate* 144
T Gate 146
$T^{\dagger}$ *Gate* 150
Rx Gate 152
Ry Gate 155
Rz Gate 157
Phase Gate 161
Conclusion 164

7. **Multi Qubit Quantum Logic Gates** **165**
Introduction 165
Structure 165
Two Qubit Quantum Gates 166
CNOT Gate 166
Bell's Inequality 169
Bell states 173
CY Gate 177
CZ Gate 180
SWAP Gate 183
CRx Gate 188
Three Qubit Quantum Gates and Beyond 191
Toffoli Gate 191
Fredkin Gate 195
Conclusion 199

8. **Qiskit Mapping and Optimization** **201**
Introduction 201
Structure 202
Dynamic Circuits 202

Repeat Until Success 203
Transpilation 207
Preset Pass Managers with Optimization Levels 209
Transpilation with Options 218
AI *Transpilation* 234
Circuit Knitting 237
Code Assistant 248
Qiskit Serverless 250
Quantification of Error Rates in Quantum Circuits 257
Conclusion 271
References 271

9. **Quantum Algorithms Part I** **275**
Introduction 275
Structure 276
Introduction to Oracle-Based Algorithms 276
Classical Oracles 277
Quantum Oracles 277
The Deutsch Algorithm 279
The Concept 279
Oracle's for Deutsch Algorithm 280
Deutsch Algorithm Steps 281
Quantum Circuit Analysis - Mathematical Derivation 282
Implementation of Deutsch Algorithm in Qiskit 284
Deutsch-Jozsa Algorithm: Scaling Deutsch Algorithm 287
The Concept 287
Quantum Circuit Analysis - Mathematical Derivation 288
Implementing the Deutsch-Jozsa Algorithm in Qiskit 290
Bernstein-Vazirani Algorithm 293
The Concept 294
Quantum Circuit Analysis - Mathematical Derivation 294
Implementing Bernstein-Vazirani Algorithm in Qiskit 296
Simon's Algorithm 298
The Concept 299
Quantum Circuit Analysis - Mathematical Derivation 300
Implementing Simon's Algorithm in Qiskit 302
Conclusion 306

10. Quantum Algorithms Part II **307**
Introduction 307
Structure 307
Quantum Fourier Transform (QFT) 308
Circuit Implementing QFT 313
Implementing QFT in Qiskit 316
Small-Scale QFT from Scratch 316
Transpilation for QFT and Utility-Scale 321
Quantum Phase Estimation (QPE) 334
QPE Circuit Analysis 334
Implementing QPE in Qiskit 336
Shor's Algorithm 342
Protocol for Shor's Algorithm 344
Quantum Circuit Analysis - Shor's Algorithm 346
Implementing Shor's Algorithm in Qiskit 350
Applications of Shor's Algorithm 354
Grover's Search Algorithm 356
Comparison with Classical algorithms 356
Grover's Search Algorithm - Pictorial Intuition 357
Step 1: Initial Superposition 357
Step 2: Oracle Operation 357
Step 3: Amplitude Amplification (Grover's Diffusion Operator) 358
Step 4: Grover Iteration 359
Implementation of Grover's Search Algorithm in Qiskit 360
Conclusion 363

11. Quantum Communication Protocols **365**
Introduction 365
Structure 366
Quantum Teleportation 367
The Protocol 368
Implementing Quantum Teleportation using Qiskit 369
Superdense Coding 377
The Protocol 377
Implementing Superdense Coding using Qiskit 379
Quantum Cryptography 382
How does quantum cryptography work? 383

Uses and examples of Quantum Cryptography 384
Benifits of Quantum Cryptography 385
Cons of Quantum Cryptography 385
Applications of Quantum Communication 386
Future of Quantum Communication 387
Conclusion 389

12. Variational Quantum Algorithms **391**
Introduction 391
Structure 392
Designing Variational Quantum Algorithms 392
Core components of VQA's 393
Detailed Working behind VQA's 394
Pros and Cons of VQA's 398
Foundation for Other Algorithms and Applications 399
VQE Algorithm and Procedure 401
Key Terms related to VQE 401
Components of VQE 404
Implementing VQE in Qiskit 407
Serverless VQE Implementation 413
Applications of VQE 423
Challenges in Implementation 424
QAOA Algorithm and Procedure 426
Implementing QAOA in Qiskit 429
Applications of QAOA 436
Challenges in Implementation 437
Conclusion 438
References 439

13. Quantum Machine Learning **441**
Introduction 441
Structure 441
Introduction to Classical Machine Learning 442
Types of Learning 443
Common Machine Learning Algorithms 445
Introduction to Quantum Machine Learning 448
Encoding Classical Data into Quantum States 449

Algorithms using Qiskit Machine Learning 451
Quantum Neural Networks (QNN) - EstimatorQNN and SamplerQNN 452
Quantum Neural Networks for Classification 457
Applications of Quantum Machine Learning 464
Quantum-enhanced Optimization 464
Data Encoding in Quantum States 465
Quantum-enhanced Feature Selection and Extraction 465
Quantum Anomaly Detection 466
Challenges and Future Directions in QML 466
Challenges 466
Future Directions 468
Conclusion 469

14. Quantum Error Mitigation **471**
Introduction 471
Structure 472
Fundamentals of Quantum Error Mitigation 472
Quantum Error Mitigation vs Quantum Error Correction . . . 473
Principles of Quantum Error Mitigation 474
Techniques and Algorithms for Quantum Error Mitigation 476
Zero-Noise Extrapolation (ZNE) 477
Probabilistic Error Cancellation (PEC) 477
Clifford Data Regression (CDR) 478
Quantum Subspace Expansion (QSE) 478
Twirled Readout Error Extinction (T-REx) 479
Readout Error Mitigation 480
Quantum Error Mitigation with Qiskit 480
Readout Error Mitigation 480
mthree based Error Mitigation 484
Qiskit Runtime based Error Mitigation Strategies 488
Applications 498
Quantum Chemistry 498
Quantum Optimization 499
Quantum Machine Learning 499
Cryptography and Security 500
Quantum Simulation 500
Error Characterization and Benchmarking 501

Quantum Metrology . . . 501
Towards Fault-Tolerant Quantum Computing . . . 501
Conclusion . . . 502

15. Qiskit Pulse for Quantum Hardware . . . **503**
Introduction . . . 503
Structure . . . 504
Introduction to Circuit QED . . . 504
The LC Oscillator . . . 504
Anharmonic Oscillator . . . 506
Introduction to Qiskit Pulser . . . 508
Motivation behind Qiskit Pulse . . . 509
Features and Components . . . 509
Applications . . . 512
Quantum Gates and Pulse Schedules . . . 513
Hadamard Gate Pulse . . . 514
Pauli X Gate Pulse . . . 517
CNOT Gate Pulse . . . 518
Measurement Gate Pulse . . . 520
Calibration of CNOT Gate - Dynamic Decoupling . . . 520
Calibration of Pauli X Gate - Qiskit Dynamics Backend . . . 525
Conclusion . . . 531

Bibliography . . . **533**

Index . . . **539**

CHAPTER 1

Foundational Mathematics

Introduction

Welcome to the exciting and fascinating realm of quantum computing, where the laws of classical computation are being questioned, and the potential for game-changing improvements in domains such as cryptography, optimization, and material science is just waiting to be explored. As you go out on this adventure into the quantum realm, it is absolutely essential that you arm yourself with a solid foundation in mathematics, as this is the language used in quantum physics.

This first chapter, titled "*Foundational Mathematics*," lays the groundwork for the rest of your journey through quantum computing. However, at its foundation, quantum computing relies on a bedrock of mathematical notions that are both elegant and profound. This is despite quantum computing being typically regarded as a realm of intricate physics and opaque algorithms. It doesn't matter if you're a seasoned mathematician or someone who hasn't touched a mathematical equation in years; this chapter aims to walk you through the fundamental mathematical tools needed to understand quantum computing and utilize its power.

Let's take a quick look at the reasons behind the widespread enthusiasm surrounding quantum computing before we go into the complexities of mathematics. Traditional computers, which have been of great service to humanity for several decades, are getting close to the point where they can no longer effectively solve certain categories of problems. Utilizing the fundamentals of quantum mechanics to perform computations in fundamentally new manners is the goal of quantum computing, which presents a potentially fruitful alternative. It has the ability to address issues that are almost hard for classical computers to handle, such as mimicking quantum systems, factoring big numbers in an efficient manner (which poses a threat to present encryption methods), and optimizing complicated systems.

However, quantum computing is about developing faster computers and rethinking the concept of computation itself. It tests our traditional intuitions, which in turn paves the way for new forms of discovery and invention. But before we can fully comprehend the power and beauty of quantum computing, we need to become proficient in its language and mathematics.

Structure

In this chapter, we are going to study:

- 2D and 3D Geometry
    - Coordinate Systems
- Basics of Trigonometry
    - Trigonometric Functions
    - Radians versus Degrees
    - Trigonometric Identities
    - Phase and Amplitude
- Complex Numbers
    - Introduction
    - Complex Number Operations
- Linear Algebra
    - Vectors
    - Matrices
    - Trace
    - Determinants
    - Eigenvalues and Eigenvectors
- Tensor Products
    - Basics of Tensor Products

- Abstract Algebra
    - Groups
    - Rings
    - Fields

2D and 3D Geometry

Geometry is the study of shapes, sizes, and the properties of space. In quantum computing, geometry plays a critical role in visualizing quantum states, understanding quantum gates, and representing quantum operations. In this section, we will explore the basics of 2D and 3D geometry, building an essential foundation for your journey through quantum mathematics.

Coordinate Systems

We'll begin with a fundamental concept: coordinate systems. Coordinate systems provide a way to locate points in space by assigning numerical values (coordinates) to them. In classical geometry, two common coordinate systems are used: the Cartesian coordinate system in two dimensions (2D) and the Cartesian coordinate system in three dimensions (3D).

2D Cartesian Coordinate System

In a 2D Cartesian coordinate system, as shown in *figure* 1.1, space is represented using two perpendicular axes: the x-axis and the y-axis. The point where these axes intersect is called the origin, denoted as (0, 0).

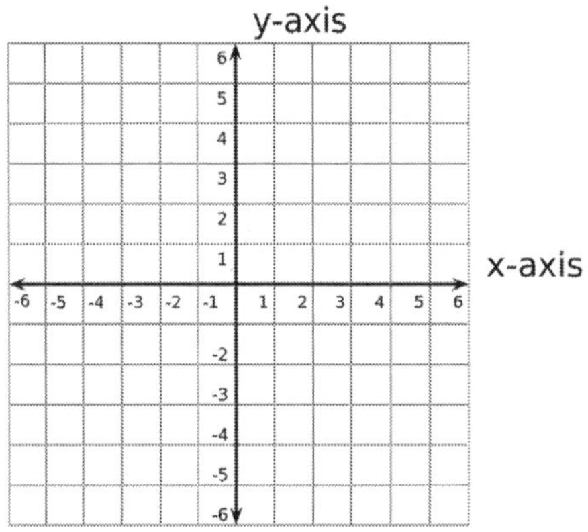

Figure 1.1: *2D Cartesian Coordinate System*

- X-Axis: The horizontal axis, typically extending to the right, is called the x-axis.
- Y-Axis: The vertical axis, typically extending upward, is called the y-axis.

Points in this system are represented as ordered pairs (x, y), where 'x' is the distance along the x-axis, and 'y' is the distance along the y-axis.

Polar Coordinates

Polar coordinates offer a unique perspective in 2D geometry by emphasizing the distance from the origin (r) and the angle (θ) relative to the positive x-axis, as shown in figure 1.2 . This representation is especially valuable when working with circular patterns, such as in physics, engineering, and navigation, where it simplifies calculations related to angles, rotations, and radial distances. Polar coordinates provide an intuitive way to describe and analyze phenomena that exhibit rotational symmetry or circular relationships, making them a powerful tool in various fields of science and mathematics.

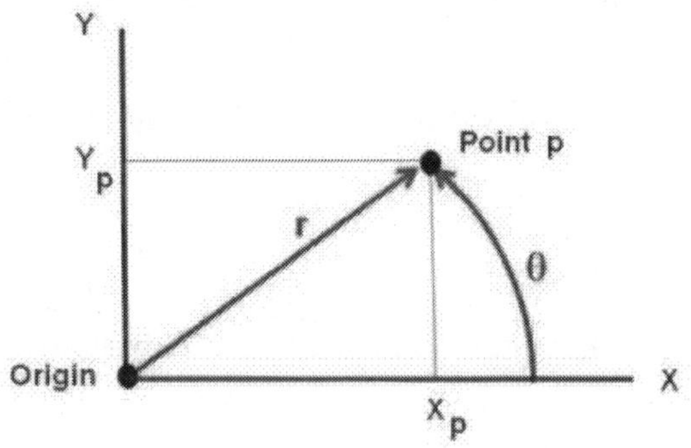

Figure 1.2: *Polar Coordinates*

3D Cartesian Coordinate System

We introduce a third axis in a 3D Cartesian coordinate system: the z-axis. This system is used to locate points in three-dimensional space. It can be clearly seen in figure 1.3 that P(x,y,z) is a point in a 3D plane.

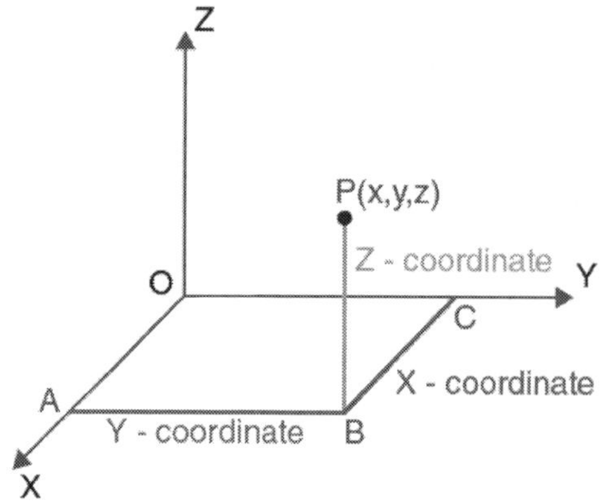

Figure 1.3: *3D Cartesian Coordinate System*

- Z-Axis: The additional axis, perpendicular to both the x and y-axes, extends outward or inward from the origin.

Points in 3D space are represented as ordered triplets (x, y, z), where ‘x’ is the distance along the x-axis, ‘y’ is the distance along the y-axis, and ‘z’ is the distance along the z-axis.

Spherical Coordinates

Spherical coordinates offer a robust method for representing points in three-dimensional space, adding an extra layer of complexity compared to their 2D polar counterparts. In spherical coordinates, a point’s position is described by three key values:

- Radial Distance (ρ): This indicates how far the point is from the origin, serving as the equivalent of distance in Cartesian coordinates. It measures how “deep” the point is located in the sphere.
- Polar Angle (θ): This angle is akin to the polar angle in 2D polar coordinates but now measures the inclination from the positive z-axis. It ranges from 0° (pointing along the positive z-axis) to 180° (pointing along the negative z-axis).
- Azimuthal Angle (ϕ): Unlike polar coordinates in 2D, spherical coordinates introduce the azimuthal angle, which measures the rotation around the positive z-axis from the positive x-axis. It spans the full 360° or 2π radians.

Spherical coordinates in figure 1.4 find extensive use in various scientific and engineering fields, particularly when dealing with objects exhibiting spherical symmetry. In physics, they simplify the description of electromagnetic fields, gravitational potentials, and atomic orbitals. Engineers employ spherical coordinates for antenna design, 3D modelling, and navigation systems, making them indispensable tools for tackling complex 3D problems with symmetry and precision.

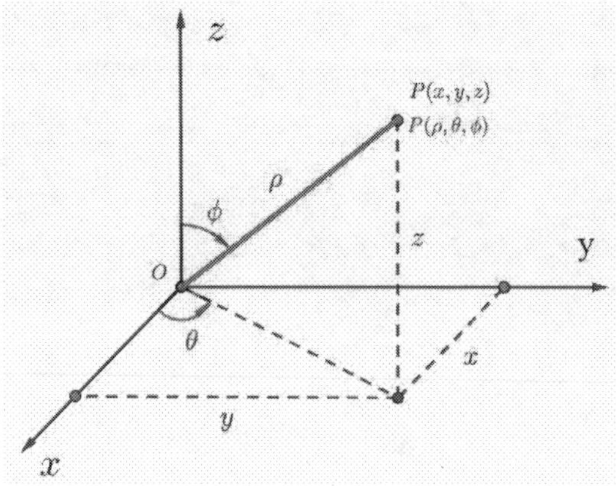

Figure 1.4: *Spherical Coordinates*

Geometry in Quantum Computing

Geometry in quantum computing serves as a powerful visual and conceptual framework for understanding the behavior of quantum systems. Quantum states, often represented as vectors in complex vector spaces, allow us to geometrically capture the intricate relationships between quantum states and operations. The geometric interpretation of quantum gates as rotations and transformations in these vector spaces enhances our ability to design and analyze quantum algorithms. Moreover, the Bloch sphere representation, a geometric model for single qubits, provides an intuitive visualization of quantum states and operations. It simplifies the understanding of qubit superposition, entanglement, and measurement outcomes. Quantum interference, a geometric consequence of superposition and phase relationships, plays a pivotal role in quantum algorithms, enabling constructive and destructive interference patterns that lead to quantum speedups.
In essence, geometry empowers quantum physicists, researchers, and quantum computing practitioners to navigate the abstract world of quantum mechanics by providing concrete and intuitive tools for quantum state manipulation, gate design, and algorithm development.
Bloch Sphere Representation The Bloch sphere in figure 1.5 is a geometric representation used to visualize the state of a single qubit in quantum computing. It provides an intuitive way to understand quantum state rotations and transformations. In this representation, a qubit's state corresponds to a point on the surface of a sphere. The azimuthal and polar angles of this point on the sphere determine the qubit's quantum state.

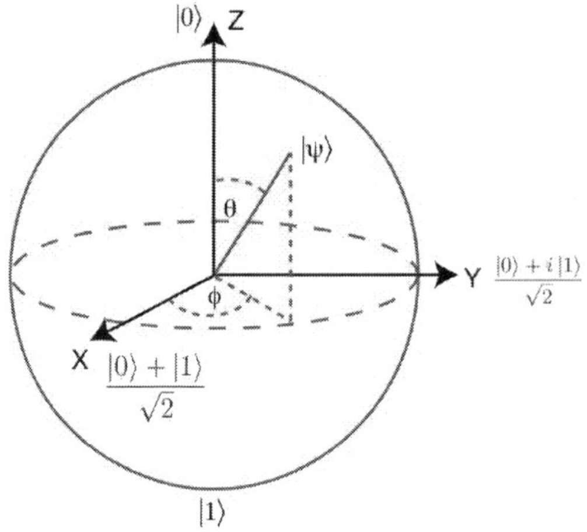

Figure 1.5: *Bloch Sphere Representation*

Quantum gates correspond to rotations around different axes in quantum state space. These rotations are fundamentally geometric operations. Understanding the geometric interpretations of these gates is essential for designing quantum algorithms and manipulating quantum states effectively. Geometry also plays a role in understanding the interference patterns that emerge during quantum computations. Quantum interference, a result of superposition and phase relationships, can be visualized geometrically and harnessed to enhance quantum algorithms and computations.
In summary, geometry is not just a mathematical tool in quantum computing; it is a visual language that allows us to grasp the behavior of quantum states and operations intuitively. By understanding the geometric foundations of quantum mechanics, researchers and practitioners can explore the full potential of quantum computing.

Basics of Trigonometry

Trigonometry is a branch of mathematics that deals with the relationships between the angles and sides of triangles. While trigonometry finds applications in various fields, its significance in quantum computing lies in its role in representing rotations and transformations applied to quantum states through quantum gates. In this section, we'll dive into the fundamental concepts of trigonometry, including trigonometric functions, radians, trigonometric identities, and their relevance in the quantum computing realm. This chapter covers the basics of trigonometry, please feel free to skip it if you are already aware of trigonometry which is covered in high school. We suggest skimming through the content as it helps you revise the topics.

Trigonometric Functions

Trigonometric functions are at the core of trigonometry and play a vital role in quantum computing. There are three primary trigonometric functions: sine (sin), cosine (cos), and tangent (tan). These functions relate the angles of a right triangle to the ratios of its sides. Let PQR be a right-angled triangle as shown in figure 1.6, where angle Q is θ and angle R is 90°. The side opposite to R is called Hypotenuse and the side that has both right-angle and θ is Adjacent and the side opposite to θ is called Opposite side.

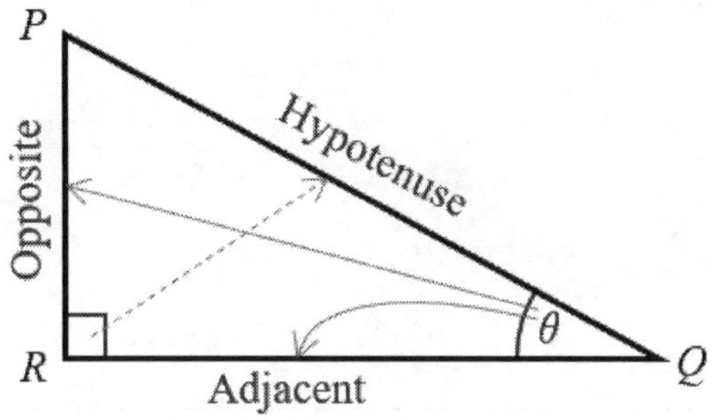

Figure 1.6: *Right Angled Triangle - PQR*

Sine (sin)

The sine of an angle in a right triangle is defined as the ratio of the length of the side opposite the angle to the length of the hypotenuse. In mathematical terms:

$$sin(\theta) = \frac{Opposite}{Hypotenuse} \tag{1.1}$$

Cosine (Cos)

The cosine of an angle is defined as the ratio of the length of the adjacent side to the length of the hypotenuse:

$$cos(\theta) = \frac{Adjacent}{Hypotenuse} \tag{1.2}$$

Tangent (tan)

The tangent of an angle is defined as the ratio of the length of the side opposite the angle to the length of the adjacent side:

$$tan(\theta) = \frac{Opposite}{Adjacent} \tag{1.3}$$

These trigonometric functions are fundamental when dealing with rotations and transformations in quantum computing. They enable us to understand how quantum gates alter quantum states by applying specific angles of rotation.

Radians versus Degrees

In trigonometry, angles can be measured in two primary units: degrees and radians. While degrees are more commonly used in everyday life, radians are the preferred choice in mathematics and quantum computing due to their convenience in expressing trigonometric functions.

Degrees

A degree is a unit of measurement where a full circle is divided into 360 equal parts, with each part being one degree (°). Degrees are familiar, especially when working with angles in geometric shapes.

Radians

Radians , on the other hand, measure angles in terms of the radius of a circle. There are approximately 2π radians in a circle, where π (pi) is approximately 3.14159. Radians are advantageous because they simplify trigonometric calculations, particularly when dealing with sine and cosine functions.

The conversion between degrees (°) and radians (rad) is given by the following formula

$$radians = \frac{\pi}{180} \times degrees \tag{1.4}$$

In quantum computing, radians are often used when specifying angles for quantum gates and rotations, as they simplify mathematical operations involving trigonometric functions.

Trigonometric Identities

Trigonometric identities are equations involving trigonometric functions that are true for all values of the variables within their domains. These identities are essential tools in simplifying trigonometric expressions and solving equations. Some of the fundamental trigonometric identities include:

Pythagorean Identities

The Pythagorean identities are a set of equations that relate the sine, cosine, and tangent functions through the Pythagorean theorem:

$$\sin^2(\theta) - 1 = -\cos^2(\theta) \tag{1.5}$$
$$\tan^2(\theta) + 1 = \sec^2(\theta) \tag{1.6}$$
$$\cot^2(\theta) + 1 = \csc^2(\theta) \tag{1.7}$$

These identities are extensively used when simplifying trigonometric expressions and verifying trigonometric relationships in quantum computations.

Double-Angle and Half-Angle Identities

Double-angle and half-angle identities express trigonometric functions of angles in terms of trigonometric functions of half-angle. These identities are particularly helpful when breaking down complex rotations into simpler components.

Double Angle Identities

$$\sin(2\theta) = 2\sin(\theta)\cos(\theta) \tag{1.8}$$
$$\cos(2\theta) = \cos^2(\theta) - \sin^2(\theta) \tag{1.9}$$
$$\tan(2\theta) = \frac{2\tan(\theta)}{1 - \tan^2(\theta)} \tag{1.10}$$

Half Angle Identities

$$\sin\left(\frac{\theta}{2}\right) = \pm\sqrt{\frac{1 - \cos(\theta)}{2}} \tag{1.11}$$
$$\cos\left(\frac{\theta}{2}\right) = \pm\sqrt{\frac{1 + \cos(\theta)}{2}} \tag{1.12}$$
$$\tan\left(\frac{\theta}{2}\right) = \pm\sqrt{\frac{1 - \cos(\theta)}{1 + \cos(\theta)}} \tag{1.13}$$

These identities provide efficient ways to manipulate quantum states' phase and amplitude, which are crucial for quantum algorithms and quantum gate operations.

Phase and Amplitude

In the context of quantum computing, trigonometric functions are closely related to the concept of phase and amplitude in complex numbers. When representing quantum states as vectors, the phase (ϕ) and amplitude (A) of a complex number are intimately linked to

the trigonometric functions of that angle.
For a complex number $z = A \cdot e^{i\phi}$, where A is the amplitude and ϕ is the phase, the trigonometric functions $\cos(\theta)$ and $\sin(\theta)$ can be related to the phase and amplitude as follows:

$$\sin(\theta) = \frac{A}{2i} \cdot (e^{i\phi} - e^{-i\phi}) \tag{1.14}$$

$$\cos(\theta) = \frac{A}{2} \cdot (e^{i\phi} + e^{-i\phi}) \tag{1.15}$$

Understanding the profound relationship between trigonometric functions and complex numbers holds paramount importance in the realm of quantum computing. Quantum circuits frequently involve phase shifts and amplitude adjustments, both of which are intricately connected to the trigonometric functions sine and cosine. These functions play a pivotal role in representing and manipulating quantum states, where the phase corresponds to the angle, and the amplitude relates to the magnitude of complex numbers. By harnessing these mathematical principles, quantum computing practitioners can precisely control and exploit the quantum phenomena of superposition and interference to develop powerful quantum algorithms and execute quantum computations with precision and efficacy. This foundational understanding bridges the gap between abstract quantum mechanics and the practical implementation of quantum circuits.
In this section, we've explored the fundamental concepts of trigonometry, including trigonometric functions, radians, trigonometric identities, and their relevance in quantum computing. These mathematical tools provide a solid foundation for understanding and manipulating quantum states and operations, allowing quantum computing practitioners to harness the power of quantum mechanics effectively.

Complex Numbers

Complex numbers , a cornerstone of mathematics, expand the realm of real numbers by introducing imaginary components, offering a rich algebraic structure for addressing problems involving squared negative numbers. Quantum computing harnesses this mathematical framework to encapsulate quantum states, operations, and probability amplitudes in a compact and expressive manner. These complex numbers empower quantum computers to simulate and manipulate quantum phenomena with exceptional precision, a capability that underpins their potential to revolutionize fields as diverse as cryptography, materials science, and optimization. In this section, we embark on a journey to explore the fundamental properties and applications of complex numbers, illuminating their indispensable role in the quantum computing landscape.

Introduction

A complex number is typically denoted as z and has the form $a + ib$, where a and b are real numbers, and i is the imaginary unit, defined as $i = \sqrt{-1}$. The real part a represents the conventional real number, while the imaginary part b is a multiple of the imaginary unit.

Complex Plane

The complex plane, also known as the Argand plane or Gauss plane, is a geometric representation that provides an intuitive and geometric understanding of complex numbers. It is a two-dimensional Cartesian coordinate system where each complex number is mapped to a unique point in the plane. The complex plane's horizontal axis represents a complex number's real part, while the vertical axis represents the imaginary part.

- **Real Axis (Horizontal)**: This axis corresponds to the real part of a complex number, usually denoted as "Re(z)." The values on this axis are real numbers. Real numbers are located exclusively along this axis in the complex plane, with no imaginary part (vertical component).
- **Imaginary Axis (Vertical)**: The vertical axis represents the imaginary part of a complex number, typically denoted as "Im(z)." The values on this axis are multiples of the imaginary unit "i," which is the square root of -1. Complex numbers with no real part (horizontal component) are located along this axis.

The complex plane as shown in figure 1.7 provides a geometric interpretation of complex numbers, allowing us to visualize their properties and relationships. The distance of a complex number from the origin (0,0) is its modulus $|z|$, which is calculated as:

$$|z| = \sqrt{a^2 + b^2} \tag{1.16}$$

The angle θ that z makes with the positive real axis, measured counterclockwise, is called the argument of z. It can be calculated using trigonometric functions:

$$\theta = arctan(\frac{b}{a}) \tag{1.17}$$

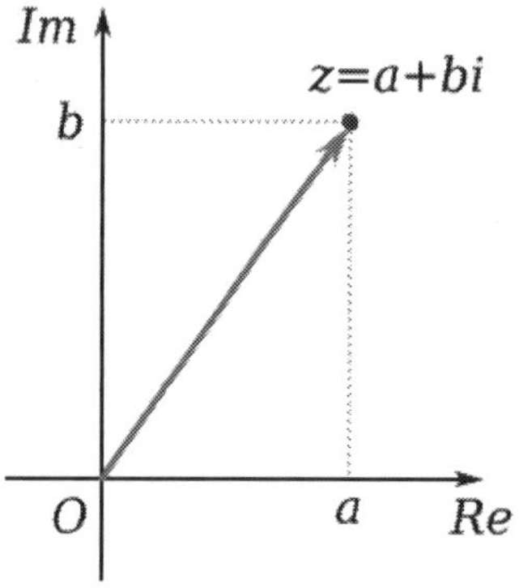

Figure 1.7:
Complex Plane Representation

Complex Number Operations

This section will explore the fundamental mathematical operations that apply to complex numbers. These operations include addition, subtraction, multiplication, and division of complex numbers, each of which has its own rules and properties. Understanding how to perform these operations is crucial not only for the manipulation of complex numbers but also for their application in various mathematical and scientific fields, including quantum computing. We will delve into the algebraic rules governing these operations and provide practical examples to illustrate their significance and utility in complex number mathematics and its applications.

Addition and Subraction

Adding or subtracting complex numbers is straightforward. You simply add or subtract the real parts and the imaginary parts separately. For two complex numbers $z_1 = a_1 + ib_1$, $z_2 = a_2 + ib_2$.

- Addition: $z_1 + z_2 = (a_1 + a_2) + (b_1 + b_2)i$
- Subtraction: $z_1 - z_2 = (a_1 - a_2) + (b_1 - b_2)i$

Multiplication

You can multiply two complex numbers using the distributive property and the fact that

$$i^2 = -1$$

. For $z_1 = a_1 + ib_1$ and $z_2 = a_2 + ib_2$, their product is given by,

$$z_1 \cdot z_2 = (a_1 + ib_1) \cdot (a_2 + ib_2) = (a_1a_2 - b_1b_2) + (a_1b_2 + a_2b_1)i$$

Divison

To divide two complex numbers, you can use the concept of the conjugate. The conjugate of a complex number $z = a + ib$ is denoted as $\bar{z} = a - ib$. For $z_1 = a_1 + ib_1$ and $z_2 = a_2 + ib_2$, their quotient is given by:

$$\frac{z_1}{z_2} = \frac{z_1}{z_2} \cdot \frac{\bar{z}_1}{\bar{z}_2} = \frac{a_1a_2 + b_1b_2}{a_2^2 + b_2^2} - \frac{a_2b_1 + a_1b_2}{a_2^2 + b_2^2}i \tag{1.18}$$

Complex Conjugate

The complex conjugate of a complex number $z = a + ib$ is denoted as $\bar{z} = a - ib$. It is obtained by changing the sign of the imaginary part. The complex conjugate of a complex number z is crucial in various mathematical operations and has significance in quantum computing, particularly in finding inner products and measuring quantum states.

Modulus and Argument

The modulus $|z|$ of a complex number $z = a + ib$ is the magnitude of **z** and is calculated as:

$$|z| = \sqrt{a^2 + b^2} \tag{1.19}$$

The argument *(arg(z))* of a complex number z is the angle θ that z makes with the positive real axis in the complex plane. It can be calculated using trigonometric functions:

$$arg(z) = arctan\frac{b}{a} \tag{1.20}$$

The modulus and argument of a complex number provide valuable information about its magnitude and direction in the complex plane.

Euler's Formula

Euler's formula is a fundamental equation that relates complex exponential to trigonometric functions. It is given by:

$$e^{i\theta} = \cos\theta + i\sin\theta \tag{1.21}$$

This formula is of paramount importance in quantum computing, where it is used to represent quantum gates that introduce phase shifts and rotations.

In quantum computing, complex numbers are used to represent amplitudes of quantum states. Quantum states are typically represented as complex vectors, and the complex numbers within these vectors denote the probabilities and phases associated with the corresponding quantum states. The probability of measuring a quantum state in a specific outcome is determined by the square of the absolute value of the complex amplitude associated with that outcome. Therefore, complex numbers in quantum computing are not just mathematical representations; they carry the essential information needed to

calculate measurement probabilities and predict quantum behaviour.
Complex numbers are a foundational concept in quantum computing, enabling the precise representation of quantum states and quantum operations. Their mathematical properties, including addition, subtraction, multiplication, division, and the use of complex conjugates, are essential tools in the quantum computing toolkit. Understanding the significance of complex numbers in quantum computing is crucial for designing quantum algorithms, quantum gates, and quantum simulations, ultimately unlocking the vast potential of quantum computing in solving complex problems efficiently and revolutionizing various industries.

Linear Algebra

In the realm of quantum computing, the language of linear algebra is the key to unlocking the incredible power of quantum systems. This section, "*Linear Algebra - Vectors, Matrices, Arithmetic operations, Trace, Determinants, Eigenvalues, Eigenvectors,*" is a comprehensive guide to the fundamental mathematical tools and concepts underpinning quantum computing's very foundation. From vectors representing quantum states to matrices defining quantum gates and from arithmetic operations manipulating quantum information to determinants and eigenvalues that unveil crucial insights, this section delves deep into the mathematical machinery that drives quantum algorithms and quantum simulations. By mastering these core principles, you'll gain a profound understanding of the quantum universe and be equipped to embark on the quantum computing journey with confidence and precision.

Vectors

Vectors are fundamental in both classical and quantum physics. In the context of geometry, vectors represent quantities that have both magnitude and direction. They can be used to describe a wide range of physical phenomena, from forces and velocities to quantum states.
Vector Notation In 2D and 3D geometry, vectors are typically represented as arrows originating from the origin (0, 0) in 2D or (0, 0, 0) in 3D. The arrow's length indicates the vector's magnitude, and its direction indicates the vector's orientation.
Mathematically, a 2D vector can be represented as:

$$V = \begin{bmatrix} V_x \\ V_y \end{bmatrix} \tag{1.22}$$

Here V represents the vector, V_x is the X component of the vector, and V_y is the Y component.
Similarly, a 3D vector is represented as:

$$V = \begin{bmatrix} V_x \\ V_y \\ V_z \end{bmatrix} \tag{1.23}$$

Here, V represents the vector, V_x is the X component of the vector, V_y is the Y component, and V_z is the Z component. In quantum computing, vectors are extensively used to represent quantum states. Quantum states can be thought of as vectors in a complex vector space. You will learn more about this in the other chapters of this book.

Vector Operations

Vectors can undergo various operations in geometry, some of which are crucial in quantum computing. These operations include vector addition , scalar multiplication , and vector normalization . In quantum computing, vector addition is used to combine quantum states, scalar multiplication adjusts the amplitudes of quantum states, and vector normalization ensures that quantum states remain in a valid probabilistic state. Understanding and mastering these operations are essential steps in manipulating and controlling quantum information effectively. Let us see some of the vector operations as follows:

Vector Magnitude

A vector's magnitude (or length) is a fundamental concept in geometry. It represents the distance from the origin to the point represented by the vector. In 2D, the magnitude of a vector V is calculated using Pythagoras theorem. Let V be a 2D vector,

$$V = \begin{bmatrix} V_x \\ V_y \end{bmatrix} \tag{1.24}$$

The magnitude of V is given by,

$$|V| = \sqrt{(V_x)^2 + (V_y)^2}$$

In 3D, the magnitude of vector V is calculated similarly,

$$|V| = \sqrt{(V_x)^2 + (V_y)^2 + (V_z^2)} \tag{1.25}$$

It is to be noted that the magnitude of a vector is always a non-negative real number.

Vector Addition

Vector addition combines two vectors to produce a third vector, often called the resultant vector. To add two vectors V and W you add their corresponding components. Let V and W be any two 2D vectors,

$$V = \begin{bmatrix} V_x \\ V_y \end{bmatrix} \tag{1.26}$$

$$W = \begin{bmatrix} W_x \\ W_y \end{bmatrix} \tag{1.27}$$

Vector addition of V and W is as follows

$$V + W = \begin{bmatrix} V_x + W_x \\ V_y + W_y \end{bmatrix} \tag{1.28}$$

Similarly, let A and B be any 3D vectors represented as follows:

$$A = \begin{bmatrix} A_x \\ A_y \\ A_z \end{bmatrix} \tag{1.29}$$

$$B = \begin{bmatrix} A_x \\ A_y \\ A_z \end{bmatrix} \tag{1.30}$$

Vector addition of A and B is as follows

$$A + B = \begin{bmatrix} A_x + B_x \\ A_y + B_y \\ A_z + B_z \end{bmatrix} \tag{1.31}$$

Vector addition is indeed fundamental in quantum computing, serving as the mathematical underpinning for combining quantum states and applying quantum gates. When quantum systems evolve, their states are represented as vectors, and quantum operations correspond to linear transformations on these vectors. By adding or superposing quantum states using vector addition, we can create complex quantum algorithms and circuits that harness quantum parallelism's power. This ability to efficiently combine states is at the core of quantum computation, allowing us to explore solutions to problems that would be computationally intractable for classical computers.

Scalar Multiplication

Scalar multiplication is a versatile operation in quantum computing, enabling precise adjustments to quantum states. By multiplying a quantum state vector by a scalar, we can control the magnitude of its amplitudes. This process allows us to apply phase shifts and amplitude scaling, which are essential for quantum algorithms and quantum gate operations. Scalar multiplication plays a pivotal role in quantum interference, where constructive and destructive interference patterns emerge, influencing the final outcome of quantum computations. Through scalar multiplication, we fine-tune the probabilities of measurement outcomes, exploiting the unique features of quantum superposition to solve specific problems efficiently.

Scalar multiplication involves multiplying a vector by a scalar (a real number). The result is a vector with the same direction but scaled in magnitude. For a vector V and a scalar c: the scalar multiplication of V and c is shown as follows

$$cV = \begin{bmatrix} cV_x \\ cV_y \end{bmatrix} \tag{1.32}$$

In 3D, scalar multiplication extends similarly

$$cV = \begin{bmatrix} cV_x \\ cV_y \\ cV_z \end{bmatrix} \tag{1.33}$$

Quantum States as Column Vectors

Quantum states are often expressed as column vectors, whether they represent qubits or quantum systems with multiple states. These vectors encapsulate the quantum information, and their components are complex numbers known as probability amplitudes. For example, a single-qubit quantum state $|\psi\rangle$ can be represented as:

$$|\psi\rangle = \begin{bmatrix} \alpha \\ \beta \end{bmatrix} \tag{1.34}$$

Where α and β are complex probability amplitudes, and the square of their magnitudes ($|\alpha|^2$ and $|\beta|^2$) represents the probabilities of measuring the corresponding basis states (eg., $|0\rangle$ and $|1\rangle$).

Vector Space

A vector space is a mathematical structure formed by a collection of vectors, which can be added together and multiplied (scaled) by numbers, called scalars. In quantum computing, vector spaces are crucial because they provide the framework for representing quantum states and operations.

Properties of Vector Spaces:

- **Vectors**: Elements in the vector space, which can represent states or directions.
- **Scalars**: Numbers (typically real or complex) that multiply vectors.

- **Vector Addition**: Combining two vectors results in another vector within the same space.
- **Scalar Multiplication**: Scaling a vector by a scalar results in another vector within the space.

Quantum states are represented by vectors in a complex vector space called the Hilbert space. Quantum operations are represented by transformations (linear operators) on these vectors. The dimension of the vector space corresponds to the number of possible states a quantum system can occupy.

Example: For a single qubit, the vector space is two-dimensional, represented as C^2 where the basis vectors are $|0\rangle$ and $|1\rangle$

Hilbert Space

A Hilbert space is a complete vector space equipped with an inner product, allowing the measurement of angles and distances between vectors. In quantum computing, it is a special kind of vector space used to describe the state space of quantum systems.

Properties of Hilbert Spaces:

- **Inner Product:** A Hilbert space $\mathcal{H}$ has an inner product $\langle\psi|\phi\rangle$ defined for any two vectors $|\psi\rangle$ and $|\phi\rangle$. This inner product is a complex number and satisfies the following properties:
  1. **Conjugate Symmetry:** $\langle\psi|\phi\rangle = \overline{\langle\phi|\psi\rangle}$.
  2. **Linearity in the First Argument:** For any scalars $\alpha, \beta \in \mathbb{C}$ and vectors $|\psi\rangle, |\phi\rangle, |\chi\rangle \in \mathcal{H}$, the inner product satisfies:

$$\langle\alpha\psi + \beta\phi|\chi\rangle = \alpha\langle\psi|\chi\rangle + \beta\langle\phi|\chi\rangle.$$

  3. **Positive-Definiteness:** $\langle\psi|\psi\rangle \geq 0$, and $\langle\psi|\psi\rangle = 0$ if and only if $|\psi\rangle = 0$.
- **Orthogonality:** Two vectors $|\psi\rangle$ and $|\phi\rangle$ are orthogonal if $\langle\psi|\phi\rangle = 0$. Orthogonal vectors represent quantum states that are completely distinguishable.
- **Normalization:** A vector $|\psi\rangle$ is normalized if its inner product with itself is equal to one:

$$\langle\psi|\psi\rangle = 1.$$

  Normalized vectors are used to represent valid quantum states.
- **Completeness:** A Hilbert space is complete, meaning that every Cauchy sequence $\{|\psi_n\rangle\}$ in $\mathcal{H}$ converges to a vector $|\psi\rangle \in \mathcal{H}$. In other words, there are no "holes" in the space.

- **Orthogonal Basis:** In a finite-dimensional Hilbert space, it is always possible to find an orthonormal basis $\{|e_i\rangle\}$ such that any vector $|\psi\rangle$ can be expressed as a linear combination:

$$|\psi\rangle = \sum_i \alpha_i |e_i\rangle,$$

where $\alpha_i \in \mathbb{C}$ and $\langle e_i|e_j\rangle = \delta_{ij}$.
- **Projection:** For any vector $|\psi\rangle$ and an orthonormal basis $\{|e_i\rangle\}$, the projection of $|\psi\rangle$ onto $|e_i\rangle$ is given by:

$$|\psi\rangle = \sum_i \langle e_i|\psi\rangle |e_i\rangle.$$

This representation is essential for calculating probabilities in quantum mechanics.

Hilbert spaces play a fundamental role in quantum computing for several reasons:

- **Representation of Quantum States:** The state of a quantum system, such as a qubit, is represented by a vector in a Hilbert space. For example, a single qubit's state is represented as a vector in the two-dimensional complex Hilbert space $\mathbb{C}^2$. For a system of n qubits, the state is represented in a 2^n-dimensional Hilbert space.
- **Quantum Operations:** Quantum operations, or gates, are represented as linear operators on the Hilbert space. These operators are unitary, preserving the inner product structure of the space, which corresponds to the conservation of probability in quantum mechanics.
- **Measurement and Probability:** The inner product in Hilbert space is used to calculate probabilities of measurement outcomes. If a system is in state $|\psi\rangle$ and we measure it in the basis $\{|\phi_i\rangle\}$, the probability of obtaining outcome $|\phi_i\rangle$ is given by $|\langle\phi_i|\psi\rangle|^2$.
- **Superposition and Entanglement:** Hilbert spaces allow the representation of superposition states, where a qubit can be in a combination of $|0\rangle$ and $|1\rangle$. They also allow the representation of entangled states, which are crucial for quantum algorithms and quantum communication.
- **Tensor Products:** The Hilbert space formalism supports tensor products, enabling the description of multi-qubit systems. If $\mathcal{H}_1$ and $\mathcal{H}_2$ are Hilbert spaces for individual qubits, the combined system is described by the tensor product space $\mathcal{H}_1 \otimes \mathcal{H}_2$.
- **Quantum Algorithms:** The evolution of quantum states through unitary transformations in Hilbert space underlies quantum algorithms. These algorithms exploit the geometric and algebraic structure of Hilbert space to solve problems more efficiently than classical algorithms.

Example: For a single qubit, the Hilbert space is a two-dimensional complex vector space, denoted as $\mathbb{C}^2$. The basis vectors are typically represented as $|0\rangle$ and $|1\rangle$, where:

$$|0\rangle = \begin{pmatrix} 1 \\ 0 \end{pmatrix} \quad \text{and} \quad |1\rangle = \begin{pmatrix} 0 \\ 1 \end{pmatrix}.$$

Any quantum state $|\psi\rangle$ of a single qubit can be written as a linear combination of these basis vectors:

$$|\psi\rangle = \alpha|0\rangle + \beta|1\rangle,$$

where α and β are complex numbers, and the normalization condition $|\alpha|^2 + |\beta|^2 = 1$ must hold to ensure that $|\psi\rangle$ represents a valid quantum state.
For example, a qubit in the state

$$|\psi\rangle = \frac{1}{\sqrt{2}}|0\rangle + \frac{1}{\sqrt{2}}|1\rangle$$

is an equal superposition of $|0\rangle$ and $|1\rangle$. This state is known as the $|+\rangle$ state and is one of the fundamental states used in quantum computing.

Matrices

Matrices are the mathematical workhorses that empower quantum computing to perform remarkable feats. In the world of quantum computation, these structured arrays of numbers serve as the language through which quantum gates, operations, and transformations are expressed. From defining the fundamental Pauli-X gate to constructing complex quantum circuits, matrices are the building blocks that govern the evolution of quantum states. In this section, we embark on a journey to unravel the intricacies of matrices, exploring their notation, operations, and significance in quantum computing. By understanding the matrix framework, quantum computing enthusiasts can dive deeper into the quantum realm, shaping the future of computation and problem-solving.

Matrix Notation

Quantum gates, the building blocks of quantum circuits, are represented as matrices. Each gate corresponds to a specific unitary matrix that describes its effect on a quantum state. These matrices dictate how the quantum state evolves as it passes through the gate. For instance, the Pauli-X gate, which flips the $|0\rangle$ state to $|1\rangle$ and vice versa, is represented as:

$$\sigma_x = \begin{bmatrix} 0 & 1 \\ 1 & 0 \end{bmatrix} \tag{1.35}$$

The application of this matrix to a quantum state results in the desired quantum transformation.

Arithmetic Operations

This subsection, "Arithmetic Operations of Matrices," delves into the essential mathematical operations that allow us to combine, adjust, and transform matrices, unveiling the intricate dance of quantum states and quantum gates. From the fundamental principles of matrix addition and subtraction to the transformative power of matrix multiplication and the profound implications of the tensor product, this exploration equips quantum computing enthusiasts with the mathematical tools to orchestrate quantum computations and explore the intriguing possibilities that quantum mechanics offers.

Matrix Addition

Matrix addition is a fundamental operation in linear algebra and quantum computing. It allows us to combine two matrices of the same dimension by adding their corresponding elements. In the context of quantum computing, matrix addition is essential for various operations, such as constructing quantum circuits and simulating quantum states.

Matrix addition is straightforward. Given two matrices of the same dimension, say A and B, their sum C is computed by adding the corresponding elements:

$$C = A + B$$

If A has dimensions mxn and B also has dimensions mxn, then each element c_{ij} of matrix C is the sum of the corresponding elements a_{ij} and b_{ij}.

$$c_{ij} = a_{ij} + b_{ij} \tag{1.36}$$

Let A and B be two matrices such that:

$$A = \begin{bmatrix} 1 & 2 & 3 \\ 4 & 5 & 6 \end{bmatrix}$$

$$B = \begin{bmatrix} -1 & -2 & -3 \\ -4 & -5 & -6 \end{bmatrix}$$

To find the sum $C = A + B$, we add the corresponding elements of A and B

$$C = \begin{bmatrix} 1 + (-1) & 2 + (-2) & 3 + (-3) \\ 4 + (-4) & 5 + (-5) & 6 + (-6) \end{bmatrix}$$

Simplifying the addition, we get

$$C = \begin{bmatrix} 0 & 0 & 0 \\ 0 & 0 & 0 \end{bmatrix}$$

In this example, matrix C is the result of adding matrices A and B. Notice that each element of C is the sum of the corresponding elements of A and B.

Matrix Multiplication

Matrix multiplication is a fundamental operation in linear algebra and quantum computing. It is used to combine two matrices in a way that represents the composition of linear transformations. In quantum computing, matrix multiplication is essential for describing the evolution of quantum states through quantum gates and circuits.

Matrix multiplication is defined for two matrices, say A and B, where the number of columns in matrix A must be equal to the number of rows in matrix B. If A is of dimension *mxn* and B is of dimension *nxp*, then the resulting matrix C will be of dimensions *mxp*. The individual elements of the resulting matrix C are calculated as follows.

$$c_{ij} = a_{i1}b_{1j} + a_{i2}b_{2j} + \cdots + a_{in}b_{nj} \tag{1.37}$$

In other words, each element c_{ij} in the resulting matrix C is obtained by taking the dot product of the ith row of the matrix A and the jth column of matrix B. Let's illustrate matrix multiplication with an example. Consider two matrices, A and B:

$$A = \begin{bmatrix} 1 & 2 \\ 3 & 4 \\ 5 & 6 \end{bmatrix}$$

$$B = \begin{bmatrix} 7 & 8 & 9 \\ 10 & 11 & 12 \end{bmatrix}$$

To find the product C = A ·B, we calculate each element of C as described earlier:

$$C = \begin{bmatrix} 1 \cdot 7 + 2 \cdot 10 & 1 \cdot 8 + 2 \cdot 11 & 1 \cdot 9 + 2 \cdot 12 \\ 3 \cdot 7 + 4 \cdot 10 & 3 \cdot 8 + 4 \cdot 11 & 3 \cdot 9 + 4 \cdot 12 \\ 5 \cdot 7 + 6 \cdot 10 & 5 \cdot 8 + 6 \cdot 11 & 5 \cdot 9 + 6 \cdot 12 \end{bmatrix}$$

Simplifying the calculations

$$C = \begin{bmatrix} 27 & 30 & 33 \\ 61 & 68 & 75 \\ 95 & 106 & 117 \end{bmatrix}$$

In this example, matrix C is the result of multiplying matrices A and B. Each element c_{ij} is calculated by taking the dot product of the corresponding row from matrix A and the corresponding column from matrix B.

Transpose and Conjugate Transpose

In linear algebra and quantum computing, a matrix's transpose and conjugate transpose (also known as the adjoint) play crucial roles in various operations and calculations. These operations involve changing the arrangement of elements in a matrix and often arise when dealing with complex numbers and quantum states. The adjoint property ensures that the norm (length) of quantum states is preserved during quantum operations, which is crucial for the validity of quantum computations.

The **transpose of a matrix** A, denoted by A^T, is obtained by switching its rows and columns. In other words, the element in the ith row and j^{th} column of the original matrix A becomes the element in the jth row and i^{th} column of the transposed matrix A^T.

The **conjugate transpose of a matrix or adjoint** A, denoted by $A^\dagger$, is similar to the transpose, but it also involves taking the complex conjugate of each element. The complex conjugate of a complex number $z = a + bi$ is $z = a - bi$, where a and b are real numbers. It should be noted that in the conjugate transpose, not only are the rows and columns switched, but the complex conjugate of each element is taken.

Let us take an example and understand the concept of transpose and conjugate transpose:

$$A = \begin{bmatrix} 2+3i & 4-2i \\ 1+5i & 6 \end{bmatrix}$$

The transpose of matrix A, denoted as A^T, is obtained by switching its rows and columns:

$$A^T = \begin{bmatrix} 2+3i & 4-2i \\ 1+5i & 6 \end{bmatrix}$$

The conjugate transpose of matrix A, denoted as $A^\dagger$ involves switching the rows and columns and taking the complex conjugate of each element:

$$A^\dagger = \begin{bmatrix} 2-3i & 1-5i \\ 4+2i & 6 \end{bmatrix}$$

Trace

The trace of a matrix is a mathematical operation that provides a scalar value representing the sum of its diagonal elements. In quantum computing and linear algebra, the trace is a fundamental concept with applications in various calculations and properties of matrices. Given a square matrix A, with dimensions *nxn*, the trace of A, denoted as *Tr*(A), is calculated as the sum of its diagonal elements.

$$Tr(A) = a_{11} + a_{22} + a_{33} + \cdots + a_{nn} \tag{1.38}$$

In other words, you simply add up the elements that lie on the main diagonal from the top-left corner to the bottom-right corner of the matrix. Let's illustrate the calculation of the trace with a simple example. Consider the following square matrix A.

$$A = \begin{bmatrix} 3 & 1 & 0 \\ 2 & 5 & 4 \\ -1 & 7 & 6 \end{bmatrix}$$

To calculate the trace *Tr*(A), we add up the diagonal elements:

$$Tr(A) = 3 + 5 + 6 = 14$$

So, the trace of matrix A is 14.

Determinants

In linear algebra, the determinant of a square matrix is a scalar value that provides crucial information about the matrix's properties and behaviour. Determinants play a fundamental role in various mathematical and scientific applications, including solving systems of linear equations, calculating areas and volumes, and understanding the invertibility of matrices. Given a square matrix A, the determinant, denoted as *det*(A) or $|A|$, is calculated using various methods, with the most common being the expansion by minors or cofactor expansion. For a 2x2 matrix

$$A = \begin{bmatrix} a & b \\ c & d \end{bmatrix}$$

The determinant *det*(A) is computed by

$$det(A) = ad - bc \tag{1.39}$$

The calculation becomes more complex for larger matrices. The expansion by minors method involves breaking down the matrix into smaller sub-matrices and calculating their determinants.

Determinants are essential in linear algebra and various fields, including quantum computing:

- **Matrix Invertibility**: A square matrix is invertible (has an inverse) if and only if its determinant is nonzero. In quantum computing, unitary matrices used for quantum gates are always invertible.
- **Volume Scaling**: Determinants are used to calculate the scaling factor of volumes in linear transformations. In quantum mechanics, this relates to the preservation of probabilities in quantum operations.
- **Cramer's Rule**: Determinants are used to solve systems of linear equations using Cramer's Rule, which expresses the solutions in terms of matrix determinants. This rule is applicable when the system's matrix (the matrix of coefficients of the linear equations) is square and invertible (i.e., has a non-zero determinant).

Properties of Determinant

The determinant of a matrix possesses several important properties that make it a valuable tool in linear algebra and various mathematical applications. Understanding these properties can help simplify computations and gain insights into the behaviour of matrices. Here are some key properties of determinants

- **Multiplicative Property**: The determinant of the product of two square matrices A and B is equal to the product of their determinants:

$$det(AB) = det(A) \cdot det(B) \tag{1.40}$$

  This property simplifies the calculation of determinants for composite transformations represented by matrices.
- **Scalar Multiplication Property**: If a square matrix A is multiplied by a scalar k, the determinant of the resulting matrix kA is equal to k^n times the determinant of A, where n is the dimension of the matrix:

$$det(kA) = k^n \cdot det(A) \tag{1.41}$$

- **Transpose Property**: The determinant of the transpose of a matrix A^T is equal to the determinant of the original matrix A: det(A^T) = det(A).

$$det(A^T) = det(A) \tag{1.42}$$

  This property shows that the orientation of the matrix's rows and columns does not affect the determinant.
- **Interchange of Rows or Columns**: Interchanging any two rows (or columns) of a

matrix changes the sign of the determinant:

$$det(P_{ij}A) = -det(A) \tag{1.43}$$

Where P_{ij} represents the permutation matrix that swaps rows i and j

Eigenvalues and Eigenvectors

Eigenvalues and eigenvectors are fundamental concepts in linear algebra with widespread applications in quantum mechanics, physics, computer science, and engineering. For any square matrix $A \in \mathbb{C}^{n \times n}$, an eigenvalue λ and its corresponding nonzero eigenvector v satisfy the equation

$$Av = \lambda v. \tag{1.44}$$

This relation indicates that the linear transformation represented by A scales the eigenvector v by the factor λ. Analyzing the eigenvalues and eigenvectors of a matrix provides insight into the intrinsic properties of the system, such as stability, spectral decomposition, and dynamical behavior. In quantum mechanics, for example, the eigenvalues of an operator correspond to measurable physical quantities, while the eigenvectors represent the associated quantum states. These concepts are essential for solving differential equations, optimizing algorithms, and modeling complex systems across various scientific disciplines.

Eigenvalues

Eigenvalues are scalar values associated with a square matrix that represent how the matrix scales or stretches space along certain directions. In other words, eigenvalues tell us how the matrix affects the magnitude of vectors without changing their direction. Given a square matrix A, an eigenvalue λ is a scalar such that there exists a non-zero vector v (eigenvector) for which the following equation holds

$$Av = \lambda v \tag{1.45}$$

In this equation, Av represents the result of multiplying matrix A by vector v, and λv represents the scaled version of vector v by the eigenvalue λ.

Eigenvectors

Eigenvectors are non-zero vectors that correspond to eigenvalues and define the directions along which a linear transformation is represented by a matrix scale or stretch space. Each eigenvalue can have multiple associated eigenvectors, and these eigenvectors form linearly independent sets. Eigenvectors are determined by solving the linear system of equations.

$$(A - \lambda I)v = 0 \tag{1.46}$$

Where A is the matrix, λ is eigenvalue, I is Identity matrix, and v is eigenvector. Lets take an example to explain eigenvalue and eigenvectors.

Matrix Definition

Consider the matrix

$$A = \begin{bmatrix} 2 & 0 \\ 0 & 3 \end{bmatrix}. \tag{1.47}$$

Finding Eigenvalues: The eigenvalues are found by solving the characteristic equation:

$$det(A - \lambda I) = 0 \tag{1.48}$$

Substituting A and I, the equation becomes:

$$det\left(\begin{bmatrix} 2-\lambda & 0 \\ 0 & 3-\lambda \end{bmatrix}\right) = 0 \tag{1.49}$$

This simplifies to:

$$(2 - \lambda)(3 - \lambda) = 0 \tag{1.50}$$

Solving this, we find:

$$\lambda_1 = 2, \quad \lambda_2 = 3 \tag{1.51}$$

Finding Eigenvectors

Eigenvector for $\lambda_1 = 2$

Set up the equation $(A - 2I)\mathbf{v} = 0$:

$$\begin{bmatrix} 0 & 0 \\ 0 & 1 \end{bmatrix} \begin{bmatrix} x \\ y \end{bmatrix} = \begin{bmatrix} 0 \\ 0 \end{bmatrix} \tag{1.52}$$

The solution gives:

$$\mathbf{v}_1 = \begin{bmatrix} 1 \\ 0 \end{bmatrix} \tag{1.53}$$

Eigenvector for $\lambda_2 = 3$

Set up the equation $(A - 3I)\mathbf{v} = 0$:

$$\begin{bmatrix} -1 & 0 \\ 0 & 0 \end{bmatrix} \begin{bmatrix} x \\ y \end{bmatrix} = \begin{bmatrix} 0 \\ 0 \end{bmatrix} \tag{1.54}$$

The solution gives:

$$\mathbf{v}_2 = \begin{bmatrix} 0 \\ 1 \end{bmatrix} \tag{1.55}$$

Practical applications of Eigenvalues and Eigenvectors

We will discuss the real life applications of Eigenvalues and Eigenvectors.
Predicting System Behaviors: Oscillations or Rotations
Example: Rotations in a Mechanical System Consider a 2D system where a point rotates around the origin. The transformation matrix for a rotation by an angle θ is:

$$R = \begin{bmatrix} \cos(\theta) & -\sin(\theta) \\ \sin(\theta) & \cos(\theta) \end{bmatrix} \tag{1.56}$$

For simplicity, let's consider a 45° rotation ($\theta = \pi/4$):

$$R = \begin{bmatrix} \frac{\sqrt{2}}{2} & -\frac{\sqrt{2}}{2} \\ \frac{\sqrt{2}}{2} & \frac{\sqrt{2}}{2} \end{bmatrix} \tag{1.57}$$

Eigenvalues and eigenvectors of R provide insights into the invariant lines under rotation and the nature of transformation. In this case, eigenvalues are complex, indicating rotational motion without real eigenvectors corresponding to invariant real directions.
Analyzing Stability: System Settling or Exploding
Example: Population Model- Consider a simple model for the population of two species with interactions described by the matrix:

$$A = \begin{bmatrix} 1.1 & 0.4 \\ 0.1 & 0.9 \end{bmatrix} \tag{1.58}$$

To analyze stability, we find the eigenvalues of A:

$$\det(A - \lambda I) = (1.1 - \lambda)(0.9 - \lambda) - (0.4)(0.1) = 0 \tag{1.59}$$

$$\lambda^2 - 2\lambda + 0.89 = 0 \tag{1.60}$$

Using the quadratic formula gives eigenvalues λ_1 and λ_2 that are greater than 1, indicating the population will exponentially grow and not settle to a stable state.
Solving Equations: Systems that Change Over Time
Example: Heat Equation Consider a discretized version of the heat equation, modeled using a matrix that describes how heat diffuses between adjacent points in a rod:

$$A = \begin{bmatrix} -2 & 1 & 0 \\ 1 & -2 & 1 \\ 0 & 1 & -2 \end{bmatrix} \tag{1.61}$$

This matrix can be used to predict temperature distribution over time. By finding the eigenvalues and eigenvectors of A, one can determine how quickly heat dissipates or stabilizes across the rod. For example, negative eigenvalues would indicate exponential decay in temperature differences, leading to a steady-state solution.

Tensor Products

The fundamental concept of the tensor product in linear algebra has far-reaching consequences for many scientific and mathematical fields. Its impact extends beyond pure mathematics to quantum computers, quantum mechanics, and other fields. The tensor product easily merges vector spaces, building composite systems from scratch. This capacity to blend and intertwine vector spaces is a powerful mathematical tool for modelling complex physical processes. In quantum computing, these systems generally feature the complex interaction of atoms, subatomic particles, or qubits.
Its foundation is the tensor product's capacity to represent and analyze composite systems. In quantum computing, vector spaces are used to describe qubits, which can exist in superpositions and entangled states. The tensor product describes how qubits interact and evolve within quantum circuits. It allows quantum algorithm construction and analysis by modelling numerous qubits in a quantum register. Quantum mechanics requires the tensor product for composite quantum systems. Imagine two entangled particles with vector spaces describing their quantum states. Tensor products must be used to capture the complicated particle correlations and interactions to understand the composite state of the entangled pair. This is crucial to understanding quantum entanglement, which has major implications for quantum physics.
Several domains use tensor products beyond quantum mechanics. They are used in machine learning, especially tensor decompositions, to analyze higher-order data structures and extract useful information from multidimensional datasets. In multilinear signal

processing, tensor products provide a strong framework for examining complex relationships in multidimensional data. The tensor product is a unifying language that spans disciplines. It allows researchers and scientists to study quantum, multidimensional, and abstract complicated systems, making it an essential tool in the ever-changing world of mathematics, science, and technology.

Basics of Tensor Products

Tensor Product of Vector Spaces Let's start by understanding the tensor product of two vector spaces V and W. The tensor product $V \otimes W$ is a new vector space formed by combining elements from both V and W.
For example, if V is a vector space spanned by v_1,v_2 and W is a vector space spanned by w_1,w_2, the tensor product $V \otimes W$ would include elements like $v_1 \otimes w_1$, $v_2 \otimes w_1$, $v_1 \otimes w_2$, $v_2 \otimes w_2$.
Notation
The tensor product is often denoted using the symbol $\otimes$, and the resulting elements are represented with this symbol. For example,
$v \otimes w$ represents an element in the tensor product of $V \otimes W$.
Composite Systems in Quantum Mechanics: In quantum mechanics, particles are often described by vector spaces, and the tensor product allows us to describe composite systems made up of multiple particles. For instance, if one particle is described by the vector space and V and another by W, the combined system is described by $V \otimes W$.
This is essential in quantum computing, where qubits are often represented as vector spaces, and tensor products model the behavior of multiple qubits in a quantum register.
Tensor Products of Matrices: Tensor products can also be applied to matrices, providing a way to describe transformations on composite systems. The tensor product of two matrices A and B, denoted as $A \otimes B$, is defined as follows: If A is *mxn* matrix and B is *pxq* matrix, then $A \otimes B$ is an *mpxnq* matrix obtained by replacing each element a_{ij} in A with a_{ij}B, resulting in a block matrix.
Let's look at an example.

$$A = \begin{bmatrix} 1 & 2 \\ 3 & 4 \end{bmatrix}$$

and

$$B = \begin{bmatrix} 0 & 5 \\ 6 & 7 \end{bmatrix}$$

The tensor product $A \otimes B$ would be a 4×4 block matrix.

$$A \otimes B = \begin{bmatrix} 1 \cdot B & 2 \cdot B \\ 3 \cdot B & 4 \cdot B \end{bmatrix} = \begin{bmatrix} 0 & 5 & 0 & 10 \\ 6 & 7 & 12 & 14 \\ 0 & 15 & 0 & 20 \\ 18 & 21 & 24 & 28 \end{bmatrix}$$

Properties of Tensor Products

The tensor product, denoted by $\otimes$, has several important properties in linear algebra and quantum mechanics:

1. **Bilinearity:**

$$(a\mathbf{u} + b\mathbf{v}) \otimes \mathbf{w} = a(\mathbf{u} \otimes \mathbf{w}) + b(\mathbf{v} \otimes \mathbf{w}), \quad \mathbf{u} \otimes (a\mathbf{v} + b\mathbf{w}) = a(\mathbf{u} \otimes \mathbf{v}) + b(\mathbf{u} \otimes \mathbf{w})$$

This property shows that the tensor product is distributive over addition and respects scalar multiplication.

2. **Associativity:**

$$(\mathbf{u} \otimes \mathbf{v}) \otimes \mathbf{w} \cong \mathbf{u} \otimes (\mathbf{v} \otimes \mathbf{w})$$

The symbol $\cong$ denotes that these spaces are canonically isomorphic, meaning that the grouping in tensor products does not affect the outcome up to a natural isomorphism.

3. **Non-commutativity:**

$$\mathbf{u} \otimes \mathbf{v} \neq \mathbf{v} \otimes \mathbf{u}$$

In general, the tensor product is not commutative, although in many contexts (e.g., finite-dimensional vector spaces over $\mathbb{C}$), there exists a natural isomorphism between $U \otimes V$ and $V \otimes U$.

4. **Dimensionality:**

$$\text{If } \dim(U) = m \text{ and } \dim(V) = n, \text{ then } \dim(U \otimes V) = m \times n.$$

5. **Universal Property:**
For any bilinear map $B : U \times V \to W$, there exists a unique linear map

$$\tilde{B} : U \otimes V \to W$$

such that

$$B(u,v) = \tilde{B}(u \otimes v).$$

6. **Basis Vectors:**

   If $\{u_i\}$ is a basis for U and $\{v_j\}$ is a basis for V, then $\{u_i \otimes v_j\}$ forms a basis for $U \otimes V$.

7. **Applications in Quantum Mechanics:** The state space of a composite quantum system is given by

$$\mathcal{H}_1 \otimes \mathcal{H}_2,$$

   where $\mathcal{H}_1$ and $\mathcal{H}_2$ are the state spaces of the component systems.

Orthonormal Properties

An orthonormal basis in the tensor product space $V \otimes W$ can be constructed from orthonormal bases of V and W.
Suppose $\{e_i\}$ is an orthonormal basis for V and $\{f_j\}$ is an orthonormal basis for W. The set $\{e_i \otimes f_j\}$ forms an orthonormal basis for $V \otimes W$. This means:
1. **Orthonormality**:

$$\langle e_i \otimes f_j, e_k \otimes f_l \rangle = \langle e_i, e_k \rangle_V \cdot \langle f_j, f_l \rangle_W = \delta_{ik}\delta_{jl}$$

Here, δ_{ik} and δ_{jl} are Kronecker deltas, which are 1 if the indices are equal and 0 otherwise.
2. **Completeness**: The set $\{e_i \otimes f_j\}$ spans $V \otimes W$, meaning any element in $V \otimes W$ can be expressed as a linear combination of these basis elements.

Example

Let $V = \mathbb{R}^2$ and $W = \mathbb{R}^2$ with standard orthonormal bases $\{e_1, e_2\}$ for V and $\{f_1, f_2\}$ for W, where:

$$e_1 = \begin{pmatrix} 1 \\ 0 \end{pmatrix}, e_2 = \begin{pmatrix} 0 \\ 1 \end{pmatrix}, f_1 = \begin{pmatrix} 1 \\ 0 \end{pmatrix}, f_2 = \begin{pmatrix} 0 \\ 1 \end{pmatrix}$$

The set $\{e_i \otimes f_j\}$ consists of:

$$\{e_1 \otimes f_1, e_1 \otimes f_2, e_2 \otimes f_1, e_2 \otimes f_2\}$$

Each tensor product in this set is a matrix:

$$e_1 \otimes f_1 = \begin{pmatrix} 1 \\ 0 \end{pmatrix} \otimes \begin{pmatrix} 1 \\ 0 \end{pmatrix} = \begin{pmatrix} 1 & 0 \\ 0 & 0 \end{pmatrix}$$

$$e_1 \otimes f_2 = \begin{pmatrix} 1 \\ 0 \end{pmatrix} \otimes \begin{pmatrix} 0 \\ 1 \end{pmatrix} = \begin{pmatrix} 0 & 1 \\ 0 & 0 \end{pmatrix}$$

$$e_2 \otimes f_1 = \begin{pmatrix} 0 \\ 1 \end{pmatrix} \otimes \begin{pmatrix} 1 \\ 0 \end{pmatrix} = \begin{pmatrix} 0 & 0 \\ 1 & 0 \end{pmatrix}$$

$$e_2 \otimes f_2 = \begin{pmatrix} 0 \\ 1 \end{pmatrix} \otimes \begin{pmatrix} 0 \\ 1 \end{pmatrix} = \begin{pmatrix} 0 & 0 \\ 0 & 1 \end{pmatrix}$$

These matrices form an orthonormal basis for $\mathbb{R}^2 \otimes \mathbb{R}^2$.

Orthogonal property

In mathematical terms, if vectors $\mathbf{u}_1$ and $\mathbf{u}_2$ are orthogonal in a vector space U, and $\mathbf{v}_1$ and $\mathbf{v}_2$ are orthogonal in another vector space V, then their tensor products are orthogonal in the tensor product space $U \otimes V$. This can be expressed as:

$$\langle \mathbf{u}_1, \mathbf{u}_2 \rangle = 0 \quad \text{and} \quad \langle \mathbf{v}_1, \mathbf{v}_2 \rangle = 0 \implies \langle \mathbf{u}_1 \otimes \mathbf{v}_1, \mathbf{u}_2 \otimes \mathbf{v}_2 \rangle = 0$$

Here, $\langle \cdot, \cdot \rangle$ denotes the inner product in the respective vector spaces. The result follows from the properties of the tensor product and the inner product:

$$\langle \mathbf{u}_1 \otimes \mathbf{v}_1, \mathbf{u}_2 \otimes \mathbf{v}_2 \rangle = \langle \mathbf{u}_1, \mathbf{u}_2 \rangle \cdot \langle \mathbf{v}_1, \mathbf{v}_2 \rangle = 0 \cdot 0 = 0$$

This property is particularly important in quantum mechanics, where the orthogonality of states is related to their distinguishability and independence.

Abstract Algebra

Abstract algebra is a branch of mathematics that investigates algebraic structures beyond familiar arithmetic operations. It provides a powerful framework for studying the properties and relationships of abstract mathematical objects. In abstract algebra, groups, rings, and fields are three fundamental algebraic structures. This exploration will delve into each of these structures and examine their essential properties and significance in mathematics and various applications.

Groups

A group is a set **G** combined with an operation "·" that satisfies four fundamental properties including,

1. **Closure:** For every a, b $\in$G, the result of the operation a·b is also in G.
2. **Associativity:** For every a, b, c $\in$G, (a·b)·c = a·(b·c)
3. **Identity Element:** There exists an element *e* $\in$G such that for every element a $\in$G, the equation e·a = a·e = a holds.
4. **Inverse Element:** For each a $\in$G, there exists an element b $\in$G such that a ·b = b ·a = e, where e is an identity element.

Groups play a crucial role in comprehending symmetries, quantum gates, and their actions in the field of quantum computing. For instance, the collection of all conceivable rotations of a quantum state constitutes a group, whereby the operation is the amalgamation of rotations, the identity element is the zero rotation (which does not alter the state), and each rotation possesses an inverse (a rotation that reverses the original rotation).

Rings

A ring is a set R equipped with two operations: addition(+) and multiplication (.) which satisfy the following properties:

1. **Addition**: forms an abelian group with R.
2. **Multiplication**: is associative. For any *a, b,* c $\in$R, *(a·b)·*c = *a·*(*b·*c)
3. **Distributive Law**: For any *a, b,* c $\in$R, *a·*(*b*+c) = *a·b* + *a·*c *and* c·(*a*+*b*) = c·*a* + c·*b*

The examination of polynomial rings holds significant importance in the field of study since they play a pivotal role in comprehending error correction codes within the realm of quantum computing. One application of polynomial rings is their utilization in the construction of quantum error-correcting codes, which serve to safeguard quantum information against faults that may arise during quantum computation and communication.

Fields

A field is a ring F in which every non-zero element has a multiplicative inverse, turning F into an abelian group under multiplication as well. Thus, a field is a set with two operations, addition and multiplication, satisfying the properties.

1. **Addition** and **multiplication** form abelian groups.
2. **Multiplicative Inverse:** For every non-zero element $a^{-1} \in F$, there exists an element a^{-1} such that a·a^{-1} = a^{-1} ·a = 1, where 1 is multiplicative identity.
3. **Distributivity** of multiplication over addition as in rings.

The utilization of fields is of utmost importance in developing quantum algorithms and establishing quantum error-correcting codes. The process of manipulating qubits, the fundamental units of quantum information, frequently entails performing operations defined within the framework of finite fields. An example of this is Shor's algorithm, which utilizes field arithmetic to determine the periods of functions. This step is crucial for efficiently factorizing numbers on a quantum computer.

Examining groups, rings, and fields can help one comprehensively comprehend the mathematical structures that underlie quantum computing. Abstract algebra principles facilitate quantum algorithms, error correction codes, and the manipulation of quantum states. Researchers and practitioners in the field of quantum computing, especially those engaged in quantum algorithms and quantum information theory, must possess a profound comprehension of these algebraic structures.

Conclusion

This chapter has examined the fundamental mathematical principles that serve as the basis of quantum computing. Through an exploration of linear algebra, complex numbers, trigonometry, and abstract algebra, we have acquired the required skills to comprehend and manipulate quantum systems. Understanding these mathematical principles is essential not only for grasping the theoretical foundations of quantum mechanics but also for executing and evaluating quantum algorithms. As we delve into more intricate subjects, the strong mathematical groundwork established in this chapter will empower us to confront the intricacies of quantum computation with assurance and exactitude. This comprehension is essential as we persist in investigating the extensive and thrilling opportunities presented by quantum technology.

In the next chapter, we will study the foundations of quantum mechanics, which will help you appreciate the principles of quantum computing taught in the book's later chapters.

CHAPTER 2

Quantum Mechanics

Introduction

Quantum mechanics is the foundational theory that governs the behavior of particles at the tiniest sizes, serving as the basis for all quantum computers. This chapter presents the fundamental ideas and concepts of quantum mechanics, which are crucial for comprehending the functioning of quantum computers. We will investigate the phenomenon of wave-particle duality, the principle of superposition, the concept of entanglement, and the probabilistic characteristics of quantum measurements. Through an exploration of the mathematical principles behind quantum mechanics, such as the Schrödinger equation, operators, and eigenstates, our goal is to provide you with the understanding needed to comprehend the complexities of quantum algorithms and how they are put into practice. Clearly, comprehending this concept is essential as we connect the disparity between theoretical quantum theory and its tangible implementations in the rapidly growing domain of quantum computing.

Structure

In this chapter, we are going to study:

- Foundations of Quantum Mechanics
    - Black-Body Radiation

    - Photoelectric Effect
    - Compton Effect
- Particles, Spins and Angular Momentum
    - Particles in Quantum Mechanics
    - Spins
    - Angular Momentum
- Postulates of Quantum Mechanics
    - Postulate 1 - The Wave Function
    - Postulate 2 - Experimental Observables
    - Postulate 3 - Individual Measurements
    - Postulate 4 - Expectation Values and Collapse of the Wavefunction
    - Time Evolution
- Quantum Bits (Qubits)
    - Classical Bits versus Qubits
    - Realization of Qubits
- Quantum Measurements
    - Basic Principles of Quantum Measurements
    - Measurement Problem and Interpretations
    - Practical Implications and No-Cloning Theorem
- Density Matrices for Mixed and Pure States
    - Density Matrices
    - Pure versus Mixed States
- Applications of Quantum Mechanics
    - MRI and NMR Spectroscopy
    - Semiconductor Technologies
    - Quantum Sensing and Metrology

Foundations of Quantum Mechanics

To explain experimental observations that were otherwise completely unexplainable, the concepts of quantum mechanics were developed. The period of innovation spanned from 1900, when Max Planck introduced the groundbreaking concept of quantization, to 1925, when Erwin Schrödinger and Werner Heisenberg independently presented two mathematically distinct but equivalent formulations of a comprehensive quantum mechanical theory. The Heisenberg method utilizes the properties of matrices, whereas the Schrödinger method employs partial differential equations. We will employ Schrödinger's methodology as it is more accessible to students who are typically more acquainted with elementary calculus rather than matrix algebra. Additionally, this approach offers a direct understanding of charge distributions in molecules, which is a fundamental aspect of chemistry.

Heisenberg and Schrödinger drew inspiration from four crucial experimental observations: the spectral distribution of black-body radiation , the properties of the photoelectric effect, the Compton effect, and the luminescence spectrum of the hydrogen atom. The elucidation of these phenomena necessitated the introduction of two groundbreaking concepts.

Physical quantities that were once believed to be continuously variable, such as energy and momentum, are actually quantized. The momentum, denoted as p, and the wavelength, denoted as λ, are related by the equation $p = h\lambda$, where h is a fundamental constant. In this chapter, we will employ a quasi-historical methodology to underscore the fact that knowledge was generated by individuals through the creation of novel ideas or concepts. What may not be immediately obvious is that these innovative concepts were initially met with significant doubt, and their adoption was delayed due to alternative suggestions that were not as groundbreaking. The inconsistencies in the counter proposals became apparent only after a certain period of time. When we say "quantized," we are referring to the fact that only specific values are possible or permitted. Money, for instance, is quantized. Money is not distributed in a continuous range of values. In India, the smallest monetary unit is a rupee, and all prices are multiples of a rupee.

Through our education in high school and introductory physics, as well as our observations in daily life, we acquire the knowledge that particles possess momentum, which is the product of their mass and velocity. The wave properties of light, such as interference, diffraction, and refraction effects, clearly illustrate its abstract nature. The fact that there is a correlation between momentum (a characteristic of particles) and wavelength (a characteristic of waves) is both astonishing and groundbreaking, and this correlation applies to both particles and light. The phenomenon known as "wave-particle duality" refers to the fact that particles exhibit wave-like characteristics, while light waves exhibit particle-like characteristics.

Black-Body Radiation

Black-body radiation was a phenomenon that classical physics failed to sufficiently explain. Objects with high temperatures release electromagnetic radiation . At their maximum setting, the burners on the majority of electric stoves emit a vibrant red glow. When a piece of metal is exposed to a flame, it undergoes a process called incandescence. Initially, it emits a dark red glow, which gradually transitions to a white or even blue glow if the temperature reaches a sufficiently high level. An object with high temperature would radiate a substantial quantity of energy in the ultraviolet range of the electromagnetic spectrum , while humans emit energy in the opposite end of the spectrum. The infrared energy can be observed through the utilization of night vision goggles. The specific spectrum is contingent upon the characteristics of the substance and the level of heat. A black-body is a theoretical object that emits radiation across all frequencies, and its spectral distribution is solely determined by its temperature, regardless of its composition. The emission of radiation by an object of this nature is referred to as black-body radiation. Experimental black-body radiation can be obtained by observing the emission of electromagnetic radiation through a small opening in a hollow chamber that is maintained at a consistent temperature.

The relationship between the observed intensity of black-body radiation and the wavelength is dependent on the temperature. Efforts to elucidate or compute this spectral distribution using classical theory were utterly unsuccessful. Rayleigh and Jeans formulated a theory which predicted that the intensity would approach infinity at shorter wavelengths. Due to the fact that the intensity decreases to zero at shorter wavelengths, the Rayleigh-Jeans result was referred to as the "ultraviolet catastrophe." There was a lack of concordance between the theoretical predictions and experimental observations in the ultraviolet portion of the black-body spectrum.

Max Planck was the pioneer in providing a successful explanation for the spectral distribution of black-body radiation. According to him, the radiation was caused by the oscillations of electrons. Likewise, the back and forth movements of electrons in an antenna generate radio waves. Planck's groundbreaking understanding and ingenuity led him to recognize that in order to account for the spectral distribution, he had to postulate that the energy E of the oscillating electrons was quantized and directly proportional to whole number multiples of the frequency v.

$$E = nhv \tag{2.1}$$

Photoelectric Effect

The photoelectric effect occurs when light illuminates a metal surface, resulting in the expulsion of electrons. The quantity of emitted electrons and their kinetic energy can be quantified in relation to the intensity and frequency of the light. At the start of the 20th century, physicists anticipated that the energy contained in a light wave (measured as its intensity in J/m^2s) would be converted into the kinetic energy of the emitted electrons.

Moreover, the quantity of electrons that detach from the metal should vary in accordance with the frequency of the light wave. The correlation between frequency and dependence was anticipated as the oscillating electric field of the light wave induces oscillations in the metal's electrons, which in turn respond at varying frequencies. Put simply, it was anticipated that the quantity of released electrons would be influenced by the frequency, while their kinetic energy would be influenced by the intensity of the light wave (at a constant wavelength).

- The relationship between the kinetic energy of the electrons and the frequency of the incident radiation is directly proportional, but only when the frequency is above a certain threshold value (v0). No current is observed when the frequency is below v0. Additionally, the kinetic energy of the electrons is not affected by the intensity of the radiation.
- The quantity of electrons, which represents the electric current, is directly related to the intensity of light at a specific wavelength. It is not affected by the frequency of the incoming radiation, as long as it exceeds a certain threshold value, denoted as v0. No current is observed when the frequency is below v0.

In 1905, Albert Einstein proposed a hypothesis that the energy carried by light exists in discrete packets of a specific amount, denoted as hv. Each packet or photon has the potential to induce the ejection of a single electron, analogous to the scenario of a moving particle colliding with a stationary particle and transferring its energy. The quantity of electrons emitted is contingent upon the quantity of photons, specifically the intensity of the light. A portion of the energy in the packet is utilized to surpass the binding energy of the electron within the metal. The energy required to remove an electron from a material is known as the work function, □. The residual energy manifests itself as the kinetic energy, 1/2mv^2, of the emitted electron.

Equations express the conservation of energy for the photoelectric process:

$$E_{photon} = K_{Electron} + W_{electron} \tag{2.2}$$

$$hv = 1/2mv^2 + \phi \tag{2.3}$$

Rearranging this equation reveals the linear dependence of kinetic energy on frequency:

$$1/2mv^2 = hv - \phi \tag{2.4}$$

Compton Effect

The Compton effect refers to the phenomenon of x-rays being scattered by electrons in an inelastic manner. Scattering refers to the dispersion of an object in various directions, while inelasticity indicates that the scattered object loses energy during this process. The scattered x-ray's intensity is quantified by measuring its wavelength shift, $\Delta\lambda$.

$$\lambda^{'} = \lambda + \lambda \tag{2.5}$$

In order to elucidate the experimental observations, it is imperative to delineate the scenario in a manner akin to the discussion of two particles, such as marbles, undergoing collision and subsequent scattering. The x-ray undergoes scattering, resulting in the ejection of an electron with mass me from the object. The direction of the ejected electron is such that the momentum of the system is conserved. The scattering angles and observed wavelength shift of the x-ray can be explained by the conservation equations of momentum and energy. In this explanation, the momentum of the x-rays is assumed to be equal to h/λ, and the energy is assumed to be hv.

These factors result in Equation , which explains the empirical observations regarding the change in $\Delta\lambda$ as a function of □. The utilization of energy and momentum conservation in the analysis of the Compton effect's experimental data provides compelling evidence that electromagnetic radiation possesses momentum akin to a particle. Furthermore, the momentum and energy of electromagnetic radiation are determined by the values of h/λ and hv, respectively.

$$\lambda = \frac{h}{m_e c}(1 - cos\theta) \tag{2.6}$$

Particles, Spins and Angular Momentum

In this section we are going to discuss in detail about particles, spin and angular momentum.

Particles in Quantum Mechanics

In the realm of classical physics, particles are commonly conceptualized as minuscule, tangible entities possessing clearly defined attributes, such as their precise position and momentum. However, within the domain of quantum mechanics, particles demonstrate wave-particle duality, indicating their ability to display characteristics of both particles and waves. The duality is represented by the wave function, symbolized as $\psi(x)$, which contains all the details regarding the particle's condition.

The Schrödinger equation dictates the dynamics of the wave function, and its solutions yield the probabilities of detecting the particle in different states. The modulus squared of the wave function, $|\psi(x)|^2$, represents the probability density of locating the particle at a specific position, x. The inherent probabilistic nature is fundamental to quantum mechanics and sets it apart from classical physics.

Spins

Spin is an intrinsic characteristic of elementary particles, such as electrons, protons, and neutrons. Although the term "spin" may bring to mind the idea of a particle physically rotating around an axis, it is important to recognize that spin is an inherent characteristic that has no classical counterpart. Instead, it refers to a type of angular momentum that is naturally present in particles, similar to their inherent rotation in the theoretical space of quantum states. Spin is quantized, meaning it can only take certain discrete values. For instance, the spin of an electron can have two values: +1/2 (spin up) or -1/2 (spin down). These values are represented by quantum numbers: m_s = +1/2 and m_s = -1/2 respectively.

Mathematically, spin is described by spin operators, which are represented by matrices. The Pauli spin matrices, σ_x, σ_y, σ_z are fundamental operators that act on the spin states of particles. These matrices govern how spin interacts with external fields and other quantum systems. The total spin operator, denoted by S is the sum of the spin operators along different axes. For instance, the z-component of the spin operator, S_z, measures the projection of spin along the z-axis.

$$S_z\,|\pm1/2\rangle = \pm1/2h\,|\pm1/2\rangle \tag{2.7}$$

The eigenvalue equations demonstrate the process of quantizing spin along the z-axis, with □ representing the reduced Planck constant.

Spin is a vital factor in dictating the behavior of particles in different physical systems. It impacts their magnetic characteristics, their interactions with electromagnetic fields, and their behavior in quantum computing systems. Comprehending the concept of spin is crucial for comprehending the complexities of quantum mechanics and its practical uses.

Angular Momentum

Angular momentum is of vital importance in both quantum mechanics and classical mechanics. Nevertheless, angular momentum in quantum mechanics is subject to quantization. The total angular momentum operator, represented as J, is the combination of the orbital angular momentum operator L and the spin angular momentum operator S:

$$J = L + S \tag{2.8}$$

where L and S satisfy the commutation relations:

$$[L_i, L_j] = ih\epsilon_{ijk}L_k[S_i, S_j] = ih\epsilon_{ijk}S_k[L_i, S_j] = 0 \tag{2.9}$$

The quantization of angular momentum arises from these commutation relations. The eigenvalues of the total angular momentum operator J^2 and one of its components J_z are provided as follows:

$$J^2 |j, m\rangle = h^2 j(j+1) |j, m\rangle \tag{2.10}$$

$$J_z |j.m\rangle = hm |j, m\rangle \tag{2.11}$$

where j is the total angular momentum quantum number and m is the magnetic quantum number. To summarize, particles in quantum mechanics have inherent characteristics such as spin, which are quantized and described by operators. These properties are essential for comprehending the behavior of quantum systems and are fundamental for applications in quantum computing and other quantum technologies.

Postulates of Quantum Mechanics

To gain a more profound comprehension of quantum mechanics, scientists have formulated a set of axioms that give rise to what are known as postulates of quantum mechanics. These assumptions are necessary for us to comprehend the connection between the observed reality and the mathematical principles of quantum mechanics. It is crucial to observe that the postulates are indispensable for understanding the theory, but they are not necessary for the mathematical calculations involved. Regardless of our interpretation, mathematics remains complete and consistent. There is a lack of consensus regarding the required number of postulates for interpreting the theory, and certain philosophical perspectives or formulations may necessitate more postulates than others. This chapter will examine the six postulates as they are commonly presented in chemistry and introductory physics textbooks, and their connection to a fundamental statistical interpretation of quantum mechanics. Irrespective of the philosophical deliberation regarding the significance and quantities of the postulate, as well as their physical source, these statements will facilitate the understanding of the theory to some extent.

Postulate 1: The Wave Function Postulate

An entire quantum mechanical system's state can be described by a function ψ(r,t) that depends on time and the particle(s)' coordinates. The function in question, known as the wave function or state function, possesses a significant characteristic whereby it is denoted as ψ*(r,t). The expression ψ(r,t) $d\tau$ represents the probability of finding the particle within the small volume element $d\tau$.

The object is situated at position r at a specific moment in time, t. The wave function must adhere to specific mathematical criteria due to its probabilistic interpretation. In the case of a single particle, the probability of locating it anywhere is 1, which satisfies the normalization condition.

$$\int_{-\infty}^{\infty} \Psi^*(r,t)\Psi(r,t)d\tau = 1 \tag{2.12}$$

Additionally, it is common practice to normalize wave functions of many particles to just one. As a result of the first postulate, it is necessary for the wave function to be both single-valued and continuous, with finite values. This allows for the definition and calculation of derivatives at every point in space. This outcome enables the application of operators (which usually involve differentiation) without encountering mathematical problems.

Postulate 2: Experimental Observables

In quantum mechanics, there is a linear Hermitian operator that corresponds to each observable in classical mechanics. This postulate is derived from the observation that the expected value of an operator representing an observable must be a real number. Consequently, the operator itself must be Hermitian. Some examples of the Hermitian Operator are:

Observable	Classical Symbol	Quantum Operator	Operation
position	r	$\hat{r}$	multiply by r
momentum	p	$\hat{p}$	$-i\hbar\left(\frac{\partial}{\partial x}\mathbf{i} + \frac{\partial}{\partial y}\mathbf{j} + \frac{\partial}{\partial z}\mathbf{k}\right)$
kinetic energy	T	$\hat{T}$	$\frac{-\hbar^2}{2m}\left(\frac{\partial^2}{\partial x^2} + \frac{\partial^2}{\partial y^2} + \frac{\partial^2}{\partial z^2}\right)$
potential energy	$V(r)$	$\hat{V}(r)$	multiply by $V(r)$
total energy	E	$\hat{H}$	$\frac{-\hbar^2}{2m}\left(\frac{\partial^2}{\partial x^2} + \frac{\partial^2}{\partial y^2} + \frac{\partial^2}{\partial z^2}\right) + V(r)$
angular momentum	l_x	$\hat{l}_x$	$-i\hbar(y\frac{\partial}{\partial z} - z\frac{\partial}{\partial y})$
	l_y	$\hat{l}_y$	$-i\hbar(z\frac{\partial}{\partial x} - x\frac{\partial}{\partial z})$
	l_z	$\hat{l}_z$	$-i\hbar(x\frac{\partial}{\partial y} - y\frac{\partial}{\partial x})$

Postulate 3: Individual Measurements

When measuring the observable associated with operator $\hat{A}$, only the eigenvalues, a, that satisfy the eigenvalue equation $\hat{A}\Psi = a\Psi$ will be observed. 1

In quantum mechanics, it is postulated that the values of dynamical variables are quantized, meaning they can only take on certain discrete values. However, in the case of unbound states, it is possible for there to be a continuum of eigenvalues. If the system is in an eigenstate of the operator $\hat{A}$ with the corresponding eigenvalue a, then any measurement of the observable A will consistently yield the value a.

While measurement will consistently produce a numerical result, the initial state does not necessarily need to be an eigenstate of $\hat{A}$. An arbitrary state can be expressed as a linear combination of the complete set of eigenvectors of $\hat{A}$, denoted as Ψ_i, where each eigenvector corresponds to an eigenvalue a_i. Mathematically, this can be represented as $\hat{A}\Psi_i = a_i\Psi_i$. The arbitrary state Ψ can then be written as the sum of the coefficients c_i multiplied by the eigenvectors Ψ_i, with n being the number of eigenvectors in the set, which can potentially be infinite. Measurement of A in this scenario will result in the determination of a single eigenvalue, a_i, without knowledge of its specific value. The probability of observing the eigenvalue a_i is determined by the magnitude of the squared coefficient, $|c_i|^2$. The third postulate of quantum mechanics also states that when the measurement of the wavefunction Ψ produces a specific value a_i, the wavefunction undergoes a phenomenon known as "collapse" and transforms into the eigenstate Ψ_i that corresponds to a_i. When a_i is degenerate, the wavefunction Ψ collapses onto the subspace that is also degenerate. Hence, the process of measurement has an impact on the condition of the system, and this phenomenon has been utilized in numerous sophisticated experimental investigations of quantum mechanics, such as Bell's theorem.

Postulate 4: Expectation Values and Collapse of the Wavefunction

If a system is in a state described by a normalized wave function ψ, then the average value of the observable corresponding to $\hat{A}$ is given by:

$$\langle A \rangle = \int_{-\infty}^{\infty} \Psi^* \hat{A} \Psi \, d\tau. \tag{2.13}$$

A significant implication of the fourth postulate is that when the wave function ψ is measured and produces an eigenvalue a_i, it instantaneously "collapses" into the matching eigenstate ψ_i.

There is no text provided. Put simply, the act of measurement has an impact on the condition of the system. This fact is utilized in several experimental tests of quantum physics, such as the Stern-Gerlach experiment. Measuring the spin along a single coordinate alters the wave function itself, changing the course of subsequent experiments rather than merely "filtering" some pre-existing property of the wave function. The collapse of the wave function, a mechanism that is still unknown, correlates to this behavior. It is worth noting that the debate does not lie in the mathematical aspects of the experiment. The challenges mostly arise due to our lack of knowledge in defining the measurement act itself, aside from its identification as a quantum mechanical technique that yields distinct and well-defined macroscopic consequences. The collapse of the wave function is commonly referred to as the measurement problem in quantum mechanics, and it continues to be a subject of investigation and discussion among contemporary scientists.

Postulate 5: Time Evolution

The wave function of a system evolves in time according to the time-dependent Schrödinger equation :

$$\hat{H}\Psi(r,t) = i\hbar \frac{\partial \Psi}{\partial t} \tag{2.14}$$

Postulate 6: Pauli Exclusion Principle

For a system including particles with spin -1/2 (also known as fermions), the entire wave function has to be antisymmetric with respect to the interchange of all the coordinates of one particle with those of another; however, for spin-1 particles (also known as bosons), the wave function is symmetric:

$$\Psi(r_1, r_2, \ldots, r_N) = -\Psi(r_2, r_1, \ldots, r_N) \qquad \text{fermions,}$$
$$\Psi(r_1, r_2, \ldots, r_N) = +\Psi(r_2, r_1, \ldots, r_N) \qquad \text{bosons.}$$

The inclusion of electronic spin is necessary in this set of coordinates. The application of mathematical principles to the concept of anti-symmetry leads to the emergence of the Pauli exclusion principle. This principle asserts that it is impossible for two or more identical fermions to occupy the same quantum state simultaneously, whereas bosons have the ability to do so without any restrictions.

Quantum Bits (Qubits)

Qubits, also known as quantum bits, serve as the basic building blocks of quantum information. They are similar to classical binary bits, but include distinct characteristics that give rise to the exceptional capabilities of quantum computing.

Classical Bits versus Qubits

In the field of classical computing, a bit is the fundamental unit of information, capable of being in either of two distinct states: 0 or 1. Nevertheless, a qubit has the ability to exist not alone in the states representing the traditional 0 or 1, but also in states that are combinations of these classical states. A qubit has the ability to exist in a state of 0, a state of 1, or a combination of both states known as a quantum superposition. The state of the qubit can be expressed as:

$$|\psi\rangle = \alpha\,|0\rangle + \beta\,|1\rangle \tag{2.15}$$

where $|0\rangle\, and\, |1\rangle$ are column operators. Here α and β are complex numbers that describe the probability amplitudes of the qubit's state. The probabilities of the qubit collapsing to either state upon measurement are $|\alpha|^2$ and $|\beta|^2$ respectively, with the condition that $|\alpha|^2 + |\beta|^2 = 1$

Realization of Qubits

Qubits can be physically realized in several ways:

- **Superconducting Circuits:** The type mentioned is extensively utilized in systems produced by prominent firms such as IBM and Google. Microscopic circuits are utilized, which facilitate the passage of currents with minimal resistance. These circuits can exist in superpositions, allowing for the simultaneous flow of currents in both clockwise and counterclockwise directions.
- **Trapped Ions:** Ions are electrically charged atoms that can be confined in electromagnetic fields and cooled using lasers. The intrinsic states of these ions represent qubits.
- **Quantum Dots:** These processes entail confining electrons within a diminutive semiconductor particle. The qubit is determined by either the spin state or the occupancy state, which refers to the presence or absence of an electron.
- **Photonic Qubits:** Qubits are encoded in the properties of photons, specifically their polarization state, in this particular method. This approach has great potential for facilitating high-speed quantum communications.

Qubits are highly fragile and susceptible to losing their quantum characteristics due to phenomena such as decoherence and dissipation. These processes include interactions with the surrounding environment, resulting in the degradation or disappearance of quantum information. Current research is primarily focused on developing methods that can effectively preserve the quantum state of qubits for extended periods of time. Qubits are the fundamental building blocks of quantum computing and possess groundbreaking capabilities that exceed the constraints of classical computing for specific problem types, such as factorization (Shor's algorithm), search algorithms (Grover's algorithm), and simulation of quantum systems. However, the implementation of these capabilities in real-world scenarios continues to be a difficulty due to the complexities associated with quantum information management and the maintenance of qubit system stability.

Quantum Measurements

Quantum mechanics is fundamentally different from classical mechanics, primarily in how we describe the state of a system and how we understand the measurement process. In this section, we will discuss various aspects of quantum measurement and its significance in quantum computing.

Basic Principles of Quantum Measurements

Quantum measurements are a fundamental aspect of quantum mechanics, in which the act of measuring can significantly change the state of the system being observed.

Postulates of Quantum Measurements

Quantum mechanics operates under several key postulates that define how measurements interact with systems:

- **State Vector:** In quantum mechanics, the state of a physical system is described by a state vector, $|\psi\rangle$, which resides in a complex vector space known as Hilbert space. This state vector contains all the information necessary to describe the system's physical properties completely.
- **Effect of Measurement:** When a measurement is made on a quantum system, the state vector $|\psi\rangle$ undergoes a reduction from a possible superposition of states to a single state, which corresponds to the eigenstate of the observable that is being measured. This process is often referred to as the "collapse" of the wave function. The postulate states that if an observable with non-degenerate eigenstates $|\phi_i\rangle$ corresponding to eigenvalues λ_i is measured, and the state of the system is $|\psi\rangle$ then:
  - The probability P_i of the system collapsing to the state $|\phi_i\rangle$ (thus yielding the measurement outcome λ_i) is given by $P_i = |\langle\phi_i|\psi\rangle|^2$.
  - Immediately after the measurement, the state of the system collapses to $|\phi_i\rangle$.

Observables and Operators

In the formalism of quantum mechanics, physical quantities are represented by observables , each associated with a mathematical operator:

- **Hermitian Operators:** Observables in quantum mechanics are represented by Hermitian (or self-adjoint) operators on Hilbert space. These operators have the special property that their eigenvalues are real numbers, which is essential because measurements of physical quantities must yield real values.
- **Eigenvalues and Eigenvectors:** The eigenvalues of a Hermitian operator represent the possible outcomes of measurements of the observable. For each eigenvalue, there corresponds an eigenvector (or a set of eigenvectors) in the Hilbert space, and these eigenvectors represent the states that the quantum system will collapse into when the corresponding eigenvalue is measured. Mathematically, if $\hat{A}$ is a Hermitian operator representing an observable A, and λ is an eigenvalue of $\hat{A}$, then the corresponding

eigenvectors $|\lambda\rangle$ satisfy:

$$\hat{A}\,|\lambda\rangle = \lambda\,|\lambda\rangle \tag{2.16}$$

This equation is known as the eigenvalue equation, and it is central to the quantum theory of measurement.

Born Rule

The Born Rule , named after physicist Max Born, provides the mathematical framework to predict a quantum system's probability distribution of measurement outcomes. It bridges the abstract mathematical description of quantum states in Hilbert space with the actual observable phenomena.

The probability that a measurement of a quantum system described by a normalized state vector $|\psi\rangle$ results in the value λ_i, which is an eigenvalue of the observable represented by operator $\hat{A}$, is given by the square of the absolute value of the projection of $|\psi\rangle$ onto the eigenvector $|\phi_i\rangle$ corresponding to λ_i:

$$P(\lambda_i) = |\langle\phi_i|\psi\rangle|^2 \tag{2.17}$$

where $|\phi_i\rangle$ are the eigenvectors of $\hat{A}$. You have already seen this previously as the effect of measurement as one of the main postulate of quantum measurement.

Example: Measurement of Spin

Consider a quantum system where the observable to be measured is the spin of a particle along the z-axis, represented by the operator $\hat{S}_z$. The eigenvalues of $\hat{S}_z$ might be $+\frac{\hbar}{2}$ and $-\frac{\hbar}{2}$, corresponding to the spin-up and spin-down states along the z-axis. If the system is in a state $|\psi\rangle = \alpha\,|+\rangle + \beta\,|-\rangle$ (where $|+\rangle$ and $|-\rangle$ are the eigenvectors corresponding to the eigenvalues $+\frac{\hbar}{2}$ and $-\frac{\hbar}{2}$ respectively), the probability of measuring the spin as $frac\hbar2$ (and the system collapsing to $|+\rangle$) is $|\alpha|^2$, and the probability of measuring $-\frac{\hbar}{2}$ (collapsing to $|-\rangle$) is $|\beta|^2$.

Measurement Problem and Interpretations

The measurement problem in quantum mechanics is one of the theory's most profound and debated issues. It concerns the nature of the wave function collapse during measurement and how or whether this collapse actually occurs.

Measurement Problem

The measurement problem arises from the dual description of quantum systems: quantum mechanics describes physical systems probabilistically and as existing in superpositions of different states, but measurement outcomes are always definite. The central question is: How does a quantum system transition from a superposition of states (described by a wave function) to a single state, as observed in measurements?

Core Issues:

- **Wave Function Collapse:** Traditional interpretations of quantum mechanics suggest that the wave function collapses upon measurement to one of the eigenstates of the observable being measured. However, this collapse is not described by the unitary evolution of quantum mechanics (as given by the Schrödinger equation), leading to a paradox: how can the deterministic and reversible evolution described by the Schrödinger equation result in the seemingly random and irreversible outcome of measurement?
- **Observer's Role:** What constitutes a "measurement"? Does the observer's interaction with the quantum system trigger the collapse? If so, how and why does this interaction have such a unique effect?

Interpretations of Quantum Mechanics

Several interpretations have been proposed to address the measurement problem, each providing a different perspective on the nature of reality, measurement, and the wave function.

1. Copenhagen Interpretation:

- Developed by Niels Bohr and Werner Heisenberg, this is the traditional "textbook" interpretation of quantum mechanics.
- It posits that the wave function does indeed collapse upon measurement. The wave function is a tool for calculating probabilities of different outcomes, and physical reality does not manifest until a measurement is made.
- The act of measurement causes the wave function to collapse to a definite state, explaining the observed outcome.

2. Many-Worlds Interpretation (MWI):

- Proposed by Hugh Everett in 1957, this interpretation eliminates the wave function collapse.
- All possible outcomes of quantum measurements are physically realized in a "multiverse", where every possible outcome of a quantum interaction is realized in a

branching, parallel universe.

- There is no collapse; instead, the universe splits into multiple universes for each possible outcome of the measurement, with the observer experiencing a different outcome in each branch.

3. **Decoherence and Consistent Histories:**
   - These related interpretations include ideas from decoherence theory , which explains the appearance of wave function collapse as a result of interactions between a quantum system and its environment.
   - Decoherence does not solve the measurement problem on its own but explains how classical-like states emerge from quantum superpositions due to the environment's effect.
   - Classical properties emerge because certain states are "selected" by their robustness against environmental disturbance, not because of a physical collapse.
4. **Pilot Wave Theory (Bohmian Mechanics):**
   - Developed by David Bohm, this theory posits that particles always have definite positions guided by a pilot wave.
   - The wave function never collapses; rather, it guides a hidden variable (the particle's exact position).
   - The apparent randomness of quantum mechanics is due to our ignorance of the hidden variables.
5. **Objective Collapse Theories:**
   - These theories suggest that wave function collapse is an objective physical process that occurs spontaneously when a quantum system reaches a specific complexity or mass.
   - These theories modify the Schrödinger equation to include non-linear terms that cause the wave function to collapse.
   - The collapse is spontaneous and does not depend on observation or measurement.

Practical Implications and No-Cloning Theorem

The no-cloning theorem is a fundamental result in quantum mechanics, imposing strict limitations on what is possible with quantum information processing. This theorem has profound implications across various domains of quantum technology, including quantum computing and quantum cryptography.

No-Cloning Theorem

Statement and Proof

- **Theorem:** It is impossible to create an exact copy of an arbitrary unknown quantum state. This was first clearly formulated by Wootters and Zurek and independently by Dieks in 1982.
- **Proof Outline:**
  - Assume the existence of a universal cloning machine that takes any arbitrary quantum state $|\psi\rangle$ and produces two copies of it. Let this machine act on an arbitrary state $|\psi\rangle$ and a standard state $|s\rangle$, leading to two copies of $|\psi\rangle$:

$$U(|\psi\rangle|s\rangle) = |\psi\rangle|\psi\rangle$$

  - Consider applying this cloning operation to two orthogonal states $|\psi\rangle$ and $|\phi\rangle$. According to the linearity of quantum mechanics, if we apply the cloning machine to a superposition of $|\psi\rangle$ and $|\phi\rangle$, it must produce a state that is the superposition of the cloned states:

$$U\left(\frac{1}{\sqrt{2}}(|\psi\rangle + |\phi\rangle)|s\rangle\right) = \frac{1}{\sqrt{2}}(|\psi\rangle|\psi\rangle + |\phi\rangle|\phi\rangle)$$

  - However, this result contradicts the expected outcome based on linear superposition, where the right side should instead be $\left(\frac{1}{\sqrt{2}}(|\psi\rangle + |\phi\rangle)\right)^2$. This contradiction implies that a universal cloner cannot exist.

Implications

- **Uniqueness:** Each quantum state is fundamentally unique and cannot be perfectly copied without a disturbance. This reflects a core principle of quantum mechanics, where the state of a system is not merely an informational property but an intrinsic nature of the system itself.
- **Information Security:** In quantum cryptography, the no-cloning theorem ensures that any attempt to eavesdrop on quantum communication would necessarily disturb the transmission, making the eavesdropping detectable.

Implications for Quantum Computing and Other Applications

- **Quantum Error Correction:** While the no-cloning theorem prohibits cloning arbitrary states, it does not prevent the development of quantum error correction, which can protect quantum information against errors without needing to know the state itself.

- **State Verification:** Quantum algorithms and protocols must often verify states without directly copying them, relying on indirect measurements and entanglement to ascertain information.
- **Quantum Key Distribution (QKD):** The security of QKD protocols like BB84 derives from the no-cloning theorem. Any attempt by an eavesdropper to intercept and measure the quantum key must irrevocably alter the state, revealing their presence.
- **Transmitting Quantum States:** Quantum teleportation uses entangled pairs to transmit quantum states between two locations without moving the physical particles themselves, circumventing the no-cloning theorem while enabling the transfer of quantum information.

Density Matrices for Mixed and Pure States

In quantum mechanics, the density matrix is a powerful mathematical tool used to describe the statistical state of a quantum system. This concept is particularly useful when dealing with mixed states, where the system may be in one of several states, each with a certain probability. It also elegantly describes pure states and provides a formalism that integrates probability with quantum mechanics.

Density Matrices

The density matrix, also known as the density operator , generalizes the concept of a state vector in quantum mechanics. It is especially useful in situations involving statistical mixtures of states, where a system may be described by multiple states with certain probabilities.

Mathematically, a density matrix ρ for a quantum system is defined such that for any quantum state represented as a vector $|\psi_i\rangle$ in a Hilbert space, the matrix elements ρ_{ij} are given by:

$$\rho_{ij} = \sum_k p_k \langle i|\psi_k\rangle\langle\psi_k|j\rangle \tag{2.18}$$

where p_k are the probabilities associated with each state $|\psi_k\rangle$.

Properties of Density Matrices

- **Hermitian:** Density matrices are Hermitian, meaning $\rho^\dagger = \rho$.
- **Unit Trace:** The trace of a density matrix is one, $\mathrm{Tr}(\rho) = 1$, reflecting the total probability of all possible states.

- **Positive Semi-definite:** All density matrix eigenvalues are non-negative, corresponding to the states' non-negative probabilities.
- **Diagonal Elements:** The diagonal elements of ρ in any basis give the probabilities of the system being found in the corresponding basis states.

Pure versus Mixed States

In this section, we will discuss about pure and mixed states in detail.

Pure States

- A pure state is a quantum state that can be described by a single state vector $|\psi\rangle$ in a complex Hilbert space, such that $\langle\psi|\psi\rangle = 1$. Normalization ensures that the total probability associated with the state is unity. The state vector encapsulates all the information about the quantum state, providing a complete and deterministic description of the system's quantum properties.
  The density matrix for a pure state is the outer product of the state vector with itself:

  $$\rho = |\psi\rangle\langle\psi|$$

  For pure states, $\rho^2 = \rho$, indicating that the matrix is idempotent (i.e., the state is not a mixture but a single state).
  Example: For a pure state $|\psi\rangle = \alpha|0\rangle + \beta|1\rangle$, the density matrix is:

  $$\rho = \begin{bmatrix} |\alpha|^2 & \alpha\beta^* \\ \beta\alpha^* & |\beta|^2 \end{bmatrix}$$

- **Deterministic Evolution:** Under isolated conditions, the evolution of a pure state $|\psi\rangle$ is described by the Schrödinger equation, a deterministic wave equation. This implies that pure states evolve into other pure states unless disturbed or measured.
- **Quantum Coherence:** Pure states maintain quantum coherence, meaning the relative phase between components of the superposition is well-defined and preserved. This coherence is crucial for quantum interference and quantum computational applications.
- **Projection Postulate:** Upon measurement of an observable represented by operator $\hat{A}$ with eigenvalues λ_i and corresponding eigenvectors $|a_i\rangle$, the state $|\psi\rangle$ collapses to one of the eigenstates $|a_i\rangle$ with probability $|\langle a_i|\psi\rangle|^2$.

- **Post-Measurement State:** The post-measurement state is thus $|a_i\rangle$, and the state vector reduction is instantaneous and random, guided by the probability distribution derived from $|\psi\rangle$.

Mixed States

- A mixed state represents a statistical ensemble of different possible states $|\psi_k\rangle$, each with a probability p_k.
- The density matrix for a mixed state is a weighted sum of the density matrices of the pure states that make up the mixture:

$$\rho = \sum_k p_k |\psi_k\rangle\langle\psi_k|$$

where $|\psi_k\rangle$ are the pure states comprising the mixture, and p_k are their respective probabilities, satisfying $p_k \geq 0$ and $\sum_k p_k = 1$.
For mixed states, $\text{Tr}(\rho^2) < 1$, and the matrix is not idempotent, reflecting the statistical mixture of states.
- **Von Neumann Entropy:** Another measure to distinguish between pure and mixed states is the von Neumann entropy, defined as:

$$S(\rho) = -\text{Tr}(\rho \log \rho)$$

For pure states, $S(\rho) = 0$ (indicating no entropy or uncertainty), while for mixed states, $S(\rho) > 0$, reflecting the presence of statistical uncertainty or entropy in the state description.
Example: Consider a mixed state composed of 50% $|0\rangle$ and 50% $|1\rangle$:

$$\rho = 0.5|0\rangle\langle 0| + 0.5|1\rangle\langle 1| = \begin{bmatrix} 0.5 & 0 \\ 0 & 0.5 \end{bmatrix}$$

- **Statistical Mixture:** Mixed states often represent either a statistical mixture of different states due to classical uncertainty about the state of the system or the reduced state of part of a larger entangled system.
- **Decoherence:** In practical scenarios, mixed states can arise due to interactions with the environment where various decoherence processes cause a system initially in a pure state to evolve into a mixed state.
- **Quantum Channels:** Quantum operations on mixed states can be described using quantum channels, which are completely positive, trace-preserving (CPTP) maps.

These maps transform density matrices according to:

$$\rho \to \mathcal{E}(\rho) = \sum_i E_i \rho E_i^\dagger$$

where E_i are operators that satisfy the completeness relation $\sum_i E_i^\dagger E_i = I$.

- **Measurement of Mixed States:** When a quantum measurement is described by a set of measurement operators $\{M_m\}$, the probability of an outcome m is $p_m = \text{Tr}(M_m^\dagger M_m \rho)$, and the state after the measurement is:

$$\rho_m = \frac{M_m \rho M_m^\dagger}{p_m}$$

Applications of Quantum Mechanics

Quantum mechanics, with its principles of superposition , entanglement , and wave-particle duality , has given rise to numerous applications across various fields. These range from technology that impacts our daily lives to sophisticated methods that promise to revolutionize computing, communication, and sensing.

MRI and NMR Spectroscopy

Magnetic Resonance Imaging (MRI) and Nuclear Magnetic Resonance (NMR) spectroscopy are quintessential examples of quantum mechanics applied in both clinical and chemical analysis contexts. These techniques rely on the magnetic properties of atomic nuclei, which can be manipulated and detected using magnetic fields, providing detailed information about the structure, dynamics, and chemical environment of molecules.

Principles of NMR Spectroscopy

Certain nuclei possess intrinsic spin, a quantum mechanical property. Associated with the spin is a magnetic moment, which interacts with external magnetic fields. The most commonly used nucleus in NMR is hydrogen (^1H), due to its abundance in organic compounds and strong magnetic properties.

Mathematical Formulation

- **Larmor Precession:** When placed in a magnetic field B_0, the magnetic moments precess around the field direction at the Larmor frequency, given by:

$$\omega_0 = \gamma B_0$$

where ω_0 is the Larmor frequency and γ is the gyromagnetic ratio, specific to each type of nucleus.

- **Hamiltonian for NMR:** The Hamiltonian describing the interaction of nuclear spins with a magnetic field is:

$$\hat{H} = -\gamma\hbar\hat{I}_z B_0$$

where $\hat{I}_z$ is the spin angular momentum operator along the z-axis (direction of B_0).

Quantum Mechanics in MRI

MRI primarily images the water and fat in the body by detecting the signal from hydrogen nuclei. The technique involves aligning the proton spins using a strong magnetic field, perturbing this alignment with radio frequency (RF) pulses, and then imaging the body by detecting the emitted RF signals as the spins return to equilibrium.

Mathematical Concepts RF Pulses and Spin Dynamics: The application of an RF pulse at the Larmor frequency can be viewed as rotating the magnetization vector away from the magnetic field axis. This is described by the Bloch equations:

$$\frac{d\vec{M}}{dt} = \gamma\vec{M} \times \vec{B}$$

where $\vec{M}$ is the magnetization vector, and $\vec{B}$ is the magnetic field vector, including both the static field B_0 and the RF field.

NMR Spectroscopy: Chemical Shifts and J-Coupling

Chemical Environment Effects

The exact magnetic field experienced by nuclei in molecules is influenced by the electronic environment surrounding them, causing shifts in the resonant frequency, known as chemical shifts. These are crucial for determining molecular structure.

J-Coupling

Coupling between nuclear spins through bond interactions leads to splitting of NMR signals into multiplets, depending on the number and orientation of neighboring spins. This effect, described by:

$$\hat{H}_\text{J} = J\hat{I}_{1z}\hat{I}_{2z}$$

where J is the coupling constant, provides detailed information about the connectivity and geometry of atoms in a molecule.

Semiconductor Technologies

Semiconductor technology is fundamentally rooted in quantum mechanics. The operation of semiconductors hinges on quantum phenomena such as band theory, electron tunneling, and quantum confinement, which govern how electrons behave in solid materials.

Band Theory and Electronic Properties

The electronic properties of semiconductors are understood through band theory, which describes the energy levels available to electrons in solids. In semiconductors, there are two critical energy bands: the valence band, which is normally filled with electrons, and the conduction band, which is higher in energy and typically empty.

Mathematical Formulation

The energy of electrons in a crystal lattice can be described by the nearly free electron model or the tight-binding model. The energy E as a function of wave vector k is given by:

$$E(k) = E_0 \pm \hbar v_F k$$

where E_0 is the energy at the band edge, $\hbar$ is the reduced Planck's constant, v_F is the Fermi velocity, and k is the wave vector describing the electron's momentum in the crystal.

The effective mass m^* of an electron is a concept from semiconductor physics that describes how the electron responds to external forces, particularly electric and magnetic fields:

$$\frac{1}{m^*} = \frac{1}{\hbar^2}\frac{d^2E}{dk^2}$$

This formulation is crucial for understanding carrier mobility in semiconductors.

Quantum Tunneling in Semiconductors

This quantum effect occurs when electrons pass through a potential barrier that they classically shouldn't be able to pass. It is essential in devices like tunnel diodes and certain types of transistors.

Mathematical Description

The probability T that an electron at energy E can tunnel through a barrier of height V_0

and width a is given by:

$$T \approx e^{-2\gamma a}$$

where $\gamma = \frac{1}{\hbar}\sqrt{2m(V_0 - E)}$ is the decay constant of the wavefunction inside the barrier.

Quantum Dots and Quantum Wells

- **Quantum Dots:** Nano-scale semiconductor particles that confine electrons in all three spatial dimensions, leading to discrete quantum states.
- **Quantum Wells**: Semiconductor structures where electrons are confined in one dimension, altering their electronic and optical properties.

Physical and Mathematical Insights

- **Energy Quantization:** In quantum dots, the energy levels are quantized, similar to atoms, and can be described as:

$$E_n = \frac{\hbar^2 \pi^2 n^2}{2m^* L^2}$$

  where L is the size of the quantum dot, and n is a quantum number.
- **Quantum Wells:** The quantization in quantum wells can be modeled by solving the Schrödinger equation for a particle in a box with finite potential walls, leading to sub-bands of energy within the conduction band.

Quantum Sensing and Metrology

Quantum sensing and metrology leverage the unique properties of quantum systems—such as superposition, entanglement, and quantum coherence—to measure physical quantities with unprecedented precision. These techniques are transforming fields like timekeeping, navigation, and diagnostics by pushing the boundaries of measurement sensitivity and accuracy.

Quantum Sensing: Principles and Applications

Foundational Concepts

- Quantum sensors utilize the superposition principle to enhance sensitivity. By placing quantum systems into superposed states, sensors can detect minute changes in the environment that affect the phase between components of the superposition.

- Enhancing measurement sensitivity and overcoming classical noise limitations often involves entangled states. Entanglement can amplify the response of quantum sensors to external perturbations, enabling precision beyond classical measurement strategies.

Applications

- **Magnetic Field Sensing:** Devices like the Nitrogen-Vacancy (NV) center in diamond are used in quantum magnetometry to detect changes in magnetic fields at the nanoscale. These sensors have applications ranging from biomedical imaging to geological exploration.
- **Atomic Clocks:** Quantum metrology is crucial in the development of highly precise atomic clocks using trapped ions or atoms. These clocks use the frequency standards from hyperfine transitions in cesium or rubidium atoms to achieve accuracy for global positioning systems and fundamental physics research.

Quantum Interferometry and Metrology

Technical Aspects

- **Quantum Interferometers:** Quantum interferometry utilizes the wave-like nature of quantum particles. Devices such as the Mach-Zehnder interferometer manipulate the paths of photons or atoms, exploiting interference effects to measure phase shifts with high precision.
- **Sagnac Effect:** This effect is used in rotational measurements and involves a setup where a beam of light (or atoms) is split along two paths that loop and recombine. Rotations of the setup cause phase shifts between the two paths, detectable through changes in the interference pattern.

Mathematical Formulation

Phase Sensitivity: In a simple quantum interferometric setup, the phase sensitivity $\Delta\phi$ can be expressed as:

$$\Delta\phi = \frac{1}{\sqrt{N}}$$

where N is the number of particles or quanta used in the measurement. This represents the standard quantum limit. However, with entangled states, sensitivity can improve to the Heisenberg limit:

$$\Delta\phi = \frac{1}{N}$$

Enhancing Techniques and Quantum Technologies

Heisenberg Limit

- The Heisenberg limit represents the ultimate bound of measurement precision allowable under quantum mechanics, which is achievable through the use of entangled states.
- Achieving this limit involves sophisticated quantum state preparation, control, and measurement techniques, often integrating error correction methods to combat decoherence and operational imperfections.

Noise and Decoherence

- Quantum sensors are sensitive not only to intentional measurements but also to unintentional interactions with their environment, which can introduce noise and loss of coherence.
- Advanced techniques such as dynamical decoupling and quantum error correction are employed to protect quantum states during sensing operations, ensuring that the quantum systems retain their coherent properties long enough to perform precise measurements.

Conclusion

This chapter has provided the necessary foundation for comprehending the intricate and captivating realm of quantum physics, which serves as the fundamental basis for quantum computing. Through the analysis of core concepts like wave-particle duality, superposition, entanglement, and the probabilistic nature of quantum measurements, we have acquired a deeper understanding of how particles behave at the quantum level. Moreover, the mathematical framework, encompassing the Schrödinger equation, operators, and eigenstates, equips us with the essential skills to elucidate and forecast quantum occurrences. Having a solid understanding of this fundamental information is essential for further exploring quantum algorithms and their practical uses. The concepts discussed in this chapter will be essential for us to understand and effectively utilize the capabilities of quantum computing.

The next chapter covers the fundamentals of computation, which will help you understand the differences between classical and quantum computation systems.

CHAPTER 3

Fundamentals of Computation

Introduction

Introducing you to the exciting realm of quantum computing: the "Fundamentals of Quantum Computation," is a crucial chapter. This chapter is intricately designed to connect classical and quantum computing, offering you a strong basis in both areas. Throughout this voyage, you will thoroughly comprehend the fundamental principles underlying computation and how they manifest in classical and quantum environments.

Our research commences by delving into the fundamental nature of computation. Our exploration focuses on the fundamental operations of a classical computer and the entangled states of quantum systems, examining the underlying mechanics that govern the processing of information. Through the analysis of the basic elements of classical computers, including algorithms, data structures, and the important function of programming languages, particularly Python, we provide the foundation for interacting with quantum technology. Python is a highly adaptable programming language that is used not only for traditional software development but also as the foundation of IBM's Qiskit, a prominent framework for quantum computing.

Gaining a clear comprehension of the characteristics and constraints of classical computing will shed light on the reasons why quantum computing signifies a substantial change in perspective. We will extensively examine computational complexity, specifically emphasizing how the efficiency of algorithms, in terms of both time and space, can significantly impact problem-solving abilities. This topic provides the foundation for understanding the concept of quantum advantage, which refers to the ability of quantum algorithms to achieve exponential improvements in speed compared to classical algorithms.

This chapter focuses on the fundamental comparison between classical and quantum computing. Our objective is to emphasize each technique's unique benefits and possible limitations, offering clear guidance on the appropriate circumstances and rationale for employing quantum computing. This comparison enhances your academic knowledge and equips you with practical applications.

Structure

In this chapter, we are going to study:

- Understanding Computation
  - Historical Context
  - Computation in Classical Computation
  - Computation in Quantum Computation
  - Theoretical Models of Computation
- Basics of Classical Computing and Circuits
  - Logic Gates and Circuits
  - From Gates to Processors
  - Programming in Classical Computing
  - Practical Application: Building a Basic Circuit
- Computational Complexity - Time and Space
  - Time Complexity
  - Polynomial versus Exponential Complexity
  - Complexity Classes
  - Practical Example: Analyzing Algorithm Complexity
- Classical Computing versus Quantum Computing
  - Theoretical Foundations and Computational Models
  - Parallelism and Entanglement
  - Practical and Technological Challenges

Understanding Computation

Computation is the act of using a predetermined set of rules to convert an input into an output. This transformation entails manipulating data or executing algorithms to solve issues, carry out calculations, or process information. Algorithms are the fundamental concept in computation. They are precise instructions that guide the processing of information step-by-step.

Historical Context

The notion of computing dates back to ancient tools like the abacus and mechanical devices like the Antikythera mechanism. The formal investigation of computation commenced in the 20th century alongside the introduction of digital computers. Alan Turing and John von Neumann were influential in establishing the fundamental theories that currently shape the discipline of computer science. One of their significant contributions was the creation of the Turing machine model , which accurately represents the core principles of algorithmic processing.

Computation in Classical Computing

In classical computing, computation is performed using classical bits with a well-defined state of 0 or 1. Bits are the fundamental data units of traditional computer systems, and they are manipulated using logical gates and circuits to carry out operations. Programming languages such as Python and Java, which are predominantly procedural and object-oriented, enable the creation of algorithms that govern these actions.

The classical model of computation entails inputting data into memory, manipulating it using a central processor based on the instructions provided by a program, and subsequently producing the desired outcomes. This sequential set of instructions is ideal for algorithmically simple jobs where each step logically proceeds from the previous one.

Computation in Quantum Computing

Quantum computing utilizes quantum bits or qubits, which can concurrently exist in various states due to the principle of superposition. This enables a more intricate and subtle type of computation capable of doing numerous calculations simultaneously. In addition, qubits can become entangled, which implies that the state of one qubit can be influenced by the state of another qubit, regardless of the distance between them. This adds a novel level of intricacy and capacity that is absent in traditional computing. Quantum algorithms exhibit inherent dissimilarities in their structure and abilities. They can effectively handle specific issue types by leveraging quantum features, including superposition, entanglement, and quantum interference.

Theoretical Models of Computation

The study of computation is facilitated through the use of well-defined theoretical models such as the Turing machine, which is employed for classical computing, and the quantum circuit model, which is utilized for quantum computing. These models assist researchers and computer scientists in comprehending the constraints and capacities of various computational paradigms.

The Turing machine paradigm, for instance, aids in delineating the problems that may be resolved using algorithms and determining the lowest resources required to solve them. The quantum circuit model elucidates the utilization of quantum gates to manipulate qubits and accomplish computation that harnesses quantum mechanical events.

Basics of Classical Computing and Circuits

Classical computing relies on the binary number system and employs classical bits , which can exist in either the state of 0 or 1. The binary system serves as the foundation for all conventional computing hardware and software, serving as the fundamental framework for computational logic and data storage in a wide range of devices, from basic calculators to advanced supercomputers. At its most basic level, a classical computer comprehends and manipulates binary codes, which are sequences consisting of 0s and 1s. Each bit corresponds to a binary state, either on or off, true or false. Multiple bits are employed to encode more intricate information, such as numbers, characters, and various data kinds. Binary logic is a simple yet potent system that enables the depiction and manipulation of all types of data.

Logic Gates and Circuits

Logic gates are the building blocks of digital circuits, the physical counterpart of Boolean functions in software. A logic gate takes one or more binary inputs and produces a binary output based on a specific rule. Common logic gates include:

- **AND Gate:** Outputs true (1) only if all inputs are true.
- **OR Gate:** Outputs true if at least one input is true.
- **NOT Gate:** Outputs the opposite of the input.

Complex operations in computing are achieved by combining these basic gates into circuits. These circuits can execute more sophisticated operations needed in computations, such as addition, multiplication, and comparison.

From Gates to Processors

Integrated circuits , or microchips, consist of millions of tiny transistors that function as logic gates. Processors are made of these microchips and serve as a computer's central processing unit (CPU), where actual computations are carried out. The CPU performs the computer's functions as dictated by the software through a sequence of operations on bits. **The Architecture of Classical Computers:** The architecture of classical computers can generally be described using the von Neumann architecture, which includes components such as:

- **Central Processing Unit (CPU):** Executes instructions from programs.
- **Memory:** Stores data and instructions needed by the CPU.
- **Input/Output Devices:** Allow the computer to communicate with the external world.
- **Storage:** Provides long-term data retention.

These components are interconnected by a system bus or a set of electrical channels that allow data to travel between them.

Programming in Classical Computing

Programming languages in classical computing exhibit significant diversity. However, their primary purpose is to facilitate human communication with computers. The spectrum of programming languages spans from low-level languages, which closely resemble the machine's binary code, to high-level languages, such as Python, which are more detached from the underlying hardware. Python is renowned for its simplicity and readability, making it ideal for both novices and experts. It functions as a versatile instrument in classical computing, capable of performing tasks ranging from simple arithmetic to overseeing extensive data systems.

Practical Application: Building a Basic Circuit

Consider building a simple digital circuit using logic gates to solidify your understanding of classical computing. For example, creating a circuit that adds two bits is an excellent exercise to apply the concepts of AND, OR, and NOT gates. This reinforces theoretical knowledge and provides practical experience in how digital logic forms the basis of more complex computations. Gaining a thorough comprehension of the fundamental principles of classical computing and circuits is essential to fully grasping how computers carry out activities at a fundamental level. As we delve into the topic of quantum computing, you will observe how these principles lay the foundation for a forthcoming era of computing characterized by enhanced capabilities and efficiencies.

Computational Complexity - Time and Space

Computational complexity is a field within theoretical computer science that aims to categorize computational problems based on their inherent level of difficulty and measure the resources required to solve them. The main factors taken into account are time and space resources, specifically the duration required to solve a problem and the amount of memory needed.

Time Complexity

Time complexity is a quantitative measure of the computational time required for an algorithm to finish based on the size of the input. It is commonly represented using big O notation, which gives an upper limit on the pace at which the runtime increases.

- **Constant Time (O(1)):** The execution time is the same regardless of the input size.
- **Linear Time (O(n)):** The execution time grows linearly with the input size.
- **Quadratic Time (O(n^2)):** The execution time grows quadratically with the input size.
- **Exponential Time (O(2^n)):** The execution time grows exponentially based on the input size.

Comprehending these categorizations aids programmers in selecting the most effective algorithms, especially in data-intensive applications where the speed of execution is crucial. Space complexity refers to the overall memory need of an algorithm, encompassing the space needed for input data, additional space for computations, and space for output. Similar to time complexity, space complexity is likewise represented using big O notation. Minimizing space complexity is essential for optimizing performance in situations with restricted memory resources, and it can also decrease time complexity in cases where accessing physical memory is a limiting factor.

Polynomial versus Exponential Complexity

- **Polynomial Time Algorithms:** These are algorithms whose time complexity can be expressed as a polynomial function of the size of the input data. They are considered efficient and feasible for practical use.
- **Exponential Time Algorithms:** These involve time complexities that grow exponentially with the input size and are generally impractical for large datasets.

The distinction between polynomial and exponential time algorithms is pivotal in understanding the potential advantages of quantum computing, as quantum algorithms can turn some classically exponential problems into polynomial ones.

Complexity Classes

The study of computational complexity also involves categorizing problems into classes based on the resources needed to solve them:

- **P (Polynomial Time):** The class of decision problems that can be solved by a deterministic Turing machine using a polynomial amount of computation time.
- **NP (Nondeterministic Polynomial Time):** Problems for which a solution can be verified in polynomial time by a deterministic Turing machine.
- **NP-Complete and NP-Hard:** These are the most difficult problems within NP, where NP-complete problems are as hard as any problem in NP, and NP-hard problems are at least as hard as any problem in NP, not necessarily being in NP themselves.

Practical Example: Analyzing Algorithm Complexity

Consider a simple sorting algorithm, like bubble sort, which has a time complexity of O(n^2) and a space complexity of O(1). Analyzing why this is the case (due to the nested loops for comparing elements and the constant space for swapping elements) helps illustrate how algorithm design impacts computational efficiency.

Gaining a thorough grasp of computational complexity in relation to time and space is crucial for developing efficient algorithms and for comprehending the quantum advantage. This knowledge not only assists in the actual construction of algorithms but also in the field of theoretical computer science, where it influences our comprehension of what can and cannot be computed effectively. As we delve into the differences between classical and quantum computing, it is important to consider these intricacies, as they emphasize the revolutionary capabilities of quantum algorithms.

Classical Computing versus Quantum Computing

In this section, we explore the differences between classical computing and quantum computing by analyzing various important factors that provide an idea of why quantum computing is an important area of study and the advantages of pursuing a career in this field.

Theoretical Foundations and Computational Models

Classical Computing

- Classical bits are the basic units of information in classical computing, representing a logical state (0 or 1).
- Classical computation uses a variety of logical gates (AND, OR, NOT, XOR, NAND, and more) to perform operations. Each gate takes one or more input bits and produces an output bit. Computations are deterministic where the output of operations is directly determined by the inputs.

Quantum Computing

- Quantum bits or qubits are the fundamental units of information, represented mathematically by normalized vectors in a two-dimensional Hilbert space. The state of a qubit is described by a linear combination of the basis states $|0\rangle$ and $|1\rangle$:

$$|\psi\rangle = \alpha|0\rangle + \beta|1\rangle$$

  where α and β are complex numbers satisfying $|\alpha|^2 + |\beta|^2 = 1$.
- Quantum gates manipulate qubits through unitary operations, represented by unitary matrices. Common quantum gates include:
  - Pauli Gate (X):equivalent to classical NOT gate.
  - Hadamard Gate (H): Creates superpositions, represented by the matrix $\frac{1}{\sqrt{2}}\begin{bmatrix}1 & 1\\ 1 & -1\end{bmatrix}$.

- Phase Shift Gate (S): Applies a phase of $\pi/2$, represented by $\begin{bmatrix} 1 & 0 \\ 0 & i \end{bmatrix}$.
- CNOT Gate: A two-qubit gate that flips the second qubit (target) if the first qubit (control) is $|1\rangle$.

Parallelism and Entanglement

- **Classical Parallelism**: Achieved through hardware (multiple processors, cores). Software approaches include parallel algorithms running on distributed systems.
- **Quantum Entanglement** : A unique quantum property where qubits become interdependent such that the state of one (no matter the distance) cannot be described independently of the state of another. Entanglement is crucial for quantum algorithms, enabling correlated computations that are not possible classically.

Algorithmic Implications

- **Shor's Algorithm**: Quantum algorithm for integer factorization runs exponentially faster than the best-known classical algorithm. Shor uses the quantum Fourier transform and relies on the ability of quantum computers to handle superpositions and entanglement.
- **Grover's Algorithm**: Provides a quadratic speedup for unstructured search problems. It uses amplitude amplification, a technique that increases the probability amplitude of the correct answer through a series of operations.

Error Correction and Decoherence

- **Classical Error Correction**:** Uses redundancy (e.g., repeating bits or using error-correcting codes like Hamming, Reed-Solomon).
- **Quantum Error Correction**: More complex due to the nature of qubit states and the no-cloning theorem. Techniques include the use of entangled qubits and syndrome measurements to detect and correct errors without directly measuring the quantum information.

Practical and Technological Challenges

- **Classical Computing**: Mature, with well-established manufacturing, programming, and application development ecosystems.
- **Quantum Computing**: Faces significant challenges, including qubit coherence, error rates, and temperature requirements (millikelvin range for superconducting qubits). Scaling up the number of qubits while maintaining fidelity is currently a major research focus.

Conclusion

This chapter serves as a bridge between the classical and quantum realms, establishing a foundation for your exploration of quantum computer science. By starting with fundamental concepts in computer science, it enables you to grasp the essence of computation in both classical and quantum contexts. The next chapter will you will be introduced to qubit modalities.

CHAPTER 4

Qubit Modalities

Introduction

This chapter explores qubit modalities, which are the physical expressions of abstract quantum notions. We commence by providing a comprehensive introduction to qubits and the fundamental components of quantum information and establish the foundation for exploring its physical manifestation.

Get ready to explore advanced quantum technologies as we dive into the details of superconducting qubits, which are well-known for their ability to scale and reliability. Furthermore, we analyze the intricacies associated with confined ion qubits, photonic qubits, topological qubits, quantum dots, and semiconductor spin qubits, each of which possesses distinct benefits and obstacles.

One will develop a comprehensive understanding of the intricate engineering principles that facilitate the operation of qubit modalities, encompassing superconducting circuits as well as laser-controlled ions. We examine the mechanisms by which qubits manipulate quantum states and engage with their immediate surroundings.

By conducting a comparison study, we highlight the merits and drawbacks associated with each qubit mode, thereby facilitating the identification of the most suitable mode for a certain quantum computing activity. Let us witness the continuous rivalry in quantum research as different modalities strive for dominance in quantum advantage.

Structure

In this chapter, we are going to study:

- Introduction to Qubits
  - Quantum Superposition
  - Quantum Entanglement
- Physical Implementation of Qubits
  - Superconducting Qubits
  - Trapped Ion Qubits
  - Photonic Qubits
  - Neutral Atom-Based Qubits
  - Nuclear Magnetic Resonance Qubits
  - Quantum Dots: Nanoscale Semiconductors for Quantum Computing
  - Semiconductor Spin Qubits: Advancing Quantum Computing with Spin States
  - Topological Qubits
- Comparing Qubit Modalities

Introduction to Qubits

The essential building units of quantum computers are known as qubits, also called quantum bits. In contrast to classical bits, which can exist in either a state of 0 or 1, qubits make use of quantum mechanics to exist in any state of 0 or 1, as well as any quantum superposition of these states. This characteristic, in conjunction with entanglement, makes it possible for quantum computers to carry out specific calculations in a manner that is significantly more effective than that of classical computers. One of the most important aspects of quantum computing is the implementation of qubits in physical systems. This allows for the utilization of a variety of quantum phenomena in order to encode and manipulate information.

Quantum Superposition

One of the most striking properties of a qubit is its ability to exist in a state of quantum superposition. This means that a qubit can be in a state of 0, 1, or any complex linear combination of those states that forms an additional quantum state apart from 0 and 1.

Mathematically, this is represented as

$$|\psi\rangle = \alpha|0\rangle + \beta|1\rangle,$$

where $|\psi\rangle$ is the state of the qubit, $|0\rangle$ and $|1\rangle$ are the basis states (analogous to the classical states 0 and 1), and α and β are complex numbers that describe the probability amplitudes of the qubit being in each state. The probabilities of measuring the state $|0\rangle$ or $|1\rangle$ are $|\alpha|^2$ and $|\beta|^2$ respectively, with the condition that

$$|\alpha|^2 + |\beta|^2 = 1.$$

This superposition principle allows quantum computers to process a vast amount of possibilities simultaneously.

Quantum Entanglement

Quantum entanglement is another key attribute of qubits. It is a phenomenon in which qubits become interconnected so that the state of one qubit can immediately change the state of another qubit, regardless of the distance between the two qubits. As a result of this entanglement, a powerful link is established between qubits, which enables quantum computers to carry out complicated calculations with an efficiency that classical computers cannot match. If two qubits are entangled in a specific manner, for example, knowing the state of one qubit instantaneously gives us the state of the other qubit, regardless of the physical distance that separates them. Aside from the fact that it is fascinating from a theoretical physics perspective, this feature also serves as an essential resource for quantum algorithms and quantum cryptography.

Qubits utilize quantum mechanics' unique and not immediately understood characteristics, such as superposition and entanglement, to carry out operations. In contrast to classical computing, which operates on deterministic and binary principles, quantum operations possess the ability to manipulate qubits in intricate manners, leveraging their superposition and entangled states. The inherent capability of quantum algorithms enables them to address certain problems significantly more efficiently than classical algorithms. As an illustration, quantum algorithms have the potential to generate exponential speedups compared to classical algorithms when applied to tasks such as factoring enormous numbers or mimicking quantum physical processes.

Physical Implementation of Qubits

Transitioning from the theoretical notion of qubits to their tangible manifestation entails encoding quantum information within the physical states of particles or systems that demonstrate quantum mechanical characteristics. Several platforms have been investigated for the realization of qubits, such as trapped ions, superconducting circuits, and photon polarization, among others. Each of these physical systems has a distinct methodology for utilizing quantum mechanics in the field of computing, accompanied by a distinct array of benefits, difficulties, and technological obstacles that must be surmounted.

Making qubits physically tangible is a crucial milestone in the advancement of quantum computing technology. A comprehensive understanding of quantum mechanics, advanced experimental methodologies, and inventive engineering approaches is necessary. As scholars persist in investigating and enhancing these technologies, the capacity of quantum computing undergoes further expansion, holding the potential to fundamentally transform computing by addressing challenges that are presently unsolvable for classical computers.

In summary, qubits play a crucial role in the field of quantum computing, leveraging the intricate and diverse realm of quantum mechanics to present novel processing opportunities. The progression from theoretical quantum bits to their tangible manifestation represents a highly captivating frontier within contemporary scientific and technological advancements. This development holds the potential to revolutionize our methodologies in computation, information processing, and problem-solving across diverse domains.

Superconducting Qubits

Superconducting qubits employ circuit fabrication techniques utilizing superconducting materials that demonstrate quantum mechanical properties under extremely low-temperature conditions. These circuits function within a domain characterized by the absence of resistance to electrical current flow, allowing for the definition of qubit states through the utilization of distinct energy levels. Microwave pulses are used to modify quantum information by causing transitions between different energy levels. Superconducting qubits are advantageous due to the well-established circuit fabrication method, which enables scalability and seamless integration with conventional electronics. Figure 4.1 shows the circuit of a superconducting qubit that has 4 qubits which can be seen in the centre as 4 grayscale boxes.

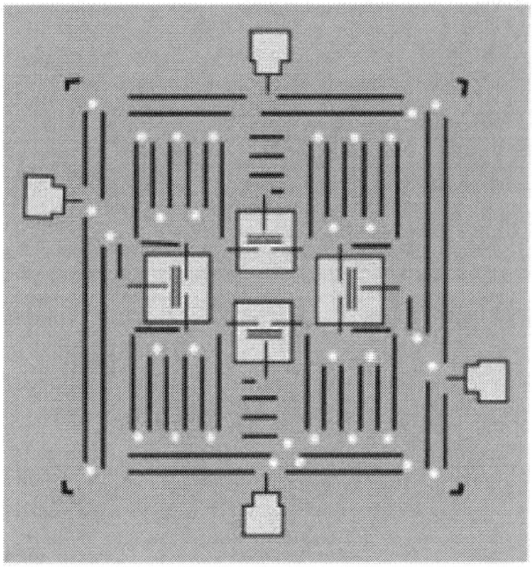

Figure 4.1:
Superconducting Qubit Circuit

Nevertheless, the maintenance of superconductivity necessitates cryogenic temperatures, hence presenting a formidable obstacle and constraint to their application. Superconducting qubits are a very promising and extensively studied technology in the pursuit of constructing a functional quantum computer. In order to encode and manipulate quantum information, these qubits leverage the quantum mechanical properties exhibited by superconducting circuits. In the following text, we explore the intricacies of superconducting qubits, encompassing their operational principles, benefits, drawbacks, existing structures, and prominent firms involved in this field.

Principles of Operation

Superconducting qubits' functionality depends on the quantum characteristics of electrical circuits that function at superconducting temperatures, which are sufficiently low to eliminate electrical resistance. At the given temperatures, it is possible for currents to flow endlessly, resulting in the manifestation of quantum phenomena in the electrical behavior of the circuit.

The Josephson junction is the fundamental element of a superconducting qubit. It is a non-linear superconducting electrical component composed of two superconductors separated by a thin insulating barrier. The junction facilitates the circuit's entry into a quantum superposition of current flows, establishing a system characterized by distinct and quantifiable energy levels that can be employed to delineate qubit states.

Advantages of Superconducting Qubits

- **Scalability:** The scalability of superconducting qubits is facilitated by the fabrication process, which closely mimics that of ordinary semiconductor devices. This similarity enables the potential utilization of existing manufacturing technology to expand the production of quantum processors.
- **Control and Readout:** Superconducting qubits has the capability to be accurately manipulated by the utilization of microwave pulses, enabling rapid readout. This characteristic renders them exceptionally well-suited for the implementation of intricate quantum algorithms.
- **Coherence Times:** The coherence times of superconducting qubits have been gradually growing due to continual advancements in materials and design. This has made them more suitable for quantum processing.
- **High-Fidelity Operations:** Superconducting qubits have exhibited exceptional gate fidelities, which are crucial for error correction and dependable quantum computation.

Disadvantages of Superconducting Qubits

- **Cryogenic Requirements:** Superconducting qubits operate at extremely low temperatures (close to absolute zero), necessitating sophisticated and expensive cryogenic equipment to maintain the operational environment.
- **Decoherence:** Despite improvements, decoherence times for superconducting qubits still pose a limitation, as qubits lose their quantum properties due to interactions with the environment.
- **Scalability Challenges:** While the technology is scalable in principle, integrating a large number of qubits while maintaining low error rates and managing heat dissipation and noise remains a significant engineering challenge.

Current Architecture

The architecture of superconducting quantum computers has evolved significantly, with several designs being explored:

- **Transmon Qubits:** Characterized by their enhanced insensitivity to charge noise, transmon qubits have become a popular design choice. They feature a Josephson junction shunted by a large capacitance to reduce sensitivity to fluctuations.
- **Flux Qubits:** These operate based on the magnetic flux threading the superconducting loop and are more sensitive to magnetic flux than charge.

- **Quantum Annealers:** Specialized quantum processors that use superconducting qubits to perform quantum annealing, a specific type of quantum computation suitable for solving optimization problems.

Leading Companies

Several key players in the tech and research fields are heavily invested in developing superconducting qubits:

- **IBM:** A pioneer in quantum computing, IBM has developed a series of quantum computers based on superconducting qubits, accessible through the cloud on the IBM Quantum Experience platform.
- **Google Quantum AI:** Google has achieved significant milestones with its superconducting quantum processors, claiming to have reached quantum supremacy with its Sycamore processor.
- **Rigetti Computing:** Rigetti focuses on building quantum integrated circuits with superconducting qubits, aiming to provide cloud-based quantum computing services.
- **D-Wave Systems:** Though distinct from general-purpose quantum computers, D-Wave specializes in quantum annealing processors based on superconducting technology, targeting optimization problems.

In summary, superconducting qubits emerge as a prominent technology in the field of quantum computing due to its ability to provide a combination of superior control accuracy, potential for scalability, and seamless integration with current production methodologies. Notwithstanding the obstacles associated with coherence times and cryogenic operation, the persistent investigation and advancement conducted by prominent corporations and research organizations persistently strive to expand the frontiers of what can be achieved through the utilization of superconducting quantum computers.

Trapped Ion Qubits

Trapped ion qubits represent a prominent advancement in the field of quantum computing, as they leverage the distinctive characteristics of ions, which are atoms that have undergone electron loss or gain, to store and manipulate quantum information effectively. This technological approach exploits the intrinsic quantum mechanical states of ions, referred to as qubits, and uses electromagnetic fields to confine and segregate them within a vacuum environment. This section delves into the operating concepts, benefits, drawbacks, existing structures, and prominent entities in the domain of trapped ion qubits.

Principles of Operation

Trapped ion quantum computing involves the confinement and suspension of individual ions in free space through the use of electromagnetic traps, such as Paul or Penning traps. The ions in question function as inherent qubits, wherein their quantum states are determined by distinct energy levels or spin states.

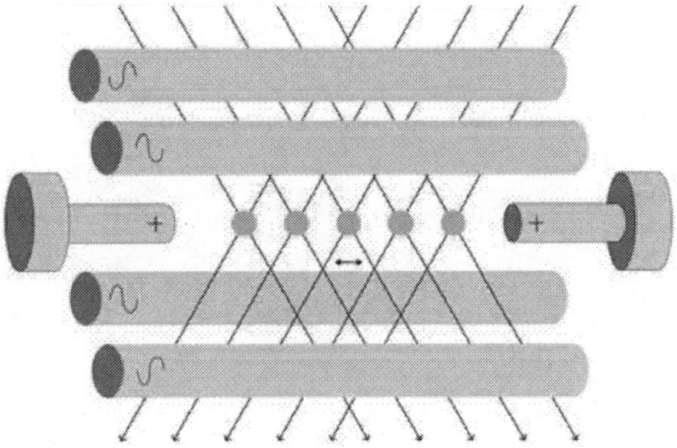

Figure 4.2: Ion Traps

The manipulation of qubit states using precise laser beams allows for the initialization, entanglement, manipulation, and readout of quantum information processing. This can be seen in Figure 4.2 where the arrows represent the laser beams acting on the ions denoted by small circles trapped in a confinement structure. The interaction between ions via Coulombic forces plays a crucial role in enabling multi-qubit operations, which are required for the execution of quantum algorithms.

Advantages of Trapped Ion Qubits

- **High Fidelity Operations:** Trapped ion qubits are renowned for their remarkably high gate fidelities and state preparation and measurement (SPAM) errors, which rank among the most minimal in all qubit technologies. This characteristic is of utmost importance in ensuring dependable quantum computation.
- **Long Coherence Times:** The qubits demonstrate prolonged periods of coherence due to the distinct internal states of the ions, enabling extensive quantum information processing prior to the onset of decoherence.
- **Fully Connected Qubit Architecture:** Trapped ion systems has the inherent capability to engage in long-range Coulomb forces, enabling them to naturally achieve completely connected qubit structures. This characteristic simplifies the design of

quantum algorithms by eliminating the necessity for several swap operations.

- **Scalability:** Contemporary developments indicate prospective avenues for the development of scalable quantum computing architectures, encompassing the utilization of microfabricated ion traps and segmented trap designs.

Disadvantages of Trapped Ion Qubits

- **Complex Laser Systems:** The precision control of trapped ion qubits requires sophisticated and stable laser systems, making the setup complex and costly.
- **Scalability Challenges:** Despite the potential for scalability, practically scaling trapped ion quantum computers to a large number of qubits poses significant engineering challenges, including managing ion heating and cross-talk between qubits.
- **Trap Instabilities:** Maintaining stable trapping conditions over long periods is challenging, as external electromagnetic fields, vacuum quality, and other factors can affect the stability of the traps.
- **Slower Gate Speeds:** Compared to some other qubit technologies, trapped ion qubits typically exhibit slower quantum gate speeds, which could impact the overall computation time for certain quantum algorithms.

Current Architecture

Trapped ion quantum computing has seen the development of various architectures aimed at enhancing scalability and fidelity:

- **Linear Paul Traps:** These are the most common architecture for small-scale trapped ion quantum processors, where ions are linearly aligned and individually addressed with lasers.
- **Micro-fabricated Chip Traps:** Advances in micro-fabrication have led to the development of chip-based ion traps, which promise greater scalability and integration capabilities.
- **Quantum CCD (Charge-Coupled Device):** This architecture proposes using a two-dimensional array of micro-traps to shuttle ions around, enabling large-scale quantum computations by reconfiguring the qubit connections dynamically.

Leading Companies and Institutions

Several companies and research institutions are pioneering the development and application of trapped ion qubits:

- **IonQ:** IonQ has been a leader in trapped ion quantum computing, developing quantum computers accessible through cloud platforms. They focus on improving the scalability and accessibility of their technology.

- **Honeywell Quantum Solutions (now part of Quantinuum):** Honeywell has achieved remarkable success with high-fidelity trapped ion qubits, focusing on creating highly connected and precise quantum computers.
- **AQT (Alpine Quantum Technologies):** AQT is leveraging trapped ion technology to build quantum computers, focusing on scalable solutions and commercial applications.

To summarize, trapped ion qubits occupy a significant role in the field of quantum computing, providing precise operations and extended coherence durations. Despite the presence of hurdles pertaining to scalability and the intricate nature of the laser systems involved, persistent research and development endeavors persist in pushing the limits, rendering trapped ion technology a captivating foundation for forthcoming quantum computers.

Photonic Qubits

Photonic qubits are an advanced kind of quantum computing that leverages the fundamental particles of light, known as photons, to encode and manipulate quantum information. The proposed approach utilizes a range of photon attributes, including polarization , phase , frequency , and route, to establish qubits' states. Photonic quantum computing has a unique array of benefits and encounters certain obstacles, so setting it apart from alternative qubit technologies. This comprehensive examination explores the operational principles, advantages, constraints, existing designs, and prominent stakeholders within the field of photonic qubits.

Principles of Operation

Photonic qubits are generated and controlled through the utilization of light. In contrast to electrons or ions, photons lack charge and exhibit less vulnerability to external interference, rendering them highly suitable for transmitting quantum information across extensive distances.

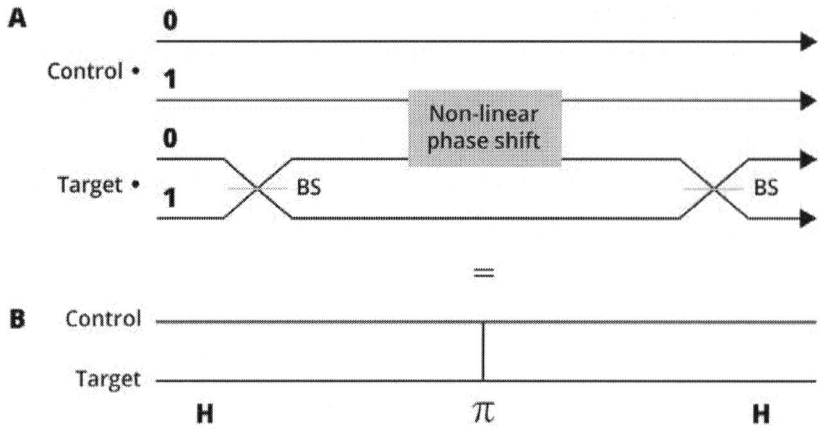

Figure 4.3: Photonic Qubits

Photonic qubits can be subjected to quantum operations through the utilization of linear optical components, including beam splitters, phase shifters, and mirrors. Additionally, non-linear mechanisms can be employed to facilitate intricate interactions. Several architectural approaches are available for the implementation of photonic quantum computing, such as bulk optics, fibre optics, and integrated photonic circuits.

Figure 4.3 depicts a quantum optical setup that utilizes linear and non-linear optics to build a Controlled-NOT (CNOT) gate. In this configuration, the upper line represents the control qubit, which stays unaltered by the optical components, while the lower line represents the target qubit. The target qubit undergoes interactions with two beamsplitters, which are optical devices capable of partially transmitting and reflecting photons. These interactions result in the creation of superpositions of photon states. Within the space defined by these beamsplitters, the system incorporates a non-linear optical interaction, denoted by the yellow box labeled "Non-linear phase shift." This interaction induces a phase shift on the wavefunction of the target qubit, contingent upon the control qubit being in the state $|1\rangle$. The phase shift alters the interference pattern of the photons upon encountering the second beamsplitter.

The second portion of the diagram displays the corresponding quantum circuit representation of this optical arrangement. In this context, the Hadamard gates are utilized to manipulate the target qubit both prior to and subsequent to the phase shift operation. The Hadamard gate is responsible for generating and annihilating superpositions, essentially transforming the state between $|0\rangle$ and $|1\rangle$ or between $|+\rangle$ and $|-\rangle$. The central section of the quantum circuit implements a conditional phase shift of π, resulting in a phase flip in the state of the target qubit. This phase flip is equivalent to the non-linear phase shift observed in the optical circuit.

Advantages of Photonic Qubits

- **High-speed and Long-distance Communication:** Photons travel at the speed of light and can transmit quantum information over long distances with minimal loss, making photonic qubits ideal for quantum communication and networking.
- **Low Decoherence:** Photons do not easily interact with their environment, leading to very low decoherence rates. This property is crucial for maintaining the integrity of quantum information over time and distance.
- **Room Temperature Operation:** Unlike many other qubit technologies that require cryogenic temperatures, photonic quantum computing can often be conducted at room temperature, simplifying the operational infrastructure.
- **Compatibility with Existing Telecommunications Infrastructure:** Photonic qubits can be integrated into existing fiber optic networks, offering a seamless transition towards quantum networking and communication.

Disadvantages of Photonic Qubits

- **Difficulty in Interacting Photons:** One of the biggest challenges in photonic quantum computing is inducing interactions between photons, which are necessary for quantum logic operations. This typically requires nonlinear optical effects, which can be difficult to achieve efficiently.
- **Complexity in Scaling:** Building large-scale photonic quantum computers requires complex optical circuits that can handle many photons simultaneously without losing coherence, posing significant engineering challenges.
- **Error Rates and Loss:** While photonic systems have low decoherence, they are susceptible to photon loss and errors during generation, manipulation, and detection, which can impact the fidelity of quantum operations.

Current Architecture

Photonic quantum computing has explored several architectures, each aiming to optimize the generation, manipulation, and measurement of photonic qubits:

- **Linear Optical Quantum Computing (LOQC):** LOQC uses linear optical elements to perform quantum computations. It relies heavily on single-photon sources, detectors, and optical circuits made from beamsplitters and phase shifters.
- **Integrated Quantum Photonics:** This approach fabricates optical circuits on a chip, allowing for more complex and scalable photonic quantum computing architectures. These integrated circuits can control large numbers of photons with high precision and low loss.
- **Quantum Dot Single-Photon Sources:** Quantum dots can generate single photons

on demand, serving as a critical resource for certain photonic quantum computing architectures. They offer a pathway to deterministic single-photon sources, which are essential for scalable quantum computing.

Leading Companies and Institutions

Several entities are making significant strides in the development and application of photonic qubits:

- **PsiQuantum:** PsiQuantum is working on building a large-scale photonic quantum computer, focusing on leveraging integrated photonics to overcome scalability challenges.
- **Xanadu Quantum Technologies:** Xanadu specializes in quantum computing based on photonic qubits, developing both hardware and software platforms aimed at harnessing the power of quantum computing for various applications.
- **QuantumCTek:** QuantumCTek is focused on quantum communication solutions, utilizing photonic qubits for secure quantum networks and cryptography.

In summary, photonic qubits present a distinctive and auspicious methodology for quantum computing and communication, characterized by their exceptional velocity, little decoherence, and ease of integration with current telecommunications infrastructure. Ongoing research and development efforts are facilitating the potential of photonic systems to assume a pivotal role in the future of quantum technology despite the inherent difficulties related to photon interaction and scale.

Neutral Atom-based Qubits

Quantum information is encoded and manipulated using qubits based on neutral atoms , which are atoms with no net electric charge . This technology uses optical traps to capture atoms, utilizing concentrated laser beams to confine and chill them near absolute zero. This process reduces their kinetic energy, thereby stabilizing their quantum states.

Qubits are based on the quantum states of atoms, which include their energy levels and spin states. Now, let's explore the operating concepts, benefits, drawbacks, existing structures, and prominent individuals involved in the domain of neutral atom-based qubits.

Principles of Operation

Neutral atom qubits are manipulated using precise laser and electromagnetic fields to induce quantum logic operations. Two primary methods are employed:

- **Optical Tweezers:** Highly focused laser beams trap single atoms in small, movable spots of light, allowing for individual control and manipulation of qubits.
- **Rydberg States:** By exciting atoms to high-energy Rydberg states , where their outermost electrons are far from the nucleus, atoms can interact over relatively large distances. This interaction enables entanglement and the execution of two-qubit gates, crucial for quantum computing.

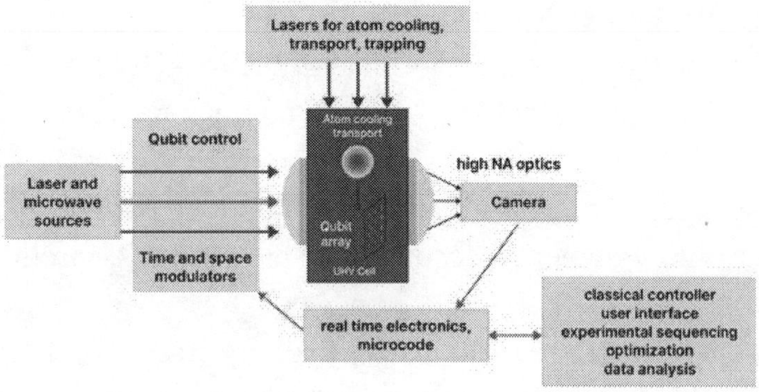

Figure 4.4: Neutral Atom Qubits

Figure 4.4 depicts the fundamental elements and interconnections of a quantum computing system based on neutral atoms. The central component of the system is the Ultra-High Vacuum (UHV) Cell, housing an array of qubits composed of individual neutral atoms. The manipulation of these atoms is achieved through the utilization of diverse laser and microwave sources, which exert control over their quantum states.

Laser technology is crucial for the processes of atom cooling, transport, and trapping, which allow for accurate manipulation of the atoms in the qubit array. This technique is crucial for initializing the qubits and preserving their coherence. The lasers used for these purposes are focused on the system, where they interact with the atoms to achieve the intended cooling and trapping effects.

The manipulation of qubit states is achieved by the utilization of both laser and microwave sources. In addition, time and space modulators are employed to precisely adjust the interactions and spatial arrangement of the qubits in the array. This enables the incorporation of quantum gates and operations that are essential for quantum computation.

The technology incorporates high Numerical Aperture (NA) optics, which are utilized in tandem with a camera to observe and quantify the qubit array. The utilization of these optics is essential for accurately observing the condition of the qubits with a high level of detail, hence offering valuable information for the control systems.

Real-time electronics and microcode are used to promptly process the signals from the optics and carry out the control instructions, guaranteeing that the quantum processes are executed with utmost accuracy.

A classical controller is responsible for overseeing the entire system. It interacts with the user and handles tasks such as experimental sequencing, optimization, and data analysis. The controller plays a crucial role in the integration of all components, ensuring efficient and accurate execution of quantum computations.

Advantages of Neutral Atom-based Qubits

- **Scalability:** The ability to trap and control large arrays of atoms with optical tweezers presents a clear path to scalability, a critical factor for building practical quantum computers.
- **Long Coherence Times:** Neutral atoms can exhibit long coherence times, as they are well isolated from environmental decoherence mechanisms, essential for maintaining quantum information.
- **High-Fidelity Quantum Gates:** The use of Rydberg state interactions allows for the implementation of high-fidelity quantum gates, which are crucial for the performance of quantum algorithms.
- **Fully Connected Qubit Architecture:** The long-range interactions between Rydberg atoms enable the realization of fully connected quantum systems, reducing the need for quantum gate decomposition and swap operations.

Disadvantages of Neutral Atom-based Qubits

- **Technical Complexity:** The technology requires sophisticated laser systems to trap, cool, and manipulate neutral atoms, presenting challenges in terms of system stability and control.
- **Sensitivity to External Fields:** Neutral atoms can be sensitive to magnetic and electric field fluctuations, potentially leading to decoherence and operational errors.
- **Laser Intensity and Stability:** Maintaining the intensity and stability of lasers used for trapping and manipulating atoms is crucial for the fidelity of quantum operations but can be technically demanding.

Current Architecture

Neutral atom-based quantum computers commonly employ a two-dimensional configuration of optical tweezers, wherein each tweezer is responsible for capturing a solitary atom. In order to accomplish quantum operations, advanced imaging technologies are employed to individually address and read the status of each atom, while lasers are utilized to alter the atomic states. Current advancements prioritize augmenting the number of confined atoms and improving the manipulation of their interactions, hence expanding the limits of what can be achieved with neutral atom quantum computing.

Leading Companies and Research Institutions

Several companies and research institutions are at the forefront of developing neutral atom-based quantum computing technologies:

- **Pasqal:** Building on research from the Institut d'Optique in France, Pasqal is developing quantum computing solutions based on neutral atom arrays to address complex computational problems across various industries.
- **Infleqtion:** Infleqtion leverages cold atom technology to develop quantum computing platforms, quantum sensing, and quantum networking applications, focusing on the precision control of neutral atoms.
- **QuEra Computing:** Emerging from research at Harvard and MIT, QuEra Computing focuses on building scalable quantum computers using neutral atoms in optical arrays to solve optimization and simulation problems unattainable by classical computers.

Overall, qubits based on neutral atoms hold significant promise in the field of quantum computing due to their scalability, extended coherence durations, and capacity for precise quantum operations. Although laser and field control pose technical obstacles, progress in this area is quickly advancing due to creative research and development endeavours. With the advancement of technology, neutral atom quantum computers have the potential to bring about significant advancements in a wide range of scientific and industrial fields, including materials science, encryption, and more.

Nuclear Magnetic Resonance Qubits

Nuclear magnetic resonance (NMR) qubits harness atomic nuclei's magnetic characteristics to encode and control quantum information. This methodology, which was among the initial approaches investigated for quantum computing, utilizes the fundamental concepts that underlie NMR spectroscopy, a widely employed tool in the field of chemistry for comprehending molecular structure. Now, let's explore the operational concepts, benefits, drawbacks, existing structures, and prominent individuals involved in the domain of NMR qubits.

Principles of Operation

The operational principle of NMR quantum computing involves the placement of molecules possessing distinct nuclear spins within a robust magnetic field, resulting in the alignment of these spins either with or against the direction of the field. The alignments between the qubit correspond to the quantum states $|0\rangle$ and $|1\rangle$. The manipulation of spin states to facilitate quantum logic operations is accomplished through the application of radio frequency (RF) pulses at specified frequencies and durations, hence enabling quantum information processing. The execution of quantum algorithms is facilitated by the superposition of spin states and the entanglement between spins of distinct nuclei within a molecule.

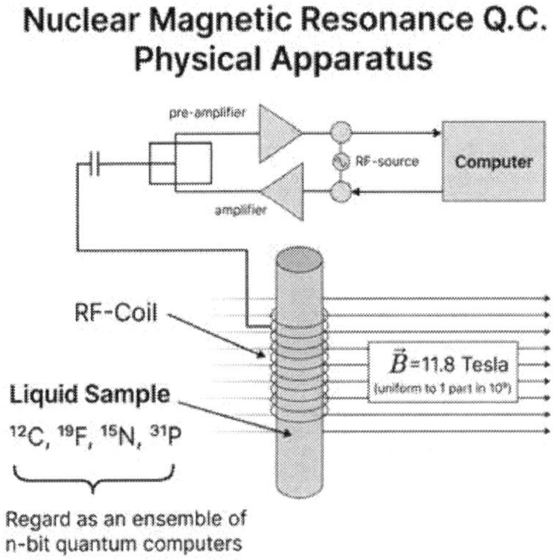

Figure 4.5: Nuclear Magnetic Resonance Qubits

Figure 4.5 illustrates the tangible equipment employed in Nuclear Magnetic Resonance (NMR) Quantum Computing. NMR quantum computing employs the principles of nuclear magnetic resonance to execute quantum computations by utilizing a collection of molecules in a liquid sample.

At the heart of the setup is the liquid sample, which contains molecules such as ^{12}C, ^{19}F, ^{15}N and ^{31}P. These molecules serve as qubits, with the nuclear spins of the atoms representing quantum states. The specimen is positioned within a robust, unchanging magnetic field referred to as $\vec{B}$, which is indicated as 11.8 Tesla in this illustration and is consistently uniform with an accuracy of 1 part in 10^9. The presence of this magnetic field induces the alignment of the nuclear spins, establishing the requisite circumstances for quantum activities.

An RF (Radio Frequency) Coil surrounds the sample and produces oscillating magnetic fields that are utilized to alter the nuclear spins. The RF pulses are utilized to execute quantum gates, namely rotations of the nuclear spins, which are crucial for quantum calculations.

An RF source generates and regulates the RF signals, which are subsequently boosted by an amplifier and directed towards the RF coil. The nuclear spins' reaction to the radio frequency (RF) pulses is identified using either the same coil or a different one and then amplified beforehand. Subsequently, the pre-amplifier processes this signal and transmits it to a computer for subsequent analysis. The computer plays a vital role in governing the sequence of RF pulses and analyzing the ensuing quantum states, so enabling computing.

In this configuration, the liquid sample can be considered as a collection of n-bit quantum computers, where each molecule in the sample executes the same quantum computation concurrently. The results of these calculations are averaged across all the molecules, offering a reliable approach to deduce the outcome of quantum algorithms.

Advantages of NMR Qubits

- **Room Temperature Operation:** Unlike many quantum computing platforms that require extreme cooling, NMR quantum computing can operate at room temperature, simplifying the experimental setup.
- **Mature Technology:** NMR spectroscopy is a well-established technique with a rich history of development, offering a solid foundation for NMR-based quantum computing.
- **Early Demonstrations of Quantum Algorithms:** NMR quantum computing was among the first to demonstrate quantum algorithms and quantum entanglement, playing a crucial role in the initial exploration of quantum computing concepts.

Disadvantages of NMR Qubits

- **Scalability Issues:** Scaling NMR quantum computers to a large number of qubits is highly challenging due to the difficulty in isolating and addressing individual spins within complex molecules as the system size increases.
- **Decoherence and Signal-to-Noise Ratio:** As the number of qubits increases, the signal-to-noise ratio decreases, making it difficult to extract clear signals from the system. This issue, combined with relatively short coherence times, limits the complexity of quantum computations that can be performed.

- **Limited to Ensemble Measurements:** NMR quantum computing measures the average behavior of an ensemble of molecules rather than individual quantum states, complicating the interpretation of quantum computation results and reducing the applicability of certain quantum algorithms.

Current Architecture

NMR quantum computers are designed using liquid-state NMR spectroscopy, in which the qubits represent the nuclear spins of atoms in dissolved molecules. Within the solution, every individual molecule functions as an identical quantum processor, facilitating parallel computations throughout the entire ensemble. The implementation of quantum gates and algorithms involves the precise timing and sequencing of RF pulses, where the collective response of the ensemble is used to infer the outcomes.

Leading Companies and Research Institutions

While NMR quantum computing played a pivotal role in the early days of quantum computing research, its challenges with scalability and the advent of more promising quantum technologies have led to a shift in focus. Consequently, few companies today are actively pursuing NMR for quantum computing. Instead, research continues primarily within academic and government research institutions, focusing on fundamental quantum mechanics studies and the development of NMR techniques that may contribute to other areas of quantum technology. For example:

- IBM and MIT have historical contributions to the development and demonstration of NMR quantum computing. Though their current focus has shifted towards other qubit technologies, the foundational work in NMR has paved the way for advancements in the field.
- National laboratories and universities worldwide continue to explore NMR for various applications, including quantum simulation and understanding quantum coherence and entanglement phenomena.

In summary, the utilization of NMR qubits has been crucial in the first investigation of quantum computing. However, the practical constraints associated with scalability and signal detection have prompted the research to investigate alternative qubit modalities. However, it is important to note that the principles and techniques derived from NMR quantum computing have had a lasting impact on the wider domains of quantum computing and quantum physics. This highlights the significance of fundamental research in propelling technological progress.

Quantum Dots: Nanoscale Semiconductors for Quantum Computing

Quantum dots (QDs) are semiconductor particles with dimensions in the nanometer range, exhibiting quantum mechanical characteristics. These minuscule particles can contain electrons or holes within a three-dimensional space of sufficiently small dimensions to exhibit noteworthy quantum mechanical features, resulting in distinct energy levels akin to atoms. The use of quantum dots has been observed in diverse domains, encompassing medical imaging, displays, and notably, as a promising quantum computing foundation. In this analysis, we explore the utilization of qubits, the underlying concepts, benefits, drawbacks, existing structures, and prominent organizations that concentrate on quantum dot technology for quantum computing.

Principles of Operation

The utilization of quantum dots in the domain of quantum computing involves the production of qubits by confining individual electrons within these minuscule structures. An electron's spin orientation, which can be either spin-up or spin-down, determines the quantum state of a qubit. In some configurations, the electron's position between dots can indicate the qubit states $|0\rangle$ and $|1\rangle$. Quantum computing is made possible by manipulating qubits through the use of electrical gates or magnetic fields, which control the spin or position of the electron.

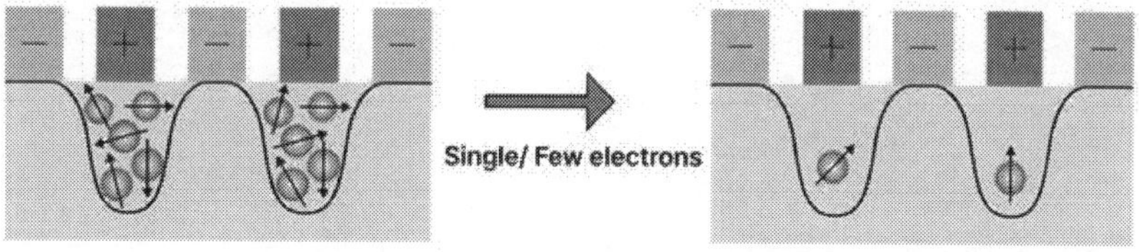

Figure 4.6: Quantum Dots as Qubits. Redrawn from [1]

Figure 4.6 shows the utilization of quantum dots in the field of quantum computing. It illustrates numerous electrons confined within potential wells created by the application of electrical potentials via gates (depicted in yellow and blue) on the left side. The "+" and "–" markings on the gates represent the respective positive and negative voltages applied, which establish the potential landscape responsible for confining the electrons. The black curves depict the potential energy profile of the quantum dots, where the electrons are initially distributed throughout these dots, and their spin states (shown by the arrows) are not yet completely regulated.

The right side of the figure depicts a more precise scenario in which the system is deliberately managed to isolate an individual or a small number of electrons within each quantum dot. The isolation is essential for quantum computing since it allows for independent control and utilization of each electron's spin as a qubit. The spin states of electrons, either up or down, correspond to the binary quantum states $|0\rangle$ and $|1\rangle$, which serve as the essential components of quantum computation.

By exerting precise control over the potential barriers through the use of gates, it becomes feasible to modify the spins of electrons within quantum dots. This enables the execution of quantum gates and operations. The capacity to manipulate individual or a small number of electrons in quantum dots serves as the foundation for scalable quantum computing platforms.

Advantages of Quantum Dots

- **Scalability:** The small size of quantum dots and the potential to integrate them into semiconductor devices using existing fabrication technologies make them an attractive option for scalable quantum computing.
- **Control and Integration:** The ability to manipulate quantum dot qubits using electric fields and to integrate them into more extensive circuits offers a path toward densely packed qubit arrays, crucial for building practical quantum computers.
- **Operation at Higher Temperatures:** Quantum dots can operate at higher temperatures than some other qubit technologies (like superconducting qubits), potentially reducing the complexity and cost of the cooling systems required for quantum computers.

Disadvantages of Quantum Dots

- **Decoherence:** While quantum dots can have relatively long coherence times, they are still susceptible to decoherence from interactions with their environment, a significant challenge for quantum computing.
- **Uniformity and Fabrication Challenges:** Producing quantum dots with uniform size and characteristics at scale is challenging, impacting the fidelity and performance of quantum dot-based qubits.
- **Complexity in Manipulation and Measurement:** Precisely controlling and measuring

the state of quantum dot qubits, particularly at scale, requires sophisticated techniques and equipment, presenting engineering challenges.

Current Architecture

Architectures for quantum computing that rely on quantum dots commonly consist of arrays of quantum dots that are manufactured on semiconductor substrates. The primary purpose of these arrays is to facilitate meticulous manipulation of individual qubits and their interconnections, which is essential for the successful implementation of quantum gates and algorithms. Current progress is centered around the development of techniques to effectively connect qubits in order to create quantum entanglement, as well as the creation of scalable designs that can be produced with exceptional accuracy.

Leading Companies and Research Institutions

Several companies and research institutions are at the forefront of research and development in quantum dot-based quantum computing:

- **Intel:** Intel has been exploring quantum computing through multiple platforms, including quantum dots, aiming to leverage its advanced semiconductor manufacturing capabilities to develop scalable quantum computing technologies.
- **Qutech:** A collaboration between TU Delft and TNO in the Netherlands, Qutech is actively researching quantum computing, including the use of quantum dots for creating qubits. Their work focuses on advancing the science and technology of quantum dots towards practical quantum computing applications.
- **University Research Labs:** Many universities worldwide, such as the University of New South Wales (UNSW) in Australia, have dedicated research groups focusing on quantum dots for quantum computing. These institutions are pushing the boundaries of what's possible with quantum dots, from achieving longer coherence times to integrating qubits into functional devices.

To summarize, quantum dots provide a compelling foundation for quantum computing, presenting benefits in terms of scalability, integration, and the capability to operate at elevated temperatures. Notwithstanding the difficulties associated with homogeneity, manufacture, and decoherence, continuous research and development endeavors are making significant progress in surmounting these barriers. With the advancement of technology, quantum dots have the potential to make a substantial contribution to the development of scalable and practical quantum computers, hence enhancing the whole quantum computing landscape.

Semiconductor Spin Qubits: Advancing Quantum Computing with Spin States

Qubits in semiconductors employ the spin of electrons or holes, which is the absence of an electron in a lattice structure, to encode quantum information. This quantum computing strategy utilizes particles' inherent spin characteristics, similar to angular momentum in quantum mechanics, to encode and manipulate qubits. The integration of quantum computing with current semiconductor technology holds great promise through the utilization of semiconductor spin qubits. Let us analyze the operational principles, benefits, drawbacks, existing architectures, and pioneering businesses in semiconductor spin qubit technology.

Principles of Operation

The functioning of semiconductor spin qubits relies on the manipulation of the spin states of electrons or holes that are restricted by quantum dots or defects in semiconductors. Quantum logic operations can be performed by manipulating spin states through the application of magnetic fields and microwave pulses. The two spin states, namely spin-up and spin-down, are representative of the qubit states $|0\rangle$ and $|1\rangle$, respectively. These states facilitate the superposition and entanglement processes that are essential for quantum computing. Quantum dots are semiconductor particles of nano-scale scale that possess the ability to confine individual electrons, with their spins functioning as qubits.

Figure 4.7: Semiconductor Spin Qubits. Redrawn from [2]

Figure 4.7 depicts a three-dimensional portrayal of the semiconductor structure, with distinct sections emphasized. The designations "SL" and "SR" correspond to the source and drain terminals (or regions), respectively, that play a crucial role in regulating the ingress and egress of electrons to and from the quantum dots. These sections facilitate the initialization, manipulation, and measurement of the qubit states.

The green structures symbolize the gates, which are commonly made of metal and positioned on a semiconductor substrate. The gates have the ability to regulate the potential landscape inside the semiconductor, enabling accurate control over the position and spin state of the electrons. By manipulating the voltage applied to these gates, it is possible to generate and manipulate quantum dots, which are regions where individual electrons are confined. Each quantum dot contains an electron with a spin that represents a qubit. The spin-up and spin-down states correspond to the logical $|0\rangle$ and $|1\rangle$ states of the qubit.

The underlying stratified arrangement beneath the gates signifies the diverse constituents present in the semiconductor hetero-structure, including silicon or gallium arsenide, in conjunction with insulating layers. The selection of these materials is done meticulously to maximize the confinement of electrons and reduce decoherence, hence guaranteeing stable qubit operation.

Advantages of Semiconductor Spin Qubits

- **Compatibility with Existing Technology:** One of the most significant advantages of semiconductor spin qubits is their compatibility with current semiconductor manufacturing processes, offering a potential pathway to leveraging existing microelectronics infrastructure for quantum computing.
- **Long Coherence Times:** Semiconductor spin qubits can exhibit long coherence times, especially when certain isotopically pure materials are used, reducing the impact of decoherence on quantum computations.
- **High-Fidelity Operations:** Advances in control and readout techniques have led to high-fidelity quantum operations with semiconductor spin qubits, crucial for implementing effective quantum error correction schemes.
- **Scalability:** The potential to integrate semiconductor spin qubits into densely packed arrays, akin to classical integrated circuits, presents a promising approach to scaling quantum computing systems.

Disadvantages of Semiconductor Spin Qubits

- **Complex Fabrication:** Fabricating quantum dots with the required precision and uniformity for high-quality qubits is challenging, requiring advanced semiconductor manufacturing techniques.

- **Sensitivity to Noise:** Semiconductor spin qubits can be sensitive to electric and magnetic field fluctuations, which can lead to decoherence and operational errors, though this can be mitigated with careful system design.
- **Scaling Challenges:** While theoretically scalable, practical implementation of large-scale systems with semiconductor spin qubits faces challenges in interconnectivity, qubit uniformity, and isolation from environmental noise.

Current Architecture

The architectural design of systems utilizing semiconductor spin qubits commonly include the incorporation of quantum dots within semiconductor materials such as silicon or gallium arsenide, forming arrays. The manipulation and quantification of electrons within quantum dots can be achieved through the utilization of adjacent metallic gates and single-electron transistors, respectively. The advancement of qubit coupling and integration is a crucial field of study that seeks to facilitate the development of intricate quantum circuits with the ability to carry out sophisticated computations.

Leading Companies and Research Institutions

- **Intel:** Intel is investing in multiple quantum computing technologies, including semiconductor spin qubits, aiming to leverage its semiconductor manufacturing prowess to develop scalable quantum computing solutions.
- **QuTech:** A collaboration between Delft University of Technology and the Netherlands Organization for Applied Scientific Research (TNO), QuTech is at the forefront of research in semiconductor spin qubits, focusing on creating scalable quantum networks and processors.
- **IBM:** While known for its work with superconducting qubits, IBM also explores semiconductor spin qubits as part of its broad research portfolio in quantum computing, aiming to harness the advantages of this technology for future quantum systems.

In summary, semiconductor spin qubits present a potentially fruitful pathway for the advancement of quantum computing, effectively integrating the realm of quantum phenomena with conventional semiconductor technology. The technology in question remains at the forefront of quantum computing research due to its compatibility with existing manufacturing techniques and potential for scalability, despite the technical constraints related to fabrication and sensitivity to noise. Semiconductor spin qubits have the potential to significantly contribute to the construction of practical and scalable quantum computers, hence facilitating the integration of quantum mechanics with classical computing infrastructure.

Comparing Quantum Computing Modalities

The field of quantum computing encompasses a diverse range of approaches, each possessing its own set of advantages and encountering certain obstacles. In the subsequent section, we provide a comprehensive examination of the principal quantum computing modalities under consideration, namely Superconducting Qubits, Trapped Ion Qubits, Photonic Qubits, Neutral Atom-based Qubits, Nuclear Magnetic Resonance (NMR) Qubits, Topological Qubits, Quantum Dots, and Semiconductor Spin Qubits. The following comparison elucidates significant characteristics such as coherence time, operating temperature, scalability, and the fundamental obstacles each method encounters.

Modality	**Coherence Time**	**Operating Temperature**	**Scalability**	**Primary Challenges**
Superconducting Qubits	Medium to High	Millikelvin	High	Cryogenic cooling, qubit connectivity
Trapped Ion Qubits	High	Room Temperature	Medium	Ion trapping and manipulation complexity
Photonic Qubits	High (inherent)	Room Temperature	Medium to High	Photon-photon interaction, integration
Neutral Atom-based Qubits	High	Room Temperature	High	Atomic arrangement precision, external field sensitivity
NMR Qubits	Medium	Room Temperature	Low	Scalability, signal-to-noise ratio
Topological Qubits	Potentially Very High	Millikelvin	Medium to High	Realization of Majorana fermions, manipulation
Quantum Dots	Medium to High	Millikelvin to Kelvin	High	Uniformity, integration with electronics
Semiconductor Spin Qubits	High	Millikelvin to Kelvin	High	Sensitivity to noise, fabrication complexity

Table 4.1: Comparison of Quantum Computing Modalities

- **Coherence Time:** Trapped Ion and Neutral Atom-based qubits, along with Topological qubits (theoritically), offer the longest coherence times.
- **Operating Temperature:** Superconducting and Topological qubits operate at millikelvin temperatures, requiring sophisticated cryogenic systems. In contrast, Trapped Ion, Photonic, and Neutral Atom-based qubits can operate at or near room temperature, simplifying the infrastructure needs.
- **Scalability:** Quantum Dots and Semiconductor Spin Qubits show high scalability potential due to their compatibility with existing semiconductor manufacturing techniques. Superconducting qubits also demonstrate considerable scalability, albeit with the challenge of maintaining coherence across large qubit arrays.
- **Primary Challenges:** Each modality faces unique hurdles. Maintaining coherence and qubit connectivity across a large array is challenging for Superconducting qubits. Trapped Ion qubits struggle with the complexity of ion trapping and manipulation. Photonic qubits must overcome the difficulty of inducing photon-photon interactions, critical for quantum logic operations. Neutral Atom-based qubits need high precision in atomic arrangements and are sensitive to external fields. NMR qubits face scalability issues and low signal-to-noise ratios. Their nascent development stage challenges topological qubits, Quantum Dots, and Semiconductor Spin Qubits, requiring breakthroughs in material science, fabrication, and qubit control techniques.

Conclusion

The selection of a modality for quantum computing is contingent upon the particular demands of the intended application, encompassing variables such as coherence time, operating temperature, and scalability potential. Superconducting and Semiconductor Spin Qubits are now at the forefront of development and utilization. However, emerging technologies such as Topological qubits and Neutral Atom-based qubits exhibit the potential to address existing constraints, providing avenues for fault-tolerant and scalable quantum computing. The continuous investigation and advancement in each of these domains are imperative for the prospective domain of quantum computing, underscoring the need for sustained ingenuity and investigation.

In the next chapter, we will start with Qiskit 1.0+, which will act as a foundation chapter for the whole book. We will cover all the primary features of the new version and highlight the important changes which have happened in the Qiskit ecosystem.

CHAPTER 5

An Introduction to Qiskit

Introduction

Qiskit has emerged as a highly adaptable and ubiquitous platform for the advancement of quantum computing. It enables researchers, developers, and quantum enthusiasts to effortlessly create, simulate, and execute quantum algorithms. With the continuous progress of quantum technology, Qiskit has transformed into a holistic package that provides much more than a mere software development kit (SDK) for quantum circuits. It has now become a diverse ecosystem with various tools and services specifically created to enhance the performance of quantum programs on different devices. The purpose of this chapter is to provide an introduction to Qiskit, including its ecosystem, SDK, runtime capabilities, and advanced features such as serverless computing and transpilation services. Moreover, it explores the rigorous patterns, primitives, and groundbreaking features of Qiskit 1.0, which enhance the efficiency, accessibility, and scalability of quantum program development.

Structure

In this chapter, we are going to study:

- Getting Started with Qiskit
  - The Qiskit Ecosystem
  - The Qiskit SDK
  - Qiskit Runtime
  - Qiskit Serverless
  - Qiskit Transpiler as a Service
- Qiskit Patterns
  - Map
  - Optimize
  - Execute
  - Post-Process
- Primitives
  - Estimator
  - Sampler
- Features and Highlights of Qiskit 1.0
  - High-Performance SDK
  - New primitive design
  - Memory usage
  - Speed
  - Native OpenQASM support
  - Stable release cycle
  - Prominent Qiskit changes

In this chapter, we will discuss the foundations of quantum computing using Qiskit software. This chapter might be overwhelming to read but the code implementation of Qiskit SDK is scattered across the whole book for different applications.

Getting Started with Qiskit

Qiskit in general refers to the collection of software tools/kits to execute programs on a quantum computer. The most notable software tools are *open-source Qiskit SDK* and *Qiskit Runtime environment*. With the help of Qiskit Runtime, one can execute operations on IBM quantum computers.

The Qiskit Ecosystem

The full form of Qiskit is **Quantum Information Science Kit** . The name Qiskit can be divided into two parts. **Qi** means Quantum Information and **kit** means toolkit or a set of tools. Qiskit is a library that offers tools for creating, simulating, and operating quantum circuits on quantum computers. Its goal is to serve as an all-inclusive toolset for quantum information science.

Qiskit is an IBM-developed open-source quantum computing framework that offers tools for interacting with quantum computers at the pulse, circuit, and algorithm levels. It provides tools for creating and manipulating quantum programs and running them on prototype quantum devices on IBM Quantum Platform or on simulators on a local computer.

Recently, IBM launched a new milestone in updating the version which is Qiskit 1.0 and it has major changes in terms of package, memory usage, speed, and more. One of the major changes is that a meta-package is installed in the earlier version of Qiskit. With the Qiskit 1.0 version, a transition was made only to a single Qiskit package, meaning the meta packages like Qiskit Terra, Aqua, Ignis, and Aer are integrated into a single unified Qiskit package. This integration reduces complexity for users who previously had to manage multiple installations and imports. If you are already a Qiskit user and using Qiskit on the local machine, it is strongly suggested to create a new virtual environment because Qiskit 1.0 will use a new packaging structure, and you will not be able to upgrade an existing Qiskit 0.x installation to Qiskit 1.0 in-place.

The Qiskit SDK

After the integration as a single unified Qiskit SDK, it has become the core component and primary package within Qiskit framework because SDK incudes the features like quantum circuit construction, Transpilation, Primitives, results and visualization, pulse level programming etc. on IBM Quantum hardware..

This library is the core component of Qiskit; it is the largest package under the Qiskit name with the broadest suite of tools for quantum computation, and many other components interface with it.

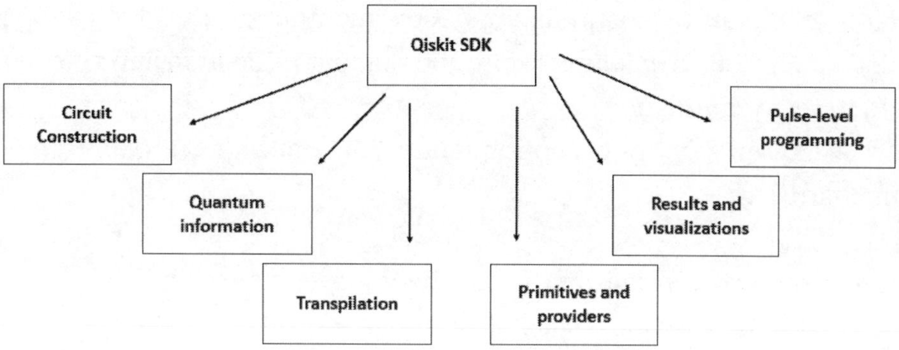

Figure 5.1: Prominent Qiskit SDK

Figure 5.1 shows the prominent Qiskit SDK tools like circuit construction, quantum information, transpilation, primitives and providers, results and visualization, pulse-level programming, etc. Each of its components plays a critical role in ensuring efficient quantum computing workflows. Circuit construction is the foundational component which enables users to design, modify, and manage circuits, which represent quantum computations. Quantum Information focuses on quantum state preparation, fidelity analysis etc. In Transpilation an input circuit must be transformed into a suitable form to execute a quantum device on real quantum hardware. Primitives refer to the fundamental building block of a certain process in a system. They can be used for quantum measurements and observable expectation calculation. Results and visualizations help users analyze quantum results using measurement data, probability distributions, and Bloch sphere visualizations. Pulse-level programming involves designing pulses that control the quantum hardware and make quantum operations possible.

While the Qiskit SDK provides the essential tools for quantum programming. it is further enhanced by a suite of extensions and services. These additional tools, including Qiskit Runtime, Qiskit Serverless, and Qiskit Patterns, extend the SDK's capabilities by optimizing execution, providing cloud-based scalability, and enabling structured quantum workflows. Next subsection explains about these extensions and services.

Qiskit Runtime

Qiskit runtime is a cloud based platform to run programs on a quantum computer. In that, the operations that needs to be executed are sent through IBM Quantum platform or IBM cloud and run in IBM Quantum Hardware.

Qiskit runtime is designed to use additional classical and quantum compute resources, including techniques such as error suppression and error mitigation, to return a higher-quality result from executing quantum circuits on quantum processors. Examples include dynamical decoupling for error suppression, and readout mitigation and zero-noise extrapolation (ZNE) for error mitigation.

Also there are three types of execution modes for running your quantum program on IBM quantum hardware.

1. *Job*

Job is a single query to a primitive that can be run over a specified number of shots. Job mode can be used when running a small experiment.

2. *Session*

Session mode provides dedicated and extended access to Quantum Processing Units (QPU). This session can be better utilized when there is a frequent interaction with classical and quantum computations.

3. *Batch mode*

This mode allows users to submit multiple primitive jobs simultaneously to shorten the processing time.

Now the main question is Qiskit Runtime open source?

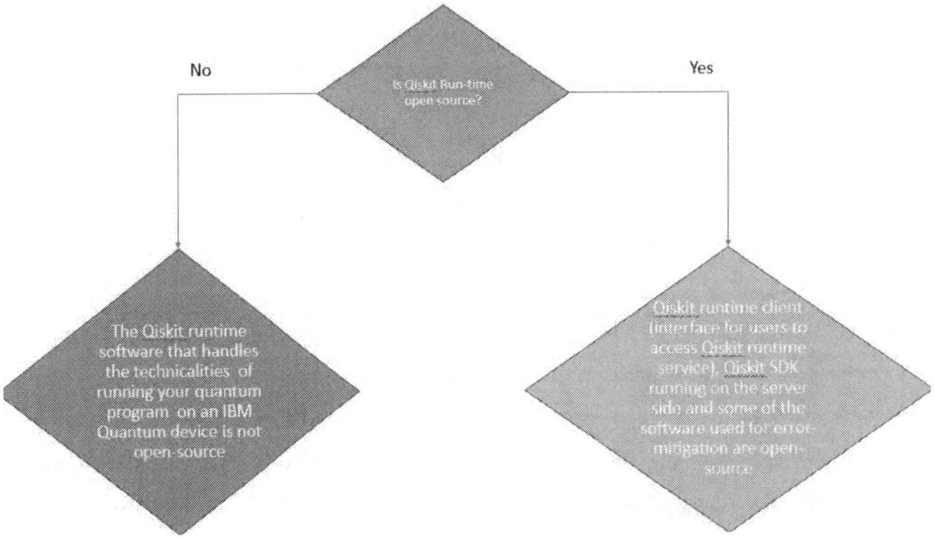

Figure 5.2: Is Runtime service open-source?

Qiskit Serverless

Qiskit Serverless makes it easy to run quantum computing tasks by managing workloads across both quantum and classical resources. Users can deploy programs to the IBM Quantum Platform and run them remotely, without worrying about setting up complex infrastructure. This service also simplifies resource management, making it useful for running quantum programs across different cloud platforms or even for advanced quantum-classical hybrid computing. Additionally, premium users have access to dedicated classical computing resources through the IBM Quantum Platform, allowing them to optimize and execute their workloads more efficiently.

Qiskit Transpiler as a Service

Transpilation is the process of rewriting the quantum circuit so that it can be efficiently applied on a quantum computer. Transpilation is done to fit the topology of a specific quantum hardware structure. Additionally, it optimizes the circuit to improve performance and reduce computational errors, especially on noisy intermediate-scale quantum (NISQ) computers.

In short, the main purpose of quantum transpilation is:

1. Adapting to specific quantum hardware structure.
2. Reducing the number of gates to match the topology of hardware (Optimization).
3. Incorporating the strategies within the circuit design to reduce the impact of errors in quantum calculations.

Transpilation involves six steps.

- **Initialization**
  Before we begin embedding the circuit onto the backend, this stage executes any necessary initial iterations. This typically entails the unrolling of custom instructions and the conversion of the circuit to solely single- and two-qubit gates.
- **Layout**
  This stage maps the virtual qubits in the circuit to the physical qubits on a backend.
- **Routing**
  After a layout has been implemented, this stage injects gates (such as swap gates) into the original circuit to ensure compatibility with the backend's connectivity.
- **Translation**
  The gates in the circuit are translated to the basis set of the intended backend during this stage.
- **Optimization**
  This phase executes the primary optimization loop repeatedly until a predetermined condition is satisfied, such as attaining a specific target depth.
- **Scheduling**
  This phase pertains to scheduling approaches that are hardware-aware. At a high level, the scheduling can be conceptualized as the introduction of delays into the circuit to

account for the inactive time on the qubits between the execution of instructions. There are four optimization levels, which range from 0 to 3. While the higher optimization levels require more time and computational effort, they may result in a superior circuit. Optimization level 0 is designed for device characterization experiments and, as such, does not conduct any optimizations; it merely maps the input circuit to the constraints of the target backend. The circuit is optimized to the greatest extent at optimization level 3. Nevertheless, the quality of the output circuit is not always enhanced by increasing computational effort, as many of the optimization techniques in the transpiler are based on heuristics.

Qiskit Patterns

The term pattern in Qiskit pattern refers to the reusable solutions or best practices that address common problems or tasks in quantum computing. These patterns are like templates or frameworks that can be adapted and used in various quantum applications to streamline development and ensure efficient implementation. To implement these patterns, Qiskit follows several key components:

- **Problem decomposition**
  Qiskit Patterns are a way to break down hard problems in a certain area into steps that are easier to handle. This organized method makes it easier to understand and work on the computer parts that are important to quantum computing.
- **Composability**
  The design makes it easy to add or combine new features, whether they were created by IBM Quantum researchers or other people in the community. This open-ended structure supports constant improvement and the use of the newest quantum computing innovations.
- **Execution environment**
  Qiskit Patterns can be used in a number of different computing settings, such as local setups, cloud services, and Quantum Serverless frameworks. This adaptability makes sure that quantum computing programs can use the best computing tools, whether those are CPUs, GPUs, or Quantum Processing Units (QPUs).
- **Tooling and SDK support**
  The Qiskit Software Development Kit (SDK) is very important because it's the base on which these models are put into action. These models can be used with the SDK and other tools and services from IBM Quantum and the open-source community as a whole.

- **Relationship between Qiskit Pattern and Qiskit serverless**
  Following best practices, developers can use Qiskit Patterns to plan and improve their quantum programs or apps. Not only does this make sure that the code works right, but it also makes sure that it runs quickly. Once these patterns are used to make quantum apps, Qiskit Serverless makes deployment easy and quick. Serverless computing can dynamically allocate resources based on the execution demand. This is especially helpful for apps that need to grow or that need flexible computing resources.

The IBM Quantum documentation outlines four primary steps in a Qiskit Pattern.These steps provide a comprehensive framework for developing quantum applications. Next subsection discusses in brief about those steps.

Map

The term map means generally refers to the process of translating or transforming a classical problem into a format that can be processed by a quantum hardware. **Mapping** is a hard problem and an active area of research

- **Understanding the problem**
  Initially, the problem must be well-understood in classical terms before any quantum operation. The problem which are solved with the help of classical computers are of no use to be implemented in a quantum hardware. Quantum computers are for problems that are classically hard.
- **Problem Encoding**
  To enable quantum computation, the classical problem needs to be encoded in a certain format. This could be creating initial quantum states, constructing a quantum circuit that represents the dynamics of the problem, or converting the problem into a set of quantum gates.
- **Qubit Mapping**
  Certain mappings may be more efficient than others, dependent upon the architecture of the quantum hardware. Early consideration of the connectivity of the heavy-hex lattice in IBM Quantum systems can result in optimizations, which could potentially enhance fidelity and reduce the necessity for SWAP gates.
- **Selecting right quantum resources**
  Depending on the intended outcome of the quantum algorithm, different Qiskit components may be utilized. For example, if you need to measure expectation values or perform state tomography, using an Estimator might be appropriate. For simpler measurements or probability distributions, a Sampler might be used.
- **Output preparation**

Output of this stage is typically a set of quantum circuits or operators ready to be executed on quantum hardware. These encapsulate all the quantum gates, initial state preparations, and measurement protocols needed to tackle the problem on a quantum computer.

- **Simulation or real hardware execution**
  Once the circuits are mapped and ready, you can use Qiskit's simulators (like Aer's) to simulate them or use the IBM Quantum Experience or other quantum processors that are available to execute the circuits on real hardware.

Optimize

Optimization for target hardware is a prominent step after Qiskit mapping because the abstract quantum circuits and operators designed during the mapping phase are properly adapted for execution on specific quantum hardware. We'll need to choose a quantum processor that has enough qubits of high enough quality that we can run our quantum circuit. There are three metrics which one can follow to choose a quantum processor.

Selecting quantum processor

- **Qubit count**
  We need to ensure the processor has a sufficient number of qubits to accommodate the circuit.
- **EPLG (Error Per Logical Gate)**
  Choose a processor with low error rates per logical gate to enhance computation accuracy.
- **CLOPS (Clock Operations Per Second)**
  Choose a processor which has high processing speed that can execute operations efficiently.

Optimizing the quantum circuit

- **Layout**
  Assign virtual qubits from your quantum circuit to specific physical qubits on the processor. This stage is essential because the performance and error rates of the circuit can be influenced by the physical layout of qubits.
- **Routing**
  Adjust the circuit to guarantee that interactions between qubits are feasible in light of the physical configuration. It is advisable to refrain from conducting long-distance interactions between qubits that are not directly connected, as these operations necessitate additional steps (such as SWAP gates) that may introduce errors.

Minimizing use of SWAP gates

Alternative routing strategies that minimize the necessity for SWAP gates, which are not only error-prone but also expensive in terms of quantum resources, should be taken into account.

Iterative process

Layout and routing should be regarded as iterative processes, with modifications being implemented in accordance with performance and error metrics.

Automation tools

- **Mapomatic**
  Suggests optimal configurations by employing approximate error rates.
- **Qiskit transpiler**
  Optimizes gate positioning and routing automatically. It can simplify and reduce the circuit by combining gates or eliminating redundant gates.
- **Manual and Automated Optimization**
  You have the option to manually tweak individual gates for more control or rely on the transpiler for automated optimizations.
- **Circuit Visualization**
  After optimization, use visualization tools in Qiskit to review the circuit's layout and timing. This helps verify that all components are correctly aligned and functioning as expected.

Error suppression

The first step in reducing errors in a circuit is optimizing the layout, routing, and minimizing the gate count. There are actually more sophisticated ways to suppress errors.

Error suppression is a collection of methods that modify a circuit during compilation to reduce the occurrence of errors. It is distinct from error mitigation. The two most common forms of error suppression are:

- **Dynamical decoupling**
  Dynamical decoupling is employed to effectively mitigate some of the environmental noise that is generated when a qubit is inactive. By implementing a sequence of gates at precise intervals, it is possible to ensure that the noise that accumulates in one portion of the inactive period is approximately balanced by the noise in the other.
- **Pauli twirling**
  Pauli twirling is a method of incorporating random gates into a circuit to simplify the noise, rather than to neutralize it, as in dynamical decoupling. The incorporation of random gates prevents the rapid accumulation of the effects of various errors and simplifies the characterization of the noise, as it now has a stochastic nature. This technique is also the foundation of a potent error mitigation method.

Execute

Execute step involves running our quantum circuit on hardware and produces the output of quantum computation. Following is the detailed breakdown of this process including the use of primitives like Sampler and Estimator in Qiskit Runtime:

Sampler

This is employed to execute quantum circuits and obtain per-shot measurement results as bitstrings. It is suitable for stochastic results that are directly obtained from quantum measurements.

Estimator

This is employed to determine the expectation values of observables. It is advantageous when one is interested in the averaged outcomes associated with physical quantities or when optimizing cost functions in algorithms such as Variational Quantum Eigensolvers (VQE).

Initialization

The Sampler and Estimator can be initialized in either a more scalable environment, such as a cloud-based cluster, or locally on your computer.

Execution modes

- **Batch execution**
  This mode enables the parallel transpilation of multiple quantum circuits. Parallel transpilation is advantageous for classical computational efficiency, as it minimizes the total time required by concurrently managing multiple circuits.
- **Session execution**
  This mode enables the parallel transpilation of multiple quantum circuits. Parallel transpilation is advantageous for classical computational efficiency, as it minimizes the total time required by concurrently managing multiple circuits.

Error mitigation

Options for configuring error suppression and mitigation techniques are available in Qiskit Runtime. The fidelity of the results derived from noisy quantum hardware is significantly enhanced by these techniques. These methods of error mitigation can vary in complexity, from straightforward techniques such as measurement error mitigation to more intricate procedures like zero-noise extrapolation.

Output differences between sampler and estimator

- **Output of estimator**
  The output of the Estimator is comprised of the calculated expectation values of the specified observables. These values are essential for the deployment of quantum algorithms such as the Quantum Approximate Optimization Algorithm (QAOA) or

Variational Quantum Eigensolvers (VQE), which aim to reduce or otherwise manipulate a cost function that is derived from these expectation values.

- **Output of sampler**
  The Sampler generates a sequence of bitstrings, each of which denotes the result of a single execution of the quantum circuit. These bitstrings are advantageous for algorithms that depend on sampling, including quantum Monte Carlo methods, as they directly correspond to the quantum state measurement results.

Post-Process

In a Qiskit pattern, the "post-process results" phase involves the manipulation and refinement of the raw outputs from quantum hardware to extract valuable data. This entails the application of a variety of traditional data-processing methods to improve the relevance and reliability of the results. The following is a comprehensive analysis of these procedures:

Visualization of results

To aid in the comprehension and analysis of the quantum computation outcomes by providing a visual interpretation. Example: Histogram, visualizing quantum state distributions, or generating graph representations of entanglement and quantum gate effects.

Readout error mitigation

To correct the errors introduced during the measurement phase of quantum computation. Example: Implementing calibration circuits that measure the error rates in advance and applying corrective algorithms to the obtained results.

Post-selection

To enhance the quality of the results, it is necessary to selectively evaluate only those outcomes that satisfy specific physical criteria that are pertinent to the issue. Example: Reduces noise and increases the relevance of the quantum simulation or computation results by discarding unphysical or erroneous outcomes.

Primitives

Computing systems are structured with several layers of abstraction, enabling the ability to concentrate on particular details based on the given task. Lower levels of computer programming include direct manipulation of hardware, whereas more intricate tasks necessitate the use of higher-level abstractions, such as programming libraries. Within this architecture, a primitive refers to the essential processing instruction at a specific level of abstraction. They are the simplest building blocks that can be given to the user to construct something useful.

Due to the swift progress in quantum computing, there is an increasing demand to work at elevated levels of abstraction. With the growth of quantum processing units (QPUs) and the increasing complexity of workflows, the emphasis has changed from handling individual qubit signals to viewing quantum devices as systems that carry out specific functions.

Quantum computers generally specialize in activities such as sampling quantum states and calculating expectation values. The Qiskit primitives, Sampler (returns shot-by-shot bit strings sampled from the probability distribution of the quantum state prepared on the device) and Estimator (computes expectation values of observables with the respective states prepared by quantum states), were created to tackle these objectives, bringing quantum programming closer to conventional programming by prioritizing the attainment of desired results rather than hardware intricacies.

Qiskit primitives streamline quantum coding by enabling users to concentrate on specific Quantum Processing Units (QPUs) without having to handle every intricate aspect, while simultaneously enhancing the accessibility of complex hardware functionalities. For example, users can readily utilize the most up-to-date error mitigation approaches by adjusting straightforward variables such as `resilience\_level`. Integrating primitives directly into their systems allows hardware providers to offer users a more direct and advantageous manner to access and utilize the top features of their technology.

Estimator

An estimator calculates the average values of observables based on the states generated by quantum circuits. The circuits can be parameterized, provided that the parameter values are also given as input to the primitive.

Both Sampler and Estimator primitives allow you to effectively construct vectorized workloads using a data structure called a Primitive Unified Bloc (PUB). The PUBs serve as the essential unit of work that a QPU requires to accomplish various workloads. The inputs for the `run()` method of the Sampler and Estimator primitives are used to execute the specified workload as a job. Subsequently, once the task has finished, the outcomes are sent in a format that relies on the PUBs employed and the runtime parameters supplied by the Sampler or Estimator primitives.

Each pub contains three values that, together, define a computation unit of work for the estimator to complete:

1. A possibly parameterized quantum circuit whose final state can be defined by $\psi(\theta)$
2. One or more observables denoted by H_j that can be defined using `ObervableArrayLike` that includes `Pauli`, `SparsePauliOp()` and `Pauli`, `PauliList` or `str` in order to

specify the expectation values for estimation.

3. A collection parameter value sets to bind the circuit against, θ_k. This can be specified as a single array-like object where the last index is over circuit `Parameter` objects, or omitted (or equivalently, set to None) if the circuit has no `Parameter` objects.
4. Optionally, a target precision for expectation values to estimate

By calling the method `result()` the expectation is calculated according to the mathematical relation which you have seen before $\langle\psi(\theta_k)|H_j|\psi(\theta_k)\rangle$. The output is a `PubResult` that contains the computed expectation values per pair, and their standard errors, in `PubResult` form. Each `PubResult` contains both data and metadata.

Each `PubResult` for the Estimator primitive contains at least an array of expectation values `PubResult.data.evs` and associated standard deviations (either `PubResult.data.stds` or `PubResult.data.ensemble\_standard\_error` depending on the `resilience\_level` used), but can contain more data depending on the error mitigation options that were specified.

Sampler

The primary responsibility of the Sampler is to sample the output register generated by the execution of quantum circuits. The input circuits can be parameterized, provided that the parameter values are also given as input to the primitive.

For the Sampler primitive, the format of the PUB tuple contains at most three values:

1. A single `QuantumCircuit`, which may contain one or more `Parameter` objects. These circuits must include the measurement instructions for each of the qubits that needs to be sampled.
2. A collection of parameter values to bind the circuit against θ_k (only needed if any `Parameter` objects are used that must be bound at runtime).
3. Optionally, a number of shots to measure the circuit with.

The Sampler primitive produces job results in a comparable style, except that each `DataBin` will have one or more `BitArray` objects that store the samples of the circuit connected to a specific `ClassicalRegister`. Typically, each shot will have one bitstring. The label property for each bit array object is determined by the `ClassicalRegisters` defined in the performed circuit. The measurement data obtained from these `BitArrays` can be transformed into a dictionary, where each bitstring measured (e.g., '1011001') is paired with the number of times (or counts) it was measured.

Features and Highlights of Qiskit 1.0

Qiskit 1.0 introduces significant enhancements, including a high-performance SDK capable of handling circuits with 100+ qubits and redesigned primitives like SamplerV2 and EstimatorV2 for efficient quantum hardware interactions. Key improvements include faster transpilation, reduced memory usage, native OpenQASM support, and a stable 12-month release cycle, ensuring a robust and scalable platform for advanced quantum computing. Some of the features are discussed are below:

High Performance SDK

With Qiskit 1.0, users will effortlessly construct and transpile circuits with 100+ qubits, establishing the foundation for future 1,000+ qubit-based workloads.

New Primitive Designs

One of the bigger changes is the redesign of the Sampler (SamplerV2) and Estimator (EstimatorV2) Primitives in the core SDK. These two interfaces are critical for facilitating user interaction with quantum hardware via Qiskit. These primitives are designed to accept vectorized input.

Memory Usage

Qiskit 1.0 has a 55% reduction in memory usage as compared to previous versions like 0.39.

Speed

Many features in Qiskit 1.0 are faster now than they were in the past. This is mostly because of ongoing internal reworking and the addition of Rust code behind the scenes. In Qiskit 1.0, the transpiler can bind and transpile circuits 39 times faster than in Qiskit 0.33. As a bonus, it can also return shorter circuit depths.

Native OpenQasm Support

OpenQASM means Open Quantum Assembly language. It is similar to classical assembly language but tailored for quantum operations. QASM is a low-level language designed to represent and control quantum operations. OpenQASM parser is written in Rust language so that it is easy to convert OpenQASM code into an internal representation that can be understood and executed by a quantum computing framework like Qiskit.

Stable Release Cycle

With Qiskit 1.0, a new 12-month release cycle for major versions began. This gives users a stable base for long-term projects and a predictable update plan.

Prominent Qiskit Changes

In this section, we highlight some of the changes in the names of the functionality between the older and the newer Qiskit versions. Please note carefully that this is not an exhaustive list and only a few relevant changes have been mentioned here, more details can be found in the references by following the Qiskit 1.0 migration guide.

Previous version	Qiskit 1.0+ version
qiskit.aer	qiskit_aer
qiskit.providers.basicaer	qiskit.providers.basic_provider
BasicAerProvider	BasicProvider
BasicAerJob	BasicProviderJob
QasmSimulatorPy	BasicSimulator
UnitarySimulatorPy	quantum_info.Operator
StatevectorSimulatorPy	quantum_info.Statevector
qiskit.providers.fake_provider.FakeQasmBackend	qiskit_ibm_runtime.fake_provider.fake_qasm_backend.FakeQasmBackend
qiskit.providers.fake_provider.FakePulseBackend	qiskit_ibm_runtime.fake_provider.fake_pulse_backend.FakePulseBackend
qiskit.qasm	qiskit.qasm2
qiskit.tools	qiskit.utils
qiskit.tools.visualization	qiskit.visualization
from qiskit import execute	from qiskit import transpile
QuantumCircuit.cnot	QuantumCircuit.cx
QuantumCircuit.toffoli	QuantumCircuit.ccx
QuantumCircuit.fredkin	QuantumCircuit.cswap
QuantumCircuit.mct	QuantumCircuit.mcx
QuantumCircuit.i	QuantumCircuit.id
QuantumCircuit.squ	QuantumCircuit.unitary
qiskit.extensions	qiskit.circuit.library

Figure 5.3: Qiskit Function Name Changes

Table 5.3 refers to the changes in the names of the essential functions that have been incorporated in the newer version.

BaseEstimator	BaseEstimatorV2
BaseSampler	BaseSamplerV2
qiskit.primitives.Estimator	qiskit.primitives.StatevectorEstimator
qiskit.primitives.Sampler	qiskit.primitives.StatevectorSampler
from qiskit import BasicAer	from qiskit.providers.basic_provider import BasicProvider

Figure 5.4: Estimator and Sampler Changes

Just like different functions having name changes, the estimator and sampler have also been upgraded and renamed as V2. In the follwing *Table* 5.4 you can find the relevant changes.

UnitarySimulatorPy	quantum_info.Operator
StatevectorSimulatorPy	quantum_info.Statevector
qiskit.qasm	qiskit.qasm2
BasicAer.backends()	BasicProvider()
qiskit.__qiskit_version__	qiskit.__version__

Figure 5.5: Backend and Version Name Changes

Finally, there have been some naming changes in the functions related to the backend and version for Qiskit which are shown in *Table* 5.5

Conclusion

The continual development of Qiskit demonstrates the increasing level of maturity in the field of quantum computing. With its robust Software Development Kit (SDK) and extensive ecosystem including serverless capabilities and superior transpilation services, Qiskit equips users with the essential tools to thoroughly investigate the potential of quantum computing. Patterns and primitives, particularly with the introduction of Qiskit 1.0, simplify the whole quantum workflow, including tasks such as mapping, optimizing, executing, and post-processing quantum circuits. By prioritizing performance enhancements, incorporating native OpenQASM support, and maintaining a consistent release cycle, the platform provides developers and researchers with the necessary conditions to effectively utilize quantum power. With Qiskit, quantum computing has transitioned from a remote future to a current and easily available technological reality.

In the next chapter, we will start with the implementation of single qubit quantum logic gates and their execution on the Aer backend and the primitives backend. Additionally, note that from the next chapter onwards, there will be a lot of coding till the end of the book. Furthermore, as you go through the book from the next chapter onwards, you will observe that some outputs have not been included and this is either because of a large figure/plot size or a large data/numeral being printed. These large outputs can be found in the open-source GitHub for this book.

References

- Qiskit 1.0 Feature Migration Guide -
  `https://docs.quantum.ibm.com/migration-guides/qiskit-1.0-features`
- Introduction to Qiskit - `https://docs.quantum.ibm.com/guides`

- Qiskit Hello World - `https://docs.quantum.ibm.com/guides/hello-world`
- Qiskit Patterns Introduction - `https://docs.quantum.ibm.com/guides/intro-to-patterns`
- Qiskit Mapping - `https://docs.quantum.ibm.com/guides/map-problem-to-circuits`
- Qiskit Optimization - `https://docs.quantum.ibm.com/guides/optimize-for-hardware`
- Qiskit Execution - `https://docs.quantum.ibm.com/guides/execute-on-hardware`
- Qiskit Post-Processing - `https://docs.quantum.ibm.com/guides/post-process-results`
- Qiskit Serverless - `https://docs.quantum.ibm.com/guides/serverless`
- Qiskit Transpilation - `https://docs.quantum.ibm.com/guides/transpile`
- Primitives - `https://docs.quantum.ibm.com/guides/primitives`

CHAPTER 6

Single Qubit Quantum Logic Gates

Introduction

Single qubit logic gates are fundamental components in the field of quantum computing, serving as the basic building blocks for quantum algorithms and operations. These gates alter the state of individual qubits, enabling us to carry out a diverse array of quantum calculations. Quantum gates, in contrast to classical logic gates, utilize the concepts of superposition and entanglement to manipulate qubits. This allows qubits to exist in numerous states concurrently and enables interactions beyond classical bits' capabilities. This chapter examines the fundamental single qubit gates, including the Pauli-X, Pauli-Y, Pauli-Z, Hadamard, and phase gates. It investigates their mathematical representations, physical realizations, and functions within quantum circuits. Comprehending these basic gates is essential for constructing more intricate quantum operations and ultimately exploiting the complete capabilities of quantum computing.

Structure

In this chapter, you are going to study:

- Single Qubit Quantum Logic Gates
  - Properties of Quantum Gates
  - Pauli X Gate
  - Pauli Y Gate
  - Pauli Z Gate
  - Hadamard Gate
  - S Gate
  - $S^\dagger$ Gate
  - T Gate
  - $T^\dagger$ Gate
  - Rx Gate
  - Ry Gate
  - Rz Gate
  - Phase Gate

Single Qubit Quantum Logic Gates

Quantum gates transform quantum states. In mathematical terms, transformation means using the matrices of a specific gate. We will discuss this in detail in the upcoming sections. Quantum gates are the only ones that can prepare a quantum state to be in superposition, which in turn creates entanglement. A few quantum logic gates took inspiration from classical logical gates. Those gates are termed Pauli gates. Apart from Pauli gates, there are multi-qubit gates, which are later used in the development of algorithms.

Once the quantum gates are applied, there is a transition to a same or different quantum state depending on the gate applied. This transition can be visualized on the computing side in various ways. One such common way is using Bloch Sphere. Bloch Sphere is a visual tool representing a single qubit's state. The north pole of the Bloch Sphere depicts $|0\rangle$ the state, and the south pole depicts $|1\rangle$. To make a transition from $|0\rangle$ to $|1\rangle$, a rotation of 180° causes a transition of states. This rotation can be implemented with the help of quantum gates.

Also, all the single-qubit , multi-qubit, Unitary, Identity, and Quantum Fourier Transform gates (QFT) are unitary in nature. We need to understand the importance of a gate being unitary and the segregation of gates as Clifford, non-Clifford, and universal gates.

Properties of Quantum Gates

There are a few prominent properties a quantum gate must satisfy.

1. **Unitary**

Quantum gates must possess the property of unitary in order to guarantee that operations can be reversed and that the overall probability of quantum states remains unchanged. A quantum operation is not unitary if it's not reversible. Non-unitary property violates the principles of quantum mechanics, especially to conserve the norm. If quantum operations are irreversible, then there is a loss in quantum information .

Unitary operation is represented as

$$U^{\dagger}U = UU^{\dagger} = I \tag{6.1}$$

where U is the unitary operator, which means it can be any gate (E.g., Pauli gates, H, S, and more). This case will be solved for the Pauli Y gate.

2. **Hermitian**

Satisfying this property, the operator has its own conjugate transpose.

This property is mathematically expressed as,

$$A^{\dagger} = A \tag{6.2}$$

In the context of quantum mechanics and linear algebra, Self-adjoint operators and Hermitian operators are used interchangeably. Both refer to an operator or matrix that is equal to its own conjugate transpose. Conjugate transpose is a mathematical operator that checks whether the operator is self-adjoint or not. An example of this case is solved for Pauli Z gate.

Importance of satisfying Hermitian property

- **Real Eigenvalues:** Self-adjoint operators are ensured to possess eigenvalues that are real. In quantum mechanics, measurements of physical observables, such as location, momentum, and energy, are essential to produce genuine values. This is because these observables are actual quantities that we perceive in the natural world. One such example is the hamiltonian operator which estimates the total energy of the system. The resultant values are of real numbers (Ex: -13 eV)
- **Orthogonal eigenvectors:** An operator is said to be hermitian when the eigenvector corresponding to its eigen values for that operators are orthogonal to each other this means when an electron is (say $|0\rangle$) one state then it can't be in other state ($|1\rangle$).

Self-adjoint operators are indispensable for describing the measurable properties of quantum systems. Their mathematical properties guarantee that they are appropriate for representing all observables in quantum theory, rendering them essential to the structure and predictions of quantum mechanics.

3. **Involutory property**

The resultant is an Identity matrix when an operator or matrix is squared. Mathematically represented as,

$$A^2 = I \tag{6.3}$$

An example of this case is explained for the Pauli X gate.

4. **Combinability**

There are two ways of computing gates. One is parallel computation and another one is series computation.

Parallel computation

Whenever the quantum gates are arranged in parallel, tensor product is used to compute two quantum gates. Here is an example.

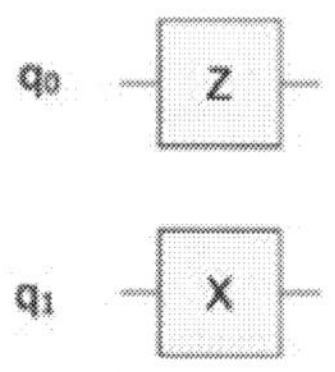

Figure 6.1: Parallel operation (tensorproduct)

Tensor Product of Pauli Z and X Gates

The tensor product which is a parallel operation is shown *Figure* 6.1.

The Pauli Z and X matrices are defined as:

$$Z = \begin{bmatrix} 1 & 0 \\ 0 & -1 \end{bmatrix}, \quad X = \begin{bmatrix} 0 & 1 \\ 1 & 0 \end{bmatrix}$$

The tensor product $Z \otimes X$ is computed by multiplying each element of Z by the entire matrix X:

$$
\begin{aligned}
Z \otimes X &= \begin{bmatrix} 1 \times X & 0 \times X \\ 0 \times X & (-1) \times X \end{bmatrix} \\
&= \begin{bmatrix} \begin{bmatrix} 0 & 1 \\ 1 & 0 \end{bmatrix} & \begin{bmatrix} 0 & 0 \\ 0 & 0 \end{bmatrix} \\ \begin{bmatrix} 0 & 0 \\ 0 & 0 \end{bmatrix} & \begin{bmatrix} 0 & -1 \\ -1 & 0 \end{bmatrix} \end{bmatrix} \\
&= \begin{bmatrix} 0 & 1 & 0 & 0 \\ 1 & 0 & 0 & 0 \\ 0 & 0 & 0 & -1 \\ 0 & 0 & -1 & 0 \end{bmatrix}
\end{aligned} \tag{6.4}
$$

This resulting matrix represents the combined operation of applying Z to the first qubit and X to the second qubit.

Remember, tensor products are non-commutative, meaning you can't reverse the order like $Z \otimes X$ to $X \otimes Z$.

Series Operation

Whenever the quantum gates are arranged one after the other, matrix multiplication is performed. This is shown in *Figure* 6.2 .

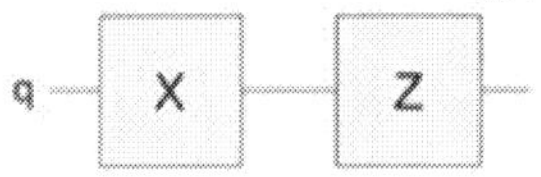

Figure 6.2: Series operation (matrix multiplication)

Matrix Multiplication of Pauli X followed by Z Gates

Define the Pauli X and Z matrices:

$$
X = \begin{bmatrix} 0 & 1 \\ 1 & 0 \end{bmatrix}, \quad Z = \begin{bmatrix} 1 & 0 \\ 0 & -1 \end{bmatrix}
$$

Perform the matrix multiplication XZ:

In quantum circuits, gates are applied from left to right. Since its a series operation, matrix multiplication is computed. The rightmost matrix acts first on the quantum state Z, and the leftmost matrix acts X last. This means if we compute XZ (multiplication of X and then Z), then Z is applied first, followed by X.

$$
ZX = \begin{bmatrix} 1 & 0 \\ 0 & -1 \end{bmatrix} \begin{bmatrix} 0 & 1 \\ 1 & 0 \end{bmatrix} = \begin{bmatrix} 1 \cdot 0 + 0 \cdot 1 & 1 \cdot 1 + 0 \cdot 0 \\ 0 \cdot 0 + (-1) \cdot 1 & 0 \cdot 1 + (-1) \cdot 0 \end{bmatrix} = \begin{bmatrix} 0 & 1 \\ -1 & 0 \end{bmatrix}
$$

The resulting matrix ZX is:

$$\begin{bmatrix} 0 & 1 \\ -1 & 0 \end{bmatrix}$$

This matrix represents the combined operation of first applying X and then Z to a quantum state.

Pauli X Gate

This is equivalent to the NOT gate used in classical computing. The quantum state is transformed when an X gate is applied to a quantum state. For example, when a qubit is in state $|0\rangle$ (default state, considered according to Qiskit) when applied X gate, the quantum state is transformed to $|1\rangle$ state. Pauli X gate can be represented as `x()` . Transformation means 180° rotation around z axis in the Bloch sphere. Z axis by default is the computational basis. This can be visualized as well as derived mathematically.

$$|0\rangle = \begin{bmatrix} 1 \\ 0 \end{bmatrix} \tag{6.5}$$

$$|1\rangle = \begin{bmatrix} 0 \\ 1 \end{bmatrix} \tag{6.6}$$

Truth Table

Input	Output
$\|0\rangle$	$\|1\rangle$
$\|1\rangle$	$\|0\rangle$

Matrix

The matrix obtained from Pauli X gate is,

$$X = \sigma_X = \begin{bmatrix} 0 & 1 \\ 1 & 0 \end{bmatrix} \tag{6.7}$$

Thus Pauli X gate is represented by 2 x 2 unitary Matrix.

$$X = \begin{pmatrix} 0 & 1 \\ 1 & 0 \end{pmatrix} \tag{6.8}$$

Now let us prove the involutory property which we discussed in the previous section.

Demonstrating the Involutory Property:

To show that the Pauli-X gate is an involution, we square the matrix:

$$X^2 = \begin{pmatrix} 0 & 1 \\ 1 & 0 \end{pmatrix} \begin{pmatrix} 0 & 1 \\ 1 & 0 \end{pmatrix} \tag{6.9}$$

By performing the matrix multiplication, we get:

$$X^2 = \begin{pmatrix} (0 \cdot 0 + 1 \cdot 1) & (0 \cdot 1 + 1 \cdot 0) \\ (1 \cdot 0 + 0 \cdot 1) & (1 \cdot 1 + 0 \cdot 0) \end{pmatrix} = \begin{pmatrix} 1 & 0 \\ 0 & 1 \end{pmatrix} = I \tag{6.10}$$

This result shows that $X^2 = I$, confirming that the Pauli-X gate is indeed an involution.

Implementing X gate

If you are using Google Colab to run the circuits provided here are the few commands to be installed prior to the import of commands. Please include the exclamation mark symbol ! before each of the the pip commands to run them without errors.

```
pip install qiskit
pip install qiskit-ibm-runtime
pip install pylatexenc
pip install qiskit-aer
pip install qiskit-algorithms
pip install qiskit-nature
pip install qiskit-machine-learning
```

One should not forgot to import libraries before implementation. Following are the necessary libraries to be implemented.

```
from qiskit import transpile
from qiskit.primitives import BackendSampler
from qiskit.qasm2 import dumps
from qiskit.qasm2 import dump
from qiskit.circuit import QuantumCircuit
from qiskit.circuit.library import DiagonalGate
from qiskit.converters import circuit_to_dag
import qiskit.qasm2
from qiskit.circuit.library import DiagonalGate
from qiskit.primitives import (
    Sampler,
    StatevectorSampler,
```

```
    Estimator,
    StatevectorEstimator,
)
from qiskit.providers.basic_provider import BasicProvider
from qiskit.quantum_info import Statevector
from qiskit.quantum_info import Operator
from qiskit.providers.basic_provider import BasicSimulator
from qiskit_ibm_runtime.fake_provider import FakeSherbrooke
from qiskit.providers.fake_provider import GenericBackendV2
from qiskit import pulse, qpy
from qiskit import pulse
from qiskit.circuit import Parameter
from math import pi
from qiskit.compiler import schedule, transpile
from qiskit.utils import parallel_map
from qiskit.visualization import plot_histogram
from qiskit.visualization import plot_state_city
from qiskit.quantum_info import Statevector
from qiskit import QuantumCircuit, QuantumRegister, ClassicalRegister
from qiskit.quantum_info import DensityMatrix
from qiskit.visualization import visualize_transition
from qiskit.visualization import array_to_latex
from qiskit.visualization import plot_bloch_multivector
from qiskit.quantum_info import DensityMatrix
from qiskit.transpiler import PassManager
from qiskit.visualization import pass_manager_drawer
from qiskit.dagcircuit import DAGCircuit
from qiskit.converters import circuit_to_dag
from qiskit.visualization import dag_drawer
from qiskit.visualization import plot_bloch_vector
from qiskit.visualization import plot_circuit_layout
from qiskit.visualization import plot_coupling_map
from qiskit.visualization import plot_distribution
from qiskit.visualization import plot_error_map
from qiskit.visualization import plot_gate_map
from qiskit.visualization import plot_state_hinton
```

```
import numpy as np
from qiskit.visualization import plot_state_paulivec
from qiskit.visualization import plot_state_qsphere
from qiskit_aer.aerprovider import AerSimulator
```

Simulators can be accessed via the BasicProvider provider. Following is the example,

```
from qiskit.providers.basic_provider import basic_simulator
BasicProvider().get_backend('basic_simulator')
```

In the following code cell, a single qubit Pauli X gate is used, and we are not measuring the circuit because we don't need Histogram visualization (probability of measuring quantum states) at present. But we are going to see it later.

```
qc =QuantumCircuit(1)
qc.x(0)
qc.draw('mpl')
```

Figure 6.3: X gate

We do the process of defining various kinds of quantum circuits or gates multiple times throughout this book. *Figure* 6.3 shows the X gate.

Plotting Bloch Sphere for X gate:

Bloch sphere visualizes the transformed state.

```
qc = QuantumCircuit(1)
qc.x(0)
qc.save_statevector()


simulator = AerSimulator(method = 'statevector')
qc = transpile(qc, simulator)
result = simulator.run(qc).result().get_statevector(qc)
plot_bloch_multivector(result)
```

From *Figure* 6.4 , its clear that the qubit state is in $|1\rangle$.

```
Quantum state is: Statevector([0.+0.j, 1.+0.j],
            dims=(2,))
```

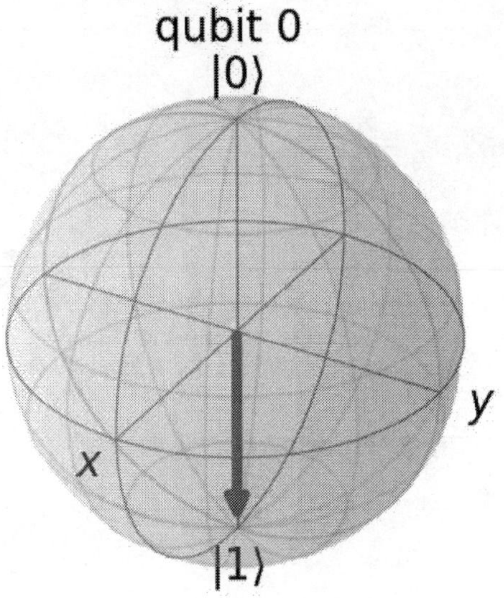

Figure 6.4: Bloch Sphere representation for X gate

- **Plotting State City**
  Plot state city graph shows the real and imaginary parts of states for X gate.
- **Real part of Amplitude**
  One part of the plot shows the real parts of the state amplitudes. In *Figure* 6.5 , Purple plot depicts Real part of Amplitude.
- **Imaginary part of Amplitude**
  The other part shows the imaginary parts of the state amplitudes. Crimson color in the folowing Image depicts Imaginary part of Amplitude.

In order to attain the state city graph **Outer product** operation is done.
The resultant state is $|11\rangle$.
A simple formula for remembering to calculate the Outer product is
Outer product = Ket ·bra
The outer product $|1\rangle\langle 1|$ is calculated as follows:

$$|1\rangle\langle 1| = \begin{bmatrix} 0 \\ 1 \end{bmatrix} \cdot \begin{bmatrix} 0 & 1 \end{bmatrix} = \begin{bmatrix} 0\cdot 0 + 1\cdot 0 & 0\cdot 1 + 1\cdot 1 \\ 1\cdot 0 + 0\cdot 0 & 1\cdot 1 + 0\cdot 0 \end{bmatrix} = \begin{bmatrix} 0 & 0 \\ 0 & 1 \end{bmatrix} \tag{6.11}$$

Always remember that the output of Outer product is a matrix .

QSphere

The next code cell is used to implement the QSphere (shown in *Figure* 6.6) for the X gate. QSpheres are used for visualizing multi-qubit states but can also be used for single-qubit

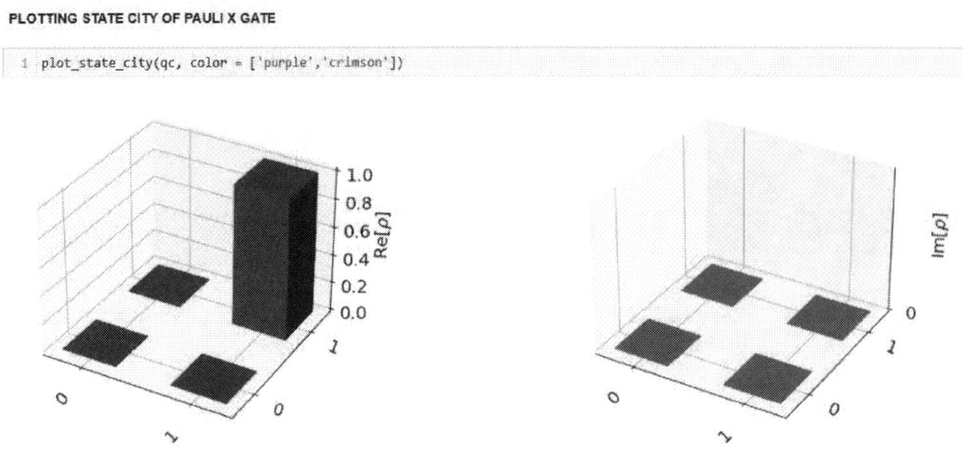

Figure 6.5: State city representation for X gate

states as well.

```
qc = QuantumCircuit(1)
qc.x(0)
plot_state_qsphere(qc)
```

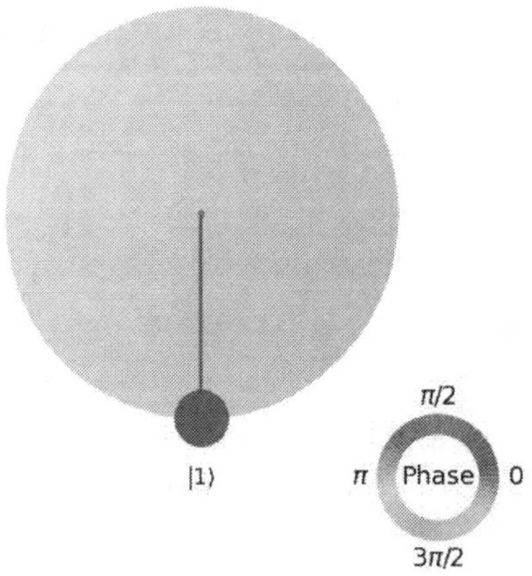

Figure 6.6: QSphere representation for X gate

Plotting Histogram for X gate

In order to plot the histogram (probability of obtaining a quantum state) for Pauli X gate one needs to measure the circuit.Other visualization methods like QSphere and State city doesn't require to measure the quantum circuit.

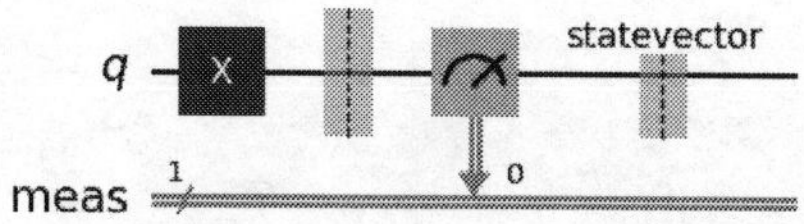

Figure 6.7: Quantum Circuit of X gate to visualize Histogram

```
qc = QuantumCircuit(1)
qc.x(0)
qc.measure_all()
qc.save_statevector()
qc.draw('mpl')
```

Figure 6.7 shows the implementation of X gate for histogram visualization.

Setting the backend simulator

Qasm simulator is used to set the backend to run the quantum circuit. We set the number of shots that describes the number of times the quantum circuit needs to run with measurement in order to accumulate the counts of the measured quantum state.

```
shots = 10000

sim_automatic = AerSimulator(method='automatic')
job_automatic = sim_automatic.run(qc, shots=shots)
counts_automatic = job_automatic.result().get_counts(qc)

plot_histogram(counts_automatic)
```

Output Histogram for X gate

Here, the probability is 100% for the output $|1\rangle$ because for all the 10,000 shots given, the same quantum state output of $|1\rangle$ is measured.

The systematic approach that has been taken to explain Pauli X gate is now employed to describe the other quantum gates as well. However, since the visualization codes used can be adapted for the other quantum gates, they have been omitted in order to reduce redundancy.

Pauli Y gate

This gate is similar to X gate but negative amplitude **i** is multiplied to the output. Else, positive amplitude is multiplied by output. In the Bloch Sphere, 180° rotation happens

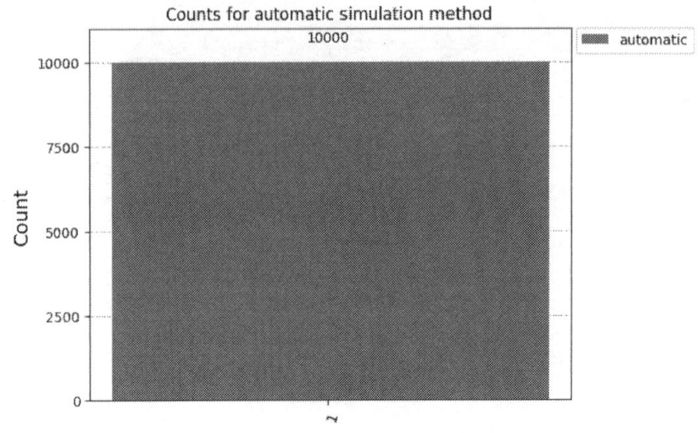

Figure 6.8: Histogram for X gate

around the Z axis. Pauli Y gate is represented as `y()`.

Truth Table

Input	Output
$\|0\rangle$	$i.\|1\rangle$
$\|1\rangle$	$-i.\|0\rangle$

```
qc = QuantumCircuit(1)
qc.y(0)
qc.draw('mpl')
```

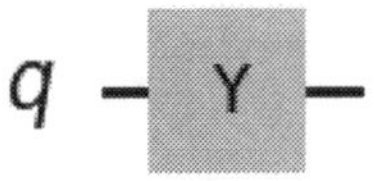

Figure 6.9: Y gate

Operator

Thus Pauli Y gate is represented by 2 x 2 unitary Matrix form as,

$$Y = \sigma_Y = \begin{bmatrix} 0 & -i \\ i & 0 \end{bmatrix} \tag{6.12}$$

Let's prove whether Y gate is unitary in nature or not. This exercise can be done for other quantum gates too and it is recommended for the reader to perform this exercise.

Proof that the Pauli-Y Gate is Unitary

The Pauli-Y gate is represented by the matrix:

$$Y = \begin{pmatrix} 0 & -i \\ i & 0 \end{pmatrix} \tag{6.13}$$

The conjugate transpose $Y^\dagger$ of the Pauli-Y gate is:

$$Y^\dagger = \begin{pmatrix} 0 & i \\ -i & 0 \end{pmatrix} \tag{6.14}$$

To prove the gate is unitary, we check if $Y^\dagger Y = I$ and $YY^\dagger = I$:

$$YY^\dagger = \begin{pmatrix} 0 & -i \\ i & 0 \end{pmatrix} \begin{pmatrix} 0 & i \\ -i & 0 \end{pmatrix} = \begin{pmatrix} 1 & 0 \\ 0 & 1 \end{pmatrix} = I \tag{6.15}$$

$$Y^\dagger Y = \begin{pmatrix} 0 & i \\ -i & 0 \end{pmatrix} \begin{pmatrix} 0 & -i \\ i & 0 \end{pmatrix} = \begin{pmatrix} 1 & 0 \\ 0 & 1 \end{pmatrix} = I \tag{6.16}$$

Both products yield the identity matrix, confirming that the Pauli-Y gate is indeed unitary.

Pauli Z Gate

In Pauli Z gate state transformation doesn't happen. Only phase flip happens. There is a specific condition for phase flip to occur. If the input qubit is in $|1\rangle$ then output qubit will be -$|1\rangle$. So a $180°$ rotation happens around Z axis. Paui Z gate can be represented as `z()`

Truth Table

Input	Output
$\|0\rangle$	$\|0\rangle$
$\|1\rangle$	$-\|1\rangle$

Operator

This Pauli Z gate is represented by a 2 x 2 unitary matrix form as,

$$Z = \sigma_Z = \begin{bmatrix} 1 & 0 \\ 0 & -1 \end{bmatrix} \tag{6.17}$$

```
qc = QuantumCircuit(1)
qc.z(0)
qc.draw('mpl')
```

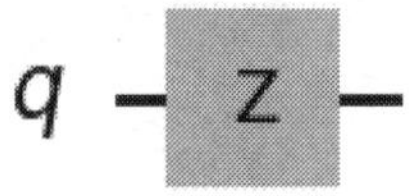

Figure 6.10: Z gate

Since we know the matrix representation of Pauli Z gate we will understand the Eigen-states and Eigenvectors of Pauli Z gate

Step 1: Finding the Eigenvalues

The characteristic equation of eigenvalue is,

$$\det(Z - \lambda I) = 0 \tag{6.18}$$

Step 2: Plugging in the Z matrix

$$\det\left(\begin{pmatrix} 1 & 0 \\ 0 & -1 \end{pmatrix} - \lambda \begin{pmatrix} 1 & 0 \\ 0 & 1 \end{pmatrix}\right) = 0 \tag{6.19}$$

Step 3; Expanding the determinant

$$\det\left(\begin{pmatrix} 1-\lambda & 0 \\ 0 & -1-\lambda \end{pmatrix}\right) = 0 \tag{6.20}$$

Step 4: Solving the quadratic equation for eigenvalues

$$(1-\lambda)(-1-\lambda) = 0 \tag{6.21}$$

Step 5: Eigenvalues

$$\lambda_1 = 1 \tag{6.22}$$

$$\lambda_2 = -1 \tag{6.23}$$

Step 6: Finding the Eigenvectors

$$\left(\begin{pmatrix} 1 & 0 \\ 0 & -1 \end{pmatrix} - 1 \begin{pmatrix} 1 & 0 \\ 0 & 1 \end{pmatrix}\right) \mathbf{v} = 0 \tag{6.24}$$

$$\begin{pmatrix} 0 & 0 \\ 0 & -2 \end{pmatrix} \mathbf{v} = 0 \tag{6.25}$$

$$\mathbf{v}_1 = \begin{pmatrix} 1 \\ 0 \end{pmatrix} \tag{6.26}$$

$$\left(\begin{pmatrix} 1 & 0 \\ 0 & -1 \end{pmatrix} + 1 \begin{pmatrix} 1 & 0 \\ 0 & 1 \end{pmatrix} \right) \mathbf{v} = 0 \tag{6.27}$$

$$\begin{pmatrix} 2 & 0 \\ 0 & 0 \end{pmatrix} \mathbf{v} = 0 \tag{6.28}$$

$$\mathbf{v}_2 = \begin{pmatrix} 0 \\ 1 \end{pmatrix} \tag{6.29}$$

$$= \begin{pmatrix} 0 \\ 1 \end{pmatrix} \tag{6.30}$$

$$\lambda_1 = 1 \text{ with eigenvector } \mathbf{v}_1 = \begin{pmatrix} 1 \\ 0 \end{pmatrix} \tag{6.31}$$

λ_2 = -1 with eigenvector $\mathbf{v}_2 = \begin{pmatrix} 0 \\ 1 \end{pmatrix}$. This represents the quantum state $|1\rangle$.

You can use the same method to find the eigenvalues and eigenvectors for Pauli X and Y gate.

Hadamard Gate

The Hadamard gate acts on a single qubit. It transforms the qubit's state from a definite state (either 0 or 1) into a complex combination of 0 and 1 states. The Hadamard gate creates an equal as well as unequal superposition of $|0\rangle$ and $|1\rangle$ if it acts on a qubit in a definite state. The Hadamard gate is represented as `h()`

In quantum computing, gates are represented by matrices. The Hadamard gate is represented by a 2x2 matrix:

Truth Table

Input	Output
$\|0\rangle$	$\frac{1}{\sqrt{2}}(\|0\rangle + \|1\rangle)$
$\|1\rangle$	$\frac{1}{\sqrt{2}}(\|0\rangle - \|1\rangle)$

By solving the output states of qubit, you will get the matrix representation,

Representing the basis states as vectors

$$|0\rangle = \begin{pmatrix} 1 \\ 0 \end{pmatrix} \quad \text{and} \quad |1\rangle = \begin{pmatrix} 0 \\ 1 \end{pmatrix} \tag{6.32}$$

Apply Hadamard to Basis States:

$$H|0\rangle = \frac{1}{\sqrt{2}}(|0\rangle + |1\rangle) = \frac{1}{\sqrt{2}}\left(\begin{pmatrix} 1 \\ 0 \end{pmatrix} + \begin{pmatrix} 0 \\ 1 \end{pmatrix}\right) = \frac{1}{\sqrt{2}}\begin{pmatrix} 1 \\ 1 \end{pmatrix} \tag{6.33}$$

$$H|1\rangle = \frac{1}{\sqrt{2}}(|0\rangle - |1\rangle) = \frac{1}{\sqrt{2}}\left(\begin{pmatrix} 1 \\ 0 \end{pmatrix} - \begin{pmatrix} 0 \\ 1 \end{pmatrix}\right) = \frac{1}{\sqrt{2}}\begin{pmatrix} 1 \\ -1 \end{pmatrix} \tag{6.34}$$

Matrix Construction

The columns of the Hadamard matrix are the resulting vectors from the preceding steps. The first column is $H|0\rangle$ and the second column is $H|1\rangle$

Hence the Hadamard matrix is,

$$H = \frac{1}{\sqrt{2}}\begin{pmatrix} 1 & 1 \\ 1 & -1 \end{pmatrix}$$

In order to implement a simple Hadamard gate the following code is as follows:

```
qc = QuantumCircuit(1)
qc.h(0)
qc.draw('mpl')
```

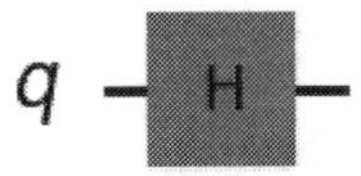

Figure 6.11: H gate

Bloch Sphere for H gate

Figure 6.11 shows the positive superposition of states.

Eigenvalues and Eigenvectors for H gate

The Hadamard matrix H is defined as:

$$H = \frac{1}{\sqrt{2}}\begin{pmatrix} 1 & 1 \\ 1 & -1 \end{pmatrix} \tag{6.35}$$

To find the eigenvalues and eigenvectors, we solve the equation $Hv = \lambda v$. Expanding

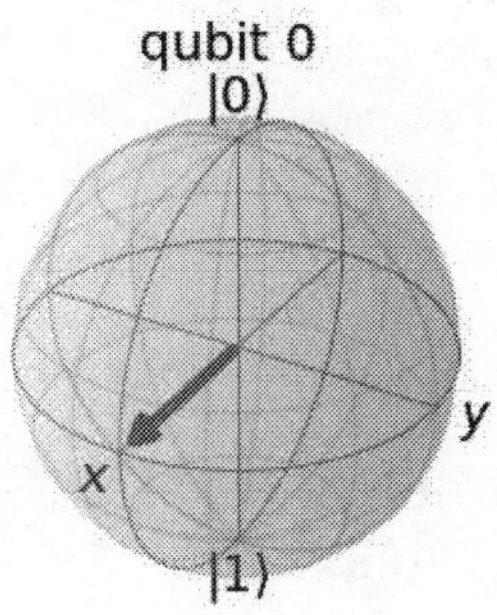

Figure 6.12: Bloch Sphere for H gate

this gives:

$$\frac{1}{\sqrt{2}}\begin{pmatrix} 1 & 1 \\ 1 & -1 \end{pmatrix}\begin{pmatrix} v_1 \\ v_2 \end{pmatrix} = \lambda \begin{pmatrix} v_1 \\ v_2 \end{pmatrix} \tag{6.36}$$

This expands to:

$$\frac{1}{\sqrt{2}}(v_1 + v_2) = \lambda v_1, \quad \frac{1}{\sqrt{2}}(v_1 - v_2) = \lambda v_2 \tag{6.37}$$

Solving for the eigenvalues, we find that $\lambda = \pm 1$.
For $\lambda = 1$, the eigenvector is:

$$v = \frac{1}{\sqrt{2}}\begin{pmatrix} 1 \\ 1 \end{pmatrix} \tag{6.38}$$

For $\lambda = -1$, the eigenvector is:

$$v = \frac{1}{\sqrt{2}}\begin{pmatrix} 1 \\ -1 \end{pmatrix} \tag{6.39}$$

Proof that H gate satisfies Hermitian property

The Hadamard gate is represented by the matrix:

$$H = \frac{1}{\sqrt{2}}\begin{pmatrix} 1 & 1 \\ 1 & -1 \end{pmatrix} \tag{6.40}$$

To prove that it is Hermitian, we compute its conjugate transpose:

$$H^\dagger = \left(\frac{1}{\sqrt{2}}\begin{pmatrix} 1 & 1 \\ 1 & -1 \end{pmatrix}\right)^\dagger = \frac{1}{\sqrt{2}}\begin{pmatrix} 1 & 1 \\ 1 & -1 \end{pmatrix}^T = \frac{1}{\sqrt{2}}\begin{pmatrix} 1 & 1 \\ 1 & -1 \end{pmatrix} \tag{6.41}$$

Comparing H and $H^\dagger$:

$$H = H^\dagger \tag{6.42}$$

Thus, the Hadamard gate is Hermitian as $H = H^\dagger$.

S Gate

S gate is called as **Phase Shift gate** , meaning shift in phase occurs. The phase shift occurs at an angle of $\pi/2$ radians. Here, probability amplitude is not disturbed, but only the phase is changed. S gate acts only on single qubit gates. This can be applied to QuantumCircuit with `s()` method.

Truth Table

Input	Output
$\|0\rangle$	$\|0\rangle$
$\|1\rangle$	$i\|1\rangle$

Matrix Representation

$$\begin{pmatrix} 1 & 0 \\ 0 & i \end{pmatrix} \tag{6.43}$$

There are a few pointers about S gate:

- **S gate is sometimes called the P gate (phase):** This reflects an aspect of naming conventions in quantum computing, particularly in relation to gates that apply phase shifts to qubits. However, it's important to clarify that while the S gate is a phase shift gate, it is not typically referred to as the "P". **The distinction lies in the specific phase shift each gate applies** .
  In short, the term **P gate** typically refers to a more **general phase shift gate** where the **phase shift angle is a variable parameter**. The S gate is a particular instance of such a phase gate with a fixed phase shift of 90 degrees.
- S **gate** $= \left(\sqrt{Z}\right)$ - the expression denotes the correlation between the S gate and the Z gate. This is an alternative representation of the S gate that highlights its relationship with the Z gate.

The matrix representation of the S gate is:

$$S = \begin{pmatrix} 1 & 0 \\ 0 & i \end{pmatrix}$$

To find the square of the S gate, we multiply the S gate matrix by itself:

$$S^2 = S \times S = \begin{pmatrix} 1 & 0 \\ 0 & i \end{pmatrix} \begin{pmatrix} 1 & 0 \\ 0 & i \end{pmatrix} \tag{6.44}$$

Performing the matrix multiplication gives:

$$S^2 = \begin{pmatrix} 1 \cdot 1 + 0 \cdot 0 & 1 \cdot 0 + 0 \cdot i \\ 0 \cdot 1 + i \cdot 0 & 0 \cdot 0 + i \cdot i \end{pmatrix} = \begin{pmatrix} 1 & 0 \\ 0 & i^2 \end{pmatrix} \tag{6.45}$$

Since $i^2 = -1$ (by the definition of the imaginary unit i)
The square of the S gate is represented by:

$$S^2 = \begin{pmatrix} 1 & 0 \\ 0 & -1 \end{pmatrix} \tag{6.46}$$

The matrix representation of the Z gate is:

$$Z = \begin{pmatrix} 1 & 0 \\ 0 & -1 \end{pmatrix} \tag{6.47}$$

Comparing the matrices, we see that:

$$S^2 = \begin{pmatrix} 1 & 0 \\ 0 & -1 \end{pmatrix} = Z \tag{6.48}$$

Thus, we have proven that the square of the S gate is indeed the Z gate.

3. **S gate is a Clifford gate**

The S gate is considered a Clifford gate because it transforms Pauli (X,Y,Z) operators into other Pauli operators under conjugation.

For example,

$$SZS^\dagger = \begin{pmatrix} 1 & 0 \\ 0 & i \end{pmatrix} \begin{pmatrix} 1 & 0 \\ 0 & -1 \end{pmatrix} \begin{pmatrix} 1 & 0 \\ 0 & -i \end{pmatrix} = \begin{pmatrix} 1 & 0 \\ 0 & -1 \end{pmatrix} = \mathbf{Z} \tag{6.49}$$

```
qc = QuantumCircuit(1)
qc.s(0)
qc.draw('mpl')
```

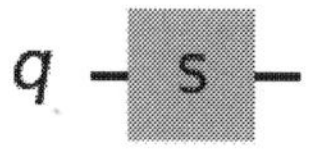

Figure 6.13: S gate

The preceding code doesn't have an effect on a qubit. In Bloch Sphere , the qubit state is in $|0\rangle$. In order to see the transition in the Bloch Sphere one needs to add X gate followed by S gate.

```
qc = QuantumCircuit(1)
qc.x(0)
qc.s(0)
qc.draw('mpl')
```

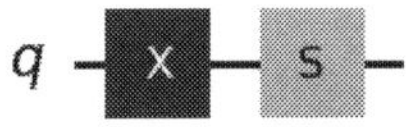

Figure 6.14: X followed by S gate

The preceding code has a qubit transition to $|1\rangle$.

Quantum circuit diagrams do not depict the state of the qubits at each stage; rather, they illustrate the sequence of operations (gates) implemented, which explains why the transition of the qubit state is not perceived visually in the circuit diagram. This type of diagram obscures the true state of the qubit, which includes any phase shifts.

In order to analyze the impact of these gates on the qubit state, it is necessary to employ a quantum simulator such as Qiskit's **StatevectorSimulator** to simulate the circuit. This would enable an examination of the qubit's state vector subsequent to each operation. This will demonstrate how the X and S gates influence the qubit's state, with the S gate introducing any phase alterations that may occur.

So basically, statevector simulator means the complex numbers associated with the qubit states. This is called as amplitude .

```
qc = QuantumCircuit(1)
qc.x(0)
qc.s(0)
qc.save_statevector()

simulator = AerSimulator(method = 'statevector')
qc = transpile(qc, simulator)
result = simulator.run(qc).result().get_statevector(qc)
plot_bloch_multivector(result)
```

The output is the following statevector.

$$\begin{aligned}\text{Statevector} = [&4.32978028e-17-4.32978028e-17j,\\ &2.77555756e-16+1.00000000e+00j],\\ \text{dims} =&(2,)\end{aligned}$$

The preceding state vector consists of two complex numbers corresponding to the amplitudes of qubit being in $|0\rangle$ and $|1\rangle$ state.

The first complex number is 4.32978028e-17 - 4.32978028e-17j . This is essentially 0 - 0j, which is approximately 0. The real and imaginary parts are extremely close to zero, indicating that the probability amplitude of the qubit being in the |0⟩ state is negligible.

The second complex number is 2.77555756e-16 + 1.00000000e+00j. This is **approximately 0 + 1j**. The real part is again close to zero, but the imaginary part is 1. This indicates that the qubit is almost entirely in the |1⟩ state.

dims=(2,) indicates the **dimensions of the quantum system**, showing it as a**single qubit system** (as two-dimensional state space).

Let's check whether the S gate satisfies the unitary and Hermitian properties

1. **Unitary** S gate is unitary in nature.

Proof of Unitarity for S Gate

$$S^{\dagger}S = \begin{pmatrix}1 & 0\\ 0 & -i\end{pmatrix}\begin{pmatrix}1 & 0\\ 0 & i\end{pmatrix} = \begin{pmatrix}1 & 0\\ 0 & 1\end{pmatrix} = I \tag{6.50}$$

2. **Non-Hermitian**

S gate is not hermitian because S gate is not equal to its conjugate transpose.

Reasoning Solve and check whether S gate is non-hermitian.

$S^{\dagger}$ Gate

$S^{\dagger}$ is the hermitian adjoint (conjugate transpose) of S gate. This applies the phase of -$\pi/2$ radians phase shift whereas S gate applies $\pi/2$ radians phase shift. Since this gate is the inverse of S gate, one can undo operations effects on qubits with the help of this gate. $S^{\dagger}$ gate can be represented as `sdg()` .

Also, $S^{\dagger}$ gate falls under the Clifford gate category and a square root of Z gate.

Truth Table

The truth table for the $S^\dagger$ gate is:

Input	Output
$\|0\rangle$	$\|0\rangle$
$\|1\rangle$	$-i\|1\rangle$

Matrix

The matrix representation of the $S^\dagger$ gate is:

$$S^\dagger = \begin{pmatrix} 1 & 0 \\ 0 & -i \end{pmatrix}$$

Implementation of Sdg gate

```
qc = QuantumCircuit(1)
qc.sdg(0)
qc.draw('mpl')
```

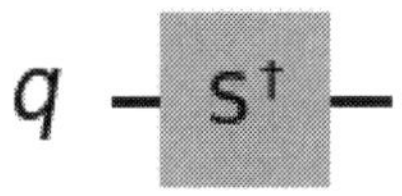

Figure 6.15: S dagger gate

The preceding code doesn't show transition on the qubit state. The state vector for this above code is:

$$\begin{aligned} \text{Statevector} = [&1. + 0.j, \\ &0. + 0.j], \\ \text{dims} = &(2,) \end{aligned}$$

Implementation of S and Sdg gate

```
qc = QuantumCircuit(1)
qc.s(0)
qc.sdg(0)
qc.draw('mpl')
```

The state vector is the same as the previous one.

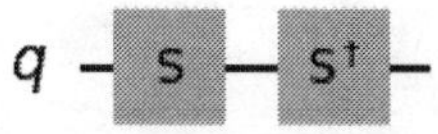

Figure 6.16: S followed by S dagger gate

Let us prove whether S dagger gate satisfies Unitary and Hermitian properties or not.

Unitary

S dagger is unitary

$$SS^\dagger = \begin{pmatrix} 1 & 0 \\ 0 & i \end{pmatrix} \begin{pmatrix} 1 & 0 \\ 0 & -i \end{pmatrix} = \begin{pmatrix} 1 & 0 \\ 0 & 1 \end{pmatrix} = I \tag{6.51}$$

Non-hermitian

The conjugate transpose (or adjoint) of $S^\dagger$, which is denoted as $(S^\dagger)^\dagger$, is calculated as follows:

$$(S^\dagger)^\dagger = \begin{pmatrix} 1 & 0 \\ 0 & i \end{pmatrix} \tag{6.52}$$

This matrix is identical to the original S gate:

$$S = \begin{pmatrix} 1 & 0 \\ 0 & i \end{pmatrix} \tag{6.53}$$

Comparing $S^\dagger$ with its adjoint:

$$S^\dagger \neq (S^\dagger)^\dagger \tag{6.54}$$

$$\begin{pmatrix} 1 & 0 \\ 0 & -i \end{pmatrix} \neq \begin{pmatrix} 1 & 0 \\ 0 & i \end{pmatrix} \tag{6.55}$$

Therefore, since $S^\dagger$ is not equal to its own conjugate transpose, it is not Hermitian. The requirement for a gate or operator to be Hermitian is that it must be equal to its own adjoint, which $S^\dagger$ does not satisfy.

T Gate

It's a single qubit gate which induces the phase shift of $\pi/4$ which means if you apply T gate 4 times you will get Z gate. This gate can be applied to QuantumCircuit object with `t()` method.

Truth Table

Input	Output
$\|0\rangle$	$\|0\rangle$
$\|1\rangle$	$e^{i\pi/4}\|1\rangle$

Matrix

$$T = \begin{pmatrix} 1 & 0 \\ 0 & e^{i\pi/4} \end{pmatrix} \tag{6.56}$$

When the T gate is applied consecutively 4 times, you get a Z gate,

$$T^4 = Z \tag{6.57}$$

Step 1
First multiplication ($T \cdot T$):

$$\begin{pmatrix} 1 & 0 \\ 0 & e^{i\pi/4} \end{pmatrix} \begin{pmatrix} 1 & 0 \\ 0 & e^{i\pi/4} \end{pmatrix} = \begin{pmatrix} 1 & 0 \\ 0 & e^{i\pi/2} \end{pmatrix} \tag{6.58}$$

Step 2:
Next, multiply this result by T again ($(T^2) \cdot T$):

$$\begin{pmatrix} 1 & 0 \\ 0 & e^{i\pi/2} \end{pmatrix} \begin{pmatrix} 1 & 0 \\ 0 & e^{i\pi/4} \end{pmatrix} = \begin{pmatrix} 1 & 0 \\ 0 & e^{i3\pi/4} \end{pmatrix} \tag{6.59}$$

Step 3:
Finally, multiply this result by T one more time ($(T^3) \cdot T$):

$$\begin{pmatrix} 1 & 0 \\ 0 & e^{i3\pi/4} \end{pmatrix} \begin{pmatrix} 1 & 0 \\ 0 & e^{i\pi/4} \end{pmatrix} = \begin{pmatrix} 1 & 0 \\ 0 & e^{i\pi} \end{pmatrix} \tag{6.60}$$

Since $e^{i\pi}$ is equivalent to -1

$$e^{i\pi} = \cos\pi + i\sin\pi \tag{6.61}$$

$$\cos\pi = -1, \sin\pi = 0 \tag{6.62}$$

Substituting in $e^{i\pi}$ we get,

$$T^4 = \begin{pmatrix} 1 & 0 \\ 0 & -1 \end{pmatrix} = Z \tag{6.63}$$

Even though T gate when multiplied 4 times gives Z gate this doesn't mean that the T gate's ability to apply a $\pi/4$ phase shift is unique and cannot be replicated by any combination of Clifford gates.

Importance of non-Clifford gate

It's important that one should recall the importance of a non-clifford gate.

1. Unique Transformations

Transformations beyond what can be accomplished by any combination of Clifford gates are introduced by non-Clifford gates, such as the T gate. The T gate transitions the quantum state through a phase shift of $\pi/4$. Clifford gates are alone is insufficient to accomplish this particular form of phase shift.

2. Universality of computation

Universal quantum computation is achieved when the T gate (or any other non-Clifford gate) is added to a quantum system's set of Clifford gates. This functionality empowers the system to execute calculations that are impracticable to simulate efficiently on classical computers, thereby capitalizing on quantum mechanics' complete potential.

Also, Clifford gates alone can't attain the universality of quantum computation. Along with non-Clifford gates such as T gate, the universality is attained.

3. Gottesman-Knill Theorem

According to this theorem, it is possible to efficiently simulate any quantum circuit composed entirely of Clifford gates on a classical computer. The inclusion of a solitary non-Clifford gate , such as the T gate, renders the circuit "universal" for quantum computing purposes. Consequently, it becomes impracticable to simulate efficiently on a classical computer in general.

```
qc = QuantumCircuit(1)
qc.t(0)
qc.draw('mpl')
```

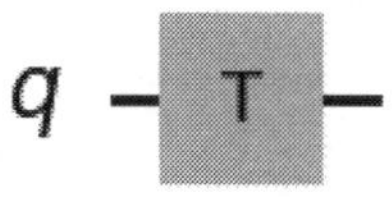

Figure 6.17: T gate

Only T gate doesn't have any visible change. Thus applying Y gate followed by T gate.

```
qc = QuantumCircuit(1)
qc.y(0)
qc.t(0)
qc.draw('mpl')
```

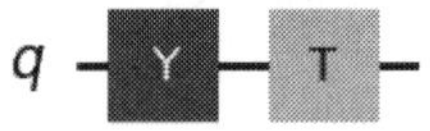

Figure 6.18: Y gate followed by T gate

The state vector for this gate is,

$$\begin{aligned}\text{Statevector} = &[0. + 0.j,\\ &- 0.70710678 + 0.70710678j],\\ \text{dims} = &(2,)\end{aligned}$$

For the first element, the magnitude is

$$0^2 + 0^2 = 0 \tag{6.64}$$

so the probability of measuring the state |0⟩ is 0%.
For the second element, the magnitude is,

$$-0.70710678^2 + 0.70710678j^2 = \text{~}1 \tag{6.65}$$

making the probability of measuring the state |1⟩ close to 100%.

Properties and Proofs of the T and $T^\dagger$ Gates

The T gate and its adjoint $T^\dagger$ have the following properties:

$T^\dagger$ **Gate:**

$$T^\dagger = \begin{pmatrix} 1 & 0 \\ 0 & e^{-i\pi/4} \end{pmatrix} \tag{6.66}$$

1. Proof of Unitarity for T Gate:

$$T^\dagger T = \begin{pmatrix} 1 & 0 \\ 0 & e^{-i\pi/4} \end{pmatrix} \begin{pmatrix} 1 & 0 \\ 0 & e^{i\pi/4} \end{pmatrix} = \begin{pmatrix} 1 & 0 \\ 0 & 1 \end{pmatrix} = I \tag{6.67}$$

2. Non-Hermitian

T gate is non-hermitian because the gate doesn't have its own conjugate transpose.

$T^\dagger$ Gate

$T^\dagger$ gate is the single qubit T-adjoint gate. Adjoint means Hermitian adjoint (conjugate transpose) of T gate. This gate is the reverse of T gate. If T gate applies $\pi/4$ phase shift, $T^\dagger$ gate applies -$\pi/4$ phase shift. This gate can be applied to QuantumCircuit object with `tdg()` method.

Truth Table

Input	Output
$\|0\rangle$	$\|0\rangle$
$\|1\rangle$	$e^{-i\pi/4}\|1\rangle$

Operator

$$T = \begin{pmatrix} 1 & 0 \\ 0 & e^{-i\pi/4} \end{pmatrix} \tag{6.68}$$

```
qc = QuantumCircuit(1)
qc.tdg(0)
qc.draw('mpl')
```

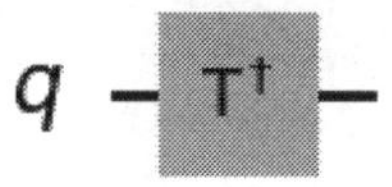

Figure 6.19: T dagger

Implementation of Tdg gate with other Clifford gates

```
qc = QuantumCircuit(1)
qc.x(0)
qc.tdg(0)
qc.draw('mpl')
```

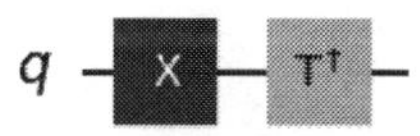

Figure 6.20: X followed by T dagger

The reason for using Clifford gates is to show the transformation in qubit states along with the change in probability.

The state vector for the preceding implementation is

$$\begin{aligned}\text{Statevector} = [0. + 0.j, \\ 0.707 - 0.707j], \\ \text{dims} = (2,)\end{aligned}$$

It's clear from the above state vector that the qubit is in $|1\rangle$ *state*, but if you observe the imaginary part of $|1\rangle$ *state*, you can see **-0.707j**. It's not a positive imaginary unit but has a negative sign. This is because of $e^{-i\pi/4}$. The real part is positive because there is no gate applied which can change the sign of the real part.

```
qc = QuantumCircuit(1)
qc.x(0)
qc.z(0)
qc.tdg(0)
qc.draw('mpl')
```

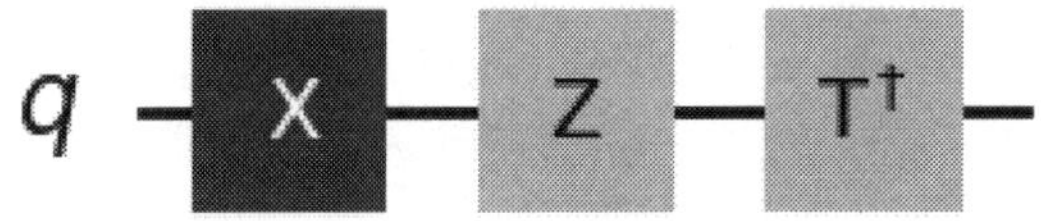

Figure 6.21: X and Z followed by Tdg

Now, the Z gate is applied. This will change the sign of the real part because the Z gate is applied after the X gate.

The state vector for the above implementation is

$$\begin{aligned}\text{Statevector} = [0. + 0.j, \\ - 0.70710678 + 0.70710678j], \\ \text{dims} = (2,)\end{aligned}$$

The real part is **-0.70710678**, which has a negative sign. This happened because **X gate followed by Z gate**. X gate changed the qubit state to $|1\rangle$ state, and Z gate changed the qubit state to -$|1\rangle$ state.

The reason to get 0.707 is

$$e^{ix} = \cos(x) + i\sin(x) \tag{6.69}$$

Applying this to $x = -\frac{\pi}{4}$ gives:

$$e^{-i\frac{\pi}{4}} = \cos\left(-\frac{\pi}{4}\right) + i\sin\left(-\frac{\pi}{4}\right) \tag{6.70}$$

$$-e^{-i\pi/4} = -(\cos(-\pi/4) + i\sin(-\pi/4)) = -\left(\frac{1}{\sqrt{2}} - i\frac{1}{\sqrt{2}}\right) = -\frac{1}{\sqrt{2}} + i\frac{1}{\sqrt{2}} \tag{6.71}$$

Properties and Proof of $T^\dagger$ gate

1.**Proof of Unitarity for $T^\dagger$ Gate:**

$$TT^\dagger = \begin{pmatrix} 1 & 0 \\ 0 & e^{i\pi/4} \end{pmatrix} \begin{pmatrix} 1 & 0 \\ 0 & e^{-i\pi/4} \end{pmatrix} = \begin{pmatrix} 1 & 0 \\ 0 & 1 \end{pmatrix} = I \tag{6.72}$$

2.**Non-Hermitian**

$T^\dagger$ is non-hermitian because the gate doesn't have its own conjugate transpose.

Reasoning Question for you

Are T and $T^\dagger$ gates involutory in nature? State the reason

Rx Gate

Rotation around the X-axis is called an Rx gate . When $\theta = \pi$, the Rx gate performs a full 180° rotation, which flips the state from $|0\rangle$ to $|1\rangle$ or vice versa, similar to the action of the Pauli-X gate. This can be applied to QuantumCircuit object using `rx()` method. Unlike Pauli gates and other phase shift gates, Rotation gates don't have any truth table because of continuous transformations.

Euler's formula states that for any real number x:

$$e^{ix} = \cos(x) + i\sin(x) \tag{6.73}$$

For the Rx gate, which performs a rotation around the x-axis, the matrix is derived as follows:

$$R_x(\theta) = e^{-i(\theta/2)X} \tag{6.74}$$

where X is the Pauli-X matrix:

$$X = \begin{pmatrix} 0 & 1 \\ 1 & 0 \end{pmatrix} \tag{6.75}$$

Applying Euler's formula, we get:

$$e^{-i(\theta/2)X} = \cos\left(-\frac{\theta}{2}\right) I - i\sin\left(-\frac{\theta}{2}\right) X \tag{6.76}$$

$$= \cos\left(\frac{\theta}{2}\right)\begin{pmatrix} 1 & 0 \\ 0 & 1 \end{pmatrix} - i\sin\left(\frac{\theta}{2}\right)\begin{pmatrix} 0 & 1 \\ 1 & 0 \end{pmatrix} \tag{6.77}$$

$$= \begin{pmatrix} \cos(\theta/2) & -i\sin(\theta/2) \\ -i\sin(\theta/2) & \cos(\theta/2) \end{pmatrix} \tag{6.78}$$

Thus, the matrix for the Rx gate is:

$$R_x(\theta) = \begin{pmatrix} \cos(\theta/2) & -i\sin(\theta/2) \\ -i\sin(\theta/2) & \cos(\theta/2) \end{pmatrix} \tag{6.79}$$

```
import math

qc = QuantumCircuit(1)
theta = math.pi / 2
qc.rx(theta, 0)
qc.draw(output='mpl')
```

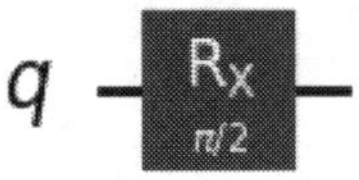

Figure 6.22: Rx gate

Bloch Sphere implementation of Rx gate

Figure 6.23 explains the visualization of transformation for Rx gate.

The Rx gate with $\theta = \frac{\pi}{2}$ has the matrix representation:

```
Quantum state is: Statevector([0.707+0.j   , 0.   -0.707j],
            dims=(2,))
```

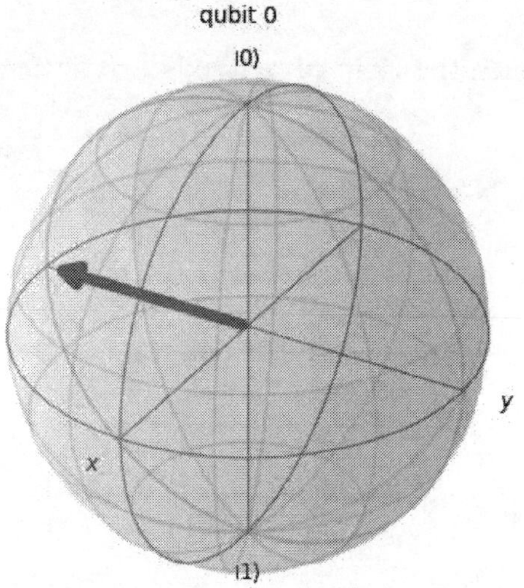

Figure 6.23: Bloch Sphere for Rx gate

$$R_x\left(\frac{\pi}{2}\right) = \begin{pmatrix} \cos\left(\frac{\pi}{4}\right) & -i\sin\left(\frac{\pi}{4}\right) \\ -i\sin\left(\frac{\pi}{4}\right) & \cos\left(\frac{\pi}{4}\right) \end{pmatrix} \tag{6.80}$$

Since $\cos\left(\frac{\pi}{4}\right) = \sin\left(\frac{\pi}{4}\right) = \frac{1}{\sqrt{2}}$, the matrix becomes:

$$R_x\left(\frac{\pi}{2}\right) = \begin{pmatrix} \frac{1}{\sqrt{2}} & -i\frac{1}{\sqrt{2}} \\ -i\frac{1}{\sqrt{2}} & \frac{1}{\sqrt{2}} \end{pmatrix} \tag{6.81}$$

The initial state of the qubit is $|0\rangle$, represented by the state vector $[1, 0]$ or $[1 + 0j, 0 + 0j]$. Applying the Rx gate to this initial state:

$$\begin{pmatrix} \frac{1}{\sqrt{2}} & -i\frac{1}{\sqrt{2}} \\ -i\frac{1}{\sqrt{2}} & \frac{1}{\sqrt{2}} \end{pmatrix} \begin{pmatrix} 1 \\ 0 \end{pmatrix} = \begin{pmatrix} \frac{1}{\sqrt{2}} \cdot 1 + -i\frac{1}{\sqrt{2}} \cdot 0 \\ -i\frac{1}{\sqrt{2}} \cdot 1 + \frac{1}{\sqrt{2}} \cdot 0 \end{pmatrix} \tag{6.82}$$

This simplifies to:

$$\begin{pmatrix} \frac{1}{\sqrt{2}} \\ -i\frac{1}{\sqrt{2}} \end{pmatrix} = \begin{pmatrix} 0.707 + 0j \\ 0 - 0.707i \end{pmatrix} \tag{6.83}$$

Thus, after applying the Rx gate with $\theta = \frac{\pi}{2}$ to the initial state $|0\rangle$, the state vector becomes $[0.707 + 0.j, 0. - 0.707j]$.

Practice

Practice these questions with the help of matrix, derive the state vector.

1. $rx = \pi$
2. $rx = 2\pi$
3. $rx = 3\pi$

Ry Gate

The Ry gate in quantum computing is a rotation around the y-axis of the Bloch sphere. Ry gate is represented as `ry()` The matrix representation of the Ry gate for a rotation by an angle θ is derived as follows:

$$R_y(\theta) = \begin{pmatrix} \cos(\theta/2) & -\sin(\theta/2) \\ \sin(\theta/2) & \cos(\theta/2) \end{pmatrix} \tag{6.84}$$

This matrix rotates the state of a qubit around the y-axis by the angle θ. The elements of the matrix are derived based on the principles of rotation in quantum mechanics.

Euler's formula can be expressed as:

$$e^{iA\theta} = \cos(\theta)I + i\sin(\theta)A$$

For the Ry gate, which represents a rotation around the y-axis, the operator A is taken to be the Pauli-Y matrix:

$$Y = \begin{pmatrix} 0 & -i \\ i & 0 \end{pmatrix} \tag{6.85}$$

Applying Euler's formula for a rotation by an angle θ around the y-axis, we have:

$$R_y(\theta) = e^{-iY\theta/2} = \cos(\theta/2)I - i\sin(\theta/2)Y \tag{6.86}$$

Expanding this expression gives:

$$\cos(\theta/2) and - \sin(\theta/2) \tag{6.87}$$

If $\theta = \pi$ (180 degrees), then:

$$\cos\left(\frac{\theta}{2}\right) = \cos\left(\frac{\pi}{2}\right) = 0 - \sin\left(\frac{\theta}{2}\right) = -\sin\left(\frac{\pi}{2}\right) = -1 \tag{6.88}$$

If $\theta = \frac{\pi}{2}$ (90 degrees), then:

$$\cos\left(\frac{\theta}{2}\right) = \cos\left(\frac{\pi}{4}\right) = \frac{1}{\sqrt{2}} \tag{6.89}$$

or approximately 0.707

$$-\sin\left(\frac{\theta}{2}\right) = -\sin\left(\frac{\pi}{4}\right) = -\frac{1}{\sqrt{2}} \tag{6.90}$$

or approximately -0.707

$$R_y(\theta) = \cos(\theta/2)\begin{pmatrix} 1 & 0 \\ 0 & 1 \end{pmatrix} - i\sin(\theta/2)\begin{pmatrix} 0 & -i \\ i & 0 \end{pmatrix} \tag{6.91}$$

$$R_y(\theta) = \begin{pmatrix} \cos(\theta/2) & -\sin(\theta/2) \\ \sin(\theta/2) & \cos(\theta/2) \end{pmatrix} \tag{6.92}$$

Qiskit Implementation of Ry gate

```
qc = QuantumCircuit(1)
theta = math.pi / 4
qc.ry(theta, 0)
qc.draw(output='mpl')
```

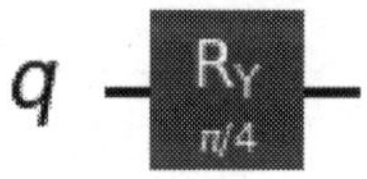

Figure 6.24: Ry gate

```
qc = QuantumCircuit(1)
theta = math.pi/4
qc.ry(theta, 0)
qc.save_statevector()
```

```
simulator = AerSimulator(method = 'statevector')
qc = transpile(qc, simulator)
result = simulator.run(qc).result().get_statevector(qc)
plot_bloch_multivector(result)
```

Bloch Sphere implementation of Ry gate

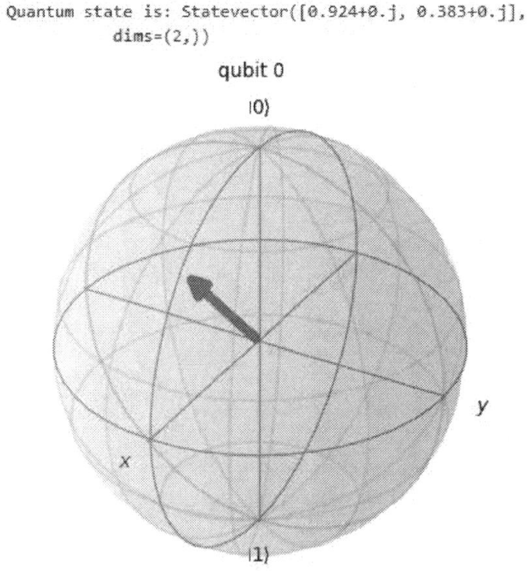

Figure 6.25: Bloch Sphere for Ry gate

Rz Gate

Rz gate is the rotation around the Z axis. Rz gate is represented as `rz()` The Rz gate rotates a qubit state around the z-axis of the Bloch sphere by a given angle θ.

Applying Euler's formula for a rotation by an angle θ around the z-axis, we have:

$$R_z(\theta) = e^{-i(\theta/2)Z} \tag{6.93}$$

where Z is the Pauli-Z matrix:

$$Z = \begin{pmatrix} 1 & 0 \\ 0 & -1 \end{pmatrix} \tag{6.94}$$

Applying Euler's formula, we get:

$$e^{-i(\theta/2)Z} = \cos\left(-\frac{\theta}{2}\right) I - i\sin\left(-\frac{\theta}{2}\right) Z \tag{6.95}$$

$$= \cos\left(\frac{\theta}{2}\right)\begin{pmatrix}1 & 0\\ 0 & 1\end{pmatrix} - i\sin\left(\frac{\theta}{2}\right)\begin{pmatrix}1 & 0\\ 0 & -1\end{pmatrix} \tag{6.96}$$

$$= \begin{pmatrix}\cos(\theta/2) - i\sin(\theta/2) & 0\\ 0 & \cos(\theta/2) + i\sin(\theta/2)\end{pmatrix} = \begin{pmatrix}e^{-i\theta/2} & 0\\ 0 & e^{i\theta/2}\end{pmatrix} \tag{6.97}$$

This matrix represents the Rz gate, which rotates the state of a qubit around the z-axis by the angle θ.

$$\cos(-\theta/2) + i\sin(-\theta/2) = e^{-i\theta/2} \tag{6.98}$$

$$\cos(\theta/2) + i\sin(\theta/2) = e^{i\theta/2} \tag{6.99}$$

The matrix representation of the Rz gate is then:

$$R_z(\theta) = \begin{pmatrix}e^{-i\theta/2} & 0\\ 0 & e^{i\theta/2}\end{pmatrix} \tag{6.100}$$

Implementation of Rz Gate

Following is the code for implementing the Rz gate

```
qc = QuantumCircuit(1)
theta = math.pi/2
qc.rz(theta, 0)
qc.draw(output='mpl')
```

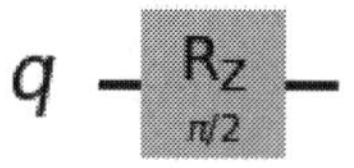

Figure 6.26: Rz gate

Bloch Sphere implementation of Rz gate

Given the implementation of the Rz code, this part explains the visualization of transformation for the Rz gate.

```
qc = QuantumCircuit(1)
theta = math.pi/2
qc.rz(theta, 0)
qc.save_statevector()

simulator = AerSimulator(method = 'statevector')
qc = transpile(qc, simulator)
result = simulator.run(qc).result().get_statevector(qc)
plot_bloch_multivector(result)
```

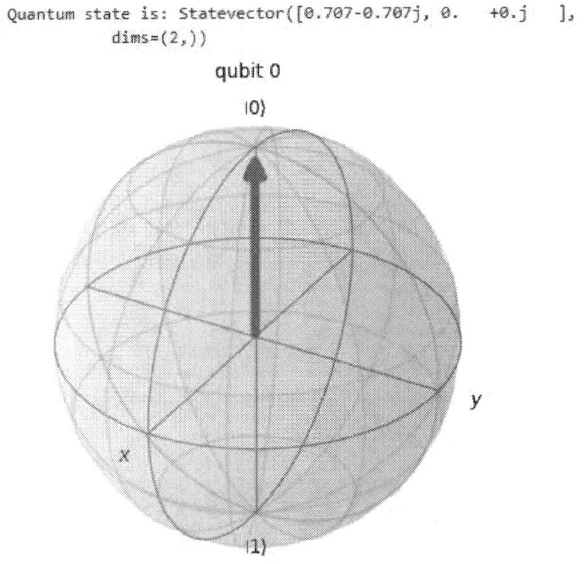

Figure 6.27: Bloch Sphere for Rz gate

Using an Rz gate to move a qubit from the north or south pole of the Bloch sphere, respectively, is not possible if the qubit begins in the state $|0\rangle$ or $|1\rangle$. Thus, no obvious transition can be observed.

Qubits must be in a superposition state where phase differences are significant in order for the effect of the Rz gate to be observed. As an illustration, the Bloch sphere's state will change if an Rz gate is applied after a Hadamard gate (H) has been utilized to generate a superposition [H].

Proof and properties of Rotation gates (R_x, R_y, R_z)

1. Unitary

All rotation gates are unitary in nature.

2. Hermitian

For a specific value of θ such as $\theta = \pi$ and $\theta = 2\pi$ rotation gates are hermitian in nature. The $Rx(\theta)$ gate is represented by:

$$Rx(\theta) = \begin{pmatrix} \cos(\theta/2) & -i\sin(\theta/2) \\ -i\sin(\theta/2) & \cos(\theta/2) \end{pmatrix} \tag{6.101}$$

This gate performs a rotation about the x-axis on the Bloch sphere. To determine when it is Hermitian, we need to check when $Rx(\theta) = Rx(\theta)^\dagger$.

The adjoint (or conjugate transpose) of $Rx(\theta)$ is:

$$Rx(\theta)^\dagger = \begin{pmatrix} \cos(\theta/2) & i\sin(\theta/2) \\ i\sin(\theta/2) & \cos(\theta/2) \end{pmatrix} \tag{6.102}$$

When $\theta = \pi$:

$$Rx(\pi) = \begin{pmatrix} \cos(\pi/2) & -i\sin(\pi/2) \\ -i\sin(\pi/2) & \cos(\pi/2) \end{pmatrix} = \begin{pmatrix} 0 & -i \\ -i & 0 \end{pmatrix} \tag{6.103}$$

This reduces to:

$$Rx(\pi) = -i \begin{pmatrix} 0 & 1 \\ 1 & 0 \end{pmatrix} \tag{6.104}$$

Here, $\begin{pmatrix} 0 & 1 \\ 1 & 0 \end{pmatrix}$ is the Pauli-X gate, thus $Rx(\pi)$ is proportional to Pauli-X by a global phase of $-i$, and it is Hermitian.

When $\theta = 2\pi$:

$$Rx(2\pi) = \begin{pmatrix} \cos(\pi) & -i\sin(\pi) \\ -i\sin(\pi) & \cos(\pi) \end{pmatrix} = \begin{pmatrix} -1 & 0 \\ 0 & -1 \end{pmatrix} \tag{6.105}$$

The adjoint $Rx(\pi)^\dagger$ is:

$$Rx(\pi)^\dagger = \left(-i \begin{pmatrix} 0 & 1 \\ 1 & 0 \end{pmatrix}\right)^\dagger = i \begin{pmatrix} 0 & 1 \\ 1 & 0 \end{pmatrix} \tag{6.106}$$

Both $Rx(\pi)$ and $Rx(\pi)^\dagger$ relate to the Pauli-X gate, demonstrating their connection through a global phase shift.

This is proportional to the identity matrix by a global phase factor of -1, making it Hermitian.

For $\theta = \pi$ and $\theta = 2\pi$, the $Rx(\theta)$ gate transforms into configurations equivalent to the

Pauli-X and the negative identity matrix, respectively, each of which is Hermitian. However, for general values of θ, $Rx(\theta)$ is not Hermitian as it does not equal its own adjoint except in these specific instances.

Phase Gate

A phase gate is a single qubit gate that rotates around the Z axis. The main difference between phase gate and S, S dagger, T, and T dagger gates is that the angle is fixed, and they are one type of Phase gate, but any angle can be fixed for a Phase gate. Phase gate is represented by `p()` method.

Truth Table

Input	Output
$\|0\rangle$	$\|0\rangle$
$\|1\rangle$	$e^{i\theta}\|1\rangle$

The matrix for the Phase gate is,

$$P = \begin{pmatrix} 1 & 0 \\ 0 & e^{i\theta} \end{pmatrix} \tag{6.107}$$

If $\theta = \pi$ Then, according to Euler's theorem,

$$e^{i\theta} = \cos(\theta) + i\sin(\theta) \tag{6.108}$$

$$e^{i\pi} = \cos(\pi) + i\sin(\pi) \tag{6.109}$$

$$\cos(\pi) = -1 and \sin(\pi) = 0 \tag{6.110}$$

So, $e^{i\pi}$ = -1

When u replace $e^{i\theta}$ with -1 you get a pauli gate.

$$P = \begin{pmatrix} 1 & 0 \\ 0 & -1 \end{pmatrix} \tag{6.111}$$

That Pauli gate is none other than **Z gate.**

There are a few more values you need to know.

$$\theta = \pi/2 \tag{6.112}$$

$$cos(\pi/2) = 0, \sin(\pi/2) = 1 \tag{6.113}$$

Then you get the matrix as,

$$P = \begin{pmatrix} 1 & 0 \\ 0 & i \end{pmatrix} \tag{6.114}$$

This matrix is equivalent to S gate if $\theta = \pi/4$

The Hadamard gate creates a superposition state from a basis state. Its matrix representation is:

$$H = \frac{1}{\sqrt{2}} \begin{pmatrix} 1 & 1 \\ 1 & -1 \end{pmatrix} \tag{6.115}$$

The Phase gate applies a phase shift to the state $|1\rangle$. For a phase of π, its matrix representation is:

$$P(\pi) = \begin{pmatrix} 1 & 0 \\ 0 & e^{i\pi} \end{pmatrix} = \begin{pmatrix} 1 & 0 \\ 0 & -1 \end{pmatrix} \tag{6.116}$$

Since $e^{i\pi} = -1$.

The overall matrix for the circuit is obtained by multiplying the matrices of the H and P gates, in the order they are applied:

$$\text{Circuit Matrix} = P(\pi) \times H \tag{6.117}$$

Calculating this:

$$\begin{pmatrix} 1 & 0 \\ 0 & -1 \end{pmatrix} \times \frac{1}{\sqrt{2}} \begin{pmatrix} 1 & 1 \\ 1 & -1 \end{pmatrix} \tag{6.118}$$

$$= \frac{1}{\sqrt{2}} \begin{pmatrix} 1 \times 1 + 0 \times 1 & 1 \times 1 + 0 \times -1 \\ 0 \times 1 - 1 \times 1 & 0 \times 1 - 1 \times -1 \end{pmatrix} \tag{6.119}$$

$$= \frac{1}{\sqrt{2}} \begin{pmatrix} 1 & 1 \\ -1 & 1 \end{pmatrix} \tag{6.120}$$

So, the complete matrix for the circuit is:

$$\frac{1}{\sqrt{2}}\begin{pmatrix} 1 & 1 \\ -1 & 1 \end{pmatrix} \tag{6.121}$$

This matrix represents the transformation that the quantum circuit applies to the state vector of a qubit. The Hadamard gate first creates a superposition, and the Phase gate then applies a π phase shift to the $|1\rangle$ component of the state.

Implementation of Phase gate

The following code implements the phase gate.

```
qc = QuantumCircuit(1)
qc.h(0)
qc.p(np.pi, 0)
qc.draw('mpl')
```

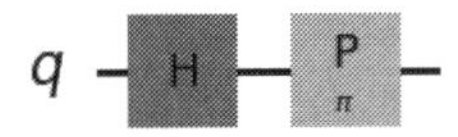

Figure 6.28: Phase gate

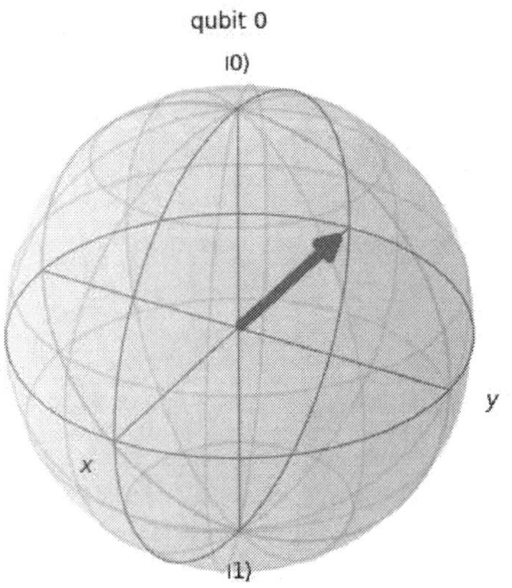

Figure 6.29: Bloch Sphere for Phase gate

Note

All the single qubit gates, multi-qubit gates, Identity gates, Unitary gates, and Quantum Fourier Transform gates (QFT) are unitary. That means the quantum state is preserved, which means the quantum information is preserved. Unitary gates are reversible in nature. If they are not unitary, then information loss occurs.

Conclusion

This chapter extensively discussed the Pauli gates, Hadamard gates, phase gates, S, $S^\dagger$, T, $T^\dagger$, phase and rotation gates, and the properties of each gate. Since you have studied the single-qubit gates, you will be comfortable in understanding the multi-qubit gates described in the next chapter.

CHAPTER 7

Multi Qubit Quantum Logic Gates

Introduction

Multi-qubit gates are quantum operations that involve two or more qubits simultaneously. They are essential for quantum computation, as they facilitate entanglement and complex state transformations. These gates enable the implementation of sophisticated quantum algorithms and operations that are not feasible with single-qubit gates alone, as they facilitate interactions between qubits. Error correction, quantum teleportation, and the generation of extremely entangled states are all tasks that require multi-qubit gates, which are fundamental to the power and potential of quantum computing.

Structure

In this chapter, you are going to study:

- Two Qubit Quantum Gates
    - CNOT Gate
    - CY Gate

- CZ Gate
- SWAP Gate
- CRx Gate

- Three Qubit Quantum Gates and Beyond
    - Toffoli Gate
    - Fredkin Gate

Two Qubit Quantum Gates

As opposed to Single qubit gates, multi-qubit gates have two qubits. Not all multi-qubit gates are Clifford gates. One example of a multi-qubit Clifford gate is the CNOT gate. An example of a non-clifford multi-qubit gate is the Toffoli gate.

The most popular gates are CNOT or CX, CY, CZ, CH, SWAP, Bell States, CRx, CRy, CRz, and more. We will discuss most of these gates in detail.

CNOT Gate

C stands for **Controlled** and NOT gate is similar to Pauli X gate. Since it's a two-qubit gate, either of the qubits acts as **control qubit** and another qubit acts as **target qubit**. This completely depends on us as to which qubit we need to fix as control and target. CNOT gate is represented as `cx()`

Implementation of CNOT gate

Now we will be implementing the CNOT gate using the **cx()** method. By default, we are considering qubit (q_0) as the control qubit and qubit (q_1) as the target qubit. This control and target qubit is user-defined.

```
qc = QuantumCircuit(2)
qc.cx(0,1) # Here. 0 is the control qubit and 1 is the target qubit
qc.draw('mpl')
```

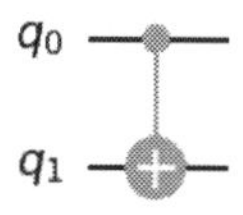

Figure 7.1: CX gate implementation

Truth Table

From quantum circuit implementation, we derive the truth table. There is a condition that when the control qubit (Input) is in $|0\rangle$ state then the target (input) will not be flipped. Only if the control (input) qubit is in $|1\rangle$ the target (input) qubit will have a bit flip. Example: You can observe that 10 becomes 11 and 11 becomes 10 (output).

Control (Input)	Target (Input)	Control (Output)	Target (Output)
0	0	0	0
0	1	0	1
1	0	1	1
1	1	1	0

Table 7.1: Truth Table for the CNOT Gate

Operator

Equation (7.1) refers to the operator (matrix) for the truth table (7.1).

$$CNOT = \begin{pmatrix} 1 & 0 & 0 & 0 \\ 0 & 1 & 0 & 0 \\ 0 & 0 & 0 & 1 \\ 0 & 0 & 1 & 0 \end{pmatrix} \tag{7.1}$$

H gate followed by CNOT creates entanglement of states.

QSphere for CX Gate

As we are aware of the QSphere implementation from the single qubit gates chapter, we can recall that QSphere is a visualization tool for multi-qubit gates.

```
plot_state_qsphere(qc)
```

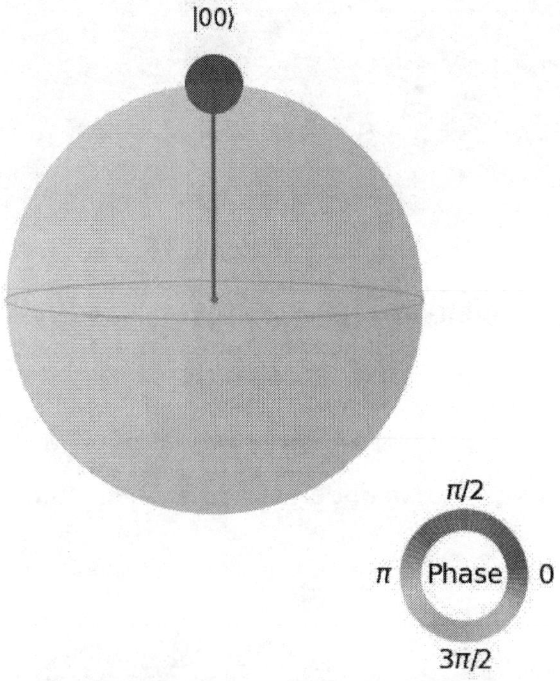

Figure 7.2: QSphere for CX gate

Histogram Implementation of CNOT Gate

In order to have histogram visualization, measuring the circuit is mandatory.

```
qc = QuantumCircuit(2)
qc.cx(0,1)
qc.measure_all()
qc.draw('mpl')
```

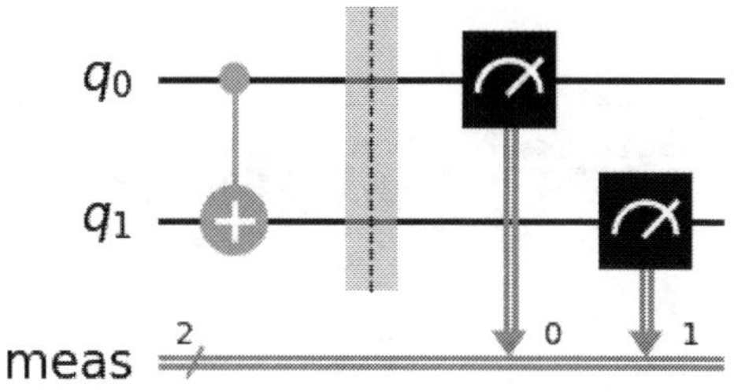

Figure 7.3: CX gate after measurement

```
shots = 10000

sim_automatic = AerSimulator(method='automatic')
job_automatic = sim_automatic.run(qc, shots=shots)
counts_automatic = job_automatic.result().get_counts(0)

plot_histogram([counts_automatic], title='Counts for automatic simulation method',
↪  legend=['automatic'])
```

The Quantum state is: **00 : 10000**

CX Gate Histogram

After running 10000 shots we can understand that the resultant is 00.

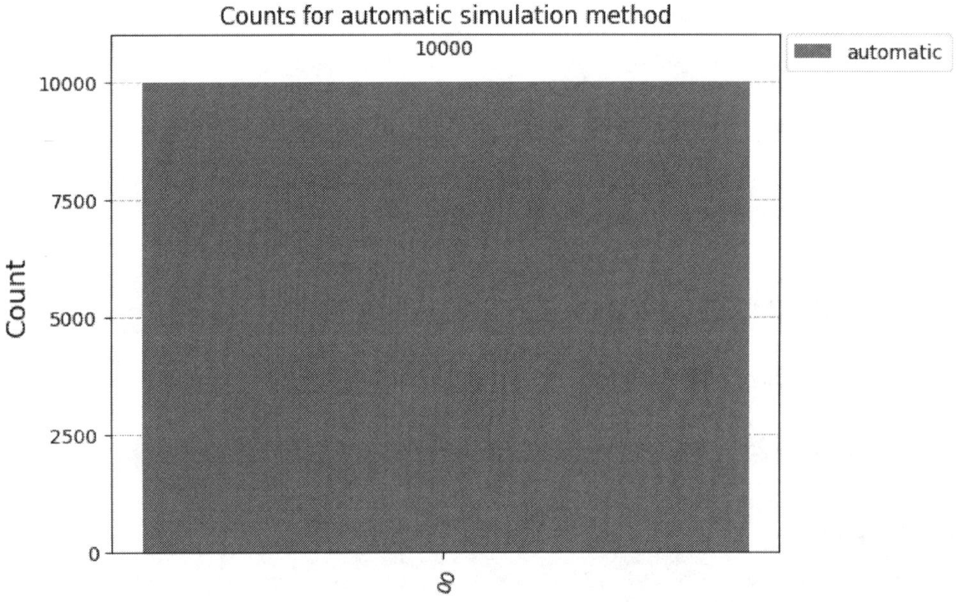

Figure 7.4: CX gate histogram

Bell's Inequality

Bell's inequality is crucial for demonstrating the fundamental differences between quantum mechanics and classical theories, highlighting the non-local nature of quantum entanglement.

Let's understand the meaning of **Non-locality**.

Non-locality

Every particle has a hidden variable (or underlying property) that determines the measurement. So, if the underlying property is known, the outcome can be deterministic.

Local hidden variable

The underlying property of a particle is said to be local if the measurement is based upon the influence of surroundings.

Quantum entanglement is explained by two theories:

1. Local hidden variable theory
2. Quantum mechanics theory

Local hidden variable theory

Under local hidden variable theory, every particle has a hidden variable (underlying property which is unknown) and the particle's entanglement is due to the underlying property (hidden variable) arising from local interactions.

Quantum mechanics

QM theory suggests that the quantum entanglement of particles is not due to the local hidden variable. So, the interaction between particles is non-local.

This means that the measurement outcome on one particle instantly affects the outcome of another irrespective of the distance thereby violating local hidden variable theory thus creating a new concept called non-locality.

The following table 7.2 shows the differentiation between local hidden variable theory and quantum mechanics theory.

Local hidden variable theory	Quantum Mechanics theory
Entanglement is due to the hidden variable and if the hidden variable is known, the outcome of the measurement is deterministic and one can know the correlation of entangled particles with non-entangled ones	Entanglement is not only because of hidden variables but is a fundamental feature of the quantum system that defies classical explanation.

Table 7.2: Short comparison between local variable theory and quantum mechanics theory

The research in locality and non-locality has evolved due to varied experiments conducted over a course of time by different physicist.

John Bell's theorem (1964)

One among the physicist to explain the locality was John Bell.

According to local hidden variable theory, entanglement between two particles occur due to the underlying properties of the particle. This is called as local interaction and the outcome of the measurements on quantum particles are determined by hidden variable that are not directly observable.

John bell derived a mathematical inequality by placing a theoretical upper bound/limit on the strength of correlations that can be predicted by local hidden variable.

Here, correlation means statistical relationship between measurement outcome on entangled particles.

For example, if you measure the spin of two entangled electrons at different axes,the result may show the correlation that are stronger than what would be expected if the particles are not entangled.

Bell's inequality refers to the maximum extent of correlation that local hidden variables account for and local hidden variables influence on measurement outcomes locally and independently. And so Bell derived an inequality that any local hidden variable theory must satisfy. If its not satisfied then local hidden variables can't fully explain entanglement. His theory challenges classical physics limitations in understanding fundamental quantum mechanical property.

Bell's original inequality is mathematically expressed as,

$$\left|P(A,B) - P(A,B')\right| + P(A',B) + P(A',B') \leq 2 \tag{7.2}$$

Original paper regarding the Bells' inequality involves two particles usually electrons or photons that are in the entangled state. If the particles are in entangled state that means their quantum properties such as spin or polarization are also linked so if you know the state of one particle, other particle state is also known. If electrons are used, their spin along certain axes (like the X-axis, Y-axis, or Z-axis) is measured. Spin is a quantum mechanical property that can be thought of as analogous to angular momentum. If photons are used, polarization (the direction in which the electric field oscillates) plays a similar role to spin in electrons and is measured instead. Different parameters such as A, B, A', and B' represent different angle or directions at which the spin or polarization is measured. The importance of measuring is because of the entangled nature of particles. We can understand in what state a particle is in.

For example, an electron is used as an entangled particle,

For particle 1

A : Measure spin along X-axis.

A' : Measure spin along Z-axis.

For particle 2

B : Measure spin along the X-axis, like A.

B': Measure spin along a different axis, say Y-axis.

Now you might have a question why using A' and B'? We should recall that if the state of one particle is changed, the other particle's state also changes. By measuring those particles at different angles or axes, modification occurs in one particle. Since they are entangled, we can also observe how far the modification of one particle has affected/ impacted the other particle so that one can observe a visible change in another particle. Thus, using multiple settings helps ensure that any observed correlations are not a result of specific experimental setup quirks but are inherent properties of the entangled states.

The outcomes of these measurements are recorded. Each measurement done at different angles results either in +1 or -1 (spin up or spin down). When these results are combined correlation function can be determined. Correlation functions show the correlation between outcomes of measurements performed on different parts of a quantum system, such as two entangled particles. The correlation value must be ≤ 2.

In classical statistics and many physical theories, correlation coefficients range from +1 to -1. From there we can fit correlation under 3 categories.

- **+1** indicates perfect correlation. If one particle is in +1 state, the other particle is also in the +1 state.
- **-1** indicates perfect anti-correlation. This means that every time one particle is measured in state +1, the other is -1.
- **0** means no correlation. When measurements between two particles are unrelated.

What if the correlation is > 2? CHSH form of inequality allows for a maximum theoretical value of $2\sqrt{2}$ known as Tsirelson's bound in quantum mechanics. Values exceeding 2 but not exceeding 2 but not exceeding $2\sqrt{2}$ are indicative of strong quantum correlations that cannot be explained by any local hidden variable theories. Not only does this prove that quantum phenomena are not classical, but it also makes us question our basic ideas about how the universe works. These discoveries were very important in creating quantum technologies, such as quantum computing and cryptography.

In order to test the Bell's experiment several experiments were conducted. One of the famous ones is CHSH inequality. Let's discuss it.

CHSH Inequality (Clauser-Horne-Shimony-Holt)

The CHSH (Clauser-Horne-Shimony-Holt) inequality , developed by John Clauser, Michael Horne, Abner Shimony, and Richard Holt, is a more generalized and experimentally feasible form of Bell's inequality. It's an extension of Bell's original idea. It is expressed as:

$$E(A, B) - E(A, B') + E(A', B) + E(A', B') \leq 2 \tag{7.3}$$

- $E(A, B)$: Correlation between measurements A and B on two entangled particles.
- $E(A, B')$: Correlation between measurement A and the alternative measurement B'.
- $E(A', B)$: Correlation between the alternative measurement A' and measurement B.

- $E(A', B')$: Correlation between the alternative measurements A' and B'.

Bell States

Bell's inequality had spurred physicists to test his work. In that way, they directly used his work and conducted experiments but later physicists started working on quantum entanglement and derived a new concept called Bell states. Bell states are a fundamental concept in the study of quantum information and quantum computing, representing the simplest and most powerful examples of quantum entanglement. They are specific types of quantum states of two qubits (quantum bits) that are maximally entangled. These states were named in honor of Bell to acknowledge his seminal contributions to the field of quantum entanglement. Bell state is a fine example of a bipartite system. A bipartite system means a quantum system having only two particles or two qubits. These particles or qubits can be entangled or non-entangled. Bell states are also called EPR states (Einstein-Podolsky-Rosen) .

Let's first define the two-qubit states, which will later help us to describe the Bell states. For state $|00\rangle$:

$$|0\rangle \otimes |0\rangle = |00\rangle = \begin{bmatrix} 1 \\ 0 \end{bmatrix} \otimes \begin{bmatrix} 1 \\ 0 \end{bmatrix} = \begin{bmatrix} 1 \\ 0 \\ 0 \\ 0 \end{bmatrix} \tag{7.4}$$

The tensor product state for $|01\rangle$ is:

$$|0\rangle \otimes |1\rangle = |01\rangle = \begin{bmatrix} 1 \\ 0 \end{bmatrix} \otimes \begin{bmatrix} 0 \\ 1 \end{bmatrix} = \begin{bmatrix} 0 \\ 1 \\ 0 \\ 0 \end{bmatrix} \tag{7.5}$$

For the $|10\rangle$ state:

$$|1\rangle \otimes |0\rangle = |10\rangle = \begin{bmatrix} 0 \\ 1 \end{bmatrix} \otimes \begin{bmatrix} 1 \\ 0 \end{bmatrix} = \begin{bmatrix} 0 \\ 0 \\ 1 \\ 0 \end{bmatrix} \tag{7.6}$$

Finally, the $|11\rangle$ state is:

$$|1\rangle \otimes |1\rangle = |11\rangle = \begin{bmatrix} 0 \\ 1 \end{bmatrix} \otimes \begin{bmatrix} 0 \\ 1 \end{bmatrix} = \begin{bmatrix} 0 \\ 0 \\ 0 \\ 1 \end{bmatrix} \tag{7.7}$$

The general description of the bell state is given in the following equation

$$|\beta_{ab}\rangle = \frac{|0b\rangle + (-1)^a|1\bar{b}\rangle}{\sqrt{2}} \tag{7.8}$$

Here, a and b can be either 0 or 1, and $\bar{b}$ is the bitwise negation of b. This formula represents a general form for the four possible Bell states, depending on the values of **a** and **b**.

$$|\beta_{00}\rangle = \frac{|00\rangle + (-1)^0|11\rangle}{\sqrt{2}} = \frac{|00\rangle + |11\rangle}{\sqrt{2}} = |\Phi^+\rangle \tag{7.9}$$

$$|\beta_{01}\rangle = \frac{|01\rangle + (-1)^0|10\rangle}{\sqrt{2}} = \frac{|01\rangle + |10\rangle}{\sqrt{2}} = |\Psi^+\rangle \tag{7.10}$$

$$|\beta_{10}\rangle = \frac{|00\rangle + (-1)^1|11\rangle}{\sqrt{2}} = \frac{|00\rangle - |11\rangle}{\sqrt{2}} = |\Phi^-\rangle \tag{7.11}$$

$$|\beta_{11}\rangle = \frac{|01\rangle + (-1)^1|10\rangle}{\sqrt{2}} = \frac{|01\rangle - |10\rangle}{\sqrt{2}} = |\Psi^-\rangle \tag{7.12}$$

Creating bell states

In order to achieve $|\beta_{00}\rangle$, following gates are applied in an order:

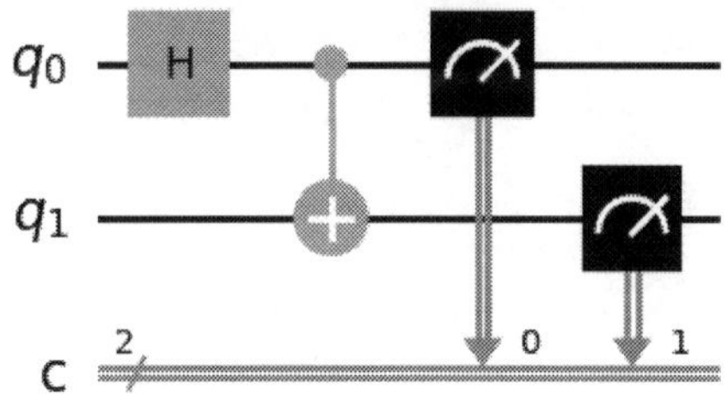

Figure 7.5: Bell state when a and b are zero

In order to achieve $|\beta_{01}\rangle$, following gates are applied in an order:

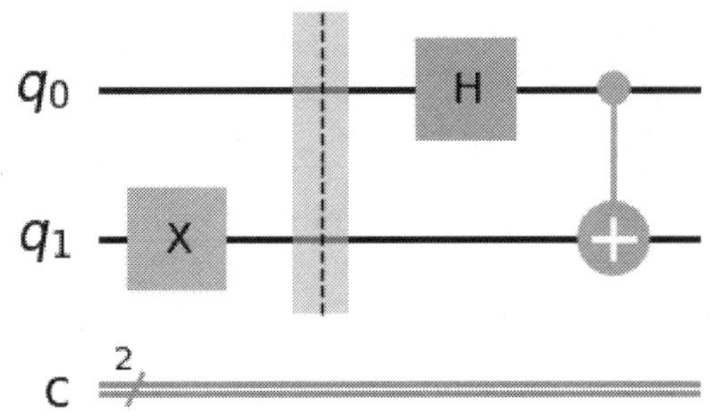

Figure 7.6: Bell states when a is zero and b is one

In order to achieve $|\beta_{10}\rangle$, following gates are applied in an order:

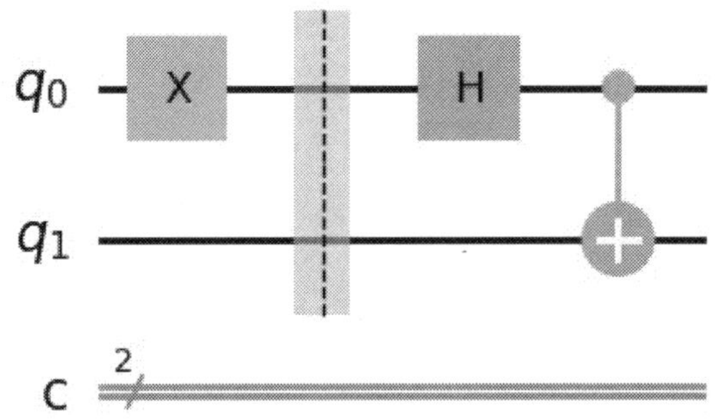

Figure 7.7: Bell state when a is one and b is zero

In order to achieve $|\beta_{11}\rangle$, following gates are applied in an order:

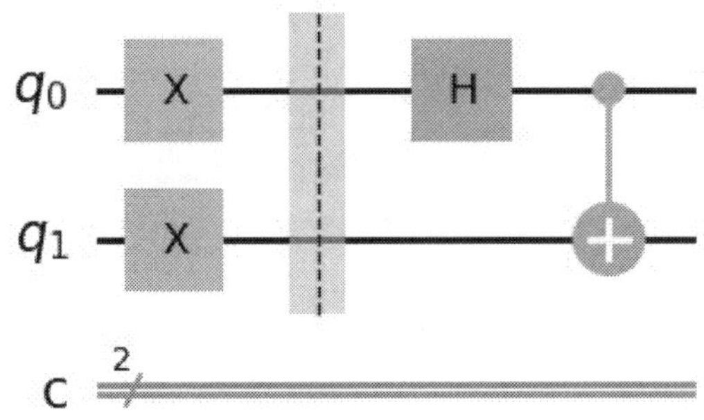

Figure 7.8: Bell state when a is one and b is one

Here the Bell states are in a superposition of two states which is classified under two categories.

- $|\Phi^+\rangle$: The symmetric superposition of $|00\rangle$ and $|11\rangle$.
- $|\Psi^+\rangle$: The symmetric superposition of $|01\rangle$ and $|10\rangle$.
- $|\Phi^-\rangle$: The antisymmetric superposition of $|00\rangle$ and $|11\rangle$.
- $|\Psi^-\rangle$: The antisymmetric superposition of $|01\rangle$ and $|10\rangle$.

A symmetric superposition of quantum states means that the combined state remains invariant under particle exchange; the coefficients of the terms in the superposition are the same, for example, $|00\rangle + |11\rangle$. An antisymmetric superposition involves quantum states where the sign of the superposition changes when particles are exchanged, usually involving a negative sign for one of the terms $|00\rangle - |11\rangle$.

The four bell states are maximally entangled states which means irrespective of distance, the two particles are maximally entangled. These states can't be factored into the product of individual states. Maximally entangled states have the highest possible entanglement entropy , meaning the entanglement between the subsystems is at its peak, making these states crucial for tasks that require strong quantum correlations , such as quantum teleportation, quantum cryptography, and certain quantum algorithms.

Least entangled states

The least entangled states are essentially the ones which have no entanglement which means there is no correlation between the states. These states are also called product states or separable states because two states can be represented in terms of a product (tensor product). They are called separable states because the system's state can be separated into individual components without losing any information.

For a two-qubit system, a product state can be written as:

$$|\psi_{\text{product}}\rangle = |\psi_1\rangle \otimes |\psi_2\rangle \tag{7.13}$$

where $|\psi_1\rangle$ and $|\psi_2\rangle$ are the quantum states of the individual qubits. The overall state of the system is just the direct product (tensor product) of the states of the individual qubits.

Examples of product states include:

$$|00\rangle = |0\rangle \otimes |0\rangle \tag{7.14}$$

$$|01\rangle = |0\rangle \otimes |1\rangle \tag{7.15}$$

$$|+\rangle \otimes |-\rangle, \text{ where } |+\rangle = \frac{1}{\sqrt{2}}(|0\rangle + |1\rangle) \text{ and } |-\rangle = \frac{1}{\sqrt{2}}(|0\rangle - |1\rangle) \tag{7.16}$$

In these states, the qubits are completely uncorrelated. If you measure one qubit, the outcome does not provide any information about the state of the other qubit.

Characteristics of least entangled states

- *No correlation*
  Measurement of one qubit doesn't give the information of another qubit.
- *Tensor product*
  The overall state is a tensor product of the individual states.
- *Entanglement entropy*
  The measure of quantum entanglement between subsystems of a quantum state.

The entanglement entropy for these states is zero, indicating no entanglement.

In order to achieve the least entangled states in a quantum system, single qubit gates are typically used. Single qubit gates don't introduce any entanglement when used individually. When you apply a single qubit gate to each qubit in a multi-qubit system, the resulting state is still a product of individual qubit states. For example,

- Applying an X gate to the first qubit in the state $|00\rangle$ will result in the state $|10\rangle$, which is a product state $|1\rangle \otimes |0\rangle$.
- Similarly, applying a Hadamard gate to the first qubit in $|00\rangle$ would result in the state

$$\frac{1}{\sqrt{2}}(|0\rangle + |1\rangle) \otimes |0\rangle$$

  which is still a separable product state.

So, if you want to create the least entangled state, avoid gates that create entanglement. Single qubit gates when used individually on each qubit don't create entanglement.

Although maximally entangled states are utilized to establish the strong correlations necessary for quantum protocols, least entangled states (product states) are frequently used as the initial point in quantum algorithms or protocols that progressively develop entanglement.

CY Gate

This is similar to Pauli Y gate. But the CY gate is a two-qubit gate. The concept is the same for all two-qubit gates, whether CX, CY, CZ, or CH gates. CY gate is represented as `cy()`.

CY gate representation

Figure 7.9 represents CY gate.

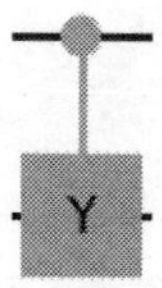

Figure 7.9: CY gate

Truth Table

CY gate is similar to Pauli Y gate but with a condition. When the control (input) qubit is in $|0\rangle$ state there is no bit flip. But if the input (control) qubit is in $|1\rangle$ state and the target (input) qubit is in $|0\rangle$ state, then the target (output) state will be bit flipped as well as an imaginary amplitude i is multiplied. If the control qubit (input) is in $|1\rangle$ state and the target (input) qubit is in $|1\rangle$ state then the target (output) will be flipped to -$|0\rangle$ state along with that an imaginary amplitude i is multiplied to it.

To summarize, the CY gate operates as follows:

- If the control qubit is 0, the target qubit remains unchanged.
- If the control qubit is 1, the target qubit transforms the Y gate, which includes a phase shift of $\pm i$.

Control (Input)	Target (Input)	Control (Output)	Target (Output)
0	0	0	0
0	1	0	1
1	0	1	$i \cdot 1$
1	1	1	$-i \cdot 0$

Table 7.3: Truth Table for the CY Gate

Operator

Equation 7.17 represents the matrix for the CY gate.

$$CY = \begin{pmatrix} 1 & 0 & 0 & 0 \\ 0 & 1 & 0 & 0 \\ 0 & 0 & 0 & -i \\ 0 & 0 & i & 0 \end{pmatrix} \tag{7.17}$$

Code Implementation of CY Gate

Implementing CY gate with default $|0\rangle$ state will not make a visible difference. Thus including the Pauli X gate followed by the CY gate.

```
qc = QuantumCircuit(2)
qc.x(0)
qc.cy(0,1)
qc.draw('mpl')
```

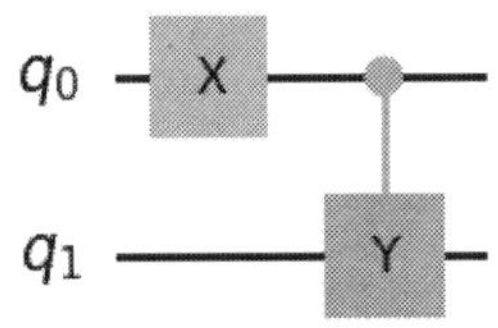

Figure 7.10: CY gate quantum circuit

QSphere for CY Gate

```
plot_state_qsphere(qc)
```

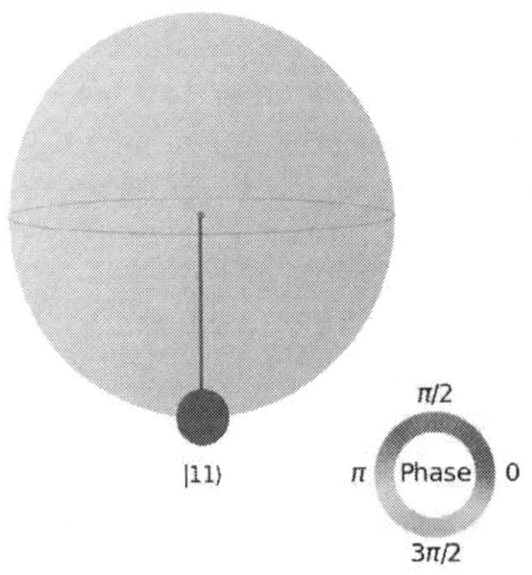

Figure 7.11: CY gate QShere

CY Gate Histogram

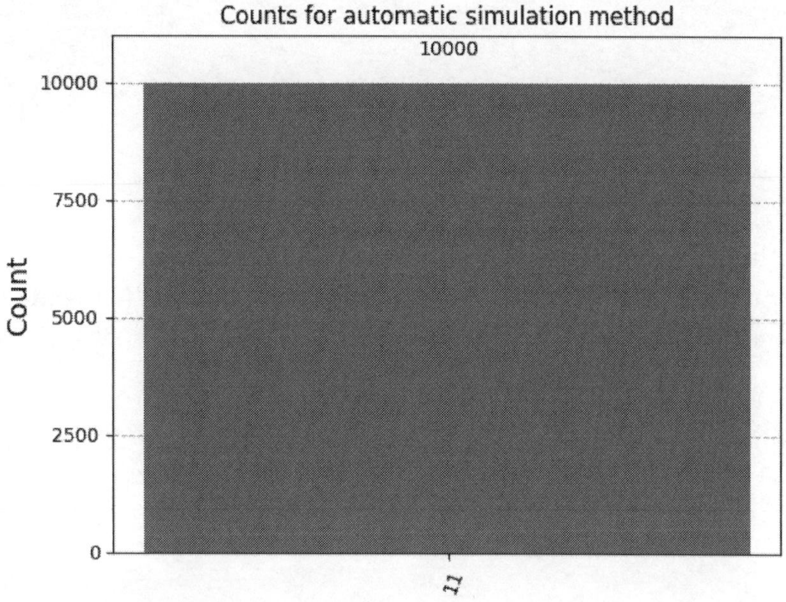

Figure 7.12: CY gate quantum circuit

The code for calculating the histogram is the same as before. So, only the histogram is given. You can refer to the previous code for implementing the histogram.

CZ Gate

This is similar to Pauli Z gate. Whatever the concepts that apply to Pauli Z will apply to CZ gate , too. But the CZ gate introduces conditional phase shift. CZ gate applies phase shift to the target qubit only when the control qubit is in $|1\rangle$ state. So, the control qubit and target qubit should be in $|1\rangle$ state. CZ gate is represented as `cz()` .

CZ gate representation

Figure 7.13 represents the CZ gate.

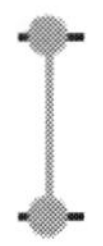

Figure 7.13: CZ gate

Truth Table

Following is the truth table for CZ gate.

Control (Input)	Target (Input)	Control (Output)	Target (Output)
0	0	0	0
0	1	0	1
1	0	1	0
1	1	1	-1

Operator

Figure 7.18 refers to the matrix of the CZ gate

$$CZ = \begin{pmatrix} 1 & 0 & 0 & 0 \\ 0 & 1 & 0 & 0 \\ 0 & 0 & 1 & 0 \\ 0 & 0 & 0 & -1 \end{pmatrix} \tag{7.18}$$

The difficulty of implementing the CZ gate by adding an extra gate and changing the control and target qubits.

Code Implementation of CZ gate

```
qc = QuantumCircuit(2)
qc.y(1)
qc.cz(1,0)
qc.draw('mpl')
```

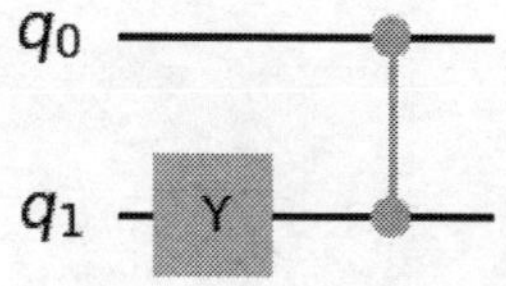

Figure 7.14: CZ quantum circuit

QSphere for CZ Gate Implementation

Since the Y gate is applied followed by the CZ gate, the visualization results came out to be $|10\rangle$.

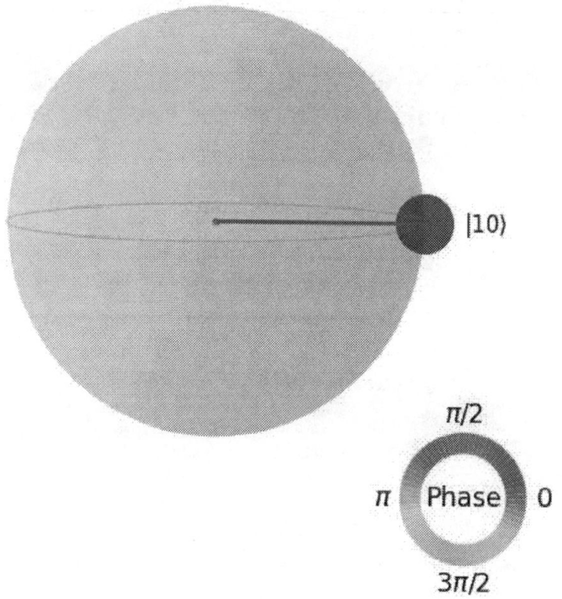

Figure 7.15: CZ gate QSphere implementation

Histogram for CZ gate

Figure 7.16 is the histogram visualization for the CZ gate.

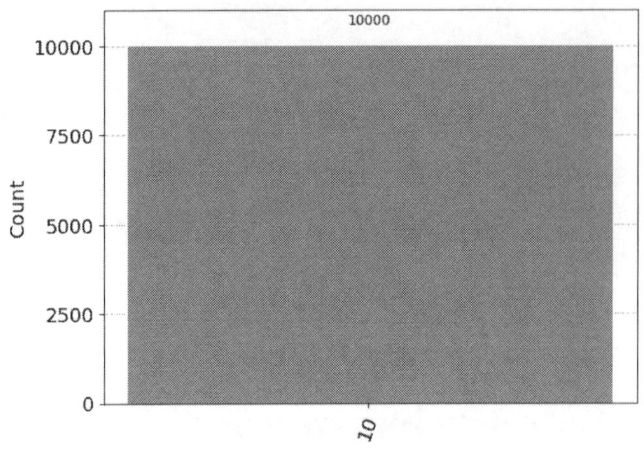

Figure 7.16: Histogram for CZ gate

To Practice

Practice the following combination of gates:

1. CH *gate*
2. X CZ
3. Y CX
4. H CH

SWAP Gate

The SWAP gate is the fundamental two-qubit gate. As the name suggests, this gate swaps the state of two qubits. This operation is useful for quantum algorithms that require rearrangement of qubits without altering the state of qubits. This gate doesn't require any condition to swap the gate. Just swapping the gate from qubit 1 (q1) to qubit 2 (q2). SWAP gate is represented as `swap()`.

SWAP Gate Representation

The SWAP gate is represented in the following *Figure* 7.17

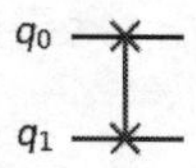

Figure 7.17: SWAP gate representation

Truth Table

SWAP gate interchanges q_1 and q_2 states.

Before SWAP		After SWAP	
q_1	q_2	q_1	q_2
0	0	0	0
0	1	1	0
1	0	0	1
1	1	1	1

Table 7.4: Truth table for the SWAP gate

Operator

The matrix for the SWAP gate is represented in *Equation* 7.19

$$SWAP = \begin{pmatrix} 1 & 0 & 0 & 0 \\ 0 & 0 & 1 & 0 \\ 0 & 1 & 0 & 0 \\ 0 & 0 & 0 & 1 \end{pmatrix} \tag{7.19}$$

There are two properties of the SWAP gate:

1. **Symmetric Property**

SWAP gate is symmetric by nature itself. It operates by exchanging the states of two qubits; if this operation is repeated in succession (a swap followed by another swap), the system returns to its initial state.

Proof

Let's consider the SWAP gate matrix:

$$U_{\text{SWAP}} = \begin{pmatrix} 1 & 0 & 0 & 0 \\ 0 & 0 & 1 & 0 \\ 0 & 1 & 0 & 0 \\ 0 & 0 & 0 & 1 \end{pmatrix}$$

The product of two SWAP matrices, representing two consecutive SWAP operations, is:

$$U_{\text{SWAP}}^2 = U_{\text{SWAP}} \cdot U_{\text{SWAP}} = \begin{pmatrix} 1 & 0 & 0 & 0 \\ 0 & 0 & 1 & 0 \\ 0 & 1 & 0 & 0 \\ 0 & 0 & 0 & 1 \end{pmatrix} \cdot \begin{pmatrix} 1 & 0 & 0 & 0 \\ 0 & 0 & 1 & 0 \\ 0 & 1 & 0 & 0 \\ 0 & 0 & 0 & 1 \end{pmatrix}$$

Calculating the product gives:

$$U_{\text{SWAP}}^2 = \begin{pmatrix} 1 & 0 & 0 & 0 \\ 0 & 1 & 0 & 0 \\ 0 & 0 & 1 & 0 \\ 0 & 0 & 0 & 1 \end{pmatrix}$$

This result is the identity matrix , indicating that applying the SWAP gate twice leaves the system in its original state, thereby proving the symmetry of the SWAP gate.

2. **Clifford gate**

Proof

To show that the SWAP gate is a Clifford gate , consider the conjugation of the X operator applied to the first qubit by the SWAP gate:

$$U_{\text{SWAP}}(X \otimes I)U_{\text{SWAP}}^\dagger$$

Given:

$$U_{\text{SWAP}} = \begin{pmatrix} 1 & 0 & 0 & 0 \\ 0 & 0 & 1 & 0 \\ 0 & 1 & 0 & 0 \\ 0 & 0 & 0 & 1 \end{pmatrix}, \quad X = \begin{pmatrix} 0 & 1 \\ 1 & 0 \end{pmatrix}, \quad I = \begin{pmatrix} 1 & 0 \\ 0 & 1 \end{pmatrix}$$

The tensor product $X \otimes I$ is:

$$X \otimes I = \begin{pmatrix} 0 & 0 & 1 & 0 \\ 0 & 0 & 0 & 1 \\ 1 & 0 & 0 & 0 \\ 0 & 1 & 0 & 0 \end{pmatrix}$$

Applying the conjugation:

$$U_{\text{SWAP}}(X \otimes I)U_{\text{SWAP}}^\dagger = U_{\text{SWAP}}(X \otimes I)U_{\text{SWAP}}$$

Since U_{SWAP} is its own inverse, $U_{\text{SWAP}}^{\dagger} = U_{\text{SWAP}}$.

Calculating this product, we find:

$$U_{\text{SWAP}}(X \otimes I)U_{\text{SWAP}} = \begin{pmatrix} 1 & 0 & 0 & 0 \\ 0 & 0 & 1 & 0 \\ 0 & 1 & 0 & 0 \\ 0 & 0 & 0 & 1 \end{pmatrix} \begin{pmatrix} 0 & 0 & 1 & 0 \\ 0 & 0 & 0 & 1 \\ 1 & 0 & 0 & 0 \\ 0 & 1 & 0 & 0 \end{pmatrix} \begin{pmatrix} 1 & 0 & 0 & 0 \\ 0 & 0 & 1 & 0 \\ 0 & 1 & 0 & 0 \\ 0 & 0 & 0 & 1 \end{pmatrix} = \begin{pmatrix} 0 & 1 & 0 & 0 \\ 1 & 0 & 0 & 0 \\ 0 & 0 & 0 & 1 \\ 0 & 0 & 1 & 0 \end{pmatrix}$$

This final matrix represents the $I \otimes X$ operator, indicating that the SWAP gate has transformed $X \otimes I$ into $I \otimes X$, thus mapping a Pauli operator to another Pauli operator. This proves that the SWAP gate is indeed a Clifford gate.

Code Implementation of SWAP Gate

The default state is $|0\rangle$. In order to swap the states, we need to have either q_1 or q_2 in $|1\rangle$ state so that there is a visible interchange in the swap operation. Thus, the X gate is given at first followed by the SWAP gate. You can use any gates before the SWAP gate or SWAP gate and observe the visualization.

```
qc = QuantumCircuit(2)
qc.x(1)
qc.swap(0,1)
qc.draw('mpl')
```

The circuit implemented in the following image shows the swap operation taking place once X gate is acted upon q_1. Following *Figure* 7.18

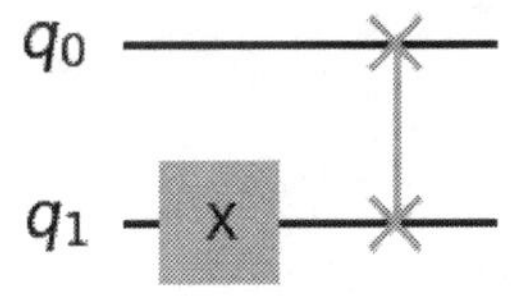

Figure 7.18: SWAP gate circuit

QSphere for SWAP Gate Implementation

You can observe the significant visualization in QSphere with $|01\rangle$ state. You can wonder how the result is $|01\rangle$ instead of $|10\rangle$. This is because of the *little endian system.*

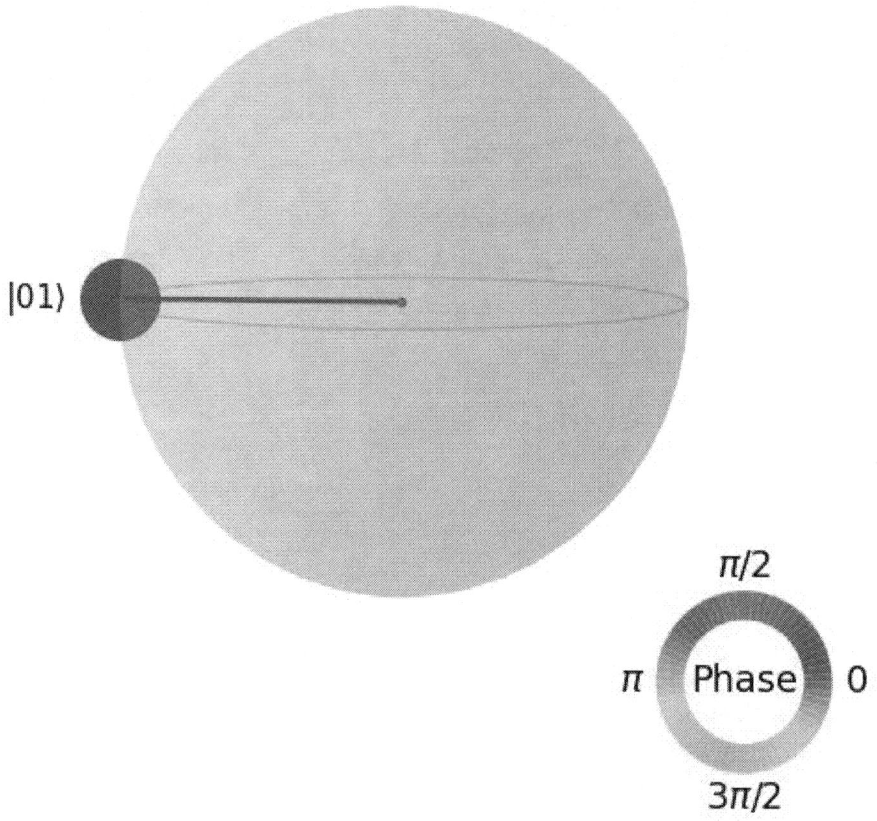

Figure 7.19: QSphere for SWAP gate

Histogram for SWAP Gate

The histogram for the SWAP gate is shown in the *Figure* 7.20.

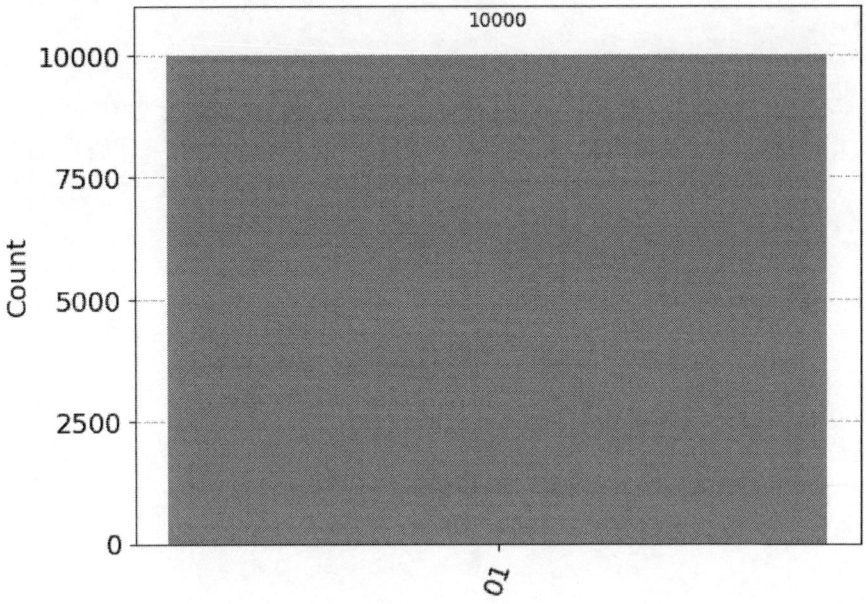

Figure 7.20: SWAP gate histogram

CRx Gate

The controlled Rx gate is a two-qubit operation in quantum computing, which applies the Rx (rotation around the x-axis) gate to the target qubit only if the control qubit is in the $|1\rangle$ state. CRx gate is represented as `crx()` .

Remember

$$Rx(\theta) = \begin{pmatrix} \cos\left(\frac{\theta}{2}\right) & -i\sin\left(\frac{\theta}{2}\right) \\ -i\sin\left(\frac{\theta}{2}\right) & \cos\left(\frac{\theta}{2}\right) \end{pmatrix} \tag{7.20}$$

CRx Gate representation

CRx gate is represented in *Figure* 7.21

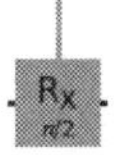

Figure 7.21: CRx gate representation

Truth Table

You can observe that when the control qubit is in $|1\rangle$ state, $Rx(\theta)$ gate is applied to the target qubit. Thus, $|10\rangle$ becomes $|1\rangle \otimes Rx(\theta)|0\rangle$ and $|11\rangle$ becomes $|1\rangle \otimes Rx(\theta)|1\rangle$.

Input (Control, Target)	Output State
$\|00\rangle$	$\|00\rangle$
$\|01\rangle$	$\|01\rangle$
$\|10\rangle$	$\|1\rangle \otimes Rx(\theta)\|0\rangle$
$\|11\rangle$	$\|1\rangle \otimes Rx(\theta)\|1\rangle$

(7.21)

Operator

The matrix representation for the CRx gate is shown in *Equation* 7.22.

$$CRx(\theta) = \begin{bmatrix} 1 & 0 & 0 & 0 \\ 0 & 1 & 0 & 0 \\ 0 & 0 & \cos\left(\frac{\theta}{2}\right) & -i\sin\left(\frac{\theta}{2}\right) \\ 0 & 0 & -i\sin\left(\frac{\theta}{2}\right) & \cos\left(\frac{\theta}{2}\right) \end{bmatrix} \tag{7.22}$$

Code Implementation of CRx Gate

X gate is added before Rx gate to increase the complexity and show the variety of implementations available to everyone reading this book.

```
qc = QuantumCircuit(2)
qc.x(1)
np.theta = pi/2
qc.crx(np.theta, 0,1)
qc.draw('mpl')
```

CRx Gate Circuit Implementation

Figure 7.22 represents the implementation of the CRx gate with increased complexity.

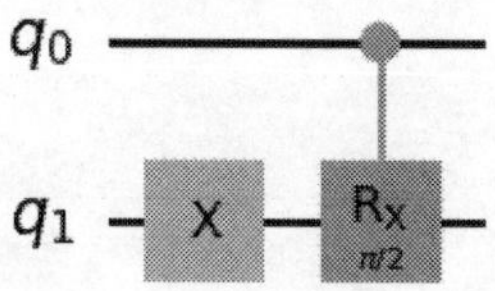

Figure 7.22: CRx gate circuit

QSphere for CRx Gate Implementation

QSphere for CRx gate is $|10\rangle$ because the circuit is X gate followed by CRx gate.

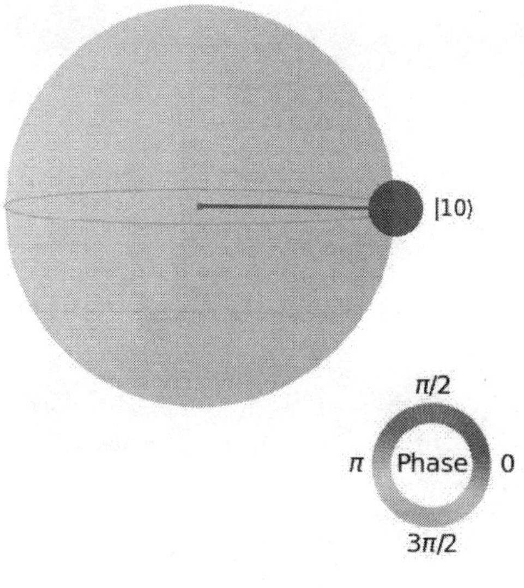

Figure 7.23: QSphere for CRx gate

Histogram for CRx Gate

Histogram visualization for the CRx gate is given in the following *Figure* 7.24.

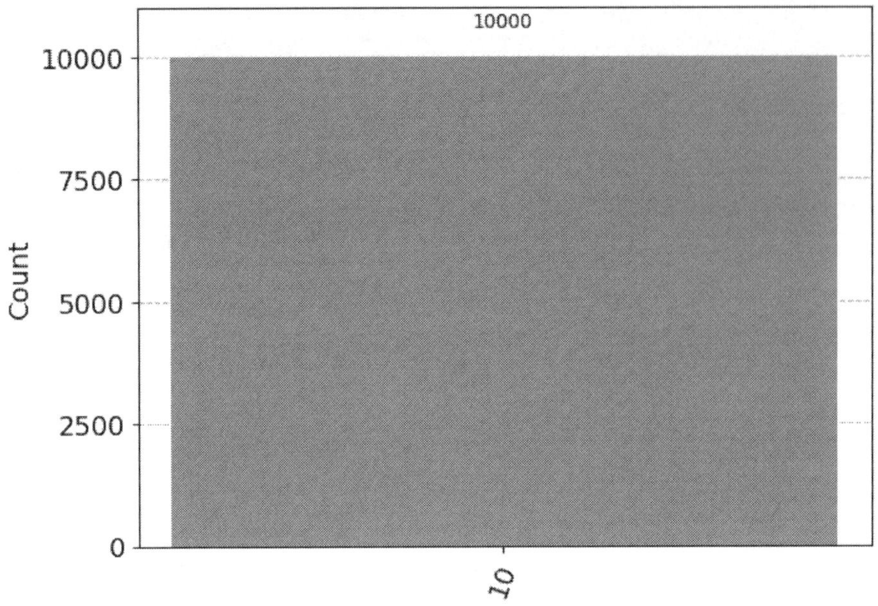

Figure 7.24: Histogram for CRx gate

To practice

1. *CRy gate*
2. *CRz gate*

Three Qubit Quantum Gates and Beyond

In contrast to single and two-qubit gates, three-qubit quantum gates concurrently process three quantum bits (qubits), thereby augmenting the intricacy and capacity of quantum computing operations.

Toffoli (CCX) and Fredkin (CSWAP) gates are three qubit quantum gates.

Toffoli Gate

Another name for Toffoli gate is CCNOT gate. Here, CC means Controlled Controlled. So, the name Controlled Controlled is NOT gate. It is similar to the Pauli X gate and CNOT gate. Here, bit flip happens to target qubits only when both control qubits are in $|1\rangle$ state. CCX gate is represented as `ccx()`.

It is profound that the Toffoli gate, when combined with single-qubit gates, is universal for quantum computation; this indicates that this collection of gates is capable of performing any quantum computation.

The Toffoli gate is analogous to the classical AND gate, but the only difference is that the Toffoli gate operation is **reversible**.

Toffoli Gate Representation

Toffoli gate is represented in the following *Figure* 7.25.

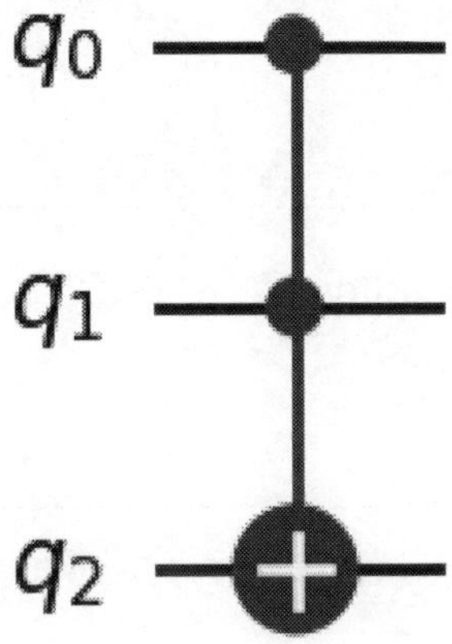

Figure 7.25: Toffoli gate representation

Truth Table

The truth table for the CCNOT gate is given here.

Control 1	Control 2	Target (before)	Target (after)
$\|0\rangle$	$\|0\rangle$	$\|0\rangle$	$\|000\rangle$
$\|0\rangle$	$\|0\rangle$	$\|1\rangle$	$\|001\rangle$
$\|0\rangle$	$\|1\rangle$	$\|0\rangle$	$\|010\rangle$
$\|0\rangle$	$\|1\rangle$	$\|1\rangle$	$\|011\rangle$
$\|1\rangle$	$\|0\rangle$	$\|0\rangle$	$\|100\rangle$
$\|1\rangle$	$\|0\rangle$	$\|1\rangle$	$\|101\rangle$
$\|1\rangle$	$\|1\rangle$	$\|0\rangle$	$\|111\rangle$
$\|1\rangle$	$\|1\rangle$	$\|1\rangle$	$\|110\rangle$

Operator

Equation 7.23 shows the 8x8 unitary matrix.

$$\begin{pmatrix} 1 & 0 & 0 & 0 & 0 & 0 & 0 & 0 \\ 0 & 1 & 0 & 0 & 0 & 0 & 0 & 0 \\ 0 & 0 & 1 & 0 & 0 & 0 & 0 & 0 \\ 0 & 0 & 0 & 1 & 0 & 0 & 0 & 0 \\ 0 & 0 & 0 & 0 & 1 & 0 & 0 & 0 \\ 0 & 0 & 0 & 0 & 0 & 1 & 0 & 0 \\ 0 & 0 & 0 & 0 & 0 & 0 & 0 & 1 \\ 0 & 0 & 0 & 0 & 0 & 0 & 1 & 0 \end{pmatrix} \tag{7.23}$$

Code Implementation of Toffoli Gate

The following code has an X gate followed by a CCX gate. X gate flips the quantum state followed by the CCX gate being applied.

```
qc = QuantumCircuit(3)
qc.x([0,1])
qc.ccx(0,1,2)
qc.draw('mpl')
```

Circuit for Toffoli Gate

In order to show the visualization of the Toffoli gate we are applying X gates in q_0, q_1 states and then the CCNOT gate is applied.

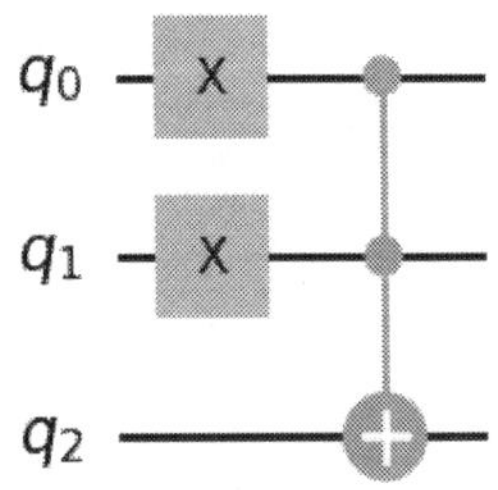

Figure 7.26: Toffoli gate circuit

QSphere for Toffoli Gate

QSphere for Toffoli gate is given in the following *Figure* 7.27

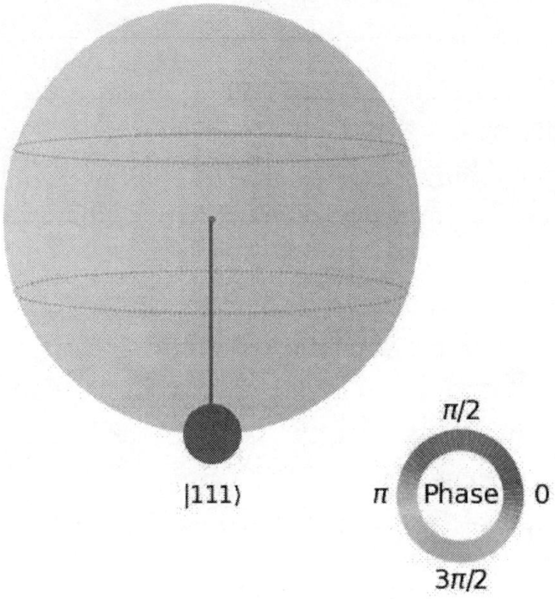

Figure 7.27: QSphere for Toffoli gate

Histogram for Toffoli Gate

Figure 7.28 shows the resultant visualization as 111 after running the circuit 10,000 times.

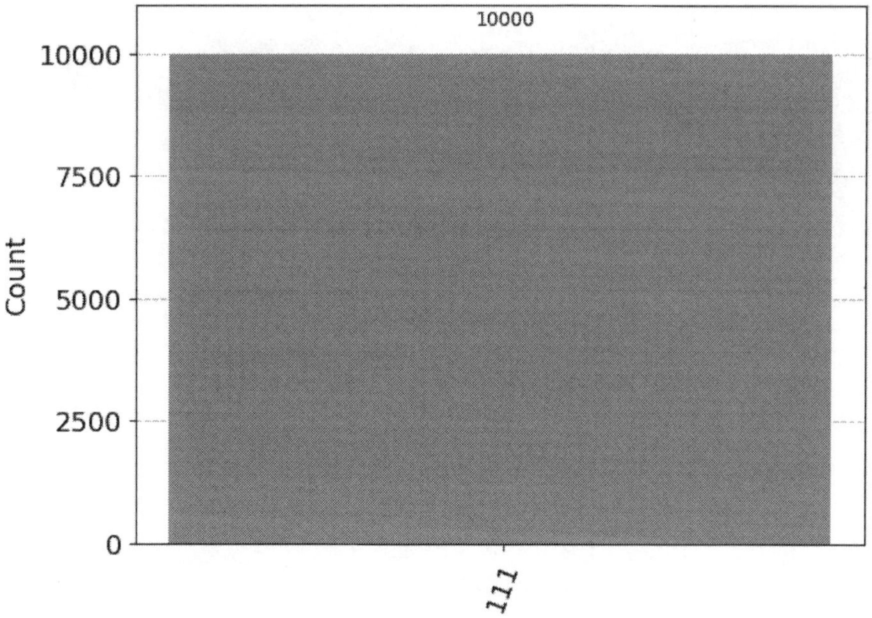

Figure 7.28: Histogram for Toffoli gate

Fredkin Gate

The Fredkin gate , also known as the controlled-SWAP (CSWAP) gate, is a three-qubit gate used in quantum computing. It performs a conditional swap between the second and third qubits based on the state of the first qubit. When combined with single-qubit gates, it is a universal gate and plays a significant role in quantum logic due to its reversible nature and the fact that it conserves quantum information.

If the control qubit (the first qubit) is in the state $|0\rangle$, the gate does nothing, and the states of the target qubits (second and third qubits) remain unchanged.

If the control qubit is in the state $|1\rangle$, the states of the two target qubits are swapped. `cswap()` method is used to implement Fredkin gate.

Fredkin Gate comes under the category of non-Clifford gates.

Fredkin Gate Representation

Fredkin Gate is represented in *Figure* 7.29

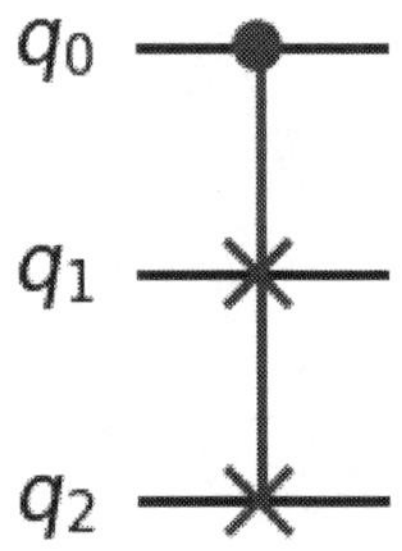

Figure 7.29: Fredkin gate representation

Truth Table

Input A (Control)	Target A (Before)	Target B (Before)	Outpust state
$\|0\rangle$	$\|0\rangle$	$\|0\rangle$	$\|000\rangle$
$\|0\rangle$	$\|0\rangle$	$\|1\rangle$	$\|001\rangle$
$\|0\rangle$	$\|1\rangle$	$\|0\rangle$	$\|010\rangle$
$\|0\rangle$	$\|1\rangle$	$\|1\rangle$	$\|011\rangle$
$\|1\rangle$	$\|0\rangle$	$\|0\rangle$	$\|100\rangle$
$\|1\rangle$	$\|0\rangle$	$\|1\rangle$	$\|110\rangle$
$\|1\rangle$	$\|1\rangle$	$\|0\rangle$	$\|101\rangle$
$\|1\rangle$	$\|1\rangle$	$\|1\rangle$	$\|111\rangle$

Table 7.5: Truth Table for the Fredkin (Controlled-SWAP) Gate

Operator

The matrix will be an 8x8 unitary matrix. Since 3 qubit gates are used.

$$F = \begin{pmatrix} 1 & 0 & 0 & 0 & 0 & 0 & 0 & 0 \\ 0 & 1 & 0 & 0 & 0 & 0 & 0 & 0 \\ 0 & 0 & 1 & 0 & 0 & 0 & 0 & 0 \\ 0 & 0 & 0 & 1 & 0 & 0 & 0 & 0 \\ 0 & 0 & 0 & 0 & 1 & 0 & 0 & 0 \\ 0 & 0 & 0 & 0 & 0 & 0 & 1 & 0 \\ 0 & 0 & 0 & 0 & 0 & 1 & 0 & 0 \\ 0 & 0 & 0 & 0 & 0 & 0 & 0 & 1 \end{pmatrix} \tag{7.24}$$

Fredkin Gate Code Implementation

Like the CCNOT gate, the X gate is applied to qubits (q_0, q_1) followed by the CSWAP gate.

```
qc = QuantumCircuit(3)
qc.x([0,1])
qc.cswap(0,1,2)
qc.draw('mpl')
```

Circuit for Fredkin Gate

Figure 7.30 shows the circuit diagram of the Fredkin gate.

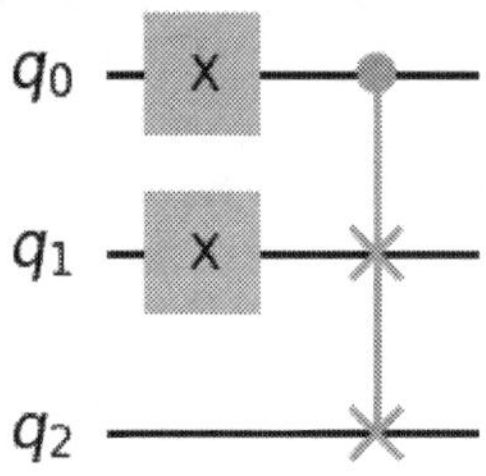

Figure 7.30: Fredkin gate circuit implementation

QSphere for Fredkin Gate

Visualization of $|101\rangle$ is represented in QSphere.

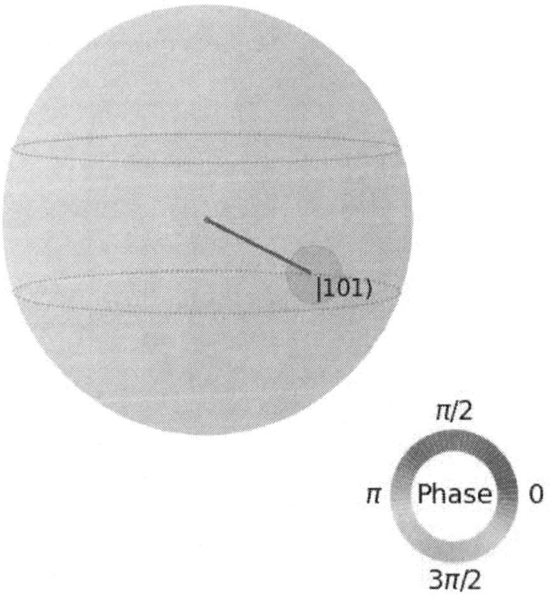

Figure 7.31: QSphere for Fredkin gate

Histogram for Fredkin Gate

Figure 7.32 shows the histogram of Fredkin gate.

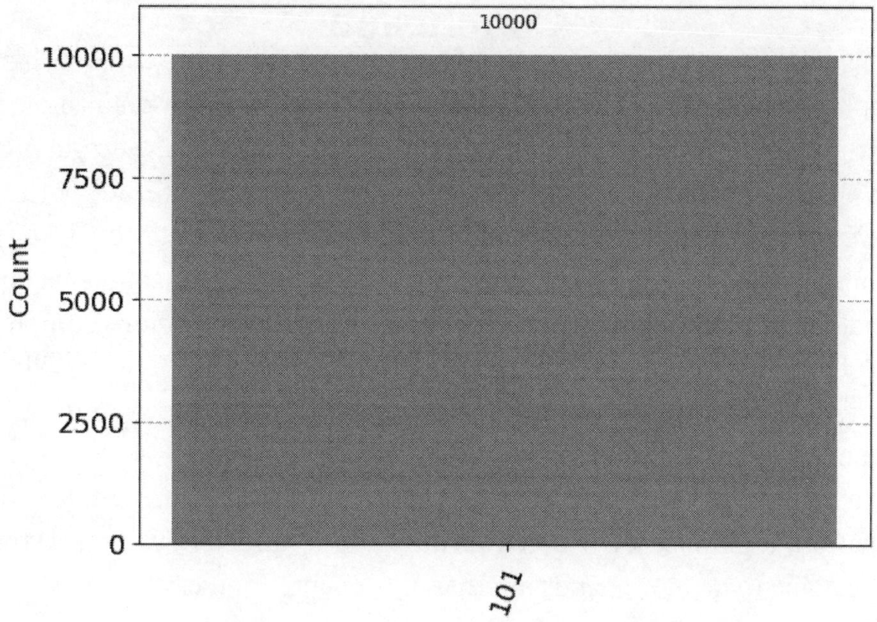

Figure 7.32: Histogram for Fredkin gate

Properties of Multi Qubit Gates

Table 7.6 explains the multi-qubit gate properties in a gist.

Gate	Hermitian	Involutory	Unitary	Clifford
CX (CNOT)	Yes	Yes	Yes	Yes
CY	Yes	Yes	Yes	No
CZ	Yes	Yes	Yes	Yes
CH (Hadamard on control)	No	No	Yes	No
SWAP	Yes	Yes	Yes	Yes
CRx (Controlled Rx)	No	No	Yes	No
Toffoli	Yes	Yes	Yes	No
Fredkin	Yes	Yes	Yes	No

Table 7.6: Properties of Multi-Qubit Gates

Conclusion

This chapter has examined the intriguing realm of multi-qubit quantum gates, which play a crucial role in facilitating intricate quantum computations. The gates mentioned, such as the CNOT, Toffoli, and swap gates, enable qubits to interact with each other, enabling the formation of entanglement and the execution of complex quantum algorithms. Gaining a comprehensive understanding of multi-qubit gates' mechanisms and practical uses is crucial for progressing from basic quantum operations to more complex quantum computing jobs. The principles and approaches covered in this chapter will be essential for harnessing the complete computational capability of quantum systems as we further advance and improve quantum technology.

In the next chapter, we will study some very important Qiskit features known as mapping and optimization, a glimpse of which you might have already studied in the previous chapters. It is going to be more hands-on than this chapter and it will cover topics such as transpilation, Qiskit AI features and error modeling.

CHAPTER 8

Qiskit Mapping and Optimization

Introduction

This present chapter explores the sophisticated methodologies and instruments that are influencing the trajectory of quantum computing. The increasing complexity of the sector necessitates the development of quantum algorithms that are more efficient, scalable, and resistant to errors. The current chapter delves into several advanced approaches, beginning with Dynamic Circuits and its novel approach to implementing quantum algorithms with conditional operations. Next, we delve into the domain of Transpilation , where we explore the significance of enhancing quantum circuits through the use of predefined pass managers, customised transpilation approaches, and the developing area of transpilation driven by artificial intelligence. Furthermore, the chapter presents Circuit Knitting, a potent method for breaking down and controlling intricate quantum circuits. Furthermore, we analyze the function of the Code Assistant in optimizing the process of developing quantum software and the capacity of Qiskit Serverless to improve the scalability and efficiency of quantum calculations. Finally, we tackle the key problem of quantifying error rates in quantum circuits, which is essential for enhancing the dependability and precision of quantum algorithms. Collectively, these sections offer a thorough summary of the tools and methodologies that are facilitating the development of practical quantum computing.

Several sections of this chapter have been adapted from the IBM Quantum challenge and the Global Summer School to showcase some very important features of the new Qiskit. We are grateful to the creators of such challenges and summer schools and due acknowledgement has been provided to them in the Acknowledgement section of this book.

Structure

In this chapter, you are going to study:

- Dynamic Circuits
    - Repeat Until Success
- Transpilation
    - Preset Pass Managers with Optimization Levels
    - Transpilation with Options
    - AI Transpilation
- Circuit Knitting
- Code Assistant
- Qiskit Serverless
- Quantification of Error Rates in Quantum Circuits

Dynamic Circuits

The circuits that you have seen in the previous chapters have *measurement* operations towards the end of the quantum circuit, these kinds of circuits are known as static circuits. In contrast, dynamic circuits integrate classical processing into the continuum of the qubits' coherence time. This implies that dynamic circuits have the capability to utilize mid-circuit measurements and execute feed-forward operations , the values generated by these measurements being used to decide the subsequent gates to be applied.

Dynamic circuits can help to overcome some constraints presented by actual hardware. Especially, dynamic circuits provide novel possibilities to balance circuit depth and width, which can determine whether a circuit functions properly or if its output is indistinguishable from noise. Dynamic circuits are demonstrably superior to static circuits in generating specific highly entangled quantum states for quantum simulation, including states that describe topological quantum order and quantum phase transitions. This section discusses the dynamic circuits and has been adapted from the IBM Quantum documentation and tutorial given online whose links can be found in the references of this chapter.

Repeat Until Success

We want to construct a theoretical quantum circuit using the basic gate set $\{H, X, S, \text{Toffoli}\}$ to implement a heralded $R_X(\theta)$ gate on a target qubit, where θ is defined such that $\cos\theta = \frac{3}{5}$. Each execution of the circuit only offers a limited probability of success. Therefore, we leverage dynamic quantum circuit techniques to repeat the procedure until successful.

We start by importing the necessary functions.

```
from qiskit.circuit import QuantumCircuit, QuantumRegister, ClassicalRegister
from qiskit_ibm_runtime import SamplerV2 as Sampler
from qiskit_ibm_runtime.fake_provider import FakeCairo
from qiskit.transpiler.preset_passmanagers import generate_preset_pass_manager
from collections import defaultdict
```

We define the different quantum, classical registers , and mid and final measurements in order to make our trial quantum circuit. We define a simple function to construct a trial quantum circuit composed of some Hadamard gates, and some controlled operations like CCX and measurement gates. The circuit is shown in *Figure* 8.1.

```
# Define quantum and classical registers
controls = QuantumRegister(2, name="control")
target = QuantumRegister(1, name="target")
mid_measure = ClassicalRegister(2, name="mid")
final_measure = ClassicalRegister(1, name="final")

# Create a quantum circuit incorporating the defined registers
circuit = QuantumCircuit(controls, target, mid_measure, final_measure)

def execute_quantum_trial(q_circuit, tgt_qubit, ctrl_qubits, measurement_bits):
    # Apply Hadamard gates to target and control qubits
    q_circuit.h(tgt_qubit)
    q_circuit.h(ctrl_qubits)

    # Controlled operations
    q_circuit.ccx(*ctrl_qubits, tgt_qubit)
    q_circuit.s(tgt_qubit)
    q_circuit.ccx(*ctrl_qubits, tgt_qubit)
```

```
    # Return qubits to their original state
    q_circuit.h(ctrl_qubits)
    q_circuit.h(tgt_qubit)

    # Measure the control qubits
    q_circuit.measure(ctrl_qubits, measurement_bits)

# Execute the function on the circuit
execute_quantum_trial(circuit, target, controls, mid_measure)

# Visualize the circuit
circuit.draw(output="mpl", style='iqp', cregbundle=False)
```

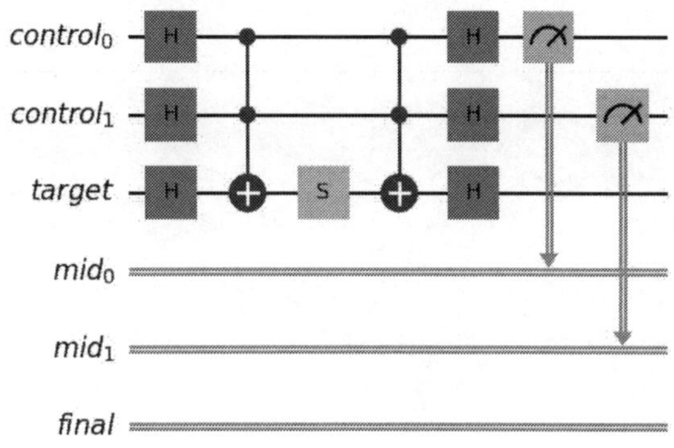

Figure 8.1: Quantum Circuit for Trial

If the measurements for both control bits are zero, the RX(θ) gate, where $\cos\theta = \frac{3}{5}$, is successfully applied. If either measurement yields a one, an X gate is executed, indicating failure. This conditional operation serves as the heralding mechanism, allowing you to deduce the correct application of the gate without disturbing the target qubit's coherence. The probability of success, P_{success}, without delving into detailed calculations, is given by:

$$P_{\text{success}} = \frac{|3+i|^2}{|3+i|^2 + |3-i|^2} = \frac{5}{8} \tag{8.1}$$

Upon a failure, the qubits are reset to their initial state for another attempt. Knowing the specific gate applied during a failure allows for an efficient reset operation without a complete hardware reset. Specifically, for two auxiliary qubits, an X gate is conditionally applied depending on the measurement output of 1. This method is especially efficient on

IBM® platforms, where qubits can be conditioned directly based on their measurement results, making this reset mechanism faster than most conventional control operations.

Qiskit does not have native support for inequality conditions directly in its programming structure, which is required for this task. To handle cases where the measurement result from the middle of the circuit does not match the bitstring '00', an alternative approach is used. Instead of checking for inequality directly, an if statement is set up to check if mid_measure equals '00'. In this setup, an empty block is passed for the if condition, and the else block is used to execute the necessary logic when the condition is not met.

You can see the full trial circuit in *Figure* 8.2.

```
def reset_control_qubits(q_circuit, ctrl_qubits, measure_bits):
    # Reset first control qubit if its corresponding measurement bit is True
    with q_circuit.if_test((measure_bits[0], True)):
        q_circuit.x(ctrl_qubits[0])
    # Reset second control qubit if its corresponding measurement bit is True
    with q_circuit.if_test((measure_bits[1], True)):
        q_circuit.x(ctrl_qubits[1])
max_trials = 2
def repeat_trials(q_circuit, tgt, ctrl, mid_meas, num_trials):
    for _ in range(num_trials - 1):
        reset_control_qubits(q_circuit, ctrl, mid_meas)
        with q_circuit.if_test((mid_meas, 0b00)) as else_block:
            # Intentionally empty block for future use with negative conditions
            pass
        with else_block:
            # Reset target and repeat the trial if conditions are not met
            q_circuit.x(tgt)
            execute_quantum_trial(q_circuit, tgt, ctrl, mid_meas)
    # Measure control qubits to capture final states due to hardware constraints
    q_circuit.measure(ctrl, mid_meas)
    # Final measurement of the target qubit to confirm the desired state
    q_circuit.measure(tgt, final_measure)
# Apply the function to the circuit
repeat_trials(circuit, target, controls, mid_measure, max_trials)
# Visualize the circuit
circuit.draw(output="mpl", style='iqp', cregbundle=False)
```

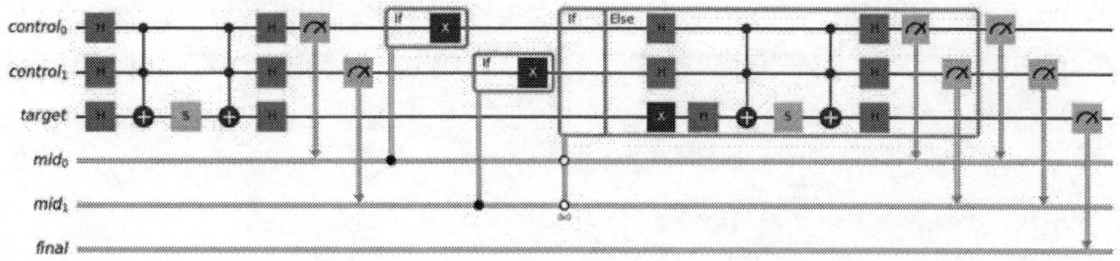

Figure 8.2: Quantum Circuit for Full Trial

We define the backend as `FakeCairo()` and then we initiate the transpilation pass managers that helps us to make the transpiled circuit with a given optimization level. This is achieved using `generate_preset_pass_manager` with optimization level 1. You will learn about transpilation in depth in the next section.

```
backend = FakeCairo()
pm = generate_preset_pass_manager(backend=backend, optimization_level=1)
isa_circuit = pm.run(circuit)
isa_circuit.draw(output="mpl", style='iqp', idle_wires=False, cregbundle=False)
```

With the help of the sampler, we ran our transpiled circuit into the fake backend we have defined earlier (you can also run on real hardware provided by IBM) and obtained the mid-circuit and final circuit measurement counts which are shown in *Figure* 8.3. Finally, we make a dictionary and combine all the data together.

```
sampler = Sampler(backend)
job = sampler.run([isa_circuit])
hardware_counts = job.result()[0]
data_mid = job.result()[0].data.mid
data_final = job.result()[0].data.final
print(f">>> Hardware counts for mid: {data_mid.get_counts()}")
print(f">>> Hardware counts for final: {data_final.get_counts()}")
merged_data = defaultdict(int)
for bs1, bs2 in zip(data_mid.get_bitstrings(), data_final.get_bitstrings()):
    merged_data[f"{bs1}-{bs2}"] += 1
print(f">>> Hardware merged data: {dict(merged_data)}")
```

```
>>> Hardware counts for mid: {'00': 773, '01': 93, '10': 81, '11': 77}
>>> Hardware counts for final: {'0': 673, '1': 351}
```

Figure 8.3: Counts of Mid Circuit and Final Circuit Measurement

We make a function that distributes counts into success or failure based on the state of the target qubit. After this we calculate the probability of success - expected and actual simulation results.

```
def separate_counts_by_qubit(count_data):
    success_counts = defaultdict(int)
    failure_counts = defaultdict(int)
    for outcome, count in count_data.items():
        if outcome[:2] == "00":  # Check if the first two qubits are in state 00
            success_counts[outcome[-1]] += count
        else:
            failure_counts[outcome[-1]] += count
    return success_counts, failure_counts
hw_successes, hw_failures = separate_counts_by_qubit(merged_data)
expected_successes = 1 - (1 - 5/8)**max_trials
actual_successes = sum(hw_successes.values()) / sum(merged_data.values())
print(f"Expected success rate {expected_successes:5.3f}.
Actual rate {actual_successes:5.3f}.")
actual_probability = hw_successes["1"] / sum(hw_successes.values())
print(f"Expected |1> probability: 0.2.  Actual probability
↪  {actual_probability:5.3f}.")
```

```
Expected success rate 0.859.  Actual rate 0.755.
Expected |1> probability: 0.2.  Actual probability 0.257.
```

Figure 8.4: Probability of Success for Simulation

From *Figure* 8.4, you can see that the actual rate we obtained is very close to the expected success rate. You might see similar values when you run on a real noisy hardware.

Transpilation

Transpilation refers to the procedure of converting a given input circuit into an equivalent circuit for a particular quantum device or enhancing the circuit for efficient run on an actual quantum system.

This requirement arises from the fact that quantum devices exhibit varying operational characteristics. Instructions transmitted to one device may not be compatible with another quantum backend. This laboratory experiment will investigate several factors such as the basis gate set of a device, the topology of the quantum chips, and time limitations that influence the operation of transpilation.

The objective of a transpiler is to optimize the results obtained by quantum hardware that exhibits noise. Most circuits need to undergo a sequence of modifications to ensure compatibility with a certain target device and to optimize them in order to minimize the impact of noise on the achieved results.

A key element of the Qiskit Software Development Kit (SDK) , the transpiler is specifically built to be flexible and easily modified. The primary objective of this project is to develop novel circuit transformations, referred to as transpiler passes, and integrate them with pre-existing passes, so significantly diminishing the overall depth and complexity of quantum circuits. The order in which passes are linked together significantly influences the ultimate result. The PassManager and StagedPassManager objects determine this pipeline specifically.

The `StagedPassManager` coordinates the execution of one or more `PassManagers` and establishes their execution order, whereas the `PassManager` object comprises one or more passes. Conceptualize the `StagedPassManager` as the conductor of an orchestra, the `PassManagers` as the several sections of instruments, and the Pass objects as the individual musicians.

Reconfiguring quantum circuits to adhere to hardware limitations and maximizing performance can be a complex task. Qiskit offers users the conventional six-stage compilation processes equipped with four pre-configured transpilation pipelines. The default configuration of the preset pass managers consists of six stages, each with distinct choices.

- `Init` : This pass performs any necessary preliminary passes previously to integrating the circuit into the system. This usually entails unwinding bespoke instructions and transforming the circuit into single- and two-qubit gates systematically. In its default state, this function only verifies the circuit instructions and converts multi-qubit gates into single- and two-qubit gates.
- `Layout` : This stage implements a layout that coordinates the virtual qubits in the circuit with the corresponding physical qubits on a backend.
- `Routing` : This stage operates subsequent to the application of a layout and will introduce gates (i.e. swaps) into the initial circuit to ensure its compatibility with the connection of the backend.
- `Translation` : Iteratively converts the gates in the circuit into the basis set of the desired backend.
- `Optimization` : This phase iterates the primary optimization loop until a predetermined condition, such as a specified depth, is satisfied.
- `Scheduling` : These stages are designated for hardware-aware scheduling passes .

Beyond the reduction of quantum circuit depth and complexity, the transpiler is specifically engineered to convert the instructions within a given `QuantumCircuit` to adhere to the Instruction Set Architecture (ISA) of a certain backend. Circuits that adhere to the Instruction Set Architecture (ISA) are comprised solely of instructions that are compatible with the backend's `Target`. These instructions include the hardware's available basis gates, measurements, resets, and control flow operations. Additionally, they must meet the limitations imposed by the hardware's connectivity, including the target's `CouplingMap`. Submitting a work to an IBM Quantum™ backend requires circuits that conform to the backend's Instruction Set Architecture (ISA).

Furthermore, Qiskit offers customers the option to select from four predetermined levels of transpilation based on their requirements. These pre-configured pass managers can be modified, and a pass manager can be constructed to create a completely bespoke pipeline for converting input circuits. Users unfamiliar with quantum circuit improvement through transpiling are advised to utilize one of the pre-existing routines. It creates and executes one of the preconfigured `StagedPassManagers` using an `optimization_level` flag that can be entered as 0, 1, 2, or 3. A higher level of optimization results in circuits that are more efficient, but at the cost of increased transpilation times.

Preset Pass Managers with Optimization Levels

In this section, let us begin a hands-on journey towards exploring different transpilation techniques offered by Qiskit in detail. The knowledge gained in this section will be immensely beneficial to your applications that require optimized quantum computing resources and scalability. Initially, our attention will be directed towards the four pre-established transpile pipelines. Subsequently, we will explore the process of constructing our own PassManager by utilizing the characteristics and choices of each pass within a pre-defined pipeline.

A pass manager is an entity that persists in a collection of transpiler passes and has the capability to carry them out on a circuit. A pass manager can be created by initializing a `PassManager` with a list of transpiler passes. To execute the transpilation on a circuit, invoke the run method with a circuit specified as the input.

An advanced pass manager, exemplified as the `StagedPassManager` class, is a unique type of pass manager that embodies a higher degree of abstraction compared to a conventional pass manager. The structure of a staged pass manager differs from that of a standard pass manager, as it consists of many transpiler passes. Because transpilation usually occurs in distinct phases, with each stage being represented by a pass manager, this abstraction is valuable.

Preset Passmanagers (`qiskit.transpiler.preset_passmanagers`) is a collection of functions that generate preset pass managers for transpiling. The preset pass managers are specific models of `StagedPassManager` that are utilized to carry out circuit changes at various optimization levels inside a predetermined transpiling pipeline. We present the functions utilized to create the complete pass manager using the `generate_preset_pass_manager` module.

Within Qiskit, the `generate_preset_pass_manager` function is employed to rapidly create a pre-configured pass manager. The provided function offers a practical and straightforward approach to creating an independent `PassManager` object that includes optimization levels and corresponding options for each pass.

The `generate_preset_pass_manager` function contains a single mandatory positional parameter, optimization_level, which determines the desired level of effort the transpiler dedicates to circuit optimization. This parameter is an integer that can only take on the values 0, 1, 2, or 3. Increased optimization levels result in the generation of more optimized circuits, but at the cost of longer compilation times, and conversely.

We begin by importing the necessary libraries for this purpose.

```
from qiskit.circuit.random import random_circuit
from qiskit.circuit.library import XGate, YGate
from qiskit_ibm_runtime.fake_provider import FakeTorino, FakeOsaka
from qiskit_ibm_runtime import QiskitRuntimeService, SamplerV2 as Sampler
from qiskit.transpiler import InstructionProperties, PassManager
from qiskit.transpiler.preset_passmanagers import generate_preset_pass_manager
from qiskit.transpiler.preset_passmanagers.plugin import list_stage_plugins
from qiskit.transpiler.timing_constraints import TimingConstraints
from qiskit.transpiler.passes.scheduling import ASAPScheduleAnalysis,
PadDynamicalDecoupling
from qiskit.visualization.timeline import draw, IQXStandard
from qiskit.transpiler import StagedPassManager
from qiskit.visualization import plot_circuit_layout
from qiskit.quantum_info.analysis import hellinger_fidelity
from qiskit.visualization import plot_distribution
from qiskit_aer import AerSimulator
import matplotlib.pyplot as plt
import numpy as np
```

With the libraries imported, we make the `transpile_scoring` function that assesses the accuracy of a quantum circuit once it has been compiled for a particular quantum backend architecture. The function systematically processes each gate in the circuit and modifies the total fidelity score (fid) according to the error rates linked to the gate operations (such as cz, ecr, measure, and delay) in the backend. The method incorporates both single-qubit and two-qubit gate errors, together with errors caused by qubit decoherence over time (measured by T1 and T2 durations) for delays. The algorithm generates a final fidelity score that quantifies the likelihood of the circuit functioning properly on the designated backend.

Using the `transpile_scoring` function, we make the `scoring` function that returns a circuit score. The closer the score is to 0, the better.

```
def transpile_scoring(circ, layout, backend):
    fid = 1

    touched = set()
    dt = backend.dt
    num_qubits = backend.num_qubits

    error=0

    t1s = [backend.qubit_properties(qq).t1 for qq in range(num_qubits)]
    t2s = [backend.qubit_properties(qq).t2 for qq in range(num_qubits)]

    for item in circ._data:
        for gate in backend.operation_names:
            if item[0].name == gate:
                if (item[0].name == 'cz') or (item[0].name == 'ecr'):
                    q0 = circ.find_bit(item[1][0]).index
                    q1 = circ.find_bit(item[1][1]).index
                    fid *= 1 - backend.target[item[0].name][(q0, q1)].error
                    touched.add(q0)
                    touched.add(q1)
                elif item[0].name == 'measure':
                    q0 = circ.find_bit(item[1][0]).index
                    fid *= 1 - backend.target[item[0].name][(q0, )].error
                    touched.add(q0)

                elif item[0].name == 'delay':
                    q0 = circ.find_bit(item[1][0]).index
```

```
                # Ignore delays that occur before gates
                # This assumes you are in ground state and errors
                # do not occur.
                if q0 in touched:
                    time = item[0].duration * dt
                    fid *= 1-qubit_error(time, t1s[q0], t2s[q0])
            else:
                q0 = circ.find_bit(item[1][0]).index
                fid *= 1 - backend.target[item[0].name][(q0, )].error
                touched.add(q0)

    return fid

def scoring( qc, backend):
    #ayout = qc.layout.final_virtual_layout()
    layout = qc.layout.final_index_layout()
    fidelity = transpile_scoring(qc, layout, backend)
    score = 1-fidelity
    return score
```

Next, we initialize some important parameter values in order to carry out our experiments. These values are seed, number of qubits and depth of the quantum circuit we want to make. We also define `FakeTorino()` as the backend and create a random quantum circuit.

```
seed = 10000
backend = FakeTorino()
num_qubits = 6
depth = 4
qc = random_circuit(num_qubits,depth,measure=False, seed=seed)
qc.draw('mpl')
```

Our objective is to systematically execute all four optimization levels and thereafter analyze and contrast our outcomes. To accomplish this, we will generate several arrays to store the collected data during our work and subsequently utilize them at a later time.

The following code cell is dedicated to the construction of these arrays. You may execute it and proceed at this time.

```
circuit_depths = {
    'opt_lv_0': None,
    'opt_lv_1': None,
    'opt_lv_2': None,
    'opt_lv_3': None,
}
gate_counts = {
    'opt_lv_0': None,
    'opt_lv_1': None,
    'opt_lv_2': None,
    'opt_lv_3': None,
}

scores = {
    'opt_lv_0': None,
    'opt_lv_1': None,
    'opt_lv_2': None,
    'opt_lv_3': None,
}
```

Now we are going to explore the various `optimization_level`. We discussed this earlier and now we are going to see this in detail. This optimization parameter is provided as a positional argument in `generate_preset_pass_manager`.

Optimization Level 0

Optimization level 0 is designed for device characterization investigations and just applies minimal optimizations to map the input circuit to the restrictions of the target backend. Using TrivialLayout, the program executes layout/routing operations by selecting the identical physical qubit values as virtual ones and inserting SWAPs to provide functionality (using StochasticSwap).

We build a pass manager with an optimization level of 0 using our FakeTorino backend and observe the outcome.

```
# Make a pass manager with our desired optimization level and backend
pm_lv0 = generate_preset_pass_manager(backend=backend, optimization_level=0,
seed_transpiler=seed)
```

```
# Run the random circuit
tr_lv0 = pm_lv0.run(qc)
# uncomment the next line to draw circuit
#tr_lv0.draw('mpl', idle_wires=False, fold=60)
```

As previously stated, `optimization_level=0` is doing a fundamental gate decomposition by mapping logical qubits to physical qubits of the same order of number utilizing basis gates of the backend. The function represents the mapping of logical qubit 0 to physical qubit 0 and logical qubit 1 to physical qubit 1.

```
circuit_depths['opt_lv_0'] =tr_lv0.depth()
gate_counts['opt_lv_0'] =sum(tr_lv0.count_ops().values())
scores['opt_lv_0'] =scoring(tr_lv0, backend)
print("Optimization level 0 results")
print("====================")
print("Circuit depth:", circuit_depths['opt_lv_0'])
print("Gate count:", gate_counts['opt_lv_0'])
print("Score:", scores['opt_lv_0'])
```

Now let us explore optimization level 1.

Optimization Level 1

Optimization level 1 performs a light optimization. The following are the techniques that are used for this optimization.

- TrivialLayout is the initial attempt at layout/routing. In the event where further SWAPs are needed, SabreSWAP is employed to identify a layout with the fewest possible SWAPs. Subsequently, VF2LayoutPostLayout is utilized to attempt to choose the optimal qubits within the graph.
- `InverseCancellation`
- 1Q gate optimization: Achieve optimality in chains of single-qubit u1, u2, u3 gates by their consolidation into a unified gate.

```
pm_lv1 = generate_preset_pass_manager(backend=backend, optimization_level=1,
seed_transpiler=seed)
tr_lv1 = pm_lv1.run(qc)
#tr_lv1.draw('mpl', idle_wires=False, fold=60)
```

One should now observe the mapping of logical qubits into distinct sets of physical qubits and a reduced number of gates.

```
circuit_depths['opt_lv_1'] = tr_lv1.depth()
gate_counts['opt_lv_1'] = sum(tr_lv1.count_ops().values())
scores['opt_lv_1'] = scoring(tr_lv1, backend)
print("Optimization level 1 results")
print("====================")
print("Circuit depth:", circuit_depths['opt_lv_1'])
print("Gate count:", gate_counts['opt_lv_1'])
print("Score:", scores['opt_lv_1'])
```

Let us see the next optimization level.

Optimization Level 2

Optimization level 2 performs a medium optimization. Let us see the operations that this includes.

- **Layout/Routing**: Optimization at level 1 (excluding trivial) with heuristic refined by increasing search depth and optimization function trials. Given that TrivialLayout is not employed, there is no endeavour to use identical physical and virtual qubit values.
- `CommutativeCancellation`: Pass for cancelling self-inverse gates/rotations. The cancellation utilizes the commutation relations in the circuit for H, X, Y, Z, CX, CY and CZ gates.

```
pm_lv2 = generate_preset_pass_manager(backend=backend, optimization_level=2,
seed_transpiler=seed)

tr_lv2 = pm_lv2.run(qc)

#tr_lv2.draw('mpl', idle_wires=False, fold=60)
```

From the first observation, it is evident that the quantity of gates has significantly reduced. The mapping of the logical qubit to the physical qubit remains constant.

```
circuit_depths['opt_lv_2'] = tr_lv2.depth()
gate_counts['opt_lv_2'] = sum(tr_lv2.count_ops().values())
scores['opt_lv_2'] = scoring(tr_lv2, backend)
```

```
print("Optimization level 2 results")
print("====================")
print("Circuit depth:", circuit_depths['opt_lv_2'])
print("Gate count:", gate_counts['opt_lv_2'])
print("Score:", scores['opt_lv_2'])
```

Next, let us take a look at the highest optimization level.

Optimization Level 3

Optimization level 3 performs a high optimization. The operations that we have at this level are the following.

- Optimization level 2 + heuristic optimized on layout/routing further with greater effort/trials.
- Resynthesis of two-qubit blocks using the KAK decomposition given in [3].
- Unitarity-breaking passes: The classical bit of the measure instruction to avoid SWAPs
  - `OptimizeSwapBeforeMeasure` : Remove swaps in front of measurements by re-targeting
  - `RemoveDiagonalGatesBeforeMeasure` : Remove diagonal gates (like RZ, T, Z, etc.) before a measurement, including diagonal 2Q gates.

```
pm_lv3 = generate_preset_pass_manager(backend=backend, optimization_level=3,
seed_transpiler=seed)

tr_lv3 = pm_lv3.run(qc)

#tr_lv3.draw('mpl', idle_wires=False, fold=60)
```

Now we have a smaller number of gates

```
circuit_depths['opt_lv_3'] = tr_lv3.depth()
gate_counts['opt_lv_3'] = sum(tr_lv3.count_ops().values())
scores['opt_lv_3'] = scoring(tr_lv3, backend)

print("Optimization level 3 results")
print("====================")
print("Circuit depth:", circuit_depths['opt_lv_3'])
print("Gate count:", gate_counts['opt_lv_3'])
```

```
print("Score:", scores['opt_lv_3'])
```

Given the whole set of results, let us plot the variations in circuit depth, gate count, and evaluation score for each optimization level.

```
colors = ['#FF6666', '#66B2FF']
ax = ["opt_lv_0", "opt_lv_1", "opt_lv_2", "opt_lv_3"]
fig, (ax1, ax2, ax3) = plt.subplots(3, 1, figsize=(10, 12))

# Plot 1: Circuit Depth
ax1.semilogy(ax, [circuit_depths[key] for key in ax],'o-',markersize=9,
↪ color='#FF6666',
label="Depth")
ax1.set_xlabel("Optimization Level", fontsize=12)
ax1.set_ylabel("Depth", fontsize=12)
ax1.set_title("Circuit Depth", fontsize=14)
ax1.legend(fontsize=10)

# Plot 2: Total Number of Gates
ax2.semilogy(ax, [gate_counts[key] for key in ax],'^-',markersize=9,
↪ color='#66B2FF',
label="Counts")
ax2.set_xlabel("Optimization Level", fontsize=12)
ax2.set_ylabel("Gate Count", fontsize=12)
ax2.set_title("Gate Count", fontsize=14)
ax2.legend(fontsize=10)

# Plot 3: Score of Transpiled Circuit
ax3.semilogy(ax, [scores[key] for key in ax],'*-',markersize=9,
label="Score")
ax3.set_xlabel("Optimization Level", fontsize=12)
ax3.set_ylabel("Score", fontsize=12)
ax3.set_title("Score", fontsize=14)
ax3.legend(fontsize=10)

fig.tight_layout()
```

```
plt.show()
```

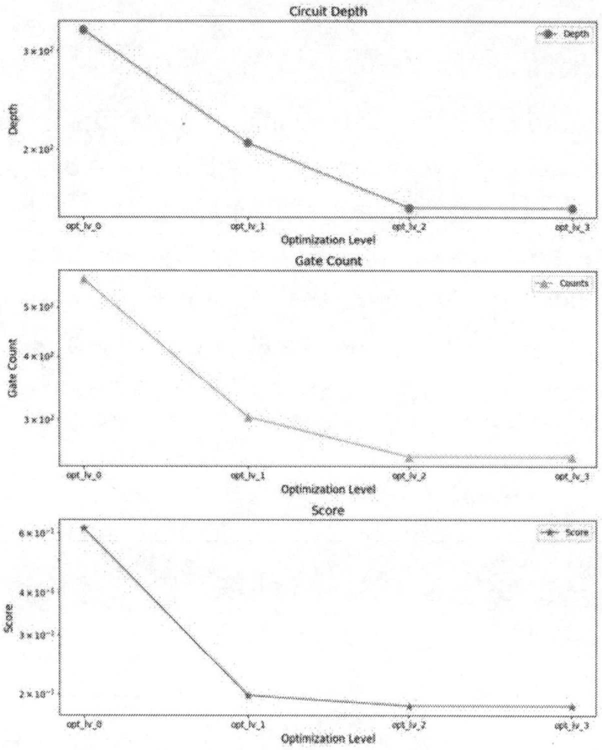

Figure 8.5: Transpiler Optimization Level Comparison

Figure 8.5 shows the comparison of different optimization levels of transpilation for circuit depth, gate count and scores.

Transpilation with Options

So far, we have examined four pre-established transpiler pipelines provided by Qiskit, which utilize random circuits. An essential characteristic of the Qiskit SDK v1.0 transpiler is its provision of a user-friendly interface for constructing and customizing a passmanager. Customize your pass manager by utilizing six standard passes in conjunction with the aforementioned optimization level, while also selecting the desired choice or plug-in for each pass. An alternative method is to generate a pass manager with any desired number of passes using `StagedPassManager`. Furthermore, it is possible to develop and launch a novel pass manager and incorporate it as a plugin in Qiskit, therefore enabling other users to get its functionality.

Let's look at all three methods in the following sections, starting with the easiest way first.

Init Stage

This initial stage has minimal default functionality and is mostly beneficial if you wish to incorporate your own initial improvements. Due to the limited design of layout and routing algorithms for single- and two-qubit gates, this stage is also employed to convert gates operating on more than two qubits into gates which function on only one or two qubits.

First, we check the possible options of the init stage we can use and you can see that without extra plugins, only default options exist. Then let's create a pass manager with init_method="default" options depending on the `optimization_level`. It gives us a list of optimization techniques for each of the levels.

```
list_stage_plugins("init")

print("Plugins run by default init stage")
print("=================================")

for i in range(4):
    print(f"\nOptimization level {i}:")
    pm = generate_preset_pass_manager(backend=backend, optimization_level=i,
    init_method="default", seed_transpiler=1000)
    for task in pm.init.to_flow_controller().tasks:
        print(" -", type(task).__name__)
```

Now let us see the next stage in this process.

Layout Stage

This stage entails determining the backend's connectivity or layout before sending a circuit there. Qubits in quantum circuits are typically *virtual* or *logical* representations of real qubits that are employed in computations; these abstract entities are known as quantum circuits. A one-to-one mapping from the *virtual* qubits to the *physical* qubits in a real quantum device is required in order to carry out a series of gates. This mapping is one of the constraints defined in the instruction set architecture (ISA) of a backend and is kept as a Layout object.

In order to minimize the number of SWAP operations required to map the input circuit onto the device topology and guarantee that the best-calibrated qubits are utilized, the mapping selection is crucial. Owing to the significance of this phase, the preset pass managers experiment with several approaches to determine the optimal configuration. This usually includes two steps: first, look for a *perfect* layout (one that doesn't require any SWAP operations); if a perfect layout can't be discovered, apply a heuristic pass to find the optimum layout to utilize. For this first stage, two Passes are usually utilized:

- **TrivialLayout**: Naively, every virtual qubit on the device is mapped to the corresponding physical qubit number (i.e., [0,1,1,3] -> [0,1,1,3]). Only at `optimization_level=1` is this historical behavior employed in an effort to discover the ideal arrangement. Next is VF2Layout if it doesn't work.
- **VF2Layout**: This AnalysisPass treats this step as a subgraph isomorphism issue, which the VF2++ algorithm solves to choose the optimal layout. A scoring heuristic is applied to choose the mapping with the lowest average error if multiple layouts are discovered.

Then for the heuristic stage, two passes are used by default:

- **DenseLayout**: If control flow operations (like IfElseOp) are present in the circuit, this sub-graph of the device with the highest connectivity and the same amount of qubits as the circuit is used for optimization level 1.
- **SabreLayout**: In order to choose a layout, this pass runs the SabreSwap algorithm repeatedly, starting with a random initial layout. This pass is only applied in optimization stages 1, 2, and 3 in the event when the VF2Layout pass is unable to identify an ideal layout. For more details refer to [4].

We can find these four passes by using the same code as the init stage with the list stage plugins for layout. Then, we run the code to see which jobs will be enabled by which `optimization_level` when `layout_method='default'` is used.

```
list_stage_plugins("layout")

print("Plugins run by default layout stage")
print("=================================")
for i in range(4):
    print(f"\nOptimization level {i}:")
    pm = generate_preset_pass_manager(backend=backend, optimization_level=i,
    layout_method='default', seed_transpiler=seed)
    qc_tr = pm.run(qc)

    for controller_group in pm.layout.to_flow_controller().tasks:
```

```
        tasks = getattr(controller_group, "tasks", [])
        for task in tasks:
            print(" - " , str(type(task).__name__))
    print(qc_tr.layout.final_index_layout())
    display(plot_circuit_layout(pm.run(qc), backend))
```

You can observe the different layouts for each of the optimization levels having honeycomb-like structures for the backend which we have selected and you can see the qubit numbers marked and numbered in black color that is being optimized for that particular level.

In order to get better clarity, we printed out the scores for each of the layouts that we discussed before. It can be seen that for the 'dense' layout, the score is closer to 0, which means it is better as compared to others like 'default', 'trivial' and 'sabre' layouts.

```
for option in list_stage_plugins("layout"):
    pm = generate_preset_pass_manager(backend=backend, optimization_level=3,
    layout_method=option, seed_transpiler=seed)
    qc_tr = pm.run(qc)
    score = scoring(qc_tr, backend)

    print(f"Layout method = {option}")
    print(f"Score: {score:.6f}")
    print(f"Layout: {qc_tr.layout.final_index_layout()}\n")
```

Now let us move on to the next stage namely the Routing stage.

Routing Stage

One or more SWAP gates must be added to the circuit to move the qubit states around until they are adjacent on the device gate map in order to build a two-qubit gate between qubits that are not directly coupled on a quantum device. Every SWAP gate is an expensive and obtrusive process to operate. Determining the bare minimum of SWAP gates required to map a circuit onto a particular device is, therefore, a crucial stage in the transpilation process. Although by default this stage is computed with the Layout stage for efficiency, they are logically separate stages. The Routing stage inserts the necessary number of SWAP gates to enable the circuits to be executed using the chosen layout, while the Layout stage chooses which hardware qubits to employ.

Finding the ideal SWAP mapping is challenging, though. The problem is actually NP-hard, which means that all but the smallest quantum devices and input circuits cannot afford to compute it. In order to get around this, Qiskit computes a good—though not always ideal—SWAP mapping using a stochastic heuristic approach known as SabreSwap . Because a stochastic method is being used, it cannot be assured that the circuits formed will remain the same after multiple iterations. In fact, there is a distribution of gate counts and circuit depths at the output when the same circuit is run repeatedly. This is the reason why a lot of users decide to repeatedly execute the routing function (or the complete StagedPassManager) and pick the outputs with the lowest depth of circuits.

First, we print out the routing stage plugins which are 'basic', 'lookahead', 'none', 'sabre' and `stochastic` . Then for each optimization level, we check the number of gates and the score for the 'basic' routing technique.

```
list_stage_plugins("routing")

print("Number of each gates of transpiled circuit and the score")
print("==================================")
for i in range(4):
    print(f"\nOptimization level {i}:")
    pm = generate_preset_pass_manager(backend=backend, optimization_level=i,
    routing_method='basic', seed_transpiler=seed)
    qc_tr = pm.run(qc)
    score = scoring(qc_tr, backend)
    for key, value in qc_tr.count_ops().items():
        print(key, ":", value)
    print(f"Score: {score:.6f}")
```

You can see that for optimization level 3, we get the lowest score. Now again for the basic routing, we can display the plugins for each optimization level.

```
print("Plugins run by basic routing stage")
print("==================================")
for i in range(4):
    print(f"\nOptimization level {i}:")
    pm = generate_preset_pass_manager(backend=backend, optimization_level=i,
    routing_method='basic', seed_transpiler=seed)

    for controller_group in pm.routing.to_flow_controller().tasks:
        tasks = getattr(controller_group, "tasks", [])
        for task in tasks:
```

```
        print(" - " , str(type(task).__name__))
    display(pm.routing.draw())
    print(pm.run(qc).layout.final_index_layout())
```

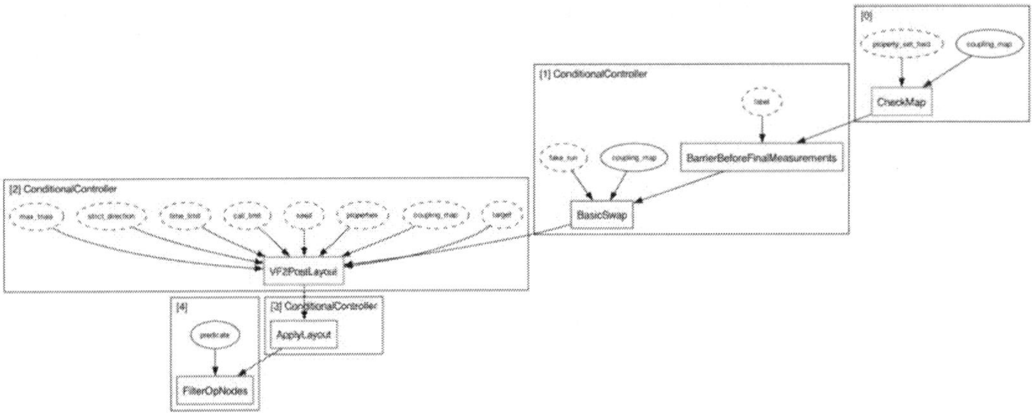

Figure 8.6: Routing Plugin Diagram

Figure 8.6 shows the plugin diagram for one of the optimization levels and you can see that for basic routing different transpiling techniques take several arguments.

In the following code cell, we set the optimization level to 3 and explore the scores of three options - `basic`, `sabre` and `stochastic`. Here we see that the scores for `sabre` are closest to 0 and the lowest compared to others.

```
options = ['basic','sabre', 'stochastic']

for option in options:
    print(f"Layout option = {option}:")
    pm = generate_preset_pass_manager(backend=backend, optimization_level=3,
    routing_method=option, seed_transpiler=seed)
    qc_tr = pm.run(qc)
    score = scoring(qc_tr, backend)

    print(f"Score: {score:.6f}")

    for key, value in qc_tr.count_ops().items():
        print(key, ":", value)
    print("\n")
```

Let us go to the translation stage now.

Translation Stage

You can utilize any quantum gate (unitary operation) that you choose when creating a quantum circuit, in addition to various non-gate operations like reset or qubit measurement instructions. Still, only a small number of quantum gate and non-gate operations are supported natively by the majority of quantum devices. The definition of a target's ISA and this step of the setup include these native gates. The gates supplied in a circuit are translated (or unrolled) by PassManagers to the native basis gates of a selected backend. This is a crucial step since it permits the backend to perform the circuit, although it usually results in a deeper and more gated circuit.

Two special cases are especially important to highlight and help illustrate what this stage does.

- Three CNOT gates are needed if a SWAP gate isn't a native gate to the destination backend. A SWAP is a costly operation to execute on noisy quantum devices since it is the result of three CNOT gates. Nevertheless, in order to integrate a circuit within the constrained gate connectivities of numerous devices, such actions are typically required. Therefore, one of the main objectives of the transpilation process is to reduce the number of SWAP gates in a circuit.
- A three-qubit gate is known as a Toffoli, or controlled-controlled-not (ccx) gate. This operation needs to be broken down because the only single- and two-qubit gates in our base gate set are present. However, the expense is high: the hardware can perform several single-qubit gates and up to six CNOT gates for each Toffoli gate in a quantum circuit. This example shows that any method using several Toffoli gates will result in a large-depth circuit, which means that noise will affect it significantly.

For translation, we have `synthesis`, `translator`, `ibm_backend`, and `ibm_dynamic_circuits` as options. The basic options in Qiskit are `translator` and `synthesis`. Let's count the total gate numbers, circuit depth, and scores of transpiled circuits with the default option (`translator`) and each optimization level. You will see the lowest number of gates for optimization level 3 with the lowest score as well.

```
list_stage_plugins("translation")

print("Number of each gates of transpiled circuit")
print("=================================")

for i in range(4):
    print(f"\nOptimization level {i}:")
```

```
    pm = generate_preset_pass_manager(backend=backend, optimization_level=i,
    translation_method='translator', seed_transpiler=seed)
    qc_tr = pm.run(qc)
    score = scoring(qc_tr, backend)
    for key, value in qc_tr.count_ops().items():
        print(key, ":", value)
    print(f"Score: {score:.6f}")
```

Let's count total gate numbers, circuit depth, and scores of transpiled circuits with each option and optimization_level=3. Here you will observe that for the 'translator' option, we have the lowest score and number of gates.

```
options = ['translator', 'synthesis']

print("Number of each gates of transpiled circuit")
print("==================================")

for option in options:
    print(f"Layout option = {option}:")
    pm = generate_preset_pass_manager(backend=backend, optimization_level=3,
    translation_method=option, seed_transpiler=seed)
    qc_tr = pm.run(qc)
    score = scoring(qc_tr, backend)
    for key, value in qc_tr.count_ops().items():
        print(key, ":", value)
    print(f"Score: {score:.6f}")
    print("\n")
```

Just like before, let us plot the graphs of circuit depth, the total number of gates and the score of the transpiled circuit against the optimization levels 0, 1, 2 and 3. You will observe that as the optimization increases, all the values decrease for both the translator and synthesis options.

```
tr_depths = []
tr_gate_counts = []
tr_scores = []

options = ['translator', 'synthesis']
```

```
for i in range(4):
    for option in options:
        pm = generate_preset_pass_manager(backend=backend, optimization_level=i,
        translation_method=option, seed_transpiler=seed)

        tr_depths.append(pm.run(qc).depth())
        tr_gate_counts.append(sum(pm.run(qc).count_ops().values()))
        tr_scores.append(scoring(pm.run(qc), backend))
```

```
colors = ['#FF6666', '#66B2FF']
markers = [ '^', '*']
linestyles = ['-.', ':']

opt_list = []
for i in range(4):
    opt_list.append(f"Optimization Level {i}")

ax = opt_list
fig, (ax1, ax2, ax3) = plt.subplots(3, 1, figsize=(10, 12))

# Plot 1: Circuit Depth
for i in range(2):
    ax1.plot(ax, tr_depths[i::2], label=options[i], marker=markers[i],
    ↪  markersize=9,
    linestyle=linestyles[i], color=colors[i], linewidth=2)
ax1.set_xlabel("translation options", fontsize=12)
ax1.set_ylabel("Depth", fontsize=12)
ax1.set_title("Circuit Depth of Transpiled Circuit", fontsize=14)
ax1.legend(fontsize=10)

# Plot 2: Total Number of Gates
for i in range(2):
    ax2.plot(ax, tr_gate_counts[i::2], label=options[i], marker=markers[i],
    ↪  markersize=9,
    linestyle=linestyles[i], color=colors[i], linewidth=2)
```

```
ax2.set_xlabel("translation options", fontsize=12)
ax2.set_ylabel("# of Total Gates", fontsize=12)
ax2.set_title("Total Number of Gates of Transpiled Circuit", fontsize=14)
ax2.legend(fontsize=10)

# Plot 3: Score of Transpiled Circuit
for i in range(2):
    ax3.plot(ax, tr_scores[i::2], label=options[i],
    ↪   marker=markers[i],markersize=9,
    linestyle=linestyles[i], color=colors[i], linewidth=2)
ax3.set_xlabel("translation options", fontsize=12)
ax3.set_ylabel("Score of Transpiled Circuit", fontsize=12)
ax3.set_title("Score of Transpiled Circuit", fontsize=14)
ax3.legend(fontsize=10)

fig.tight_layout()
plt.show()
```

This concludes the translation stage discussion. Let us now move on to the next stage which is the optimization stage.

Optimization Stage

The depth and gate count of quantum circuits are increased by breaking down the circuits into the basis gate set of the target device and by adding swap gates to fit the hardware topology. Thankfully, there are numerous algorithms available for combining or removing gates to optimize circuits. These techniques can sometimes be so successful that the output circuits are shallower than the inputs. In other situations, not much can be done, and using noisy equipment to execute the computation could be challenging. With varying `optimization_level` settings, different gate optimizations are enabled.

- For `optimization_level=1`, this stage prepares `Optimize1qGateDecomposition` and `CXCancellation`, which combine chains of single-qubit gates and cancel any back-to-back CNOT gates.
- For `optimization_level=2`, this stage uses the `CommutativeCancellation` pass instead of `CXCancellation`, which removes redundant gates by exploiting commutation relations.

- For `optimization_level=3`, this stage prepares the following passes- `Collect2qBlocks`, `ConsolidateBlocks`, `UnitarySynthesis`, `Optimize1qGateDecomposition`, `CommutativeCancellation`. Additionally, this stage also executes a few final checks to make sure that all instructions in the circuit are composed of the basis gates available on the target backend.

We currently have two choices to set up:

- `approximation_degree` (float, in the range 0-1 | None): Heuristic dial used for circuit approximation (1.0 = no approximation, 0.0 = maximal approximation). The default value is 1.0. Specifying None sets the approximation degree to the reported error rate.
- `optimization_method (str)`: The name of the plugin to employ during the optimization phase. An external plugin is not used by default. Using `list_stage_plugins()` with optimization for the stage_name input, you can view a list of installed plugins.

To indicate how closely you want the output circuit to resemble the intended (input) circuit, you might use the approximation degree. This float is in the (0.0 - 1.0) range, where 1.0 (the default) indicates no approximation and 0.0 represents the largest approximation. Lower values give up output precision in favor of the simplicity of execution (fewer gates). 1.0 is the default value.

This number indicates the desired amount of output decomposition fidelity in two-qubit unitary synthesis, which is utilized in the first stages of all levels and for the optimization stage with optimization level 3. That is, the amount of error that results from translating a circuit's matrix representation into discrete gates. The output circuit from synthesis will deviate more from the input matrix if the approximation degree is smaller (greater approximation). However, it will also probably contain fewer gates and be simpler to operate because any given two-qubit operation can be completely decomposed with at most three CX gates.

Circuits with one or two CX gates may be synthesized when the approximation degree is less than 1.0, which results in less inaccuracy from the hardware and more from the approximation. Reduce the amount of CX gates in synthesis, even at the expense of fidelity, since they are the most costly gates in terms of error (this method was employed to boost quantum volume on IBM® systems).

Now considering different `approximation_degree` values ranging like [0, 0.1, 0.2,...,0.9, 1] in the X axis, we again plot the parameters - total gate number, circuit depth and score of the transpiled circuit.

```
tr_depths = []
tr_gate_counts = []
tr_scores = []
```

```
approximation_degree_list = np.linspace(0,1,10)
for i in range(4):
    for j in approximation_degree_list:
        pm = generate_preset_pass_manager(backend=backend, optimization_level=i,
        approximation_degree=j, seed_transpiler=seed)
        tr_depths.append(pm.run(qc).depth())
        tr_gate_counts.append(sum(pm.run(qc).count_ops().values()))
        tr_scores.append(scoring(pm.run(qc), backend))
```

```
colors = ['#FF6666', '#FFCC66', '#99FF99', '#66B2FF']
markers = ['o', 's', '^', '*']
linestyles = ['-', '--', '-.', ':']

ax = approximation_degree_list
fig, (ax1, ax2, ax3) = plt.subplots(3, 1, figsize=(10, 12))

# Plot 1: Circuit Depth
for i in range(4):
    ax1.plot(ax, tr_depths[i*10:i*10+10], label=f"Optimization Level {i}",
    marker=markers[i],
    markersize=9, linestyle=linestyles[i], color=colors[i], linewidth=2)
ax1.set_xlabel("Approximation Degree", fontsize=12)
ax1.set_ylabel("Depth", fontsize=12)
ax1.set_title("Circuit Depth of Transpiled Circuit", fontsize=14)
ax1.legend(fontsize=10)

# Plot 2: Total Number of Gates
for i in range(4):
    ax2.plot(ax, tr_gate_counts[i*10:i*10+10], label=f"Optimization Level {i}",
    marker=markers[i],
    markersize=9, linestyle=linestyles[i], color=colors[i], linewidth=2)
ax2.set_xlabel("Approximation Degree", fontsize=12)
ax2.set_ylabel("# of Total Gates", fontsize=12)
ax2.set_title("Total Number of Gates of Transpiled Circuit", fontsize=14)
ax2.legend(fontsize=10)
```

```
# Plot 3: Score of Transpiled Circuit
for i in range(4):
    ax3.plot(ax, tr_scores[i*10:i*10+10], label=f"Optimization Level {i}",
    marker=markers[i],
    markersize=9, linestyle=linestyles[i], color=colors[i], linewidth=2)
ax3.set_xlabel("Approximation Degree", fontsize=12)
ax3.set_ylabel("Score of Transpiled Circuit", fontsize=12)
ax3.set_title("Score of Transpiled Circuit", fontsize=14)
ax3.legend(fontsize=10)

fig.tight_layout()
plt.show()
```

Like before, you can see that with increasing `approximation_degree` values, all the parameters decrease with some minor fluctuations. Additionally, it seems like `approximation_degree=0.5` returns the best performance.

In order to understand this, let's compare the ideal simulation result of this target circuit to transpiled circuits using Hellinger fidelity, which returns fidelity between two counts distributions, using circuits having the approximation degrees as follows `approximation_degree=[0, 0.5, 1]`.

The fidelity is defined as $\left(1 - H^2\right)^2$ where H is the Hellinger distance. This value is bounded in the range $[0, 1]$.

This is equivalent to the standard classical fidelity $F(Q, P) = \left(\sum_i \sqrt{p_i q_i}\right)^2$ that in turn is equal to the quantum state fidelity for diagonal density matrices.

First, let's compute the ideal noiseless measurement, by using `AerSimulator` with the state vector method.

```
aer_sim = AerSimulator(method='statevector')
sampler = Sampler(backend=aer_sim)
sampler.options.default_shots = 20000

qc_m = qc.measure_all(inplace=False)

pm_sim = generate_preset_pass_manager(backend=aer_sim, optimization_level=3,
seed_transpiler=seed)

result = sampler.run([pm_sim.run(qc_m)]).result()[0]
```

```
ideal_counts = result.data.meas.get_counts()
```

Next, let's create 3 circuits by using optimization_level=3 and `approximation_degree=[0, 0.5, 1]` with our `FakeTorino()` and get counts with 20000 shots.

Now let's compute the fidelity of each count by using Hellinger fidelity .

```
pm_0 = generate_preset_pass_manager(backend=backend, optimization_level=3,
approximation_degree=0, seed_transpiler=seed)
pm_05 = generate_preset_pass_manager(backend=backend, optimization_level=3,
approximation_degree=0.5, seed_transpiler=seed)
pm_1 = generate_preset_pass_manager(backend=backend, optimization_level=3,
approximation_degree=1, seed_transpiler=seed)

noisy_sampler = Sampler(backend=backend)
noisy_sampler.options.default_shots = 20000

noisy0 = noisy_sampler.run([pm_0.run(qc_m)]).result()[0].data.meas.get_counts()
noisy05 = noisy_sampler.run([pm_05.run(qc_m)]).result()[0].data.meas.get_counts()
noisy1 = noisy_sampler.run([pm_1.run(qc_m)]).result()[0].data.meas.get_counts()

print("approximation_degree = 0 fidelity", round(hellinger_fidelity(ideal_counts,
noisy0), 4))
print("approximation_degree = 0.5 fidelity",
↪  round(hellinger_fidelity(ideal_counts,
noisy05), 4))
print("approximation_degree = 1 fidelity", round(hellinger_fidelity(ideal_counts,
noisy1), 4))
```

It shows even if we can get the smallest circuit by using `approximation_degree=0.5` , the transpiled circuit is too much approximated from the original circuit.

It is important to note that while creating or customizing a transpiler that impacts the enrollment circuit, there are additional factors to consider.

Let us see the last stage of transpilation with options - The scheduling stage.

Scheduling Stage

This last phase is executed only when specifically requested, analogous to the init stage , and is not active by default (although a method can be defined by using the 1scheduling_method1 parameter when invoking `generate_preset_pass_manager`). Typically, the scheduling stage is employed after the circuit has been converted to the target basis, mapped to the device, and thoroughly optimized. The primary objective of these passes is to allocate all the idle time inside a circuit. Broadly speaking, the scheduling pass can be conceptualized as the deliberate inclusion of delay instructions to accommodate the periods of inactivity between gate executions and to assess the duration of circuit operation on the backend.

There are three options in scheduling - 'alap', 'asap' and 'default'.

Prior to using scheduling options, it is necessary to establish `timing_constraints` , which encompass relevant details about the backend in order to obtain the most efficient pulse schedule.

We initialize pass managers for both 'alap' and 'asap' in order to compare their scores later.

```
list_stage_plugins("scheduling")

backend_timing = backend.target.timing_constraints()
timing_constraints = TimingConstraints(
    granularity=backend_timing.granularity,
    min_length=backend_timing.min_length,
    pulse_alignment=backend_timing.pulse_alignment,
    acquire_alignment=backend_timing.acquire_alignment )

pm_asap = generate_preset_pass_manager(
    optimization_level=3,
    backend=backend,
    timing_constraints=timing_constraints,
    scheduling_method="asap",
    seed_transpiler=seed,
)

my_style = {
    'formatter.general.fig_width': 40,
```

```
    'formatter.general.fig_unit_height': 1,
}

draw(pm_asap.run(qc), style=IQXStandard(**my_style), show_idle=False,
↪   show_delays=True)
```

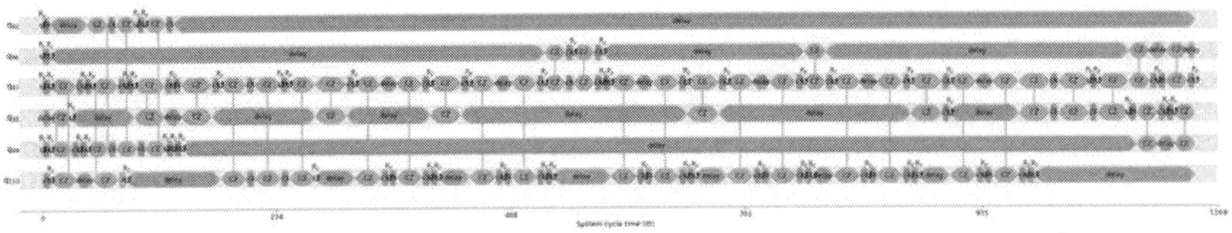

Figure 8.7: asap Pulse Diagram

```
pm_alap = generate_preset_pass_manager(
    optimization_level=3,
    backend=backend,
    timing_constraints=timing_constraints,
    scheduling_method="alap",
    seed_transpiler=seed,
)
draw(pm_alap.run(qc), style=IQXStandard(**my_style), show_idle=False, \\
↪   show_delays=True)
```

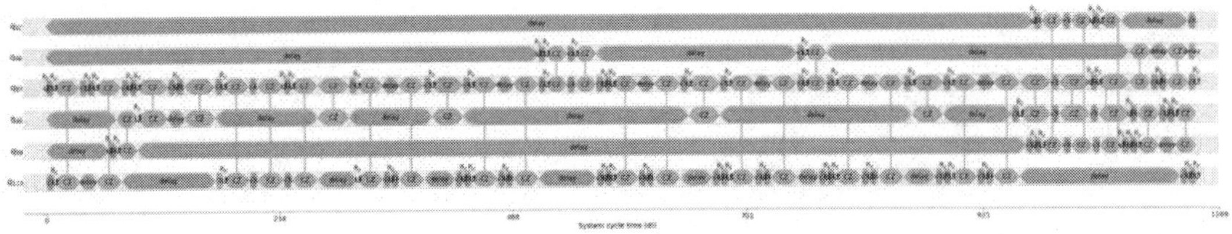

Figure 8.8: alap Pulse Diagram

As you can see, there are significant delays in these two circuits, but they differ in terms of position and order. Performance variations may result from this schedule, depending on the circuit and backend. Let's examine and contrast these two circuits' scores.

```
def qubit_error(time, t1, t2):
    t2 = min(t1, t2)
    rate1 = 1/t1
    rate2 = 1/t2
    p_reset = 1-np.exp(-time*rate1)
    p_z = (1-p_reset)*(1-np.exp(-time*(rate2-rate1)))/2
    return p_z + p_reset

print("Score")
print("===============")
print(f"asap: {scoring(pm_asap.run(qc), backend):.6f}")
print(f"alap: {scoring(pm_alap.run(qc), backend):.6f}")
```

You will see that you get scores for asap: 0.212772 and for alap: 0.177097 where alap is better performing than asap.

AI Transpilation

A very important part of quantum computing is translating general quantum circuits to fit the limits and features of specific quantum devices. Through the previous hands-on transpiler coding you saw that this process usually uses heuristic algorithms. However, the new transpiler passes driven by AI could make the process more efficient and produce better results while still being fast enough for real-world use. Here we use the Qiskit Transpiler Service to carry out AI Transpilation. The technique has been described in [5].

First, we make the necessary imports.

```
import numpy as np
import matplotlib.pyplot as plt
from qiskit.circuit.library import EfficientSU2
from qiskit.transpiler.preset_passmanagers import generate_preset_pass_manager
from qiskit_ibm_runtime import QiskitRuntimeService
from qiskit_transpiler_service.transpiler_service import TranspilerService
from qiskit_ibm_runtime import QiskitRuntimeService
```

We define the number of qubits and construct an `EfficientSU2()` circuit having circular entanglement.

```
NUM_QUBITS = 61
circuit = EfficientSU2(NUM_QUBITS, entanglement="circular", reps=1).decompose()
print(f"Original circuit -> Depth: {circuit.depth()}, CNOTs:
{circuit.num_nonlocal_gates()}")
#circuit.draw(fold=-1, output="mpl", style="iqp", scale=0.2)
```

We get a circuit of depth 65 and 61 CNOT gates or non-local gates.

Using the Qiskit Transpiler Service, you will transpile and optimize your circuit in this stage. This procedure will be carried out twice: once without AI and once with transpiler passes enabled by AI. For this section, the Qiskit Transpiler Service will be used. On the cloud, heuristic and AI-powered transpilation capabilities are offered via the Qiskit Transpiler Service.

First, save your IBM Quantum account details by using the QiskitRuntimeService and initialize it. Then we define the TranspilerService without the AI functionality.

```
QiskitRuntimeService.save_account(
    channel="ibm_quantum",
    token="PASTE YOUR TOKEN FROM IBM QUANTUM ACCOUNT",
    set_as_default=True,
    overwrite=True,
)
service = QiskitRuntimeService()
transpiler_ai_false = TranspilerService(
    backend_name="ibm_brisbane",
    ai=False,
    optimization_level=3,
)
circuit_ai_false = transpiler_ai_false.run(circuit)
print(f"Transpiled without AI -> Depth: {circuit_ai_false.depth()},
CNOTs: {circuit_ai_false.num_nonlocal_gates()}")
#circuit_ai_false.draw(fold=-1, output="mpl", scale=0.2)
```

We get a Depth of 1313 and a number of CNOTs as 364 by not using the AI transpilation. Now let us see what happens when we enable the AI transpilation as the following code cell shows.

```
transpiler_ai_true = TranspilerService(
    backend_name="ibm_brisbane",
    ai=True,
    optimization_level=3,
)
circuit_ai_true = transpiler_ai_true.run(circuit)
print(f"Transpiled with AI -> Depth: {circuit_ai_true.depth()},
CNOTs: {circuit_ai_true.num_nonlocal_gates()}")
#circuit_ai_true.draw(fold=-1, output="mpl", scale=0.2)
```

As expected we get Depth: 276 and the CNOTs: 64 with AI transpilation.

In order to make a better comparison, let us plot a graph between the number of CNOT gates against the different number of qubits to check the performance of AI-based transpilation and non-AI-based transpilation.

```
# Transpiling locally using Qiskit SDK
service = QiskitRuntimeService()
backend = service.backend("ibm_sherbrooke")
pm = generate_preset_pass_manager(backend=backend, optimization_level=3)

# Run and compile results
num_qubits = [11, 21, 41, 61, 81]
num_cnots_local = []
num_cnots_with_ai = []
num_cnots_without_ai = []

for nq in num_qubits:
    circuit = EfficientSU2(nq, entanglement="circular", reps=1).decompose()

    # Using the Transpiler locally on Qiskit
    circuit_local = pm.run(circuit)
    # Using the transpiler service without AI
    circuit_without_ai = transpiler_ai_false.run(circuit)
    # Using the transpiler service with AI
    circuit_with_ai = transpiler_ai_true.run(circuit)

    num_cnots_local.append(circuit_local.num_nonlocal_gates())
```

```
    num_cnots_without_ai.append(circuit_without_ai.num_nonlocal_gates())
    num_cnots_with_ai.append(circuit_with_ai.num_nonlocal_gates())

plt.plot(num_qubits, num_cnots_with_ai, '.-')
plt.plot(num_qubits, num_cnots_without_ai, '.-')
plt.plot(num_qubits, num_cnots_local, '--')
plt.xlabel("Number of qubits")
plt.ylabel("CNOT count")
plt.legend(["Qiskit Transpiler Service with AI", "Qiskit Transpiler Service
↪  without AI",
"Qiskit SDK"])
```

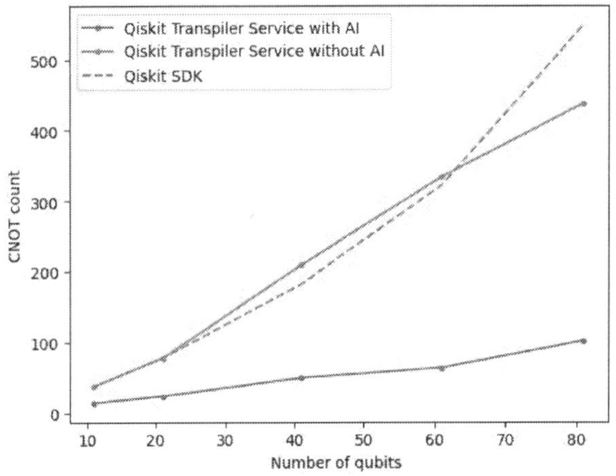

Figure 8.9: AI vs Non-AI Transpilation

From the graph, it is clear that as the number of qubits increases, AI transpilation is much more effective in reducing the number of CNOT gates.

In order to explain transpilation, here we considered a random quantum circuit. However, in *Chapter 10, Quantum Algorithms Part II*, you will see how Quantum Fourier Transform can be transpiled efficiently using the transpilation techniques you learnt here and running those at a utility scale.

Circuit Knitting

In the previous section on transpilation, you saw that applying gates between distant qubits would require a large swap overhead. Circuit cutting is a process wherein a large quantum circuit's gates and/or wires are cut, hence reducing the requirement for swap gates. By doing this, the circuit is broken down into smaller pieces that can be implemented with the limitations of the current quantum technology. The solution to the initial problem is then reconstructed using the output of these smaller circuits.

Therefore, circuit cutting allows us to run larger circuits on quantum hardware at the cost of additional sampling overhead.

A quantum channel $\mathcal{E}$ can be decomposed into a linear combination of several channels $\mathcal{E}_i$ with coefficients a_i. Therefore, a virtual gate is also implemented by a sum over several circuits:

$$\mathcal{E}(\cdot) = \sum_i a_i \mathcal{E}_i(\cdot) \tag{8.2}$$

The a_i do not form a valid probability decomposition since some $a_i < 0$ cannot sample. We transform to a valid probability distribution via:

$$\gamma = \sum_i |a_i| \tag{8.3}$$

So, $\sum \frac{|a_i|}{\gamma} = 1$. Therefore, $\frac{|a_i|}{\gamma}$ forms a valid probability distribution:

$$\mathcal{E}(\rho) = \gamma \sum_i \frac{|a_i|}{\gamma} \text{sign}(a_i)\mathcal{E}_i(\cdot) \tag{8.4}$$

This is Quasi-Probability Decomposition and it allows us to cut gates.

First we make the necessary imports.

```
import numpy as np
import matplotlib.pyplot as plt
from qiskit import QuantumCircuit
from qiskit.transpiler.preset_passmanagers import generate_preset_pass_manager
from qiskit.visualization import plot_gate_map
from qiskit.quantum_info import SparsePauliOp
from qiskit_aer import AerSimulator
from qiskit_ibm_runtime import QiskitRuntimeService, SamplerV2 as Sampler
from circuit_knitting.cutting import generate_cutting_experiments, cut_gates
```

Now let us create a Bell-pair and see how we can cut a CNOT gate using the Circuit Knitting Toolbox in this. After constructing the Bell circuit, define the QiskitRuntimeService since we will be running this code in one of the quantum hardware provided by IBM Quantum. We select the ibm_kyoto as our backend for this purpose.

```
# create a bell pair
bell_state = QuantumCircuit(2)
bell_state.h(0)
bell_state.cx(0,1)
bell_state.draw("mpl")

service = QiskitRuntimeService(
   channel='ibm_quantum',
   instance='ibm-q/open/main',
   token='PASTE YOUR TOKEN FROM IBM QUANTUM ACCOUNT'
)
service = QiskitRuntimeService(channel="ibm_quantum")
backend = service.backend("ibm_kyoto")
```

We now select a layout that necessitates numerous swaps in order to implement the gates between qubits 122 and 126 and to move the qubits back to their starting places.

```
layout=[122, 126]
qubit_color = []
for i in range(127):
    if i in layout:
        qubit_color.append("#ff0066")
    else:
        qubit_color.append("#6600cc")
plot_gate_map(backend, qubit_color=qubit_color, qubit_size=60, font_size=25,
figsize=(8,8))
```

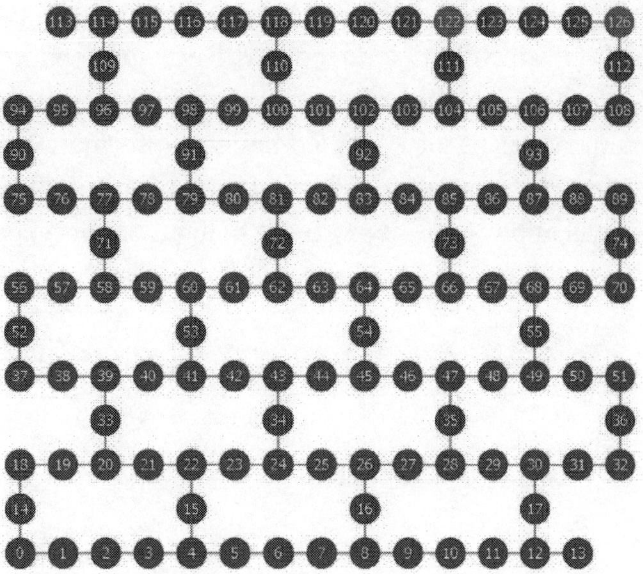

Figure 8.10: Qubits 122 and 126 marked in Red

We transpile the Bell pair circuit to get the Instruction Set Architecture (ISA) circuit, which the device can understand and execute.

```
# transpile the circuit
pm = generate_preset_pass_manager(backend=backend, optimization_level=1,
initial_layout=layout, seed_transpiler=0)
isa_qc = pm.run(bell_state)
# original circuit depth
isa_qc_depth = isa_qc.depth()
print(f"Transpiled circuit depth: ", isa_qc_depth)
#isa_qc.draw("mpl", scale=0.6, idle_wires=False, fold=False)
```

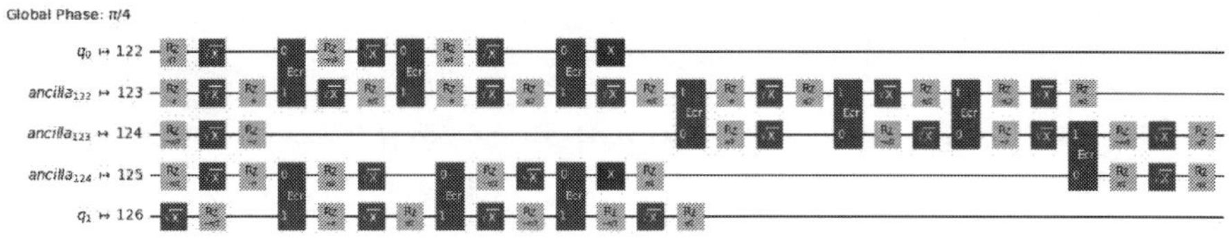

Figure 8.11: Depth 27 Quantum Circuit

We see that many ancilla qubits are used and the depth of the transpiled circuit is 27. This is the case if we don't use the Qiskit Circuit Knitting Toolbox.

By defining their indices, we will swap out the distant gates—that is, the gates that connect the non-local qubits, 122 and 126—with `TwoQubitQPDGates` (QPD stands for quasi-probability decomposition, which is introduced in the previous chapters). Also, `cut_gates` will provide a list of `QPDBasis` objects, one for each gate decomposition, and substitute `TwoQubitQPDGates` for the gates in the specified indices. Information about breaking down the cut gates into single-qubit operations can be found in the `QPDBasis` object.

In the next cell, we will apply `cut_gates` to the bell circuit with specified indices to cut then get the circuit in which the CNOT gate is cut.

```
# Find the indices of the distant gates
cut_indices = [
    i
    for i, instruction in enumerate(bell_state.data)
    if {bell_state.find_bit(q)[0] for q in instruction.qubits} == {0, 1}
]
# Decompose distant CNOTs into TwoQubitQPDGate instances
qpd_circuit, bases = cut_gates(bell_state, cut_indices)
#qpd_circuit.draw("mpl", scale=0.6)
```

Many sub-experiments are constructed from the joint quasiprobability distribution of the decomposed gates and then run on one or more backends to replicate the expected value of the full-sized circuit. The `num_samples` controls how many samples are drawn from the distribution; for each distinct sample, a single combined coefficient is provided.

In the next cell, `generate_cutting_experiments` accepts a circuit containing `TwoQubitQPDGates` instances and observables as a `PauliList`.

```
observable = SparsePauliOp(["ZI"])
# Generate the sub-experiments and sampling coefficients
sub_experiments, coefficients = generate_cutting_experiments(
    circuits=qpd_circuit, observables=observable.paulis, num_samples=np.inf
)
```

This is an illustration of a sub-experiment that was selected at random using the QPD circuit. Its depth dropped dramatically from 27 to 7. Reconstructing an expectation value of the deeper circuit requires the generation and evaluation of numerous probabilistic sub-experiments. To reconstruct this circuit, six sub-experiments are required.

```
# Transpile the circuit
pm = generate_preset_pass_manager(backend=backend, optimization_level=1,
initial_layout=layout, seed_transpiler=0)
```

```
isa_qpd_circuit = pm.run(sub_experiments[5])
# depth using circuit cutting
isa_qpd_depth = isa_qpd_circuit.depth()
print(f"Original circuit depth after transpile: ", isa_qc_depth)
print(f"QPD sub-experiment depth after transpile: ", isa_qpd_depth)
print(f"Number of sub-experiments:", len(sub_experiments))
isa_qpd_circuit.draw("mpl", scale=0.6, idle_wires=False, fold=False)
x = np.array([c.depth() for c in pm.run(sub_experiments)])
print(x)
```

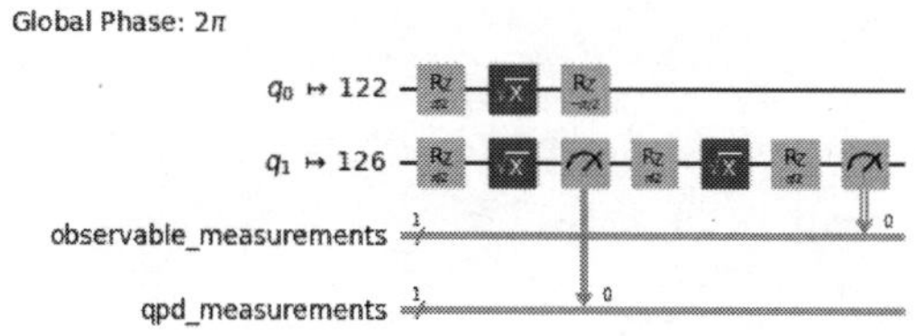

Figure 8.12: Depth 7 Quantum Circuit

The circuit shown previously was the 5th circuit out of the 6 sub-experiments. For all the experiments we get the depths as a list: [4 3 3 3 7 7].

The expected value of the original circuit must be determined by carrying out several sub-experiments. In this instance, sub-observables and sample coefficients must be used to execute and reconstruct the six circuits. As a result, circuit trimming drastically reduces the depth of each circuit while still requiring the execution of numerous circuits.

Let us try to minimize the circuit depth of Toffoli gate. Let us choose the qubit numbers 122, 124 and 126 where each Toffoli qubit can be located on the ibm_kyoto device. We use the `generate_preset_pass_manager()` with the arguments `optimization_level=1` and `seed_transpiler=0`.

```
toffoli_layout = [122, 124, 126]
toffoli = QuantumCircuit(3)
toffoli.ccx(0, 1, 2)
#toffoli.draw("mpl")
# Transpile the circuit
pm = generate_preset_pass_manager(backend=backend, optimization_level=1,
initial_layout=toffoli_layout, seed_transpiler=0)
isa_toffoli =  pm.run(toffoli)
# Calculate original circuit depth
```

```
isa_toffoli_depth = isa_toffoli.depth()
print(f"Transpiled circuit depth: ", isa_toffoli_depth)
isa_qc.draw("mpl", scale=0.6, idle_wires=False, fold=False)
```

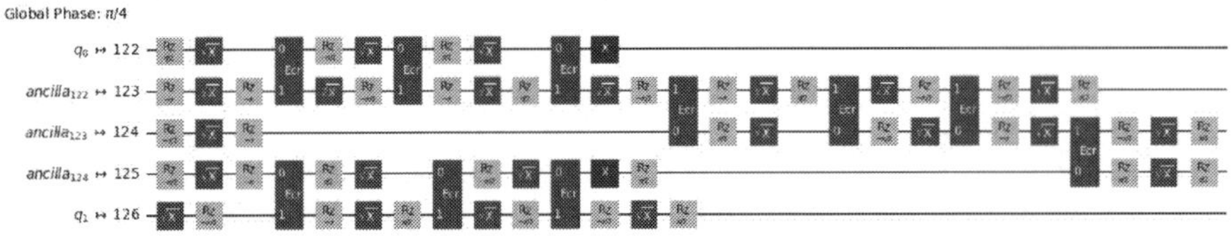

Figure 8.13: Toffoli Transpiled Depth 62 Quantum Circuit

We get a transpiled depth of 62 for the Toffoli gate. To cut the circuit, we use the decomposed toffoli circuit, not ISA circuit.

```
# Decompose the toffoli circuit
toffoli_ = toffoli.decompose()
# Find the indices of the distant gates
gates_connecting_to_cut = {0,2}
cut_indices =[
    i
    for i, instruction in enumerate(toffoli_.data)
    if {toffoli_.find_bit(q)[0] for q in instruction.qubits} == \\
    ↪ gates_connecting_to_cut
]
# Decompose distant CNOTs into TwoQubitQPDGate instances
qpd_circuit, bases = cut_gates(toffoli_, cut_indices)
qpd_circuit.draw("mpl", scale=0.6)
```

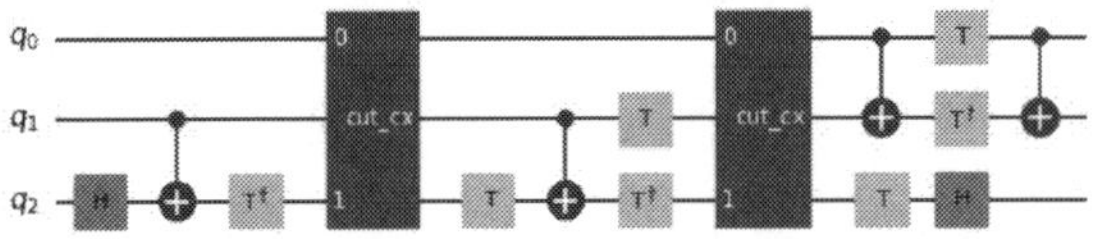

Figure 8.14: Toffoli Decomposed Quantum Circuit

```
# set the observables
observable = SparsePauliOp(["ZZZ"])
# Generate the sub-experiments and sampling coefficients
sub_experiments, coefficients = generate_cutting_experiments(
    circuits=qpd_circuit, observables=observable.paulis, num_samples=np.inf
)
# Transpile the circuit
pm = generate_preset_pass_manager(backend=backend, optimization_level=1,
initial_layout=toffoli_layout, seed_transpiler=0)
isa_qpd_toffoli =  pm.run(sub_experiments[0])
# Depth using circuit cutting
isa_qpd_toffoli_depth =isa_qpd_toffoli.depth()
print(f"Transpiled circuit depth: ", isa_toffoli_depth)
print(f"QPD sub-experiment depth after transpile: ", isa_qpd_toffoli_depth)
print(f"Number of sub-experiments:", len(sub_experiments))
#isa_qpd_circuit.draw("mpl", scale=0.6, idle_wires=False, fold=False)
# mean of the depth of all sub-experiments
depth_list = np.array([c.depth() for c in pm.run(sub_experiments)])
isa_qpd_toffoli_depth_mean =depth_list.mean()
print(isa_qpd_toffoli_depth_mean)
```

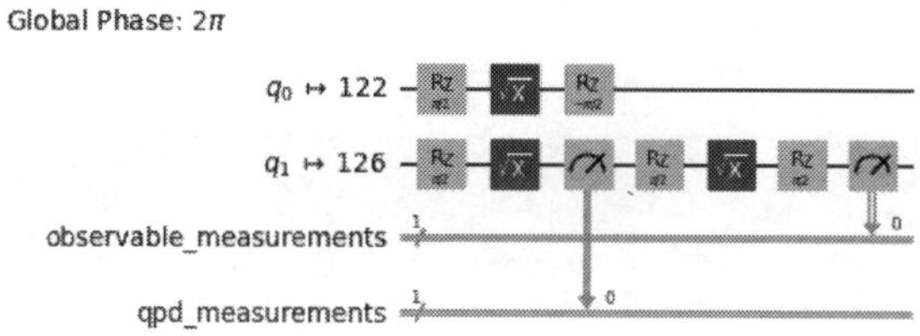

Figure 8.15: Toffoli QPD Quantum Circuit

We can see that QPD sub-experiment depth after transpile is 35 and the number of sub-experiments is 36. The mean depth QPD Toffoli comes out to be 35.333333333333336.

In order to reduce the depth further we can explore to cut two gate connections.

```
# Find the indices of the distant gates
gates_connecting_to_cut_1 = {0,2} # Hint: Expected type: set {int, int}
gates_connecting_to_cut_2 = {1,2} # Hint: Expected type: set {int, int}
cut_indices = [
```

```
    i
    for i, instruction in enumerate(toffoli_.data)
    if {toffoli_.find_bit(q)[0] for q in instruction.qubits} == \\
    ↪  gates_connecting_to_cut_1
    or {toffoli_.find_bit(q)[0] for q in instruction.qubits} == \\
    ↪  gates_connecting_to_cut_2
]
# Decompose distant CNOTs into TwoQubitQPDGate instances
qpd_circuit_2, bases = cut_gates(toffoli_, cut_indices)
qpd_circuit_2.draw("mpl", scale=0.6)
```

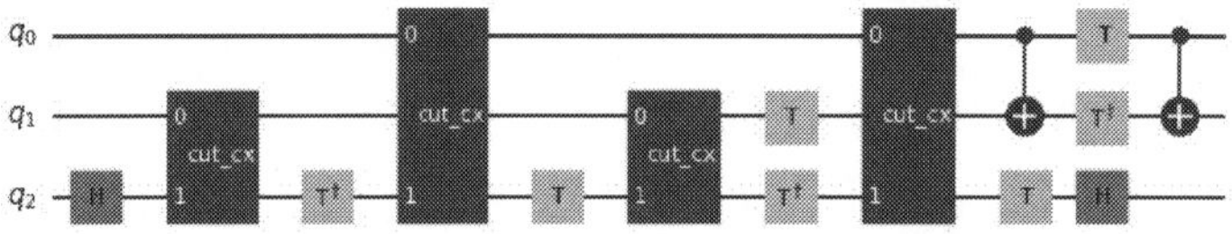

Figure 8.16: Toffoli QPD Two Cut Quantum Circuit

```
# set the observables
observable = SparsePauliOp(["ZZZ"])
# Generate the sub-experiments and sampling coefficients
sub_experiments_2, coefficients = generate_cutting_experiments(
    circuits=qpd_circuit_2, observables=observable.paulis, num_samples=np.inf
)
# Transpile the circuit
# Note: Use optimization_level=1 and seed_transpiler=0
pm = generate_preset_pass_manager(backend=backend, optimization_level=1,
initial_layout=toffoli_layout, seed_transpiler=0)
isa_qpd_circuit_2 = pm.run(sub_experiments_2[0])
# Depth using circuit cutting
isa_qpd_toffoli_depth_2 = isa_qpd_circuit_2.depth()
print(f"QPD sub-experiment depth after transpile: ", isa_qpd_toffoli_depth_2)
print(f"Number of sub-experiments:", len(sub_experiments_2))
#isa_qpd_circuit_2.draw("mpl", scale=0.6, idle_wires=False, fold=False)
# mean of the depth of all sub-experiments
depth_list_2 = np.array([c.depth() for c in pm.run(sub_experiments_2)])
```

```
isa_qpd_toffoli_depth_2_mean = depth_list_2.mean()
print(isa_qpd_toffoli_depth_2_mean)
```

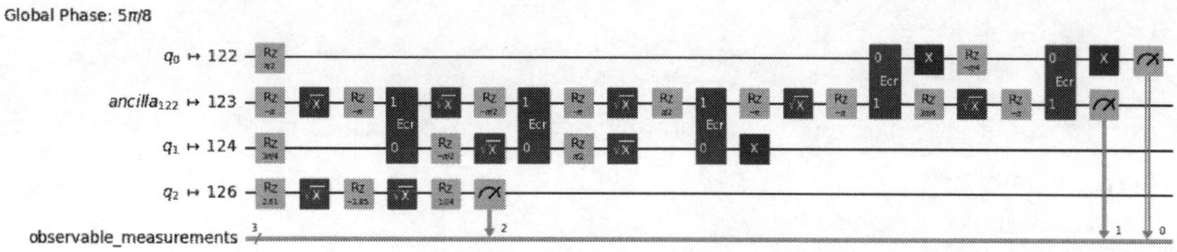

Figure 8.17: Toffoli QPD Two Cut Transpiled Quantum Circuit

We can see that the QPD sub-experiment depth of the two-cut circuit after transpile is 21 and the number of sub-experiments is 1296. The mean depth QPD Toffoli comes out to be 21.246913580246915. Let us plot the results before the circuit cutting and the results for first and second cuts for the Toffoli gate.

```
# Number of sub-experiments
num_sub_experiments_1_cut = len(sub_experiments)
num_sub_experiments_2_cut = len(sub_experiments_2)
# Data for plotting
categories = ['Before Cutting', 'After 1 Cut', 'After 2 Cuts']
depth_values = [isa_toffoli_depth, isa_qpd_toffoli_depth_mean,
isa_qpd_toffoli_depth_2_mean]
num_sub_experiments = [1, num_sub_experiments_1_cut, num_sub_experiments_2_cut]
# Create figure and axis
fig, ax1 = plt.subplots()
# Plot depth values
color = 'tab:blue'
ax1.set_xlabel('Number of Cuts')
ax1.set_ylabel('Circuit Depth', color=color)
bars = ax1.bar(categories, depth_values, color=color, alpha=0.6)
ax1.tick_params(axis='y', labelcolor=color)
# Add value labels on bars
for bar in bars:
    yval = bar.get_height()
    ax1.text(bar.get_x() + bar.get_width() / 2, yval + 1, round(yval, 2),
    ↪ ha='center',
```

```
    color=color, fontsize=10)
# Create a second y-axis to plot the number of subexperiments
ax2 = ax1.twinx()
color = 'tab:green'
ax2.set_ylabel('Number of Sub-experiments', color=color)
ax2.plot(categories, num_sub_experiments, color=color, marker='o')
ax2.tick_params(axis='y', labelcolor=color)
# Add value labels on points
for i, num in enumerate(num_sub_experiments):
    ax2.text(i, num + 0.1, num, ha='center',
    color=color, fontsize=10)
# Add titles and labels
plt.title('Circuit Knitting Toolbox Results')
fig.tight_layout()  # Adjust layout to make room for both y-axes
# Show plot
plt.show()
```

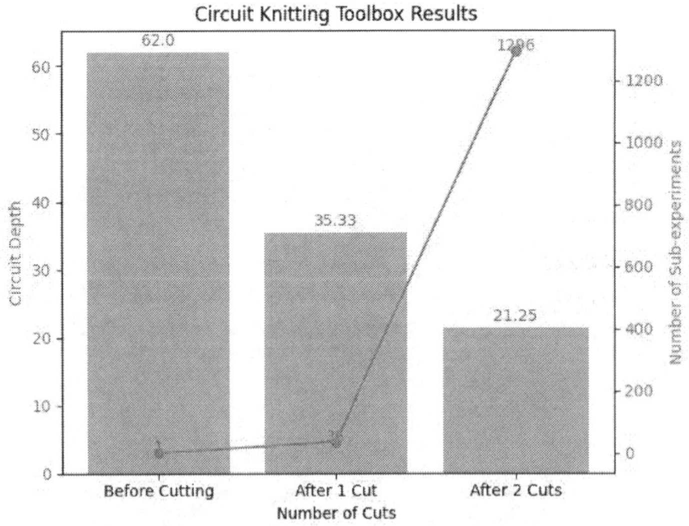

Figure 8.18: Toffoli QPD Before and After Cut Circuit Depth Comparison

From *Figure* 8.18, it can be seen that after 2 cuts the circuit depth reduces drastically and the number of sub-experiments shoots up significantly.

Code Assistant

The Qiskit Code Assistant is a cutting-edge tool specifically created to optimize the effectiveness and user-friendliness of quantum computing development utilizing the Qiskit framework. This technology incorporates artificial intelligence (AI) into the development environment, enabling users to write, troubleshoot, and enhance quantum code with more efficiency. The Qiskit Code Assistant is an artificial intelligence solution integrated into the Qiskit environment, designed to help developers write quantum circuits and algorithms more efficiently and accurately. Utilizing sophisticated natural language processing (NLP) methods, this system comprehends the user's intents and offers context-aware recommendations, code completions, and explanations for commands and constructions specific to Qiskit. The command pip install qiskit-code-assistant-jupyterlab can be used to install the Qiskit code assistant. Some of the notable characteristics are as follows:

- **Code Completion and Recommendations:** The Qiskit Code Assistant provides sophisticated code completions while editing, particularly beneficial for novices who may lack familiarity with all the functions and classes in the Qiskit library. By offering recommendations for quantum gates, operations, and even more advanced algorithms, it guarantees that the code strictly follows the accurate grammar and structure.
- **Contextual Explanations:** This functionality enables users to hover over particular Qiskit commands or lines of code in order to obtain comprehensive explanations regarding their usage. In order to facilitate comprehension of intricate quantum ideas, the explanations incorporate usage examples, best practices, and possible dangers.
- **Detection and Debugging of Errors:** This assistant has the ability to detect prevalent faults in quantum circuits or algorithms, such as erroneous gate sequences or improper qubit indices. Furthermore, it offers recommendations on how to rectify these mistakes, therefore assisting users in effectively troubleshooting their code. Moreover, it has the capability to identify logical mistakes that may not manifest as syntactical mistakes but have the potential to produce inaccurate outcomes.
- **Quantum Circuit Visualization:** The Qiskit Code Assistant has the capability to automatically produce schematic depictions of quantum circuits in real-time throughout the writing process. The provision of real-time visualization facilitates users in comprehending the structure and flow of their quantum programs, thereby simplifying the identification of mistakes or the optimization of circuit geometry.
- **Integration of Documentation:** The helper is intricately linked to the documentation of Qiskit. By directly accessing pertinent areas of the documentation from their code editor, users are able to efficiently retrieve definitions, examine illustrative code

samples, or delve into the theoretical foundation of quantum algorithms.

- **Mode of Learning:** Furthermore, the assistant incorporates a "learning mode" that adjusts to the user's coding style and level of expertise as time progresses. As the user gains deeper expertise with Qiskit, the assistant can provide increasingly sophisticated recommendations or direct them towards more streamlined coding methodologies.

Designed for novice learners, the Qiskit Code Assistant mitigates the challenging learning process linked to quantum programming by offering prompt feedback and direction. This facilitates learners in directing their attention towards comprehending quantum mechanics rather than on grammar. Experienced developers derive advantages from the accelerated speed and enhanced efficiency provided by the assistance, resulting in increased productivity. The reduction of time allocated to debugging and code optimization enables a greater emphasis on the development of intricate and groundbreaking quantum algorithms.

The assistant facilitates the early detection and rectification of flaws in the development process, a critical aspect in quantum computing because even marginal errors can result in substantial consequences in the final result. The Qiskit Code Assistant is specifically developed to provide smooth integration into widely used Integrated Development Environments (IDEs) such as Visual Studio Code (VS Code) and Jupyter Notebooks. Incorporating quantum-specific intelligence amplifies the inherent capabilities of these settings, therefore transforming them into formidable instruments for the development of quantum software.

With the ongoing advancement of quantum computing, the Qiskit Code Assistant will also progress. Potential future versions could have more sophisticated artificial intelligence functionalities, such as automated optimization of quantum circuits, immediate simulation feedback, and enhanced integration with quantum hardware infrastructure. These technological developments will progressively narrow the divide between classical and quantum computers, therefore facilitating the involvement of a wider spectrum of developers in quantum technology.

The Qiskit Code Assistant marked a notable advancement in enhancing the accessibility and user-friendliness of quantum computing. By incorporating artificial intelligence (AI)-based support into the development process, it enables both inexperienced and seasoned developers to produce superior quantum code, with increased speed and low error rates. As an integral component of the Qiskit ecosystem, it assumes a pivotal function in the continuous endeavors to democratize quantum computing and expedite the advancement of quantum applications.

The following extensive explanation aims to offer a thorough overview of the Qiskit Code Assistant for your book, emphasizing its significance and usefulness in the field of quantum software development.

Qiskit Serverless

You will learn how to deploy quantum algorithms on serverless in *Chapter 12, Variational Quantum Algorithms*, where you will delve into how Qiskit's serverless infrastructure can supercharge your quantum workflows. In this section, we will demonstrate how to concurrently transpile quantum circuits using various configurations of the Qiskit transpiler and Qiskit transpiler service to identify the optimal circuit for a specific quantum backend. The serverless framework developed by Qiskit is intended to facilitate the seamless execution of distributed parallel computing tasks. The management of the underlying infrastructure is not a concern with serverless computing. Resources are dynamically allocated, parallelized, and scaled to meet your requirements, enabling you to concentrate on the quantum duties at hand. The process of transpilation is essential for the preparation of quantum circuits for execution on quantum hardware. It entails the transformation of a high-level quantum circuit into a format that a quantum computer can comprehend and execute with efficiency. This process can become more time-consuming as circuits become more complex. The methodology of parallel transpilation illustrated in this example distributes the task across multiple computational resources, enabling the simultaneous exploration of a variety of optimization strategies. We begin by importing the necessary libraries as follows:

```
import numpy as np
import matplotlib.pyplot as plt
from timeit import default_timer as timer
import warnings
from qiskit import QuantumCircuit
from qiskit.transpiler.preset_passmanagers import generate_preset_pass_manager
from qiskit.circuit.random import random_circuit
from qiskit.quantum_info import SparsePauliOp
from qiskit.circuit.library import TwoLocal, EfficientSU2
from qiskit_ibm_runtime import QiskitRuntimeService, Estimator, Session, Options
from qiskit_serverless import QiskitFunction, save_result, get_arguments,
↪   save_result, distribute_task, distribute_qiskit_function, IBMServerlessClient,
↪   QiskitFunction
from qiskit.transpiler.preset_passmanagers import generate_preset_pass_manager
from qiskit_transpiler_service.transpiler_service import TranspilerService
from qiskit_aer import AerSimulator
```

We initiate the optimization process by establishing the quantum circuits that we wish to optimize. The transpilation process will be founded on these circuits. Our abstract circuits will be optimized for operation on the backend.

```
num_qubits = [41, 51, 61]
circuits = [EfficientSU2(nq, su2_gates=["rz","ry"], entanglement="circular",
↪  reps=1).decompose()
for nq in num_qubits]
service = QiskitRuntimeService(channel="ibm_quantum")
backend = service.backend("ibm_brisbane")
```

We establish a variety of transpiler configurations with varying optimization levels and strategies. Each configuration denotes a distinct method of transpiling the circuit. The configurations that we are selecting are `optimization_level` values of 1, 2, and 3 for local Qiskit transpilation and `optimization_level` of 3 for the Qiskit Transpiler Service with `ai=False` and `ai=True`. Each circuit will undergo each of these transpilation stages, and the optimal circuit will be determined by the circuit that yields the most favorable results.

```
# Define Configs
optimization_levels = [1,2,3]
pass_managers = [{'pass_manager':
↪  generate_preset_pass_manager(optimization_level=level,
backend=backend), 'optimization_level': level} for level in optimization_levels]

transpiler_services = [
        {'service': TranspilerService(backend_name="ibm_brisbane", ai="false",
        optimization_level=3), 'ai': False, 'optimization_level': 3},
        {'service': TranspilerService(backend_name="ibm_brisbane", ai="true",
        optimization_level=3), 'ai': True, 'optimization_level': 3}
    ]

configs = pass_managers + transpiler_services
```

Before distributing the duties, we should perform the transpilation locally to compare the results and establish a baseline. This procedure will guarantee that our configurations function as anticipated.

```
# Local transpilation setup
def transpile_parallel_local(circuit: QuantumCircuit, config):
    """Transpilation for an abstract circuit into an ISA circuit for a given \\
    ↪  config."""
    transpiled_circuit = config.run(circuit)
    return transpiled_circuit
# Run local transpilation
warnings.filterwarnings("ignore")
start = timer()
# Run transpilations locally for baseline
results = []
for circuit in circuits:
    for config in configs:
        if 'pass_manager' in config:
            results.append(transpile_parallel_local(circuit,
            ↪  config['pass_manager']))
        else:
            results.append(transpile_parallel_local(circuit, config['service']))

end = timer()
# Record local execution time
execution_time_local = end - start
print("Execution time locally: ", execution_time_local)
```

In order to distribute these transpilation tasks across numerous computational nodes, we will now leverage the capabilities of the Qiskit Serverless module. Starting from this point, we will configure Qiskit Serverless to execute and deploy distributed tasks.

Initially, we will establish an authentication with the Qiskit Serverless service on the IBM Quantum Platform. This employs your default IBM Quantum Platform API Token.

```
serverless = IBMServerlessClient("PASTE YOUR TOKEN FROM IBM QUANTUM ACCOUNT")
```

Let us further explore the novel concepts that have been incorporated into this pattern: The `distribute_task` decorator converts a function into a distributed task, enabling it to execute asynchronously and in parallel with the primary context on distinct compute resources.

A reference to the function execution is returned when a function decorated with distribute_task is invoked, rather than the actual result. The get function must be invoked on this reference in order to obtain the result. The result of the function is returned by the get function after the task has been completed.

The transpile_parallel function has been decorated with the distribute_task decorator in the aforementioned pattern. This function accepts a QuantumCircuit and a transpiler configuration as inputs and returns the circuit transpiled in accordance with the configuration supplied. The save_result function can be employed to save the results once they have been obtained.

In essence, this pattern reads the circuits from the pattern arguments, executes the transpile_parallel function on each circuit and config in parallel, accumulates the results from the function executions, and saves the results.

```
from qiskit import QuantumCircuit
from qiskit.transpiler.preset_passmanagers import generate_preset_pass_manager
from qiskit_transpiler_service.transpiler_service import TranspilerService
from qiskit_serverless import get_arguments, save_result, distribute_task, get
from qiskit_ibm_runtime import QiskitRuntimeService
from timeit import default_timer as timer

@distribute_task(target={"cpu": 2})
def transpile_parallel(circuit: QuantumCircuit, config):
    """Distributed transpilation for an abstract circuit into an ISA circuit for
    ↪ a given
    backend."""
    transpiled_circuit = config.run(circuit)
    return transpiled_circuit
# Get program arguments
arguments = get_arguments()
circuits = arguments.get("circuits")
backend_name = arguments.get("backend_name")
# Get backend
service = QiskitRuntimeService(channel="ibm_quantum")
backend = service.get_backend(backend_name)
# Define Configs
optimization_levels = "# Add your code here"
pass_managers = [generate_preset_pass_manager(optimization_level=level, backend=
↪ \\ backend)
```

```
for level in optimization_levels]
transpiler_services = [
        TranspilerService( "# Add your code here" ),
        TranspilerService( "# Add your code here" ),
    ]
configs = pass_managers + transpiler_services
# Start process
print("Starting timer")
start = timer()
# run distributed tasks as async function
# we get task references as a return type
sample_task_references = []
for circuit in circuits:
    sample_task_references.append([transpile_parallel(circuit, config)
    for config in configs])
# now we need to collect results from task references
results = get([task for subtasks in sample_task_references for task in subtasks])
end = timer()
# Record execution time
execution_time_serverless = end-start
print("Execution time: ", execution_time_serverless)
save_result({
    "transpiled_circuits": results,
    "execution_time" : execution_time_serverless

})
```

Complete initialization of the `QiskitFunction` template below.

```
transpile_parallel_function = QiskitFunction(
    title="transpile_parallel",
    entrypoint="transpile_parallel.py",
    working_dir="./transpile_parallel",
    dependencies=["qiskit-transpiler-service"]
)
serverless.upload(transpile_parallel_function)
```

We will execute our transpilation duties in a serverless environment and capitalize on Qiskit's serverless capabilities to efficiently distribute and execute them now that we have uploaded our QiskitFunction. Furthermore, we have the ability to retrieve any function that we have previously uploaded. We can accomplish this by following these steps:

```
# Get list of functions
serverless.list()
# Fetch the specific function titled "transpile_parallel"
transpile_parallel_serverless = serverless.get('transpile_parallel')
# Run the "transpile_parallel" function in the serverless environment
job = transpile_parallel_serverless.run(
    circuits= circuits,
    backend_name= backend
    )
```

Once the execution is complete, we retrieve and analyze the results.

```
result = job.result()
result_transpiled = result["transpiled_circuits"]
# Compare execution times:
execution_time_serverless = result["execution_time"]
from utils import plot_execution_times
plot_execution_times(execution_time_serverless, execution_time_local)
```

The bar graph shown in *Figure* 8.19 illustrates the differential execution times of a quantum computing activity carried out in a serverless environment as opposed to a local one. The horizontal axis denotes the two distinct execution modes, namely *Serverless* and *Local* while the vertical axis displays the duration of operation in seconds. The execution time of serverless applications is considerably shorter, typically around 154.5 seconds, in comparison to the local execution time, which is roughly 405.90 seconds. These findings indicate that the serverless method is more effective, resulting in a quicker completion time for the identical activity. The observed disparity in execution durations underscores the prospective advantages in performance that serverless computing offers for quantum algorithms.

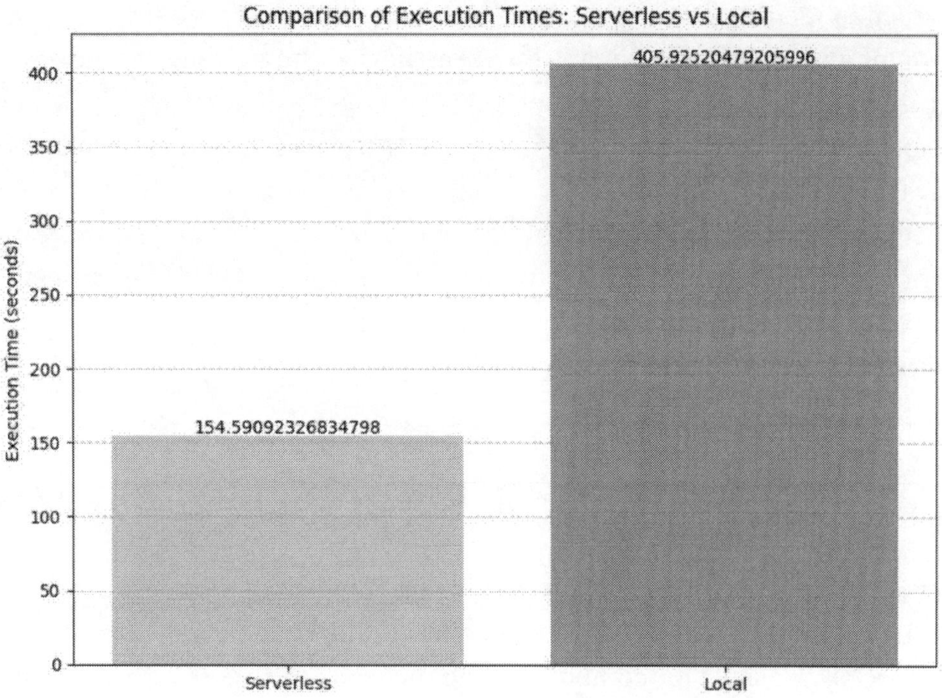

Figure 8.19: Comparison of Local and Serverless times

Upon completion of the transpilation jobs, collect the findings and compare the transpiled circuits. In this experiment, we assess the performance of different circuits by analyzing the shortest depth of the transpiled circuit data.

```
from utils import process_transpiled_circuits
best_circuits, best_depths, best_methods = process_transpiled_circuits(configs,
result_transpiled)
```

```
# Display the best circuits, depths, and methods
for i, (circuit, depth, method) in enumerate(zip(best_circuits, best_depths,
best_methods)):
    print(f"Best result for circuit {i + 1}:")
    print(f"  Depth: {depth}")
    print(f"  Method: {method}")
    # Display or process the best circuit as needed
    # e.g., circuit.draw(output="mpl")
```

Congratulations on successfully finishing the Qiskit Serverless module! You have effectively investigated the robust functionalities of Qiskit Serverless, acquiring knowledge on the deployment and execution of quantum algorithms without concerns associated with infrastructure administration. By utilizing this serverless architecture, you can concentrate more on your code and effectively maximize the use of both quantum and classical resources. The experience has furnished you with invaluable knowledge on executing quantum operations seamlessly and scalablely on cloud platforms. Furthermore, you have acquired knowledge on how to execute parallel processes on Qiskit Serverless in order to optimize efficiency and performance. Engage in ongoing experimentation with Qiskit Serverless to go deeper into other possibilities.

Quantification of Error Rates in Quantum Circuits

Presented here is a systematic approach for calculating the Error Per Layered Gate (EPLG) and Layer Fidelity (LF). Error rates in a circuit are quantified by these measures, which are especially valuable for comprehending the overhead needed to implement error mitigation at utility-scale workloads.

Consult the Quantum Research Blog entry or the related scientific publication, Benchmarking Quantum Processor Performance at Scale, for further information on the context of these measures. An implementation of the Layer Fidelity experiment may be found here that utilizes the qiskit-experiments module. However, in this section, we shall directly use Qiskit Runtime Primitives for circuit execution.

The latter sections of this topic provide a detailed tutorial on how to use the Qiskit Runtime for performing utility-scale computations. As usual, let us start by importing all the necessary libraries.

```
import os
from qiskit_ibm_runtime import QiskitRuntimeService
from qiskit.circuit import Parameter
from qiskit.transpiler.preset_passmanagers import generate_preset_pass_manager
import numpy as np
from qiskit.primitives.containers.bindings_array import BindingsArray
from itertools import product
from qiskit.quantum_info import SparsePauliOp
from qiskit.primitives.containers.observables_array import ObservablesArray
from qiskit.primitives.containers.estimator_pub import EstimatorPub
from qiskit_ibm_runtime import EstimatorV2
```

```
import lmfit
import pandas as pd
```

Begin by selecting a backend. Feel free to select any desired backend.

To determine the EPLG and LF, it is necessary to select a sequence of qubits on the device for use in characterization. Let us establish the following definitions:

- An acyclic sequence of qubits on the device, represented as a path graph of their connections. Specifically, we offer a list `PATH_ANSWER: list[int]` that consists of physical qubits on the device. The neighbouring members of the list are linked on the coupling map by edges. A minimum of three elements should be included in the list.
- The selected backend: BACKEND: IBM Backend application.

```
os.environ['QXToken'] = 'PASTE YOUR TOKEN FROM IBM QUANTUM ACCOUNT'
QiskitRuntimeService.save_account(channel='ibm_quantum', token=os.environ['QXToken'])
service = QiskitRuntimeService()
BACKEND = service.backend('ibm_sherbrooke')
cmap = BACKEND.configuration().coupling_map
 # Search a simple connected path of at least 3 qubits
def find_path(coupling_map, length):
    path = []
    for edge in coupling_map:
        if not path:
            path.append(edge[0])
            path.append(edge[1])
        elif path[-1] == edge[0]:
            path.append(edge[1])
        elif path[-1] == edge[1]:
            path.append(edge[0])
        if len(path) >= length:
            break
    return path if len(path) >= length else None
# Get a path of at least 3 qubits
PATH_ANSWER = find_path(cmap, 5)
```

Subsequently, it is necessary to create two sets of edges that correspond to the distinct layers in the benchmarking process, namely `LAYER_1_ANSWER` and `LAYER_2_ANSWER`. Each set should be of the type `list[tuple[int, int]]`. Each of these layers must possess the following characteristics:

- Each `LAYER_i_ANSWER` exhibits edges on separate sets of qubits. For example, the pairs (0, 1) and (1, 2) cannot coexist in `LAYER_i_ANSWER`, as they both include the value of 1.
- Each individual qubit in the `PATH_ANSWER` must be present in at least one of the `LAYER_is`.

```
PATH_ANSWER = [0, 1, 2, 3, 4]
# Function to create pairs from a path
def make_pairs(path):
    return [(path[i], path[i+1]) for i in range(len(path)-1)]
# Function to create layers from pairs
def make_layers(pairs, coupling_map):
    layer_1 = []
    layer_2 = []
    # Create a set for quick lookup of valid edges
    valid_edges = set(tuple(edge) for edge in coupling_map)
    for i, pair in enumerate(pairs):
        if tuple(pair) not in valid_edges:
            pair = tuple(reversed(pair))
        if i % 2 == 0:
            layer_1.append(pair)
        else:
            layer_2.append(pair)
    return layer_1, layer_2
# Generate pairs from PATH_ANSWER
pairs = make_pairs(PATH_ANSWER)
# Generate the layers
LAYER_1_ANSWER, LAYER_2_ANSWER = make_layers(pairs, cmap)
print(f"PATH_ANSWER: {PATH_ANSWER}")
print(f"LAYER_1_ANSWER: {LAYER_1_ANSWER}")
print(f"LAYER_2_ANSWER: {LAYER_2_ANSWER}")
```

The `LAYER_i` from the preceding problem may now be utilized to generate the QuantumCircuits for each layer, which will be employed in the EPLG tests. We will proceed with the construction of two circuits, namely `CIRC_1_ANSWER` and `CIRC_2_ANSWER`.

- Each pair in `LAYER_1_ANSWER` and `LAYER_2_ANSWER` from earlier should inherently include a two-qubit Clifford gate.
- The two-qubit Clifford gate (`GATE_NAME`) in question must be a gate that is supplied by

the selected backend, namely within the backend. The value of `basis_gates` should be either 'ecr', 'cz', or 'cx', depending on your backend.

```
GATE_NAME = None
basis_gates = BACKEND.configuration().basis_gates
if 'ecr' in basis_gates:
    GATE_NAME = 'ecr'
elif 'cz' in basis_gates:
    GATE_NAME = 'cz'
elif 'cx' in basis_gates:
    GATE_NAME = 'cx'
else:
    raise ValueError("None of the required two-qubit Clifford gates are
    ↪  available on the
    backend.")
# Function to create a circuit from a layer of pairs
def create_circuit(layer, gate_name):
    # Find the maximum qubit index to define the number of qubits in the circuit
    max_qubit = max(max(pair) for pair in layer)
    circuit = QuantumCircuit(max_qubit + 1)
    for pair in layer:
        if gate_name == 'ecr':
            circuit.ecr(pair[0], pair[1])
        elif gate_name == 'cz':
            circuit.cz(pair[0], pair[1])
        elif gate_name == 'cx':
            circuit.cx(pair[0], pair[1])
    return circuit
# Create the circuits
CIRC_1_ANSWER = create_circuit(LAYER_1_ANSWER, GATE_NAME)
CIRC_2_ANSWER = create_circuit(LAYER_2_ANSWER, GATE_NAME)
print(f"LAYER_1_ANSWER: {LAYER_1_ANSWER}")
print(f"LAYER_2_ANSWER: {LAYER_2_ANSWER}")
print(f"CIRC_1_ANSWER:\n{CIRC_1_ANSWER}")
print(f"CIRC_2_ANSWER:\n{CIRC_2_ANSWER}")
print(f"GATE_NAME: {GATE_NAME}")
```

We will utilize the circuits built to construct the complete EPLG circuit models . These circuits incorporate the layers from the previous stages between layers of arbitrary Clifford gates. `example_circuit_1` and `example_circuit_2` are examples of the EPLG circuits for depth d=4. In a later part, we will use this function to construct circuits for varying depths.

- Discrepancies exist between the circuits developed in this study and those specified in the EPLG report. In the case of a circuit with a depth of d (where d is even), we stochastically select 1-qubit Clifford gates for $d/2$ layers, then thereafter reverse the circuit for the remaining $d/2$ layers. This offers a straightforward implementation for our objectives.
- We use 1-qubit Clifford sampling to exploit the property that in backends with single qubit gates consisting of $R_z(\theta_1)\sqrt{X}R_z(\theta_2)\sqrt{X}R_z(\theta_3)$, if θ_i is a component of the interval $\pm\frac{\pi}{2}, \pm\pi, 0\}$, the resultant single qubit gate is a Clifford. This enables us to randomly select 1-qubit Clifford gates by simple modification of parameters.

```
def eplg_circuit(num_qubits: int, depth: int, layer: QuantumCircuit, qubits:
tuple[int, ...]) -> QuantumCircuit:
    if depth % 2 != 0:
        raise ValueError(f"The depth must be even, got {depth}")

    def parameters():
        _depth = 0
        while True:
            for zi in range(3):
                for q in range(num_qubits):
                    yield Parameter(f"d{_depth}_q{q}_z{zi}")
            _depth += 1
    _parameters = parameters()

    circ = QuantumCircuit(num_qubits)

    def _1q_layer():
        for j in range(3):
            for k in qubits:
                circ.rz(next(_parameters), k)
            if j == 2:
                continue
            circ.sx(qubits)
```

```
    for _depth in range(depth // 2):
        circ.barrier(qubits)
        _1q_layer()
        circ.barrier(qubits)
        circ.compose(layer, inplace=True)
    circ.barrier(qubits)
    _1q_layer()
    circ.barrier(qubits)

    # Assuming mirroring is fine
    circ = circ.compose(circ.inverse())

    circ.measure_active()

    pm = generate_preset_pass_manager(basis_gates=
    ["ecr", "sx", "rz"], optimization_level=0)
    circ = pm.run(circ)

    circ.metadata["layer_depth"] = depth
    circ.metadata["qubits"] = qubits
    circ.metadata["num_qubits"] = num_qubits

    return circ

example_circuit_1 = eplg_circuit(
    num_qubits=BACKEND.num_qubits,
    depth=4,
    layer=CIRC_1_ANSWER,
    qubits=PATH_ANSWER,
)

example_circuit_2 = eplg_circuit(
    num_qubits=BACKEND.num_qubits,
    depth=4,
    layer=CIRC_2_ANSWER,
    qubits=PATH_ANSWER,
```

```
)
```

In the preceding section, we have designed circuits that are parameterized in a manner that, when sampled with the suitable values, consistently generate random single-qubit Clifford gates.

In order to perform our EPLG calculations, it is necessary to sample numerous sets of parameters. This is succinctly represented using the `BindingsArray`. A `BindingsArray` is an array where each element represents a collection of parameters and their corresponding bound values.

For instance, if we own a circuit with k parameters and require the sampling of all parameters m times, the `BindingsArray` that does this may be defined as (m,). Likewise, if we desire a more intricate collection of bindings to execute, our `BindingsArray` can provide any form and facilitate numpy-like reshaping operations, slicing, and so on.

This part will outline the construction of a function that takes a `QuantumCircuit`, the desired amount of samples, and a numpy RNG to execute the single-qubit Clifford sampling . This will be utilized subsequently to generate our `EstimatorPubs`. Notice that despite a large number of parameters, the `BindingsArray` has shape (10,), meaning it has 10 entries. As we discussed before, this is because its elements correspond to sets of parameters and their bound values.

```
def get_clifford_rz_samples(
    circ: QuantumCircuit,
    num_samples: int,
    rng: np.random.Generator,
) -> BindingsArray:
    """Uniformly sample the Rz parameters in a `QuantumCircuit`
    from -pi, -pi/2, 0, +pi/2, +pi.
    """

    _allowed_ops = {'rz', 'sx', 'sxdg', 'ecr', 'barrier', 'measure'}
    if (_other := set(circ.count_ops().keys()) - _allowed_ops):
        raise ValueError(f"Circuit must only contain ops: {_allowed_ops}, \\ got
        ↪ {_other}")

    sampled_pars = rng.integers(-2, 3, size=(num_samples, len(circ.parameters)))
    ↪ *
    (np.pi/2)
```

```
    return BindingsArray({
        tuple(circ.parameters): sampled_pars
    })
num_samples = 10
ARRAY_1_ANSWER = get_clifford_rz_samples(
    circ=example_circuit_1,
    num_samples=num_samples,
    rng=np.random.default_rng(42))
```

The sole need for generating a `EstimatorPub` is a `ObservablesArray`. The `ObservablesArray` is an array consisting of data elements that can be observed. In our scenario, the designated operators will be `SparsePauliOps`.

To determine the EPLG and LF, we must calculate the expectation values given by $\mathrm{Tr}(\rho\,|00\rangle_{i,j}\,\langle 00|_{i,j})$ and $\mathrm{Tr}(\rho\,|0\rangle_i\,\langle 0|_i)$. The quantization of qubits i and j is contingent upon the previously selected layers.

An alternative approach would be to use the `SamplerV2` instead of the `EstimatorV2`. This method has the drawback of necessitating further post-processing. However, we can do this by utilizing the `EstimatorV2` to generate the projectors $|0\rangle_i\,\langle 0|_i$ and $|00\rangle_{i,j}\,\langle 00|_{i,j}$ and employing them as observables.

This implies that the expectation values obtained from the estimator V2 will accurately represent the process fidelities that are of interest to us. We also need to produce ObservablesArrays which correspond to the projectors we are interested in, that is, the process fidelities for subsets of our path. The shape of the `LAYER_i_OBSERVABLES` array is determined by the number of subsystems in each layer.

Given that all the observables in our ObservablesArrays are diagonal in the computational basis, meaning they only include Paulis with I and Z coefficients, the `EstimatorV2` does not require the computation of expectation values in other bases.

```
def process_fidelity_observable(num_qubits: int, qubits: tuple[int, ...])
-> SparsePauliOp:
    """Produces the all 0 projector on `qubits` tensored with the identity
    on all other qubits"""
    pauli_strings = []

    for p_sub_str in product(["I", "Z"], repeat=len(qubits)):
```

```
        p_str = ["I"] * num_qubits
        for qi, pi in zip(qubits, p_sub_str):
            p_str[qi] = pi
        pauli_strings.append("".join(p_str[::-1]))

    return SparsePauliOp(pauli_strings, np.ones(len(pauli_strings)) /
    ↪   2**len(qubits))
LAYER_1_SUBSYSTEMS = LAYER_1_ANSWER + [(q,) for q in set(PATH_ANSWER)
- set(item for sublist in LAYER_1_ANSWER for item in sublist)]
LAYER_2_SUBSYSTEMS = LAYER_2_ANSWER + [(q,) for q in set(PATH_ANSWER)
- set(item for sublist in LAYER_2_ANSWER for item in sublist)]
LAYER_1_OBSERVABLES = ObservablesArray([process_fidelity_observable(BACKEND
.num_qubits, qubits) for qubits in LAYER_1_SUBSYSTEMS])
LAYER_2_OBSERVABLES = ObservablesArray([process_fidelity_observable(BACKEND
.num_qubits, qubits) for qubits in LAYER_2_SUBSYSTEMS])
LAYER_1_OBSERVABLES.shape == (len(LAYER_1_SUBSYSTEMS),)
LAYER_2_OBSERVABLES.shape == (len(LAYER_2_SUBSYSTEMS),)
```

At last, we can build our estimator pubs. The `EstimatorPub` can be represented as a tuple including a fractional quantum circuit, an observables array, a bindings array, and possibly a precision. Provided a `EstimatorPub` of a certain form, the `EstimatorV2` will generate arrays of expectation values (along with their standard deviations) that have the same form as the original `EstimatorPubs`.

To formulate the `EstimatorPubs` required for conducting the EPLG computations, we require `EstimatorPubs` that exhibit variations in.

Initiate the itemization process by specifying the input circuit, which consists of two distinct sets of edges. Additionally, specify the depth of the circuit, which has been set to 6 depths by default. Terminate itemization.

Thus, the total number of estimator pods will be $2 \times 6 = 12$. Within each of these, there are 10 spinning samples and k fidelities (which are determined by the selected path and should be approximately half of the track length). Each of the 12 estimator pubs consists of 10,000 pieces.

Thus, the anticipated total number of expectation values is \$120,000. A chain of length 30 with a value of $k = 15$ should yield approximately 1,800 expectation values in total, contingent upon the edges of the chain.

```
rng = np.random.default_rng(42)
num_samples = 10
depths = [2, 4, 8, 16, 32, 64]
estimator_pubs = []
for depth in depths:
    for layer, name, observables in [(CIRC_1_ANSWER, "circ_1",
    ↪  LAYER_1_OBSERVABLES),
    (CIRC_2_ANSWER, "circ_2", LAYER_2_OBSERVABLES)]:
        circ = eplg_circuit(
            num_qubits=BACKEND.num_qubits,
            depth=depth,
            layer=layer,
            qubits=PATH_ANSWER,
        )
        circ.metadata["layer_idx"] = name
        bindings_array = get_clifford_rz_samples(
            circ=circ,
            num_samples=num_samples,
            rng=rng,
        )
        # We need to reshape the `ObservablesArray`s and `BindingsArray`s so they
        # can be broadcasted.
        # https://numpy.org/doc/stable/user/basics.broadcasting.html#basics-broa
        ↪  dcasting
        estimator_pubs.append(EstimatorPub(
            circuit=circ,
            observables=observables.reshape((*observables.shape, 1)),
            parameter_values=bindings_array.reshape((1, *bindings_array.shape)),
        ))
num_evs_expected = 0
for pub in estimator_pubs:
    num_evs_expected += np.prod(estimator_pubs[0].shape)
num_evs_expected
```

The `EstimatorPubs` have been successfully transferred to the `EstimatorV2`.
Given the SPAM-robust nature of EPLG calculation, it is advisable to disable the mea-

surement mitigation feature, which is already activated by default. Proceed to execute the `EstimatorV2` using our `EstimatorPubs` and await the outcome. Furthermore, we can obtain the `PrimitiveResult`.

Assuming the default parameters in this section, the completion time should not exceed 10 minutes (excluding queue time).

```
estimator = EstimatorV2(backend=BACKEND)
estimator.options.resilience.measure_mitigation = False
estimator_job = estimator.run(estimator_pubs)
primitive_result = estimator_job.result()
primitive_result
```

Executing the fits of the decay curves is the last stage in doing the EPLG analysis.

Firstly, let us extract some pertinent data from the `PrimitiveResult` column. We may now reorganize the expectation values into an array in a systematic manner, and get the average across the randomized Cliffords. The resultant shape has two axes: one representing the depth (axis 0 in shape 6) and another representing the number of subsystem fidelities (axis 1, which varies depending on the chosen path).

```
data_out = {
    "evs": [pub_res.data.evs for pub_res in primitive_result],
    "stds": [pub_res.data.stds for pub_res in primitive_result],
    "result_metadata": primitive_result.metadata,
    "pub_metadata": [pub_res.metadata for pub_res in primitive_result]
}
evs_at_depth = np.zeros((len(depths), data_out['evs'][0].shape[0]*2))
for i in range(len(depths)):
    layer1_evs = np.average(data_out['evs'][2*i], axis=-1)
    layer2_evs = np.average(data_out['evs'][2*i+1], axis=-1)
    evs_at_depth[i,:] = np.array([item for pair in zip(layer1_evs, layer2_evs)
    for item in pair])
evs_at_depth.shape
```

Now we can plot the decay curves for the different subsystems.

```
ax = plt.gca()
for i in range(evs_at_depth.shape[1]):
    ax.plot(depths, evs_at_depth[:,i])
```

```
ax.set_ylabel("Ground State Population")
ax.set_xlabel("Depth")
ax.grid()
```

The next step is to apply exponential decay to these results. This task can be accomplished using the `lmfit` Python library. Exponential decay is expressed as follows:

$$A\alpha^L + B$$

The error rate is denoted by α, the number of cycles (depth) in the EPLG circuits is denoted by L, and the fitting parameters A and B are specified to capture the SPAM (state preparation and measurement) errors. We can finally use the expressions in the EPLG paper to compute process fidelities. α is related to the average gate error via

$$\epsilon = \frac{D-1}{D}(1-\alpha)$$

where D denotes the dimension of the Hilbert space, e.g., $D = 4$ for two-qubit processes. The average gate fidelity is $F_g = 1 - \epsilon$. The process fidelity is related to the average gate fidelity via

$$F_g = \frac{DF_p + 1}{D + 1}.$$

```
model= lmfit.models.ExpressionModel(
            expr="a * alpha ** x + b",
            name="rb_decay")

params_dict = {
    'a': {'value': 1.0,
            'min': -1.0,
            'max': 1.0,
            },
    'b': {'value': 0.0,
            'min': -1.0,
            'max': 1.0,
            },
    'alpha': {'value': 0.9,
              'min': 0.0,
              'max': 1.0
```

```
            },
}
p = model.make_params(**params_dict)
alphas = []
for i in range(evs_at_depth.shape[-1]):
    result = model.fit(evs_at_depth[:,i], p, x=depths)
    alphas.append(result.params['alpha'].value)
def cal_process_fid(alpha, D=4):
    epsilon = (D-1) * (1 - alpha)/D
    Fg = 1 - epsilon
    Fp = ((D+1) * Fg -1)/D
    return Fp
```

And with a little data-wrangling in Pandas, we can apply this to our data.

```
qubit_pairs = [item for pair in zip(LAYER_1_ANSWER, LAYER_2_ANSWER) for item in
↪   pair]
pfs = [cal_process_fid(alpha) for alpha in alphas]
df = pd.DataFrame(zip(qubit_pairs, alphas, pfs),
columns=['qubit pair', 'alpha', 'process fidelity'])
df
```

We shall now use the 2-qubit process fidelity `pfs` that was computed earlier to calculate the Layer Fidelity. For each chain size value, we select the highest Layer Fidelity among all the measured subchains. The 1-qubit process fidelity at both ends of the supply chain is estimated by taking the square root of the 2-qubit process fidelity. Now we can present the Layer Fidelity as a function of our chain length. This should decrease for larger chains.

```
chain_lens = np.arange(2, len(pfs), 1)
chain_fids = []
for length in chain_lens:
     w = length + 1  # window size
     fid_w = max(
          np.sqrt(pfs[s]) * np.prod(pfs[s + 1 : s + w - 1]) * np.sqrt(pfs[s + w
          ↪  - 1])
          for s in
          range(len(pfs) - w + 1))
```

```
    chain_fids.append(fid_w)
plt.title(f"Backend: {BACKEND.name}")
plt.plot(
    chain_lens,
    chain_fids,
    marker="o",
    linestyle="-",
)
plt.xlim(0, chain_lens[-1] * 1.05)
plt.ylim(0.95 * min(chain_fids), 1)
plt.ylabel("Layer Fidelity")
plt.xlabel("Chain Length")
plt.grid()
plt.show()
```

Then, at long last, we can calculate the EPLG as a function of chain length. EPLG is defined as

$$EPLG = 1 - LF^{1/n_{2q}}$$

where n_{2q} is the number of two-qubit gates in all the layers.

```
num_2q_gates = [length - 1 for length in chain_lens]
chain_eplgs = [
    1 - (fid ** (1 / num_2q)) for num_2q, fid in zip(num_2q_gates, chain_fids)
]
plt.title(f"Backend: {BACKEND.name}")
plt.plot(
    chain_lens,
    chain_eplgs,
    marker="o",
    linestyle="-",
)
plt.xlim(0, chain_lens[-1] * 1.05)
plt.ylabel("Error per Layered Gates")
plt.xlabel("Chain Length")
plt.grid()
```

```
plt.show()
```

This analysis is very useful in diagnosing which qubits and devices to use for utility-scale workloads.

Conclusion

Given the ongoing progress in quantum computing, the methods explored in this chapter will be crucial in addressing the obstacles related to constructing resilient and expandable quantum systems. From the adaptability provided by dynamic circuits to the optimization capabilities of transpilation methods, every instrument and methodology helps to improve the efficiency and results of quantum calculations. Circuit knitting and the code assistant are revolutionary advancements in streamlining the creation and implementation of intricate quantum algorithms. Meanwhile, serverless computing frameworks such as Qiskit Serverless provide new opportunities for expanding quantum workloads. Furthermore, it is crucial to comprehend and reduce error rates in order to attain the necessary accuracy in quantum computing applications. Developing proficiency in these sophisticated methodologies enables researchers and practitioners to expand the limits of what can be achieved in quantum computing, so approaching the realization of its whole capabilities.

In this next chapter, we will start studying quantum algorithms, which extensively use single and multi-qubit quantum gates.

References

- Classical Control Flow in Quantum Circuits - `https://docs.quantum.ibm.com/guides/classical-feedforward-and-control-flow`
- Dynamic Circuits Blog by IBM - `https://www.ibm.com/quantum/blog/quantum-dynamic-circuits`
- Dynamic Circuits Blog by Dr Derek Wang, YouTube - `https://www.youtube.com/watch?v=QDPtcwhpQkE`
- Trivial Layout - `https://docs.quantum.ibm.com/api/qiskit/qiskit.transpiler.passes.TrivialLayout#triviallayout`
- Stochastic Swap - `https://docs.quantum.ibm.com/api/qiskit/qiskit.transpiler.passes.StochasticSwap#stochasticswap`
- Sabre Swap - `https://docs.quantum.ibm.com/api/qiskit/qiskit.transpiler.passes.SabreSwap#sabreswap`

- VF2 Post Layout - `https://docs.quantum.ibm.com/api/qiskit/qiskit.transpiler.passes.VF2PostLayout`
- Inverse Cancellation - `https://docs.quantum.ibm.com/api/qiskit/qiskit.transpiler.passes.InverseCancellation#inversecancellation`
- Optimize1qgates - `https://docs.quantum.ibm.com/api/qiskit/qiskit.transpiler.passes.Optimize1qGates#optimize1qgates`
- Commutative Cancellation - `https://docs.quantum.ibm.com/api/qiskit/qiskit.transpiler.passes.CommutativeCancellation#commutativecancellation`
- Unitary Synthesis - `https://docs.quantum.ibm.com/api/qiskit/qiskit.transpiler.passes.UnitarySynthesis#unitarysynthesis`
- High Level Synthesis - `https://docs.quantum.ibm.com/api/qiskit/qiskit.transpiler.passes.HighLevelSynthesis#highlevelsynthesis`
- Basis Translator - `https://docs.quantum.ibm.com/api/qiskit/qiskit.transpiler.passes.BasisTranslator#basistranslator`
- RemoveDiagonalGatesBeforeMeasure - `https://docs.quantum.ibm.com/api/qiskit/qiskit.transpiler.passes.RemoveDiagonalGatesBeforeMeasure`
- Optimize1qGatesDecomposition - `https://docs.quantum.ibm.com/api/qiskit/qiskit.transpiler.passes.Optimize1qGatesDecomposition`
- Collect2qBlocks - `https://docs.quantum.ibm.com/api/qiskit/qiskit.transpiler.passes.Collect2qBlocks`
- ConsolidateBlocks - `https://docs.quantum.ibm.com/api/qiskit/qiskit.transpiler.passes.ConsolidateBlocks`
- Approximation Degree - `https://docs.quantum.ibm.com/guides/common-parameters#approximation-degree`
- Hellinger Fidelity - `https://docs.quantum.ibm.com/api/qiskit/0.31/qiskit.quantum_info.hellinger_fidelity`
- Transpiler Plugins - `https://docs.quantum.ibm.com/api/qiskit/transpiler_plugins`
- UnitarySynthesisPlugin - `https://docs.quantum.ibm.com/api/qiskit/qiskit.transpiler.passes.synthesis.plugin.UnitarySynthesisPlugin`
- HighLevelSynthesisPlugin - `https://docs.quantum.ibm.com/api/qiskit/qiskit.transpiler.passes.synthesis.plugin.HighLevelSynthesisPlugin`
- AI Transpiler Passes Blog by IBM - `https://www.ibm.com/quantum/blog/ai-transpiler-passes`
- AI Practical and efficient quantum circuit synthesis and transpiling with Reinforcement Learning - `https://arxiv.org/abs/2405.13196`
- Qiskit Transpiler Service - `https://docs.quantum.ibm.com/guides/qiskit-transpiler-service`

- Circuit Cutting as a Quasiprobability Decomposition - https://qiskit-extensions.github.io/circuit-knitting-toolbox/circuit_cutting/explanation/index.html#circuit-cutting-as-a-quasiprobability-decomposition-qpd
- Circuit Knitting Generate Cutting Experiments - https://qiskit-extensions.github.io/circuit-knitting-toolbox/stubs/circuit_knitting.cutting.generate_cutting_experiments.html#circuit_knitting.cutting.generate_cutting_experiments
- Gate Cutting to Reduce Circuit Depth - https://qiskit-extensions.github.io/circuit-knitting-toolbox/circuit_cutting/tutorials/02_gate_cutting_to_reduce_circuit_depth.html
- Quantum Metric Layer Fidelity - IBM Quantum Blog - https://www.ibm.com/quantum/blog/quantum-metric-layer-fidelity
- Benchmarking Quantum Processor Performance at Scale - https://arxiv.org/abs/2311.05933
- Layer Fidelity - https://github.com/qiskit-community/qiskit-device-benchmarking/blob/main/notebooks/layer_fidelity.ipynb
- Qiskit Serverless Distributed Workloads - https://qiskit.github.io/qiskit-serverless/getting_started/basic/04_distributed_workloads.html
- Qiskit Function - https://qiskit.github.io/qiskit-serverless/stubs/qiskit_serverless.core.QiskitFunction.html#qiskit_serverless.core.QiskitFunction
- IBM Serverless Client - https://qiskit.github.io/qiskit-serverless/stubs/qiskit_serverless.core.IBMServerlessClient.html#qiskit_serverless.core.IBMServerlessClient

CHAPTER 9

Quantum Algorithms Part I

Introduction

This chapter delves into the fundamental algorithms that form the basis of quantum computing, using the robust framework of Qiskit to demonstrate and execute these innovative ideas. Quantum algorithms signify a fundamental change in computational thought by utilizing the laws of quantum mechanics to solve issues that are unsolvable for classical computers. We start by exploring quantum oracles and enigmatic black boxes that empower quantum algorithms to execute their operations. We explore the Deutsch and Deutsch-Jozsa algorithms, which are early examples of quantum computing's ability to surpass classical methods. The chapter discusses Bernstein-Vazirani and Simon's algorithms, revealing distinct perspectives on quantum problem-solving and its benefits. We want to offer a thorough grasp of how quantum algorithms utilize superposition, entanglement, and interference principles to pave the way for advanced quantum computing applications.

Structure

In this chapter, you are going to study:

- Introduction to Oracle-Based Algorithms
    - Classical Oracles
    - Quantum Oracles
- The Deutsch Algorithm
    - The Concept
    - Oracle's for Deutsch Algorithm
    - Deutsch Algorithm Steps
    - Quantum Circuit Analysis - Mathematical Derivation
- Implementing Deutsch Algorithm in Qiskit
- Deutsch-Jozsa Algorithm: Scaling Deutsch Algorithm
    - The Concept
    - Quantum Circuit Analysis - Mathematical Derivation
- Implementing Deutsch-Jozsa Algorithm in Qiskit
- Bernstein-Vazirani Algorithm
    - The Concept
    - Quantum Circuit Analysis - Mathematical Derivation
- Implementing Bernstein-Vazirani Algorithm in Qiskit
- Simon's Algorithm
    - The Concept
    - Quantum Circuit Analysis - Mathematical Derivation
- Implementing Simon's Algorithm in Qiskit

Introduction to Oracle-Based Algorithms

An **oracle**, in the context of computational theory and quantum computing, serves as an abstract mechanism or mathematical construct that provides external information to an algorithm, effectively acting as a*black box* . This concept is instrumental in both classical and quantum computational models for analyzing algorithmic processes' limits and constructing proofs of computational complexity.

Classical Oracles

In classical computing, an oracle is depicted as a black box that executes a certain operation on input data to generate an output. The user is only concerned with the input-output relationship defined by the black box, as the internal workings are unknown to them. An example of a classical oracle could be a function that receives a number as input and indicates whether the number is prime. The oracle conceals the intricacy of deciding the result, and the user engages with it solely through its inputs and outputs.

The oracle abstraction enables theorists to investigate issues of computability and complexity without getting into the details of how specific computations are executed. Oracles in classical contexts are commonly employed to articulate problems related to decision-making, search, or optimization. The oracle promptly offers a solution to a particular problem instance, regardless of the computing complexity involved in finding that solution.

Mathematical View

An oracle can be thought of as a function $f : X \to Y$, where X is the set of possible inputs and Y is the set of possible outputs. For instance, a function $f(x)$ might map a set of integers X to $\{0, 1\}$, indicating whether each integer is even (0) or odd (1).

Mathematically, we can represent a classical oracle's action on an input x as:

$$f(x) = y \tag{9.1}$$

where $x \in X$ and $y \in Y$. This representation is deterministic, meaning for a given input x, the output y is fixed.

Quantum Oracles

Quantum oracles apply the classical oracle idea in the quantum realm by working with quantum bits (qubits) and leveraging superposition and entanglement concepts. A quantum oracle is a unitary operation that operates on a group of qubits, altering quantum states according to the oracle's fundamental function. Quantum oracles may handle several inputs at the same time due to the notion of quantum superposition, unlike classical oracles. This enables a type of parallelism that is not present in classical computing.

Mathematical View

A quantum oracle operates on quantum bits (qubits) and is represented by a unitary operator U_f that acts on a quantum state. If we consider a function $f : \{0, 1\}^n \to \{0, 1\}$, the quantum oracle for f can be represented as:

$$U_f |x\rangle |y\rangle = |x\rangle |y \oplus f(x)\rangle \tag{9.2}$$

Here, $|x\rangle$ is a quantum state representing the input, $|y\rangle$ is an auxiliary qubit (often initialized to $|0\rangle$ or $|1\rangle$), and $\oplus$ denotes bitwise XOR. This operation illustrates how a quantum oracle can entangle the input and output states, allowing for the superposition principle to evaluate f on multiple inputs simultaneously.

Quantum Parallelism and Superposition

Quantum superposition allows a single quantum state to represent multiple classical states simultaneously. If we prepare a quantum state in a superposition of all possible inputs and apply U_f, the system evolves to:

$$U_f(\sum_{x=0}^{2^n-1} |x\rangle |0\rangle) = \sum_{x=0}^{2^n-1} |x\rangle |f(x)\rangle \tag{9.3}$$

This equation showcases the parallelism inherent in quantum computing as U_f acts on each component of the superposition, effectively computing $f(x)$ for all x in a single operation.

Entanglement

The quantum oracle's ability to produce entangled states is crucial for algorithms like Simon's, where the goal is to find a hidden string s that satisfies $f(x) = f(x \oplus s)$ for all x. The entanglement generated by U_f facilitates the extraction of information about s through quantum interference effects.

Quantum operations are unitary and reversible, unlike conventional operations that might discard information, such as irreversible functions. This attribute is essential for quantum computation as it guarantees the preservation of information, preventing any loss of quantum information throughout the computation process.

Importance of Oracles

Oracles are crucial in theoretical computer science, especially in analyzing computational complexity and the distinctions among complexity classes. Oracles are utilized to create theoretical situations where problems can be handled with the help of an oracle that can immediately determine membership in a particular class. This results in the formation of relativized worlds where the connection between complexity classes (such as P vs. NP) can be investigated based on various assumptions. Oracles in quantum computing showcase the quantum advantage by illustrating instances where quantum algorithms surpass classical ones, revealing valuable information about the capabilities and constraints of quantum computation.

The Deutsch Algorithm

David Deutsch devised the Deutsch algorithm in 1985, which is a fundamental quantum algorithm. It illustrates the capacity of quantum computing to resolve issues more effectively than classical computers. Using a single evaluation of the function, the algorithm ascertains whether a binary function, which generates either 0 or 1, is constant (emits the same output for all inputs) or balanced (emits equal quantities of 0s and 1s for all inputs). By demonstrating a quantum speed-up over classical methods, this demonstrates the power of quantum superposition and interference.

The Concept

The Deutsch Algorithm is a significant example in the field of quantum computing, showcasing quantum benefit despite its simplicity. Introduced by David Deutsch in 1985, this technique efficiently distinguishes between two types of black box functions (oracles) by addressing a fundamental difficulty. The Deutsch Algorithm is essential not only for its immediate use but also as a fundamental concept for grasping the wider significance of quantum computing. It eloquently demonstrates how a quantum computer may determine features of a function with fewer queries than classical computers using the principles of superposition and interference. This algorithm represents a significant shift from theoretical concepts to practical quantum algorithms, highlighting the potential of quantum computing to transform information processing. The Deutsch Algorithm provides an initial understanding of quantum parallelism and quantum logic, paving the way for more intricate quantum algorithms that capitalize on these quantum phenomena.

Deutsch Algorithm tackles the following problem $\rightarrow$ Given an oracle, U_f, implementing some unknown function $f : \{0,1\} \rightarrow \{0,1\}$, determine whether f is *constant* (returns the same output for all inputs) or *balanced* (returns 0 for half of the inputs and 1 for the other half).

- In a **Constant** function, its output is the same for all possible inputs. Constant functions remain consistent regardless of the input and demonstrate consistent behaviour throughout the function's domain. In the Deutsch Algorithm, identifying a function as constant indicates that the oracle behaves the same way for all input states, allowing for the function's overall behaviour to be determined with just one quantum query.
- In a **Balanced** function, if it produces an equal number of outputs of 0 and 1 for all possible inputs. This implies that for the two possible inputs (0 and 1), the function yields one 0 and one 1. Balanced functions display symmetry in their output distribution,

which contrasts with constant functions. Within the realm of quantum computing, the Deutsch Algorithm identifies a function as balanced by highlighting the oracle's input-dependent operation. This enables the algorithm to utilize quantum superposition and interference to distinguish between balanced and constant functions more efficiently.

- Deutsch's algorithm illustrates key ideas of quantum parallelism and quantum quantum interference that are used in all useful quantum algorithms
- It is one of the first quantum algorithms which showed quantum algorithms may be more efficient than their classical counterparts

Let $f : \{0,1\} \rightarrow \{0,1\}$ be a binary function (digital function), then there are four possible functions as follows:

- **Constant:** $f_0 : 0 \rightarrow 0, 1 \rightarrow 0$ signifying $f(0) = 0$ and $f(1) = 0$
- **Constant:** $f_1 : 0 \rightarrow 1, 1 \rightarrow 1$ signifying $f(0) = 1$ and $f(1) = 1$
- **Balanced:** $f_2 : 0 \rightarrow 0, 1 \rightarrow 1$ signifying $f(0) = 0$ and $f(1) = 1$
- **Balanced:** $f_3 : 0 \rightarrow 1, 1 \rightarrow 0$ signifying $f(0) = 1$ and $f(1) = 0$

The problem is to determine if an unknown binary function f is

- Constant: $f(0) \oplus f(1) = 0$; $f(0) = f(1)$; Algorithm output $\rightarrow 0$
- Balanced: $f(0) \oplus f(1) = 1$; $f(0) \neq f(1)$; Algorithm output $\rightarrow 1$

The Deutsch algorithm is capable of determining the value of $f(0) \oplus f(1)$ by making only a single query to the oracle implementing f.

Classically, two queries are necessary: Two evaluations of functions f for input 0 and input 1

Oracle's for Deutsch Algorithm

Here, we see the Oracle implementations in terms of quantum circuits for the Constant and Balanced cases in the Deutsch algorithm. It is important to note that the states $|x\rangle$ and $|y\rangle$ that are input to to the circuit are in superposition as Hadamards are applied before the oracle is applied. This becomes more clear in the next sections.

Constant; $f(x) = 0$

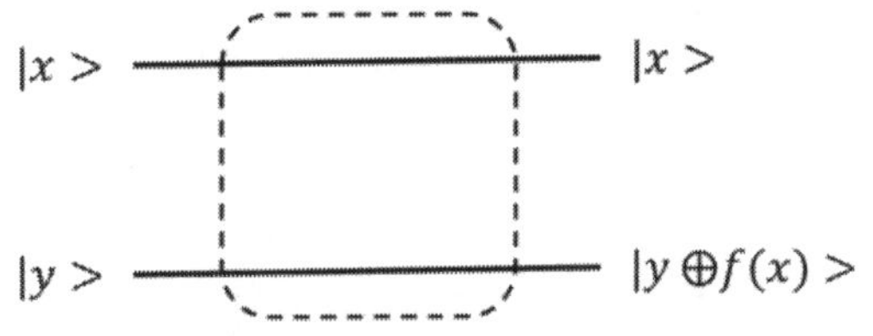

Figure 9.1: Oracle for $f(x) = 0$

Constant; $f(x) = 1$

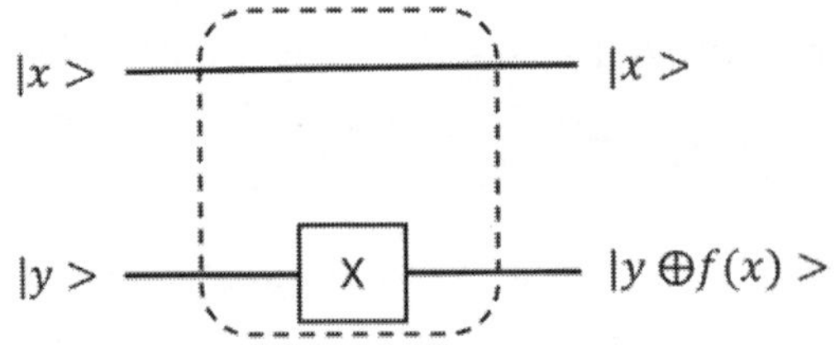

Figure 9.2: Oracle for $f(x) = 1$

Balanced; $f(x) = x$

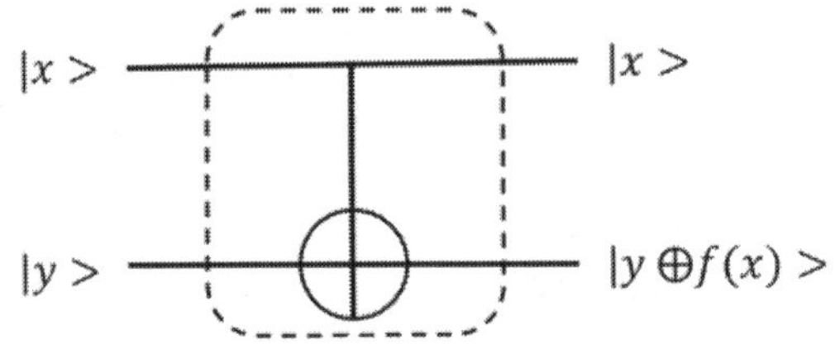

Figure 9.3: Oracle for $f(x) = x$

Balanced; $f(x) = x \oplus 1$

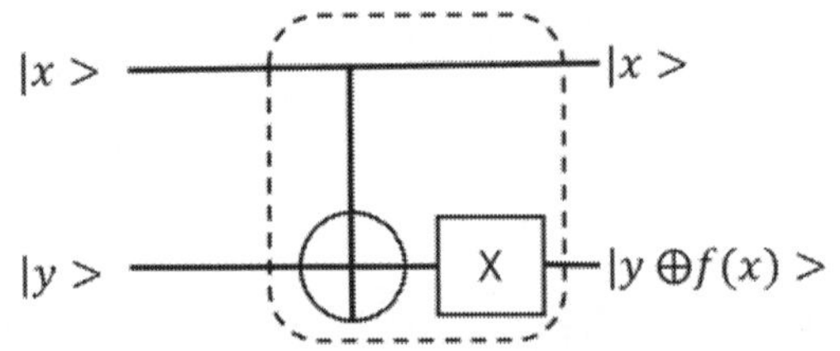

Figure 9.4: Oracle for $f(x) = x \oplus 1$

Deutsch Algorithm Steps

Before deriving the quantum circuit analysis for the Deutsch algorithm, it is important to highlight the steps so as to make it easier to grasp the analysis.

- Step 1: Apply Hadamard gates to the input states $|0\rangle, |1\rangle$ to produce a two-quantum state superposition.
- Step 2: Apply U_f to that superposition state ($U_f : |x, y\rangle \rightarrow |x, y \oplus f(x)\rangle$)
- Step 3: Apply Hadamard gate to the 1st qubit, leaving the 2nd qubit alone
- Step 4: Make a measurement on the 1st qubit, and the result obtained is the output of the algorithm

Quantum Circuit Analysis - Mathematical Derivation

After covering the algorithm's steps, we will now rigorously examine the mathematical quantum circuit analysis of the Deutsch algorithm.

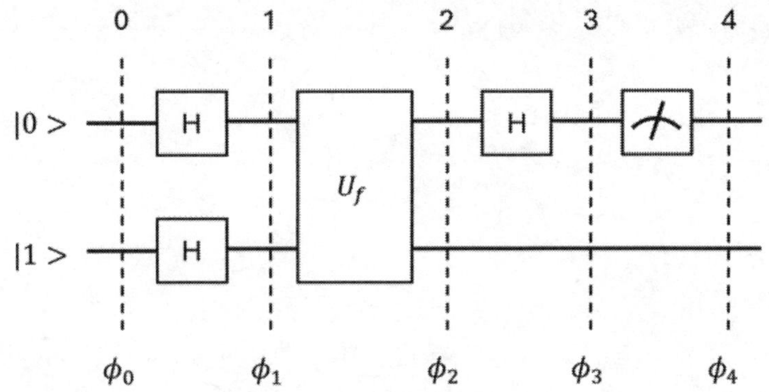

Figure 9.5: Quantum Circuit for Deutsch Algorithm

We will analyze the circuit step by step. From *Figure* 9.5 , the step numbers have been written on the top of the dotted lines and the quantum state of each of the steps by applying the gates have been denoted by ϕ with the subscript indicating the step number. Let us begin.

Step 0:

Initially, we prepare the state.

$$|\phi_0\rangle = |0\rangle |1\rangle = |01\rangle \tag{9.4}$$

Step 1:

Apply Hadamard gates to $|\phi_0\rangle$ to create superposition state

$$|\phi_1\rangle = (H \otimes H) |0\rangle |1\rangle = \left(\frac{|0\rangle + |1\rangle}{\sqrt{2}}\right) \left(\frac{|0\rangle - |1\rangle}{\sqrt{2}}\right) = |+\rangle |-\rangle \tag{9.5}$$

$$|\phi_1\rangle = \frac{1}{2}(|00\rangle - |01\rangle + |10\rangle - |11\rangle) \tag{9.6}$$

Step 2:

Apply the oracle U_f to $|\phi_1\rangle$ (Quantum Parallelism) $\rightarrow$ applies U_f to each term of $|\phi_1\rangle$

Recall that $U_f : |x, y\rangle = |x, y \oplus f(x)\rangle$ and we are now going to use the same to derive the result of each of the terms in $|\phi_1\rangle$. We will ignore the factor $\frac{1}{2}$ for the time being.

- $U_f |00\rangle = |0, 0 \oplus f(0)\rangle$
  - If $f(0) = 0$, then $U_f |00\rangle = |00\rangle = (1 - f(0)) |00\rangle$

- If $f(0) = 1$, then $U_f |00\rangle = |01\rangle = f(0)|01\rangle$

$\Rightarrow U_f |00\rangle = (1 - f(0))|00\rangle + f(0)|01\rangle$

- $U_f |01\rangle = |0, 1 \oplus f(0)\rangle$
  - If $f(0) = 0$, then $U_f |01\rangle = |01\rangle = (1 - f(0))|01\rangle$
  - If $f(0) = 1$, then $U_f |01\rangle = |00\rangle = f(0)|00\rangle$

$\Rightarrow U_f |01\rangle = f(0)|00\rangle + (1 - f(0))|01\rangle$

- $U_f |10\rangle = |1, 0 \oplus f(1)\rangle$
  - If $f(1) = 0$, then $U_f |10\rangle = |10\rangle = (1 - f(1))|10\rangle$
  - If $f(1) = 1$, then $U_f |10\rangle = |11\rangle = f(1)|11\rangle$

$\Rightarrow U_f |10\rangle = (1 - f(1))|10\rangle + f(1)|11\rangle$

- $U_f |11\rangle = |1, 1 \oplus f(1)\rangle$
  - If $f(1) = 0$, then $U_f |11\rangle = |11\rangle = (1 - f(1))|11\rangle$
  - If $f(1) = 1$, then $U_f |11\rangle = |10\rangle = f(1)|10\rangle$

$\Rightarrow U_f |11\rangle = f(1)|10\rangle + (1 - f(1))|11\rangle$

Now, arranging all the terms together and bringing the $\frac{1}{2}$ factor back, we will have

$$|\phi_2\rangle = U_f |\phi_1\rangle = \frac{1}{2}(U_f |00\rangle - U_f |01\rangle + U_f |10\rangle - U_f |11\rangle) \tag{9.7}$$

$$|\phi_2\rangle = \frac{1}{2}[(1 - 2f(0))|00\rangle - (1 - 2f(0))|01\rangle + (1 - 2f(1))|10\rangle - (1 - 2f(1))|11\rangle] \tag{9.8}$$

Step 3:

Apply Hadamard gate to the 1st qubit that is, we perform the operation $(H \otimes I)|\phi_2\rangle$

$$(H \otimes I)\left(\frac{1 - 2f(0)}{2}\right)|00\rangle = \left(\frac{1 - 2f(0)}{2}\right)\left(\frac{|0\rangle + |1\rangle}{\sqrt{2}}\right)|0\rangle = \left(\frac{1 - 2f(0)}{2\sqrt{2}}\right)(|00\rangle + |10\rangle) \tag{9.9}$$

$$(H \otimes I)\left(\frac{1 - 2f(0)}{2}\right)|01\rangle = \left(\frac{1 - 2f(0)}{2}\right)\left(\frac{|0\rangle + |1\rangle}{\sqrt{2}}\right)|1\rangle = \left(\frac{1 - 2f(0)}{2\sqrt{2}}\right)(|01\rangle + |11\rangle) \tag{9.10}$$

$$(H \otimes I)\left(\frac{1 - 2f(1)}{2}\right)|10\rangle = \left(\frac{1 - 2f(1)}{2}\right)\left(\frac{|0\rangle - |1\rangle}{\sqrt{2}}\right)|0\rangle = \left(\frac{1 - 2f(1)}{2\sqrt{2}}\right)(|00\rangle - |10\rangle) \tag{9.11}$$

$$(H \otimes I)\left(\frac{1 - 2f(1)}{2}\right)|11\rangle = \left(\frac{1 - 2f(1)}{2}\right)\left(\frac{|0\rangle - |1\rangle}{\sqrt{2}}\right)|1\rangle = \left(\frac{1 - 2f(1)}{2\sqrt{2}}\right)(|01\rangle - |11\rangle) \tag{9.12}$$

With some simple algebraic manipulation and separating out the 1st and 2nd qubit states, the final output state ϕ_3 is

$$|\phi_3\rangle = (H \otimes I)\,|\phi_2\rangle = (1 - f(0) - f(1))\,|0\rangle \left(\frac{|0\rangle - |1\rangle}{\sqrt{2}}\right) + (f(1) - f(0))\,|1\rangle \left(\frac{|0\rangle - |1\rangle}{\sqrt{2}}\right) \quad (9.13)$$

Step 4:

The 1st qubit is measured, and the results are as follows:

- If f is constant, $f(0) \oplus f(1) = 0$
  - $f(0) = f(1) = 0 \Rightarrow |\phi_3\rangle = |0\rangle\,|-\rangle$
  - $f(0) = f(1) = 1 \Rightarrow |\phi_3\rangle = -\,|0\rangle\,|-\rangle$

  $\Rightarrow |\phi_3\rangle = \pm\,|0\rangle\,|-\rangle \Rightarrow |\phi_4\rangle = 0$
- If f is balanced, $f(0) \oplus f(1) = 1$
  - $f(0) = 0, f(1) = 1 \Rightarrow |\phi_3\rangle = |1\rangle\,|-\rangle$
  - $f(0) = 1, f(1) = 0 \Rightarrow |\phi_3\rangle = -\,|1\rangle\,|-\rangle$

  $\Rightarrow |\phi_3\rangle = \pm\,|1\rangle\,|-\rangle \Rightarrow |\phi_4\rangle = 1$

Implementation of Deutsch Algorithm in Qiskit

Before we begin implementing the Deutsch Algorithm in Qiskit, let us first import all the necessary libraries that are required for this purpose:

```
from qiskit import QuantumCircuit
from qiskit.providers.basic_provider import BasicSimulator
from qiskit import transpile
from qiskit.visualization import plot_histogram
```

In the first step, we create a 2 qubit circuit with qubit1 set to $|0\rangle$ and qubit2 set to $|1\rangle$. For that, we apply an identity gate to qubit1 and a Hadamard gate to qubit2.

```
qc=QuantumCircuit(2,1)
qc.id(0)
qc.x(1)
qc.draw(output='mpl')
```

The output of the preceding code is as follows:

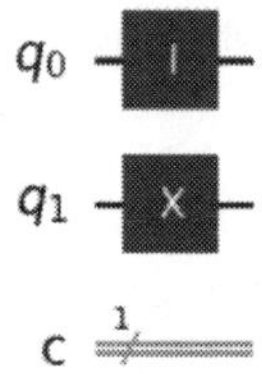

Figure 9.6: Output of step1

In the next step, using Hadamard Gates, we create a superposition state that allows us to simultaneously iterate through all four states of the two qubit system.

```
qc.h(0)
qc.h(1)
qc.draw(output='mpl')
```

The output of the above code is shown here:

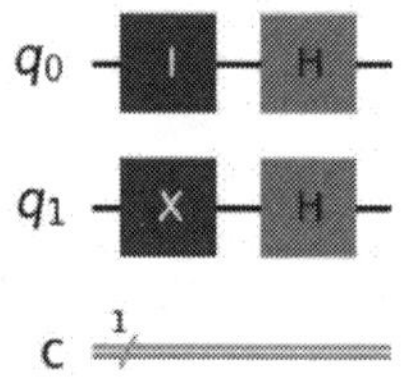

Figure 9.7: Output of step2

Next we apply the oracle, in our case to simplify the code, we are using a CNOT gate which operates on q0 and q1. Depending upon the state of q0 it acts either as a not on q1 or does not change the state of q1.

```
qc.cx(0,1)
qc.draw(output='mpl')
```

The output of this code is shown as:

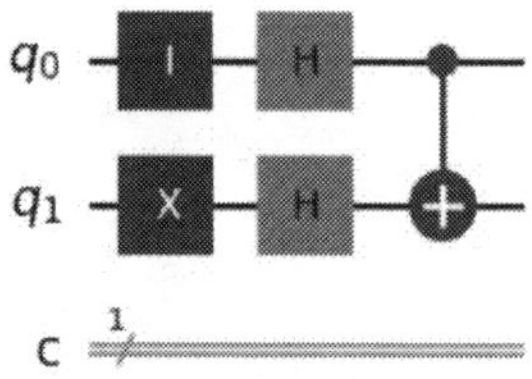

Figure 9.8: Output of step3

In the next step, we add Hadamard gates to all the qubits and create a superposition.

```
qc.h(0)
qc.h(1)
qc.draw(output='mpl')
```

The output of this code is shown as:

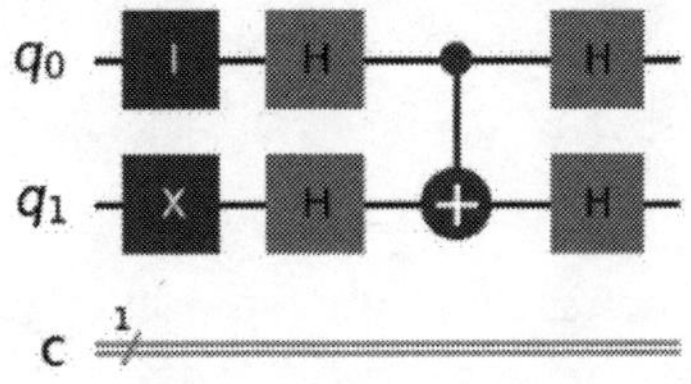

Figure 9.9: Output of step4

In the last step, we take the measurement of qubit0, if the output of this qubit is 0 then the function is a constant function. If the output of the qubit is 1 then the function is a balanced function.

```
qc.measure(0,0)
backend = BasicSimulator()
tqc = transpile(qc, backend)
counts = backend.run(tqc).result().get_counts()
plot_histogram(counts)
```

Final Circuit of Deutsch Algorithm:

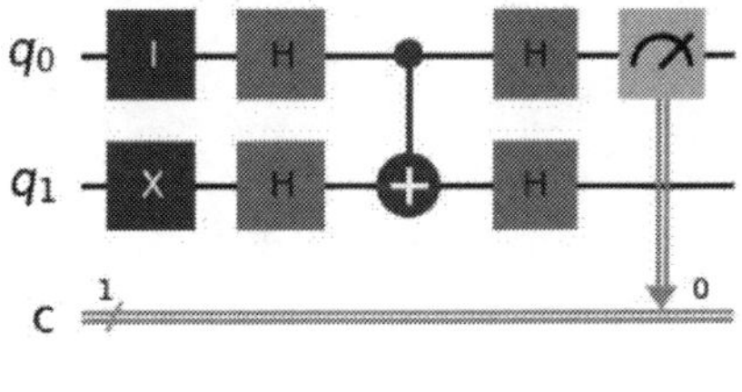

Figure 9.10: Final Circuit of Deutsch Algorithm

Final output of Deutsch Algorithm:

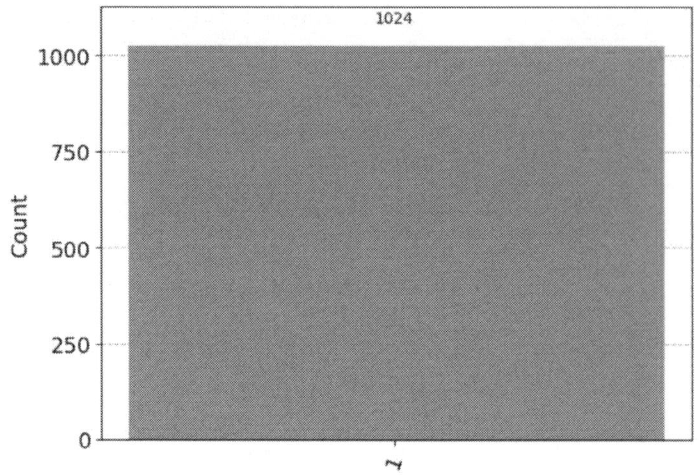

Figure 9.11: The histogram shows the result of the Deutsch algorithm, indicating a single outcome with 100% probability. This confirms that the given function is either constant or balanced, as determined by the quantum interference in the circuit. The algorithm efficiently identifies the function type using just one query.

Since the output in figure 9.11 is 1, the function is a balanced function.

Deutsch-Jozsa Algorithm: Scaling Deutsch Algorithm

Let us start with the Deutsch-Jozsa algorithm which is a scaled up version of the Deutsch algorithm that you saw in the previous section.

The Concept

The Deutsch-Jozsa algorithm is a straightforward generalization of the problem solved by the Deutsch algorithm. It has the same structure as the Deutsch algorithm, and again, it allows us to determine whether a function is constant or balanced. However, this time, the function has multiple input values, i.e., multiple qubits can be used to represent the input. For instance, a two-qubit input will have the bitstrings 00, 01, 10 and 11.

Input: Black box for computing an unknown function, $f : \{0, 1\}^n \rightarrow \{0, 1\}$

Problem: Determine whether f is constant or balanced by making queries to f.

Algorithm Output: $|000...0\rangle \rightarrow$ Constant, otherwise Balanced.

Using a classical algorithm, we cannot decide with certainty (worst case) whether f is constant or balanced using any less than $2^{n-1} + 1$ queries. As for the Deutsch-Jozsa algorithm takes advantage of quantum superposition and interference to determine the global property of f, i.e., constant or balanced. This algorithm will determine the result by making only a single query, and it provides a deterministic exponential speed-up over the classical case.

Constant versus Balanced Oracles

As you are aware, Deutsch-Jozsa is a scalable version of the Deutsch algorithm, and in order to achieve this scalable aspect, two registers have been introduced in the quantum circuit for this algorithm. The 1st register has multiple input qubits, all of which are initialized to the $|0\rangle$ state, and the 2nd register has a single input qubit initialized to $|1\rangle$ state similar to that of the Deutsch algorithm.

- **Constant Oracle:** Input has no effect on the output; therefore, to implement this, randomly flipping the 2nd register by applying Pauli X gate works. The output will be $|000...0\rangle$ state taken by measuring the 1st register.
- **Balanced Oracle:** For implementing this, perform the CNOT operation with the 1st register qubits as control and the 2nd register qubit as target. For different input values such as 01, 10, 11, and more (considering 1st register has two qubits), wrap the selected controls (where one is present) of 1st register with Pauli X gates.
  For example, 01 has the 2nd qubit as 1, so we only wrap the CNOT gates by applying X gates for the 2nd qubit. This becomes clear during the Qiskit implementation stage.

Quantum Circuit Analysis - Mathematical Derivation

Similar to the mathematical derivation for the Deutsch algorithm, we will now study the general mathematical details of the Deutsch-Jozssa algorithm. *Figure* 9.12 shows the quantum circuit for the Deutsch-Jozsa highlighting the n qubits in the 1st register, whereas in Deutsch, there was a single qubit.

Step 0:

Initially, we prepare the state.

$$|\phi_0\rangle = |0\rangle^{\otimes n} |1\rangle \tag{9.14}$$

Step 1:

We apply the Hadamard gates to both 1st and 2nd registers, we get

$$|\phi_1\rangle = \left(H^{\otimes n} |0\rangle^{\otimes n}\right) \otimes (H |1\rangle) = \frac{1}{\sqrt{2^n}} \sum_{x=0}^{2^n-1} |x\rangle |-\rangle \tag{9.15}$$

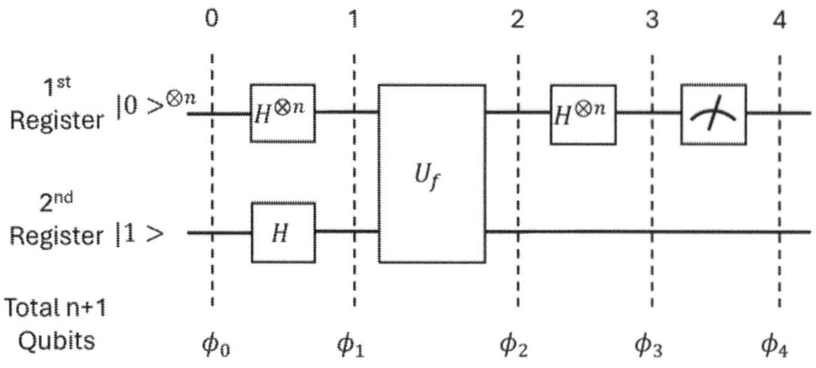

Figure 9.12: Quantum Circuit for Deutsch-Jozsa Algorithm

Step 2:

The U_f unitary is applied to all the qubit states simultaneously.

$$|\phi_2\rangle = U_f |\phi_1\rangle = \frac{1}{\sqrt{2^n}} \sum_{x_1,x_2,\ldots x_n \in \{0,1\}} (-1)^{f(x)} |x\rangle |-\rangle \tag{9.16}$$

Step 3:

Apply Hadamard gates on the 1st register qubits, leaving the 2nd register as it is.

$$|\phi_3\rangle = \left(H^{\otimes n} \otimes I\right) |\phi_2\rangle = \left(\frac{1}{\sqrt{2^n}} \sum_{x\in\{0,1\}^n} (-1)^{f(x)} \frac{1}{\sqrt{2^n}} \sum_{z\in\{0,1\}^n} (-1)^{x\cdot z} |z\rangle \right) (|-\rangle) \tag{9.17}$$

From *Equation*9.17, we can see that inside the big bracket there are two terms. The term $\left(\frac{1}{\sqrt{2^n}} \sum_{z\in\{0,1\}^n} (-1)^{x\cdot z} |z\rangle\right)$ is the operation $H^{\otimes n} |x\rangle$.

After the rearrangement of the terms, we will have the following.

$$|\phi_3\rangle = \frac{1}{2^n} \sum_{z\in\{0,1\}^n} \left(\sum_{x\in\{0,1\}^n} (-1)^{f(x)+x\cdot z} \right) |z\rangle (|-\rangle) \tag{9.18}$$

Step 4:

Finally, the first n qubits (1st register) is measured on a computational basis.

We consider the probability of measuring zero on every qubit, which corresponds to the term in the superposition where $|z\rangle$ is $|0\rangle^{\otimes n}$.

Constant f

We can factor out the term $(-1)^{f(x)}$ in $|\phi_3\rangle$, then we have

$$|\phi_3\rangle = (-1)^{f(x)} \sum_{z\in\{0,1\}^n} \left(\frac{1}{2^n} \sum_{x\in\{0,1\}^n} (-1)^{x\cdot z} \right) |z\rangle \left(|-\rangle\right) \tag{9.19}$$

For $|z\rangle = |0\rangle^{\otimes n}$, we have

$$\frac{1}{2^n} \sum_{x\in\{0,1\}^n} (-1)^{x\cdot 0\ldots 0} = \frac{1}{2^n} \sum_{x\in\{0,1\}^n} (-1)^0 = \frac{1}{2^n} \sum_{x\in\{0,1\}^n} 1 = \frac{1}{2^n} \cdot 2^n = 1(-1)^{f(x)} = \pm 1 \tag{9.20}$$

This means state $|0\rangle^{\otimes n} |-\rangle$ has amplitude 1 and it can be concluded that $|\phi_3\rangle = (-1)^{f(x)} |0\rangle^{\otimes n} |-\rangle$ has all the weight.

So, measuring the first n qubits in a computational basis yields the outcome $|0\rangle^{\otimes n}$ with certainty of amplitude ± 1

Balanced f

We cannot factor out $(-1)^{f(x)}$ as it takes different values depending on input x. So for $|z\rangle = |0\rangle^{\otimes n}$

$$\frac{1}{2^n} \sum_{x\in\{0,1\}^n} (-1)^{f(x)+x\cdot 0\ldots 0} = \frac{1}{2^n} \sum_{x\in\{0,1\}^n} (-1)^{f(x)} \tag{9.21}$$

As f is balanced, precisely half the terms in the summation, $f(x) = 0$ (yielding a +1 factor) and the other half $f(x) = 1$ (yielding a -1 factor), so they cancel, and the sum equals 0. We conclude that the amplitude $|0\rangle^{\otimes n}$ is 0, and we will never see $|0\rangle^{\otimes n}$ state in the measurement.

In conclusion

- If the function f is **constant**, the measurement of the first n qubits will yield $|0\rangle^{\otimes n}$ with certainty.
- If the function f is **balanced**, there is zero probability of measuring $|0\rangle^{\otimes n}$, indicating that at least one of the measurements will yield a state different from $|0\rangle^{\otimes n}$.

Implementing the Deutsch-Jozsa Algorithm in Qiskit

In this section, let us implement the Deutsch-Jozsa Algorithm in Qiskit. Let us first import all the necessary libraries that are required:

```
import numpy as np
from qiskit import QuantumCircuit, ClassicalRegister, QuantumRegister
from qiskit.providers.basic_provider import BasicSimulator
from qiskit import transpile
```

```
from qiskit.visualization import plot_histogram
```

Let's define the variable n to represent the number of qubits we want in our first register. The value of $2n$ represents the total number of potential inputs that our function can accommodate. In our case let us take n to be 3, which means the length of the first register for querying the oracle is 3.

```
n = 3
```

Select an oracle type at random. There is a 50% chance that it is constant, and an equal 50% chance that it is balanced.

```
oracleType, oracleValue = np.random.randint(2), np.random.randint(2)
if oracleType == 0:
    print("The oracle returns a constant value ", oracleValue)
else:
    print("The oracle returns a balanced function")
    a = np.random.randint(1,2**n) # this is a hidden parameter for balanced oracle.
```

To create registers, we need to allocate n qubits for querying the oracle and one additional qubit for storing the answer. All qubits are initially set to zero. The first register is used to record the measurement.

```
qr = QuantumRegister(n+1)
cr = ClassicalRegister(n)
circuitName = "DeutschJozsa"
djCircuit = QuantumCircuit(qr, cr)
```

Apply the Hadamard gate to each qubit in the first register to create the superposition of all input queries.

```
for i in range(n):
    djCircuit.h(qr[i])
```

Flip the second register and apply the Hadamard gate.

```
djCircuit.x(qr[n])
djCircuit.h(qr[n])
```

Apply barrier to mark the beginning of the oracle. If the oracleType is "0", the oracle returns oracleValue for all input. Otherwise, it returns the inner product of the input with a (non-zero bitstring)

```
djCircuit.barrier()
if oracleType == 0:
    if oracleValue == 1:
        djCircuit.x(qr[n])
    else:
        djCircuit.id(qr[n])
else:
    for i in range(n):
        if (a & (1 << i)):
            djCircuit.cx(qr[i], qr[n])
```

Apply barrier to mark the end of the oracle. Apply Hadamard gates after querying the oracle. Final step would be to measure all the qubits.

```
djCircuit.barrier()
for i in range(n):
    djCircuit.h(qr[i])
djCircuit.barrier()
for i in range(n):
    djCircuit.measure(qr[i], cr[i])
```

Final circuit of Deutsch-Jozsa algorithm is shown in the following figure Code to run the

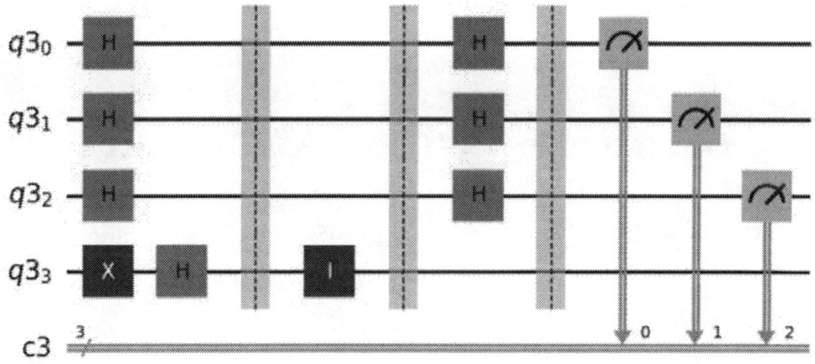

Figure 9.13: Quantum Circuit for Deutsch-Jozsa Algorithm

algorithm and the output is shown here:

```
backend = BasicSimulator()
tqc = transpile(djCircuit, backend)
```

```
counts = backend.run(tqc).result().get_counts()
plot_histogram(counts)
```

Figure 9.14 shows that by running the circuit 1024 times, with 100% accuracy the output is $|000\rangle$.

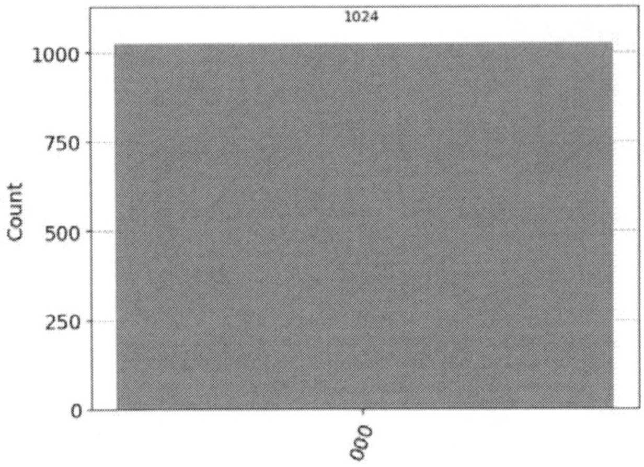

Figure 9.14: The histogram shows a single output state with 100% probability, indicating the result of the Deutsch-Jozsa algorithm. This confirms that the given function is constant, as the algorithm determines whether a function is constant or balanced with a single quantum query, demonstrating an exponential speedup over classical methods.

Bernstein-Vazirani Algorithm

The Bernstein-Vazirani algorithm is a quantum protocol specifically developed to ascertain a concealed binary sequence within a given function, which is presented as an oracle. In the conventional scenario, the process of obtaining the string would necessitate the execution of several queries, as each bit of the string would need to be resolved separately. However, the Bernstein-Vazirani approach exploits quantum superposition and interference to efficiently discover the concealed string with a single query. The proposed method effectively uncovers the binary string by generating a quantum state in superposition, implementing the oracle function, and doing a final measurement. The aforementioned showcases the efficacy of quantum computing in expediting the resolution of particular problems beyond the capabilities of classical approaches.

The Concept

The Bernstein-Vazirani algorithm is a special case of the Deutsch-Jozsa algorithm in which the function $f(x) = a \cdot x$ rather than a general function, where $a = a_{n-1}a_{n-2}...a_0$ is an n-bit binary number.

Problem:

Given an unknown function linear function $f(x_{n-1}x_{n-2}...x_1x_0)$ of n inputs that are known to be defined by the mod 2 dot product with an n (binary) digit constant, a, $f(x) = a \cdot x$. Find a in one query of the quantum oracle U_f

Quantum Circuit Analysis - Mathematical Derivation

The quantum circuit of the Bernstein-Vazirani is the same as that of the Deutsch-Jozsa algorithm, which is a particular case. Therefore, the mathematical analysis is similar to that of the Deutsch-Jozsa algorithm. The 1st register or top register provides the quantum parallelism, and the $|1\rangle$ in the bottom or 2nd register offers a phase kickback that transfers information about f from target output to data output.

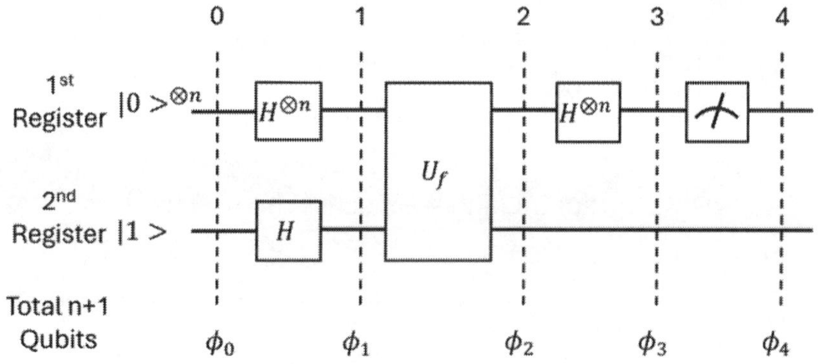

Figure 9.15: Quantum Circuit for Bernstein-Vazirani Algorithm

Step 0:

Initially, we prepare the state.

$$|\phi_0\rangle = |0\rangle^{\otimes n} |1\rangle \tag{9.22}$$

Step 1:

We apply the Hadamard gates to both the 1st and 2nd registers, and we get

$$|\phi_1\rangle = \left(H^{\otimes n} |0\rangle^{\otimes n}\right) \otimes (H|1\rangle) = \frac{1}{\sqrt{2^n}} \sum_{x=0}^{2^n-1} |x\rangle |-\rangle \tag{9.23}$$

Step 2:

The U_f unitary is applied to all the qubits.

$$|\phi_2\rangle = U_f |\phi_1\rangle = \left(\frac{1}{\sqrt{2^n}} \sum_{x=0}^{2^n-1} (-1)^{a \cdot x} |x\rangle\right) |-\rangle \tag{9.24}$$

Step 3:

Apply Hadamard gates to the 1st register qubits to interfere with the superposed states. The interference pattern is such that it directly encodes the unknown n-bit string a in the computational basis states of the first register.

$$|\phi_3\rangle = \left(H^{\otimes n} \otimes I\right) |\phi_2\rangle = \frac{1}{2^n} \sum_{z \in \{0,1\}^n} \left(\sum_{x \in \{0,1\}^n} (-1)^{a \cdot x + x \cdot z} \right) |z\rangle (|-\rangle) \tag{9.25}$$

Now, let $C(z) = \sum_{x \in \{0,1\}^n} (-1)^{a \cdot x + x \cdot z} |z\rangle$ so that it is easier to do further explanations in the next step.

Step 4:

Finally, the 1st register is measured on a computational basis. Now, we consider the term.

$$C(z) = \sum_{x \in \{0,1\}^n} (-1)^{a \cdot x + x \cdot z} |z\rangle \tag{9.26}$$

Now, two cases arise at this point, and we discuss them as follows.

- $z = a$

  $$C(a) = \sum_{x=0}^{2^n-1} (-1)^{a \cdot x + x \cdot a} = \sum_{x=0}^{2^n-1} 1 = 2^n \tag{9.27}$$

  Therefore,

  $$\frac{C(a)}{2^n} = \frac{2^n}{2^n} = 1 \tag{9.28}$$

- $z \neq a$

  There will be the same number of x such that $a \cdot x = 0$ and x such that $a \cdot x = 1$ in the summation. This causes the corresponding positive and negative phases to cancel each other out. As a result, the probability amplitude vanishes as follows.

$$\sum_{x\in\{0,1\}^n} (-1)^{a\cdot x}(-1)^{x\cdot z} = 0, z \neq a \tag{9.29}$$

Let us see an example to understand how the calculation happens -
Consider $a = 01$ and $z = 00$
Then, we will have

$$\sum_{x\in\{0,1\}^n} (-1)^{a\cdot x}(-1)^{x\cdot z} = (-1)^{0\cdot 0\oplus 1\cdot 0}(-1)^{0\cdot 0\oplus 0\cdot 0} \tag{9.30}$$

$$+(-1)^{0\cdot 0\oplus 1\cdot 1}(-1)^{0\cdot 0\oplus 1\cdot 0} \tag{9.31}$$

$$+(-1)^{0\cdot 1\oplus 1\cdot 0}(-1)^{1\cdot 0\oplus 0\cdot 0} \tag{9.32}$$

$$+(-1)^{0\cdot 1\oplus 1\cdot 1}(-1)^{1\cdot 0\oplus 1\cdot 0} \tag{9.33}$$

$$= (-1)^0(-1)^0 + (-1)^1(-1)^0 + (-1)^0(-1)^0 + (-1)^1(-1)^0 = 1 - 1 + 1 - 1 = 0 \tag{9.34}$$

Implementing Bernstein-Vazirani Algorithm in Qiskit

Suppose we possess a confidential numerical value, and your task is to conjecture the exact value of that number. What is your estimated number of attempts required?

For illustration purposes, let's choose a binary string **1011001** consisting of 7 bits. Traditionally, a computer would necessitate 7 queries to achieve accuracy. First, the 7th bit will undergo an AND operation with the value "1". If the output is 1, the computer can confidently determine that the 7th bit is set to 1. Conversely, if the output is 0, the computer can deduce that the last bit is set to 0. Similarly, the computer will need to conduct a number of queries equal to the number of bits (n) in the string to retrieve the secret value, starting with the last bit. Nevertheless, quantum computers provide the potential to determine the correct number accurately in a single attempt. Ethan Bernstein and Umesh Vazirani first proposed the quantum algorithm in 1992, which goes into more detail about the viability of doing this.

This section will guide you through the Qiskit implementation of the Bernstein-Vazirani algorithm.

Let us first import all the required libraries from qiskit.

```
from qiskit import QuantumCircuit
from qiskit.providers.basic_provider import BasicSimulator
from qiskit import transpile
from qiskit.visualization import plot_histogram
```

In the next step, we choose a binary number that needs to be guessed in a string format.

```
secret_number = input("Input a Binary String of your choice")
#In this example, we took it to be 1010
```

We initialize the qubits in the $|+\rangle$ state by applying n (in this case, it is 4) Hadamard gates. We will apply an X-gate on the last qubit before the Hadamard gate.

```
circ = QuantumCircuit(len(secret_number)+1,len(secret_number))
circ.h(range(len(secret_number)))
circ.x(len(secret_number))
circ.h(len(secret_number))
circ.barrier()
circ.draw("mpl")
```

Now let us construct an oracle, which performs the following transformation:

$$|x\rangle \rightarrow (-1)^{f(x)}|x\rangle \tag{9.35}$$

The Oracle applies a CX-gate to the qubit for every "1" in the bit-string. However, in this case, we will not have knowledge of when to utilize the C-NOT gate. Instead, we will create a program that will perform the task on our behalf. Here, the CX gate represents a modulo 2 operation. The oracle function, in contrast to Deutsch's approach, does not need to be balanced.

```
for digit, query in enumerate(reversed(secret_number)):
    if query == "1":
        circ.cx(digit, len(secret_number))
circ.barrier()
circ.draw("mpl")
```

Following the oracle inquiry, it is necessary to implement Hadamard gates for the purpose of performing a unitary operation. Once we perform the unitary operation, we measure the qubits.

```
circ.h(range(len(secret_number)))
circ.barrier()
circ.measure(range(len(secret_number)),range(len(secret_number)))
circ.draw("mpl")
```

Now, let us check if our circuit is working well. The output we get in the histogram should also be the same secret number we took above which is 1010.

```
backend = BasicSimulator()
tqc = transpile(circ, backend)
counts = backend.run(tqc).result().get_counts()
plot_histogram(counts)
```

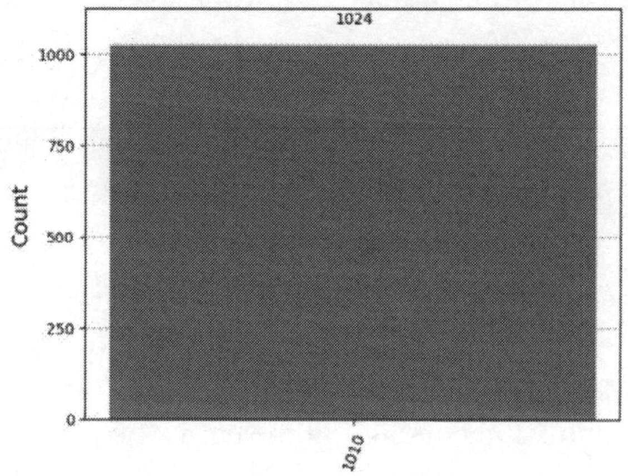

Figure 9.16: The histogram shows a single output state with 100% probability, indicating the result of the Bernstein-Vazirani algorithm. This suggests that the hidden bitstring (oracle's encoded number) is 1010, as the algorithm efficiently determines the secret string in a single query, showcasing quantum advantage over classical approaches.

This clearly shows that all the 1024 default shots are in the '1010' state. This indicates that we have found the secret number using the Bernstein Vazirani Algorithm running the circuit on the BasicSimulator.

Simon's Algorithm

Simon's Algorithm is an essential quantum computing algorithm introduced by Daniel Simon in 1994, which demonstrates the power of quantum computers to solve certain problems exponentially faster than classical computers. It was the first algorithm to show an exponential speed-up compared to the best classical algorithm in solving a specific problem.

The Concept

Simon's algorithm is particularly significant as it inspired Peter Shor's work on quantum factoring and discrete logarithms. Both Simon's and Shor's algorithms are well-known prime factorization algorithms solving a similar problem: Given a function f, find the period of that function. Simon's algorithm can also be applied to solve the hidden bitstring problem, which we will explore with Qiskit later.

Simon's Problem Statement

Given an unknown black box function $f : \{0,1\}^n \rightarrow \{0,1\}^n$ which can be:

- **One-to-One:** Maps exactly one unique output for every input. For example, $f(1) \rightarrow 1$, $f(2) \rightarrow 2$, $f(3) \rightarrow 3$, $f(4) \rightarrow 4$. The algorithm outputs $00....0$ bitstring only.
- **Two-to-One:** Maps exactly two inputs to every unique output. For example, $f(1) \rightarrow 1$, $f(2) \rightarrow 2$, $f(3) \rightarrow 1$, $f(4) \rightarrow 2$. The algorithm outputs our hidden bitstring only.

This Two-to-One mapping is according to a hidden bitstring s.

Given x_1, x_2: $f(x_1) = f(x_2)$ if $x_1 = x_2$ or

it is guaranteed: $x_1 \oplus x_2 = s$ or $x_1 = x_2 \oplus s$

If $s = 000....0$, it represents One-to-One f.

Some important points regarding Simon's algorithm are the following.

- The best classical algorithms, including probabilistic ones, require an exponential $\Omega(2^{n/2})$ queries to the black box function in order to determine s. This exponential query complexity arises because, without any prior information about s, classical computers must essentially perform a randomized or exhaustive search to distinguish between a one-to-one and a two-to-one mapping, especially in worst-case scenarios.
- Simon's algorithm solves this problem in polynomial time, performing an optimal $\mathcal{O}(n)$ queries. Each query enriches the dataset of results by leveraging superposition, which means every individual query is exponentially informative compared to its classical counterpart. This stark contrast in the number of queries underscores the potential of quantum computing to revolutionize fields where query complexity is a significant bottleneck.
- Simon's algorithm requires some processing at the end, solving a system of linear equations in order to determine the find the solution. This step can be efficiently performed using Gaussian elimination, which operates in polynomial time with respect to the number of equations and unknowns.

Simon's oracle implements the unitary operation -

$$U_f |x\rangle |y\rangle = |x, y \oplus f(x)\rangle$$

If $y = 0$, then

$$U_f |x\rangle |0\rangle = |x, f(x)\rangle$$

We are going to use this result obtained in the circuit analysis for Simon's algorithm.

Quantum Circuit Analysis - Mathematical Derivation

To better understand Simon's algorithm, let us go through the quantum circuit analysis of the algorithm step by step, just as we have done for other algorithms. You will observe here that the steps are a bit different from those you have already learned.

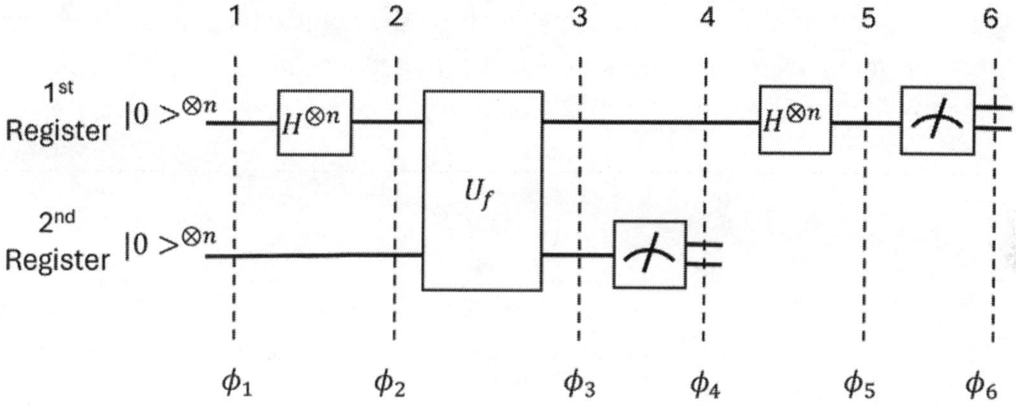

Figure 9.17: Quantum Circuit for Simon's Algorithm

Step 1:

Initially, two n-qubit registers are initialized to the zero state.

$$|\phi_1\rangle = |0\rangle^{\otimes n} |0\rangle^{\otimes n} \tag{9.36}$$

Step 2:

Apply Hadamard gates to the 1st register.

$$|\phi_2\rangle = \frac{1}{\sqrt{2^n}} \sum_{x \in \{0,1\}^n} |x\rangle |0\rangle^{\otimes n} \tag{9.37}$$

Step 3:

Apply the oracle function U_f.

$$|\phi_3\rangle = \frac{1}{\sqrt{2^n}} \sum_{x \in \{0,1\}^n} |x\rangle |f(x)\rangle \tag{9.38}$$

Step 4:

Measure the 2nd register. This measurement collapses the second register to a specific value, say $|f(x_0)\rangle$. According to the properties of f specified in Simon's algorithm, if f is two-to-one, exactly one other input $y_0 = x_0 \oplus s$ such that $f(y_0) = f(x_0)$ exists. For simplicity, we will keep the notations as x and y rather than x_0 and y_0, but the concept explained before remains the same.

Mathematically, The domain of f is $\{0,1\}^n$, tells us that the domain can be partitioned into two disjoint sets $\mathbb{R}$ and $\mathbb{R} \oplus s$ where $\mathbb{R}$ is any subset of the domain and $\mathbb{R} \oplus s$ is its coset by s.

$$\mathbb{Z}_{2^n} = \mathbb{R} \cup (\mathbb{R} \oplus s) \tag{9.39}$$

Now, $\mathbb{R} \oplus s$ is a coset of set $\mathbb{R}$. The cosets partition the domain into two sets where every element in one set maps to the same value under f as its partner in the other set.

This means that an element $x \in \mathbb{R}$ has a unique partner in $\mathbb{R} \oplus s$ satisfying

$$\begin{cases} x \\ x \oplus s \end{cases} \overset{f}{\leftrightarrow} f(x) \tag{9.40}$$

Each element in one coset pairs uniquely with an element from the other, both mapping to the same output; therefore, the value of $f(x)$ could correspond to x and $y = x \oplus s$ and the 1st register is collapsed to

$$|\phi_4\rangle = \frac{1}{\sqrt{2}}(|x\rangle + |y\rangle) \tag{9.41}$$

Step 5:

Apply Hadamard gates to the 1st register.

$$|\phi_5\rangle = \frac{1}{\sqrt{2^{n+1}}} \sum_{z\in\{0,1\}^n} [(-1)^{x\cdot z} + (-1)^{y\cdot z}]\,|z\rangle \tag{9.42}$$

Step 6:

Measuring the 1st register will give an output only if

$$(-1)^{x\cdot z} = (-1)^{y\cdot z} \tag{9.43}$$

The equation $(-1)^{x\cdot z} = (-1)^{y\cdot z}$ ensures that only those z values that are orthogonal to s (i.e., $s \cdot z = 0$ (mod 2)) will have constructive interference and thus a non-zero probability of being observed.

The condition leads to the following derivations.

$$x \cdot z = y \cdot z \tag{9.44}$$
$$x \cdot z = (x \oplus s) \cdot z \tag{9.45}$$
$$x \cdot z = x \cdot z \oplus s \cdot z \tag{9.46}$$
$$s \cdot z = 0(mod2) \tag{9.47}$$

A string z will be measured, whose inner product $s \cdot z = 0$. Thus, repeating the algorithm $\approx n$ times, we will be able to obtain n different values of z, and the following system of linear equations can be written.

$$s \cdot z_1 = 0 \tag{9.48}$$
$$s \cdot z_2 = 0 \tag{9.49}$$
$$\vdots \tag{9.50}$$
$$s \cdot z_n = 0 \tag{9.51}$$

The secret string s can be determined by the Gaussian Elimination technique.

Some important points to consider are

- A unique non-zero solution for s is only achievable under the condition that the measured vectors $z_1, z_2, .., z_n$ are linearly independent.
- The probability that $z_1, z_2, .., z_n$ are linearly independent is at least $\prod_{k=1}^{\infty}(1 - \frac{1}{2^k}) \cong 0.2888 > \frac{1}{4}$
- If we run the algorithm $3n$ times, the probability that we will obtain n linearly independent equations is at least $\frac{2}{3}$.

These probabilistic elements underscore the algorithm's quantum nature. The quantum measurements provide data that is inherently stochastic yet statistically sufficient to deduce s with high confidence under the framework of quantum mechanics.

Implementing Simon's Algorithm in Qiskit

Let us implement simon's algorithm using the above mentioned steps. Before we start, let us import all the necessary libraries from qiskit:

```
from qiskit import QuantumCircuit, transpile, assemble, QuantumRegister,
            ClassicalRegister
```

```
from qiskit.visualization import plot_histogram
from qiskit_aer import Aer
from qiskit.providers.basic_provider import BasicSimulator
import numpy as np
```

Let us assume the hidden bitstring to be '001'. In the following code we define the bitstring with 's', it should be also noted that lenght of s must be between 2 and 10. The above restriction in length of the bitstring in not universal and we use it for easy computational purpose. Also, all the numbers of the bitstring must be of either 0's or 1's.

```
s = "10" # the hidden bitstring

assert 1 < len(s) < 10, "The length of s must be between 2 and 19"

for c in s:
    assert c == "0" or c == "1", "s must be a bitstring of '0' and '1'"

n = len(s) #the length of the bitstring
```

In the next step, let us create the simon circuit to find the bitstring s. The number of qubits is 2*n, where n is the length of the bitstring, whereas the number of bits to measure the circuit is n. As suggested in equation 9 we start by applying hadamard gates to the qubits.

```
Step 1
# Creating registers
# qubits for querying the oracle and recording its output
qr = QuantumRegister(2*n)
# for recording the measurement on the first register of qr
cr = ClassicalRegister(n)

circuitName = "Simon"
simonCircuit = QuantumCircuit(qr, cr)

# Step 2
# Apply Hadamard gates before querying the oracle
for i in range(n):
    simonCircuit.h(qr[i])
```

```
# Apply barrier to mark the beginning of the blackbox function
simonCircuit.barrier()
simonCircuit.draw('mpl')
```

We now detail the construction of 1-to-1 and 2-to-1 permutation circuits of the blackbox function. Let us assume the blackbox function receives $|x\rangle|0\rangle$ as input. With regards to a predetermined s, the blackbox function writes its output to the second register so that it transforms the input to $|x\rangle|f_s(x)\rangle$ such that $f(x) = f(x \oplus s)$ for all $x \in \{0,1\}^n$.

Such a blackbox function can be realized by the following procedures.

- Copy the content of the first register to the second register.

$$|x\rangle|0\rangle \rightarrow |x\rangle|x\rangle \tag{9.52}$$

- (Creating 1-to-1 or 2-to-1 mapping) If s is not all-zero, then there is the least index j so that $s_j = 1$. If $x_j = 0$, then XOR the second register with s. Otherwise, do not change the second register.

$$|x\rangle|x\rangle \rightarrow |x\rangle|x \oplus s\rangle \text{ if } x_j = 0 \text{ for the least index } j \tag{9.53}$$

- (Creating random permutation) Randomly permute and flip the qubits of the second register.

$$|x\rangle|y\rangle \rightarrow |x\rangle|f_s(y)\rangle \tag{9.54}$$

Given here is the circuit of the blackbox function based on the above procedures.

```
# Create the oracle function of our secret string
# Since we are only setting the first qubit to be 1,
# we will only apply cx gates to the first qubit.
for idx in range(n):
    if(s[idx] == '1'):
        for count in range(n):
            simonCircuit.cx(idx, n + count)

simonCircuit.barrier()

simonCircuit.draw('mpl')
```

Next, we proceed with the sequential execution of the Simon algorithm by implementing the Hadamard gates on the first register and subsequently performing a measurement.

```
# Step 4 apply Hadamard gates to the first register
for i in range(n):
    simonCircuit.h(qr[i])

# Step 5 perform measurement on the first register
for i in range(n):
    simonCircuit.measure(qr[i], cr[i])

#draw the circuit
simonCircuit.draw('mpl')
```

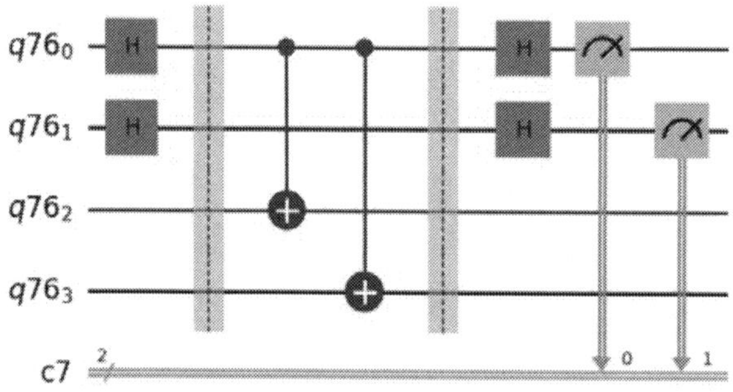

Figure 9.18: Circuit of Simons Algorithm

Now the final step is to execute the circuit on the BasicSimulator provided by Qiskit.

```
backend = BasicSimulator()
tqc = transpile(simonCircuit, backend)
counts = backend.run(tqc, shots=1000).result().get_counts()
plot_histogram(counts)
```

As we can see in the graph shown in *Figure* 9.19, we have two input register results - 00 and 01- for our secret string (s=10). String values are reversed in Qiskit, so 01 is actually '10', our secret string. If we had only '00' as the result then this would have meant that f is a one-to-one function. This would have been possible if s='00'. Since we have s='10', we know that f is a two-to-one function.

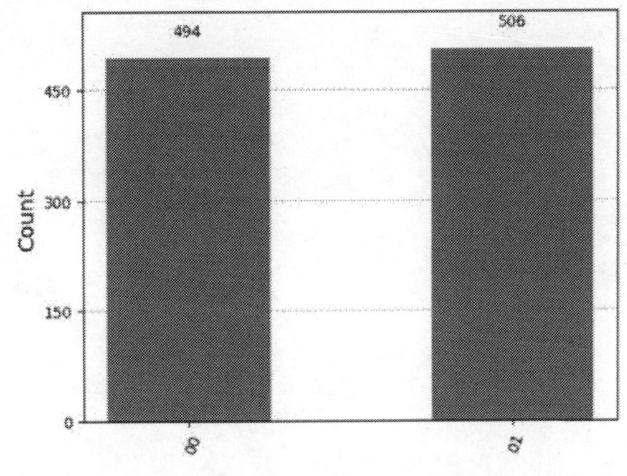

Figure 9.19: The histogram shows two equally probable outcomes, indicating the result of Simon's algorithm for the hidden string s=10. The algorithm identifies pairs of bitstrings differing by revealing the secret period with an exponential speedup over classical approaches. The two observed states confirm the periodic structure required for solving the problem efficiently.

Conclusion

This chapter has explored several fundamental algorithms in quantum computing, including Deutsch, Deutsch-Jozsa, Bernstein-Vazirani, and Simon's algorithms. By examining both the theoretical foundations and practical applications utilizing Qiskit, we have shown how these algorithms illustrate the superiority of quantum computing over classical computing. Every algorithm demonstrates distinct features of quantum computation, ranging from basic problem-solving to intricate oracle-based challenges, emphasizing the potency of quantum parallelism and interference. Gaining proficiency in these algorithms and their implementations establishes a strong basis for comprehending more sophisticated quantum algorithms and facilitates further investigation into the extensive capabilities of quantum computing.

In the next chapter, we will dive into more complex algorithms which form part of useful applications in quantum computing. We will also see an example of using transpilation for a complex quantum procedure.

CHAPTER 10

Quantum Algorithms Part II

Introduction

This chapter will examine several highly sophisticated and influential algorithms in the field of quantum computing, such as the Quantum Fourier Transform (QFT), Shor's algorithm, and Grover's search method. These algorithms demonstrate the revolutionary capacity of quantum computation, providing answers to problems that are impossible for traditional computers to solve. In addition, we will explore the process of designing and implementing variational quantum algorithms. These algorithms utilize a combination of quantum and classical methods to address intricate optimization issues. By comprehending the fundamental principles and practical uses of these sophisticated algorithms, we may fully grasp the significant consequences they have for various domains, such as cryptography and data retrieval, among others.

Structure

In this chapter, we are going to study:

- Quantum Fourier Transform (QFT)
    - Circuit Implementing QFT
- Implementing QFT using Qiskit
- Quantum Phase Estimation (QPE)
    - QPE Circuit Analysis
- Implementing QPE using Qiskit
- Shor's Algorithm
    - Protocol for Shor's Algorithm
    - Quantum Circuit Analysis - Shor's Algorithm
- Implementing Shor's Algorithm using Qiskit
- Applications of Shor's Algorithm
- Grover's Search Algorithm
    - Comparison with Classical Algorithms
    - Mathematical Derivation
- Grover's Search Algorithm - Pictorial Intuition
    - Step 1: Initial Superposition
    - Step 2: Oracle Operation
    - Step 3: Amplitude Amplification (Grover's Diffusion Operator)
    - Step 4: Grover's Iteration
    - Mathematical Derivation of Amplitude Amplification
- Implementation of Grover's Search Algorithm using Qiskit

Quantum Fourier Transform (QFT)

Quantum Fourier Transform is analogous to classical Fourier transform. In classical Fourier transform , converting the signal from the time domain to the frequency domain is the main concept. In Quantum Fourier transform, there is no signal involved. Usually the computations are performed in computational basis (bloch sphere) but these computations must be changed to Fourier basis , and that change from one basis to another is Quantum Fourier transform.

What is Computational basis?

Computational basis consists of all possible states that can be formed by arranging the qubits in states $|0\rangle$ and $|1\rangle$ states. The computational basis states for single qubits are $|0\rangle$ and $|1\rangle$. For a system of n qubits, computational basis include 2^n possible arrangements of n qubits in state $|0\rangle$ and $|1\rangle$ such as $|00\rangle$, $|01\rangle$, $|10\rangle$, $|11\rangle$ for two qubits. Depending upon the number of qubits, the states differ.

Every state in the computational basis corresponds directly to a binary number. This facilitates the translation between quantum states and the binary data often employed in classical computing.

What is Fourier basis?

In quantum computing, the Fourier basis is a set of states utilized in Quantum Fourier Transform (QFT) operations, which are the quantum equivalent of the discrete Fourier transform. This foundation is crucial for algorithms such as Shor's algorithm for factorizing huge numbers and the quantum phase estimation algorithm. It enables the representation and manipulation of quantum states in a manner that simplifies the extraction of periodicity and phase information.

For a n-qubit system, the computational basis are labeled as $|0\rangle$, $|1\rangle$ .... $2^n - 1$. The Fourier basis states for this system are obtained from the computational basis states via the quantum Fourier transform and are represented as $|u_k\rangle$ for k = 0,1,2..$2^n - 1$ where each $|u_k\rangle$ is a superposition of of all computational basis states with different amplitudes that depend on k.

Applications of QFT

The Fourier basis is crucial in quantum algorithms that involve analyzing periodic characteristics of functions for estimating phases.

In Shor's approach, the quantum Fourier transform is utilized to determine the period of a function, a crucial step in integer factorization.

The quantum phase estimation approach utilizes the Quantum Fourier Transform (QFT) to approximate the phase (eigenvalue) linked to an eigenvector of a unitary operator, with relevance in quantum simulations and various algorithms.

Key characteristics of Fourier Basis state

Let us see some of the key characteristics of the Fourier basis state

- **Superposition**
  Every Fourier basis state is a combination of all computational basis states, with complex coefficients that store phase information in a manner beneficial for quantum algorithms focusing on periodicity and phases.
- **Global Phase information**
  The Fourier basis is ideal for encoding and manipulating global phase information, which is essential to many quantum algorithms.
- **Amplitude**
  In simple QFT, the amplitudes are the same but vary by a phase that changes on the value of the Fourier basis state.

The general form of a Fourier basis state $|u_k\rangle$ in an n-qubit system can be expressed as:

$$|x_k\rangle = \frac{1}{\sqrt{N}} \sum_{y=0}^{N-1} e^{\frac{2\pi ixy}{N}} |y\rangle \tag{10.1}$$

Here, $|j\rangle$ represents the j-th computational basis state and the coefficient $e^{\frac{2\pi ijk}{2^n}}$ is a complex exponential determining the amplitude and phase of each $|j\rangle$ component in the superposition. The factor $\frac{1}{\sqrt{2^n}}$ ensures that the state $|u_k\rangle$ is properly normalized.

This represents the quantum state after applying the quantum Fourier transform to the basis state

$|x_k\rangle$ = This represents the quantum state after applying the quantum Fourier transform to the basis state. $|x_k\rangle$ is the superposition of all the basis states with coefficients determined by fourier transform.

$\frac{1}{\sqrt{N}}$ = This is a normalization factor that ensures the total probability amplitude of the state $|x_k\rangle$ sums to 1, making it a valid quantum state. Here, $N = 2^n$ where n is the number of qubits.

$\sum_{y=0}^{N-1}$ = This summation indicates that the state $|x_k\rangle$ is a superposition of all N basis states $|y\rangle$. Here, $|y\rangle$ ranges from 0 to N-1.

$e^{\frac{2\pi ixy}{N}}$ = This exponential term represents the complex amplitude of each $|y\rangle$ basis state in the superposition. The phase of this amplitude is determined by the fraction $\frac{2\pi ixy}{N}$ where i is the imaginary unit.

$|y\rangle$= These are the computational basis states of the system. In an n-qubit quantum computer, these states represent all possible configurations of n qubits, ranging from $|0\rangle$ to $|2^n - 1\rangle$.

Now, let us consider an example having 1 qubit. So, n = 1 which means $N = 2^1$. So, N = 2. Let us substitute this value in equation 10.1

$$|x_k\rangle = \frac{1}{\sqrt{2}} \sum_{y=0}^{2-1} e^{\frac{2\pi ixy}{2}} |y\rangle \tag{10.2}$$

$$|x_k\rangle = \frac{1}{\sqrt{2}} \sum_{y=0}^{1} e^{\frac{2\pi ixy}{2}} |y\rangle \tag{10.3}$$

Consider the Quantum Fourier Transform applied to a 1-qubit system, where $N = 2$. The QFT operation for a state $|x\rangle$ in this context is given by:

$$|x_k\rangle = \frac{1}{\sqrt{2}} \sum_{y=0}^{1} e^{\frac{2\pi ixy}{2}} |y\rangle \tag{10.4}$$

For a 1-qubit system ($N = 2$), there are two possible values of x = 0 and 1. The QFT transforms these basis states as follows:

For $x = 0$ (the state $|0\rangle$), the phase factor $e^{\frac{2\pi i \cdot 0 \cdot y}{2}} = e^0 = 1$. For, x=1, the phase becomes $e^{\pi i x}$

$$|x_k\rangle = \frac{1}{\sqrt{2}}(|0\rangle + e^{\pi i x} \cdot |1\rangle) \tag{10.5}$$

From *Equation* 10.5, if we apply x = 0 and 1 , the results are mind blowing.

For $x = 0$ (the state $|0\rangle$), the phase factor $e^{\frac{2\pi i \cdot 0 \cdot y}{2}} = e^0 = 1$ for all y, leading to the transformed state:

$$|0_k\rangle = \frac{1}{\sqrt{2}}(|0\rangle + |1\rangle) \tag{10.6}$$

For $x = 1$ (the state $|1\rangle$), the phase factor $e^{\frac{2\pi i \cdot 1 \cdot y}{2}}$ introduces a phase of $e^{\pi i y}$, which equals $+1$ for $y = 0$ and -1 for $y = 1$. This results in the transformed state:

$$|1_k\rangle = \frac{1}{\sqrt{2}}(|0\rangle - |1\rangle) \tag{10.7}$$

This transformation demonstrates the QFT's effect on a single qubit, mapping the computational basis states to their Fourier counterparts, which are superpositions of the computational basis states with specific phase relations.

Now, think for 3 qubits. The phase value will be changing but the value of y will be in the range $|0\rangle$, $|1\rangle$, $|2\rangle$ ...$|7\rangle$. Writing $|0\rangle$, $|1\rangle$ is the standarad form of representation but for $|3\rangle$, $|4\rangle$ how can one represent?

Compact form of fractional binary notation

$$y = y_1 y_2 \cdots y_n = \sum_{k=1}^{n} y_k 2^{-k} \tag{10.8}$$

Example, for $y_1 = 1$, $y_2 = 0$, $y_3 = 1$, $y_4 = 1$, we get the following

$$y = \frac{1}{2} + \frac{0}{4} + \frac{1}{8} + \frac{1}{16} = \frac{8}{16} + \frac{2}{16} + \frac{1}{16} = \frac{11}{16} \tag{10.9}$$

This can be written as 0.1011_2, which equals 0.6875 in decimal. The fractional binary notation will now be utilized to derive the mathematical expression of the QFT.

We start with the n-qubit QFT that is given by

$$|x_k\rangle = \frac{1}{\sqrt{N}} \sum_{y=0}^{N-1} e^{2\pi i x y / N} |y\rangle \tag{10.10}$$

Expanding *Equation* (10.10) using the binary fraction given in

$$|x\rangle = \frac{1}{\sqrt{N}} \sum_{y=0}^{N-1} e^{2\pi i (\sum_{k=1}^{n} y_k 2^{-k}) x} |y_1 y_2 \ldots y_n\rangle \tag{10.11}$$

Expanding the exponential of a sum to a product of exponentials:

$$\frac{1}{\sqrt{N}} \bigotimes_{k=1}^{n} \left(|0\rangle + e^{\frac{2\pi i x}{2^k}} |1\rangle\right) \tag{10.12}$$

After expanding the sum and products and employing the simplification of the sums:

$$\frac{1}{\sqrt{N}} \left(|0\rangle + e^{\frac{2\pi i x}{2}} |1\rangle\right) \otimes \left(|0\rangle + e^{\frac{2\pi i x}{2^2}} |1\rangle\right) \otimes \ldots \otimes \left(|0\rangle + e^{\frac{2\pi i x}{2^n}} |1\rangle\right) \tag{10.13}$$

Observe that $|x\rangle$ has a binary representation corresponding to the pattern $10\ldots0$ and so on.

By observing the expression, we can understand that each qubit went from

$$|x_k\rangle \text{ to } |0\rangle + e^{\frac{2\pi i x}{2^k}} |1\rangle \tag{10.14}$$

Two gates to construct QFT

1. Hadamard gate
2. U Rotation gate (UROT)

The Hadamard gate is necessary:

For $x_k = 0$:

$$H|x_k\rangle = \frac{1}{\sqrt{2}}(|0\rangle + |1\rangle)$$

This can be compactly written as:

$$|+\rangle$$

For $x_k = 1$:

$$H|x_k\rangle = \frac{1}{\sqrt{2}}(|0\rangle - |1\rangle)$$

This can be compactly written as:

$$|-\rangle$$

Applying the Hadamard gate to $|x_k\rangle$:

$$H|x_k\rangle = \frac{1}{\sqrt{2}}(|0\rangle + e^{\frac{2\pi i x_k}{2}}|1\rangle)$$

$$= \left(|0\rangle + e^{\frac{2\pi i x_k}{2}}|1\rangle\right) \cdot \frac{1}{\sqrt{2}}$$

So, for $e^{\frac{2\pi i x_k}{2}}$: When $x_k = 0$:

$$e^{\frac{2\pi i \cdot 0}{2}} = e^0 = 1 = |+\rangle$$

When $x_k = 1$:

$$e^{\frac{2\pi i \cdot 1}{2}} = e^{\pi i} = -1 = |-\rangle$$

The U_{ROT} gate is the 'controlled' rotation gate (applies phase):

$$U_{\text{ROT}_k}|x_j\rangle = e^{\frac{2\pi i}{2^k}x_j}|x_j\rangle$$

For $x_j = 0$:

$$e^{\frac{2\pi i}{2^k}\cdot 0}|0\rangle = e^0|0\rangle \Rightarrow |0\rangle$$

For $x_j = 1$:

$$e^{\frac{2\pi i}{2^k}\cdot 1}|1\rangle = e^{\frac{2\pi i}{2^k}}|1\rangle$$

Thus, the matrix representation of U_{ROT_k} is:

$$U_{\text{ROT}_k} = \begin{bmatrix} 1 & 0 \\ 0 & e^{\frac{2\pi i}{2^k}} \end{bmatrix}$$

The job of the matrix is to apply the phase $e^{\frac{2\pi i}{2^k}}$ for state $|1\rangle$.

Circuit Implementing QFT

We are going to study the quantum circuit that implements the QFT. As you have already seen, we need only two quantum gates to implement the full circuit, and therefore, it is very straightforward as we follow the original QFT mathematical derivation.

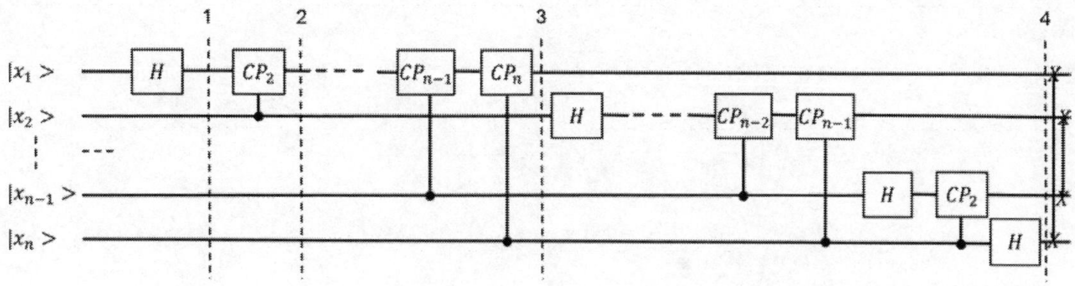

Figure 10.1: Quantum Circuit for Quantum Fourier Transform

Figure 10.1 shows the full QFT circuit with the Hadamard and the CP gates applied in a specific arrangement.

Step 1

Applying H-gate to $|x_1\rangle$

$$H|x_1\rangle \otimes |x_2x_3\dots x_n\rangle = \frac{1}{\sqrt{2}}\left(|0\rangle + e^{\frac{2\pi i x_1}{2}}|1\rangle\right) \otimes |x_2x_3\dots x_n\rangle \tag{10.15}$$

where $N = 2^n$, $N' = 2^{n-1}$, and $N'' = 2^{n-2}$.

Step 2

Applying CP gate with $|x_2\rangle$ as control and $|x_1\rangle$ as target

$$\frac{1}{\sqrt{2}}\left(|0\rangle + \exp\left(\frac{2\pi i x_2}{2^2} + \frac{2\pi i x_1}{2}\right)|1\rangle\right) \otimes |x_2x_3\dots x_n\rangle \tag{10.16}$$

Here, $\frac{2\pi i x_2}{2^2}$ phase is added to the existing phase.

Step 3 Applying the sequences of CP gates till the control is $|x_n\rangle$ with target on $|x_1\rangle$:

$$\frac{1}{\sqrt{2}}\left(|0\rangle + \exp\left(\frac{2\pi i}{2^n}x_n + \frac{2\pi i}{2^{n-1}}x_{n-1} + \dots + \frac{2\pi i}{2^2}x_2 + \frac{2\pi i}{2}x_1\right)|1\rangle\right) \otimes |x_2x_3\dots x_n\rangle \tag{10.17}$$

Also note that:

$$x = 2^{n-1}x_1 + 2^{n-2}x_2 + \dots + 2^0 x_n$$

Therefore:

$$\frac{1}{\sqrt{2}}\left(|0\rangle + \exp\left(\frac{2\pi i x}{2^n}\right)|1\rangle\right) \otimes |x_2x_3\dots x_n\rangle$$

Step 4

Performing steps 1 to 3 for qubits starting from $|x_2\rangle$ up to $|x_n\rangle$, we will get the following expression.

$$\frac{1}{\sqrt{2}}\left(|0\rangle + \exp\left(\frac{2\pi i x_1}{2^n}\right)|1\rangle\right) \otimes \frac{1}{\sqrt{2}}\left(|0\rangle + \exp\left(\frac{2\pi i x_2}{2^{n-1}}\right)|1\rangle\right) \otimes \cdots \tag{10.18}$$

$$\otimes \frac{1}{\sqrt{2}}\left(|0\rangle + \exp\left(\frac{2\pi i x_{n-1}}{2^2}\right)|1\rangle\right) \otimes \tag{10.19}$$

$$\frac{1}{\sqrt{2}}\left(|0\rangle + \exp\left(\frac{2\pi i x_n}{2}\right)|1\rangle\right) \tag{10.20}$$

The above is the final state in which the order of qubits are reversed in output state.

3 Qubit QFT

The steps to creating the circuit for $|y_3y_2y_1\rangle = QFT_8|x_3x_2x_1\rangle$ are as follows:

1. Apply a Hadamard gate to $|x_1\rangle$

$$|\psi_1\rangle = |x_3\rangle \otimes |x_2\rangle \otimes \frac{1}{\sqrt{2}}\left(|0\rangle + \exp\left(\frac{2\pi i}{2}x_1\right)|1\rangle\right) \tag{10.21}$$

2. Apply a $UROT_2$ gate to $|x_1\rangle$ depending on $|x_2\rangle$

$$|\psi_2\rangle = |x_3\rangle \otimes |x_2\rangle \otimes \frac{1}{\sqrt{2}}\left(|0\rangle + \exp\left(\frac{2\pi i}{2^2}x_2 + \frac{2\pi i}{2}x_1\right)|1\rangle\right) \tag{10.22}$$

3. Apply a $UROT_3$ gate to $|x_1\rangle$ depending on $|x_3\rangle$

$$|\psi_3\rangle = |x_3\rangle \otimes |x_2\rangle \otimes \frac{1}{\sqrt{2}}\left(|0\rangle + \exp\left(\frac{2\pi i}{2^3}x_3 + \frac{2\pi i}{2^2}x_2 + \frac{2\pi i}{2}x_1\right)|1\rangle\right) \tag{10.23}$$

4. Apply a Hadamard gate to $|x_2\rangle$

$$|\psi_4\rangle = |x_3\rangle \otimes \frac{1}{\sqrt{2}}\left(|0\rangle + \exp\left(\frac{2\pi i}{2}x_2\right)|1\rangle\right)$$
$$\otimes \frac{1}{\sqrt{2}}\left(|0\rangle + \exp\left(\frac{2\pi i}{2^3}x_3 + \frac{2\pi i}{2^2}x_2 + \frac{2\pi i}{2}x_1\right)|1\rangle\right) \tag{10.24}$$

5. Apply a $UROT_2$ gate to $|x_2\rangle$ depending on $|x_3\rangle$

$$|\psi_5\rangle = |x_3\rangle \otimes \frac{1}{\sqrt{2}}\left(|0\rangle + \exp\left(\frac{2\pi i}{2^2}x_3 + \frac{2\pi i}{2}x_2\right)|1\rangle\right)$$
$$\otimes \frac{1}{\sqrt{2}}\left(|0\rangle + \exp\left(\frac{2\pi i}{2^3}x_3 + \frac{2\pi i}{2^2}x_2 + \frac{2\pi i}{2}x_1\right)|1\rangle\right) \tag{10.25}$$

6. Apply a Hadamard gate to $|x_3\rangle$

$$|\psi_6\rangle = \frac{1}{\sqrt{2}}\left(|0\rangle + \exp\left(\frac{2\pi i}{2}x_3\right)|1\rangle\right) \otimes \frac{1}{\sqrt{2}}\left(|0\rangle + \exp\left(\frac{2\pi i}{2^2}x_3 + \frac{2\pi i}{2}x_2\right)|1\rangle\right) \otimes \frac{1}{\sqrt{2}}\left(|0\rangle + \exp\left(\frac{2\pi i}{2^3}x_3 + \frac{2\pi i}{2^2}x_2 + \frac{2\pi i}{2}x_1\right)|1\rangle\right) \tag{10.26}$$

Please remember that we need to reverse the qubits according to the little-endian system .

Implementing QFT in Qiskit

Now we focus on implementing QFT using Qiskit. First, we will see the coding of a simple QFT circuit. Then, we see a utility-scale and better-transpiled version of QFT and since the transpilation has already been covered in one of the previous chapters, therefore we will be focusing on the scaling up of QFT and coding it with better transpilation schemes.

Small-Scale QFT from Scratch

Let us first import all the necessary libraries before we start implementing QFT.

```
from qiskit import QuantumCircuit, transpile
from qiskit.visualization import plot_histogram, plot_bloch_multivector
from numpy import pi
from qiskit_aer import Aer
```

Now as we imported all the necessary libraries, let us define the function or circuit upon which QFT acts.

```
# Function to compute the QFT

def qft_rotations(circuit, n):
    if n == 0: # Exit function if circuit is empty
        return circuit
    n -= 1 # Indexes start from 0
    circuit.h(n) # Apply the H-gate to the most significant qubit
    for qubit in range(n):
        # For each less significant qubit, we need to do a
```

```
        # smaller-angled controlled rotation:
        circuit.cp(pi/2**(n-qubit), qubit, n)

    qft_rotations(circuit, n)
```

As we defined the fucntion `qft_rotations` above which takes quantum circuit and number of qubits as input, let us build the quantum circuit using the above defined function. In this example we take three qubits as an example. Please feel free to change it as required.

```
qc = QuantumCircuit(3)
qft_rotations(qc,3)
qc.draw('mpl')
```

The output of the preceding circuit is shown in the following image:

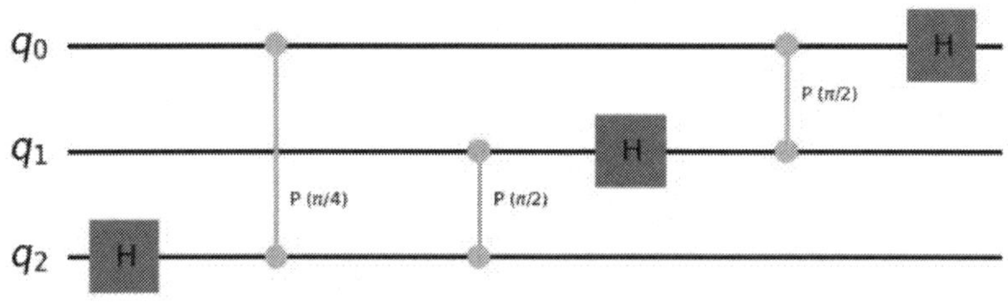

Figure 10.2: 3 Qubit QFT Circuit

Now, we write another function to swap the registers after QFT computation.

```
def swap_registers(circuit, n):
    for qubit in range(n//2):
        circuit.swap(qubit, n-qubit-1)
    return circuit
```

As we defined both the necessary functions above, let us club them to form a Quantum Fourier Transform. We write a separate function for this:

```
def qft(circuit, n):
    """QFT on the first n qubits in circuit"""
    qft_rotations(circuit, n)
    swap_registers(circuit, n)
    return circuit
```

Let us apply our QFT to a simple state, i.e., $|000\rangle$. The output state should be $|+++\rangle$. Let us examine whether the QFT written above is working:

We build a quantum circuit of three qubits and states initialized to 0's.

```
# QFT circuit for a 3 Qubit case at state |000>
qc = QuantumCircuit(3)
qft(qc,3)
qc.draw('mpl')
```

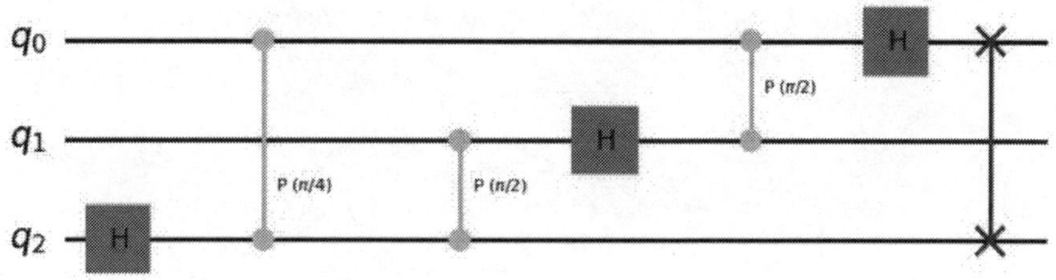

Figure 10.3: QFT applied to $|000\rangle$

Now, we run the above circuit on `statevector_simulator` . We shall also see the Bloch sphere of the three qubits so that we can verify the output.

```
backend = Aer.get_backend('statevector_simulator')
job = backend.run(transpile(qc, backend))
result = job.result()
statevector = result.get_statevector(qc, decimals=3)
print("\nQuantum state is:",statevector)
plot_bloch_multivector(statevector)
```

Result

So, the state received after applying QFT to $|000\rangle$ is $|+++\rangle$.

Bonus: Let us also code Inverse Quantum Fourier Transform. Inverse Quantum Fourier Transform , as the name suggests, is the inverse of Quantum Fourier Transform. To explain explicitly, let us take the output of the above Quantum Fourier Transform, which is $|+++\rangle$ and apply the inverse Fourier transform. The output which should be obvious is $|000\rangle$. Let us write the code and verify.

Let us build the inverse Fourier circuit.

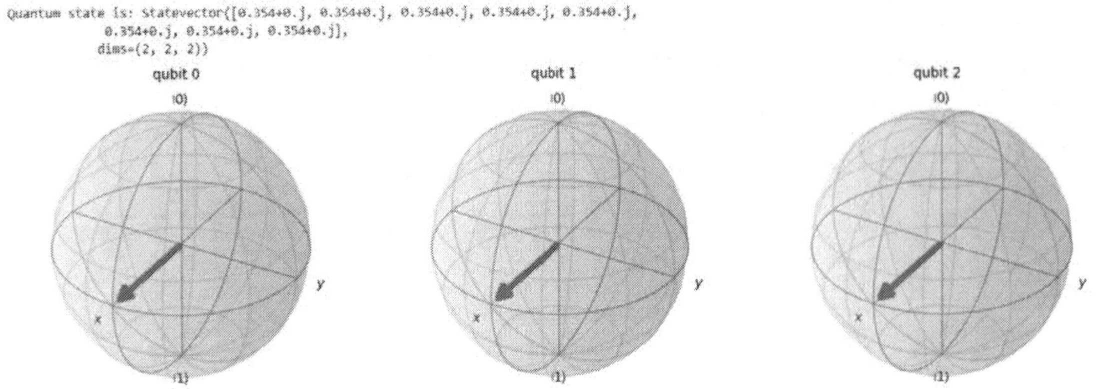

Figure 10.4: Output Bloch sphere of three qubits

```
def inverse_qft(circuit, n):
    """Does the inverse QFT on the first n qubits in circuit"""
    # First we create a QFT circuit of the correct size:
    qft_circ = qft(QuantumCircuit(n), n)
    # Then we take the inverse of this circuit
    invqft_circ = qft_circ.inverse()
    # And add it to the first n qubits in our existing circuit
    circuit.append(invqft_circ, circuit.qubits[:n])
    return circuit.decompose() # .decompose() allows us to see the individual
     ↪  gates
```

Now let us create the state $|+++\rangle$, which is the output of quantum Fourier transform:

```
nqubits = 3
qc = QuantumCircuit(nqubits)
for qubit in range(nqubits):
    qc.h(qubit)
qc.draw('mpl')
```

Now, let us apply inverse quantum fourier transform function that we built above 'inverse_qft' to the circuit we just designed.

```
# Calling the inverse QFT Function
qc = inverse_qft(qc, nqubits)
qc.measure_all()
qc.draw('mpl')
```

The final circuit is shown in the following figure:

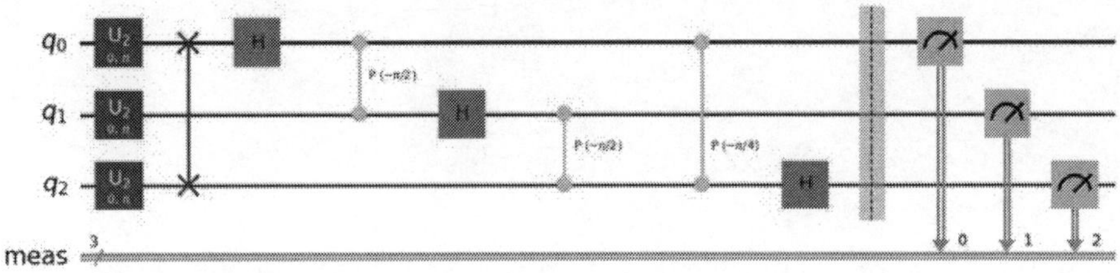

Figure 10.5: Inverse Quantum Fourier Transform

Let us now run this circuit on qasm simulator and validate the result ourselves. The output should be $|000\rangle$.

```
backend = Aer.get_backend('qasm_simulator')
job = backend.run(transpile(qc, backend))
result = job.result()
counts = result.get_counts(qc)
plot_histogram(counts)
```

Output after running the cirucit on qasm simulator is shown below:

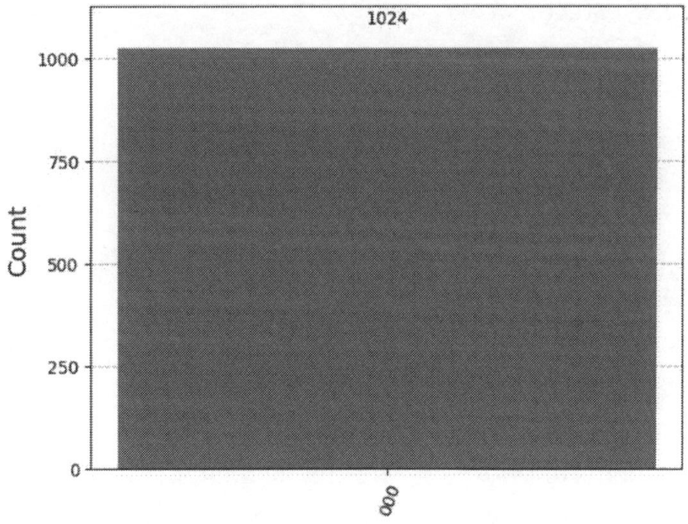

Figure 10.6: Inverse Quantum Fourier Transform Ouput

So, the state received after applying IQFT to $|+++\rangle$ is $|000\rangle$

In the latest version of qiskit, implementing QFT has become even more simpler. QFT has a separate class which makes our lives easier while using the algorithm. Let us take a look at another way of using QFT:

```
from qiskit.circuit.library import QFT
qft = QFT(num_qubits=3, do_swaps=True)
```

Given here are all the parameters of the QFT class:

- `num_qubits` - The number of qubits on which the QFT acts.
- `approximation_degree` - The degree of approximation (0 for no approximation).
- `do_swaps` - Whether to include the final swaps in the QFT.
- `inverse` - If True, the inverse Fourier transform is constructed.
- `insert_barriers` - If True, barriers are inserted as visualization improvement.
- `name` - The name of the circuit

Please run the following code yourself to check the result of the above defined qft using QFT class:

```
backend = Aer.get_backend('statevector_simulator')
job = backend.run(transpile(qft, backend))
result = job.result()
statevector = result.get_statevector(qft, decimals=3)
print("\nQuantum state is:",statevector)
plot_bloch_multivector(statevector)
```

The output states of all the three qubits should be $|+\rangle$ which means the overall output of the circuit is $|+++\rangle$.

Transpilation for QFT and Utility-Scale

Here we will go through the step-by-step implementation of transpilation for QFT and also see the code for utility scale. The steps mentioned here are closely related to what you have already learnt in one of the previous chapters where you saw the process of transpilation in full detail. Therefore, we are not again going to describe all the steps of transpilation but rather show how it is incorporated for QFT circuits. This will serve as an example for you to construct your circuit required in any kind of application and then transpile it efficiently to optimize quantum resources.

As always, first, we import the necessary functionalities that will be required later on.

```
from math import pi
from qiskit.circuit.library import QFT
from qiskit.providers.fake_provider import GenericBackendV2, generic_backend_v2
generic_backend_v2._NOISE_DEFAULTS["cx"] = (5.99988e-06, 6.99988e-06, 1e-5, 5e-3)

from qiskit import transpile, QuantumCircuit
from qiskit.circuit import Gate
from qiskit.converters import circuit_to_dag
from qiskit.transpiler import CouplingMap, StagedPassManager, PassManager,
↪  AnalysisPass,
TransformationPass
from qiskit.transpiler.preset_passmanagers import generate_preset_pass_manager
from qiskit.transpiler.preset_passmanagers.common import generate_unroll_3q,
generate_embed_passmanager
from qiskit.quantum_info import hellinger_fidelity
from qiskit.providers.basic_provider import BasicSimulator
from qiskit.dagcircuit import DAGCircuit
from qiskit_ibm_runtime.fake_provider import FakeTorino

# Transpiler Passes
## Layout passes
from qiskit.transpiler.passes.layout.csp_layout import CSPLayout
from qiskit.transpiler.passes.layout.dense_layout import DenseLayout
from qiskit.transpiler.passes.layout.sabre_layout import SabreLayout
from qiskit.transpiler.passes.layout.vf2_layout import VF2Layout
from qiskit.transpiler.passes.layout.trivial_layout import TrivialLayout

## Routing passes
from qiskit.transpiler.passes.routing.basic_swap import BasicSwap
from qiskit.transpiler.passes.routing.lookahead_swap import LookaheadSwap
from qiskit.transpiler.passes.routing.sabre_swap import SabreSwap
from qiskit.transpiler.passes.routing.stochastic_swap import StochasticSwap
from qiskit.transpiler.passes.routing.star_prerouting import StarPreRouting

## Synthesis passes (passes for the translation stage)
from qiskit.circuit import SessionEquivalenceLibrary
```

```
from qiskit.circuit.equivalence_library import SessionEquivalenceLibrary
from qiskit.transpiler.passes.basis.basis_translator import BasisTranslator
from qiskit.transpiler.passes.synthesis.high_level_synthesis import
↪  HighLevelSynthesis
### The next pass could also be considered an optimization pass.
from qiskit.transpiler.passes.synthesis.unitary_synthesis import UnitarySynthesis

## Optimization passes
from qiskit.transpiler.passes.optimization.collect_1q_runs import Collect1qRuns
from qiskit.transpiler.passes.optimization.collect_2q_blocks import
↪  Collect2qBlocks
from qiskit.transpiler.passes.optimization.consolidate_blocks import
↪  ConsolidateBlocks
from qiskit.transpiler.passes.optimization.commutative_cancellation import
CommutativeCancellation
```

In order to keep the computations simple, let us work on a small QFT circuit that can be scaled later on as per necessity.

First, we define the QFT circuit of 10 qubits with no swaps. Then, we have defined a function `get_qc_characteristics()` that determines the number of qubits needed by a quantum circuit (to be stored in the variable `num_qubits`, the quantity and kind of quantum gates (to be stored in the variable ops), the depth of a quantum circuit (to be stored in the variable `depth`, and the number of multi-qubit operations (to be stored in the variable textbf `num_multi_qubit_ops`. The longest chain of quantum gates from the beginning to the end of a quantum circuit that must be computed sequentially is known as the depth of a quantum circuit, and it represents the amount of time needed to execute a quantum circuit on a quantum computer.

Finally, we define a function `print_qc_characteristics()` in order to print the relevant characteristics of our QFT circuit.

```
# get an abstract quantum circuit from Qiskit's library of circuits
num_qubits = 10
qc = QFT(num_qubits, do_swaps=False)
#qc.draw()
def get_qc_characteristics(qc):
    # determine the quantum circuit depth of `qc` and assign it to `depth`
```

```
    depth = qc.depth()
    # determine the number of qubits in `qc` and assign it to `num_qubits`
    num_qubits = qc.num_qubits
    # determine the operations in `qc` and assign it to `ops`
    ops = qc.count_ops()
    # determine the number of n-qubit operations (with n larger than 1) in `qc`
    ↪  and
    assign it to
    #`num_multi_qubit_ops`,
    num_multi_qubit_ops = qc.num_nonlocal_gates()
    return {"depth": depth, "num_qubits": num_qubits, "ops": ops,
    ↪  "num_multi_qubit_ops":
    num_multi_qubit_ops}
def print_qc_characteristics(qc):
    characteristics = get_qc_characteristics(qc)
    print("Quantum circuit characteristics")
    print("  Depth:", characteristics['depth'])
    print("  Number of qubits:", characteristics['num_qubits'])
    print("  Operations:", dict(characteristics['ops']))
    print("  Number of multi-qubit Operations:",
    ↪  characteristics['num_multi_qubit_ops'])
print_qc_characteristics(qc)
```

Since this quantum circuit only has one operation—QFT—that is defined over `num_qubits` qubits with a depth of one gate, it is not hardware-compliant. Because the quantum circuit requires one QFT operation, which requires `num_qubits` qubits to interact simultaneously, to be supported by a target quantum computer, it is not hardware-compliant. As of right now, no quantum computer has a basis gate set that includes such a QFT operation. Rather, this kind of operation needs to be converted to the target quantum computer's basis gate set.

Now let us see the decomposition of the QFT circuit that is offered by Qiskit. Hadamard (H) gates and a single controlled-phase two-qubit gate, placed in a specific structure that repeats from the bottom qubit to the top qubit, are included in the default QFT quantum circuit decomposition between each pair of qubits. One way to conceptualize this structure would be a harp or star; a two-qubit gate connects the 'center' qubit to the first qubit above it, and so on until the top qubit is reached. Since not all quantum computers enable the controlled-phase gate and because the default QFT quantum circuit decomposition necessitates unrestricted qubit-connectivity, quantum circuit transpilation is necessary.

Next, we make the `GenericBackendV2` as our primary backend and by printing the basis gate sets we can see that it supports 'cx', 'id', 'rz', 'sx', 'x', 'reset', 'delay' and 'measure' basis gates. This universal set of basis quantum gates is sufficient to perform any quantum computation in principle. As you might have observed that the QFT operation is not directly supported by the quantum computer backend and this is where transpilation is a very important step to perform.

Once you draw and print out the characteristics of `qc_synth` you can see that every pair of qubits in a quantum circuit created by transpilation has a two-qubit quantum gate between them. By default, a coupling map with all-to-all connected qubits is included in the description of the `backend`. Transpile a quantum circuit with a linear coupling map `cm` of type `CouplingMap` for the same basis gate set and qubit count as the backend. A qubit with index i is only coupled to its immediate neighbour, a qubit with index i+1, in a coupling map. There are multiple ways to pass the coupling map to Qiskit's transpilation. It should be noted that the `basis_gates` and `coupling_map` arguments in `generate_preset_pass_manager` are subordinate to the `backend` parameter; that is, if the `backend` is set, the latter parameters are disregarded.

```
qc_dec = qc.decompose()
get_qc_characteristics(qc_dec)
#qc_dec.draw(fold=-1)
backend = GenericBackendV2(num_qubits)
#print("Supported basis gates:", backend.operation_names)
qc_synth = generate_preset_pass_manager(2, backend=backend).run(qc)
qc_synth.draw(fold=-1)
#print_qc_characteristics(qc_synth)
# assign a 10-qubit linear `CouplingMap` to the variable cm
cm = CouplingMap([[0, 1], [1, 2], [2, 3], [3, 4], [4, 5], [5, 6], [6, 7], [7, 8],
[8, 9]])
qc_routed = transpile(qc, coupling_map=cm, basis_gates=['u1', 'u2', 'u3', 'cx'])
```

Our objective is to demonstrate a hardware-compliant Quantum Field Theory (QFT) quantum circuit that has a minimum of 20% fewer two-qubit quantum gates compared to the quantum circuit generated by Qiskit's default transpilation.

To this end, we implement a staged pass manager and systematically fill the separate stages to direct and construct the quantum circuit. However, we also select one or more appropriate passes for each stage later in order to reduce the number of two-qubit quantum gates in the output circuit by 20% compared to Qiskit's default transpilation.

We commence the routing process by allocating a routing pass to a suitable stage of `pm_staged`.

```
pm_staged = StagedPassManager()
# replace the n-qubit QFT operation with its decomposition in two-qubit gates
pm_staged.init = generate_unroll_3q(None)
# initialize the layout stage with an empty pass manager
pm_staged.layout = PassManager()
# set a 'trivial' initial layout, i.e. each qubit in the quantum circuit with
↪ index i
# is mapped to the physical qubit on a device with the same index
pm_staged.layout += TrivialLayout(cm)
pm_staged.layout += generate_embed_passmanager(cm)
routing_pass = StochasticSwap(coupling_map=cm)
pm_staged.routing = PassManager((routing_pass))
qc_routed = pm_staged.run(qc)
print_qc_characteristics(qc_routed)
qc_routed.draw(fold=-1)
```

It should be noted that the two-qubit quantum gates in the QFT quantum circuit are only present between adjacent qubits. In other words, the quantum circuit can only be run on qubits that are linked in a linear array.

A quantum circuit must be designed using the basis gate set of the backend in order to ensure hardware compatibility with a quantum computer specified by the backend. It is possible to achieve this by allocating a suitable pass to a stage of `pm_staged`.

The quantum circuit `qc_routed_synth` is now compatible with the quantum computer as specified in the backend implementation and can be operated directly. Yet, by printing the characteristics we see that `qc_routed_synth` is far larger than Qiskit's default transpiler.

Within a physical device, this disparity in circuit size can determine whether a quantum circuit is executed successfully or produces an incorrect result. Using Qiskit, we can simulate the noise present in actual devices to compare the performance of Qiskit's default transpiler with our transpiler, as measured by the Hellinger fidelity.

We get our own transpiler fidelity of 0.231 and the Qiskit transpiler fidelity of 0.5694.

```
basis_gates = ['cx', 'id', 'rz', 'sx', 'x', 'reset', 'delay', 'measure']
translation_pass = BasisTranslator(SessionEquivalenceLibrary, basis_gates)
```

```
pm_staged.translation = PassManager(translation_pass)
qc_routed_synth = pm_staged.run(qc)
#print_qc_characteristics(qc_routed_synth)
#qc_routed_synth.draw(fold=-1)
qk_qc = generate_preset_pass_manager(2, backend=backend).run(qc)
#print_qc_characteristics(qk_qc)

def noisy_sim(qc, backend):
    return backend.run(qc.measure_all(inplace=False), shots=7 * 1024).result()
    .get_counts()
own_transpiler_sim = noisy_sim(qc_routed_synth, backend)
qiskit_transpiler_sim = noisy_sim(qk_qc, backend)
reference_sim = noisy_sim(transpile(qc.decompose(), backend=backend), \\
↪  BasicSimulator())
print("Own transpiler fidelity", round(hellinger_fidelity(own_transpiler_sim,
reference_sim), 4))
print("Qiskit transpiler fidelity", round(hellinger_fidelity
(qiskit_transpiler_sim, reference_sim), 4))
```

We try to reduce the QFT quantum circuit size after transpilation by at least 20% compared to Qiskit's default transpilation. Note that you can achieve this reduction in circuit size by only using a suitable selection of passes included in Qiskit. It is not necessary to create a new pass.

We start by creating the `StagedPassManager()` and defining the init stage as the decomposition of QFT in terms of two-qubit gates. Then we initialize the layout stage with an empty pass manager and set the layout as `TrivialLayout` with the coupling map of our backend. Considering our circuit is star-shaped we use `StarPreRouting()` for routing purpose. After this we we perform the translation operation based on our backend basis gate set.

It should be noted that a block consisting of two-qubit and single-qubit gates constructed on a pair of qubits requires a maximum of three CX gates and up to eight single-qubit gates. Since our quantum circuit has two-qubit blocks with more CX gates, we apply `Collect2qBlocks()`, `ConsolidateBlocks()` and `UnitarySynthesis()` to rectify it. We run our quantum circuit and print out the relevant characteristics and Hellinger fidelity values.

```
pm_opt = StagedPassManager()
pm_opt.init = generate_unroll_3q(None)
pm_opt.layout = PassManager()
pm_opt.layout += TrivialLayout(cm)
pm_opt.layout += generate_embed_passmanager(cm)
pm_opt.routing = PassManager(StarPreRouting())
pm_opt.translation = PassManager(BasisTranslator(SessionEquivalenceLibrary,
['cx', 'id', 'rz', 'sx', 'x', 'reset', 'delay', 'measure']))
pm_opt.optimization = PassManager(
    [
        Collect2qBlocks(),
        ConsolidateBlocks(),
        UnitarySynthesis(basis_gates)
    ]
)
print_qc_characteristics(qc_opt)
reduction_ratio =
↪   round(100-100*(get_qc_characteristics(qc_opt)['num_multi_qubit_ops']/
get_qc_characteristics(qk_qc)['num_multi_qubit_ops']), 3)
print("Reduction in two-qubit gates compared to qiskit
↪   {}%!".format(reduction_ratio))
qc_opt.draw(fold=-1)
opt_transpiler_sim = noisy_sim(qc_opt, backend)
print("Own transpiler fidelity",
↪   round(hellinger_fidelity(own_transpiler_sim,reference_sim)
, 4))
print("Qiskit transpiler fidelity",
↪   round(hellinger_fidelity(qiskit_transpiler_sim,
reference_sim), 4))
print("Own optimized transpiler fidelity", round(hellinger_fidelity
(opt_transpiler_sim,
reference_sim), 4))
```

After printing the Hellinger scores, we see that our transpilation has now a value of 0.9034 which is far greater than the default Qiskit transpilation. Now as an exercise, increase the number of qubits to 100, apply some more transpilation optimization techniques and run this QFT on a real quantum backend.

Now let us try to extend the transpilation capabilities of Qiskit by developing our transpiler passes. Once a transpiler pass is included in Qiskit, other users have the ability to include it into their own custom transpiler, resulting in hardware-compliant quantum circuits with a smaller size, similar to the prior exercise. Transpiler passes can be categorized into two main types: analysis passes, which are used to determine a certain property or quantity of a given quantum circuit, and transformation passes, which are used to modify or transform a selected quantum circuit.

Transpiler passes in general executes calculations on a graph data structure known as the `DAGCircuit` and save information in a `property_set`. Transformation passes yield a `DAGCircuit`, whereas analysis passes only store the identified information in a `property_set` without generating a `DAGCircuit` representation.

First, we make an analysis pass that determines the number of two-qubit gates and single-qubit gates on each qubit and stores it in the `property_set` using the keys `one_q_op` and `two_q_op` respectively. For each of these keys, a dictionary is added to the `property_set` where the dictionary contains each qubit as a key and the respective gate count of the qubit as a value which means the type of both dictionaries should be `Dict[Qubit,int]`.

```
class GatesPerQubit(AnalysisPass):
    def run(self, dag):
        # Initialize dictionaries for one-qubit and two-qubit gate counts
        one_q_op = {qubit: 0 for qubit in dag.qubits}
        two_q_op = {qubit: 0 for qubit in dag.qubits}
        # Iterate over all operation nodes in the DAG
        for node in dag.op_nodes():
            if node.op.num_qubits == 1:
                # Increment the count for the corresponding qubit
                one_q_op[node.qargs[0]] += 1
            elif node.op.num_qubits == 2:
                # Increment the count for both qubits involved in the two-qubit
                ↪ gate
                two_q_op[node.qargs[0]] += 1
                two_q_op[node.qargs[1]] += 1
        # Store the counts in the property set
        self.property_set["one_q_op"] = one_q_op
        self.property_set["two_q_op"] = two_q_op
        # Return the unmodified DAG
```

```
        return dag
# The QFT circuit
qc = QFT(4, do_swaps=False)
# Run the preset pass manager to transpile the circuit
qc = generate_preset_pass_manager(2, backend=backend).run(qc)
# An instance of the custom analysis pass
gpq = GatesPerQubit()
# Run the custom analysis pass on the transpiled circuit
pm = PassManager(gpq)
pm.run(qc)
qc = QFT(4, do_swaps=False)
qc = generate_preset_pass_manager(2, backend=backend).run(qc)
gpq = GatesPerQubit()
gpq(qc)
print("single-qubit gates on qubit", gpq.property_set["one_q_op"])
print("two-qubit gates on qubit", gpq.property_set["two_q_op"])
qc.draw(fold=-1, idle_wires=False)
```

Furthermore, our objective is to not only collect data on a quantum circuit but also modify it to ensure alignment with the hardware requirements of an IBM quantum computer.

Now we write the `TransformationPass` to define a quantum circuit transformation and run it on a certain input circuit that includes 'Peres' quantum gates.

Peres quantum gates are not included by default in Qiskit and cannot be used directly on an IBM quantum computer. Rather, they need to be swapped out in the input quantum circuit for gates from the destination quantum computer's basis gate set, or
`backend.operation_names=['reset', 'delay', 'measure', 'cx', 'id', 'rz', 'sx', 'x']`

The 'Peres' quantum gate (PG) is defined on three qubits as

$$PG = \begin{pmatrix} 1 & 0 & 0 & 0 & 0 & 0 & 0 & 0 & 0 & 0 \\ 0 & 1 & 0 & 0 & 0 & 0 & 0 & 0 & 0 & 0 \\ 0 & 0 & 1 & 0 & 0 & 0 & 0 & 0 & 0 & 0 \\ 0 & 0 & 0 & 1 & 0 & 0 & 0 & 0 & 0 & 0 \\ 0 & 0 & 0 & 0 & 0 & 0 & 0 & 0 & 1 & 0 \\ 0 & 0 & 0 & 0 & 0 & 0 & 0 & 0 & 0 & 1 \\ 0 & 0 & 0 & 0 & 0 & 0 & 0 & 1 & 0 & 0 \\ 0 & 0 & 0 & 0 & 0 & 0 & 1 & 0 & 0 & 0 \end{pmatrix} \quad (10.27)$$

and within Qiskit as a `Gate` object.

With the use of Peres gates (PG), controlled-X (CX) swap gates, and a Quantum Fourier Transform (QFT), the `get_qc_in` function builds a quantum circuit. To start, the circuit builds a QFT on nq qubits without swaps and adds it to the circuit as a whole `qc_in`. Subsequently, it applies a number of CX gates that effectively switch pairs of qubits to the qubits, after which it applies a series of Peres gates, a kind of three-qubit gate. The circuit incorporates an additional set of Peres gates and repeats the CX swap operations after applying a phase rotation (RZ gate) to the final qubit. In the end, the circuit applies the inverse QFT to close it. For jobs involving quantum phase estimation or other algorithms requiring QFT and qubit swaps, the function returns the entire quantum circuit.

```
pg = Gate('Peres', 3, params=[], label='PG')
qc_pg = QuantumCircuit(3)
qc_pg.append(pg, [0, 1, 2])
#qc_pg.draw()
def get_qc_in(nq):
    # QFT circuit
    qc_qft = QFT(nq, do_swaps=False)
    # part of the circuit including the Peres gate
    qc_inner = QuantumCircuit(nq)
    for i in range(1, nq - 1):
        qc_inner.append(pg, [nq - i - 2, nq - i - 1, nq - 1])
    qc_in = QuantumCircuit(nq)
    # add QFT circuit to qc_in
    qc_in.compose(qc_qft, range(nq), inplace=True)
    # perform swap gates
    for i in range(nq // 2):
        qc_in.cx(i, nq - i - 1)
        qc_in.cx(nq - i - 1, i)
        qc_in.cx(i, nq - i - 1)
    qc_in.rz(pi, nq - 1)
    # add circuit with peres gates
    qc_in.compose(qc_inner, range(nq), inplace=True)
    # perform swap gates
    for i in range(nq // 2):
        qc_in.cx(i, nq - i - 1)
        qc_in.cx(nq - i - 1, i)
```

```
        qc_in.cx(i, nq - i - 1)
    # add inverse QFT circuit
    qc_in.compose(qc_qft.inverse(), range(nq), inplace=True)
    return qc_in
nq = 5
qc_in = get_qc_in(nq)
qc_in.draw(fold=-1)
```

We looked into how to make the QFT circuit consistent with the target quantum computer's basis gate set in the earlier code cell. We will create a transformation pass for the remaining `qc_in` gates in this experiment. To construct the TransformationPass, use the decomposition found in the method `get_peres_decomposition`.

```
class PeresGateTranslation(TransformationPass):
    def get_peres_decomposition(self):
        qcsx = QuantumCircuit(2)
        qcsx.rz(math.pi / 4, 0)
        qcsx.rz(math.pi / 2, 1)
        qcsx.sx(1)
        qcsx.rz(math.pi / 2, 1)
        qcsx.cx(0, 1)
        qcsx.rz(-math.pi / 4, 1)
        qcsx.cx(0, 1)
        qcsx.rz(3 * math.pi / 4, 1)
        qcsx.sx(1)
        qcsx.rz(math.pi / 2, 1)

        qcsx_inv = QuantumCircuit(2)
        qcsx_inv.rz(math.pi / 4, 1)
        qcsx_inv.cx(0, 1)
        qcsx_inv.rz(-math.pi / 4, 1)
        qcsx_inv.cx(0, 1)
        qcsx_inv.rz(math.pi / 2, 0)
        qcsx_inv.rz(math.pi / 2, 1)
        qcsx_inv.cx(0, 1)
        qcsx_inv.rz(math.pi / 2, 1)
        qcsx_inv.sx(1)
```

```
        qcsx_inv.rz(-3 * math.pi / 4, 1)
        qcsx_inv.sx(1)
        qcsx_inv.cx(0, 1)
        qcsx_inv.sx(1)
        qcsx_inv.rz(-3 * math.pi / 4, 1)
        qcsx_inv.sx(1)
        qcsx_inv.rz(-3 * math.pi / 4, 1)
        qcsx_inv.cx(0, 1)
        qcsx_inv.rz(-math.pi / 4, 1)
        qcsx_inv.cx(0, 1)
        qcsx_inv.rz(math.pi / 4, 0)

        qc_dec = QuantumCircuit(3)
        qc_dec.cx(0, 1)
        qc_dec.cx(1, 0)
        qc_dec.cx(0, 1)
        qc_dec.compose(qcsx, [1, 2], inplace=True)
        qc_dec.cx(0, 1)
        qc_dec.cx(1, 0)
        qc_dec.cx(0, 1)
        qc_dec.compose(qcsx, [1, 2], inplace=True)
        qc_dec.cx(0, 1)
        qc_dec.compose(qcsx_inv, [1, 2], inplace=True)
        qc_dec.cx(0, 1)
        qc_dec.cx(0, 1)
        return qc_dec
    def run(self, dag: DAGCircuit) -> DAGCircuit:
        for node in dag.op_nodes():
            if node.op.name == 'Peres':
                # Get the Peres gate decomposition
                qc_dec = self.get_peres_decomposition()
                dag_dec = circuit_to_dag(qc_dec)
                # Replace the Peres gate with its decomposition
                dag.substitute_node_with_dag(node, dag_dec)
        return dag
# Instantiate the custom transformation pass
```

```
peres_gate_translation = PeresGateTranslation()
# Apply the custom transformation pass to the circuit
pm = PassManager(peres_gate_translation)
qc_transformed = pm.run(qc_in)
# Verify the transformation
qc_transformed.draw(fold=-1)
```

With this, we have now finished the hands-on coding of QFT transpilation and now you will be confident to apply and explore these techniques in your own quantum applications.

Quantum Phase Estimation (QPE)

One of the applications of QFT is Quantum Phase estimation (QPE). Quantum Phase Estimation (QPE) is a technique designed to calculate the phase (or eigenvalue) of an eigenstate produced by a unitary operator. Accurate estimates are essential for numerous quantum algorithms that rely on understanding the eigenvalues of a unitary operation. The technique utilizes the Quantum Fourier Transform (QFT) as a subprogram to translate the phase information encoded in the quantum state into a legible format. Quantum Phase Estimation (QPE) extends the use of Quantum Fourier Transform (QFT) to calculate phases, which can be applied to tasks such as factoring and computing discrete logarithms.

QPE Circuit Analysis

Here, we mathematically derive the results of the quantum phase estimation circuit step-by-step, as we have done previously for other algorithms.

Figure 10.7 shows the quantum circuit of the QPE. The first register, referred to as the auxiliary/counting register, is initialized to $|0\rangle$ and the second register, known as the target register, stores the quantum state $|\psi\rangle$.

Step 0: Preparation

We start with an n-qubit auxiliary register initialized to $|0\rangle^{\otimes n}$ and a target register in the state $|\psi\rangle$, an eigenvector of U. The initial state is:

$$|\Psi_0\rangle = |0\rangle^{\otimes n} \otimes |\psi\rangle$$

Step 1: Applying Hadamard Gates

Apply a n-bit Hadamard gate operation $H^{\otimes n}$ on the counting register:

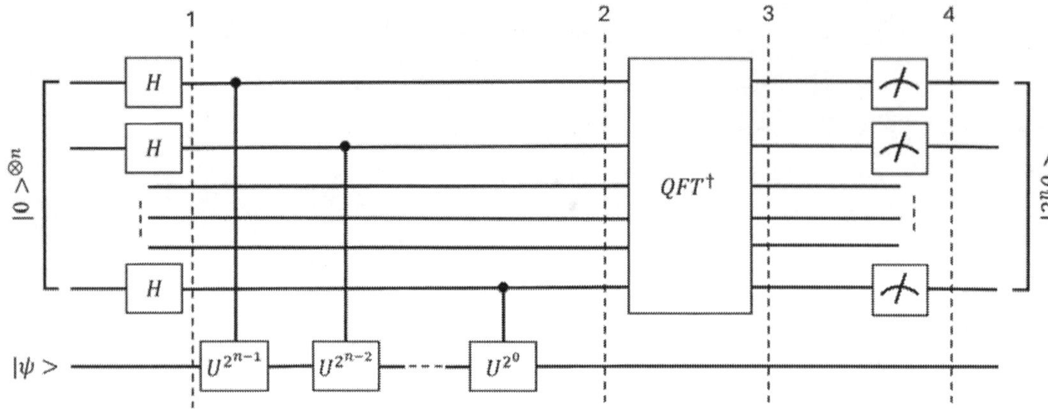

Figure 10.7: Quantum Circuit for Quantum Phase Estimation

$$|\psi_1\rangle = \frac{1}{2^{\frac{n}{2}}} \left(|0\rangle + |1\rangle\right)^{\otimes n} |\psi\rangle$$

Step 2: Controlled-U Operation

Remember that phase estimation algorithm doesn't give accurate estimation of θ unless you take high powers of U.

We can assume that we have some kind of circuit that will compute U^{2^j} in polynomial time in j.

We need to introduce the controlled unitary CU that applies the unitary operator U on the target register only if its corresponding control bit is $|1\rangle$. Since U is a unitary operator with eigenvector $|\psi\rangle$ such that $U|\psi\rangle = e^{\mathbf{2\pi i\theta}}|\psi\rangle$, this means:

$$U^{2^j}|\psi\rangle = U^{2^j-1}U|\psi\rangle = U^{2^j-1}e^{2\pi i\theta}|\psi\rangle = \cdots = e^{2\pi i 2^j \theta}|\psi\rangle$$

Applying all the n controlled operations CU^{2^j} with $0 \leq j \leq n-1$, and using the relation $|0\rangle \otimes |\psi\rangle + |1\rangle \otimes e^{2\pi i\theta}|\psi\rangle = \left(|0\rangle + e^{2\pi i\theta}|1\rangle\right) \otimes |\psi\rangle$:

$$|\psi_2\rangle = \frac{1}{2^{\frac{n}{2}}} \left(|0\rangle + e^{\mathbf{2\pi i\theta 2^{n-1}}}|1\rangle\right) \otimes \cdots \otimes \left(|0\rangle + e^{\mathbf{2\pi i\theta 2^1}}|1\rangle\right) \otimes \left(|0\rangle + e^{\mathbf{2\pi i\theta 2^0}}|1\rangle\right) \otimes |\psi\rangle$$

$$= \frac{1}{2^{\frac{n}{2}}} \sum_{k=0}^{2^n-1} e^{\mathbf{2\pi i\theta k}}|k\rangle \otimes |\psi\rangle$$

where k denotes the integer representation of n-bit binary numbers.

Step 3: Inverse Quantum Fourier Transform (QFT)

Following is the action of QFT on $|x\rangle$

$$QFT|x\rangle = \frac{1}{2^{\frac{n}{2}}}\left(|0\rangle + e^{\frac{2\pi i}{2}x}|1\rangle\right) \otimes \left(|0\rangle + e^{\frac{2\pi i}{2^2}x}|1\rangle\right) \otimes \ldots \otimes \left(|0\rangle + e^{\frac{2\pi i}{2^{n-1}}x}|1\rangle\right) \otimes \left(|0\rangle + e^{\frac{2\pi i}{2^n}x}|1\rangle\right)$$

Replacing x by $2^n\theta$ in the given expression gives exactly the expression derived in step 2 above. Therefore, to recover the state $|2^n\theta\rangle$, apply an inverse Fourier transform on the auxiliary register. Doing so, we find

$$|\psi_3\rangle = \frac{1}{2^{\frac{n}{2}}}\sum_{k=0}^{2^n-1} e^{\mathbf{2\pi i\theta k}}|k\rangle \otimes |\psi\rangle \xrightarrow{\mathcal{QFT}_n^{-1}} \frac{1}{2^n}\sum_{x=0}^{2^n-1}\sum_{k=0}^{2^n-1} e^{-\frac{2\pi ik}{2^n}(x-2^n\theta)}|x\rangle \otimes |\psi\rangle$$

Step 4: Measurement

The above expression peaks near $x = 2^n\theta$. For the case when $2^n\theta$ is an integer, measuring in the computational basis gives the phase in the auxiliary register with high probability:

$$|\psi_4\rangle = |2^n\theta\rangle \otimes |\psi\rangle$$

For the case when $2^n\theta$ is not an integer, it can be shown that the above expression still peaks near $x = 2^n\theta$ with probability better than $4/\pi^2 \approx 40\%$

The essence of the QPE algorithm lies in encoding the phase θ into the amplitudes of the quantum state through controlled operations and then using the inverse QFT to decode this phase into a readable binary format. The final measurement collapses the superposition into a state that, with high probability, directly relates to the phase θ we're estimating.

Implementing QPE in Qiskit

Let's take a gate we know well, the T-gate, and use Quantum Phase Estimation to estimate its phase. You will remember that the T-gate adds a phase of $e^{i\frac{\pi}{4}}$ to the state $|1\rangle$:

$$T|1\rangle = \begin{bmatrix} 1 & 0 \\ 0 & e^{i\frac{\pi}{4}} \end{bmatrix} \begin{bmatrix} 0 \\ 1 \end{bmatrix} = e^{i\frac{\pi}{4}}|1\rangle$$

Since QPE will give us θ where:

$$T|1\rangle = e^{2\pi i\theta}|1\rangle$$

We expect to find:

$$\theta = \frac{1}{8}$$

In this example we will use three qubits and obtain an *exact* result (not an estimation!).

Let us import all the required libraries before we start implementing quantum phase estimation in qiskit.

```
#initialization
import matplotlib.pyplot as plt
import numpy as np
import math

# importing Qiskit
from qiskit import transpile, assemble
from qiskit import QuantumCircuit, ClassicalRegister, QuantumRegister
from qiskit_aer import Aer
# import basic plot tools
from qiskit.visualization import plot_histogram
```

Now, set up the quantum circuit. We will use four qubits – qubits 0 to 2 as counting qubits, and qubit 3 as the eigenstate of the unitary operator (T).

We start $|\psi\rangle = |1\rangle$ by applying an X gate:

```
qpe = QuantumCircuit(4, 3)
qpe.x(3)
qpe.draw('mpl')
```

The following step involves the application of Hadamard gates to the counting qubits:

```
for qubit in range(3):
    qpe.h(qubit)
qpe.draw('mpl)
```

Subsequently, we execute the controlled unitary operations. Please note that Qiskit arranges its qubits in the reverse order compared to depicted image that we get above.

```
repetitions = 1
for counting_qubit in range(3):
    for i in range(repetitions):
        qpe.cp(math.pi/4, counting_qubit, 3); # This is CU
```

```
    repetitions *= 2
qpe.draw('mpl')
```

The state of the counting register is converted using the inverse quantum Fourier transformation. The code for the QFT dagger is provided as follows:

```
def qft_dagger(qc, n):
    """n-qubit QFTdagger the first n qubits in circ"""
    # Don't forget the Swaps!
    for qubit in range(n//2):
        qc.swap(qubit, n-qubit-1)
    for j in range(n):
        for m in range(j):
            qc.cp(-math.pi/float(2**(j-m)), m, j)
        qc.h(j)
```

We then measure the counting register:

```
qpe.barrier()
# Apply inverse QFT
qft_dagger(qpe, 3)
# Measure
qpe.barrier()
for n in range(3):
    qpe.measure(n,n)

qpe.draw('mpl')
```

Let us now run the QPE circuit on `qasm_simulator` with 1000 shots and plot the results on histogram.

```
simulator = Aer.get_backend('qasm_simulator')
tqc = transpile(qpe, simulator)
counts = simulator.run(tqc, shots=1000).result().get_counts()
plot_histogram(counts)
```

We see we get one result (001) with certainty, which translates to the decimal: 1. We now need to divide our result (1) by 2^n to get θ:

$$\theta = \frac{1}{2^3} = \frac{1}{8}$$

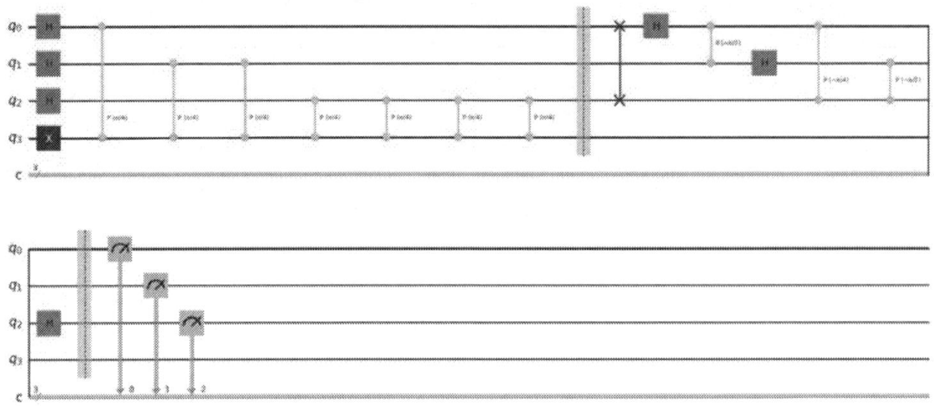

Figure 10.8: Quantum Phase Estimation Circuit in Qiskit

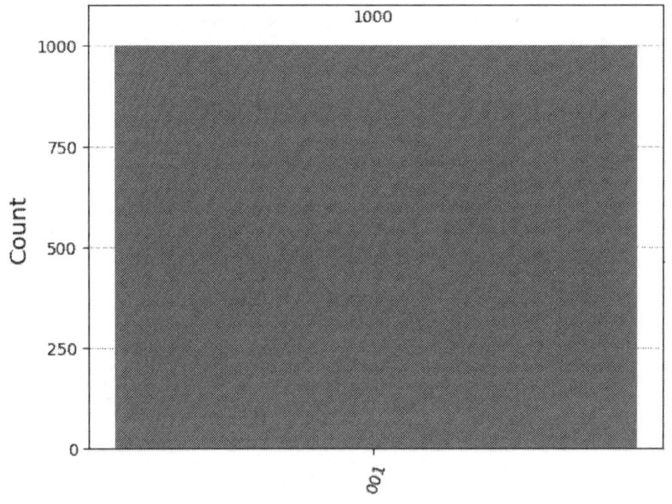

Figure 10.9: Histogram of QPE

This is exactly the result we expected!

Instead of T let us assume a gate with $\theta = 1/3$. Let us first design the circuit:

```
# Create and set up circuit
qpe2 = QuantumCircuit(4, 3)

# Apply H-Gates to counting qubits:
for qubit in range(3):
    qpe2.h(qubit)

# Prepare our eigenstate |psi>:
```

```
qpe2.x(3)

# Do the controlled-U operations:
angle = 2*math.pi/3
repetitions = 1
for counting_qubit in range(3):
    for i in range(repetitions):
        qpe2.cp(angle, counting_qubit, 3);
    repetitions *= 2

# Do the inverse QFT:
qft_dagger(qpe2, 3)

# Measure of course!
for n in range(3):
    qpe2.measure(n,n)

qpe2.draw('mpl')
```

Now let us simulate the circuit on the aer simulator with 100 shots. Let us also look at the probabilities of all the 8 possible outcomes.

```
simulator = Aer.get_backend('qasm_simulator')
tqc = transpile(qpe2, simulator)
counts = simulator.run(tqc, shots=1000).result().get_counts()
plot_histogram(counts)
```

The previous *Figure 10.10*, counts versus all possible outcomes,illustrates that the most likely outcomes '010' and '011', when converted to decimal are 2 and 3 respectively. For the two results we got, θ as 0.25(2/23) and 0.37(3/23) respectively. The exact amswer lies in between these two values as the actual θ we used is 0.33(1/3). To get more precision we simply add more counting qubits. We are going to add two more counting qubits:

```
# Create and set up circuit
qpe3 = QuantumCircuit(6, 5)

# Apply H-Gates to counting qubits:
for qubit in range(5):
```

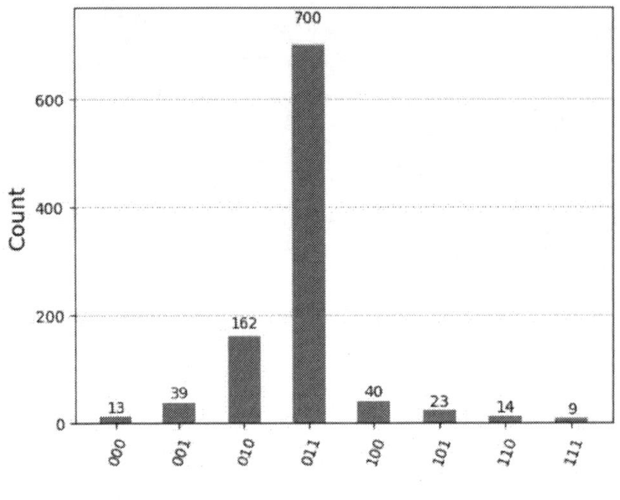

Figure 10.10: Quantum Phase Estimation Circuit ($\theta = 1/3$) in Qiskit

```
    qpe3.h(qubit)

# Prepare our eigenstate |psi>:
qpe3.x(5)

# Do the controlled-U operations:
angle = 2*math.pi/3
repetitions = 1
for counting_qubit in range(5):
    for i in range(repetitions):
        qpe3.cp(angle, counting_qubit, 5);
    repetitions *= 2

# Do the inverse QFT:
qft_dagger(qpe3, 5)

# Measure of course!
qpe3.barrier()
for n in range(5):
    qpe3.measure(n,n)

qpe3.draw('mpl')
```

Let us run this circuit on qasm simulator and check the precision(how close is the θ compared to 0.33).

```
simulator = Aer.get_backend('qasm_simulator')
tqc = transpile(qpe3, simulator)
counts = simulator.run(tqc, shots=1000).result().get_counts()
plot_histogram(counts)
```

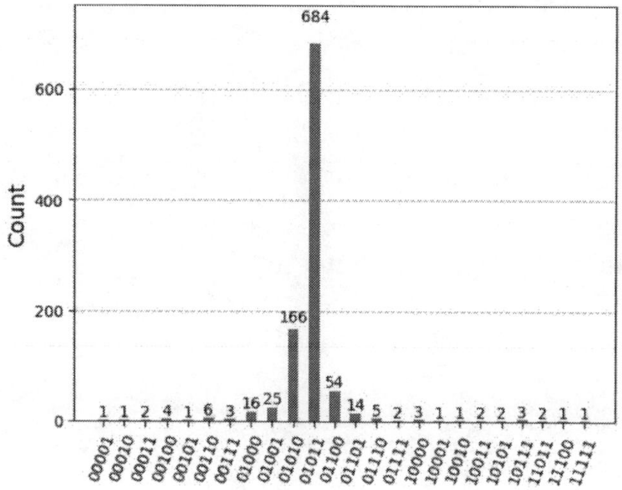

Figure 10.11: Quantum Phase Estimation Circuit with 5 Counting Qubits in Qiskit

The two most likely measurements in *Figure* 10.11 are now 01011 (decimal 11) and 01010 (decimal 10). Measuring these results would tell us θ is:

$$\theta = \frac{11}{2^5} = 0.344, \quad \text{or} \quad \theta = \frac{10}{2^5} = 0.313$$

These two results differ from $\frac{1}{3}$ by 3% and 6% respectively. A much better precision!

Shor's Algorithm

Before diving into Shor's algorithm , we would like to provide motivation for its study and its significance by examining the classical cryptographic algorithm, the RSA algorithm.

RSA - Classical Encryption Scheme

RSA, known as Rivest-Shamir-Adleman , is a popular public-key cryptographic technique that ensures safe data transmission. The concept relies on the challenging nature of factorizing huge integers, a problem without a known effective classical solution. The majority of applications working on the internet depend on the difficulty of factoring prime numbers.

The technique begins by generating keys - encryption and decryption using two large prime numbers; then, the message is encrypted using modular arithmetic , and it can be decrypted only using the decrypted key generated before.

Key Generation

1. Choose two large prime numbers, p and q.
2. Compute $n = pq$ (the modulus).
3. Compute the totient function, $\phi(n) = (p-1)(q-1)$.
4. Choose an encryption key, e, that is coprime to $\phi(n)$.
5. Compute the decryption key, d, as the modular inverse of e modulo $\phi(n)$.

Encryption

For a message M, the ciphertext C is computed as:

$$C = M^e \mod n$$

Decryption

The original message is recovered by computing:

$$M = C^d \mod n$$

The above is the generic method used in the RSA encryption scheme.

Breaking RSA with Shor's

Shor's technique weakens RSA security by offering a polynomial-time approach to factor huge integers, directly challenging the fundamental complexity that RSA security relies on. Following are the ways that Shor's algorithm compromises RSA encryption:

- **Factoring Modulus (n)**
  Shor's approach can efficiently determine the prime factors p and q of an RSA modulus n. This is the main point of the technique, as the process of factoring n is deemed difficult using traditional computers for sufficiently high integers.
- **Computing Private Key**
  Once the attacker has p and q, they can compute $\phi(n) = (p-1)(q-1)$. With (n) and the public encryption key e, it's straightforward to calculate the private decryption key d using the modular inverse operation, as d is the modular inverse of e modulo

(n).

- **Decrypting messages**
  With the private key d in hand, any encrypted message can be decrypted, effectively breaking the RSA encryption scheme.

Small Comparison of Big-O Notation Between Classical and Quantum Algorithm

There is no better classical algorithm for breaking encryption. The best-known classical algorithms are the General Number Field Sieve (GNFS) and the Elliptical Curve method (ECM). The GNFS is a subexponential algorithm that can factor any number N in $O\left(\exp\left((\log N)^{\frac{1}{3}}(\log\log N)^{\frac{2}{3}}\right)\right)$ time, which is faster than exponential but slower than polynomial. The ECM is a probabilistic algorithm that can factor numbers with small prime factors faster than the GNFS but slower for large prime factors. Both algorithms use complex mathematical techniques and require a lot of memory and processing power. The run time of best classical algorithm takes $O\left(\exp\left(c \cdot n^{\frac{1}{3}}(\log n)^{\frac{2}{3}}\right)\right)$ big O notation.

But, Shor's algorithm is a bit more efficient than classical, which is proved in terms of Big O notation as $O((\log N)^3)$. Here, there is **no exponential term**, which is not the case in classical algorithm notation. The reason for better notation in Shor's is due to the quantum mechanical property. Whenever the run time is exponential for an algorithm, there is an exponential increase in operation time making it inefficient. Because if the input size is changed even a bit, there is a visible shift in time taken for the computation to occur.

Protocol for Shor's Algorithm

Let N be a number that is formed by multiplying two prime numbers P and Q.

- $N = PQ \quad (P, Q$ are prime numbers)

Before knowing more technicality, let Us recall modular arithmetic we studied in high school.

The modular arithmetic calculations are used to perform modular exponentiation, a process that's pivotal in the period-finding step of Shor's algorithm. Once the period is found then factoring integers becomes easy. The crucial step is to find the Period. This operation is quantum mechanical in nature, and its result is later transformed into classical information via the inverse Quantum Fourier Transform (IQFT).

Modular arithmetic

Consider an example $\frac{5}{3}$. Here, Quotient = 1 and Remainder = 2. This can be written in a proper mathematical format as $5 \equiv 2 \pmod 3$ (pronounce it as 5 equivalent to 2 mod 3).

Now, let's find the period/pattern/repetition of numbers for that consider x, and it has a series of values ranging from 1,2,3...9. Take mod 3 for each value of x. Once it's done, you can find the repetition/period:

Let x be:

$$x \in \{1, 2, 3, 4, 5, 6, 7, 8, 9\}$$
$$x \mod 3 \in \{1, 2, 0, 1, 2, 0, 1, 2, 0\} \pmod 3$$

This is how the period is found. The same concept is applied to Shor's algorithm.

Step 1: Pick a number a that is co-prime with N (no common divisor).

Step 2: Find the *order* r of the function $a^r \mod N$.

If we could find period r, then it is comparatively easier to find the factors.

Order r means the smallest r such that:

$$a^r \equiv 1 \pmod N$$

Step 3: If r is even and $x = a^{r/2} \pmod N$ and if x $\not\equiv \pm 1 \pmod N$ then P or Q, which we are looking for (either P or Q) is contained in gcd$(x + 1, N)$ and gcd$(x - 1, N)$.

If the above case is not applicable, then find another a.

Example of Shor's Protocol

Let's factor $N = 15$. In binary, '15' is written as '1111' (4 bits).

Just follow the Shor's protocol

Step 1: Pick a number a that is co-prime with N.

Let $a = 13$

Step 2 Find the period/order r of the function $a^r \mod N$.

$$13^r \mod 15$$

Given $N = 15$, we can find values of $13^r \mod 15$ for different r as follows:

$$r \in \{0, 1, 2, 3, 4, 5, 6, 7\}$$
$$13^r \in \{1, 13, 4, 7, 1, 13, 4, 7, 0\} \pmod{15}$$

Let r be the smallest number such that:

$$a^r \equiv 1 \pmod{N}$$

We have found that:

$$r = 4$$

In the context of Shor's algorithm, **r** refers to the order of a modulo N, which is the smallest positive integer for which $a^r \equiv 1(modN)$. While r =1 can satisfy the above equation $a^1 \equiv 1(modN)$ unless $a^1 \equiv 1(modN)$ to start with which is not the general case for Shor's algorithm.

Step 3 Fortunately, r is even.

Let $x = a^{r/2} \mod N$. Given that $a = 13$ and $N = 15$, we have:

$$x = 13^{4/2} \mod 15 = 13^2 \mod 15 = 4$$

Then, we compute $x + 1$ and find its greatest common divisor with N:

$$x + 1 = 4 + 1 = 5 \mod 15$$

$$\gcd(x + 1, N) = \gcd(5, 15) = 5$$

Similarly, we compute $x - 1$ and find its greatest common divisor with N:

$$x - 1 = 4 - 1 = 3 \mod 15$$

$$\gcd(x - 1, N) = \gcd(3, 15) = 3$$

Therefore, the factors p, q are:

$$\{p, q\} = \{5, 3\}$$

This is how the factors are obtained.

Quantum Circuit Analysis - Shor's Algorithm

Equipped with an understanding of Shor's protocol, we are now ready to dive into the detailed quantum circuit analysis of Shor's algorithm and the classical post-processing steps. *Figure* 10.12 shows the quantum circuit for Shor's algorithm.

Step 0

First, we initialize our qubits to all zeros for both the $|x\rangle$ and $|w\rangle$ registers.

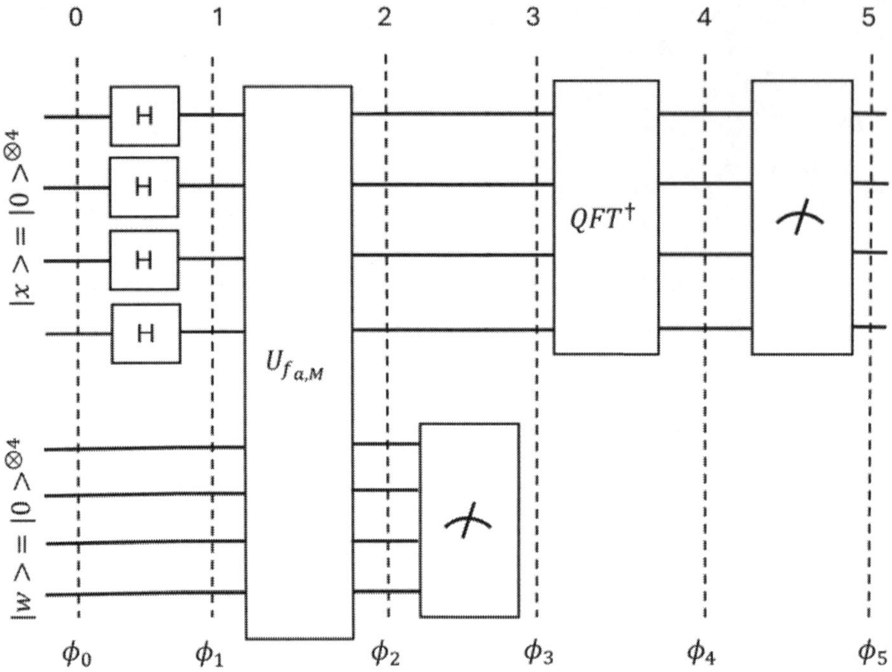

Figure 10.12: Quantum Circuit for Shor's Algorithm

$$|0\rangle^{\otimes 4} \otimes |0\rangle^{\otimes 4} \tag{10.28}$$

Here $|x\rangle = |0\rangle^{\otimes 4}$ and $|w\rangle = |0\rangle^{\otimes 4}$

Step 1

Hadamard gate is applied to all the qubits of $|x\rangle$

$$H|x\rangle|w\rangle = \left[H^{\otimes 4} \otimes |0\rangle^{\otimes 4}\right]|0\rangle^{\otimes 4} \tag{10.29}$$

$$\frac{1}{4}\left[|0\rangle_4 + |1\rangle_4 + |2\rangle_4 + \ldots + |15\rangle_4\right]|0\rangle_4 \tag{10.30}$$

Step 2

The oracle $U_{f_{a,M}}$ is applied to the states of the registers $|x\rangle$ and $|w\rangle$ which performs the operation $|x\rangle|w\rangle = |x\rangle|w \oplus f_{a,M}(x)\rangle$ where $f_{a,M}(x) = a^x(modM)$.

$$\frac{1}{4}\left[|0\rangle_4 \otimes (|0 \oplus 13^0(mod15)\rangle_4) + |1\rangle_4 \otimes (|1 \oplus 13^1(mod15)\rangle_4) + \ldots\right] \tag{10.31}$$

$$= \frac{1}{4}[|0\rangle_4 |1\rangle_4 + |1\rangle_4 |13\rangle_4 + |2\rangle_4 |4\rangle_4 + |3\rangle_4 |7\rangle_4$$
$$+ |4\rangle_4 |1\rangle_4 + |5\rangle_4 |13\rangle_4 + |6\rangle_4 |4\rangle_4 + |7\rangle_4 |7\rangle_4$$
$$+ |8\rangle_4 |1\rangle_4 + |9\rangle_4 |13\rangle_4 + |10\rangle_4 |4\rangle_4 + |11\rangle_4 |7\rangle_4$$
$$+ |12\rangle_4 |1\rangle_4 + |13\rangle_4 |13\rangle_4 + |14\rangle_4 |4\rangle_4 + |15\rangle_4 |7\rangle_4]$$

By applying the oracle, we receive states $|1\rangle$, $|13\rangle$, $|4\rangle$ and $|7\rangle$ in the $|w\rangle$ register in superposition with the states of $|x\rangle$.

Step 3

After measuring w register, let's say we measured $|7\rangle$. Then the state $|x\rangle$ collapses to the following state:

$$|x\rangle = \frac{1}{2}[|13\rangle_4 + |7\rangle_4 + |11\rangle_4 + |15\rangle_4] \otimes |7\rangle_4 \tag{10.32}$$

Note that $\frac{1}{2}$ is normalization constant.

Step 4

Apply $QFT^\dagger$ on the x register

Recall:

$$QFT|x\rangle = |\tilde{x}\rangle = \frac{1}{\sqrt{N}} \sum_{y=0}^{N-1} e^{\frac{2\pi i}{N}xy} |y\rangle$$

$$QFT^\dagger |\tilde{x}\rangle = |x\rangle = \frac{1}{\sqrt{N}} \sum_{y=0}^{N-1} e^{-\frac{2\pi i}{N}xy} |y\rangle \tag{10.33}$$

$$QFT^\dagger |3\rangle_4 = \frac{1}{\sqrt{16}} \sum_{y=0}^{15} e^{-\frac{2\pi i}{16}3y} |y\rangle = \frac{1}{4} \sum_{y=0}^{15} e^{-\frac{\pi i}{8}3y} |y\rangle \tag{10.34}$$

$$QFT^\dagger |7\rangle_4 = \frac{1}{4} \sum_{y=0}^{15} e^{-\frac{\pi i}{8}7y} |y\rangle \tag{10.35}$$

$$QFT^\dagger |11\rangle_4 = \frac{1}{4} \sum_{y=0}^{15} e^{-\frac{\pi i}{8}11y} |y\rangle \tag{10.36}$$

$$QFT^\dagger |15\rangle_4 = \frac{1}{4} \sum_{y=0}^{15} e^{-\frac{\pi i}{8}15y} |y\rangle \tag{10.37}$$

$$QFT^{\dagger}|x\rangle = \frac{1}{8}\sum_{y=0}^{15}\left[\exp\left(-i\frac{3\pi}{8}y\right) + \exp\left(-i\frac{7\pi}{8}y\right) + \exp\left(-i\frac{11\pi}{8}y\right) + \exp\left(-i\frac{15\pi}{8}y\right)\right]|y\rangle$$

$$= \frac{1}{8}\left[4|0\rangle_4 + 4i|4\rangle_4 - 4|8\rangle_4 - 4i|12\rangle_4\right] \tag{10.38}$$

Step 5

In this step, we will now perform the measurement of the $|x\rangle$ register and apply some classical post-processing in order to extract the factors based on the measured states.

When we measure the $|x\rangle$ register we will get $|0\rangle$, $|4\rangle$, $|8\rangle$, or $|12\rangle$ with equal probability of $\frac{1}{4}$.

We will now analyze the measured result step-by-step for each of the states. These measured results must peak near $\frac{j}{r}N$ for some $j \in \mathbb{Z}$. Let us begin.

- $|4\rangle$: $j \cdot \frac{16}{r} = 4$ so $r = 4$ if $j = 1$. $r = 4$ is even
  $x = a^{r/2} \mod N = 13^2 \mod 15 = 4$
  $x + 1 = 5$; $\gcd(x+1, N) = 5$
  $x - 1 = 3$; $\gcd(x-1, N) = 3$
- $|8\rangle$: $j \cdot \frac{16}{r} = 8$ so $r = 2$ and $j = 1$ or $r = 4$ and $j = 2$
  $x = 13^4 \mod 15 = 2$
  $x + 1 = 3$; $\gcd(x+1, N) = 3$ (partial)
  $x - 1 = 1$; $\gcd(x-1, N) = 1$
- $|12\rangle$: $j \cdot \frac{16}{r} = 12$ so $r = 4$ and $j = 3$

We can observe that for $|4\rangle$, we were able to extract both factors successfully; however, for $|8\rangle$ and $|12\rangle$, we were only able to extract the factors partially. This means that based on the states measured at a certain instance, we are able to extract the factors successfully.

Modular Exponentiation

Implementation of $U_{f_{a,N}}$

Recall: $f_{a,N}(x) \equiv a^x \mod N$

$x = [x_{n-1}, x_{n-2}, \ldots, x_0] = 2^{n-1}x_1 + 2^{n-2}x_2 + \ldots + 2^0 x_n$

$f_{a,N}(x) \equiv a^x \mod N$

$$= a^{2^{n-1}x_1 + 2^{n-2}x_2 + \ldots + 2^0 x_n} \mod N$$

$$= a^{2^{n-1}x_1} a^{2^{n-2}x_2} \ldots a^{2^0 x_n} \mod N$$

Implementing Shor's Algorithm in Qiskit

In this section we will implement the circuit shown in *Figure* 10.12. Let us start by importing all the necessary libraries required:

```
import matplotlib.pyplot as plt
import numpy as np
from qiskit import QuantumCircuit, transpile
from qiskit_aer import Aer
from math import gcd
import pandas as pd
from qiskit.visualization import plot_histogram
from qiskit.circuit.library import QFT
```

Step 1

The circuit will be constructed by initializing a set of n qubits. A qubit can exist in a superposition of 2n̂ computational base states. To generate a superposition state with n qubits, a Hadamard gate is applied to the measurement qubits. The Figure 10.12 (0-1) part illustrates the initialization of n qubits in the state (0), followed by the application of the Hadamard gate to these n qubits resulting in the state $|0\rangle^{\otimes n}$.

It is important to note that the Hadamard gate converts a qubit from its computational basis $|0\rangle$ or $|1\rangle$ to the Fourier basis $|+\rangle$ or $|-\rangle$. We must apply a tensor product, as we are performing this for all n measurement bases.

There are n measurement qubits and m qubits that will be initialized as target qubits. The eigenstate of the target qubits will be $|1\rangle$, and a unitary operator U will be applied to it. The X gate is applied to the final qubit $(n + m - 1)$ as the enumeration commences at the 0th qubit.

```
def initialize_qubits(given_circuit, n, m):

    given_circuit.h(range(n))
    given_circuit.x(n+m-1)
```

Step 2

It is important to remember that any prime number N can be expressed as the product of two primes p and q or $N = pq$. Please be advised that Shor's algorithm is equivalent to determining the period of a periodic function $f(x) = a^x \mod N$. The smallest integer r that satisfies the equation $a^r \mod N = 1$ and the equation

$$f(x) = f(y),\ |x - y| = k \cdot r \text{ where } k \text{ is an integer}$$

is known as the period.

A function $U(x) = a^x \mod 15$ is defined to factor the number 15. The qubits will be subjected to the norm-preserving unitary operator U. Controlled by the n measurement qubits, the unitary operator will execute modular exponentiation on the target qubits.

As Shor's algorithm employs quantum phase estimation on the unitary operator,

$$U|y\rangle = |ay \mod N\rangle$$

Classical Steps to Shor's Algorithm

Since $a^r \equiv 1 \mod N$

$$a^r = (a^{r/2})^2 \equiv 1 \mod N$$

$$(a^{r/2})^2 - 1 \equiv 0 \mod N$$

$$(a^{r/2} + 1)(a^{r/2} - 1) \equiv 0 \mod N$$

The product $(a^{r/2} + 1)(a^{r/2} - 1)$ is an integer multiple of N.

If we compute the greatest common divisor of $\gcd(a^{r/2} + 1, N)$ and $\gcd(a^{r/2} - 1, N)$, we will get a factor of N and the gcd can be calculated using the Euclidean Algorithm.

If we consider $N = 15$, we will look at values of $1 < a < 15$ where a is coprime with 15.

a	Power Sequence of a^x	$a^x \mod 15$	Period r	$\gcd(a^{r/2} - 1, 15)$	$\gcd(a^{r/2} + 1, 15)$
2	1,2,4,8,16,32...	1,2,4,8,1,2...	4	3	5
4	1,4,16,64,256...	1,4,1,4...	2	3	5
7	1,7,49,343,2401...	1,7,4,13,1,7...	4	3	5
8	1,8,64,512,4096...	1,8,4,2,1,8...	4	3	5
11	1,11,121,1331,14641...	1,11,1,11...	2	5	3
13	1,13,169,2197,28561...	1,13,4,7,1,13...	4	3	5
14	1,14,196,2744,38416...	1,14,1,14...	2	1	15

Table 10.1: Classical Steps to Shor's Algorithm for $N = 15$

The factors of 15 are returned for any value of a that is not equal to 14. We will employ $a = 7$ to evaluate Shor's algorithm.

The function `c_amod15` will be defined to return a controlled-U gate for a repeated x

times. `c_amod15` will be a 4-qubit unitary regulated by a 5th qubit that will be appended to the circuit.

```
def c_amod15(a, x):
    if a not in [2,7,8,11,13]:
        raise ValueError("'a' must be 2,7,8,11,13")
    U = QuantumCircuit(4)
    for iteration in range(x):
        if a in [2,13]:
            U.swap(0,1)
            U.swap(1,2)
            U.swap(2,3)
        if a in [7,8]:
            U.swap(2,3)
            U.swap(1,2)
            U.swap(0,1)
        if a == 11:
            U.swap(1,3)
            U.swap(0,2)
        if a in [7,11,13]:
            for q in range(4):
                U.x(q)
    U = U.to_gate()
    U.name = "%i^%i mod 15" % (a, x)
    c_U = U.control()
    return c_U
```

Next, we will perform modular exponentiation on the circuit and add the fifth qubit by applying the control qubit followed by four target qubits.

```
def modular_exponentiation(circuit, n, m, a):
  for x in range(n):
    exponent = 2**x
    circuit.append(c_amod15(a, exponent),
                   [x] + list(range(n, n+m)))
```

Step 3

We will create a function. The function `inverse_qft` requires two parameters: the circuit on which the inverse Quantum Fourier transform will be executed, and the set of measurement qubits onto which the Inverse Fourier transform will be applied. The `.inverse()` function is then applied to obtain the inverse QFT function.

```
def inverse_qft(circuit,measurement_qubits):
    circuit.append(QFT( len(measurement_qubits), do_swaps=False).inverse(),
    measurement_qubits)
```

Step 4

Let us write the code that implements the circuit in qiskit and we shall also visualize the same shors circuit that we implement.

```
def shors_algorithm(n, m, a):

    qc = QuantumCircuit(n+m, n)
    initialize_qubits(qc, n, m)
    qc.barrier()

    modular_exponentiation(qc, n, m, a)
    qc.barrier()

    inverse_qft(qc, range(n))
    qc.measure(range(n), range(n))

    return qc

n = 4; m = 4; a = 7
final_circuit = shors_algorithm(n, m, a)
final_circuit.draw('mpl')
```

Step 5

Now let us run the circuit on 'qasm simulator' with 1000 shots and plot the histogram or the measurement results.

```
simulator = Aer.get_backend('qasm_simulator')
tqc = transpile(final_circuit, simulator)
counts = simulator.run(tqc, shots=1000).result().get_counts()
plot_histogram(counts)
```

Step 6

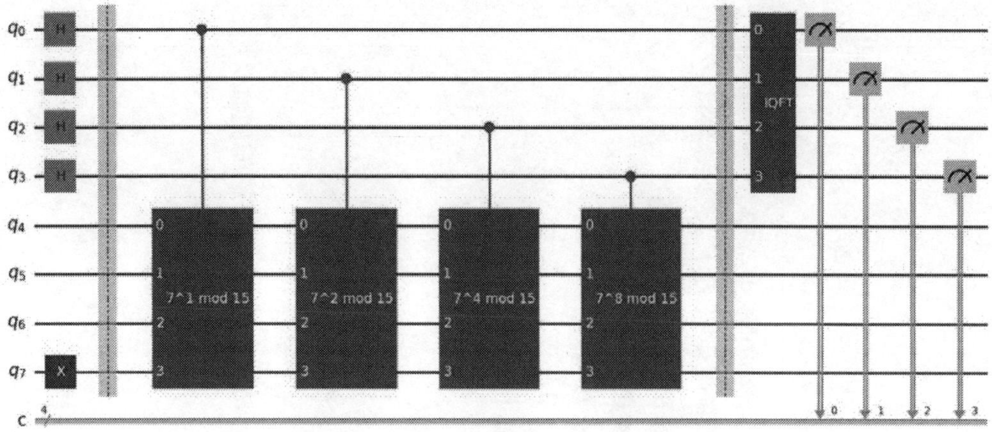

Figure 10.13: Shors Circuit in Qiskit

Now let us classically process these quantum results to obtain the factors of 15.

```
for i in counts:
    measured_value = int(i[::-1], 2)


    if measured_value % 2 != 0:
        print("Measured value not even")
        continue
    x = int((a ** (measured_value/2)) % 15)
    if (x + 1) % 15 == 0:
        continue
    factors = gcd(x + 1, 15), gcd(x - 1, 15)
    print(factors)
```

The output of the preceding code will give the following output: (5, 3) (1, 15)

The resulting pairs obtained for the greatest common divisor of (x+1,15) and (x-1,15) are (1,15) and (5,3), respectively. These pairings represent the factors of 15 factorial. Therefore, we employed Shor's Algorithm to factorize the integer 15.

Applications of Shor's Algorithm

- **Cryptography**

  Shor's algorithm possesses the capability to factorize huge integers with efficiency, so

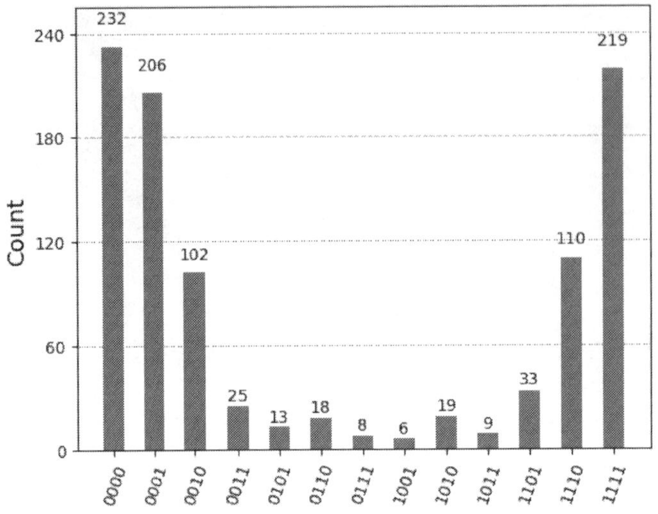

Figure 10.14: The histogram represents the probability distribution of measured states from Shor's algorithm. Peaks correspond to high-probability measurement outcomes, revealing the period of the modular exponentiation function used in the algorithm. The periodicity helps determine the factors of the given composite number using quantum Fourier transform.

serving as a fundamental element in its influence on cryptography. Several commonly employed encryption schemes, such as RSA, depend on the challenge of factoring huge composite integers. Shor's technique has the potential to compromise RSA encryption by efficiently factoring the product of two large prime numbers that serve as the RSA modulus, provided that a quantum computer of sufficient size is constructed.

- **Cryptanalysis of Cryptosystems**
  Furthermore, Shor's algorithm can be modified to effectively address the discrete logarithm problem . This issue is fundamental to the security of various cryptographic systems, such as the Diffie-Hellman key exchange , the Digital Signature Algorithm (DSA) , and elliptic curve cryptography (ECC). The Shor's algorithm has the ability to compromise these systems, hence posing a threat to existing digital security infrastructures.
- **Mathematical Research** Shor's algorithm is primarily an algorithm used for finding the order of elements, and it has wider applications in the fields of number theory and group theory. It is applicable in diverse mathematical issues that require determining the order of an element within a group.

Grover's Search Algorithm

Imagine you found your grandmother's telephone directory which she used in her childhood. You have a list of names and corresponding numbers associated with it. It definitely takes a lot of time to go through the book and find the number of your grandmother's friend. Now let us see how classical algorithms and Grover's algorithm acts differently.

Comparison with Classical Algorithms

Binary Search

Binary search is a highly effective algorithm for locating an item within a list of things that is already sorted. The process involves iteratively halving the segment of the list that may contain the item until just one viable position remains. Binary search is advantageous due of its efficiency. Binary search can locate an object in a list of N items in a maximum of $log_2 N$ steps, significantly quicker than sequentially scanning each element.

Brute Force Search

Brute force search , on the other hand, is a straightforward approach that involves checking each entry in the list until you find the match. Using the phone book analogy, if you're given a phone number and need to find the corresponding name but the phone numbers are unsorted, you might have to look through every single number until you find the one that matches.

The primary disadvantage of brute force search is its inefficiency, as it takes O(N) queries or checks—where N is the entire number of entries—to locate the object. This implies that, in the worst situation, you might need to go through the entire list of entries in order to locate your match.

Grover's algorithm

Few steps which are not followed by classical algorithm but followed by Grover algorithm is Quantum superposition, Oracle usage, Amplitude amplification, Quantum parallelism and more. By the mentioned methods, Grovers algorithm search the database consisting of N items in $0(\sqrt{N})$ run time. This run time is called as **quadratic speedup** . This algorithm developed by Lov Grover in 1996 proved to be advantageous over classical algorithms like Brute Force Search.

Grover's Search Algorithm - Pictorial Intuition

Grover's Search technique uses amplitude amplification and quantum superposition to search an unsorted database quadratically faster. Consider every potential database entry as a circle with points to help you visualize the method. To give each entry an equal amplitude, Grover's technique first creates an equal superposition across all points. The next steps are to reflect the amplitude of the solution and increase it while decreasing the amplitude of the incorrect solutions. The likelihood of measuring the right response is progressively increased by repeated reflections, which are represented as rotations in the direction of the right answer. These geometric rotations in quantum state space demonstrate how Grover's algorithm guarantees that the chance of obtaining the intended result reaches a maximum after a predetermined number of rounds.

Step 1: Initial Superposition

Consider a quantum system with $N = 2^n$ states, where n is the number of qubits. The goal is to find a specific state $|w\rangle$ (the *winner*) out of these N states. We start by preparing all qubits in the □0⟩ state and then apply a Hadamard transform H to each qubit to create a superposition of all possible states with equal amplitude:

$$|s\rangle = H^{\otimes n}|0\rangle^n = \frac{1}{\sqrt{N}}\sum_{x=0}^{N-1}|x\rangle \tag{10.39}$$

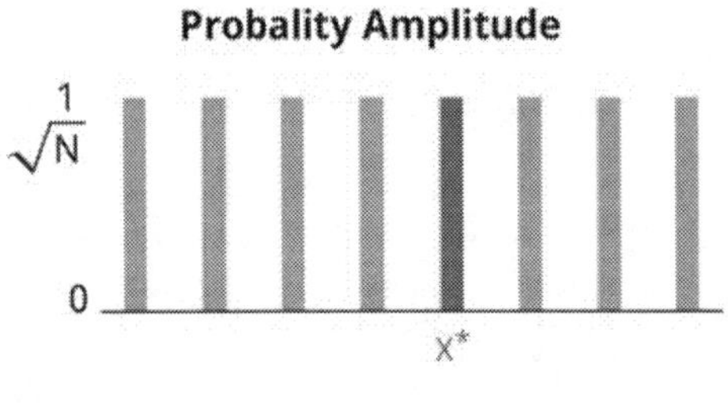

Figure 10.15: Initial Superposition of States

This state $|s\rangle$ represents a uniform superposition of all possible states $|x\rangle$ in our search space.

Step 2: Oracle Operation

The oracle U_w is a unitary operation that marks the target item $|w\rangle$ by flipping its phase, leaving all other states unchanged. The action of the oracle can be expressed as:

$$U_w|x\rangle = \begin{cases} -|x\rangle & \text{if } x = w \\ |x\rangle & \text{otherwise} \end{cases} \tag{10.40}$$

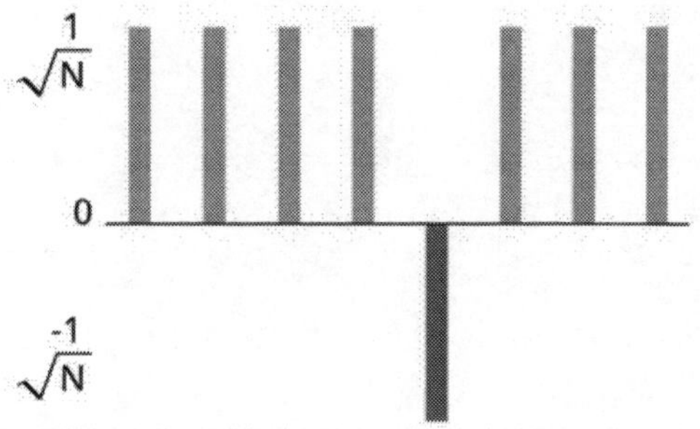

Figure 10.16: Oracle Operation

Applying U_w to $|s\rangle$ results in,

$$U_w|x\rangle = (-1)^{f(x)}|x\rangle \tag{10.41}$$

where $f(x) = 1$ if $x = w$ and 0 otherwise. Applying U_w to $|s\rangle$, we get:

$$U_w|s\rangle = \frac{1}{\sqrt{N}}\left(-|w\rangle + \sum_{x\neq w}|x\rangle\right) \tag{10.42}$$

Step 3: Amplitude Amplification (Grover's Diffusion Operator)

After applying the oracle, algorithm uses the diffusion operator D to amplify the amplitude of the state $|w\rangle$. The diffusion operator is defined as:

$$D = 2|s\rangle\langle s| - I \tag{10.43}$$

where I is the Identity matrix

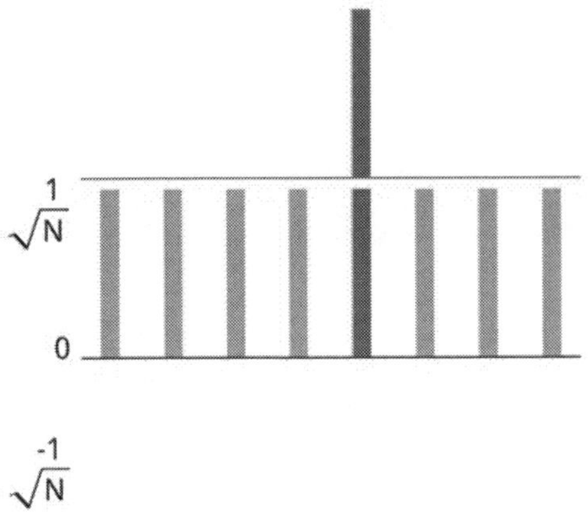

Figure 10.17: Amplitude Amplification

The operator D performs an inversion about the average amplitude of all states. When applied to the state after the oracle operation, it increases the amplitude of $|w\rangle$ and decreases the amplitude of other states.

Applying D to any state vector $|\psi\rangle$ results in:

$$D|\psi\rangle = 2\langle s|\psi\rangle|s\rangle - |\psi\rangle \tag{10.44}$$

Step 4: Grover Iteration

A single Grover iteration combines the oracle and diffusion steps:

$$G = D \cdot U_w$$

After k iterations, the state of the system is,

$$|\psi_k\rangle = (DU_w)^k|s\rangle$$

The number of iterations k needed to maximize the probability of measuring $|w\rangle$ is approximately $\frac{\pi}{4}\sqrt{N}$.

Mathematical Derivation of Amplitude Amplification

The action of G on the state vector can be understood by looking at the state vector in a two-dimensional space spanned by $|w\rangle$ and the uniform superposition of all other states. Each iteration rotates the state vector close to $|w\rangle$. The amplitude of $|w\rangle$ and it's probability increases with each iteration until it reaches its maximum. To find the optimal number of iterations, consider the angle θ by which the state vector is rotated towards $|w\rangle$ in each iteration. This angle is determined by the initial amplitude of $|w\rangle$ which is $\frac{1}{\sqrt{N}}$ leading to,

$$\sin\theta = \frac{1}{\sqrt{N}} \tag{10.45}$$

After k iterations, the state vector is rotated by an angle of approximately $2k\theta$ and the probability of observing $|w\rangle$ is maximized when $2k\theta \approx \frac{\pi}{2}$ giving,

$$k \approx \frac{\pi}{4\theta} = \frac{\pi}{4}\sqrt{N} \tag{10.46}$$

This derivation shows the core of Grover's algorithm by iteratively applying the oracle and the diffusion operator, it amplifies the amplitude of the *winner* state, making it much more likely to be observed when measuring the quantum state, all while maintaining the quantum superposition of all possible solutions

Implementation of Grover's Search Algorithm in Qiskit

Initially, we import the standard Python modules, including Matplotlib , a module specifically created for generating plots, and NumPy , a module intended to streamline intricate computations with its pre-existing functions (such as computing the dot product of vectors). For this particular situation, we are exclusively utilizing the pyplot *sub-module* of MatPlotLib. We employed the acronyms *plt* and *np* to refer to the matplotlib library *Pyplot* and *NumPy*, respectively. We also import all the modules that we require from qiskit.

```
import matplotlib.pyplot as plt
import numpy as np
from qiskit import QuantumCircuit, transpile, QuantumRegister, ClassicalRegister
from qiskit.visualization import plot_histogram
from qiskit_aer import Aer
from qiskit.providers.basic_provider import BasicSimulator
```

Upon importing all necessary components, we proceed to establish a function that initializes all the qubits by placing them in an equal superposition through the utilization of Hadamard gates. The function accepts two parameters: GC, which represents a quantum circuit, and qubits, which indicates the number of qubits we are initializing. Next, employing a for-each loop, we iterate through each qubit and apply the Hadamard gate to it. Next, we will return the newly created quantum circuit, thereby concluding our initialization procedure.

```
# Function to Initialize Quantum States for N Qubits
# Two parameters: GC: a quantum circuit, and qubits: the number of qubits
def Initialize(GC, qubits):
    # Apply a Hadamard (H) Gate to the Qubits
    # Hadamard gate just puts the qubit in a superposition
    for q in qubits: # iterates through all the qubits,
        GC.h(q) # applying a H gate to each individually
    return GC # returns the new quantum circuit with the H gates applied
```

Let's begin with a straightforward implementation of Grover's Algorithm, using a simplified version with two qubits. For this illustration, we will employ the state *winner* represented as $|x\rangle$=$|11\rangle$. This implies that we desire the quantum computer to identify and disregard all states except for the one specified.

We declare an integer variable n of type int and initialize it with the value 2. Additionally, we establish a variable `grover_circuit` of type QuantumCircuit , which represents a quantum circuit with 2 qubits. To begin, we initiate our circuit by utilizing the Initialize function that we have recently developed. Next, we generate a graphical depiction of the circuit. Here is a visual representation of the setup, featuring two Hadamard gates.

```
# Grover's Algorithm with 2 qubits
# |x> = |11>
n = 2 # number of qubits

grover_circuit = QuantumCircuit(n) # create a Quantum Circuit with the name
'grover_circuit'
grover_circuit = Initialize(grover_circuit, [0, 1]) # initialize said circuit
grover_circuit.draw('mpl') # draw the circuit
```

Once the circuit has been established, we proceed to implement the Oracle Matrix. For our specific example, the gate that we need to use is the controlled-Z gate. We will incorporate this gate into our quantum circuit, which we have named `grover\_circuit` . Once more, we can generate a graphical depiction of the circuit. In addition to the two H gates, we have now introduced the CZ gate.

```
#Apply the oracle specific to 2 qubits
grover_circuit.cz(0, 1) #Oracle is a CZ gate
grover_circuit.draw('mpl') #draw the circuit
```

Afterward, we proceed to apply the Diffuser. Here, the H gate is applied to both qubits, followed by the Z gate on both qubits, then the CZ gate on both qubits, and lastly, the H gate on both qubits. Similarly, we can display the circuit on the screen. The newly erected gates are readily seen, collectively forming the Diffuser.

```
# Apply the Diffuser
# [0,1] means apply the gate to qubits q0 and q1
grover_circuit.h([0,1]) # applies H gate
grover_circuit.z([0,1]) # applies Z gate
grover_circuit.cz(0,1) # applies CZ gate
grover_circuit.h([0,1]) # applies H gate
grover_circuit.measure_all() # measure all the qubits
grover_circuit.draw('mpl')
```

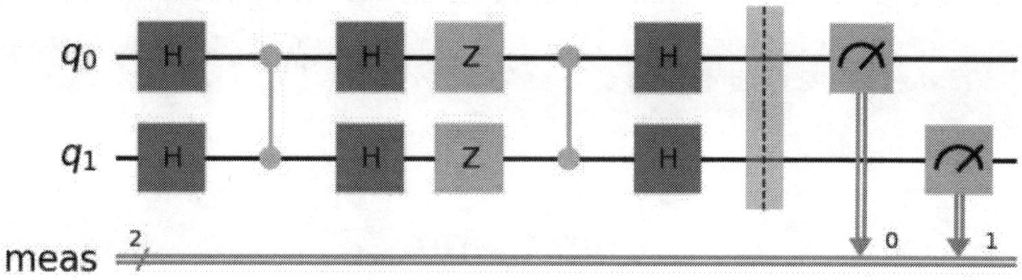

Figure 10.18: Quantum Circuit for Two Qubit Grover's Algorithm

Surprisingly, that was the only requirement for us to develop a two-qubit Grover's algorithm! Subsequently, we can employ a quantum simulator to replicate the method and obtain an approximation of the anticipated outcomes. The desired outcome is for the state $|x\rangle$=$|11\rangle$ to have a probability of 1.000 of being seen, aligning with my objective.

We simulate the circuit and get the results. Next, we store the probabilities of measuring each qubit state using the get_counts function and storing the value in answers. Finally, we plot a histogram of these probabilities.

```
backend = BasicSimulator()
tqc = transpile(grover_circuit, backend)
counts = backend.run(tqc, shots=1000).result().get_counts()
plot_histogram(counts)
```

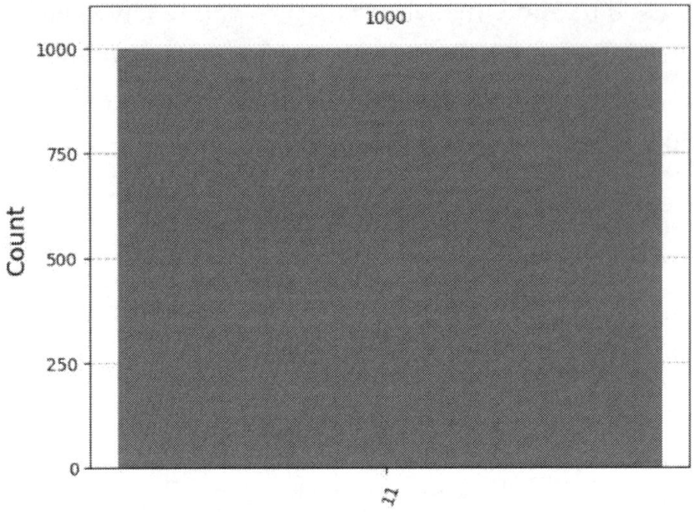

Figure 10.19: This result from Grover's algorithm for a 2-qubit system shows that the quantum search successfully amplified the target state $|11\rangle$ to near certainty (1000 counts out of 1000 total measurements). Grover's algorithm is designed to find a marked element in an unstructured database with quadratic speedup compared to classical search. The output confirms that the algorithm correctly identified the desired state after the required number of iterations.

Conclusion

This chapter has provided a detailed exploration of the sophisticated algorithms that utilize the capabilities of quantum computing. By studying the Quantum Fourier Transform (QFT) and Quantum Phase Estimation (QPE), we have established the foundation for comprehending the quantum advancements that make algorithms such as Shor's and Grover's very innovative. Shor's approach demonstrates the capacity of quantum computing to efficiently address traditionally unsolvable problems, such as integer factorization, that are difficult to solve using classical methods. However, Grover's technique showcases the effectiveness of quantum search algorithms by achieving quadratic speed improvements. We also explored the intricacies of designing and executing Variational Quantum Algorithms (VQAs), a highly promising method for addressing intricate optimization issues and mimicking quantum systems. By actively applying Qiskit, we have observed the functioning of these algorithms and acquired actual expertise in quantum programming. As we finish this chapter, we find ourselves at the point where theory and practice meet, armed with the understanding and resources to investigate the immense possibilities of quantum algorithms in addressing practical issues.

In the next chapter, we will study various quantum communication protocols that can be used to study various quantum mechanical phenomena and realize quantum networking applications.

CHAPTER 11

Quantum Communication Protocols

Introduction

In today's digital age, ensuring the security of our communications has become of utmost importance, as they serve as the foundation of our interconnected global society. Conventional approaches are becoming more susceptible to the advanced techniques cybercriminals and eavesdroppers use. Nevertheless, introducing quantum physics in communication presents a revolutionary resolution to these difficulties. This chapter explores the innovative realm of quantum communication protocols, where the laws of quantum physics are not merely abstract concepts but tangible instruments for transforming how we safeguard and transfer data.

Quantum communication utilizes phenomena such as quantum entanglement and superposition to accomplish tasks that are not achievable using classical physics. The core of this technology lies in the capability to transmit quantum states between remote entities via quantum entanglement, a phenomenon that may appear reminiscent of a plot in a science fiction book. You will investigate how this entanglement serves as more than just a unique characteristic of quantum theory but rather as a strategic method to accomplish secure and immediate communication across vast distances.

Superdense coding is a highly notable protocol in quantum communication. This approach enables a single qubit to encode two classical bits of information when entangled. This feature increases the data stored in a given space and establishes the basis for more effective quantum networks. Comprehending superdense coding is crucial for fully comprehending the capabilities of quantum communication technology.

Quantum Key Distribution (QKD) is essential to quantum communication, particularly in quantum cryptography. The BB84 protocol is a secure communication method that enables the exchange of a cryptographic key between parties while ensuring that any effort at eavesdropping can be detected. This protocol illustrates how quantum mechanics offers security that is not solely reliant on mathematical complexity but rather on the underlying principles of physics.

In addition to discussing the protocols, this chapter will explore the practical implementations of quantum communication. Implementing quantum communication has wide-ranging and diverse ramifications, including secure messaging, financial transactions, and robust data protection. We will examine how these technologies are not just hypothetical but are currently being implemented to safeguard data and communications in ways that were previously considered unattainable.

Finally, the chapter will examine the future prospects of quantum communication and its potential to transform further and redefine our digital environment. As you progress through the chapter, you will acquire a more profound comprehension of the mechanics of quantum communication and a recognition of its capacity to safeguard our digital world from emerging dangers.

Upon completing this chapter, you will thoroughly understand quantum communication's fundamental principles, protocols, and applications. This knowledge will enable you to recognize its potential and anticipate its future influence on worldwide communication networks. Here, we initiate our investigation by closely examining quantum teleportation, which serves as a foundation for delving further into the complex realm of using quantum mechanics to communicate.

Structure

In this chapter, you are going to study:

- Quantum Teleportation
    - The Portal
    - Implementing Quantum Teleportation Using Qiskit
- Superdense Coding
    - The Protocol
    - Implementing Superdense Coding Using Qiskit
- Quantum Cryptography
    - How does Quantum Cryptography Work?
    - Uses and Examples of Quantum Cryptography
    - Advantages of Quantum Cryptography
    - Disadvantages of Quantum Cryptography
- Applications of Quantum Communications
- Future of Quantum Communications

Quantum Teleportation

Quantum teleportation is a highly fascinating phenomenon that arises from the field of quantum mechanics. In contrast to its science fiction equivalent, quantum teleportation does not entail the physical displacement of items between different locations. Instead, it emphasizes the transmission of quantum information, which are the basic components of the quantum realm, over long distances without physically crossing the intervening space.

Quantum teleportation is based on the remarkable and deep-seated characteristics of quantum entanglement, which Einstein originally referred to as *spooky action at a distance.*Entanglement is a phenomenon where quantum particles are connected such that the state of one particle immediately affects the state of its entangled partner, regardless of the distance between them.

This procedure involves transmitting quantum information encoded in the state of a qubit from one site to another. It allows for the accurate reproduction of quantum states across different quantum systems. This feature has great potential for quantum communication, cryptography, and computation, leading to a future when the secure and efficient transport of quantum information becomes possible.

This exploration focuses on the complexities of quantum teleportation, examining its mathematical foundations and detailed processes. By comprehending quantum teleportation, we delve into the captivating realm of quantum mechanics, where the distinctions of classical intuition become indistinct, and novel opportunities for information processing and communication arise.

The Protocol

Let us assume there are two people named Alice and Bob. Alice wants to send her qubit state to Bob, which can be achieved through quantum teleportation. Now let us see the step-by-step procedure for how Alice is able to send her qubit state to Bob.

Entanglement Creation

Alice and Bob first establish a shared entangled state. One commonly used entangled state is the Bell state $|\Phi^+\rangle_{AB}$, which is given by,

$$|\Phi^+\rangle_{AB} = \frac{1}{\sqrt{2}}(|00\rangle + |11\rangle) \tag{11.1}$$

This state implies that the particles are perfectly correlated; if one is measured to be in state $|0\rangle$ the other is also in $|0\rangle$ and similarly for $|1\rangle$.

Initial State Preparation

Alice has a qubit **C** whose state $|\psi\rangle$ she wants to teleport to Bob. The state $|\psi\rangle$ is represented as:

$$|\psi\rangle_C = \alpha|0\rangle_C + \beta|1\rangle_C$$

Here, α and β are complex numbers representing the probability amplitudes of the qubit's state.

Combined System

The total initial state of the system, considering the entangled pair and Alice's qubit, can be represented as:

$$|\Psi\rangle_{ABC} = |\psi\rangle_C \otimes |\Phi^+\rangle_{AB} \tag{11.2}$$

Bell State Measurement

Alice performs a measurement on her qubit **C** and her part of the entangled pair **A** in the Bell basis. The system's state before measurement can be expanded in terms of Bell states for qubits **A** and **C**:

$$|\Psi\rangle_{ABC} = \frac{1}{2}\left(|\Phi^+\rangle_{AC}(\alpha|0\rangle_B + \beta|1\rangle_B) + |\Phi^-\rangle_{AC}(\alpha|0\rangle_B - \beta|1\rangle_B) + \cdots\right) \tag{11.3}$$

The measurement collapses the state into one of the Bell states, correlating Bob's qubit

B with the state $|\psi\rangle$ Alice wishes to teleport.

Transmitting the Measurement

Alice sends the result of her Bell measurement to Bob using classical communication. This result is essential for Bob to know how to transform his qubit to achieve the state $|\psi\rangle$.

Recreating the State

Depending on Alice's measurement result, Bob applies the corresponding unitary transformation to his qubit **B** to convert it into the state $|\psi\rangle$. These transformations are:

- If $|\Phi^+\rangle_{AC}$, then U = I (identity)
- If $|\Phi^-\rangle_{AC}$, then U = $\sigma_z(PauliZgate)$
- If $|\Psi^+\rangle_{AC}$, then U = $\sigma_x(PauliXgate)$
- If $|\Psi^-\rangle_{AC}$, then U = $i\sigma_y(PauliYgate)$

After applying the transformation, Bob's qubit is now in the quantum state $|\psi\rangle$ successfully completing the teleportation process.

Implementing Quantum Teleportation Using Qiskit

Let us first import all the neccessary libraries.

```
import numpy as np
from qiskit import QuantumCircuit, QuantumRegister, ClassicalRegister
from qiskit import transpile
from qiskit.providers.basic_provider import BasicProvider
from qiskit.visualization import plot_histogram, plot_bloch_multivector
import matplotlib.pyplot as plt
%matplotlib inline
from qiskit.visualization import plot_histogram
```

Before starting the implementation, there are two things that one should keep in mind, they are:

- To transfer a qubit, Alice and Bob must use a third party (Eve) to send them an entangled qubit pair.
- Alice performs some operations on her qubit, sends the results to Bob over a classical communication channel, and Bob then performs some operations on his end to receive Alice's qubit.

Since the quantum teleportation protocol uses 3 qubits, and 2 classical bits (stored in different registers), we will initialize the Quantum Registers and make our teleportation circuit.

```
qr = QuantumRegister(3)
cr1 = ClassicalRegister(1)
cr2 = ClassicalRegister(1)
teleportation_circuit = QuantumCircuit(qr, cr1, cr2)
```

Step 1: Eve creates an Entangled Pair

A third party, Eve, needs to create an entangled pair of qubits. She will give one to Bob and one to Alice. The pair Eve creates is a special pair called a Bell pair. In order to create a bell pair between two qubits she must first transfer one of them to the X-basis ($|+\rangle$ and $|-\rangle$) using a Hadamard gate (the default basis used in Qiskit is the computational basis), and apply a CNOT gate onto the other qubit controlled by the one in the X-basis. The CNOT gate is a binary gate that is applied on two qubits. It is the way used to create an entangled pair. We will write code to create a circuit and apply the CNOT gate.

```
    def entanglement_bell_pair(qc, a, b):

    qc.h(a) # Put qubit a into state |+> or |-> using hadamard gate
    qc.cx(a,b) # CNOT with a as control and b as target

#  Eve entangles qubits q1 and q2

entanglement_bell_pair(teleportation_circuit, 1, 2)
teleportation_circuit.draw('mpl')
```

The output of the preceding code is as shown as follows:

Step 2: Alice applies quantum gates to her bits

Alice needs to apply a CNOT gate to q1 , controlled by $|\psi\rangle$ (the qubit she sends to Bob which is q0). Then Alice applies a Hadamard gate to $|\psi\rangle$.

```
def alice_state_qubits(qc, psi, a):
qc.cx(psi, a) #psi is the state of q0
qc.h(psi)
```

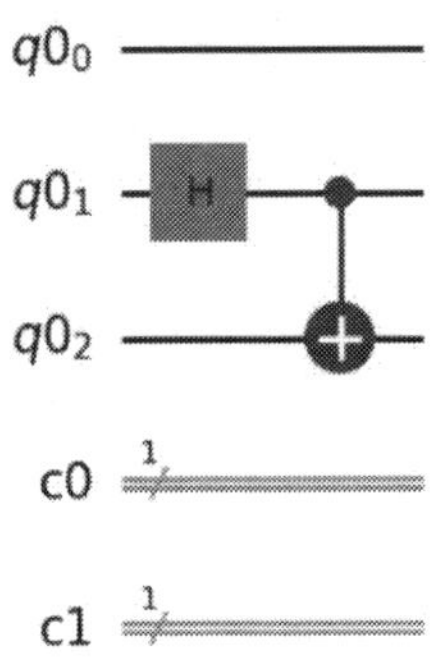

Figure 11.1: Entanglement Bell Pair

```
# call the function to our circuit
teleportation_circuit.barrier()
alice_state_qubits(teleportation_circuit, 0, 1)
teleportation_circuit.draw(output='mpl')
```

The output of the preceding code is shown here:

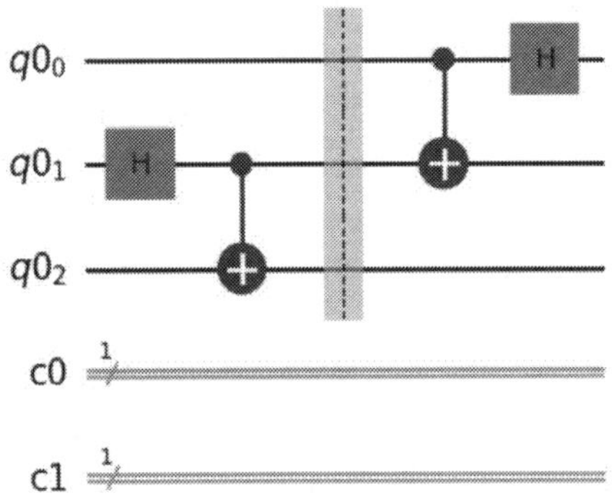

Figure 11.2: Alice applies quantum gates to her bits

Step 3: Alice measures the state of qubits, stores results in classical bits and sends it to Bob

Next, Alice applies a measurement to both qubits that she owns, q1 and $|\psi\rangle$, and stores this result in two classical bits. She then sends these two bits to Bob as we know that this will not violate the no-cloning theorem.

```
    def measure_classical_send(qc, a, b):

    qc.barrier()
    qc.measure(a,0)
    qc.measure(b,1)

measure_classical_send(teleportation_circuit, 0 ,1)
teleportation_circuit.draw(output='mpl')
```

The output of the preceding code is shown here:

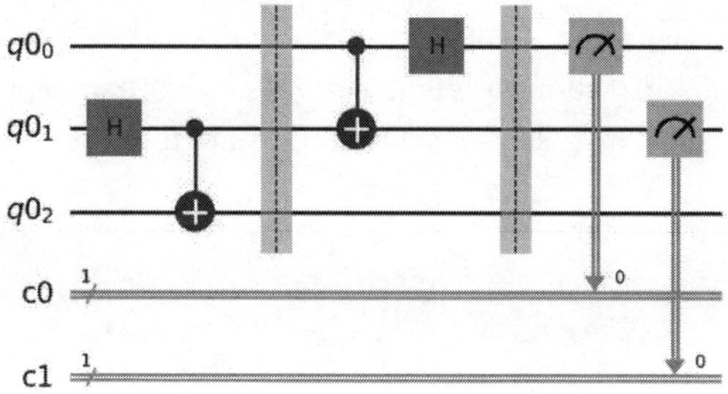

Figure 11.3: Alice measures state of qubits

Step 4: Bob Decodes

Bob, who already has the qubit q2, applies quantum gates based on the bits he receives:

- If 00, then apply I gate.
- If 01, then apply Pauli X gate.
- If 10, then apply Pauli Z gate.
- If 11, then apply Pauli ZX gate.

```
#based on cr1 and cr2 which store the classical bits
def bob_apply_gates(qc, qubit, cr1, cr2):

    qc.z(qubit).c_if(cr1, 1)  #if cr1 is 1 apply Z gate
    qc.x(qubit).c_if(cr2, 1) #if cr2 is 1 apply x gate, look at table above
# Let's apply this to our circuit:
teleportation_circuit.barrier() # Use barrier to separate steps
bob_apply_gates(teleportation_circuit, 2, cr1, cr2)
teleportation_circuit.draw(output='mpl')
```

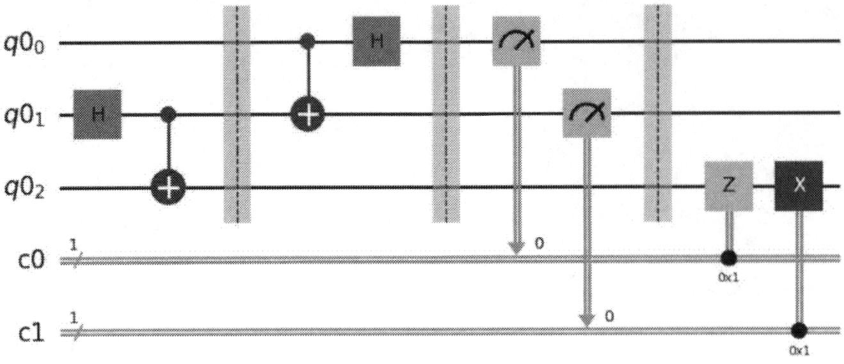

Figure 11.4: Bob Decodes

Step 5: Using a quantum simulator to test the protocol

We will initialize Alice's qubit in a random state $|\psi\rangle$. This state will be created using an Initialize gate on $|q0\rangle$. First, we will create a random state function.

```
    def random_state(nqubits):
    """Creates a random nqubit state vector"""
    from numpy import append, array, sqrt
    from numpy.random import random
    real_parts = array([])
    im_parts = array([])
    for amplitude in range(2**nqubits):
        real_parts = append(real_parts, (random()*2)-1)
        im_parts = append(im_parts, (random()*2)-1)
    # Combine into list of complex numbers:
    amps = real_parts + 1j*im_parts
    # Normalise
    magnitude_squared = 0
    for a in amps:
        magnitude_squared += abs(a)**2
    amps /= sqrt(magnitude_squared)
    return amps
# specify a random state
psi = random_state(1)
```

Define initialization gate to create $|\psi\rangle$ from the state $|0\rangle$:

```
from qiskit.circuit.library import Initialize
init_gate = Initialize(psi)
```

Step 6: Test the quantum teleportation protocol

Now, we will call all the functions we have created so far and test our quantum teleportation protocol.

```
qr = QuantumRegister(3)
cr1 = ClassicalRegister(1)
cr2 = ClassicalRegister(1)
qc = QuantumCircuit(qr, cr1, cr2)

#let's initialise Alice's q0
qc.append(init_gate, [0])
qc.barrier()

# teleportation protocol
entanglement_bell_pair(qc, 1, 2)
qc.barrier()
# Send q1 to Alice and q2 to Bob
alice_state_qubits(qc, 0, 1)

# alice sends to Bob
measure_classical_send(qc, 0, 1)

# Bob decodes qubits
bob_apply_gates(qc, 2, cr1, cr2)

qc.draw(output='mpl')
```

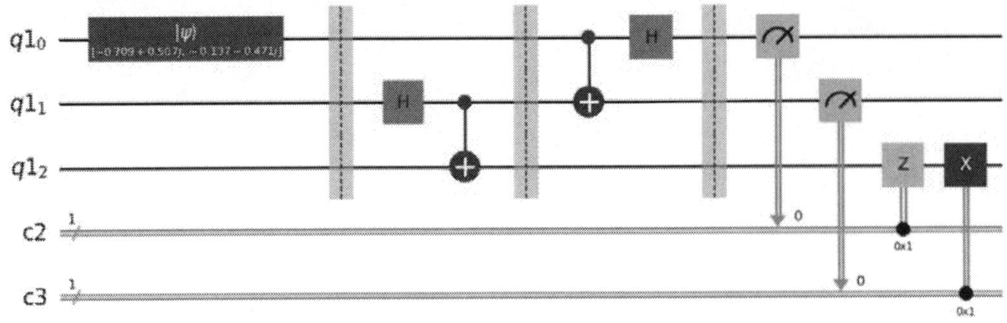

Figure 11.5: Quantum Teleportation Circuit

```
from qiskit_aer import Aer
backend = Aer.get_backend('statevector_simulator')
result = backend.run(qc).result()
sv = result.get_statevector(qc)
plot_bloch_multivector(sv)
```

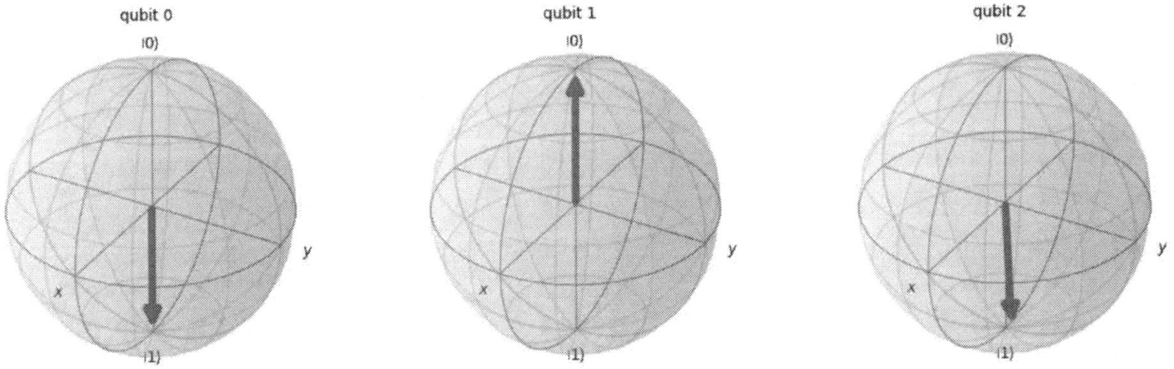

Figure 11.6: Bloch Sphere Visualization

Step 7: Execute on Backend

Quantum teleportation is designed to send qubits between two parties. We would not be able to use the state vector on a quantum computer, so to check that the teleportation circuit is working, we need to do things slightly differently. You will remember that we used Initialize to turn our $|0\rangle$ qubit into the state $|\psi\rangle$.

$|0\rangle \longrightarrow$ Initialize $|\psi\rangle$

Since all quantum gates are reversible, we can find the inverse of Initialize using:

```
inverse_init_gate
init_gate.gates_to_uncompute()
qc.append(inverse_init_gate, [2])
qc.draw(output='mpl')
```

```
#add a new classical register to see the result
cr_result = ClassicalRegister(1)
qc.add_register(cr_result)
qc.measure(2,2)
qc.draw(output='mpl')
```

Plot the histogram of the results:

```
from qiskit.providers.basic_provider import BasicSimulator
backend = BasicSimulator()
tqc = transpile(qc, backend)
counts = backend.run(tqc).result().get_counts()
plot_histogram(counts)
```

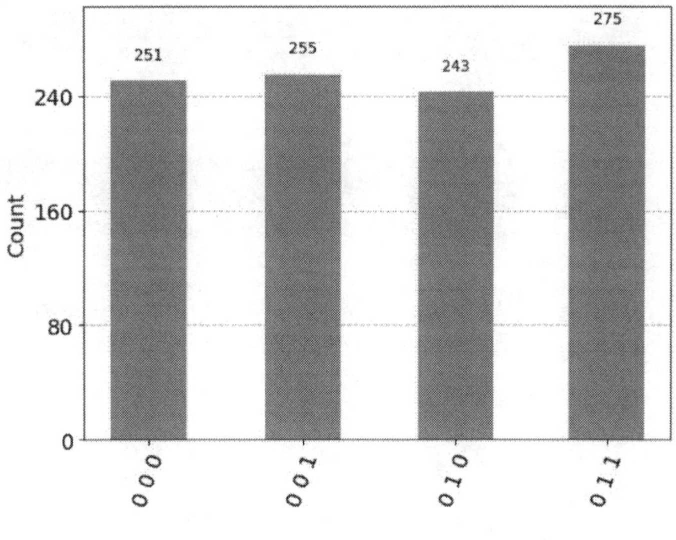

Figure 11.7: Histogram plot

We can see that we have a 100% chance of measuring q2 (the leftmost bit in the string) in the state $|0\rangle$. This is the expected result and indicates the teleportation protocol has worked properly.

Superdense Coding

The concepts of quantum teleportation and superdense coding are closely connected, yet to avoid confusion, it is necessary to differentiate between the two.

Using two bits of classical communication and a Bell pair, quantum teleportation is a procedure that allows the state of a qubit $|\psi\rangle$ to be sent from one location to another. This is accomplished through the use of conventional communication. In other terms, we may say that it is a protocol that uses shared entanglement to destroy the quantum state of a qubit in one site and then reconstruct it on a qubit in a different location. This is accomplished by destroying the qubit's quantum state there. The process of superdense coding is a method that enables one person to convey two classical bits to another party while only utilizing a single qubit of transmission. To put it another way, the teleportation protocol can be compared to a reversed version of the superdense coding protocol. This is because Alice and Bob just "swap their equipment" in order to use the teleportation protocol.

Teleportation	**Superdense Coding**
Transmit one qubit using two classical bits	Transmit two classical bits using one qubit
Information flows from sender to receiver	Information is encoded by the sender into the entangled state and then decoded by the receiver
Useful in scenarios where direct transmission of quantum states is difficult or impossible	Useful in maximizing the efficiency of data transfer over quantum networks, making it suitable for high-density information transmission scenarios.

Table 11.1: Teleportation and Superdense coding

Table 11.1 shows the difference between teleportation and superdense coding.

The Protocol

Here, we will describe the superdense coding protocol step by step.

Step 1

We will refer to this individual as Charlie, and he is the first step in the process. The preparation of two qubits in an entangled state is carried out by Charlie. Initially, he begins the process of starting the two qubits in the basic state $|0\rangle$. For the purpose of generating superposition, he applies the Hadamard gate to the first qubit. The CNOT gate is then applied, with the first qubit serving as the control and the second qubit doing the work of the target. The entangled state, also known as the Bell pair, is what we were referring to earlier.

We start with the state:

$$|00\rangle = |0\rangle_A \otimes |0\rangle_B \tag{11.4}$$

where the qubit to be sent to Alice is labeled with A and the qubit to be sent to Bob is labeled B. Charlie first applies a Hadamard gate to the first qubit, which creates superposition and we get the state:

$$|{+0}\rangle = \frac{1}{\sqrt{2}}(|00\rangle + |10\rangle) \tag{11.5}$$

Then Charlie applies the CNOT gate. The CNOT gate entangles both qubits, i.e., it flips the target if the control is 1. Note that the control qubit is our leftmost qubit.

$$\text{CNOT}\left(\frac{1}{\sqrt{2}}(|00\rangle + |10\rangle)\right) = \frac{1}{\sqrt{2}}(|00\rangle + |11\rangle) \tag{11.6}$$

Step 2

The first qubit is delivered to Alice by Charlie, and the second qubit is delivered to Bob by Charlie. In order to accomplish the protocol's objective, Alice must use her qubit to transmit two classical bits of information to Bob. However, before she can proceed, she must first apply a set of quantum gates to her qubit, making sure that the gates are appropriate for the two bits of information that she wishes to transmit:

Table 11.2 shows the encoding rules for superdense coding (Alice protocol):

Intended Message	Applied Gate	Resulting State
00	I	$\|00\rangle + \|11\rangle$
01	X	$\|10\rangle + \|01\rangle$
10	Z	$\|00\rangle - \|11\rangle$
11	ZX	$-\|10\rangle + \|01\rangle$

Table 11.2: Encoding rules for superdense coding

Thus if she wants to send a 00, she does nothing to her qubit (apply the identity (I) gate). If she wants to send a 01, then she applies the X gate. Depending on what she wants to send, she applies the appropriate gate, then sends her qubit to Bob for the final step in the process.

Step 3

Bob obtains Alice's qubit, which is the leftmost qubit, and then uses his own qubit to decipher the message that Alice sent. It should be brought to your attention that in order to decode it, he does not require any prior knowledge of the state; rather, he merely employs the restoration operation. Bob applies a CNOT gate, with the qubit on the left as the control and the right as the target. He then applies a Hadamard gate and, to recover Alice's message, measures both qubits individually.

Bob Receives $\left(-\frac{1}{\sqrt{2}}\right)$	**After CNOT-gate** $\left(-\frac{1}{\sqrt{2}}\right)$	**After H-gate**
$\|00\rangle + \|11\rangle$	$\|00\rangle + \|10\rangle$	$\|00\rangle$
$\|10\rangle + \|01\rangle$	$\|11\rangle + \|01\rangle$	$\|01\rangle$
$\|00\rangle - \|11\rangle$	$\|00\rangle - \|10\rangle$	$\|10\rangle$
$-\|10\rangle + \|01\rangle$	$-\|11\rangle + \|01\rangle$	$\|11\rangle$

Table 11.3: Quantum state transformations involving Bob's operations

Table 11.3 shows bob decoding process.

Implementing Superdense Coding Using Qiskit

Now, let us see how superdense coding is implemented using qiskit. It starts with a third party (say, Charlie) who prepares a pair of entangled states at |0⟩. Applying Hadamard gates to both the initialized qubits, a CX gate is applied in order to create an entangled state. (The first is the control, and the second is the target).

```
def preparation(qc):
    qc.h(0)
    qc.cx(0,1)
```

Sender takes q0 and receiver takes q1, they travel far apart.

```
def seperation(qc):
    qc.barrier()
```

Next, we encode as we discussed in step 2.

```
def state_00(qc):
    pass


def state_01(qc):
    qc.z(0)
```

```
def state_10(qc):
    qc.x(0)

def state_11(qc):
    qc.x(0)
    qc.z(0)

def encoding(qc):
    message = input('Enter your intended message from 00, 01, 10 and 11 :   ')
    if message == '00':
        state_00(qc)
    elif message == '01':
        state_01(qc)
    elif message == '10':
        state_10(qc)
    elif message == '11':
        state_11(qc)
    else:
        print('Invalid message: Sending 00')
```

The sender physically sends h(is/er) encoded qubit to the receiver.

```
def transmission(qc):
    qc.barrier()
```

Now, we decode as discussed in step 3 above.

```
from qiskit.providers.basic_provider import BasicSimulator
from qiskit import transpile
from qiskit.visualization import plot_histogram
def bell_measure(qc):
    qc.cx(0,1)
    qc.h(0)
    qc.measure(range(2),range(2))
    display(qc.draw('mpl'))
    backend = BasicSimulator()
    tqc = transpile(qc,backend)
    counts = backend.run(tqc).result().get_counts()
```

```
    received = dict([(value,key) for key,value in counts.items()])
    display(plot_histogram(counts))
```

The complete protocol in a simulator.

```
from qiskit import QuantumCircuit
## Initializing:
qc_test = QuantumCircuit(2,2)

## Preparing entangled state:
preparation(qc_test)

## Sender Receiver moves apart:
seperation(qc_test)

## Sender encodes h(is/er) qubit:
encoding(qc_test)

## Sender transmits h(is/er) encoded qubit physically to receiver:
transmission(qc_test)

# Receiver performs bell-measurement on both qubits :
bell_measure(qc_test)
```

```
Enter your intended message from 00, 01, 10 and 11 :   11
```

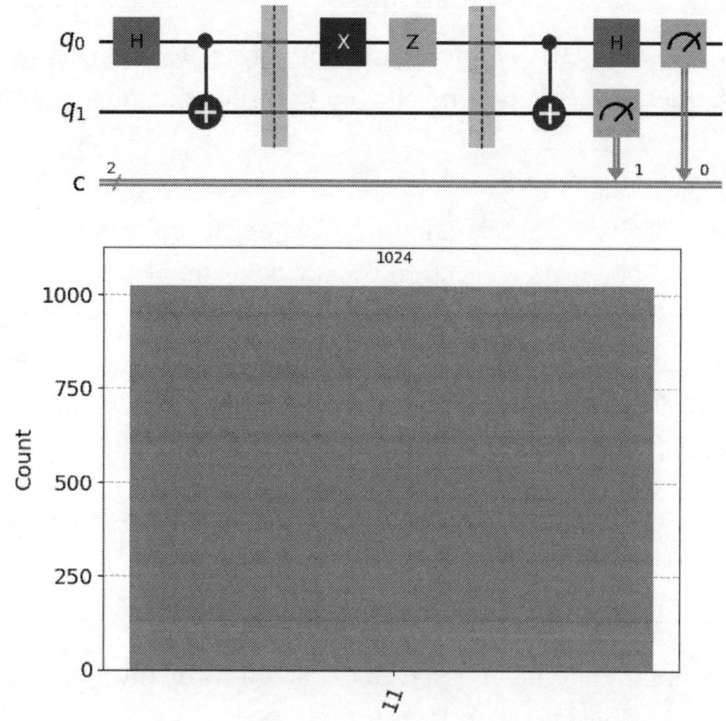

Figure 11.8: Superdense Coding Output

Quantum Cryptography

Quantum cryptography is an encryption technique that leverages the inherent characteristics of quantum physics to safeguard and transmit data in an impervious manner to hacking.

Cryptography is the method of encoding and safeguarding data so that only individuals possessing the correct secret key may decode it. Quantum cryptography diverges from conventional cryptographic systems by placing physics, rather than mathematics, at the core of its security framework.

Quantum cryptography is an inherently secure system that cannot be hacked without the awareness of both the message sender and the receiver. Specifically, it is not feasible to replicate or access information stored in a quantum state without notifying the sender or recipient. Quantum cryptography must also maintain its security against adversaries utilizing quantum computing.

Quantum cryptography employs photons, which are individual particles of light, to convey data across fiber optic cables. The photons serve as binary units. The system's security is dependent on the principles of quantum physics. The following properties are secure:

- Particles have the ability to occupy several locations or states simultaneously.
- A quantum characteristic cannot be viewed without causing a change or disruption to it.
- It is not possible to duplicate entire particles.

The inherent characteristics of these features render it unfeasible to accurately determine the quantum state of any given system without causing disruption to that system.

Photons are employed in quantum cryptography because they possess all the requisite characteristics: Their activity is comprehensively understood, and they serve as conveyors of information in optical fibre cables. Quantum key distribution (QKD) is a well-known and highly regarded form of quantum cryptography that offers a reliable means of exchanging secure keys.

Functioning of Quantum Cryptography

A model that was created in 1984 is used to explain how quantum cryptography should work. The model thinks that Alice and Bob are two people who want to send a message safely to each other. Alice sends Bob a key to start the message. A stream of photons moving in one way is the key. Each photon is a single bit of information, either a 0 or a 1. These photons are moving in a straight line, but they are also oscillating, or quivering, in a certain way.

The photons go through a polarizer before Alice, the source, starts the message. Polarizers are like filters; they let some photons pass through with the same vibrations while letting other photons pass through with different vibrations. The split states could be 45 degrees to the right (1 bit), 45 degrees to the left (0 bit), or 45 degrees to the right (1 bit). There are two possible polarizations for the transmission: either 0 or 1. This means that the bit can be either 0 or 1.

Now, the photons are moving from the polarizer along the optical line to Bob, the receiver. For this process, a beam splitter is used to read the polarization of each photon. Bob does not know which phase of the photons to use when he gets the photon key, so he picks one at random. Now Alice checks to see what Bob did to polarize the key and then tells Bob which polarizer she used to send each photon. After that, Bob checks to make sure he used the right filter. The photons that were read with the wrong splitter are then thrown away, and the sequence that is left is thought to be the secret.

It's possible that someone is listening in. Let's call her Eve. Eve tries to listen in, and she has the same tools that Bob does. But, while Eve can't, Bob can talk to Alice to find out what kind of filter was used for each photon. Eve makes a mistake when she writes the last key. Eve is also discovered by Alice and Bob. If Eve watched how the photons moved, it would change where Alice and Bob think the photons are.

Figure 11.9: The case of Alice, Bob and Eve

In the *Figure* 11.9, it can be clearly seen that the photons Alice sent have been changed due to Eavesdropping.

Uses and Examples of Quantum Cryptography

Compared to standard cryptography, quantum cryptography makes it safer for people to talk to each other. Once the parties involved have traded keys, there isn't much chance that someone bad could read the data without the key. If someone looks at the key while it's being made, the intended result changes, which lets both the sender and the receiver know.

This type of encryption hasn't been fully worked out yet, but it has been used successfully in the following ways:

- The University of Cambridge and Toshiba Corp. used the BB84 quantum cryptography protocol to make a high-bit rate QKD device.
- The Defense Advanced Research Projects Agency Quantum Network was a 10-node QKD network built by Boston University, Harvard University, and IBM Research. It was in use from 2002 to 2007.
- Quantum Xchange set up the first quantum network in the United States. It has 1,000

kilometres (km) of fibre optic line.

- Business firms like ID Quantique, Toshiba, Quintessence Labs, and MagiQ Technologies Inc. also made business QKD systems.

Besides QKD, these are some of the most well-known protocols and quantum methods used in quantum cryptography:

- Quantum coin tossing;
- Quantum cryptography based on position;
- Quantum key distribution with BB84 Protocol.

Benefits of Quantum Cryptography

Quantum cryptography has several advantages, including:

- Ensures encrypted and protected communication. Quantum cryptography relies on the principles of physics rather than complex numerical codes, making it a highly advanced and secure kind of encryption.
- Identifies the presence of unauthorized interception of communication. When an unauthorized individual tries to access the encrypted data, the quantum state is altered, resulting in a different expected result for the users.
- Provides a variety of security options. Multiple quantum cryptography protocols are utilized. For instance, techniques such as QKD can be integrated with classical encryption methods to enhance security.

Cons of Quantum Cryptography

The potential drawbacks and constraints associated with quantum cryptography are as follows:

- Modifications in polarization and error rates: Photons can alter their polarization during transmission, potentially leading to an increase in error rates.
- Quantum cryptography normally has a maximum range of approximately 400 to 500 km, except with Terra Quantum, which has a different range.
- Quantum cryptography necessitates a dedicated infrastructure, employing fibre optic cables and repeaters.
- Number of destinations: Sending keys to several locations in a quantum channel is not feasible.

Applications of Quantum Communication

Quantum communication is at the forefront of secure communication technology, utilizing the principles of quantum mechanics to achieve unparalleled levels of privacy and security. Its applications cover a broad spectrum of fields, including data encryption, networking, and more. Here's a brief summary of several important applications:

Quantum Key Distribution

A widely recognized application of quantum communication stands out among the rest. QKD enables the creation of cryptographic keys that are highly secure against any attempts to eavesdrop, thanks to the fundamental principles of quantum mechanics. Unlike traditional cryptographic methods that depend on solving mathematical problems, QKD is based on the principles of quantum mechanics, including the uncertainty principle and the no-cloning theorem. Using the principles of quantum mechanics, QKD guarantees that any unauthorized attempt to intercept the communication will disrupt the delicate quantum state, immediately notifying the communicating parties of a potential eavesdropper. This allows for the creation of extremely secure communication channels to transmit sensitive information, like financial transactions or government communications.

Quantum Teleportation

Quantum teleportation involves the transfer of the quantum state of one system to another system located far away without the need for physical transportation of the system itself. Although quantum teleportation has not been achieved for larger objects, it has been effectively demonstrated for quantum bits (qubits) of information. This capability has a wide range of potential applications in the fields of quantum computing, quantum networking, and quantum communication. It allows for the efficient transfer of quantum information over long distances, ensuring high fidelity in the process.

Quantum Cryptography

The realm of quantum cryptography expands beyond QKD to include a wider array of cryptographic protocols and techniques rooted in quantum principles. Some examples of these are quantum secure direct communication (QSDC), quantum coin flipping, and quantum digital signatures, among others. Quantum cryptography tackles the security hurdles in modern communication systems by utilizing quantum states and processes to ensure provable security guarantees. It focuses on key distribution, authentication, and integrity verification.

Quantum Internet

It is a network infrastructure that allows for the secure transmission of quantum information between connected nodes. Expanding on quantum communication technologies such as QKD and quantum teleportation, a quantum internet would enable a variety of applications, including secure communication, distributed quantum computing, and quantum sensor networks. Scientists are diligently working to bring the concept of a quantum internet to life. Through experiments and demonstrations, they are making progress in creating quantum communication protocols and infrastructure that are scalable and dependable.

Exploring the Realm of Quantum Sensors and Metrology

Applying quantum communication techniques can greatly improve sensing and metrology capabilities across different fields, such as precision measurement, navigation, and imaging. Quantum sensors utilize the fascinating properties of quantum mechanics to achieve remarkable levels of sensitivity and precision. This opens up a wide range of applications, including the detection of gravitational waves, mapping magnetic fields, and imaging biological systems. By incorporating quantum communication technologies into sensor networks, scientists can improve the durability and safety of distributed sensing systems, while also unlocking new possibilities for scientific research and technological advancement.

Simply put, quantum communication has the potential to completely transform secure communication and unlock a whole new world of possibilities in various fields, including cryptography, networking, sensing, and metrology. With the ongoing progress in quantum communication research and development, we can anticipate the emergence of more advanced applications and infrastructure that utilize the principles of quantum mechanics to revolutionize our methods of communication and interaction with the world.

Future of Quantum Communication

The future of quantum communication holds immense potential to completely transform the way we transmit, secure, and process information. As advancements in quantum technologies continue to unfold, a number of significant trends and directions are becoming apparent:

Scalability and Integration

One of the main obstacles to achieving practical quantum communication systems is the issue of scalability. Quantum communication protocols, such as Quantum Key Distribution (QKD), have been successfully tested over shorter distances and with a smaller number of users. Nevertheless, expanding these systems to encompass larger networks and cover longer distances poses considerable technical obstacles. In the future, our main focus will be on creating architectures that can be scaled up and incorporating quantum communication protocols into the current telecommunications infrastructure. This involves the creation of quantum repeaters that can expand the reach of quantum communication links and the incorporation of quantum devices into fibre-optic networks.

The Concept of a Quantum Internet

It involves creating a network of interconnected quantum nodes to facilitate secure quantum communication and distributed quantum computing, which is quickly transitioning from a theoretical idea to a tangible possibility. Scientists are making remarkable progress in the development of the essential technologies and protocols for constructing a quantum internet. Important elements of the quantum internet consist of quantum repeaters for transmitting information over long distances, quantum routers for directing quantum data, and quantum memories for retaining quantum states. Efforts are also being made to standardize quantum communication protocols and establish international collaborations to speed up the development of a global quantum internet infrastructure.

Quantum Computing and Simulation

Quantum communication and quantum computing are closely connected. Understanding quantum communication protocols is crucial for the development of quantum computing systems. With the advancement of quantum computing technologies, the importance of quantum communication cannot be overstated. It will serve as a vital link between distributed quantum processors, facilitating secure communication among them. In addition, quantum communication can be utilized for quantum simulation, where quantum systems are employed to simulate intricate physical phenomena. Quantum communication networks enable the distribution of entangled states to support distributed quantum simulations and problem-solving in fields like materials science, chemistry, and fundamental physics.

Quantum-Secure Cryptography

Given the rise of advanced quantum computers, traditional cryptographic algorithms will be at risk of being compromised by quantum algorithms like Shor's algorithm, which can efficiently factor large numbers. Utilizing quantum communication can effectively address this issue by implementing cryptographic protocols that are resistant to quantum attacks. Utilizing mathematical problems that pose a challenge even for quantum computers, post-quantum cryptography can be implemented with the help of quantum communication techniques. This ensures long-term security against potential quantum attacks. Understanding the principles of quantum-resistant cryptography and how it can be combined with quantum communication is essential in order to safeguard upcoming communication networks from potential quantum risks.

Commercialization and Applications

With the advancement and increased availability of quantum communication technologies, it is inevitable to witness their extensive adoption and integration into diverse industries. Industries such as finance, healthcare, government, and defence can greatly benefit from quantum communication's heightened security and privacy. Utilizing quantum communication networks will provide high security for various applications such as financial transactions, confidential healthcare communication, and secure government communications. In addition, quantum sensors and metrology devices that utilize quantum communication techniques will have practical applications in various fields, including environmental monitoring, infrastructure inspection, and precision agriculture.

Ultimately, the future of quantum communication appears promising, as continuous research and development are driving the advancement of revolutionary technologies and applications. As we explore the depths of quantum science and engineering, quantum communication will be instrumental in shaping the future of secure and efficient information transmission in the digital age.

Conclusion

This chapter has examined the captivating realm of quantum communication protocols, specifically focusing on the complexities of quantum teleportation and superdense coding. Using Qiskit, we have directly observed the effectiveness of quantum entanglement in facilitating the transfer of information in manners that are beyond the capabilities of classical systems. Quantum teleportation enables the accurate transmission of quantum states over long distances. At the same time, superdense coding demonstrates the exceptional efficiency of quantum communication by conveying two classical bits with only one qubit. In addition, we have analyzed the fundamental principles of quantum cryptography, emphasizing its capacity to transform secure communication by utilizing protocols such as quantum key distribution. These technological breakthroughs offer the potential to improve the security and effectiveness of our communication networks, establishing a solid foundation for future innovations.

The next chapter will deal with the variational quantum eigensolver algorithm, a significantly used algorithm for quantum chemistry and material science simulations. This algorithm enables the usage of quantum computers for industrial applications.

CHAPTER 12

Variational Quantum Algorithms

Introduction

Variational Quantum Algorithms (VQAs) are a type of hybrid quantum-classical algorithms that make use of the advantages of quantum computing while effectively addressing its existing constraints. These algorithms play a crucial role in numerous quantum applications soon, since they provide a viable method for addressing intricate optimization issues by progressively improving the parameters of quantum circuits. This chapter focuses on the detailed structure of VQAs, examining their fundamental elements, many categories, and the benefits and inherent difficulties they present. Additionally, we will analyze how these algorithms function as fundamental instruments for diverse quantum applications, such as quantum chemistry and machine learning.

The chapter proceeds to provide an in-depth examination of the Variational Quantum Eigensolver (VQE), an innovative technique inside the VQA framework that has shown considerable promise in estimating the ground-state energies of molecular systems. The following topics will be discussed: fundamental ideas of Variational Quantum Eigensolver (VQE), its implementation using Qiskit, and the difficulties involved in deploying it on existing quantum hardware. Next, we will go into the Quantum Approximate Optimization

Algorithm (QAOA), which is specifically designed for solving combinatorial optimization problems. The chapter ends by analyzing the practical applications, different forms, and difficulties connected to QAOA, offering a thorough comprehension of the present status and future possibilities of VQAs in quantum computing.

Structure

In this chapter, you are going to study:

- Designing Variational Quantum Algorithms
  - Core Components of VQA's
  - Types of VQA's
  - Advantages
  - Disadvantages
  - Foundation for Other Algorithms and Applications
- VQE Algorithm and Procedure
  - Key terms related to VQE
  - Implementing VQE in Qiskit
  - Variants of VQE
  - Applications of VQE
  - Challenges in Implementation
- QAOA Algorithm and Procedure
  - Implementing QAOA in Qiskit
  - Variants of QAOA
  - Applications of QAOA
  - Challenges in Implementation

Designing Variational Quantum Algorithms (VQA's)

In this decade, research is focused on different areas like Quantum Key Distribution (QKD), Quantum Error Correction (QEC), Quantum Machine learning (QML), Quantum hardware like topological quantum computing, Superconducting circuits, Quantum dots, Trapped ions, neutral atoms and more. However current quantum devices have serious constraints like limitations to use qubits, environmental noise and decoherence.

This problem is solved efficiently by VQAs. The term **variational** refers to the use of variational principles, which are methods for finding the minimum (or maximum) of a function. In the context of VQAs, this typically involves finding the minimum of a cost function, which is a way to measure how far off a quantum algorithm's output is from the desired result. This approach is used in several quantum algorithms to solve optimization problems, among other things. VQA uses a Classical Optimizer to train parameterized Quantum circuits. VQAs leverage Classical optimization and use parameterized Quantum circuits that run on quantum computers and then outsource parameter optimization to a classical optimizer. This makes the quantum circuit depth shallow, if the circuit depth is shallow then the noise is mitigated.

In short, VQAs are hybrid algorithms that combine quantum and classical computing and are designed to find approximate solutions to optimization problems on quantum computers.

Core components of VQA's

Let us see briefly some of the core components that are involved in a VQA architecture. This will also help us to understand the inner workings of the VQAs in the next section.

1. **Variational Circuit (Ansatz)**

This quantum circuit has tuneable parameters. Circuit design is vital and typically adapted to the problem. Ansatz selection can greatly impact algorithm efficiency and solution quality.

2. **Classical Optimizer**

This component adjusts variational circuit parameters to reduce (or maximize) a given objective function, which is commonly measured by executing the circuit on a quantum computer. The optimizer iterates through parameter adjustments based on quantum computation results in a classical computation environment.

3. **Cost function**

The cost function quantifies the degree of similarity between the desired outcome and the output of the quantum circuit based on a certain parameter set. The evaluation is conducted by measuring the quantum state generated by the circuit. The precise formulation of the cost function varies depending on the specific challenge at hand, such as determining ground state energies or solving optimization problems. The classical optimizer aims to identify the parameters that reduce or maximize the cost function.

4. **Encoding problem**

Before applying a VQA, the problem must be encoded in a manner compatible with the processing capabilities of the quantum circuit. This entails converting the problem into a quantum Hamiltonian or an alternative representation that can be expressed within a quantum system. The method by which problems are encoded can greatly affect the efficiency and effectiveness of the algorithm.

5. **Parameter selection**

The initial condition for the optimization process might impact its rate of convergence and whether it reaches a global minimum or merely a local minimum. The initial parameters might be selected randomly, based on heuristics, or by utilizing knowledge from the issue domain.

Detailed Working behind VQA's

In this section, you will learn about the detailed working and design of variational quantum algorithms step-by-step by considering sequential VQA architecture block diagrams. The diagrams and explanations of this section have been redrawn and adapted from Michał Stęchły's Musty Thoughts blog respectively. The links to the blog articles have been provided in the references section of this chapter.

Indeed, quantum computers in the present day are inherently flawed technologies. Certainly, there is no justification to believe that these flaws have not affected the measurement procedure. Measurement of a qubit can result in the occurrence of several mistakes. It is often indeterminate if an error has happened, but at other times we may identify its presence by analyzing the behavior of the physical system. It is therefore possible to either discard such a sample or rectify it. It is important to note that measurement errors might be significantly larger than compared to other forms of errors.

Another important aspect to consider is the inclusion of various forms of error mitigation or error correction. At its most fundamental level, it is not necessary to utilize it for Variational Quantum Algorithms (VQAs), as they are specifically engineered to have a certain level of resistance to noise. Although they may derive advantages from it. The inclusion of error correction is a sophisticated enhancement of the fundamental VQA techniques. One further complexity arises from the fact that, depending on the implementation, it may be located in various positions within our diagram, such as ansatz or compilation.

Typically, in order to obtain measurements for each Pauli term of a given Hamiltonian, it is necessary to run a separate circuit. Nevertheless, this approach is very simplistic - in fact, there exist specific grouping techniques that enable the simultaneous measurement of many parameters. Thus, selecting a certain grouping approach can impact the appearance of the circuit, especially its last segment.

Determining the desired number of samples, sometimes referred to as "shots," is a complex and essential matter. While a single sample may be insufficient for a certain problem, a sample size of one million may be much excessive. Typically, we just choose a certain numerical value, such as 1000. To further complicate matters, it may be advisable to employ different quantities of shots for separate groups or modify it in different iterations of the optimization loop.

Accordingly, this is the current appearance of our picture shown in *Figure* 12.1.

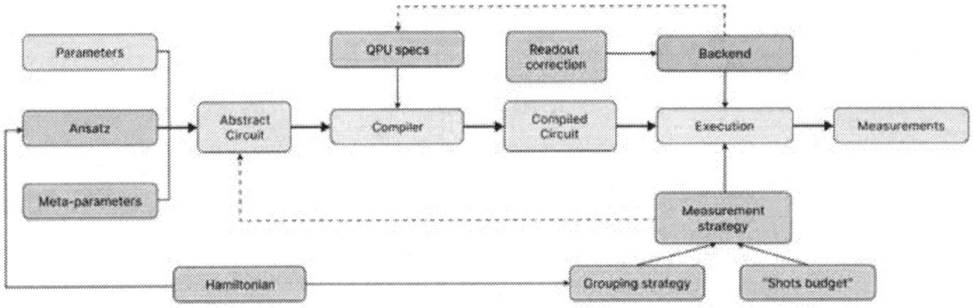

Figure 12.1: The image depicts a quantum workflow pipeline for executing a variational quantum algorithm

As evident, we have also included a Hamiltonian box. While it may impact the appearance of our ansatz (e.g. in QAOA) or determine the necessity for state rotation before measurement (in VQE), it also directs the grouping approach.

These measurements obtained at the conclusion raise the question of whether they are of significant importance to us. They serve only as a method to achieve a goal. Indeed, they are! The objective in the case of Variational Quantum Eigensolver (VQE) is to determine the expected value of an operator. This involves analyzing the measurements for each term to identify the eigenvector they represent and calculate the related eigenvalue. For further information, please refer to the VQE article. In the context of QAOA, it is unnecessary to employ such procedures. We can simply input the bitstring we have obtained, substitute it into the cost function, and obtain the cost value. Given the potential variability in the specific method described, let us refer to this section as *postprocessing* and acknowledge that it converts all the obtained data into *energy* or *cost value.*

Figure 12.2 thus far can be partitioned into two sections. One encompasses all the actions we take to create a circuit that will be executed on quantum devices. The second category encompasses all our actions and activities related to this circuit, including its operation and the results obtained from measurements.

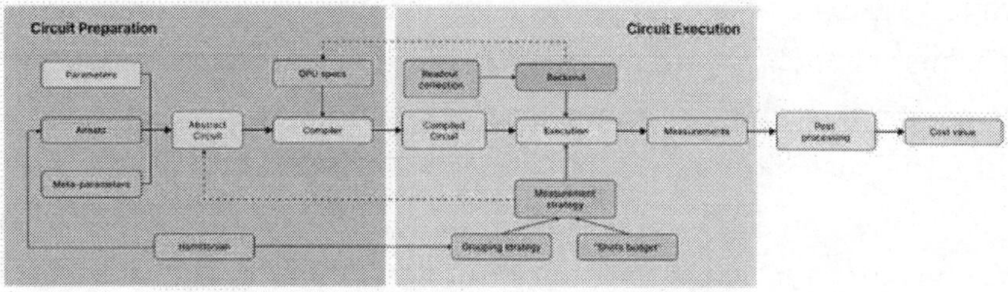

Figure 12.2: The image represents the workflow of a variational quantum algorithm (VQA), divided into Circuit Preparation and Circuit Execution phases

Given some parameters, we construct a circuit, execute it, measure its performance, compute the energy value, and input it to the optimizer together with the initial parameters. Given that the optimizer may require previous values in order to function correctly, there is also a dashed loop around it.

This new block is titled *Optimizer*, but, we have not yet adequately addressed the topic of *Parameters*. Therefore, let us begin with that.

Given that the optimizer modifies parameters according to the cost function value, it is unclear from whence the initial set of parameters originates. Those originate from a *parameter initialization* process. To initialize them, we require empirical knowledge of a few specific factors:

- What is the total number of parameters?
- Are they subject to any form of constraint?
- Which approach should we employ for the initialization?

The answers to the first two questions are contingent upon the methodology employed and the specific problem being addressed. In the case of QAOA, the number of parameters is determined totally by the number of layers, not by the problem at hand. Each layer consists of a single pair of (β, γ). Furthermore, considering the periodic nature of our ansatz with relation to these angles, it may be advisable to restrict them to the range of $(0, 2\pi)$. There remains one final point to be addressed - how to select optimal initial angles. The most fundamental approach is to randomly select them, but, there exist several alternative method to obtain more optimal beginning values, which ultimately impact the algorithm's effectiveness.

A first consideration is that an optimizer may possess several hyperparameters, such as the desired magnitude of the steps in a gradient approach or the desired number of iterations. These hyperparameters may vary during the optimization process.

Furthermore, separate from the parameters of the optimizer, there are also its limitations. Sometimes it may be necessary to impose restrictions on the parameters, such as requiring them to total to 1, which affects the behavior of the optimizer. One conceivable scenario is an issue in which we are aware that our quantum state must have a predetermined number of particles and our quantum circuit should not include states with other numbers, despite the possibility using the ansatz we employ.

Finally, an optimizer may alter certain components within the *Circuit preparation/circuit execution* box, particularly the measurement technique. The most straightforward example is altering the quantity of shots implemented during the training session. It may be contended that during the initial iterations of exploring the optimization landscape, a high level of precision may not be necessary, and hence, a reduced number of shots can be executed to save some QPU time. Nevertheless, when we approach the minimum, even a slight variation in parameters can have significant repercussions, so we rather aim for greater precision. Thus, this is the current architecture of VQA is shown in *Figure* 12.3.

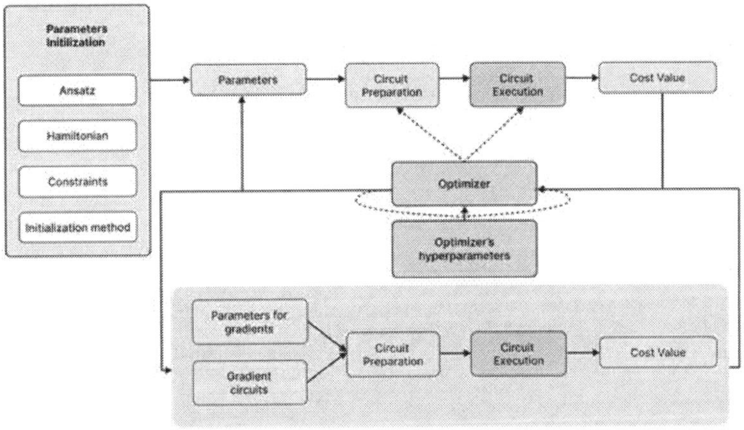

Figure 12.3: The image illustrates the workflow of a Variational Quantum Algorithm (VQA) with an optimization loop.

Situated at the lower part, the gradient computation loop is visible. To avoid unnecessary complexity, we will conceal this visualization within the optimizer. *Figure* 12.4 is highly precise for the generic variants of VQAs that are commonly encountered.

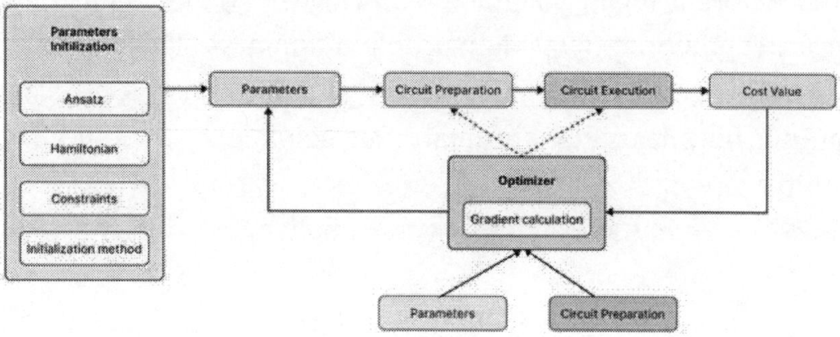

Figure 12.4: The image presents a Variational Quantum Algorithm (VQA) workflow with gradient-based optimization.

Now let us see some of the common advantages and disadvantages of VQAs.

Pros and Cons of VQA's

There are several advantages and disadvantages of variational quantum algorithms and it is helpful to be aware of this since it aids in the development of novel techniques and provides insights about the practical applicability of these algorithms.

Advantanges

Some of the advantages of VQAs are

- **NISQ Compatibility:**
  VQAs are specifically engineered for Noisy Intermediate-Scale Quantum (NISQ) devices. They operate using relatively shallow circuits and a modest number of qubits, making them well-suited to current hardware constraints. This enables the exploration of quantum computing potential without the need for full quantum error correction, thereby leveraging the capabilities of existing quantum processors.
- **Error Tolerance:**
  By integrating classical optimization techniques within a hybrid quantum-classical framework, VQAs can partially mitigate the impact of hardware noise and gate imperfections. The variational principle allows the optimization process to adjust circuit parameters in response to experimental errors, enhancing the overall robustness and reliability of the computed outcomes despite the inherent noise in current quantum devices.
- **Flexibility:**

The VQA framework is highly adaptable, allowing the design of custom parameterized circuits (Ansätze) tailored to specific problem domains. This flexibility makes VQAs applicable to a wide range of tasks, including combinatorial optimization, quantum simulation, machine learning, and materials science. The ability to fine-tune the circuit architecture and cost function enables researchers to balance expressibility with resource efficiency, addressing diverse challenges effectively.

Disadvantages

Some of the disadvantages of VQAs are

- **Barren Plateaus:**
  VQAs can suffer from the *barren plateau* phenomenon in their optimization landscapes. In these regions, the gradient of the cost function decays exponentially with the system size or circuit depth, making it exceedingly difficult for classical optimizers to identify a descent direction. To mitigate this challenge, researchers are exploring advanced initialization methods, structured ansatz designs, and layer-wise training protocols.
- **Noise Sensitivity:**
  Although VQAs are designed for the Noisy Intermediate-Scale Quantum (NISQ) era, they remain vulnerable to noise from various sources such as gate imperfections, decoherence, and measurement errors. Noise can obscure the evaluation of the cost function, leading to inaccurate gradient estimates and, consequently, suboptimal parameter updates. Techniques like zero-noise extrapolation, probabilistic error cancellation, and other error mitigation strategies are under active investigation to alleviate these issues.
- **Limitations in Scalability:**
  As the number of qubits increases and circuit architectures become more complex, the challenges of controlling noise and ensuring high-fidelity operations escalate. The exponential growth of the Hilbert space further complicates the optimization landscape, making the training process more arduous. Moreover, the resource overhead required for error mitigation—and eventually for full error correction—scales unfavorably, which currently limits the practical scalability of VQAs to large-scale, real-world problems.

Foundation for Other Algorithms and Applications

Variational Quantum Algorithms are the foundation to several useful quantum algorithms that are significant for the growth of quantum machine learning and other applications spanning life sciences to materials to finances.

- **Quantum Chemistry**
  Variational Quantum Eigensolvers (VQAs), like the VQE, are employed to determine molecules' ground state energies. This is essential for comprehending chemical reactions and developing novel materials.
- **Quantum Approximation Optimization Algorithm (QAOA)**
  The Quantum Approximate Optimization Algorithm (QAOA) is a type of Variational Quantum Algorithm (VQA) specifically developed to address combinatorial optimization problems.
- **Variational Quantum EigenSolver (VQE)**
  The primary objective of VQE is to determine the lowest possible energy state of a Hamiltonian, a crucial challenge in quantum chemistry and physics. Variational Quantum Eigensolver (VQE) is a method used to estimate the lowest eigenvalue of the Hamiltonian. By doing so, VQE can forecast the ground state energies of molecules, which is crucial for advancements in materials research and drug discovery.
- **Quantum Variational Classifier (QvC)**
  QVCs are a modification of the VQA concept specifically designed for quantum machine learning. They are utilized for supervised learning tasks, including as classification and regression. Within this particular framework, the variational quantum circuit is fine-tuned to minimize a loss function that quantifies the discrepancy between the predicted and actual labels of a training dataset.
- **Variational Quantum Simulation**
  QS algorithms are specifically developed to replicate the behavior of quantum systems. While VQE primarily concerns itself with stationary characteristics such as ground state energy, VQS seeks to simulate the temporal progression of quantum states. Understanding the behavior of quantum systems over time is essential, with implications in physics and other fields.
- **Quantum Neural Network (QNN)**
  Although VQAs do not have a direct application like VQE or QAOA, the ideas underlying VQAs inspire the creation of QNNs. Within this framework, the variational circuit functions as a layer in a neural network, where its parameters are optimized to carry out tasks such as pattern recognition and data classification within the context of quantum computing.

VQE Algorithm and Procedure

In this section, we are going to learn about the key terms used in VQE, its algorithm and its Qiskit implementation. Towards the end of this section, we also see the serverless VQE implementation. Recall that you have studied about serverlesss implementation in previous chapters.

Key Terms related to VQE

There are certain keywords that are used in VQE if you are aware about this in advance, it will make it easier for you to understand the algorithm later. Let us go ahead and learn about these terms.

Physical System

A *physical system* in quantum mechanics is any entity to which quantum laws are applied to understand its behavior at the microscopic level. Such systems can range from a single elementary particle to complex molecular assemblies. For instance:

Single-Particle Systems

When considering an isolated particle—such as an electron—the system is characterized by its Hamiltonian operator, which represents the total energy. The Hamiltonian is typically expressed as

$$H = T + V, \tag{12.1}$$

where T is the kinetic energy operator (commonly given by

$$T = -\frac{\hbar^2}{2m}\nabla^2 \tag{12.2}$$

for a non-relativistic particle) and V is the potential energy function that encapsulates interactions with external fields or potentials. Solving the Schrödinger equation,

$$H\psi = E\psi, \tag{12.3}$$

yields the energy eigenstates ψ and corresponding eigenvalues E.

Molecular Systems

For a molecule, the Hamiltonian becomes more complex because it must account for multiple interacting components. In such cases, the Hamiltonian includes:

- The kinetic energy of the electrons.
- Electron-nuclear attraction terms.
- Electron-electron repulsion terms.
- Nuclear-nuclear repulsion terms.

To simplify the problem, the **Born-Oppenheimer approximation** is often employed, which separates the fast electronic motion from the slower nuclear dynamics. This allows the electronic Hamiltonian to be solved independently, thereby providing insights into molecular electronic structures, chemical bonding, reaction mechanisms, and stability.

Hamiltonian

Hamiltonian is a mathematical operator (often represented as a matrix) that encapsulates the total energy of a physical system (we have discussed what a physical system is in the previous section). Once the Hamiltonian of the system is determined, we can analyze how the energies are distributed within the system and predict how the system evolves over time.

Let's consider a simple example of a Hamiltonian for a single, non-relativistic particle—such as an electron—moving in a one-dimensional potential. For simplicity, we assume the electron is moving in *free space* (i.e., without any external forces acting upon it, corresponding to a constant potential). Although this is a highly simplified model, it serves to introduce the basic concept.

In quantum mechanics, the Hamiltonian H for a particle in terms of its momentum p and mass m is given solely by its kinetic energy when no potential energy is present. In classical mechanics, the kinetic energy T is expressed as

$$T = \frac{p^2}{2m}, \tag{12.4}$$

where p is the momentum of the particle and m is its mass.

Translating this into quantum mechanics, we replace the classical momentum with the quantum mechanical operator. In the position representation, the momentum operator is defined as

$$\hat{p} = -i\hbar\frac{\partial}{\partial x}, \tag{12.5}$$

where i is the imaginary unit, $\hbar$ is the reduced Planck's constant, and $\frac{\partial}{\partial x}$ denotes the partial derivative with respect to position. The hat over p signifies that it is an operator.

Thus, the Hamiltonian operator for a free particle in one dimension becomes

$$\hat{H} = -\frac{\hbar^2}{2m}\frac{\partial^2}{\partial x^2}. \tag{12.6}$$

This Hamiltonian governs the time evolution of the electron's quantum state and allows us to compute its energy levels. In this case, since there is no potential energy, the energy derived from this Hamiltonian is purely kinetic.

By substituting this Hamiltonian into the Schrödinger equation

$$\hat{H}\psi = E\psi, \tag{12.7}$$

where ψ is the wave function of the electron and E is the energy of the system, we can find solutions that describe the behavior of the electron. For a free particle, the solutions are plane waves, which indicate that the particle can have any energy (within the non-relativistic regime) and that its position is completely delocalized.

This simple example illustrates the foundational role of the Hamiltonian in quantum mechanics. In more complex, real-world scenarios, Hamiltonians include additional potential energy terms that account for external forces or interactions with other particles.

Eigenvalues

As we discussed, a physical system can possess various types of energies, corresponding to different quantum states. In quantum mechanics, each state is represented by an eigenvector of the Hamiltonian operator, and the associated energy is given by the corresponding eigenvalue. Mathematically, if $\hat{H}$ is the Hamiltonian, then the eigenvalue equation is

$$\hat{H}\,\psi_i = E_i\,\psi_i, \tag{12.8}$$

where ψ_i is the eigenvector representing a state, and E_i is the energy corresponding to that state. In particular, the lowest eigenvalue, E_0, represents the ground state energy of the system.

Ground State

When a state is in the *ground state*, it means that the system (for example, an atom or a molecule) is in its lowest energy configuration—the minimum energy level permitted by quantum mechanics. The ground state is considered the most stable state of a system, and systems naturally evolve toward lower energy states. Once in the ground state, the system achieves its highest possible stability at a given temperature.

Purpose of Knowing the Ground State of a System

- **Chemical Reactions:** The ground state energy is crucial for understanding chemical reactions. Molecules in their ground states possess specific electron configurations that determine how they interact with other molecules. Transitions involving electrons moving from ground states to excited states (and vice versa) are fundamental to chemical bonding and reactivity.
- **Computational Accuracy:** The ground state energy is a foundational parameter for calculating various molecular properties, including reaction rates, binding strengths, and reaction pathways. In computational chemistry, many methods consist of sequential steps; thus, any error in the initial estimation of the ground state energy can propagate through subsequent calculations. A more accurate determination of the ground state energy leads to improved reliability in the overall computational outcome.

In quantum mechanics, the ground state ψ_0 of a system is defined as the eigenvector of the Hamiltonian $\hat{H}$ corresponding to the lowest eigenvalue E_0. This relationship is expressed by the eigenvalue equation

$$\hat{H}\psi_0 = E_0\psi_0, \tag{12.9}$$

where E_0 represents the ground state energy.

Relevance of VQE:

The Variational Quantum Eigensolver (VQE) is a hybrid quantum-classical algorithm designed to estimate the ground state energy of a physical system efficiently. By leveraging quantum processors for state preparation and classical optimizers for parameter adjustment, VQE addresses the challenges of accurately determining the ground state energy. Understanding the ground state is a crucial first step in applying VQE to various problems in chemistry, materials science, and beyond.

Components of VQE

Now, comes the major part of VQE which are the components needed to utilize this algorithm.

Ansatz

Earlier, when discussing the concept of the ground state, we examined the different energy states of a quantum system. To effectively apply the variational principle and target the correct energy state, we employ parameterized quantum circuits known as **Ansatz**.

An ideal Ansatz should satisfy the following conditions:

- **Simplicity:** The Ansatz should be simple, meaning it should have a minimal number of parameters. A smaller parameter set generally results in a simpler optimization landscape, thereby reducing the computational complexity during the variational optimization process.
- **Expressibility:** The Ansatz must be sufficiently expressive to generate all relevant quantum states. This ensures that the variational procedure can adequately explore the Hilbert space and identify the true ground state (or the state of interest).

Classical Optimizer

:

This component is responsible for optimizing the parameters of the quantum circuit. After each evaluation of the circuit, the optimizer adjusts the parameters with the goal of minimizing a cost function. Typically, this cost function is defined as the expectation value of the Hamiltonian with respect to the quantum state prepared by the circuit. Formally, if we denote the cost function as

$$C(\boldsymbol{\theta}) = \langle \psi(\boldsymbol{\theta}) | \hat{H} | \psi(\boldsymbol{\theta}) \rangle, \tag{12.10}$$

where $\boldsymbol{\theta}$ represents the set of circuit parameters and $\psi(\boldsymbol{\theta})$ is the parameterized quantum state, then the optimizer updates $\boldsymbol{\theta}$ in order to reduce $C(\boldsymbol{\theta})$.

Various optimization techniques can be employed, including:

- **Gradient Descent Methods:** Techniques such as stochastic gradient descent or Adam, which use the gradient $\nabla_{\boldsymbol{\theta}} C(\boldsymbol{\theta})$ to iteratively update the parameters.
- **Genetic Algorithms:** Population-based methods that explore the parameter space by mimicking the process of natural selection.
- **Bayesian Optimization:** A probabilistic approach that builds a model of the cost function and selects parameter values based on the expected improvement.

Quantum Measurement

:

Once the parameterized quantum circuit is executed, measurements are performed to gather statistical data about the quantum state. This measurement data is then used to compute a cost (or objective) function, $C(\boldsymbol{\theta})$, where $\boldsymbol{\theta}$ represents the set of circuit parameters. Typically, the objective function is defined as the expectation value of a chosen observable, for example,

$$C(\boldsymbol{\theta}) = \langle \psi(\boldsymbol{\theta}) | \hat{O} | \psi(\boldsymbol{\theta}) \rangle, \tag{12.11}$$

where $\hat{O}$ is the observable of interest (such as the Hamiltonian in VQE) and $\psi(\boldsymbol{\theta})$ is the state prepared by the circuit. Depending on the specific challenge, the algorithm then endeavors to either minimize or maximize $C(\boldsymbol{\theta})$ to optimize the performance of the quantum circuit.

Cost or Objective Function

:

This classical function quantifies how close the current solution is to the optimal one based on quantum observations. In the framework of variational quantum algorithms (VQAs), the objective function is typically defined as

$$C(\boldsymbol{\theta}) = \langle \psi(\boldsymbol{\theta}) | \hat{O} | \psi(\boldsymbol{\theta}) \rangle, \tag{12.12}$$

where $\boldsymbol{\theta}$ represents the parameters of the quantum circuit, $\psi(\boldsymbol{\theta})$ is the quantum state prepared by the circuit, and $\hat{O}$ is the observable of interest (for example, the Hamiltonian in VQE). The goal of the VQA is to optimize the parameters $\boldsymbol{\theta}$ in order to minimize (or maximize, depending on the problem) this function, thereby steering the quantum system toward the optimal solution.

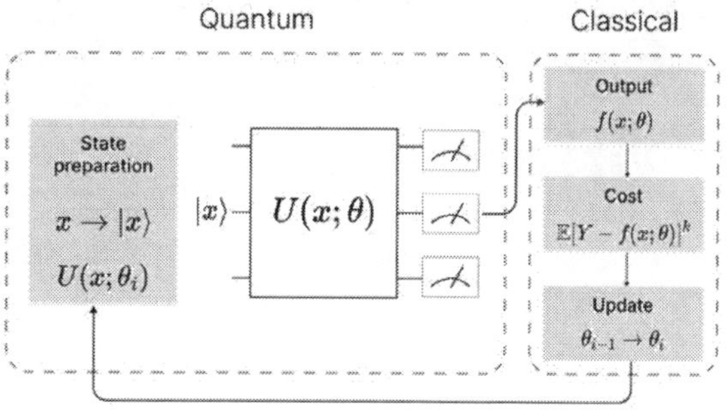

Figure 12.5: VQE Architecture

Figure 12.5 represents the workflow of the Variational Quantum Eigensolver (VQE), a hybrid quantum-classical algorithm designed to find the ground state energy of a quantum system.

The procedure commences with state preparation, in which an initial quantum state $|x\rangle$ is readied. The state in question is usually a basic quantum state, such as a Hartree-Fock state commonly used in quantum chemistry applications. The state preparation is accomplished by employing a parameterized quantum circuit, represented as $U(x;\theta_i)$, where θ_i denotes the initial parameters of the circuit. These characteristics are essential as they determine the configuration of the quantum state that will be transformed by the circuit.

After the initial state is prepared, the quantum state $|x\rangle$ is inputted into a more intricate quantum circuit called $U(x;\theta)$, which is parameterized. This circuit implements a series of quantum gates, where the values of the parameters □ can be optimized. The objective of this circuit is to modify the initial state in a manner that closely resembles the ground state of the quantum system being studied. The circuit produces a quantum state which is then measured. The quantum circuit measurements provide expectation values for specific observables, usually the system's Hamiltonian. The expectation values are utilized to assess the energy of the system based on the specified parameters θ.

Subsequently, the measurement outcomes obtained from the quantum circuit are transferred to the classical component of the algorithm. In this context, the output evaluation entails calculating a cost function by considering the expected value of the Hamiltonian, which represents the energy of the system given the current parameters θ. The VQE algorithm aims to minimize the cost function, represented as $\mathbb{E}[H(\theta)]$.

The conventional optimizer subsequently modifies the parameters θ utilizing techniques such as gradient descent, Nelder-Mead, SPSA, COBYLA, SLSQP or alternative optimization methods. The objective of this optimization is to systematically modify the parameters in order to minimize the cost function, hence bringing the quantum circuit closer to generating the actual ground state of the system.

Implementing VQE in Qiskit

In this section, let us implement VQE in Qiskit's latest version where we will leverage Qiskit Runtime and a Variational Quantum Eigensolver (VQE). We will use the Qiskit Runtime Estimator to find the expected values for different sets of qubits, and the Qiskit Runtime Sessions to make running a VQE algorithm easier. Let us import all the necessary libraries.

```
import numpy as np
from typing import List, Callable
from scipy.optimize import minimize
from scipy.optimize._optimize import OptimizeResult
```

```
import matplotlib.pyplot as plt

from qiskit import QuantumCircuit
from qiskit.quantum_info import Statevector, Operator, SparsePauliOp
from qiskit.primitives import StatevectorSampler, PrimitiveJob
from qiskit.circuit.library import TwoLocal
from qiskit.transpiler.preset_passmanagers import generate_preset_pass_manager
from qiskit.visualization import plot_histogram
from qiskit_ibm_runtime.fake_provider import FakeSherbrooke
from qiskit_ibm_runtime import Session, EstimatorV2 as Estimator
from qiskit_aer import AerSimulator
```

Let us start by creating a Pauli operator, which is a matrix that denotes a quantum mechanical observable that corresponds to a measurement of spin along a specific axis (x, y, z).

```
pauli_op = SparsePauliOp(['ZII', 'IZI', 'IIZ'])
print(pauli_op.to_matrix())
```

We will commence the process of establishing our VQE algorithm. Variational quantum eigensolvers (VQEs) are hybrid algorithms that employ both quantum and classical techniques to determine the ground state of a specific physical system. They are frequently employed in quantum chemistry and optimization problems, and they are promising candidates for hybrid algorithms in NISQ devices.

VQEs are distinguished by the iterative enhancement of a parameterized experimental solution, referred to as an *ansatz*, through the application of a classical optimization algorithm. The objective is to determine the ground state of a Hamiltonian that is represented as a linear combination of Pauli terms.

We follow three important steps to execute VQE in Qiskit. They are as follows:

- Establishing the Hamiltonian and the Ansatz based on the problem statement
- The Qiskit runtime estimator is implemented.
- Incorporating the classical optimizer and executing the program

Our first step will be to create our ansatz or experimental solution for the problem, which we will then compare to. This can be accomplished by employing Qiskit's `TwoLocal` circuit, a prebuilt circuit that is capable of generating experimental wave functions for variational quantum algorithms or classification circuits for machine learning. `TwoLocal` circuits are parameterized circuits that are composed of alternating entangled layers and rotational layers. Using Ry and Rz rotations, we will establish a 3-qubit TwoLocal circuit.

The entanglement blocks will utilize the CZ gate, and the entanglement will be set to full.

```
num_qubits = 3
rotation_blocks = ['ry','rz']
entanglement_blocks = 'cz'
entanglement = 'full'

ansatz = TwoLocal(num_qubits, rotation_blocks,
entanglement_blocks, entanglement, reps=1, insert_barriers=True)

ansatz.decompose().draw('mpl')
```

The ansatz circuit we created above is defined by a vector of parameters θ. The total number of parameters is given by:

```
num_params = ansatz.num_parameters
num_params
```

In this instance, we will utilize the FakeSherbrooke, a simulated 127-qubit backend, which serves the purpose of testing the transpiler and other functionalities related to the backend.

The `transpile()` function use preset pass managers as its default pass managers. The `transpile()` function offers an easy and straightforward approach to create a standalone `PassManager` object that replicates the optimization and transformation process performed by the transpile function. This is done to prepare a quantum circuit for execution on a particular backend.

```
backend_answer = FakeSherbrooke()
optimization_level_answer = 2
pm = generate_preset_pass_manager(backend=backend_answer,
optimization_level=optimization_level_answer)
isa_circuit = pm.run(ansatz)
```

Qiskit Runtime's latest version requires that all circuits sent to a backend adhere to the limitations imposed by the backend's Target. These circuits are typically expressed using the Instruction Set Architecture (ISA) of the backend, which refers to the set of instructions that the device can comprehend and carry out. The Target limitations are determined by elements such as the device's inherent basis gates, its qubit connectivity, and, if applicable, its pulse and other instruction timing specifications. In order to generate visual representations of our Instruction Set Architecture (ISA) circuits, we can execute the following commands:

```
isa_circuit.draw('mpl', idle_wires=False,)
```

After transpilation, the circuit exclusively comprises the native basis gates of the backend. The following code defines the Hamiltonian.

```
hamiltonian_isa = pauli_op.apply_layout(layout=isa_circuit.layout)
```

Similar to numerous classical optimization problems, the resolution of a VQE problem can be expressed as the act of minimizing a scalar cost function. The cost function for our Variational Quantum Eigensolver (VQE) is defined as the energy of the system. The cost function is established by the utilization of the Qiskit Runtime Estimator, which determines the energy of a parameterized state in relation to our Hamiltonian.

```
def cost_func(params, ansatz, hamiltonian, estimator, callback_dict):
    """Return estimate of energy from estimator

    Parameters:
        params (ndarray): Array of ansatz parameters
        ansatz (QuantumCircuit): Parameterized ansatz circuit
        hamiltonian (SparsePauliOp): Operator representation of Hamiltonian
        estimator (EstimatorV2): Estimator primitive instance

    Returns:
        float: Energy estimate
    """
    pub = (ansatz, [hamiltonian], [params])
    result = estimator.run(pubs=[pub]).result()
    energy = result[0].data.evs[0]

    callback_dict["iters"] += 1
    callback_dict["prev_vector"] = params
    callback_dict["cost_history"].append(energy)
    print(energy)
    return energy, result
```

Callback functions serve as a conventional method for users to acquire further information regarding the progress of an iterative algorithm, such as VQE. Nevertheless, it is feasible to accomplish significantly more than this. In this context, a mutable object (namely, a dictionary) is employed to store the resulting vector at each iteration of our method. This is done to facilitate the possibility of restarting the routine in the event of failure or to retrieve the vector at a different iteration number.

```
callback_dict = {
    "prev_vector": None,
    "iters": 0,
    "cost_history": [],
}
```

At this point, we have the option to using a conventional optimizer to reduce the cost function. When using actual quantum hardware, the selection of an optimizer is crucial because not all optimizers perform equally well in dealing with noisy cost function landscapes. SciPy routines can be utilized here. To initiate the procedure, we designate a stochastic initial collection of parameters:

```
x0 = 2 * np.pi * np.random.random(num_params)
x0
```

In the next steps, we will utilize the latest QiskitRuntimeService V2 components, namely EstimatorV2 and SamplerV2.

The updated Estimator interface allows you to define a singular circuit together with various observables and parameter value sets for that circuit. This enables fast specification of sweeps over different parameter value sets and observables. In the past, it was necessary to repeatedly indicate the same circuit in order to accommodate the amount of data that needed to be merged. In addition, although you can still utilize `optimization_level` and `resilience_level` as basic controls, V2 primitives provide you with the versatility to enable or disable certain error mitigation and suppression mechanisms in order to tailor them to your specific requirements.

SamplerV2 has been streamlined to prioritize its primary function of sampling the quantum register during the execution of quantum circuits. The software returns the samples of a specific type, without any associated weights. The output data is segregated according to the output register names specified in the application. This modification allows for future assistance of circuits that use classical control flow.

In addition, we will utilize Qiskit's 1.0 local testing mode. The local testing mode, which requires qiskit-ibm-runtime version 0.22.0 or later, enables the development and testing of programs prior to fine-tuning and deployment on actual quantum hardware.

```
backend = FakeSherbrooke()
def cost_func_2(*args, **kwargs):
    energy, result = cost_func(*args, **kwargs)
    return energy

with Session(backend=backend) as session:
    estimator = Estimator(session=session)

    res = minimize(
        cost_func_2,
        x0,
        args=(isa_circuit, hamiltonian_isa, estimator, callback_dict),
        method="cobyla",
        options={'maxiter': 100})
```

Let's look at our results:

```
fig, ax = plt.subplots()
plt.plot(range(callback_dict["iters"]), callback_dict["cost_history"])
plt.xlabel("Iteration")
plt.ylabel("Cost")
plt.draw()
```

As expected our VQE algorithm minimized our energy across iterations, until reaching the ground state that can be seen in the next *Figure* 12.6. We have now successfully implemented a VQE algorithm.

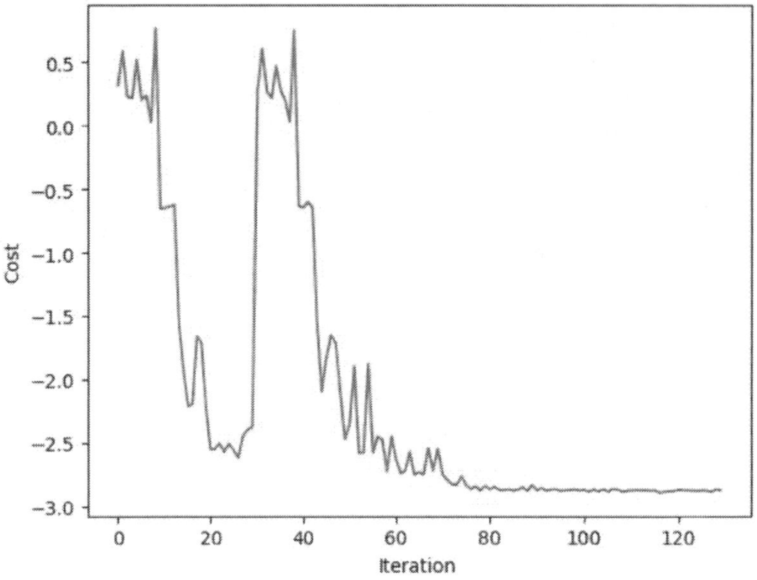

Figure 12.6: Final output of VQE cost versus iterations

Serverless VQE Implementation

In this section, we will review the deployment of the Variational Quantum Eigensolver (VQE) as a QiskitFunction utilizing Qiskit Serverless technology. The Qiskit Serverless framework is a user-friendly technology that facilitates the execution of intricate quantum computing operations. This software enables the execution of Qiskit programs as long-running jobs, allowing for their distribution across several CPUs, GPUs, and QPUs systems. This enables you to handle more intricate quantum-classical programs and execute them effortlessly. Users need not be concerned about the configuration or scaling of computing resources, since Qiskit Serverless assumes responsibility for all tasks on their behalf. Development of utility-scale quantum applications often necessitates a range of computational resource parameters. The Qiskit Serverless framework enables the convenient submission of quantum workflows for remote and controlled execution on the IBM Quantum Platform. It is a common practice to implement these quantum operations using a widely used pattern known as a Qiskit Pattern.

The following section will provide guidance on how to use the Qiskit Serverless capabilities for executing VQE. Upon completion of this module, you will have hands-on experience in implementing and operating a quantum algorithm in a serverless environment, therefore deepening your comprehension of quantum computing processes. Let us commence by importing all the necessary libraries.

```
import numpy as np
import matplotlib.pyplot as plt
from timeit import default_timer as timer
import warnings

from qiskit import QuantumCircuit
from qiskit.transpiler.preset_passmanagers import generate_preset_pass_manager
from qiskit.circuit.random import random_circuit
from qiskit.quantum_info import SparsePauliOp
from qiskit.circuit.library import TwoLocal, EfficientSU2
from qiskit_ibm_runtime import QiskitRuntimeService, Estimator, Session, Options
from qiskit_serverless import QiskitFunction, save_result, get_arguments,
save_result, distribute_task,
distribute_qiskit_function, IBMServerlessClient, QiskitFunction
from qiskit.transpiler.preset_passmanagers import generate_preset_pass_manager
from qiskit_transpiler_service.transpiler_service import TranspilerService
from qiskit_aer import AerSimulator
```

The experiment will be established using the VQE example provided in the preceding section. We shall employ the identical ansatz, parameters, and Hamiltonian operator as that previously defined. In order to facilitate a thorough comparison of outcomes, we shall adhere to the aforementioned section.

```
QiskitRuntimeService.save_account(
    channel="ibm_quantum",
    token="PASTE YOUR IBM TOCKEN HERE",
    set_as_default=True,
    overwrite=True,
)

service = QiskitRuntimeService(channel="ibm_quantum")

# Specify a system to use for transpilation
real_backend = service.backend("ibm_brisbane")
```

Let us establish the problem definition. The problem definition is identical to that of the preceding section. Please feel free to revisit the preceding section for a reminder.

```
# Qiskit Pattern Step 1: Map quantum circuits and operators (Define Ansatz and \\
operators)
num_qubits = 3
rotation_blocks = ['ry','rz']
entanglement_blocks = 'cz'
entanglement = 'full'

# Define Ansatz
ansatz = TwoLocal(num_qubits, rotation_blocks, entanglement_blocks, entanglement,
reps=1, insert_barriers=True)

# Define parameters
num_params = ansatz.num_parameters

# Qiskit Pattern Step 2: Optimize the circuit for quantum execution
optimization_level = 2
pm = generate_preset_pass_manager(backend=real_backend,
optimization_level=optimization_level)
isa_circuit = pm.run(ansatz)

# Define Hamiltonian for VQE
pauli_op = SparsePauliOp(['ZII', 'IZI', 'IIZ'])
hamiltonian_isa = pauli_op.apply_layout(layout=isa_circuit.layout)
```

We should guarantee that our environment is configured for Qiskit Serverless. If you have not already done so, install the Qiskit Serverless utility. Set up the IBMServerlessClient to utilize your IBM Quantum account and define your token. This will grant you access to the serverless capabilities. For this exercise, we will implement QiskitRuntime without service, as we will be employing local testing mode. In order to operate on genuine backends, set the `USE_RUNTIME_SERVICE` indicator to True. Ensure that you have your IBM Quantum token readily available for authentication and authorization.

```
# Setup Qiskit Serverless Client and Qiskit Runtime client
client = IBMServerlessClient("YOUR_IBM_QUANTUM_TOKEN")

Change to True only if you wish to use real backend.
USE_RUNTIME_SERVICE = False
```

```
if USE_RUNTIME_SERVICE:
    service = QiskitRuntimeService(
        channel='ibm_quantum',
        verify=False
    )
else:
    service = None
```

The code commences by integrating the requisite libraries and defining functions that facilitate the execution of the VQE algorithm. The `run` function functions as a subroutine that computes the energy of the quantum system using the Estimator primitive, monitors the optimization process, and stores pertinent data, including the cost history and the time taken per iteration. The energy estimate for a specific set of parameters is returned by the `cost_func` function, which functions as a container to the `run` function.

The actual VQE operation is executed in the `run_vqe` function. It initializes a dictionary to store callback data and subsequently employs the 'minimize' function from the `scipy.optimize` library to conduct the classical optimization over the quantum circuit's parameters. The optimization method is specified, with COBYLA serving as the default; however, this can be modified. The script is capable of supporting both cloud-based and local quantum simulations. If a cloud service is available, it will select the least active backend. Otherwise, it will default to a local simulator that utilizes the AerSimulator. The script captures the optimization results, which include the optimal parameters, minimum energy value, total optimization time, number of iterations, and the history of cost function values after the VQE is executed. This structure enables the code to be highly adaptable to a variety of quantum backends and optimization methodologies.

```
from qiskit_aer import AerSimulator
import logging
from typing import Optional
import time
import numpy as np
from scipy.optimize import minimize

from qiskit import QuantumCircuit
from qiskit_ibm_runtime import (
    EstimatorV2 as Estimator,
```

```
    SamplerV2 as Sampler,
    QiskitRuntimeService,
    Session,
)
from qiskit.transpiler.preset_passmanagers import generate_preset_pass_manager
from qiskit_serverless import (
    distribute_task,
    get_arguments,
    get,
    save_result,
)

def run(params, ansatz, hamiltonian, estimator, callback_dict):
    """Return callback function that uses Estimator instance,
    and stores intermediate values into a dictionary.

    Parameters:
        params (ndarray): Array of ansatz parameters
        ansatz (QuantumCircuit): Parameterized ansatz circuit
        hamiltonian (SparsePauliOp): Operator representation of Hamiltonian
        estimator (Estimator): Estimator primitive instance
        callback_dict (dict): Mutable dict for storing values

    Returns:
        Callable: Callback function object
    """
    result = estimator.run([(ansatz, [hamiltonian], [params])]).result()
    energy = result[0].data.evs[0]

    # Keep track of the number of iterations
    callback_dict["iters"] += 1
    # Set the prev_vector to the latest one
    callback_dict["prev_vector"] = params
    # Compute the value of the cost function at the current vector
    callback_dict["cost_history"].append(energy)
    # Grab the current time
```

```
    current_time = time.perf_counter()
    # Find the total time of the execute (after the 1st iteration)
    if callback_dict["iters"] > 1:
        callback_dict["_total_time"] += current_time -
        ↪  callback_dict["_prev_time"]
    # Set the previous time to the current time
    callback_dict["_prev_time"] = current_time
    # Compute the average time per iteration and round it
    time_str = (
        round(callback_dict["_total_time"] / (callback_dict["iters"] - 1), 2)
        if callback_dict["_total_time"]
        else "-"
    )
    # Print to screen on single line
    print(
        "Iters. done: {} [Avg. time per iter: {}]".format(
            callback_dict["iters"], time_str
        ),
        end="\r",
        flush=True,
    )

    return energy, result


def cost_func(*args, **kwargs):
    """Return estimate of energy from estimator

    Parameters:
        params (ndarray): Array of ansatz parameters
        ansatz (QuantumCircuit): Parameterized ansatz circuit
        hamiltonian (SparsePauliOp): Operator representation of Hamiltonian
        estimator (Estimator): Estimator primitive instance

    Returns:
        float: Energy estimate
```

```
    """
    energy, result = run(*args, **kwargs)
    return energy


def run_vqe(initial_parameters, ansatz, operator, estimator, method):
    callback_dict = {
        "prev_vector": None,
        "iters": 0,
        "cost_history": [],
        "_total_time": 0,
        "_prev_time": None,
    }

    result = minimize(
        cost_func,
        initial_parameters,
        args=(ansatz, operator, estimator, callback_dict),
        method=method,
    )
    return result, callback_dict


if __name__ == "__main__":
    arguments = get_arguments()

    service = arguments.get("service")

    ansatz = arguments.get("ansatz")
    operator = arguments.get("operator")
    method = arguments.get("method", "COBYLA")
    initial_parameters = arguments.get("initial_parameters")

    if initial_parameters is None:
        initial_parameters = 2 * np.pi * np.random.rand(ansatz.num_parameters)
```

```
if service:
    backend = service.least_busy(operational=True, simulator=False)
else:
    backend = AerSimulator(method='density_matrix')

if initial_parameters is None:
    initial_parameters = 2 * np.pi * np.random.rand(ansatz.num_parameters)

if service:
    with Session(service=service, backend=backend) as session:
        estimator = Estimator(session=session)
        vqe_result, callback_dict = run_vqe(
            initial_parameters=initial_parameters,
            ansatz=ansatz,
            operator=operator,
            estimator=estimator,
            method=method,
        )
else:
    estimator = Estimator(backend=backend)
    vqe_result, callback_dict = run_vqe(
        initial_parameters=initial_parameters,
        ansatz=ansatz,
        operator=operator,
        estimator=estimator,
        method=method,
    )


save_result(
    {
        "optimal_point": vqe_result.x.tolist(),
        "optimal_value": vqe_result.fun,
        "optimizer_time": callback_dict.get("_total_time", 0),
         "iters": callback_dict["iters"],
```

```
            "cost_history" : callback_dict["cost_history"]
        }
    )
```

```
# Define the Qiskit Function
if USE_RUNTIME_SERVICE:
    function = QiskitFunction(title="vqe")
else:
    function = QiskitFunction(title="vqe", dependencies=["qiskit_aer"])
# Upload the Qiskit Function using IBMServerlessClient
client.upload(function)
```

We are prepared to execute the VQE algorithm using Qiskit Serverless now that we have uploaded our QiskitFunction. Execute these procedures and specify the essential variables to execute the algorithm and retrieve the results:

Utilize the COBYLA method for the optimizer parameters.

```
# Define input_arguments
input_arguments = {
    "ansatz": isa_circuit, # Replace with your transpiled ansatz
    "operator": hamiltonian_isa, # Replace with the hamiltonian operator
    "method": "COBYLA", # Using COBYLA method for the optimizer
    "service": service, # Add your code here
}

# Qiskit Pattern Step 3: Run the payload on backend
job = client.run("vqe", arguments=input_arguments) # Pass the arguments dict here)
```

Continue to monitor the execution's progress and await its conclusion. To obtain the most recent status, it is possible to resume the cell.

```
job.status()
```

Once the execution is complete, retrieve and analyze the results.

```
# Return result from QiskitFunction job
job.result()
```

To acquire a deeper understanding of the quantum algorithm's efficacy, retrieve and analyze the results of the VQE execution. Contrast these findings with the results of the preceding section and your expectations. Assess the optimal energy and parameters derived from the Qiskit Serverless execution and compare them to the previous section results.

```
# Qiskit Pattern Step 4: Postprocess and analyze the Estimator V2 results
result = job.result()


fig, ax = plt.subplots()
plt.plot(range(result["iters"]), result["cost_history"])
plt.xlabel("Energy")
plt.ylabel("Cost")
plt.draw()
```

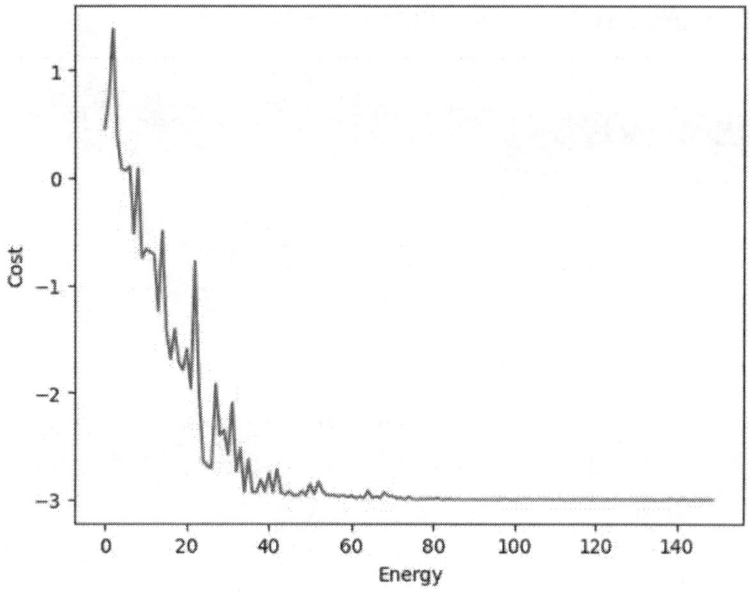

Figure 12.7: Cost versus Energy

The Variational Quantum Eigensolver (VQE) algorithm's convergence behavior over iterations is illustrated in the *Figure* 12.7 . The iteration number, which is frequently referenced as "Energy" in this context, is represented by the x-axis. However, it may be more accurately labeled as "Iteration Number." The cost function value, which is the estimated energy of the quantum system in this instance, is represented by the y-axis.

- **Initial Fluctuations:** The cost function demonstrates substantial fluctuations at the outset of the optimization process (left side of the graph). This is a common occurrence in VQE, as the optimizer investigates the parameter space to identify the region where the energy is reduced.

- **Convergence:** The cost function value gradually decreases as the iterations progress, approaching a minimum value, and the fluctuations decrease. This suggests that the optimizer is focusing on the optimal parameters for the quantum circuit, which is equivalent to the ground state energy of the Hamiltonian under investigation.
- **Final Stabilization:** The cost function value stabilizes around a minimum value during the final iterations (right side of the graph), with only minimal fluctuations. This implies that the VQE algorithm has likely reached a solution that approximates the ground state energy.

The final stabilization of the cost function and the overall downward trend suggest that the VQE algorithm has effectively reduced the energy and has likely identified an optimal or near-optimal solution to the problem it is addressing. The small residual fluctuations in the cost function at the end are common and may be attributed to the inherent stochastic character of quantum measurements or numerical noise.

Applications of VQE

The Variational Quantum Eigensolver (VQE) is a computational method that combines quantum and conventional techniques to efficiently determine the lowest energy state of quantum systems. This algorithm has significant implications in various domains. These are some of the main uses:

- **Molecular Energy Calculations:** VQE is extensively applied to compute the ground state energies of molecules—a key step in elucidating chemical properties, reaction mechanisms, and molecular stability. In practice, molecular Hamiltonians are mapped onto qubit representations using transformations such as Jordan-Wigner or Bravyi-Kitaev, and an appropriate ansatz (e.g., Unitary Coupled Cluster Singles and Doubles (UCCSD) or hardware-efficient circuits) is employed. These techniques are vital for advancing research in pharmaceuticals, materials science, and catalysis.
- **Simulation of Complex Molecules:** Classical computational methods often struggle with the exponential scaling of Hilbert space dimensions when simulating large molecules. VQE provides a quantum alternative that can handle the simulation of intricate and extensive molecular systems, offering detailed insights into electronic structures and reactivity patterns that are otherwise computationally intractable.
- **Design of Novel Materials:** In materials science, VQE is used to compute the electronic configurations and energy landscapes of various compounds. Such simulations

inform the design of materials with specific properties—such as superconductivity, magnetism, or enhanced thermal conductivity—by accurately predicting their ground state characteristics. This capability is crucial for the development of next-generation functional materials.

- **Investigation of New Phases:** VQE aids in exploring exotic quantum phases of matter by simulating many-body Hamiltonians that characterize systems like topological insulators, quantum magnets, and quantum spin liquids. By determining the ground state properties, researchers can map phase diagrams and study quantum phase transitions, thereby uncovering new phases and critical phenomena in condensed matter physics.
- **Nuclear Structure Calculations:** VQE is leveraged to compute the ground and low-lying excited state energies of atomic nuclei. These calculations are fundamental for understanding nuclear structure, binding energies, and decay mechanisms, which have implications for both theoretical nuclear physics and practical applications such as nuclear reactor design.
- **Investigation of Nuclear Reactions:** The algorithm also facilitates the simulation of complex nuclear reactions by providing approximate solutions to many-body nuclear problems. Through these simulations, VQE contributes to a deeper understanding of reaction dynamics and cross-sections, which are pertinent to fields ranging from energy generation to astrophysical processes like nucleosynthesis.

Challenges in Implementation

The implementation of the Variational Quantum Eigensolver (VQE) presents numerous obstacles, encompassing both quantum and classical aspects. These are the primary obstacles:

- **Choosing the Right Ansatz:** The performance of VQE critically depends on the choice of ansatz—the parameterized quantum circuit that prepares the trial state. An ideal ansatz must balance expressibility (its ability to represent the true ground state) with trainability (ensuring efficient convergence during optimization).
  - A simplistic ansatz may lack the expressiveness needed to capture complex correlations in the target state.
  - An overly complex ansatz, such as those with excessive circuit depth or entanglement, can require more quantum resources than are available on near-term devices and may exacerbate noise and decoherence effects.
  - Modern strategies include problem-inspired ansätze (e.g., unitary coupled cluster for quantum chemistry) and hardware-efficient ansätze that align with the native

gate set of the device.

- **Barren Plateaus:** In high-dimensional parameter spaces, the cost function gradients can vanish exponentially with the number of qubits or circuit depth—a phenomenon known as barren plateaus.
    - Such flat landscapes hinder the progress of classical optimizers by making it difficult to discern a descent direction.
    - Mitigation strategies include careful circuit initialization, layer-wise training, and designing ansätze that incorporate problem structure to reduce the randomness in parameter space.
- **Circuit Depth and Qubit Count:** The scalability of VQE is severely limited by hardware constraints:
    - As problem size increases, both the required number of qubits and the circuit depth escalate, potentially exceeding current quantum device capabilities.
    - Deeper circuits are more susceptible to noise and decoherence, reducing the fidelity of the prepared state.
    - Error mitigation techniques and circuit compression methods are actively researched to address these limitations.
- **Classical-Quantum Communication Overhead:** VQE inherently relies on a hybrid workflow, where the quantum processor evaluates the cost function while a classical optimizer updates the circuit parameters.
    - Frequent exchanges between the quantum and classical components introduce communication latency, which can significantly slow down the overall optimization, especially when real-time feedback is required.
    - Strategies such as batching measurements, asynchronous optimization routines, or integrating more efficient communication protocols are being investigated to reduce this overhead.
- **Classical Optimizer Performance:** The classical optimization step in VQE is challenging due to the following factors:
    - The optimization landscape is typically non-convex and high-dimensional, containing numerous local minima that can trap the optimizer.
    - Noise in the cost function evaluations—stemming from quantum measurement uncertainties—further complicates convergence.
    - A variety of optimization algorithms (e.g., gradient-based methods, derivative-free techniques, or hybrid approaches) are being explored to improve convergence robustness and efficiency.
- **Large Number of Measurements:** Accurate estimation of the expectation values of Hamiltonian terms is essential for VQE, which necessitates:

- A large number of measurements (shots) to reduce statistical noise, especially as the system size grows.
- Techniques such as grouping commuting observables and employing variance reduction methods can help alleviate the measurement overhead.
- Nonetheless, for complex Hamiltonians, the measurement requirement remains a significant bottleneck, directly affecting the total runtime.

QAOA Algorithm and Procedure

In this section we provide a practical demonstration of implementing the Quantum Approximate Optimization Algorithm (QAOA) [6], which is a hybrid quantum-classical iterative method, within the framework of Qiskit patterns. The tutorial initially focuses on solving the Maximum-Cut (or Max-Cut) problem for a small-scale graph and subsequently extends the approach to a utility-scale application.

The Max-Cut problem is a well-known NP-hard optimization problem, meaning it is computationally intractable for large instances. This problem has significant applications across various domains, including clustering, network science, and statistical physics. The objective of the Max-Cut problem is to partition the nodes of a given graph, connected by edges, into two distinct sets such that the total number of edges between nodes in different sets (the cut) is maximized. In essence, the goal is to divide the graph into two subsets where the number of edges that cross the partition is as large as possible.

The initial segment of this section delves into a small-scale instance of the Max-Cut problem, serving as a demonstrative example to outline the procedure for resolving an optimization problem via quantum computing techniques.

To contextualize this problem before mapping it onto a quantum algorithm, one can conceptualize the Max-Cut problem as a classical combinatorial optimization challenge. The problem can be framed as the minimization of a function $f(\mathbf{x})$, where

$$\min_{\mathbf{x}\in\{0,1\}^n} f(\mathbf{x}), \tag{12.13}$$

with the input $\mathbf{x}$ represented as a vector. Each component of this vector corresponds to a node within a graph, with the constraint that each component x_i can assume binary values of 0 or 1, denoting whether a node is included in the cut or not, respectively. For this example, we consider a graph with $n = 5$ nodes.

The function $f(\mathbf{x})$ can be further detailed by considering the function between pairs of nodes (i, j), which determines whether the corresponding edge is included in the cut.

For instance, the expression $x_i + x_j - 2x_ix_j$ evaluates to 1 only if one of the nodes x_i or x_j is included in the cut (i.e., the edge (i, j) is traversed by the cut), otherwise, it evaluates to zero. Consequently, the problem of maximizing the number of edges in the cut can be mathematically expressed as:

$$\max_{\mathbf{x}\in\{0,1\}^n} \sum_{(i,j)} (x_i + x_j - 2x_ix_j)\,, \tag{12.14}$$

which, equivalently, can be reformulated into a minimization problem:

$$\min_{\mathbf{x}\in\{0,1\}^n} \sum_{(i,j)} (2x_ix_j - x_i - x_j)\,. \tag{12.15}$$

In this specific case, the minimum value of $f(\mathbf{x})$ corresponds to the configuration where the number of edges traversed by the cut is maximized. At this stage, the problem remains within the domain of classical computation, as the quantum computational framework has yet to be introduced. The challenge now is to reformulate this classical problem into a form that is amenable to quantum computation.

The initial step in this process involves transforming the classical problem, represented by a graph, into a quantum framework comprising circuits and operators. This transformation is achieved through the following three primary steps:

1. Employ a sequence of mathematical reformulations to express the problem using the Quadratic Unconstrained Binary Optimization (QUBO) formulation.
2. Reformulate the optimization problem into a Hamiltonian, where the ground state of this Hamiltonian corresponds to the solution that minimizes the cost function.
3. Design a quantum circuit that prepares the quantum state corresponding to the ground state of this Hamiltonian, using techniques analogous to quantum annealing.

Note: *In the Quantum Approximate Optimization Algorithm (QAOA) framework, the goal is to define an operator, specifically a Hamiltonian, that encapsulates the cost function of the hybrid quantum-classical algorithm. Concurrently, a parameterized quantum circuit, often referred to as an Ansatz, is designed to generate quantum states representing candidate solutions. These candidate states can be sampled and evaluated based on the defined cost function.*

The first phase in this mapping process involves a change in notation. The problem can be succinctly expressed in the QUBO formalism as follows:

$$\min_{\mathbf{x}\in\{0,1\}^n} \mathbf{x}^T Q\mathbf{x}, \tag{12.16}$$

where Q is an $n \times n$ matrix of real numbers, n corresponds to the number of nodes in the graph, $\mathbf{x}$ is a vector of binary variables corresponding to the nodes, and $\mathbf{x}^T$ denotes the transpose of the vector $\mathbf{x}$.

To illustrate how the QAOA problem can be reformulated, we first introduce a new set of variables $z_i \in \{-1, 1\}$ by redefining the binary variables x_i as:

$$x_i = \frac{1 - z_i}{2}. \tag{12.17}$$

In this transformation, note that if $x_i = 0$, then z_i must be 1. Substituting x_i in terms of z_i within the quadratic form $\mathbf{x}^T Q\mathbf{x}$, the optimization problem can be re-expressed as:

$$\mathbf{x}^T Q\mathbf{x} = \sum_{ij} Q_{ij} x_i x_j \tag{12.18}$$

$$= \frac{1}{4}\sum_{ij} Q_{ij}(1 - z_i)(1 - z_j) \tag{12.19}$$

$$= \frac{1}{4}\sum_{ij} Q_{ij} z_i z_j - \frac{1}{4}\sum_{ij}(Q_{ij} + Q_{ji}) z_i + \frac{n^2}{4}. \tag{12.20}$$

At this stage, by defining $b_i = -\sum_j (Q_{ij} + Q_{ji})$ and discarding the constant terms and prefactor that do not affect the optimization, we arrive at two equivalent forms of the original optimization problem:

$$\min_{\mathbf{x}\in\{0,1\}^n} \mathbf{x}^T Q\mathbf{x} \iff \min_{\mathbf{z}\in\{-1,1\}^n} \mathbf{z}^T Q\mathbf{z} + \mathbf{b}^T\mathbf{z}. \tag{12.21}$$

Here, the vector $\mathbf{b}$ is dependent on the matrix Q. Note that in deriving the expression $\mathbf{z}^T Q\mathbf{z}+\mathbf{b}^T\mathbf{z}$, we neglected the prefactor $\frac{1}{4}$ and the constant offset $\frac{n^2}{4}$ as they do not influence the optimization result.

Next, to translate this classical optimization problem into a quantum formalism, we replace the variables z_i with Pauli-Z matrices, denoted as Z_i, which are 2×2 matrices of the form:

$$Z_i = \begin{pmatrix} 1 & 0 \\ 0 & -1 \end{pmatrix}. \tag{12.22}$$

Substituting these matrices into the reformulated optimization problem yields the corresponding Hamiltonian:

$$H_C = \sum_{ij} Q_{ij} Z_i Z_j + \sum_i b_i Z_i. \tag{12.23}$$

Additionally, it is crucial to recall that these Z matrices are embedded within the quantum computer's computational space, specifically within a Hilbert space of dimension $2^n \times 2^n$. Consequently, terms such as $Z_i Z_j$ should be interpreted as tensor products $Z_i \otimes Z_j$ within the $2^n \times 2^n$ Hilbert space. For instance, in a scenario involving five decision variables, the term $Z_1 Z_3$ is understood as $I \otimes Z_3 \otimes I \otimes Z_1 \otimes I$, where I is the 2×2 identity matrix.

This Hamiltonian, denoted as the cost function Hamiltonian H_C, is characterized by the property that its ground state corresponds to the solution minimizing the cost function $f(\mathbf{x})$. Consequently, to address the optimization problem, one must prepare the ground state of H_C (or a quantum state that exhibits a significant overlap with the ground state) on the quantum computer. By sampling from this quantum state, the solution to min $f(\mathbf{x})$ can be obtained with high probability.

The Hamiltonian H_C encodes the quantum description of the optimization problem. The next step is to design a quantum circuit capable of sampling optimal solutions using a quantum computer. The QAOA technique is inspired by quantum annealing and employs alternating layers of operators within the quantum circuit.

The core concept involves initializing the system in the ground state of a known configuration, denoted as $H^{\otimes n} |0\rangle$. From this initial state, the system is gradually evolved towards the ground state of the Hamiltonian H_C, which represents the cost function. This evolution is achieved by successively applying the unitary operators $\exp\{-i\gamma_k H_C\}$ and $\exp\{-i\beta_k H_m\}$, where the angles $\gamma_1, \ldots, \gamma_p$ and $\beta_1, \ldots, \beta_p$ are tunable parameters.

The quantum circuit constructed in this manner is parametrized by the angles γ_i and β_i, allowing for the exploration of different configurations by varying these parameters and sampling from the resulting quantum state.

Implementing QAOA in Qiskit

This section showcases the utilization of the Quantum Approximate Optimization Algorithm (QAOA) to solve a graph partitioning problem, namely finding the maximum cut. It also includes a comparison with a solution obtained by the brute-force method.

Let us first import all the necessary libraries to run the algorithm sucessfully.

```
import numpy as np
import networkx as nx

from qiskit.quantum_info import Pauli, SparsePauliOp
from qiskit.primitives import Sampler
from qiskit.quantum_info import Pauli
```

```
from qiskit.result import QuasiDistribution

from qiskit_algorithms import QAOA
from qiskit_algorithms.optimizers import COBYLA

from qiskit_algorithms.utils import algorithm_globals

from qiskit_algorithms import NumPyMinimumEigensolver
from qiskit.quantum_info import Operator
from qiskit.circuit.library import TwoLocal
from qiskit_algorithms import SamplingVQE
```

The objective is to divide the vertices of the graph into two sets that complement each other, maximizing the number of edges between the sets. Initially, we establish the graph by utilizing an adjacency matrix, which precisely determines the interconnections between the nodes. We employ this technique to visually represent the vertices and edges of the graph.

```
num_nodes = 4
w = np.array(
    [[0.0, 1.0, 1.0, 0.0], [1.0, 0.0, 1.0, 1.0], [1.0, 1.0, 0.0, 1.0],
    [0.0, 1.0, 1.0, 0.0]]
)
G = nx.from_numpy_array(w)

layout = nx.random_layout(G, seed=10)
colors = ["r", "g", "b", "y"]
nx.draw(G, layout, node_color=colors)
labels = nx.get_edge_attributes(G, "weight")
nx.draw_networkx_edge_labels(G, pos=layout, edge_labels=labels);
```

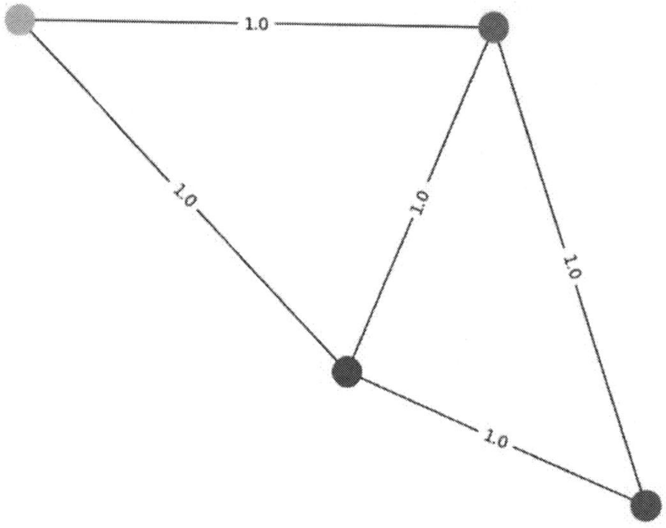

Figure 12.8: Graph on which we apply QAOA for maxcut

Here is how the brute-force approach works. In essence, we attempt each binary assignment in its entirety. A vertex's entry in a binary assignment can be either 0 (indicating that it is in the first partition) or 1 (indicating that it is in the second partition). We output the binary assignment that minimizes the number of crossing edges while satisfying the graph partition's definition.

```
def objective_value(x, w):
    """Compute the value of a cut.
    Args:
        x: Binary string as numpy array.
        w: Adjacency matrix.
    Returns:
        Value of the cut.
    """
    X = np.outer(x, (1 - x))
    w_01 = np.where(w != 0, 1, 0)
    return np.sum(w_01 * X)


def bitfield(n, L):
    result = np.binary_repr(n, L)
    return [int(digit) for digit in result]  # [2:] to chop off the "0b" part
```

```python
# use the brute-force way to generate the oracle
L = num_nodes
max = 2**L
sol = np.inf
for i in range(max):
    cur = bitfield(i, L)

    how_many_nonzero = np.count_nonzero(cur)
    if how_many_nonzero * 2 != L:  # not balanced
        continue

    cur_v = objective_value(np.array(cur), w)
    if cur_v < sol:
        sol = cur_v

print(f"Objective value computed by the brute-force method is {sol}")
```

As seen in the accompanying cell, the graph partition issue can be transformed into an Ising Hamiltonian. This conversion module is used to generate the operator without additional explanation because the objective is to demonstrate QAOA. The Qiskit Optimization package is a resource you may want to look into since it has the ability to perform this conversion automatically for a number of optimization situations.

```python
def get_operator(weight_matrix):
    r"""Generate Hamiltonian for the graph partitioning
    Notes:
        Goals:
            1 Separate the vertices into two set of the same size.
            2 Make sure the number of edges between the two set is minimized.
        Hamiltonian:
            H = H_A + H_B
            H_A = sum\_{(i,j)\in E}{(1-ZiZj)/2}
            H_B = (sum_{i}{Zi})^2 = sum_{i}{Zi^2}+sum_{i!=j}{ZiZj}
            H_A is for achieving goal 2 and H_B is for achieving goal 1.
    Args:
        weight_matrix: Adjacency matrix.
```

```
    Returns:
        Operator for the Hamiltonian
        A constant shift for the obj function.
    """
    num_nodes = len(weight_matrix)
    pauli_list = []
    coeffs = []
    shift = 0

    for i in range(num_nodes):
        for j in range(i):
            if weight_matrix[i, j] != 0:
                x_p = np.zeros(num_nodes, dtype=bool)
                z_p = np.zeros(num_nodes, dtype=bool)
                z_p[i] = True
                z_p[j] = True
                pauli_list.append(Pauli((z_p, x_p)))
                coeffs.append(-0.5)
                shift += 0.5

    for i in range(num_nodes):
        for j in range(num_nodes):
            if i != j:
                x_p = np.zeros(num_nodes, dtype=bool)
                z_p = np.zeros(num_nodes, dtype=bool)
                z_p[i] = True
                z_p[j] = True
                pauli_list.append(Pauli((z_p, x_p)))
                coeffs.append(1.0)
            else:
                shift += 1

    return SparsePauliOp(pauli_list, coeffs=coeffs), shift


qubit_op, offset = get_operator(w)
```

So let us use the QAOA algorithm to find the solution.

```
sampler = Sampler()

def sample_most_likely(state_vector):
    """Compute the most likely binary string from state vector.
    Args:
        state_vector: State vector or quasi-distribution.

    Returns:
        Binary string as an array of ints.
    """
    if isinstance(state_vector, QuasiDistribution):
        values = list(state_vector.values())
    else:
        values = state_vector
    n = int(np.log2(len(values)))
    k = np.argmax(np.abs(values))
    x = bitfield(k, n)
    x.reverse()
    return np.asarray(x)


algorithm_globals.random_seed = 10598

optimizer = COBYLA()
qaoa = QAOA(sampler, optimizer, reps=2)

result = qaoa.compute_minimum_eigenvalue(qubit_op)

x = sample_most_likely(result.eigenstate)

print(x)
print(f"Objective value computed by QAOA is {objective_value(x, w)}")
```

It is evident that the result matches the value determined using brute force above. However, we can also perform the computation using the traditional 'NumPyMinimumEigensolver', which could be helpful as a guide instead of using brute force.

```
npme = NumPyMinimumEigensolver()
result = npme.compute_minimum_eigenvalue(Operator(qubit_op))

x = sample_most_likely(result.eigenstate)

print(x)
print(f"Objective value computed by the
NumPyMinimumEigensolver is {objective_value(x, w)}")
```

An additional option for solving the issue is to utilize SamplingVQE, as seen here:

```
algorithm_globals.random_seed = 10598

optimizer = COBYLA()
ansatz = TwoLocal(qubit_op.num_qubits, "ry", "cz", reps=2, entanglement="linear")
sampling_vqe = SamplingVQE(sampler, ansatz, optimizer)

result = sampling_vqe.compute_minimum_eigenvalue(qubit_op)

x = sample_most_likely(result.eigenstate)

print(x)
print(f"Objective value computed by SamplingVQE is {objective_value(x, w)}")
```

We investigated three distinct quantum methods to solve the MaxCut problem, a basic combinatorial optimization problem: SamplingVQE, QAOA, and NumPyEigensolver. Our implementations offer insightful information about how well they functioned in situations involving small to medium-sized problems.

SamplingVQE used classical optimizers and variational methods to estimate the problem Hamiltonian's ground state. This approach demonstrated how hybrid quantum-classical algorithms can solve NP-hard problems, however, their effectiveness will vary depending on the optimizer and ansatz selected. Because the ansatz may be easily customized to meet the needs of a given situation, SamplingVQE is a flexible tool for quantum optimization.

A more structured method was provided by QAOA, which established a direct correlation between the quantity of layers (p) and the solution's quality. This approach showed that it is a strong choice for near-term quantum devices since it can produce good approximate solutions with relatively thin circuits. But it's important to carefully balance the trade-off between circuit depth and solution quality, especially when working with hardware limitations.

A classical exact solver, NumPyEigensolver, was used as a reference to assess how well the quantum algorithms performed. Its application is constrained by the exponential scaling of traditional resources needed for huge problem instances, even though it ensures finding the optimal solution. However, it offered a crucial benchmark that enabled us to evaluate the precision of the quantum solutions.

Applications of QAOA

- **Portfolio Optimization:** The Quantum Approximate Optimization Algorithm (QAOA) can be applied to portfolio optimization by mapping the asset selection problem to a combinatorial optimization framework (e.g., as a Quadratic Unconstrained Binary Optimization (QUBO) problem). In this formulation, qubits represent asset inclusion decisions, and the cost function encodes returns, risks, and additional constraints such as budget limits and risk tolerance via penalty terms. This approach enables the identification of an optimal or near-optimal asset allocation that balances return maximization with risk minimization. Advanced encoding techniques and tailored penalty functions are crucial to ensure that the quantum Hamiltonian faithfully represents the underlying financial problem while remaining resource-efficient for near-term quantum devices.
- **Quantum neural networks:** Variational quantum circuits, including QAOA-inspired architectures, are increasingly being explored as quantum analogs of classical neural networks. In this context, QAOA-like layers can be employed during the training phase to optimize circuit parameters analogous to weights and biases in classical neural networks. These circuits leverage the variational principle to minimize a cost function that reflects the network's performance on a given task (e.g., classification or regression). Integrating such quantum layers may lead to hybrid models where classical optimization routines (e.g., gradient descent or adaptive methods) interface with quantum circuits to potentially exploit quantum-enhanced feature representations or decision boundaries. However, careful design is required to ensure that the non-convex optimization landscape, similar to that observed in standard QAOA, does not impede convergence.
- **The Traveling Salesman Problem (TSP):** The TSP, which seeks the most efficient route visiting a set of cities and returning to the origin, can be encoded as a combinatorial optimization problem suitable for QAOA. In this application, cities and routes are mapped onto qubit configurations, while constraints—such as ensuring each city is visited exactly once—are embedded into the problem Hamiltonian through penalty

terms. Although QAOA is designed to yield approximate solutions, its performance depends on the quality of the encoding, the choice of mixer operators, and the depth of the quantum circuit. Current research focuses on developing improved ansätze and optimization strategies that can effectively handle the complex constraint structures inherent in TSP formulations, thereby enhancing solution quality and scalability.

Challenges in Implementation

- **Parameter Optimization:** Optimizing the set of rotation angles in the QAOA circuit is critical, as these parameters dictate the performance of the algorithm. The optimization landscape is typically non-convex, often featuring a high density of local minima and potential barren plateau regions, where gradients vanish exponentially with system size. These characteristics challenge classical optimizers, which may become trapped in suboptimal configurations. Strategies to mitigate these issues include:
  - *Initialization Heuristics:* Using informed or warm-start strategies based on problem structure or previous layers can help avoid poor local minima.
  - *Advanced Optimization Methods:* Techniques such as stochastic gradient descent, adaptive methods (e.g., Adam), Bayesian optimization, or derivative-free methods (e.g., Nelder-Mead, genetic algorithms) may improve convergence.
  - *Layer-wise Training:* Gradually increasing the circuit depth while reusing optimized parameters from previous layers can alleviate optimization difficulties.

  As the number of parameters increases, so does the computational cost of each optimization iteration, making efficient optimization algorithms a crucial component of practical QAOA implementations.
- **Optimization Loop Efficiency:** The performance of the QAOA hybrid algorithm heavily depends on the efficiency of the optimization loop—the iterative process that integrates quantum circuit evaluations with classical parameter updates. Key factors include:
  - *Quantum-Classical Communication Overhead:* Minimizing latency and ensuring synchronization between the quantum processor and classical optimizer is essential, especially when real-time feedback is required.
  - *Measurement Noise and Shot Complexity:* Since expectation values are estimated from finite sampling (shots), statistical noise can slow convergence; employing variance reduction techniques or adaptive shot allocation strategies can help.
  - *Parallelization:* When possible, parallel evaluation of multiple parameter sets can improve overall throughput and mitigate bottlenecks.

Optimizing these factors is crucial for scaling QAOA to solve more complex and large-scale problems efficiently.

- **Encoding the Problem:** A fundamental step in QAOA is the precise mapping of a classical optimization problem to a corresponding quantum Hamiltonian. This encoding must:
  - *Faithfully Represent the Original Problem:* The Hamiltonian should incorporate all constraints and objectives, often by mapping classical variables to qubit states (e.g., via Pauli-Z operators) and embedding problem constraints as penalty terms.
  - *Be Resource-Efficient:* The encoding must minimize the number of qubits and quantum gates required, which is particularly important given the limitations of NISQ devices.
  - *Maintain Favorable Spectral Properties:* A well-designed Hamiltonian should preserve a reasonable spectral gap to ensure that the QAOA circuit can effectively transition between ground and excited states.

  Research into advanced encoding strategies—such as parity encoding, domain wall encoding, or problem-specific ansätze—can significantly enhance QAOA's performance, particularly for complex and combinatorial optimization problems.

Conclusion

Ultimately, Variational Quantum Algorithms (VQAs) play a crucial role in the progress of quantum computing, particularly in the context of noisy intermediate-scale quantum (NISQ) devices. Variational Quantum Algorithms (VQAs) offer a practical approach to solving optimization problems that would otherwise be impossible for classical methods alone by efficiently combining quantum and classical resources. This chapter provides a thorough examination of the VQE and QAOA algorithms, emphasizing the possibilities and difficulties of implementing VQAs in real-world situations.

The Variational Quantum Eigensolver (VQE) showcases the capabilities of quantum algorithms in accurately estimating molecule energies, providing a preview of the potential of quantum chemistry and materials research. Upon analyzing the several versions and practical uses of VQE, it becomes evident that although it holds immense potential, it also poses substantial challenges, notably in relation to hardware noise and scalability.

Moreover, the Quantum Approximate Optimization Algorithm (QAOA) highlights the suitability of Variational Quantum Algorithms (VQAs) for solving combinatorial optimization problems. Examining many variations of QAOA and its practical uses uncovers its advantages as well as its present constraints, specifically in terms of the complexity of its layers and the vulnerability of optimization landscapes.

As we further improve and optimize these algorithms, by tackling their difficulties through advancements in both quantum hardware and algorithmic design, VQAs are expected to become the fundamental building blocks of numerous future quantum applications. This chapter has presented a thorough and detailed examination of VQAs, including their design, implementation, and potential. As a result, readers are now equipped with the necessary knowledge to delve deeper into and make contributions to this dynamic and quickly advancing field of quantum computing.

We will be studying quantum machine learning in the next chapter.

References

- Musty Thoughts - How VQA's Work - `https://www.mustythoughts.com/vqas-how-do-they-work`
- Musty Thoughts - VQA Challenges and State of Research - `https://www.mustythoughts.com/vqas-challenges`

CHAPTER 13

Quantum Machine Learning

Introduction

The proliferation of classical computers across industries and applications has led to a significant increase in data generation in recent years. The emergence of robust classical computing, including Graphics Processing Units (GPUs), has allowed several businesses to process vast volumes of data quickly and effectively. We have noticed a significant increase in the amount of data, which is expected to continue expanding in the future. This will result in classical computing methods requiring more time to process and extract valuable information from the data. Quantum machine learning (QML) explores potential advantages by leveraging quantum superposition and interference to enhance pattern recognition and optimization beyond classical capabilities.

Structure

In this chapter, you are going to study:

- Introduction to Classical Machine Learning

- Types of Learning
- Common Machine Learning Algorithms
- Introduction to Quantum Machine Learning
    - Encoding Classical Data into Quantum States
- Algorithms Using Qiskit Machine Learning
    - Quantum Neural Networks (QNN) - EstimatorQNN and SamplerQNN
    - Quantum Neural Networks for Classification
- Applications of Quantum Machine Learning
    - Quantum-enhanced Optimization
    - Data Encoding in Quantum States
    - Quantum-Enhanced Feature Selection and Extraction
    - Quantum Anomaly Detection
- Challenges and Future Directions in QML
    - Challenges
    - Future Directions

Introduction to Classical Machine Learning

Machine learning involves creating intelligent computers capable of performing various tasks without explicit programming. It is a study of algorithms and statistical models that may address a specific issue without explicit programming, instead relying on data patterns and inferences. Classical machine learning refers to using classical computers, which operate on classical bits, to perform machine learning tasks.

The definition of machine learning implies that the computer does not learn but instead seeks a mathematical relationship within input data to provide a prediction as an output. Arthur Samuel from IBM coined the marketing phrase *machine learning* in 1959 to promote the application of this technology to businesses and customers. Machine learning is essentially a combination of mathematical concepts from several fields like statistics, probability, linear algebra, calculus, and optimization. Machine learning is frequently referred to as statistical learning due to the fact that machine learning algorithms are based on statistical approaches. Therefore, it is essential to have a good understanding of statistics and other mathematical concepts.

This book does not focus on machine learning, thus we will not explore this topic extensively or delve into its mathematical intricacies. We shall concentrate solely on particular classical machine learning methods, with their quantum counterparts being addressed in subsequent sections.

Types of Learning

Various categories of learning exist within machine learning algorithms. The learning process is determined by the nature of the data used to train the machine learning algorithms. There are four types of learning, as follows:

- **Supervised Learning:** This learning method involves datasets with labels assigned to each data point. Labels serve as overseers for the machine learning algorithm, aiding in the efficient learning of the data. Supervised learning can be categorized into two types: classification learning and regression learning. If you have many photographs of dogs and cats, assign the labels *dog* and *cat* to the respective images for classification by your algorithm. The case including dogs and cats has a finite number of classes, making it an instance of classification learning. Having labels represented as numerical values, which are continuous, is referred to as regression learning. Supervised algorithms such as linear regression, logistic regression, artificial neural networks, support vector machines, decision trees, and random forests are commonly used in data analysis.
- **Unsupervised Learning:** This learning method involves datasets without labels. The machine learning method aims to identify patterns and distributions within the dataset rather than focusing on making predictions. Unsupervised learning examples include principal component analysis, K-means clustering, autoencoder-based recommender systems, and outlier detection.
- **Semi-Supervised Learning:** The dataset contains both labeled and unlabeled samples. The machine learning method constructs a model from the unlabeled data points, similar to supervised learning.
- **Reinforcement Learning:** Reinforcement learning involves a machine acting as an agent inside an environment. The environment's state is represented as a feature vector, allowing the agent to conduct different actions that may lead to rewards or punishments. The agent aims to optimize its policy by selecting behaviors that yield the highest average reward. The common examples of reinforcement learning algorithms include Q-learning, deep Q-learning, Monte Carlo, SARSA, trusted region policy optimization (TRPO), proximal policy optimization (PPO), twin delayed deep deterministic (TD3) policy gradient, and the asynchronous advantage actor-critic (A3C) algorithm.

Now, let's examine the types of machine learning models depending on the quantity of parameters in a machine learning algorithm. Every algorithm has a unique set of parameters that can be adjusted to improve predictions and accuracy for a specific dataset. The types of machine learning models based on the number of parameters are categorized as follows:

- **Parametric Models:** This model contains a finite, constant set of parameters in the method that does not increase with the size of the training data. Regardless of the quantity of training data provided to the parametric algorithm, the number of parameters will remain constant, and only those specific parameters will be utilized for making predictions. These models are straightforward, need minimal training data to learn, and have a fast training process. Nevertheless, these models are constrained by restricted functional forms and inadequate data fitting. Parametric algorithms such as linear regression, logistic regression, perceptrons, naïve Bayes, and artificial neural networks are commonly used in data analysis.
- **Non-Parametric Models:** In this approach, the number of parameters for a machine learning algorithm increases as the training dataset size expands. Non-parametric techniques can capture more information as the dataset size increases. As the number of parameters increases, these models offer flexibility, power, and performance but have decreased training speeds and overfitting problems. Non-parametric techniques such as K-nearest neighbours, decision trees, random forests, and support vector machines are commonly used in machine learning.

We will now examine algorithms that rely on simulating the distribution of data, commonly used phrases in research literature.

- **Discriminative Models:** Let X represent the data and Y represent the corresponding labels. A discriminative model directly learns the conditional probability distribution P(Y|X) from the training data. These models represent the decision border that separates different categories or classes within the dataset. Discriminative models are cost-effective, robust against outliers, and suitable for supervised machine-learning tasks. These models typically do not handle missing data well and necessitate a larger amount of training data to learn effectively. Discriminative models encompass logistic regression, support vector machines, K-nearest neighbours, artificial neural networks, decision trees, and random forests.
- **Generative Models:** Generative models are designed to understand and learn the joint probability distribution P(X, Y) = P(X|Y) P(Y) of the given data. They derived the parameters P(X|Y) and P(Y) directly from the training data and then applied Bayes' theorem to determine P(Y|X). It is akin to converting P(X, Y) to P(Y|X) by Bayes' theorem. Generative models represent the actual distribution of each class in the dataset. Generative models are computationally intensive, sensitive to outliers in the dataset, and require less training data than discriminative models. These models are suitable for handling missing data and are effective for unsupervised learning tasks. Generative models such as linear discriminant analysis (LDA), naïve Bayes, Bayesian networks, hidden Markov models, and Markov random fields are commonly used in data analysis.

Common Machine Learning Algorithms

In the following section, we will study some well-known classical machine learning algorithms and compare them to their quantum counterparts. Understanding classical algorithms will enable you to grasp the basics of quantum machine learning methods.

Artificial Neural Networks

Artificial neural networks are machine learning models that mimic the structure and function of organic neurons seen in the human brain. Biological neurons and artificial neural networks both function as information processing units. Artificial neural networks are composed of computing units called neurons that calculate the average of all incoming data. Synapses are the connections between neurons, each with associated weights that can be adjusted to facilitate learning in the neural network.

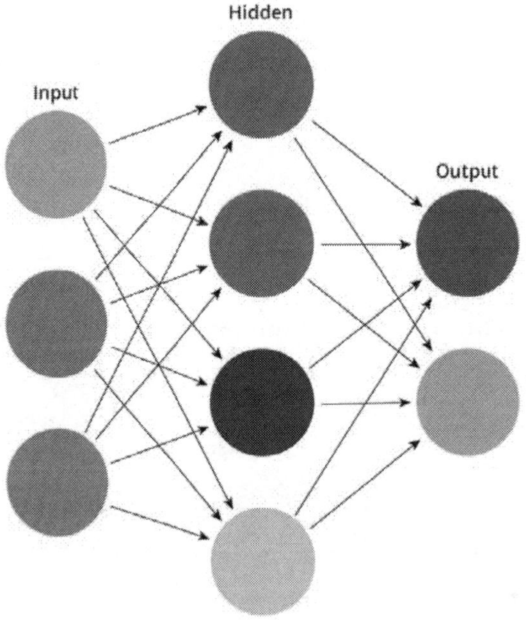

Figure 13.1: Artificial Neural Network

Figure 13.1 displays a visual representation of a basic neural network using a solitary, hidden layer. Increasing the number of hidden layers in a neural network results in a deeper network, which is referred to as a deep neural network. A neural network consisting of two or more layers is called a deep neural network.

Activation functions are utilized in neural networks to introduce non-linearity. Activation functions assist a neural network in representing intricate, non-linear data commonly present in ordinary datasets. Common activation functions for neural networks include sigmoid, threshold, rectified linear unit (ReLU), and hyperbolic tangent functions. The ReLU activation function is utilized in the hidden layers of a neural network for deep networks. It aids in representing intricate mathematical functions more effectively for the provided dataset.

The output layer predicts classes or continuous regression values depending on the dataset. The forecasted classes are inputted into a loss function, which compares them with the true labels from the dataset. The loss function value quantifies the network's mistake rate. The error value is used to adjust the neural network weights through optimization techniques like gradient or stochastic gradient descent. The optimization algorithm aims to minimize the discrepancy between the anticipated and actual labels, and there are several optimization procedures beyond gradient descent approaches. Calculating derivatives is called backpropagation, sometimes called backprop or BP. Backpropagation entails calculating the gradient of the loss function concerning the weights. Optimization procedures, like gradient descent, update the weights using derivatives determined through backpropagation to minimize the loss. Weights in neural networks are the adjustable parameters that are optimized by backpropagation to improve prediction accuracy.

Support Vector Machines

Support vector machines (SVM) is a supervised learning method for classification and regression tasks. We will use Support Vector Machine (SVM) as a classification technique to demonstrate its functionality. SVM aims to identify the best hyperplane that effectively separates different classes. In a two-dimensional scenario, a simple line is a hyperplane to separate the data points.

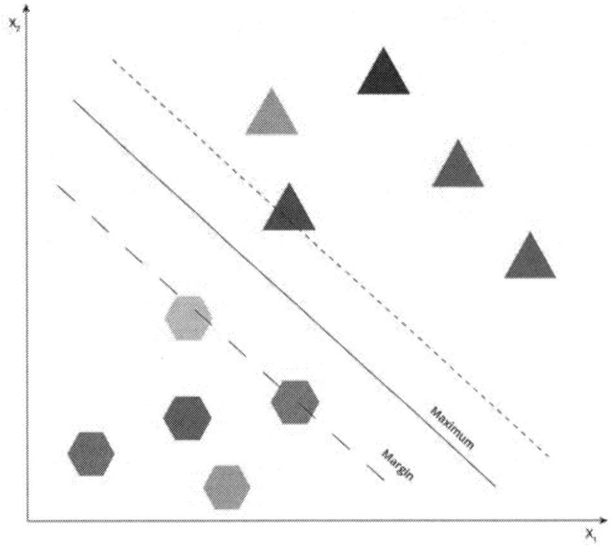

Figure 13.2: Linear SVM Binary Classification

Figure 13.2 displays a 2D plane with three lines. The central line is the decision boundary, while the two other lines are the margins (the dotted lines at the bottom and top) that should be maximally distanced for the most precise forecasts.

Margin lines are formed using support vectors, which are data points representing the classes in a dataset. Two boxes are in contact with the bottom margin line, while a circle is in contact with the top margin lines. The support vectors consist of these two boxes and the circle.

Every data point in the 2D space is treated as a vector since all SVM computations occur in the 2D plane, which is a vector space. The margin lines can alter if the position of the support vectors changes.

The SVM algorithm identifies two margin lines with no data points in between. The algorithm first maximizes the distance between the margins and then establishes the decision boundary (positioned halfway between the margins) for classification. The linear SVM approach we have covered is not suitable for differentiating classes in high-dimensional datasets due to the complexity of higher-dimensional feature spaces and large amounts of data points in real-world scenarios.

When dealing with non-linear data, like the one displayed in *Figure* 13.4 on the left graph, we employ a mathematical technique called a kernel trick to simplify our classification task.

A circle can separate the boxes based on the circle data points, but it is not a linear boundary. By utilizing the kernel method in the right-hand graph, it is possible to divide the boxes and circles using a 2D hyperplane in a 3D coordinate vector space. This 2D-to-3D transformation is simulated, not actual!

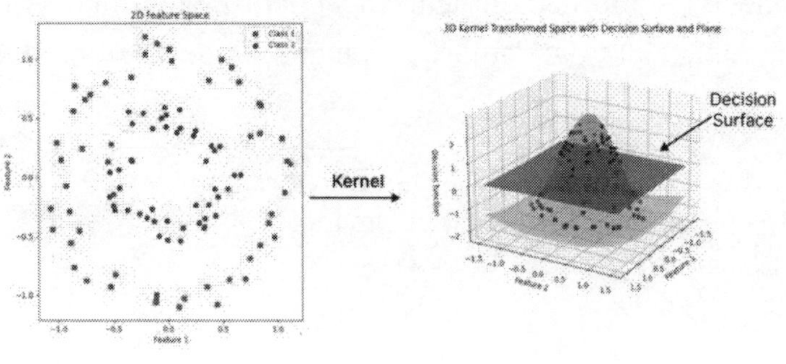

Figure 13.3: Kernel SVM Binary Classification

The kernel method of Support Vector Machine (SVM) is a mathematical methodology used for classifying high-dimensional data without the need to compute the data's coordinates in higher dimensions. The kernel approach aids in identifying similarities within data that exist in high-dimensional spaces. The need to transform data into a higher-dimensional space for classification is eliminated, as the kernel trick enables computations to be performed in the original feature space. Available kernel types include radial basis functions (RBFs), Gaussian kernels, polynomial kernels, sigmoid kernels, and Laplace RBF kernels.

Introduction to Quantum Machine Learning

You were introduced to the topic of machine learning and the two most commonly employed algorithms by researchers and industries to boost growth in the previous part. Each year, we observe a substantial increase in global data volume; this growth rate is expected to escalate more in the next few years. Approximately 60 zettabytes (10^{21}) of data have been amassed on our planet.

The capabilities of classical computers are being constrained by the increasing volume of data and its related characteristics. Current classical computers can effectively process high-dimensional data, but they will eventually struggle with very high-dimensional data, at which point quantum machine learning techniques will be necessary.

Lloyd, Mohseni, and Rebentrost introduced the phrase *quantum machine learning* in their 2013 study titled "Quantum algorithms for supervised and unsupervised machine learning." Subsequently, extensive research and advancements have occurred in this innovative subject. Quantum machine learning combines quantum algorithms with conventional machine learning techniques, commonly called quantum-enhanced machine learning. There are numerous advancements in quantum machine learning, such as solving linear equations, quantum-enhanced reinforcement learning, quantum neural networks, and quantum sampling techniques, which are particularly applied in finance-related sectors.

Type of Data	Type of Processing Device	
	Classical Device	Quantum Device
Classical Data	CC	CQ
Quantum Data	QC	QQ

Table 13.1: Approaches to QML

Quantum machine learning approaches can be classified into four primary types based on the type of data and the data-processing equipment. The categories are outlined in *Table* 13.1 given previously, displaying the classical elements.

In the CC (Classical Data, Classical Device) approach, classical computers process classical data, as demonstrated in the previous section. These are your traditional machine learning algorithms. The QC case involves the application of classical machine learning to quantum data, namely in differentiating different quantum states and understanding phase transitions in complex quantum systems.

CQ and QQ are forms of quantum machine learning, where a quantum computer is used as the primary processing unit for both classical and quantum input. We are focusing on the CQ situation, where we utilize quantum computers to analyze big classical datasets to uncover hidden patterns and extract valuable information for making judgments.

You may be curious about how classical data can be utilized on a quantum computer, even though it is classical in nature and not in a quantum state. Encoding mechanisms are available that can assist in converting classical data into a quantum state for processing by a quantum computer.

Encoding Classical Data into Quantum States

Multiple methods exist for encoding classical information into a quantum state. We shall briefly review the encoding approaches. We will cover basis encoding, amplitude encoding, angle encoding, higher-order embedding, and variational/trained embedding approaches. Let's begin with basis encoding.

Basis Encoding

Basis encoding is a scheme where binary data (using 0s and 1s) is encoded as a superposition of the quantum states. For example, if we have the data points $\begin{bmatrix}1\\0\\0\\0\end{bmatrix}$ and $\begin{bmatrix}0\\0\\0\\1\end{bmatrix}$ as quantum states $|00\rangle$ and $|11\rangle$, we can make a superposition state of 2 qubits as $\frac{1}{2}(|00\rangle + |01\rangle + |10\rangle + |11\rangle)$, from which we can form the amplitude vector as $\left[\frac{1}{\sqrt{2}}, 0, 0, \frac{1}{\sqrt{2}}\right]$. Therefore, the superposition state of encoding becomes $\frac{1}{\sqrt{2}}|00\rangle + \frac{1}{\sqrt{2}}|11\rangle$. As the number of qubits increases, the amplitude vector gets more sparse, containing many zeros, which is inefficient.

Amplitude Encoding

Amplitude encoding involves encoding classical information as the probability amplitude linked to quantum states. For example, if we have the classical data, $\begin{bmatrix}0.41\\-0.94\end{bmatrix}$ and $\begin{bmatrix}0.38\\-0.62\end{bmatrix}$ then the quantum state vector will be $\frac{1}{2}(0.41\,|00\rangle - 0.94\,|01\rangle + 0.38\,|10\rangle - 0.62\,|11\rangle)$. Amplitude encoding may lead to data corruption during quantum processing in quantum states. Corruption can provide faulty data and lead to erroneous predictions during the training of the quantum model. Let's examine a more effective and user-friendly method of data encoding called angle encoding.

Angle Encoding

The angle encoding method is widely utilized in numerous quantum machine learning models. Angle encoding stores data values as rotations of quantum states, where the angle value of the rotation corresponds to the classical data value. The number of qubits can match the number of features in the dataset. For example, the data $\begin{bmatrix}0.41\\-0.94\end{bmatrix}$ and $\begin{bmatrix}0.38\\-0.62\end{bmatrix}$ can be stored using angle encoding with X, Y, and Z-axis rotations around the Bloch sphere, such as $R_y(0.41)$, $R_z(-0.94)$ and $R_y(0.38)$, $R_z(-0.62)$ separated by Hadamard gates.

Higher-Order Encoding

Quantum feature maps serve as quantum analogs of classical kernels, enabling non-linear transformations in quantum-enhanced machine learning models. To achieve a quantum advantage, these maps must encode transformations that are classically intractable. Higher-order encoding maps classical data into high-dimensional quantum Hilbert spaces using quantum feature maps, leveraging entanglement and superposition to enhance expressivity and separability in quantum machine learning models.

Variational/Trained Encoding

This encoding approach closely resembles higher-order encoding. Quantum feature maps are used to represent classical data points as quantum states. This is referred to as quantum embedding. The embedding process involves utilizing a parameterized quantum circuit, where the parameters can be adjusted or optimized similarly to a neural network. This data encoding method is known as variational data encoding.

Algorithms using Qiskit Machine Learning

Qiskit Machine Learning provides a versatile framework for quantum machine learning that is accessible to both novices and experts. The framework provides fundamental computational components such as Quantum Kernels and Quantum Neural Networks for use in classification and regression tasks. The `FidelityQuantumKernel` class uses the `BaseStateFidelity` technique to calculate kernel matrices. It supports the Quantum Support Vector Classifier and Regressor for addressing classification and regression issues, respectively. It integrates smoothly with traditional kernel-based machine-learning algorithms.

The platform establishes a universal neural network interface through the implementation of `EstimatorQNN` and `SamplerQNN`.
textbf `EstimatorQNN` utilizes parameterized quantum circuits and observables to produce outputs, while `SamplerQNN` converts quasi-probabilities of bitstrings into outputs, aiding in class interpretation. These networks facilitate input evaluation and gradient computation, crucial for enhancing training efficiency. Qiskit Machine Learning provides `NeuralNetworkClassifier` and `NeuralNetworkRegressor` for utilizing quantum neural networks in classification and regression tasks. It also offers user-friendly implementations such as the Variational Quantum Classifier and Regressor.

The TorchConnector combines quantum neural networks with the PyTorch library, allowing for automatic differentiation and including quantum networks in backpropagation. This adaptable structure allows for future extensions to be made to other software programs.

We are now going to discuss a few Qiskit Machine Learning tutorials in detail that are available on the Qiskit Ecosystem website in order to provide better familiarity with the new functionalities that the Qiskit team has introduced in their new 1.0 package.

Quantum Neural Networks (QNN) - EstimatorQNN and SamplerQNN

Let us begin by importing the necessary functions.

```
from qiskit_algorithms.utils import algorithm_globals

algorithm_globals.random_seed = 42

from qiskit.circuit import Parameter
from qiskit import QuantumCircuit
from qiskit.quantum_info import SparsePauliOp
from qiskit_machine_learning.neural_networks import EstimatorQNN
from qiskit.circuit import ParameterVector
from qiskit_machine_learning.neural_networks import SamplerQNN
```

We begin by creating the parameterized circuit. The quantum circuit contains two parameters: one for a Quantum Neural Network (QNN) input and the other for a trainable weight.

```
params_est = [Parameter("input_est"), Parameter("weight_est")]
qc_est = QuantumCircuit(1)
qc_est.h(0)
qc_est.ry(params_est[0], 0)
qc_est.rx(params_est[1], 0)
qc_est.draw("mpl", style="clifford")
```

The `EstimatorQNN` receives a parameterized quantum circuit and an optional quantum mechanical observable as input and calculates expectation value computations for the forward pass. The `EstimatorQNN` can also process lists of observables to create more intricate QNNs.

By default, `EstimatorQNN` creates the quantum mechanical observable $Z^{\otimes n}$, but we create the observable $Y^{\otimes n}$ with the help of sparse Pauli operator representation and define the `EstimatorQNN` parameters. This instantiates the estimator.

```
observable_est = SparsePauliOp.from_list([("Y" * qc_est.num_qubits, 1)])
estimator_qnn = EstimatorQNN(
    circuit=qc_est, observables=observable_est, input_params=[params_est[0]],
    weight_params=[params_est[1]]
)
estimator_qnn
```

It is important to note that the `EstimatorQNN` also takes an optional `estimator` argument, which the user can define as per the application.

The `SamplerQNN` is created in a manner akin to the `EstimatorQNN`, but it does not need a customized observable as it directly uses samples obtained from measuring the quantum circuit.

The output samples are automatically interpreted as the probability of measuring the integer index associated with a bitstring. The `SamplerQNN` also enables us to define an interpret function for post-processing the samples. Define this function to accept an integer value derived from a bitstring and transform it into a non-negative integer.

We define the following parameterized quantum circuit for the `SamplerQNN`.

```
inputs_sam = ParameterVector("input_sam", 2)
weights_sam = ParameterVector("weight_sam", 4)

qc_sam = QuantumCircuit(2)
qc_sam.ry(inputs_sam[0], 0)
qc_sam.ry(inputs_sam[1], 1)
qc_sam.cx(0, 1)
qc_sam.ry(weights_sam[0], 0)
qc_sam.ry(weights_sam[1], 1)
qc_sam.cx(0, 1)
qc_sam.ry(weights_sam[2], 0)
qc_sam.ry(weights_sam[3], 1)

qc_sam.draw("mpl", style="clifford")
```

The process for creating `SamplerQNN` is similar to that of the `EstimatorQNN`, and the arguments taken by the `SamplerQNN` function are also similar. Just like the estimator argument, an optional argument is a `sampler` primitive instance that can be provided, too.

```
sampler_qnn = SamplerQNN(circuit=qc_sam, input_params=inputs_sam,
weight_params=weights_sam)
sampler_qnn
```

As discussed previously, the codes for the `EstimatorQNN` and `SamplerQNN` are similar. Therefore, here we only discuss the next steps for `EstimatorQNN`, and we leave the `SamplerQNN` coding as a practice for the reader.

Let us explore the forward and backward passes for the `EstimatorQNN`. We start by defining random inputs and weights, but please note that inputs should be replaced with input dataset values, and the weights will be tuned by the training algorithm or defined by a pre-trained model.

```
estimator_qnn_input = algorithm_globals.random.random(estimator_qnn.num_inputs)
estimator_qnn_weights = algorithm_globals.random.random(estimator_qnn.num_weights)

print(
    f"Number of Input features for EstimatorQNN: {estimator_qnn.num_inputs}
    \nInput: {estimator_qnn_input}"
)
print(
    f"Number of trainable weights for EstimatorQNN: {estimator_qnn.num_weights}
    \nWeights: {estimator_qnn_weights}"
)
```

The output of the previous code will be

```
Number of Input features for EstimatorQNN: 1
Input: [0.77395605]
Number of trainable weights for EstimatorQNN: 1
Weights: [0.43887844]
```

The intended output shape for the forward pass of the `EstimatorQNN` is
`(1, num_qubits * num_observables)`,
where 1 represents the number of samples. Since, the inputs and weights have been defined, we can create a non-batched forward pass as follows

```
estimator_qnn_forward = estimator_qnn.forward(estimator_qnn_input,
↪  estimator_qnn_weights)
```

```
print(
    f"Forward Pass result for EstimatorQNN: {estimator_qnn_forward}.
    \nShape: {estimator_qnn_forward.shape}"
)
```

where the result is given as

```
Forward Pass result for EstimatorQNN: [[0.2970094]].
Shape: (1, 1)
```

The batched forward pass and its output can be generated by

```
estimator_qnn_forward_batched = estimator_qnn.forward(
    [estimator_qnn_input, estimator_qnn_input], estimator_qnn_weights
)

print(
    f"Forward pass result for EstimatorQNN: {estimator_qnn_forward_batched}.
    \nShape: {estimator_qnn_forward_batched.shape}"
)
```

```
Forward Pass result for EstimatorQNN: [[0.2970094]
 [0.2970094]].
Shape: (2, 1)
```

Utilize the inputs and weights previously defined to demonstrate the process of the backward pass. The function returns a tuple, including input gradients and weight gradients. The default setting is for the backward pass to compute gradients alone in relation to the weight parameters.

If you want to enable gradients with respect to the input parameters, you should set the following flag during the QNN instantiation: `qnn=...QNN(..., input_gradients=True)`

This is compulsory for the Torch connector so as to use PyTorch functionalities.

For the `EstimatorQNN`, the expected output shape for the weight gradients is `(batch_size,num_qubits*num_observables,num_weights)`

```
estimator_qnn_input_grad, estimator_qnn_weight_grad = estimator_qnn.backward(
    estimator_qnn_input, estimator_qnn_weights
)
```

```
print(
    f"Input gradients for EstimatorQNN: {estimator_qnn_input_grad}.
    \nShape: {estimator_qnn_input_grad}"
)
print(
    f"Weight gradients for EstimatorQNN: {estimator_qnn_weight_grad}.
    \nShape: {estimator_qnn_weight_grad.shape}"
)
```

```
Input gradients with EstimatorQNN: None.
Shape: None
Weight gradients with EstimatorQNN: [[[0.63272767]]].
Shape: (1, 1, 1)
```

With the gradients enabled, we will have

```
estimator_qnn.input_gradients = True
#sampler_qnn.input_gradients = True

estimator_qnn_input_grad, estimator_qnn_weight_grad = estimator_qnn.backward(
    estimator_qnn_input, estimator_qnn_weights
)

print(
    f"Input gradients EstimatorQNN: {estimator_qnn_input_grad}.
    \nShape: {estimator_qnn_input_grad.shape}"
)
print(
    f"Weight gradients EstimatorQNN: {estimator_qnn_weight_grad}.
    \nShape: {estimator_qnn_weight_grad.shape}"
)
```

```
Input gradients EstimatorQNN: [[[0.3038852]]].
Shape: (1, 1, 1)
Weight gradients EstimatorQNN: [[[0.63272767]]].
Shape: (1, 1, 1)
```

We have covered several important aspects of the estimator and sampler QNNs. Feel free to experiment with the problem setup to observe how varying circuit sizes, input lengths, and weight parameter values impact the output shapes.

Quantum Neural Networks for Classification

In this part, we explore the intriguing overlap between quantum computing and machine learning, specifically emphasizing utilizing Quantum Neural Networks (QNNs) for classification purposes. We will use the sophisticated features of Qiskit to help you understand how to improve traditional classification algorithms using quantum computing. This section seeks to explain how Quantum Neural Networks (QNNs) may be built and utilized with Qiskit to solve classification problems. It provides insight into the potential future of computing, where quantum and classical approaches combine to address intricate obstacles. By providing practical examples and extensive explanations, readers will acquire practical experience in developing quantum-based classification models, establishing a strong basis for delving deeper into quantum machine learning. As mentioned before, we are using the codes from the Qiskit Machine Learning tutorials to provide detailed explanations of the features that could be utilized for different kinds of projects.

EstimatorQNN Based Classification

We create a simple dataset for performing binary classification of two classes $\{-1, +1\}$

```
num_inputs = 2
num_samples = 20
X = 2 * algorithm_globals.random.random([num_samples, num_inputs]) - 1
y01 = 1 * (np.sum(X, axis=1) >= 0)  # in { 0,  1}
y = 2 * y01 - 1  # in {-1, +1}
y_one_hot = np.zeros((num_samples, 2))
for i in range(num_samples):
    y_one_hot[i, y01[i]] = 1

for x, y_target in zip(X, y):
    if y_target == 1:
        plt.plot(x[0], x[1], "mo")
    else:
        plt.plot(x[0], x[1], "yo")
```

```
plt.plot([-1, 1], [1, -1], "--", color="black")
plt.show()
```

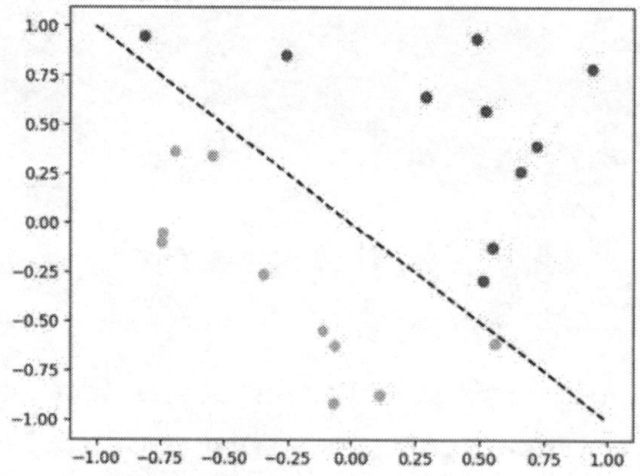

Figure 13.4: Binary Classification Data

Now, we utilize the default `QNNCircuit()` function containing ZZFeatureMap and Real Amplitudes ansatz for constructing a simple parameterized quantum circuit. With the circuit constructed, we define the QNN estimator and perform a forward pass where inputs are mapped to $\{-1, +1\}$.

```
qc = QNNCircuit(num_qubits=2)
qc.draw("mpl", style="clifford")

estimator_qnn = EstimatorQNN(circuit=qc)
estimator_qnn.forward(X[0, :],
algorithm_globals.random.random(estimator_qnn.num_weights))
```

In order to generate a live plot, a callback function is defined that takes the current weights and the value of the objective function at those weights.

```
def callback_graph(weights, obj_func_eval):
    clear_output(wait=True)
    objective_func_vals.append(obj_func_eval)
    plt.title("Objective function value against iteration")
    plt.xlabel("Iteration")
    plt.ylabel("Objective function value")
    plt.plot(range(len(objective_func_vals)), objective_func_vals)
    plt.show()
```

```
estimator_classifier = NeuralNetworkClassifier(
    estimator_qnn, optimizer=COBYLA(maxiter=60), callback=callback_graph
)

objective_func_vals = []
plt.rcParams["figure.figsize"] = (12, 6)
estimator_classifier.fit(X, y)
plt.rcParams["figure.figsize"] = (6, 4)
estimator_classifier.score(X, y)
```

We use this function inside the `NeuralNetworkClassifier()` function along with the QNN estimator and the optimizer. Next, the classifier is fitted to the data, and its true values and the score are calculated, which is 0.8.

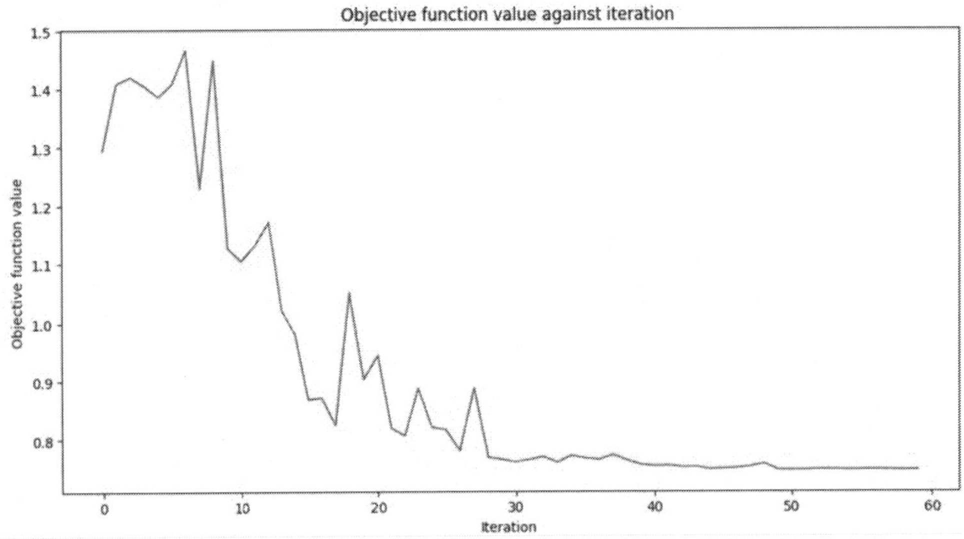

Figure 13.5: Binary Classification Convergence

Once the training process converges, we perform a prediction on the training dataset, and we get the plot as shown in *Figure* 13.6.

```
y_predict = estimator_classifier.predict(X)

for x, y_target, y_p in zip(X, y, y_predict):
    if y_target == 1:
        plt.plot(x[0], x[1], "mo")
```

```
    else:
        plt.plot(x[0], x[1], "yo")
    if y_target != y_p:
        plt.scatter(x[0], x[1], s=200, facecolors="none", edgecolors="r",
        ↪ linewidths=2)
plt.plot([-1, 1], [1, -1], "--", color="black")
plt.show()
```

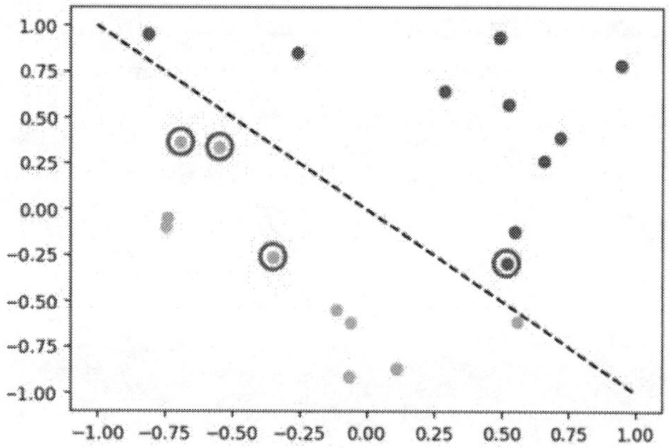

Figure 13.6: Binary Classification Predictions

The red circles around the data points represent the wrongly classified points. As an exercise, try to implement the same kind of classification using the `SamplerQNN` technique. You can take inspiration from the example solved in the Qiskit ML tutorial and experiment with different parameters and values to check for convergence and classification results. Furthermore, you can explore multi-class classification with both `SamplerQNN` and `EstimatorQNN`. We now move on to the variational quantum classifier (VQC) being applied to a real-world dataset for classification problems.

Variational Quantum Classifier on Real-World Dataset

The Variational Quantum Classifier approach integrates the principles of quantum physics with variational algorithms to address classification problems, which are crucial to the field of machine learning. By utilizing Qiskit to develop Variational Quantum Circuits (VQCs) on real-world datasets, this study not only demonstrates the effectiveness of quantum algorithms in addressing intricate data-driven challenges but also offers readers a firsthand opportunity to connect quantum theory with real-world applications. This sub-section provides a comprehensive tutorial on the process of developing, training, and evaluating a Variational Quantum Classifier. Its purpose is to equip readers with the necessary knowledge and skills to apply quantum computing principles in practical situations effectively.

We start by loading the IRIS flower dataset containing 150 data points of three different flower species (Iris-Setosa, Iris-Versicolour and Iris-Virginica) characterized by four attributes. This dataset is well balanced, i.e., it has 50 data points per class. As a next step, we store these features as the main data along with their class labels that we need to predict.

Initially, we will standardize the features. Specifically, we will employ a straightforward conversion to standardize all features to a uniform scale. In our particular situation, we compress or condense all the characteristics or attributes onto the range or span of values between 0 and 1. This process is called Normalization and is a widely used method in machine learning that frequently results in improved numerical stability and algorithm convergence.

```
iris_data = load_iris()
features = iris_data.data
labels = iris_data.target
features = MinMaxScaler().fit_transform(features)
```

Once we have the dataset and labels set up, we first run a simple support vector classifier (SVC) on these data. But before doing that, we split our dataset into 80% training data and 20% test data. The SVC is trained on the training data, and to check its accuracy on unseen data, we use the test data points. Once the SVC model gets trained on the data, we can calculate the score or accuracy of the predictions, which comes out to be 99% and 97% for the training and testing data, respectively.

```
algorithm_globals.random_seed = 123
train_features, test_features, train_labels, test_labels = train_test_split(
    features, labels, train_size=0.8, random_state=algorithm_globals.random_seed
)
svc = SVC()
_ = svc.fit(train_features, train_labels)

train_score_c4 = svc.score(train_features, train_labels)
test_score_c4 = svc.score(test_features, test_labels)
```

We will conduct training for a variational quantum classifier (VQC). The Variational Quantum Classifier (VQC) is the most basic classification algorithm offered in Qiskit Machine

Learning. It serves as an excellent entry point for individuals new to quantum machine learning, particularly those with prior experience in classical machine learning. Before training a model, let's analyze the components of the VQC class. The feature map and ansatz are two key components. The following will explain these.

The nature of our data is classical, indicating that it is composed of a collection of bits rather than qubits. We require a method to convert the data into qubits. This approach is essential if we desire to get an efficient quantum model. The process of mapping data is commonly known as data encoding, data embedding, or data loading, and the feature map performs it. The different encoding schemes have already been explained in the *Introduction to Quantum Machine Learning* section. Although feature mapping is a widely used mechanism in machine learning, the process of loading data into quantum states is not present in classical machine learning, which exclusively acts in the classical world.

Upon loading the data, it is imperative to implement a parameterized quantum circuit promptly. This circuit is an exact analogue to the layers seen in standard neural networks, again, which has been discussed previously. The system possesses a collection of adjustable parameters or weights. The weights are adjusted in order to minimize an objective function. The objective function quantifies the discrepancy between the predictions and the labelled data that is already known. A parameterized quantum circuit is alternatively referred to as a parameterized trial state, variational form, or ansatz. Arguably, the latter is the most commonly employed phrase.

We use a standard encoding technique called the `ZZFeatureMap()`, which is a second-order Pauli-Z evolution circuit. This takes the four features of our dataset encoded in each qubit. Therefore, a 4-qubit circuit is formed.

```
num_features = features.shape[1]
feature_map = ZZFeatureMap(feature_dimension=num_features, reps=1)
feature_map.decompose().draw(output="mpl", style="clifford", fold=20)
```

After the feature encoding step, we define the ansatz. Here, we use the `RealAmplitudes()` circuit. The circuit consists of alternating layers of Y rotations and CX entanglements. The user can tailor the entanglement pattern or select from a previous assortment. The term `RealAmplitudes` is employed to describe quantum states that possess solely real amplitudes, with the imaginary component consistently equal to zero.

```
ansatz = RealAmplitudes(num_qubits=num_features, reps=3)
ansatz.decompose().draw(output="mpl", style="clifford", fold=20)
```

```
optimizer = COBYLA(maxiter=100)

objective_func_vals = []
plt.rcParams["figure.figsize"] = (12, 6)


def callback_graph(weights, obj_func_eval):
    clear_output(wait=True)
    objective_func_vals.append(obj_func_eval)
    plt.title("Objective function value against iteration")
    plt.xlabel("Iteration")
    plt.ylabel("Objective function value")
    plt.plot(range(len(objective_func_vals)), objective_func_vals)
    plt.show()

sampler = Sampler()
vqc = VQC(
    sampler=sampler,
    feature_map=feature_map,
    ansatz=ansatz,
    optimizer=optimizer,
    callback=callback_graph,
)

# clear objective value history
objective_func_vals = []

start = time.time()
vqc.fit(train_features, train_labels)
elapsed = time.time() - start

print(f"Training time: {round(elapsed)} seconds")
```

After the VQC training had concluded, we checked the model's accuracy, which was 88% and 98% for the training and testing data, respectively. A better model can increase accuracy in different ways. Firstly, you can tweak the parameters present in the feature map and the ansatz. A higher number of parameters makes the model complex and increases

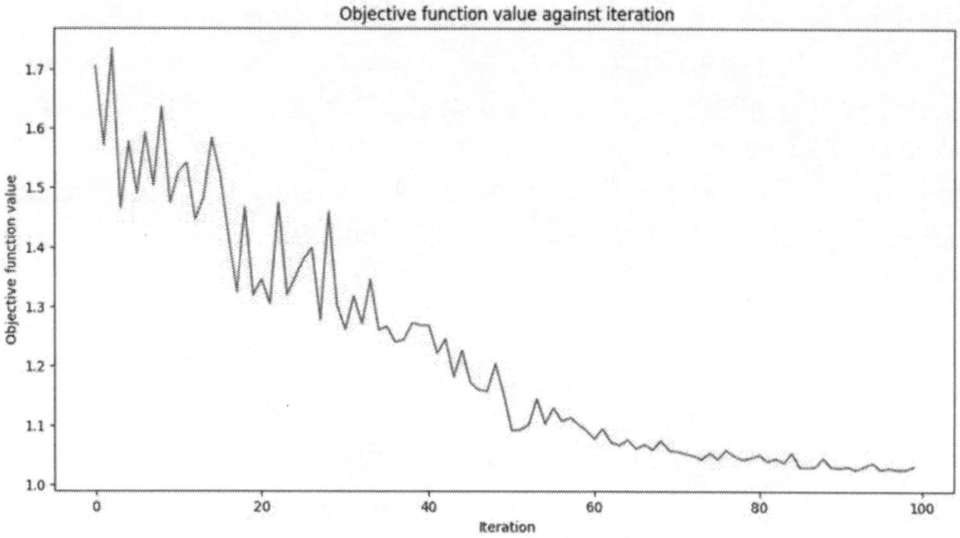

Figure 13.7: IRIS Data Classification Convergence

training time, but it becomes flexible. Different optimizers can be experimented upon, and additionally, efficient feature selection strategies such as Principal Component Analysis can also be applied to train the model only on those features which contribute to the improvement of the QML model.

Applications of Quantum Machine Learning

QML has a wide range of applications across various sectors where conventional ML has already made substantial progress. This section explores the practical uses of QML, highlighting the meticulousness and profound impact of quantum improvements in machine learning.

Quantum-Enhanced Optimization

Optimization underpins machine learning, focusing on minimizing cost functions to determine optimal model parameters. Classical methods rely on gradient-based optimizers such as Stochastic Gradient Descent (SGD) and Adam to efficiently navigate high-dimensional loss landscapes. Quantum Approximate Optimization Algorithm (QAOA) and Variational Quantum Eigensolver (VQE) provide hybrid quantum-classical frameworks for combinatorial and continuous optimization, respectively. QAOA encodes optimization problems into quantum circuits, iteratively refining solutions via parameterized ansätze and classical feedback, while VQE approximates ground states of Hamiltonians for continuous optimization. These approaches leverage quantum superposition, interference, and entanglement to explore rugged cost landscapes, potentially outperforming classical heuristics in specific cases. However, current quantum hardware limitations, including noise and qubit connectivity constraints, necessitate Quantum Error Mitigation (QEM) techniques such as Zero-Noise Extrapolation (ZNE) and Clifford Data Regression (CDR) to enhance computational reliability.

Data Encoding in Quantum States

Quantum Machine Learning (QML) leverages quantum states for high-dimensional data representation, utilizing encoding techniques such as amplitude encoding and quantum feature mapping. Amplitude encoding efficiently encodes classical data into quantum amplitudes, reducing memory overhead by representing 2^n features with only n qubits. Quantum feature mapping embeds data into high-dimensional quantum Hilbert spaces, enhancing separability for classification and regression tasks. Quantum algorithms perform key linear algebra operations, such as inner products and kernel evaluations, in logarithmic time for structured datasets, offering potential speedups over classical methods in high-dimensional data analysis. These advantages improve supervised and unsupervised learning tasks, including classification (Quantum Support Vector Machines), clustering (Quantum k-Means), and regression (Variational Quantum Regression), enabling more efficient processing in big data analytics.

Quantum-Enhanced Feature Selection and Extraction

Feature selection identifies key variables for a model, while feature extraction transforms data into more informative representations, reducing dimensionality and enhancing efficiency. Quantum algorithms exploit superposition and entanglement to evaluate feature relevance efficiently, potentially surpassing classical exhaustive search in high-dimensional datasets. Quantum feature extraction employs parameterized quantum circuits (PQCs) to encode data into high-dimensional Hilbert spaces, enabling representations inaccessible to classical methods. These quantum techniques may enhance anomaly detection, clustering, and classification by uncovering complex patterns and correlations in large datasets.

Quantum Anomaly Detection

Anomaly detection identifies data points that deviate significantly from expected patterns, often signaling fraud, system faults, or novel insights. Quantum anomaly detection encodes data into quantum states, leveraging quantum feature mapping and similarity measures to highlight deviations in complex datasets. Quantum interference enhances detection sensitivity by amplifying anomalies while suppressing background noise, potentially improving accuracy and efficiency in large-scale anomaly detection tasks.

Challenges and Future Directions in QML

Quantum Machine Learning (QML) poses notable difficulties and holds great potential for future advancements as it aims to exploit the transformative capabilities of quantum computing to revolutionize machine learning. A significant obstacle arises from the hardware constraints of existing Noisy Intermediate-Scale Quantum (NISQ) systems, characterized by elevated error rates and restricted qubit coherence durations. These limitations need the implementation of strong quantum error mitigation and correction strategies in order to guarantee the reliability of quantum machine learning algorithms. Furthermore, the exploration of effective quantum algorithms that can surpass classical counterparts in real-world applications continues to be a subject of ongoing research. Potential future paths involve investigating hybrid quantum-classical architectures, in which quantum computers are utilized to perform specific sub-tasks within broader classical frameworks, capitalizing on the advantages of both paradigms. Significant performance improvements will rely heavily on advancements in quantum hardware, including error-corrected qubits and scalable quantum systems. Moreover, the integration of knowledge from quantum physics, machine learning, and information theory in interdisciplinary research will stimulate innovation by tackling key inquiries regarding the computational intricacy and potential of QML. In order to evaluate and compare the performance of QML algorithms on various platforms and in diverse scenarios, it will be crucial to establish common benchmarks and create open-source frameworks.

Challenges

Quantum Machine Learning (QML) is an innovative combination of quantum computing and machine learning. However, it is still a relatively new topic that faces both theoretical and practical difficulties. Here, we discuss some of the challenges in the field of QML.

Hardware Limitations

The main obstacle in QML is the constraint imposed by quantum hardware. Quantum computers are now operating in the Noisy Intermediate-Scale Quantum (NISQ) era, which is marked by a limited number of qubits and substantial quantum noise. The limitations imposed by these constraints restrict the level of intricacy achievable in quantum algorithms, hence affecting the scalability of QML models and their suitability for real-world datasets.

- **Qubit Coherence Time:** The limited timeframe during which qubits maintain their quantum state imposes constraints on the complexity and execution time of quantum algorithms.
- **Error Rates:** The presence of significant error rates in quantum processes necessitates the use of advanced error correction techniques. However, implementing these approaches requires a significant increase in the number of physical qubits, which in turn reduces the available computing space for quantum machine learning applications.

Algorithmic Efficiency and Scalability

Demonstrating a quantum advantage in real-world QML tasks remains challenging due to hardware limitations and algorithmic constraints. While certain quantum algorithms show theoretical speedups in noiseless settings, achieving these advantages on practical NISQ devices remains difficult due to noise, decoherence, and classical pre-processing overhead.

- **Barren Plateaus:** Variational quantum algorithms, such as those in quantum neural networks and QAOA, suffer from barren plateaus, where cost function gradients vanish exponentially as system size grows. This hinders classical gradient-based optimization, requiring strategies like layer-wise training, adaptive learning rates, and quantum-specific ansätze to mitigate the issue.
- **Scalability:** The benefits of quantum algorithms must be maintained or strengthened when problems increase in size. It is essential for the future success of Quantum Machine Learning (QML) to make sure that the benefits of quantum speedups are not nullified by the additional time and resources required for data encoding and error correction.

Data Encoding and Quantum Feature Spaces

Optimizing classical-to-quantum data encoding is crucial for reducing overhead and maximizing quantum advantage in machine learning applications. Quantum feature maps define data embeddings in high-dimensional Hilbert spaces, directly impacting the expressivity and separability of QML models. Selecting an optimal feature map remains a non-trivial challenge due to computational complexity and problem-specific dependencies.

- **Encoding Complexity:** The ongoing study focuses on devising effective methods to encode high-dimensional classical data into quantum states without incurring excessive computing expenses.
- **Feature Space Exploration:** It is essential to comprehend the characteristics of quantum feature spaces and their potential utilization in machine learning jobs. There is a requirement for methodical techniques to create and choose quantum feature maps that are customized for specific machine learning challenges.

Quantum Software and Interoperability

For the expansion of Quantum Machine Learning (QML), it is crucial to have quantum software frameworks and tools that are easily accessible, efficient, and compatible with classical machine learning pipelines.

- **Software Development:** Advancing quantum programming languages, compilers, and development environments is essential for handling complex QML applications. This includes improving debugging capabilities, quantum circuit optimizations, and efficient parameter tuning in variational quantum algorithms.
- **Hybrid Systems:** Developing hybrid quantum-classical frameworks requires optimized interfaces for efficient data transfer, quantum-classical model co-processing, and seamless workflow execution. This is critical for near-term QML implementations, where quantum processors handle computational subroutines within larger classical machine learning pipelines.

Future Directions

The domain of QML, notwithstanding its difficulties, is abundant, with prospects for notable advancements and implementations. To overcome the existing constraints, it is necessary to make focused and coordinated efforts in multiple areas:

- **Advancements in Quantum Hardware:** Enhancing qubit coherence times, gate fidelities, and connectivity—along with scaling up the number of qubits—is essential.

Equally important is the development of robust quantum error correction and noise mitigation techniques. Improvements in the integration of quantum processors with classical control systems will also play a pivotal role in executing more complex QML algorithms.

- **Innovative Algorithm Design:** Designing novel variational quantum algorithms and hybrid quantum-classical approaches is crucial. Addressing challenges such as barren plateaus through methods like adaptive circuit design, improved parameter initialization, and layerwise training can significantly enhance scalability and efficiency. These innovations will facilitate the development of algorithms that are both resilient to noise and capable of leveraging quantum parallelism.
- **Theory of Quantum Learning:** Developing a rigorous theoretical framework is imperative. This includes establishing bounds on expressivity, sample complexity, and generalization capabilities of quantum models. A deeper theoretical understanding of when and how quantum algorithms outperform classical methods will guide the design of more effective QML systems, especially under realistic noise and decoherence conditions.
- **Cross-Disciplinary Collaboration:** Effective progress in QML requires close collaboration among quantum physicists, computer scientists, applied mathematicians, and domain experts. Such interdisciplinary efforts can drive the development of standardized benchmarks, integrated software-hardware co-design, and hybrid architectures that seamlessly combine quantum and classical computing resources to tackle complex real-world problems.

Conclusion

Quantum Machine Learning (QML) is an interdisciplinary field that merges the principles of quantum computing with advanced machine learning approaches to solve intricate computational issues. In this chapter, we have examined the fundamental principles, algorithms, and possible uses of QML, emphasizing its distinct benefits and existing constraints.

The main advantage of QML is its capability to use quantum phenomena like superposition and entanglement, allowing for the simultaneous processing of large volumes of data and the investigation of intricate solution spaces. Algorithms such as Quantum Neural Networks (QNNs) offer substantial improvements in speed for classification and pattern recognition tasks by utilizing the unique features of quantum systems.

However, QML encounters significant obstacles mainly because of the constraints imposed by the present Noisy Intermediate-Scale Quantum (NISQ) devices. Significant obstacles to fully fulfilling the potential of QML include high error rates, short coherence durations, and restricted qubit connections. To deal with these problems, it is crucial to employ strong quantum error mitigation and correction algorithms. Furthermore, advancing effective quantum algorithms that may clearly surpass classical algorithms in practical applications continues to be a crucial field of study.

The future of QML relies on several crucial advances. Hybrid quantum-classical architectures involve integrating quantum processors into conventional machine learning workflows. This method allows for the utilization of quantum benefits while addressing current hardware limits. Advancements in quantum hardware, including creating error-corrected qubits and scalable quantum systems, are crucial for reaching the processing power necessary for major advancements in QML.

Moreover, integrating several academic disciplines would be essential in promoting the progress of QML. Integrating quantum physics, machine learning, and information theory will be important in addressing current obstacles and unleashing novel opportunities. It is crucial to provide consistent standards and create open-source frameworks to assess and compare the effectiveness of QML algorithms. This will help promote wider acceptance and collaboration among researchers.

To summarize, although QML is still in its early phases of development, it has the potential to greatly impact machine learning and computational sciences. By tackling present obstacles and exploring novel research paths, QML has the potential to open up new possibilities in artificial intelligence and other areas. This will ultimately drive progress in both quantum computing and machine learning.

In the next chapter, we will explore one of the most important concepts in quantum computing - Error Mitigation. While studying the algorithms in this book, you may have noticed that on noisy simulators or hardware, we cannot achieve accurate results of the probabilities. To address these results, we will study quantum error mitigation.

References

- Training a Quantum Model on a Real Dataset - `https://qiskit-community.github.io/qiskit-machine-learning/tutorials/02a_training_a_quantum_model_on_a_real_dataset.html`

CHAPTER 14

Quantum Error Mitigation

Introduction

This chapter delves into Quantum Error Mitigation (QEM), a crucial aspect of quantum computing focused on improving the dependability and precision of quantum calculations. Quantum computing has the potential to solve intricate problems that classical computers cannot. However, this capability is currently hindered by quantum mistakes. The flaws stem from external interference, faults in quantum gate operations, and the inherent fragility of quantum states. Developing and implementing error mitigation measures is crucial to fully harnessing the potential of quantum computing. We start by establishing the fundamental notions of Quantum Error Mitigation, presenting the principles and methods to minimize the effects of mistakes on quantum computations without requiring complete correction. We then explore applying these techniques in the Qiskit framework, an open-source quantum computing software development kit that offers practical tools for implementing QEM. We discuss the difficulties involved in Quantum Error Correction, emphasizing the intricacies and constraints encountered when adapting these solutions for real-world quantum computing purposes. We will examine many scenarios and applications in various fields where quantum error mitigation is essential for quantum algorithms to realize their theoretical potential. This exploration of Quantum Error Mitigation will highlight the challenges and novel strategies being developed to overcome obstacles in achieving quantum computing.

Structure

In this chapter, you are going to study:

- Fundamentals of Quantum Error Mitigation
    - Quantum Error Mitigation versus Quantum Error Correction
    - Principles of Quantum Error Mitigation
- Techniques and Algorithms for Quantum Error Mitigation
    - Zero-Noise Extrapolation (ZNE)
    - Probabilistic Error Cancellation (PEC)
    - Clifford Data Regression (CDR)
    - Quantum Subspace Expansion (QSE)
    - Twirled Readout Error Mitigation (T-Rex)
    - Readout Error Mitigation
- Quantum Error Mitigation with Qiskit
    - Readouot Error Mitigation
    - mthree Based Error Mitigation
    - Qiskit Runtime-Based Error Mitigation Strategies
- Applications
    - Quantum Chemistry
    - Quantum Optimization
    - Quantum Machine Learning
    - Cryptography and Security
    - Quantum Simulation
    - Error Characterization and Benchmarking
    - Quantum Metrology
    - Towards Fault-Tolerant Quantum Computing

Fundamentals of Quantum Error Mitigation

Quantum Error Mitigation (QEM) refers to a collection of strategies and procedures that aim to minimize the effects of mistakes in quantum computing, particularly in the context of Noisy Intermediate-Scale Quantum (NISQ) devices. Quantum error correction normally necessitates a substantial surplus of extra qubits and operations to encode and rectify faults. In contrast, QEM strives to enhance the precision of quantum algorithms without the requirement for such large resources. Zero-noise extrapolation techniques exploit the relationship between noise effects and scale to extend the results to a limit where there is no noise, hence eliminating inaccuracies. Probabilistic error cancellation utilizes a comprehensive noise model to reverse the impact of noise on quantum operations, reconstructing the desired result by probabilistically combining noisy observations. Quantum subspace expansion is a crucial approach that involves enlarging the Hilbert space of interest to incorporate error states. This enables the identification and reduction of mistakes inside the specific subspace of the solution. In conjunction with progress in hardware characterization and noise modelling, these techniques are the foundation of QEM, facilitating more accurate and dependable quantum computing.

Quantum Error Mitigation versus Quantum Error Correction

Developing techniques to mitigate quantum mistakes is essential for the progress of quantum computing. Two main strategies have been developed: Quantum Error Correction (QEC) and Quantum Error Mitigation (QEM). These techniques fundamentally vary in their goals, execution, and resource needs. Comprehending these distinctions is crucial for understanding their individual functions in the realm of present and future quantum computing technology.

Differences in Approach

Quantum Error Correction (QEC) is focused on fixing faults in quantum states to maintain the accuracy of quantum information. It entails storing logical quantum information over several physical qubits to establish redundancy for error detection and repair without directly measuring the quantum information. Prominent QEC protocols like the Shor, Steane, and surface codes utilize ancilla qubits and syndrome measurements to detect and rectify faults. Quantum error correction relies on fault-tolerance theory, which states that quantum calculations can be performed with high accuracy by raising the level of encoding if the error rate is below a specific threshold.

Mathematically, QEC can be described using the stabilizer formalism for certain codes. For a simple example, consider a three-qubit bit-flip code that encodes a logical qubit state $|\psi\rangle = \alpha|0\rangle + \beta|1\rangle$ into $|\psi_L\rangle = \alpha|000\rangle + \beta|111\rangle$. The stabilizer generators for this code might be Z_1Z_2 and Z_2Z_3, where a measurement of +1 for both indicates no error, and any other outcome indicates a specific bit-flip error that can then be corrected.

Quantum Error Mitigation (QEM) does not aim to rectify faults directly. It aims to minimize their influence on the computation's result, either by using post-processing methods or modifying the quantum operations to account for the expected defects. Quantum error mitigation (QEM) is especially important for Noisy Intermediate-Scale Quantum (NISQ) devices, as they are unable to execute full QEC due to their restricted qubit count and high error rates. This approach includes techniques like error extrapolation, probabilistic error cancellation, and symmetry verification. Error extrapolation involves conducting computations numerous times with different levels of noise and then extending the findings to the zero-noise limit based on an expected correlation between noise and error.

Resource Requirements

Quantum error correction (QEC) necessitates a substantial amount of extra qubits for encoding logical qubits and ancillas for syndrome measurement, along with intricate gate operations for encoding, syndrome extraction, and repair. The amount of overhead is contingent upon the specific code utilized and the intended degree of error correction. Implementing a surface code may necessitate hundreds of physical qubits for each logical qubit to ensure fault tolerance based on the physical error rates.

On the other hand, QEM usually demands fewer supplementary resources. Several quantum error mitigation approaches can be used using the current technology without requiring additional qubits. Error extrapolation and probabilistic error cancellation use classical computation to modify the outcomes of quantum calculations, eliminating the need for quantum resource overhead in QEC. Yet, QEM methods may increase the computational burden or require more measurements to achieve the intended mitigation impact.

Principles of Quantum Error Mitigation

Quantum Error Mitigation (QEM) relies on comprehending and strategically addressing quantum faults. It utilizes several methods to minimize the influence of errors on quantum computations, playing a crucial role in the pursuit of dependable quantum computing, particularly in the age of Noisy Intermediate-Scale Quantum (NISQ) devices. Effective QEM relies on accurately identifying mistakes and utilizing targeted mitigation methods.

Error Characterization

It is crucial to analyze and understand the flaws to effectively mitigate quantum defects. It is crucial to comprehend the characteristics, extent, and statistical attributes of errors while choosing and creating suitable mitigation strategies. Error characterization entails measuring the extent to which quantum processes differ from their ideal executions and how these differences impact the computation's results.

Techniques for Error Modeling and Characterization:

- **Quantum Process Tomography (QPT):** Quantum Process Tomography (QPT) is a technique employed to analyze quantum processes comprehensively. By generating a specific group of input states and observing the resulting output states following the quantum process, it is possible to create the process matrix (or Choi matrix) that characterizes the quantum operation. This matrix offers comprehensive details on the procedure, including its error introduction mechanism. QPT is resource-intensive and does not scale well with the amount of qubits.
- **Randomized Benchmarking (RB):** RB is a method employed to quantify the average error rate of quantum gates. RB offers a more efficient method to assess the overall fidelity of quantum processes by executing random gate sequences and measuring the degradation of the system's fidelity, unlike QPT, which provides a full error model. Randomized benchmarking (RB) is especially valuable for evaluating the effectiveness of quantum gates in a manner that is less affected by errors in state preparation and measurement.
- **Gate Set Tomography (GST):** GST extends the idea of QPT and RB, aiming to simultaneously characterize the quantum gates, state preparation, and measurement processes. GST provides a comprehensive error model that accounts for all aspects of the quantum process, offering a detailed understanding of the sources of error.

By utilizing various characterization approaches, one can pinpoint mistakes and use mitigation strategies that directly address the shortcomings in quantum processes.

Mitigation Strategies

Understanding error characterisation allows for the implementation of several solutions to reduce the effects of errors. Each strategy approaches the issue from a unique perspective, and their efficacy may differ based on the quantum system's distinct error traits.

- **Error Extrapolation:** This method entails deliberately altering the noise level in quantum operations and then projecting the outcomes to a setting with no noise. One may predict the computation's result without any noise interference by conducting calculations at various regulated noise levels. If the connection between the observable O and the noise parameter λ is polynomial, measurements can be taken at various λ values to extrapolate the value of O at $\lambda = 0$ using regression analysis.

- **Probabilistic Error Cancellation:** This approach considers errors as reversible operations that may be corrected with a specific probability despite being noisy. It requires the use of a quasi-probability distribution to reverse the impact of noise, which then necessitates a classical post-processing of measurement outcomes. The effectiveness of this approach depends on appropriately representing errors as reversible operations, which can be computationally demanding due to the need to sum over numerous noise scenarios.
- **Symmetry Verification:** Symmetry verification uses the symmetries of the quantum system or program to identify and address faults. Encoding quantum information in a manner that maintains specific symmetries allows errors to be identified as any departure from these symmetries. Measurement results that do not adhere to the anticipated symmetries are disregarded, essentially picking only error-free outcomes. This method is based on the concept that some faults can disrupt specific symmetries. By recognizing and eliminating these cases, the accuracy of the computation can be enhanced.

Each strategy provides a distinct method for minimizing the effects of errors in quantum calculations. The success and impact of quantum error mitigation techniques rely on the specific flaws found in the system, underscoring the significance of detailed error analysis as an initial stage in the process.

Techniques and Algorithms for Quantum Error Mitigation

Quantum error mitigation (QEM) utilizes several methods to minimize the effects of mistakes on quantum computing. These methods, such as error extrapolation and virtual distillation, provide approaches to improve the precision of quantum algorithms when dealing with unavoidable noise and flaws. Every technique is based on unique concepts and algorithms to tackle the issues caused by quantum mistakes.

Zero-Noise Extrapolation

Zero-noise extrapolation (ZNE) is a method of error extrapolation that aims to reduce noise to a theoretical zero-noise level.

Methodology

- **Noise Scaling:** Perform quantum computations while intentionally amplifying noise using techniques such as modifying hardware parameters or inserting redundant operations that increase decoherence effects.
- **Data Collection:** Execute the quantum circuit at different noise levels and systematically collect measurement results to study how noise affects the computed observables.
- **Extrapolation to Zero Noise:** Construct a mathematical model that describes the dependence of the result on noise strength and use it to extrapolate the noiseless expectation value, providing an estimate of the ideal quantum computation.

ZNE is adaptable and can be utilized in different quantum computations, provided that the noise can be regulated.

Probabilistic Error Cancellation

Probabilistic error cancellation (PEC) is the process of simulating the reverse of quantum faults in a system to eliminate their impact. This method involves representing the errors as identifiable, reversible actions and thereafter making adjustments according to a quasi-probability distribution.

Algorithmic Framework

- **Error Modeling:** Noise in the quantum circuit is modeled as a linear combination of ideal operations and error terms, allowing a probabilistic correction strategy to mitigate errors.
- **Quasi-Probability Distribution:** A quasi-probability distribution is created, representing an optimal combination of ideal and error-mitigating operations. The weights in this distribution can be positive or negative, meaning some operations contribute with "negative probabilities" (which do not correspond to physical probabilities but are a mathematical tool for cancellation).
- **Statistical Sampling:** The quantum circuit is executed multiple times, with each execution randomly sampling operations from the quasi-probability distribution. The results are combined using statistical weighting to reconstruct an error-mitigated expectation value.

PEC transforms the quantum error mitigation issue into a statistical problem, where the precision of the mitigation is weighed against the rise in the required number of samples to reach a specific level of accuracy.

Clifford Data Regression

Clifford Data Regression (CDR) is a method that uses the stability and simple simulation of Clifford circuits to reduce mistakes in advanced quantum computations that are not based on Clifford gates.

Implementation Overview

- **Circuit Simplification:** Replace non-Clifford parts of a quantum circuit with Clifford-only circuits that are classically simulable and less sensitive to noise.. These Clifford circuits approximate the structure of the original circuit but exclude computationally hard non-Clifford operations.
- **Data Collection:** We run both the original quantum circuit with non-Clifford operations and multiple modified versions of it that contain only Clifford operations. The measurement results from these Clifford-only circuits provide a reference dataset.
- **Regression Analysis:** Use the measurement data from the noise-free Clifford circuits to build a regression model that approximates the expected outputs. This model generalizes the expected error-free result of the full circuit, including non-Clifford operations.
- **Error Mitigation:** Apply the regression model to the noisy results from the original quantum circuit, reducing the impact of noise and improving the accuracy of the computed results.

CDR is particularly effective for computations where non-Clifford gates are sparse and can be isolated within primarily Clifford circuits.

Quantum Subspace Expansion

Quantum Subspace Expansion (QSE) seeks to improve the precision of quantum measurements by extending the calculation into a broader Hilbert space, allowing for easier detection and reduced mistakes.

Process

- **State Preparation:** Prepare the desired quantum state and apply structured transformations to expand it into a larger Hilbert space. These transformations help create a set of related quantum states that preserve key properties of the original state while allowing error detection.

- **Measurement:** Measure relevant observables within the expanded Hilbert space, extracting additional information that can be used to detect and characterize errors.
- **Error Mitigation:** Use the additional measurement data from the expanded space to construct error-resilient estimators for the desired observables, improving accuracy while mitigating the effects of noise.

QSE is particularly useful for quantum simulations and quantum chemistry applications, where the precise measurement of observables is critical.

Twirled Readout Error Extinction (T-REx)

The Twirled Readout Error Extinction (T-REx) technique aims to reduce measurement errors in quantum computers. Measurement error mitigation is important it can directly impact the ultimate result of a quantum computation, potentially resulting in inaccurate conclusions or interpretations of the quantum state. T-REx seeks to minimize errors by utilizing a sequence of operations that manipulate the error channels, ultimately averaging out specific sorts of errors.

How it Works

1. **Twirling Operations:** The term "twirling" refers to applying randomized quantum operations to transform errors into a form that is easier to handle. Prior to measuring a qubit, a series of quantum gates (usually Pauli gates X, Y, Z) are applied in a random sequence, called Pauli twirling. The gates are selected for their ability to to randomize errors, ensuring that readout errors become symmetrically distributed across all possible outcomes.
2. **Measurement and Inversion:** The qubit is measured after the twirling operations are applied. Statistical post-processing is performed on the measurement outcomes to counteract systematic readout errors..
3. **Error Extinction:** Applying twirling operations and their inversion helps to not completely eliminate readout errors but randomizes them, effectively reducing systematic biases.. The term *extinction* is employed to describe The statistical nature of twirling that helps in averaging out errors, leading to a more accurate probability distribution of measurement outcomes.
4. **Statistical Analysis:** By repeating the application of different randomized sequences of twirling operations and evaluating the statistical distribution of the results using Bayesian inference or Maximum Likelihood Estimation (MLE), one can better identify and reduce remaining errors.

The T-REx system is valuable for quantum investigations requiring accurate measurements, such as quantum error correction methods, quantum algorithm benchmarking, and quantum sensing.

Readout Error Mitigation

Readout error mitigation is a series of strategies designed to minimize errors arising during qubit state measurement. Quantum measurements in quantum computing are essential but susceptible to mistakes caused by inadequate detector efficiency, qubit crosstalk, and ambient noise. These inaccuracies can greatly skew the observed results, resulting in erroneous depictions of the quantum state.

How it Works

1. **Error Characterization:** Perform calibration experiments to quantify readout errors by preparing qubits in known states ($|0\rangle$ and $|1\rangle$), measuring them, and constructing confusion matrices that describe how measurement errors occur.
2. **Correction Matrix:** Using the confusion matrices, construct a global correction matrix that represents the readout error model. The inverse of this matrix is later applied to correct for systematic readout errors.
3. **Result Adjustment:** After quantum computation, the recorded measurement outcomes are post-processed using the correction matrix, allowing for an error-mitigated estimate of the actual quantum state probabilities.

Readout error reduction is crucial for activities that need high measurement fidelity in quantum computing, such as quantum algorithm verification, quantum simulation, and quantum cryptography. It is widely used in several quantum computing platforms.

Quantum Error Mitigation with Qiskit

We are now going to implement some basic error mitigation strategies based on Qiskit that will help correct errors after the quantum operations have been performed successfully. It is important to note that the codes discussed in this section have been taken from some of the IBM Quantum documentation available online, which used old Qiskit versions. Here, the codes have been modified according to the newer Qiskit version.

Readout Error Mitigation

Readout errors significantly contribute to mistakes in quantum computing, particularly during the measurement phase when the state of a qubit is identified. These inaccuracies can distort the distribution of outcomes and impact the accuracy of expectation values generated for different observables. Understanding and reducing readout errors can improve the dependability of quantum calculations.

Readout mistakes occur when the measuring method inaccurately represents the actual state of the qubits. For example, a qubit in the state $|1\rangle$ could be mistakenly measured as $|0\rangle$ and vice versa. To reduce these errors, it is crucial to identify and classify them first, usually achieved by constructing an assignment matrix.

The assignment matrix A is a $2^n \times 2^n$ matrix, where n is the number of qubits, and the matrix elements, $A_{y,x}$ represent the probability of observing the outcome y when the true outcome is x. This matrix captures the probabilities of all possible measurement errors across the qubit system.

The mitigation matrix, obtained from the assignment matrix, is utilized in the readout error mitigation process. This matrix aids in modifying the observed result distributions to approximate what they would have been without readout errors.

The Local Readout Mitigator assumes that readout errors are mainly local, meaning that the readout errors for separate qubits are not dependent on each other. The independence permits a simplified description of the assignment matrix as the tensor product of $n 2 \times 2$ matrices, each corresponding to a qubit. A 2×2 matrix describes the readout errors for a single qubit by showing the odds of correctly measuring the qubit's state and the likelihood of different types of mistakes.

Advantages of Local Readout Mitigation:

- **Scalability:** Scalability is achieved by representing the assignment matrix as the tensor product of smaller 2×2 matrices, which decreases complexity and storage needs, allowing it to handle larger numbers of qubits.
- **Practicality:** This approach is suitable for systems in which readout errors are mostly independent among qubits. It streamlines the creation of the assignment matrix and, thereafter, the mitigation matrix.

Implemetation using Qiskit

The `LocalReadoutMitigator` class in Qiskit enables efficient readout error mitigation on quantum devices. It effectively mitigates readout imperfections by keeping only the individual 2×2 assignment matrices for each qubit, leveraging the assumption of local errors.

Firstly, we import the necessary libraries

```
import numpy as np
import jax
```

```
import mthree
import scipy.optimize as opt
from qiskit import QuantumCircuit, pulse, transpile, schedule
from qiskit.primitives import BackendSampler
from qiskit.pulse.library import Gaussian
from qiskit.pulse.library import Drag
from qiskit_dynamics import DynamicsBackend, Solver
from qiskit_dynamics.array import Array
from qiskit.providers.basic_provider import BasicProvider
from qiskit_ibm_runtime.fake_provider import FakeProvider, FakeValencia,
FakeSherbrooke, FakeKolkata, FakeAthens
from qiskit_ibm_provider import IBMProvider
from qiskit.circuit.library import XGate, SXGate, RZGate, CXGate, TwoLocal
from qiskit.circuit import Gate, Parameter
import qiskit_ibm_provider.jupyter
from qiskit.visualization import plot_histogram, plot_distribution
from qiskit.primitives import (
    Sampler, # V1
    StatevectorSampler, #V2
    Estimator, #V1
    StatevectorEstimator, #V2
)
from qiskit_experiments.library import LocalReadoutError, CorrelatedReadoutError
from qiskit.result.mitigation.utils import (
    expval_with_stddev,
    str2diag,
    counts_probability_vector
)
```

Now we create a simple quantum circuit having an X gate and check for the number of times we achieve 0 and 1 for ideal and fake backend simulations.

```
circ = QuantumCircuit(1, 1)
circ.x(0)
circ.measure(0, 0)
circ.draw('mpl')
```

```
sampler_v2 = StatevectorSampler()
result = sampler_v2.run([circ], shots=1024).result()
data_pub = result[0].data
# Get counts for the classical register "c"
noiseless_counts = data_pub.c.get_counts()
print(f"The counts are: {noiseless_counts}")

backend2 = FakeSherbrooke()
transpiled_circ = transpile(circ, backend2)
# Run the transpiled circuit using the simulated fake backend
job_fake = backend2.run(transpiled_circ, shots=1024)
noisy_counts = job_fake.result().get_counts()
print(f"The counts are: {noisy_counts}")
```

For the state vector sampler, which is an ideal simulation, the output is `{'1': 1024}` and for the fake hardware simulation backend, we receive `{'0': 17, '1': 1007}`. The noise in the fake backend has given an incorrect output state for the execution of X gate on a $|0\rangle$ qubit. This means error mitigation can be used to mitigate this issue.

```
qubits = [0]
exp = LocalReadoutError(qubits)
for c in exp.circuits():
    print(c)

exp.analysis.set_options(plot=True)
result = exp.run(backend2)
mitigator = result.analysis_results("Local Readout Mitigator").value

shots = 1024
unmitigated_probs = {label: count / shots for label, count in
↪  noisy_counts.items()}
mitigated_quasi_probs = mitigator.quasi_probabilities(noisy_counts)
mitigated_stddev = mitigated_quasi_probs._stddev_upper_bound
mitigated_probs = (mitigated_quasi_probs.nearest_probability_distribution()
.binary_probabilities())

legend = ['Mitigated Probabilities', 'Unmitigated Probabilities']
```

```
plot_distribution([mitigated_probs, unmitigated_probs], legend=legend, \\
↪  sort="value_desc",
bar_labels=False)
```

From the previous code, firstly, the qubits that we want for the characterization of the errors are defined. In the next step, the local readout error is applied to the qubits, which generate several quantum circuits. These circuits are designed to help characterize the readout errors by preparing different states and measuring the outcomes. Then, the experiments are run on the fake backend, and the mitigator retrieves the readout error mitigator from the experiment results. This mitigator is an object that can be used to correct readout errors in subsequent measurements. After this, we recover the mitigated and unmitigated probabilities and plot them as a histogram.

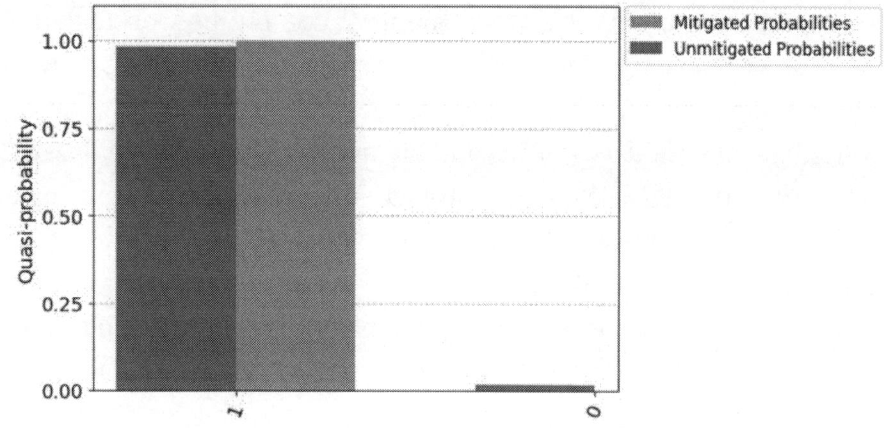

Figure 14.1: Readout Mitigation of X Gate for Noisy Backend

As shown in *Figure 14.1*, after mitigating errors, the X gate returns correct probability counts when applied to the $|0\rangle$ state.

Now, we are going to explore the M3 error mitigation provided by Qiskit and an example of an error mitigated VQE using M3.

mthree Based Error Mitigation

The mthree library provides an advanced method for mitigating quantum measurement errors called matrix-free measurement mitigation (M3). This approach tackles scaling issues encountered by conventional error mitigation methods.

- **Matrix-Free Approach:** Conventional error mitigation techniques typically include creating an assignment matrix that describes readout errors and its inverse to rectify errors in measured bitstrings. This method can be resource-intensive, particularly for systems with numerous qubits, because the matrix size grows exponentially with the number of qubits. M3 does not necessitate the explicit creation of these matrices. It immediately processes the noisy bitstrings acquired from quantum experiments, enhancing scalability and efficiency.

- **Reduction to Subspace:** M3 concentrates on a diminished subspace determined by the distinct noisy bitstrings that are seen, rather than the complete multi-qubit Hilbert space. This method greatly simplifies the issue by leveraging the fact that the quantity of distinct bitstrings is frequently less than the overall number of potential states within the Hilbert space. Therefore, the linear system of equations that must be solved to fix the errors becomes more manageable.

When the number of distinct bitstrings is limited, LU decomposition can efficiently solve the linear system of equations. This efficient approach uses minimal computational resources, making it appropriate for various quantum computing workloads.

M3 utilizes iterative linear solution methods when handling numerous distinct bitstrings or working within strict memory limitations without the need to create matrices. Methods like Generalized Minimal Residual (GMRES) and Biconjugate Gradient Stabilized (BiCGSTAB) are utilized. These iterative algorithms can solve linear systems without storing or inverting massive matrices, saving memory and processing resources.

Applications and Limitations of mthree

- **Quasi-Probabilities:** M3 is ideal for tasks that include quasi-probabilities, such as computing expectation values or determining the most likely bitstring. Quasi-probabilities, which can be negative, help to adjust for reading errors while calculating these values. These quasi-probabilities can be modified to create an actual probability distribution. However, this modification may complicate error analysis.
- **Mid-Circuit Measurements:** M3 additionally provides error mitigation for mid-circuit measurements, focusing on ensemble averages rather than addressing mistakes in individual single-shot observations. This feature is important for specific quantum algorithms and simulations that depend on sensing quantum states during the computation process.
- **Limitation on Single-Shot Measurements:** M3 cannot correct faults in one-time measurements used for conditional-gate logic in quantum devices. This limitation arises from the M3 approach's method of correcting faults collectively rather than individually per shot.

Error Mitigated VQE with mthree

We have seen a simple example of error mitigation that shows the significance of the technique and the power to correct the errors that occur in quantum computing processes. Now, we are ready to explore the M3 for a more real problem, which is for the calculation of a ground state using VQE with error mitigation. This application can then be extended to any other algorithm that you are using for your project or research. As mentioned before, we take up an example from the M3 Qiskit documentation available online and explain the operations step by step.

Since all the necessary libraries have already been imported, we go ahead and define a simple Hamiltonian with coefficients and operator strings. We create a `TwoLocal` ansatz that will be used for the VQE operation. Then, we extract the coefficients and the operator strings and store them separately.

```
H_op = [(0.39793742484318045, 'YZ'), (-0.39793742484318045, 'ZI'),
        (-0.01128010425623538, 'ZZ'), (0.18093119978423156, 'XX')]

ansatz = TwoLocal(2, rotation_blocks='ry', entanglement_blocks='cx')

coeffs = np.array([item[0] for item in H_op], dtype=float)
op_strings = [item[1] for item in H_op]
```

We need to define a function that creates a list of quantum circuits that apply designated post-rotation operations to qubits before measurement using a list of operator strings. The operator strings define the measurement type for each qubit in a quantum circuit. For the X operator, a Hadamard gate is applied and for the Y operator a $S^\dagger$ followed by Hadamard is applied.

```
def opstr_to_meas_circ(op_str):
    num_qubits = len(op_str[0])
    circs = []
    for op in op_str:
        qc = QuantumCircuit(num_qubits)
        for idx, item in enumerate(op):
            if item == 'X':
                qc.h(num_qubits-idx-1)
            elif item == 'Y':
                qc.sdg(num_qubits-idx-1)
```

```
            qc.h(num_qubits-idx-1)
        circs.append(qc)
    return circs

meas_circs = opstr_to_meas_circ(op_strings)

full_circs = [ansatz.compose(meas_circs[kk]).measure_all(inplace=False) for kk in
range(len(meas_circs))]

meas_strings = [string.replace('X', 'Z').replace('Y', 'Z') for string in op_strings]
meas_strings
```

The function created helps us get the measurement circuits and combine them with the ansatz that was defined earlier. We require the strings that specify the diagonal operators to be used by the expectation value function. Post-rotations have been added to each circuit for X and Y measurements, so these strings must be translated to Z. This is done by the last few lines of the code shown previously.

Once we get the full circuits, we transpile them over the `FakeAthens()` backend and define some parameters which are needed to be passed into the parameterized circuit required by the VQE algorithm. In the next step, we apply the M3 error mitigation on the backend and retrieve the calibration data for the backend only for the first two qubits 0 and 1 since they are the ones that are measured.

```
backend = FakeAthens()
trans_circs = transpile(full_circs, backend)

num_params = ansatz.num_parameters
params = np.array([1.22253725, 0.39053752, 0.21462153, 5.48308027,
                   2.06984514, 3.65227416, 4.01911194, 0.35749589])
params += 0.05*(np.random.random(params.shape[0])-0.5)

mit = mthree.M3Mitigation(backend)
mit.cals_from_system([0,1])
```

With this, we are ready to create our VQE function. The parameters defined previously are assigned to the transpiled circuits to create a list of binded circuits. Then, these binded circuits are executed on the backend and measurement error mitigation is applied to the probabilities of the result considering qubits 0 and 1 only. We retrieve the energy by adding over the product of coefficients and the expectation value of the measured strings obtained previously.

```
def vqe_func(params, *args):
    # Attach parameters to the transpiled circuit variables
    bound_circs = [circ.assign_parameters(params) for circ in trans_circs]
    # Submit the job and get the resultant counts back
    counts = backend.run(bound_circs, shots=4096).result().get_counts()
    # Apply mitigation to get quasi-probabilities
    quasis = mit.apply_correction(counts, [0,1])
    # Evaluate the coefficients times each expectation value obtained from
    # quasi-probabilities and sum.
    energy = np.sum(coeffs*quasis.expval(meas_strings))
    return energy

res = opt.minimize(vqe_func, params, method = 'COBYLA')

print(res.fun)
```

The optimized result is obtained with the help of SciPy's optimize function, and then we receive the mitigated ground state energy value as `-0.43276573777861704`.

Qiskit Runtime Based Error Mitigation Strategies

In *Chapter* 5, *An Introduction to Qiskit*, you saw that the new Qiskit Runtime offers essential features for running quantum circuits and applications on simulators and on the hardware available in the IBM Quantum cloud. Some of the useful features include quantum error mitigation techniques and we are now going to delve into this section.

As you are already aware Qiskit Primitives can support different types of quantum error mitigation techniques by configuring the parameter known as `resilience_level`. The resilience level determines the degree of robustness must be developed in order to mitigate errors. Increasing the levels leads to more precise outcomes, but this comes at the cost of longer processing durations. Resilience levels can be utilized to adjust the balance between cost and accuracy when implementing error mitigation for your basic query. Error mitigation is a technique that minimizes errors (bias) in outcomes by analyzing the outputs of a group, or ensemble, of interconnected circuits.
There are three resilience levels for the V2 Estimator. Note that the Sampler does not support error mitigation techniques.

- **Level 0**: There is no error mitigation at this level.
- **Level 1**: Here TREX measurement twirling is applied to mitigate readout errors at minimal mitigation costs. To minimize measurement error, the noise channel linked to the measurement is diagonalized by randomly applying X gates to qubits just before the measurement process. A scaling factor is obtained by evaluating the performance of randomly initialized circuits in the zero state, using the diagonal noise channel. This enables the service to eliminate any bias in the anticipated values that arise from readout noise.
- **Level 2**: TREX + ZNE + Gate twirling are used together to reduce bias in estimators with medium mitigation costs. ZNE calculates the average value of a observable for various levels of noise (amplification stage) and then uses these measured average values to estimate the ideal average value when there is no noise present (extrapolation stage). This method has a tendency to decrease errors in the anticipated values, while it is not certain to yield an unbiased outcome. The computational burden of this strategy increases proportionally with the quantity of extraneous variables. The default settings measure the expected value at three levels of noise, resulting in approximately three times the additional workload when using this degree of resilience. During Level 2, the TREX approach introduces random qubit flips using X gates just before measurement. If an X gate is applied, the corresponding measured bit is flipped.

Qiskit Implementation of Error Mitigation Techniques for Circuit and Observables

Now, we are going to implement all levels of error mitigation using the `EstimatorOptions()` functionality since it provides more flexibility in customizing different mitigation parameters. However, please note that setting `resilience_level` will also provide proper output.

We start by importing the necessary libraries that will be required to execute the different functions.

```
import os
import numpy as np
from qiskit_ibm_runtime import QiskitRuntimeService
from qiskit.circuit.library import EfficientSU2, UnitaryOverlap
from qiskit.quantum_info import SparsePauliOp
from qiskit_ibm_runtime.fake_provider import FakeOsaka
from qiskit.transpiler.preset_passmanagers import generate_preset_pass_manager
```

```
from qiskit_ibm_runtime import EstimatorV2 as Estimator, EstimatorOptions, Batch
import matplotlib.pyplot as plt
```

For this experiment, we will be utilizing the IBM Quantum cloud hardware. First we store the token by copying it from the IBM Quantum account dashboard. Secondly, we save the credentials using the Qiskit Runtime service and initialize it.

```
os.environ['QXToken'] = 'PASTE YOUR TOKEN FROM IBM QUANTUM ACCOUNT'

QiskitRuntimeService.save_account(channel='ibm_quantum',
↪  token=os.environ['QXToken'])
service = QiskitRuntimeService()
```

Since Qiskit 1.0+ is for quantum computing at utility-scale, so we choose the number of qubits as 50 with two repetitions and pairwise entanglement of the `EfficientSU2()` circuit.

Next, we assign randomly initialized parameters to the `EfficientSU2()` circuit. Towards the end of this experiment, your objective is to juxtapose the output of the quantum computer with the optimal solution. To determine this value for small quantum circuits, one can simulate the circuit on a classical computer. However, this approach is not feasible for larger utility-scale circuits. To address this problem, one might employ the *mirror circuit* technique (sometimes referred to as *compute-uncompute*), which proves to be valuable in evaluating the efficiency of quantum devices.

The mirror circuit technique involves concatenating a circuit with its inverse, which is created by inverting each gate of the circuit in the opposite order. The circuit that is produced implements the identity operator, which can easily be mimicked. By maintaining the structure of the original circuit, the mirror circuit provides insight into the performance of the quantum device on the original circuit.

The following code cell utilizes the `UnitaryOverlap` class from Qiskit's circuit library to create the mirror circuit. Before mirroring the circuit, add a barrier instruction to prevent the transpiler from combining the two sections of the circuit located on each side of the barrier. In the absence of the barrier, the transpiler would combine the initial circuit with its opposite, leading to a transpiled circuit devoid of any gates.

```
num_qubits = 50
reps = 2
abstract_circuit = EfficientSU2(num_qubits, reps=reps, entanglement="pairwise")
num_parameters = abstract_circuit.num_parameters
```

```
param_values = np.random.uniform(-np.pi, np.pi, size=num_parameters)
abstract_circuit.assign_parameters(param_values, inplace=True)
abstract_circuit.barrier()
abstract_circuit = UnitaryOverlap(abstract_circuit, abstract_circuit)
```

With the circuit constructed, now we focus on creating the observables that can be used with the Qiskit estimator. To keep the process simple, we create weight-1 $\langle Z_i \rangle$ observables for each qubit in the circuit. As an example, if you have a 3-qubit abstract circuit, then the weight-1 observables will be IIZ, IZI and ZII where the $\langle Z \rangle$ operator acts on different qubits at a time while the other qubits have the identity operator applied to them. This is then wrapped into `SparsePauliOp()` for efficient implementation.

Once the observables are defined, we initialize the backend service using the `least_busy()` method so that we can fetch the hardware that is least busy in the IBM Quantum cloud and finally we print its name.

If you find all the backends to be busy or they are unavailable, then you can also use the fake quantum hardware simulators like `FakeOsaka()` that has already been imported and has 127 qubits. Please note that simulating 30 or more qubits is going to take a lot of RAM and time, therefore, you can test your code with qubits less than 30.

```
paulis = ["".join("Z" if i == q else "I" for i in range(num_qubits)) for q in
range(num_qubits)]
abstract_observables = [SparsePauliOp(pauli) for pauli in paulis]
backend = service.least_busy(min_num_qubits=127)
backend.name
```

Since we have our abstract observables, we need to optimize these into the quantum hardware backend qubit layout which can done using transpilation. You can transpile your circuit by creating a pass manager and then running the pass manager on the circuit. We do this by using the `general_preset_pass_manager()` with a heavier optimization level of 3. Then we create the target circuit by running the abstract circuit using the preset pass manager and making a layout from the target circuit. This layout is then utilized to construct the target observables for each of the abstract observables we obtained earlier.

```
pm = generate_preset_pass_manager(backend=backend, optimization_level=3)
target_circuit = pm.run(abstract_circuit)
layout = target_circuit.layout
target_observables = [abs_obs.apply_layout(layout=layout)
for abs_obs in abstract_observables]
```

In the following code, we submit the jobs to the IBM Quantum backend. We do the submission in Batch execution mode so as to leverage the parallel processing capabilities offered by the Qiskit Runtime service. We kept the optimization and resilience levels zero for all the jobs.

The jobs that we experiment with are

- Job 1: No Mitigation
- Job 2: Dynamical Decoupling (DD)
- Job 3: TREX Measurement Mitigation
- Job 4a: ZNE with exponential extrapolation
- Job 4b: ZNE with linear extrapolation
- Job 5: Gate Twirling + ZNE
- Job 6: Using all the mitigation techniques together

The code has intuitive variable names and comments which will help you to understand the functioning. For each of the error mitigation jobs, there are certain parameters provided via `EstimatorOptions()` that help configure each of the mitigation techniques. We run each of the jobs on the IBM Quantum backend by using `Estimator()` and then append all the results in a list called `primitive_results`.

```
# Define the primitive unified bloc (PUB) for Estimator jobs
pub = (target_circuit, target_observables)
default_shots = 10_000

# list for saving job results
primitive_results = []

# Submit Jobs 1 to 3 inside a Batch execution mode
with Batch(backend=backend) as batch:
    # Job 1: No mitigation
    options_ex1 = EstimatorOptions() # some suppression and mitigation are
    ↪ enabled by
    default
    options_ex1.optimization_level = 0
    options_ex1.resilience_level = 0
    options_ex1.default_shots = default_shots

    # Instantiate `Estimator` with options
    estimator = Estimator(options=options_ex1)
```

```
    # Submit job
    job_ex1 = estimator.run(pubs=[pub])

    # Job 2: Dynamical Decoupling (DD)
    options_ex2 = EstimatorOptions()
    options_ex2.default_shots = default_shots
    options_ex2.optimization_level = 0
    options_ex2.resilience_level = 0
    options_ex2.dynamical_decoupling.sequence_type = "XX"
    options_ex2.dynamical_decoupling.enable = True

    estimator = Estimator(options=options_ex2)
    job_ex2 = estimator.run(pubs=[pub])

    # Job 3: Measurement mitigation (TREX)
    options_ex3 = EstimatorOptions()
    options_ex3.default_shots = default_shots
    options_ex3.optimization_level = 0
    options_ex3.resilience_level = 0


    options_ex3.resilience.measure_mitigation = True
    estimator = Estimator(mode = batch, options=options_ex3)
    job_ex3 = estimator.run(pubs=[pub])

# Wait for first 3 jobs to complete. Fetch results when done
primitive_results.append(job_ex1.result())
primitive_results.append(job_ex2.result())
primitive_results.append(job_ex3.result())

# Submit Jobs 4a, 4b, and 5 inside another Batch execution mode
with Batch(backend=backend) as batch:
    # Job 4a: Zero Noise Extrapolation (extrapolator="exponential" |
    ↪ noise_factors=
    (1, 3, 5))
    options_ex4a = EstimatorOptions()
```

```
options_ex4a.default_shots = default_shots
options_ex4a.optimization_level = 0
options_ex4a.resilience_level = 0
options_ex4a.resilience.zne_mitigation = True
options_ex4a.resilience.zne.noise_factors = (1, 3, 5)
options_ex4a.resilience.zne.extrapolator = 'exponential'

estimator = Estimator(options=options_ex4a)
job_ex4a = estimator.run(pubs=[pub])

# Job 4b: Zero Noise Extrapolation (extrapolator="linear" and noise_factors=
(1, 3, 5))
options_ex4b = EstimatorOptions()
options_ex4b.default_shots = default_shots
options_ex4b.optimization_level = 0
options_ex4b.resilience_level = 0
options_ex4b.resilience.zne_mitigation = True
options_ex4b.resilience.zne.noise_factors = (1, 3, 5)
options_ex4b.resilience.zne.extrapolator = 'linear'

estimator = Estimator(options=options_ex4b)
job_ex4b = estimator.run(pubs=[pub])

# Job 5: Gate Twirling + Zero Noise Extrapolation (extrapolator=
# ("exponential", "linear") and noise_factors=(1, 3, 5))
options_ex5 = EstimatorOptions()
options_ex5.default_shots = default_shots

options_ex5.optimization_level = 0
options_ex5.resilience_level = 0

# Gate Twirling
options_ex5.twirling.enable_gates = True
options_ex5.twirling.enable_measure = False
options_ex5.twirling.num_randomizations = 'auto'
options_ex5.twirling.shots_per_randomization = 'auto'
```

```
    options_ex5.twirling.strategy = 'active-accum'

    # ZNE
    options_ex5.resilience.zne_mitigation = True
    options_ex5.resilience.zne.noise_factors = (1, 3, 5)
    options_ex5.resilience.zne.extrapolator = ("exponential", "linear")

    estimator = Estimator(options=options_ex5)
    job_ex5 = estimator.run(pubs=[pub])

# Wait for next 3 jobs to complete. Fetch results when done
primitive_results.append(job_ex4a.result())
primitive_results.append(job_ex4b.result())
primitive_results.append(job_ex5.result())

# Job 6: All
options_ex6 = EstimatorOptions()
options_ex6.default_shots = default_shots

# Dynamical Decoupling
options_ex6.dynamical_decoupling.enable = True
options_ex6.dynamical_decoupling.sequence_type = 'XX'
options_ex6.dynamical_decoupling.extra_slack_distribution = 'middle'
options_ex6.dynamical_decoupling.scheduling_method = 'alap'

# Twirling
options_ex6.twirling.enable_gates = True
options_ex6.twirling.enable_measure = True
options_ex6.twirling.num_randomizations = 'auto'
options_ex6.twirling.shots_per_randomization = 'auto'
options_ex6.twirling.strategy = 'active-accum'

# Measurement Error Mitigation
options_ex6.resilience.measure_mitigation = True
options_ex6.resilience.measure_noise_learning.num_randomizations =  32
options_ex6.resilience.measure_noise_learning.shots_per_randomization = 'auto'
```

```
# ZNE
options_ex6.resilience.zne_mitigation = True
options_ex6.resilience.zne.noise_factors = (1, 3, 5)
options_ex6.resilience.zne.extrapolator = 'exponential'

# Note: explicitly set `mode=backend` in Job execution mode.
# Inside Batch context manager, `Estimator` knows the context/backend implicitly
# However, without the context manager, we must set `mode` explicitly
estimator = Estimator(mode=backend, options=options_ex6)
job_ex6 = estimator.run(pubs=[pub])
primitive_results.append(job_ex6.result())
```

Once we have all the results, we can analyze them by plotting some data. Each `PrimitiveResult` is a list with a single single `PubResult` since we have submitted single PUB. Now for each `PubResult`, it contains an array of expectation values each corresponding to an observable inside its `data` container `pub_result.data.evs`. For each qubit in the `abstract_circuit` we have one weight 1 $\langle Z \rangle$ observable.

We compute the average of expectation values in each `PubResult` and plot a bar chart of average expectation values to analyze how different error suppression and mitigation methods are improving results. Note that due to the compute-uncompute structure of the circuit, the ideal average expectation value is 1.0 for each job respectively.

```
# List to store the averages of expectation values
averages = []

# Iterate over each PrimitiveResult
for primitive_result in primitive_results:
    for pub_result in primitive_result:
        # Extract the expectation values
        evs = pub_result.data.evs
        # Compute the average
        average = np.mean(evs)
        averages.append(average)

# Labels for the different methods
labels = ['No Mitigation', 'DD', 'TREX', 'ZNE Exp', 'ZNE Lin', 'ZNE + Twirling', 'All']
```

```
ideal_value = 1

# Plotting
plt.figure(figsize=(8, 4))
plt.bar(labels, averages, color='green')
plt.axhline(y=ideal_value, color='g', linestyle='--', label='ideal')
plt.xlabel('Experiments')
plt.ylabel('Avg Expectation Value')
plt.title('Bar Chart of Experiment Results')
plt.legend()
plt.show()

# Analyze the results
for label, avg in zip(labels, averages):
    print(f"{label}: Average Expectation Value = {avg:.4f} (Difference from ideal:
    {abs(1.0 - avg):.4f})")
```

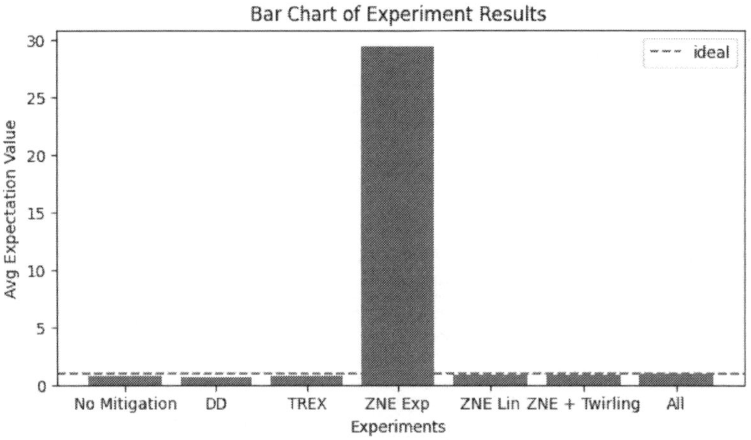

Figure 14.2: Qiskit Error Mitigation Techniques Comparison

From the graph shown in *Figure* 14.2, you can observe that the ZNE with exponential extrapolation performs exceedingly well for the given circuit and observables. Additionally, applying all the error mitigation techniques does not guarantee a great result as confirmed by the graph. It is also essential to note that DD usually does not perform well for denser circuits as there are very less gaps present in the quantum circuits due to which the DD pulses interfere with different gate operations present in the circuit.

As an exercise, run the same exercise for a lesser number of qubits such as 8 qubits and compare the graphs obtained for the 8-qubit case and the 50-qubit case that has been discussed here. Additionally, try to implement the error mitigation techniques for a circuit and observable of your choice by adjusting the `resilience_level` and plotting the results for comparison between the different levels.

Applications

Quantum Error Mitigation (QEM) is crucial in the Noisy Intermediate-Scale Quantum (NISQ) era, where quantum systems are limited in size and affected by noise. This makes full error correction impossible but allows calculations surpassing conventional computers. QEM applications include a wide range of industries, showcasing the extensive possibilities of quantum computing.

Quantum Chemistry

Quantum chemistry applies quantum mechanics to study molecular and atomic behavior by solving the Schrödinger equation. It employs computational techniques such as Hartree-Fock, Density Functional Theory (DFT), and Coupled Cluster to determine electronic structures, bonding interactions, and reaction mechanisms.

In quantum computing, quantum chemistry enables more efficient modeling of complex molecular systems compared to exact classical methods like Full Configuration Interaction (FCI). This has implications for drug discovery, materials science, and catalysis. However, quantum noise and gate errors necessitate error mitigation techniques such as Zero-Noise Extrapolation (ZNE) and Probabilistic Error Cancellation (PEC) to improve computational accuracy.

- **Ground State Calculation:** Variational Quantum Eigensolver (VQE) estimates ground state energies by minimizing the expectation value of the molecular Hamiltonian. Accurate ground state determination is vital for chemical bonding, material design, and drug discovery.
- **Excited State Calculation:** Quantum algorithms such as Variational Quantum Deflation (VQD) and Quantum Subspace Expansion (QSE) compute excited states, essential for modeling photoactivated processes, fluorescence, and electronic transitions. Quantum error mitigation (QEM) techniques like Zero-Noise Extrapolation (ZNE) and Clifford Data Regression (CDR) enhance computational accuracy.

Quantum Optimization

Quantum optimization applies quantum algorithms to efficiently explore solution spaces in combinatorial and constrained problems, with applications in logistics, finance, and machine learning. The Quantum Approximate Optimization Algorithm (QAOA) leverages quantum superposition and interference to evaluate multiple solutions in parallel, potentially improving performance over classical heuristics. While quantum speedup depends on the problem type, hybrid quantum-classical methods show promise for large-scale optimization. However, quantum noise and decoherence require error mitigation techniques such as Zero-Noise Extrapolation (ZNE) and Probabilistic Error Cancellation (PEC) to enhance computational reliability.

- **Combinatorial Optimization:** QAOA and other quantum algorithms address optimization problems in logistics, finance, and operations research, including the Traveling Salesman Problem (TSP) and portfolio optimization. Quantum Error Mitigation (QEM) reduces quantum noise, enhancing solution feasibility and accuracy.
- **Quantum Approximate Optimization Algorithm (QAOA):** QAOA approximates solutions to combinatorial optimization problems by leveraging quantum interference to explore solution spaces efficiently. Error mitigation techniques, such as Zero-Noise Extrapolation (ZNE) and Clifford Data Regression (CDR), improve result precision, increasing quantum optimization's competitiveness.

Quantum Machine Learning

Quantum Machine Learning (QML) explores the potential for enhanced machine learning using quantum superposition, entanglement, and interference, though speed improvements remain problem-dependent. Key QML approaches include Quantum Support Vector Machines (QSVM) for classification, Variational Quantum Classifiers (VQC) for supervised learning, and Quantum Neural Networks (QNNs) for pattern recognition. Variational Quantum Algorithms (VQAs) optimize parameterized quantum circuits through classical feedback, enabling hybrid quantum-classical learning. However, quantum noise and decoherence pose challenges, requiring error mitigation techniques such as Zero-Noise Extrapolation (ZNE) and Probabilistic Error Cancellation (PEC) to improve computational accuracy.

- **Data Classification:** Quantum machine learning algorithms, such as Variational Quantum Classifiers (VQC) and Quantum Support Vector Machines (QSVM), explore potential advantages in classification tasks like image recognition and natural language processing. Quantum Error Mitigation (QEM) techniques reduce misclassification errors, improving performance on Noisy Intermediate-Scale Quantum (NISQ) devices.

- **Quantum Feature Spaces:** Quantum feature maps enable high-dimensional embeddings for clustering and regression, leveraging quantum kernels to capture complex data relationships. Quantum Error Mitigation (QEM) enhances precision in feature space manipulations, improving QML model reliability.

Cryptography and Security

Quantum cryptography leverages quantum mechanics to develop cryptographic protocols with security guarantees rooted in quantum physics. Quantum Key Distribution (QKD) enables secure communication by allowing two parties to establish a shared secret key over a quantum channel. The no-cloning theorem and quantum measurement principles detect eavesdropping attempts, ensuring key integrity. Post-quantum cryptography (PQC) develops classical encryption schemes resistant to quantum decryption, complementing quantum cryptographic efforts. However, practical challenges such as entanglement distribution, quantum repeater development, and scalable quantum networks limit widespread implementation. Quantum error mitigation (QEM) enhances QKD reliability by reducing noise in quantum hardware, improving security against adversarial attacks.

Quantum Simulation

Quantum simulation leverages quantum computers to model complex quantum systems beyond classical computational feasibility. Quantum simulators efficiently replicate molecular structures, materials, and many-body quantum systems using tailored quantum algorithms. Variational Quantum Eigensolver (VQE) and Quantum Phase Estimation (QPE) compute ground and excited state energies, enabling the study of electronic structures and quantum dynamics. However, quantum noise and hardware limitations require advanced error mitigation techniques, such as Zero-Noise Extrapolation (ZNE) and Probabilistic Error Cancellation (PEC), to improve simulation accuracy.

- **Material Science:** Quantum simulators model quantum properties of materials, aiding in the discovery of novel compounds such as high-temperature superconductors. Quantum Error Mitigation (QEM) enhances simulation accuracy, accelerating material innovation.
- **High-Energy Physics:** Quantum algorithms simulate particle interactions in quantum chromodynamics (QCD), enabling exploration of non-perturbative phenomena. Quantum Error Mitigation (QEM) reduces noise in quantum field theory simulations, improving insights into fundamental forces.

Error Characterization and Benchmarking

Error characterization and benchmarking identify, quantify, and analyze error types and rates in quantum systems. Techniques include Randomized Benchmarking (RB) for assessing average gate fidelity, Quantum Process Tomography (QPT) for reconstructing quantum operations, and Gate Set Tomography (GST) for full gate error characterization. Benchmarking results inform hardware improvements and optimize quantum error correction (QEC) and mitigation strategies. Accurate error characterization ensures reliable hardware performance, enhancing the scalability and fault tolerance of quantum systems.

- **Device Characterization:** Error characterization techniques, combined with Quantum Error Mitigation (QEM), provide insights into quantum processor error profiles, guiding qubit design, error correction strategies, and device optimization.
- **Quantum Process Tomography:** Quantum Process Tomography (QPT) reconstructs quantum operations to validate gate implementations. Quantum Error Mitigation (QEM) enhances accuracy by reducing noise in the reconstructed process data.

Quantum Metrology

Quantum metrology leverages superposition and entanglement to achieve precision beyond classical limits, approaching the Heisenberg limit. Quantum interferometry and quantum sensors enhance measurement sensitivity in timekeeping, magnetometry, and gravitational wave detection. Quantum entanglement reduces measurement uncertainty through correlated states, while quantum squeezing redistributes noise to improve precision. However, environmental noise and decoherence hinder implementation, requiring techniques such as error mitigation, quantum feedback control, and dynamical decoupling to ensure measurement reliability.

Quantum sensors exploit quantum coherence and entanglement to achieve high-precision measurements of time, acceleration, and magnetic fields. Quantum error mitigation (QEM) techniques reduce noise, enhancing accuracy in applications such as navigation, atomic clocks, and fundamental physics experiments.

Towards Fault-Tolerant Quantum Computing

Fault-tolerant quantum computing ensures reliable quantum computations by suppressing errors below a critical threshold. Quantum error correction (QEC) encodes logical qubits across multiple physical qubits, enabling error detection and correction without disrupting quantum coherence. Surface codes and Bacon-Shor codes protect quantum information, while fault-tolerant gate designs and syndrome-based error detection maintain computational stability. While full fault tolerance is the ultimate goal, Quantum Error Mitigation (QEM) enhances near-term quantum computations by reducing noise in Noisy Intermediate-Scale Quantum (NISQ) devices, informing the development of scalable QEC protocols.

Conclusion

Quantum Error Mitigation is an essential element in the progress of quantum computing, specifically for Noisy Intermediate-Scale Quantum (NISQ) devices. QEM approaches greatly improve the precision and dependability of these devices, which are currently hindered by noise and decoherence. QEM utilizes advanced techniques such as zero-noise extrapolation, probabilistic error cancellation, and quantum subspace expansion to correct and minimize errors effectively. This is achieved without the need for extensive quantum error correction codes.

This feature is crucial for researchers and industry experts alike, as it allows for investigating and utilizing intricate quantum algorithms and applications that were previously unattainable due to significant error rates. For example, QEM can greatly enhance the efficiency of variational quantum algorithms like the Variational Quantum Eigensolver (VQE) and the Quantum Approximate Optimization Algorithm (QAOA). These algorithms are crucial for solving problems in quantum chemistry, materials science, and optimization.

Furthermore, the utilization of QEM also encompasses improving the precision of quantum simulations, which are essential for comprehending and forecasting the behaviour of quantum systems. QEM enhances the reliability of simulation findings by reducing mistakes, hence expediting the development of new materials and pharmaceuticals.

Essentially, QEM addresses the limits of existing quantum hardware and facilitates future progress by enabling more precise and dependable quantum computations. Consequently, this phenomenon propels the quantum computing revolution, propelling innovation and exploration in many scientific and technical domains.

In the next chapter, we will deviate from the high-level manipulation of quantum gates and circuits and dive into the low-level details of their implementation. This is done using a technique known as pulse-level programming, where users can define and rectify the pulses that create the quantum gate/circuit operations in real quantum hardware. This helps to incorporate quantum error mitigation efficiently on the hardware level.

CHAPTER 15

Qiskit Pulse for Quantum Hardware

Introduction

Qiskit Pulse is an advanced component of the Qiskit framework that offers precise manipulation of the quantum hardware at the level of individual pulses. This chapter examines the technical complexities of Qiskit Pulse, investigating its fundamental elements and their capabilities. Pulse-level programming enables the precise manipulation of qubits by using bespoke control pulses, providing unparalleled precision in quantum operations. Readers will get insight into optimizing quantum gates and mitigating errors by comprehending the structure, implementation, and programming structures of pulse schedules and pulse libraries. This chapter aims to provide you with the necessary information to effectively utilize Qiskit Pulse for advanced quantum computing research and development. By doing so, you will be able to improve the accuracy and efficiency of quantum algorithms on actual hardware.

Structure

In this chapter, you are going to study:

- Introduction to Circuit QED
  - The LC Oscillator
  - Anharmonic Oscillator
- Introduction to Qiskit Pulse
  - Motivation Behind Qiskit Pulse
  - Features and Components
  - Applications
- Quantum Gates and Pulse Schedules
  - Hadamard Gate Pulse
  - Pauli X Gate Pulse
  - CNOT Gate Pulse
  - Measurement Gate Pulse
- Calibration of CNOT Gate - Dynamic Decoupling
- Calibration of Pauli X Gate - Qiskit Dynamics Backend

Introduction to Circuit QED

A revolutionary paradigm known as Circuit Quantum Electrodynamics (cQED) [7] has emerged in the intriguing field of quantum mechanics due to the interaction between circuits and quantum systems. A quantum physicist's sandbox for exploring and modifying the behavior of quantum bits, or qubits, inside clearly specified electrical topologies, cQED extends the study of traditional quantum electrodynamics to include superconducting circuits. This chapter explores the core ideas of cQED while highlighting its importance in the larger quantum context. A key study in the search for next-generation quantum technologies, cQED, has led the path for improvements in quantum computing, quantum simulation, and even quantum metamaterials by utilizing the advantages of electrical circuits.

The LC Oscillator

Superconductivity was discovered in 1911 [8], and since then, it has been a topic of ongoing research due to its applicability in several industries. In a superconductor, the electrons flow in pairs, known as Cooper pairs [9] that behave as a resistance-less condensate [10]

[11]. One of the primary applications of superconductors is in superconducting quantum circuits, specifically, the LC oscillator consisting of an inductor in parallel with a capacitor shown in Fig. 15.1a. A dissipationless current flow describes a single degree of freedom [12] for a superconducting circuit.

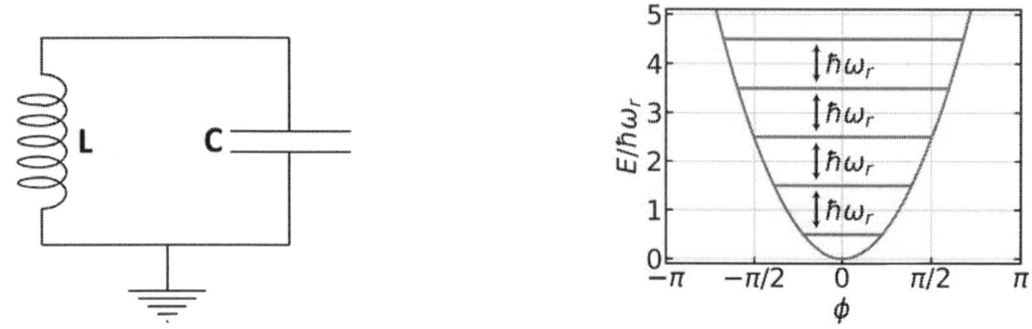

(a) (b)

Figure 15.1: LC circuit schematic and potential. (a) An electrical schematic of an LC oscillator with an inductor of inductance L in parallel with a capacitor of capacitance C. (b) Harmonic potential of the LC oscillator with energy levels (shown by horizontal blue lines) and transition energies (shown by double-sided arrows). The energy scale is normalized to $\hbar\omega_r = \frac{\hbar}{\sqrt{LC}}$. Figure adapted from [13].

The derivation for the Hamiltonian of the LC oscillator is carried out in this section to understand the system's behaviour and the potential energy landscape with the energy levels. In Fig. 15.1a, suppose that $I = \frac{dq}{dt} = \dot{q}$, current flows through the inductor, which gives the kinetic energy across the inductor by,

$$K.E. = \frac{LI^2}{2} = \frac{L\dot{q}^2}{2} \tag{15.1}$$

where $\dot{q}$ is the time derivative of the charge associated with one of the capacitor plates q. Similarly, the potential energy of the capacitor is given by,

$$P.E. = \frac{q^2}{2C} \tag{15.2}$$

The K.E. and the P.E. allow us to write the Lagrangian of the system given as,

$$\mathcal{L} = \frac{L\dot{q}^2}{2} - \frac{q^2}{2C} \tag{15.3}$$

The conjugate momentum from the Lagrangian is given as follows,

$$\frac{\partial \mathcal{L}}{\partial \dot{q}} = L\dot{q} = LI = \Phi \tag{15.4}$$

where Φ is the magnetic flux flowing through the inductor, and therefore, we get the Hamiltonian as,

$$H = \Phi \dot{q} - \mathcal{L} = \frac{\Phi^2}{2L} + \frac{q^2}{2C} \tag{15.5}$$

Equation 15.5 can be compared to a classical spring-mass mechanical system with L (inductance) as mass and $\frac{1}{C}$ as the spring constant. The resonance frequency,

$$\omega = \frac{1}{\sqrt{LC}} \tag{15.6}$$

The derivation carried out is consistent with the classical LC oscillator system. In order to derive the quantum mechanical version of the oscillator, we perform a change of operators of the coordinate (q) and momentum (Φ) to $\hat{q}$ and $\hat{\Phi}$ that satisfies the commutation relation,

$$[\hat{q}, \hat{\Phi}] = i\hbar \tag{15.7}$$

where $\hbar$ is the reduced Planck's constant. With this, the Hamiltonian can now be written in terms of the Cooper pair number operator $\hat{n} = \frac{\hat{q}}{-2e}$ and the phase operator $\hat{\phi} = 2\pi \frac{\hat{\Phi}}{\Phi_0}$, we obtain,

$$H = \frac{\hat{q}^2}{2C} + \frac{\hat{\Phi}^2}{2L} = 4E_C \hat{n} + \frac{E_L}{2} \hat{\phi} \tag{15.8}$$

where $E_C = \frac{e^2}{2C}$, $E_L = \frac{(\frac{\Phi_0}{2\pi})^2}{L}$ is the characteristic inductive energy and $\Phi_0 = \frac{h}{2e}$ is the flux quantum. Fig. 15.1b shows the Hamiltonian solutions that give the potential energy landscape along with the energy levels and transition energies between each energy level. LC oscillators are crucial in cQED, acting as resonators for readout and measurement.

Anharmonic Oscillator

As discussed in the previous section, superconducting harmonic oscillators, such as the LC oscillator, have equally spaced energy levels in their potential energy landscape. Therefore, individual energy transitions cannot be conducted, which is compulsory for qubit operations. Indeed, non-linearly spaced energy levels are required to carry out a successful qubit operation, and it can be achieved with a Josephson junction (JJ) [14].
A Josephson junction is created using two superconducting electrodes with a non-superconducting material in between the superconductors. The most commonly used Josephson junction is the superconductor-insulator-superconductor (SIS) [15] which is

described the sinusoidal current phase relation [16],

$$I_s = I_c sin\phi \tag{15.9}$$

where I_s denotes the supercurrent or the switching current of the junction, ϕ denotes the superconducting phase difference across the JJ, and I_c is the critical current, that is, the largest current that the JJ can sustain before turning non-superconducting.

Comparing both *Figure* 15.2*a* with *Figure* 15.1*a*, it can be seen that the Josephson junction is substituted for the inductor, and it is in parallel with the capacitor, similar to an LC circuit. The Lagrangian of the circuit from *Figure* 15.2*a* is,

$$\mathcal{L} = \frac{C_J}{2}\dot{\Phi}^2 + E_J cos(2\pi\frac{\Phi}{\Phi_0}) \tag{15.10}$$

from which the Hamiltonian is given by,

$$H = 4E_C\hat{n}^2 - E_J cos(\hat{\phi}) \tag{15.11}$$

Considering our JJ system has a discrete flow of charges across the junction (integer number of Cooper pairs), the Hamiltonian can be written with an offset charge n_g, which is controlled by a gate voltage V_g,

$$H = 4E_C(\hat{n} - n_g)^2 - E_J cos(\hat{\phi}) \tag{15.12}$$

It is also worth noting that the potential energy landscape which is the numerical solution of *Equation* 15.11 shown in *Figure* 15.2*b* is non-linear, and unequal-spaced energy levels help to describe proper qubit operations. *Figure* 15.3 displays the energy levels against the charge offset, n_g, as a transition from a Cooper pair (charge carrier) based Josephson device towards a transmon-based Josephson device.

To understand the anharmonic behaviour of the qubit, qubit anharmonicity is a crucial parameter of interest that describes the maximum speed of qubit rotations. It is defined as,

$$E_{12} - E_{01} = \alpha \approx -E_C \tag{15.13}$$

where $E_{01} \approx E_1 - E_0 = \sqrt{8E_JE_C} - E_C$ and $E_{12} \approx E_2 - E_1 = \sqrt{8E_JE_C} - 2E_C$. As $\frac{E_J}{E_C}$ increases, the anharmonicity is sufficiently large for fast operations while eliminating the charge noise by suppressing charge dispersion. Typically, qubits are operated in frequencies $f \approx 5$ GHz. This means microwave pulses of frequencies comparable to that of the energy level spacing of the states in the potential energy plot can be utilised to drive qubit state transitions. This can be achieved using Pulse-level programming kits such as Qiskit Pulse.

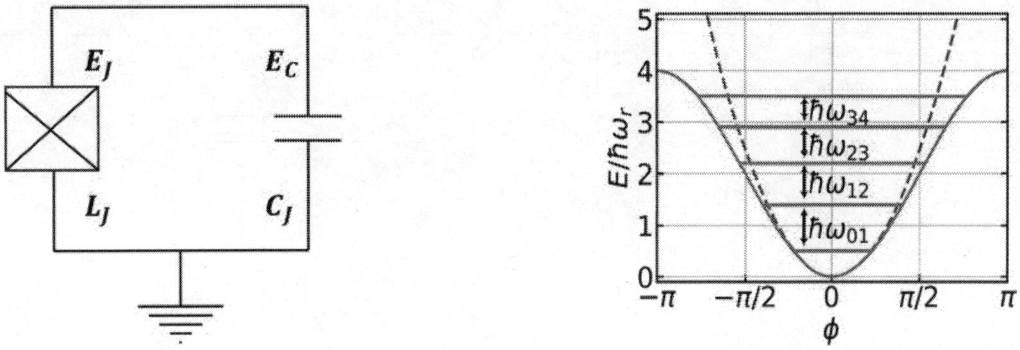

(a) (b)

Figure 15.2: Josephson circuit schematic and potential. (a) An electrical schematic of a Josephson junction with Josephson energy E_J in parallel with a capacitor of capacitance C_J. (b) The potential of an insulator-based Josephson junction with energy levels (shown by horizontal blue lines) and transition energies (shown by double-sided arrows). The dotted line shows the harmonic potential of the LC oscillator. The energy scale is normalized to $\hbar\omega_r = \frac{\hbar}{\sqrt{L_J C_J}} = \sqrt{8E_J E_C}$. Figure adapted from [13].

Having covered the foundations of circuit QED, we are now ready to dive into the functionalities of Qiskit Pulse for the rest of this chapter.

Introduction to Qiskit Pulse

Qiskit Pulse is a lower-level programming package allowing the user to control the quantum hardware using microwave pulses directly. Qiskit pulse enables the user to bypass the abstraction layer of quantum gates and define customized pulses for direct manipulation of the qubits or quantum states. Users have the ability to generate pulse schedules, which consist of a series of pulses and operations that are carried out on the quantum hardware. These schedules can be meticulously adjusted to maximize performance and investigate novel quantum computing strategies. **Pulses** refer to waveforms specifically specified in the time domain and distinguished by their shape, amplitude, and length. Users have the option to explicitly define pulses by specifying the waveform point by point. Alternatively, they can utilize pre-defined forms like Gaussian or Square pulses that are available in Qiskit Pulse's libraries. Pulses are crucial for implementing precise quantum gate operations by accurately manipulating the qubit's state.

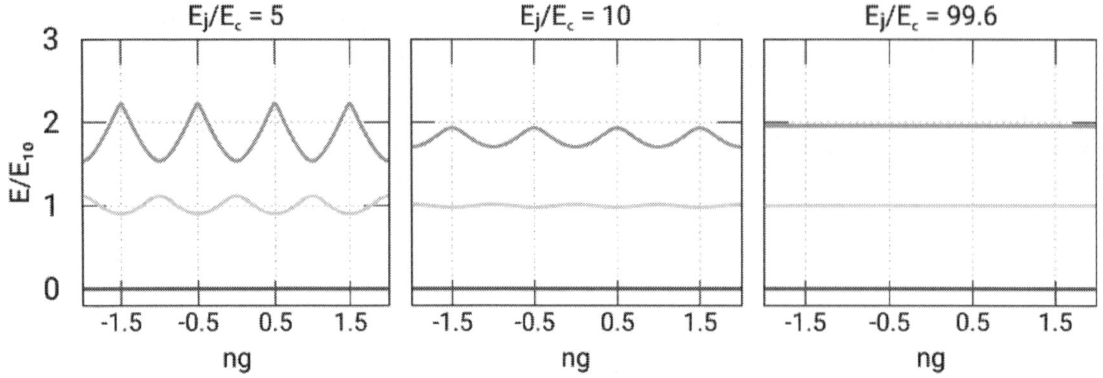

Figure 15.3: Numerical solutions to transmon Hamiltonian. Numerical solutions to Eq. (15.12) for three different $\frac{E_J}{E_C}$ showcasing the three lowest energy levels, E_0, E_1, E_2 (red, green, blue) as a function of offset charge n_g. As the ratio $\frac{E_J}{E_C}$ increases from 5 - 99.6, the charge dispersion, defined as the amplitude of the charge fluctuations in E_n, is substantially reduced. This figure is inspired by Ref. [17].

Motivation Behind Qiskit Pulse

So far in this book, you have learned about implementing quantum gates and their features on a high level without having to think about the underlying processes of their actual operations. It is easier to design algorithms in that way. However, with the high-level implementation, we cannot control the physical qubits to mitigate certain errors, increasing gate-fidelities and devising new measurement strategies. Since, in real quantum hardware, most of the quantum operations are implemented as precise sequences of pulses, it becomes necessary to have direct control over these pulses to generate more accurate quantum algorithms. Additionally, pulse level controls allow us to have dynamic decoupling (Dynamic decoupling is a quantum error correction technique that employs accurately timed pulse sequences to minimize decoherence and noise in qubit systems. This technique efficiently maintains the quantum states of qubits for longer durations. It improves the accuracy of quantum computations.) and constructs custom gate operations unavailable in the standard gate set.

Features and Components

The fundamental elements of Qiskit Pulse comprise the Schedule and Instruction classes, which provide the meticulous coordination of pulse sequences, and the PulseLibrary, which serves as a repository for reusable pulse forms. These qualities empower researchers and developers to fine-tune quantum operations and customize them to the unique attributes of their quantum devices, thereby improving the efficiency and accuracy of quantum calculations.

Pulse Instructions

Pulse Instructions serve as the basic components for building quantum operations in Qiskit Pulse. The users manipulate the quantum hardware by precisely setting the shape and timing of signals transmitted to the qubits. The main categories of Pulse Instructions are as follows:

- **Play**: The Play command is utilized to generate a pulse on a designated channel. It effectively executes the specified pulse waveform, directing it towards a qubit or a group of qubits to carry out quantum operations. The Play command is the main method used to implement quantum gates in the Pulse programming style.
- **Delay**: Delay instructions impose a predetermined period of inactivity on a channel, thereby halting any operation on the qubit or qubits linked to that channel for the duration of the delay. Timing control and synchronization between actions on distinct qubits can be paramount.
- **ShiftPhase (FrameChange)**: involve altering the phase reference for future pulses on a channel without physically modifying the states of the qubits. This action is similar to altering the framework in which the following operations are described, enabling intricate manipulation of qubit phases, a fundamental feature of numerous quantum algorithms.
- **Acquire**: The Acquire command initiates the measurement process on one or more qubits, directing the system to retrieve and display the states of the qubits. This command collaborates with MeasureChannels to transform the quantum state of the qubits into classical information that may be utilized for subsequent computing or analysis.

Channels

Channels in Qiskit Pulse encompass the diverse means by which control signals can engage with the qubits and their surroundings, encompassing:

- **DriveChannel**: Drive channels are utilized to directly manipulate qubits, specifically to transition their state from $|0\rangle$ to $|1\rangle$, or to perform superpositions or rotations within the qubit's state space. Usually, every qubit is linked to its own DriveChannel. .
- **ControlChannel**: Control channels are utilized for executing tasks that entail interactions between qubits, such as implementing two-qubit gates. They possess the ability to regulate the connection between qubits, a crucial aspect in generating entanglement and executing quantum logic operations that go beyond individual qubit manipulations.
- **MeasureChannel**: These channels are specifically designed for the purpose of mea-

suring the quantum information stored in qubits and transforming it into classical bits that an external device may read. MeasureChannel procedures frequently require intricate signal processing to precisely determine the qubit's state.

- **AcquireChannel**: Enables the essential procedures for accurately timed and regulated retrieval of qubits. The role of quantum measurements is crucial in achieving precise execution of quantum algorithms and reliable characterization of quantum hardware.

Pulse Libraries

Qiskit Pulse incorporates libraries that offer pre-defined pulse forms, streamlining the process of generating commonly used waveform patterns.

- **Predefined Pulse Shapes**: These waveforms, such as Gaussian, Square, or Drag pulses, are commonly employed in quantum operations due to their standardized and distinct features. For instance, Gaussian pulses are frequently employed due to their low power bandwidth product, which decreases the likelihood of stimulating undesired transitions in the qubits.
- **Custom Waveforms**: In addition to the pre-established shapes, users have the ability to create customized waveforms, allowing them to adjust the pulse according to the exact requirements of their quantum activities. Researchers can utilize this freedom to conduct experiments with innovative pulse forms in order to enhance gate fidelities, reduce mistakes, or investigate new quantum control approaches.

Pulse Schedules

In Qiskit Pulse, a Schedule is a fundamental object that signifies a series of commands to be carried out on the control hardware of a quantum computer. These instructions are not quantum gates used in gate-based quantum computing. Instead, they are pulses of microwave radiation that directly affect the quantum states of the qubits.

Features of Schedules:

- **Time Tracking**: Every schedule in Qiskit Pulse is cognizant of the timing of each instruction. Timing and order of pulses are critical since they can impact the quantum state and the results of quantum processes. Precise timing control aids in synchronizing processes among several qubits and channels.
- **Parallel Operations**: Schedules can coordinate simultaneous instructions across several channels. Various channels in quantum hardware, such as drive channels for qubits, control channels for coupling qubits, and measurement channels for qubit state readout, can be modified concurrently. This parallelism is crucial for effective quantum computation.
- **Low-Level Control**: Researchers and developers can optimize quantum operations by working at the pulse level. This involves personalized pulse forms, frequencies, amplitudes, and durations, providing a detailed level of control over qubit manipulation

that cannot be achieved only with high-level quantum gates.

Components of Schedule:

- **Channels**: These are the pathways through which pulses are sent to the qubits or readout devices. Each channel type serves a different purpose, such as driving qubit transitions, controlling interactions between qubits, or measuring qubit states.
- **Instructions**: The schedule's fundamental components consist of pulse instructions (defining pulse characteristics, duration, and channel), delay instructions (for time intervals), and other control instructions essential for quantum processes.
- **Duration and Timing**: The schedule monitors the timing of each instruction's start and end times to ensure that operations are carried out in the correct sequence, maintaining accurate timing relationships between parallel and sequential pulses.

Applications

Gate Calibration

Accurate gate calibration is essential for maximizing the efficiency of quantum gates, which serve as the fundamental components of quantum algorithms. Through the process of modifying the pulse forms and durations that control quantum gates, researchers have the ability to:

- **Minimize Gate Errors**: Customize the pulses' properties to match a quantum system's unique attributes, thereby minimizing operational mistakes and enhancing the precision of quantum computations.
- **Enhance Qubit Coherence**: Optimize pulse parameters to execute operations more rapidly than the qubit's decoherence time, thus maintaining quantum information.

Error Mitigation

Implementing error mitigation techniques is crucial for enhancing the dependability of quantum computations when confronted with noise and flaws in quantum hardware. Qiskit Pulse enables:

- **Dynamic Decoupling**: Deploy pulse sequences specifically engineered to nullify noise and maintain qubit coherence for extended durations, improving quantum process accuracy.
- **Custom Correction Sequences**: Create and implement pulse sequences that selectively target identified error sources in the quantum hardware, thereby minimizing their influence on quantum algorithms.

Exploratory Research

- **Implement Novel Quantum Gates**: Explore unconventional quantum gate configurations by directly programming the underlying pulses, potentially uncovering more efficient or potent quantum computations.

- **Quantum Sensing and Metrology**: Harness the exact manipulation of qubits to perform accurate measurements of external physical processes, thereby pushing the boundaries of quantum sensing.

Hamiltonian Engineering

- **Simulate Complex Quantum Systems**: Utilize the manipulation of qubit interactions to replicate the behavior of intricate quantum systems, facilitating the examination of quantum physics and the advancement of novel materials and pharmaceuticals.
- **Implement Quantum Simulations**: Facilitate the development of customized interactions that are inherently challenging or unattainable in natural settings, hence creating novel opportunities for study in quantum simulation.

Quantum Control Theory

- **Optimal Control**: Create pulse sequences that are theoretically optimal to achieve specific objectives, such as decreasing the duration of operations while maximizing accuracy.
- **Feedback Control**: Enable adaptive quantum computing by swiftly measuring the states of qubits and making prompt adjustments to control pulses, thereby implementing real-time feedback control systems.

Qubit Characterization

- **Spectroscopy**: Observe the response of qubits by applying pulses of different frequencies to determine their energy levels and transition frequencies.
- **T1 and T2 Measurements**: Quantify the relaxation (T1) and dephasing (T2) durations of qubits, fundamental indicators of qubit excellence.

State Preparation and Measurement (SPAM) Optimization

- **Custom State Preparation**: Create customized pulse sequences to generate intricate quantum states with a high level of accuracy, which is crucial for specific quantum algorithms and experimental purposes.
- **Enhanced Readout Fidelity**: Enhance the efficiency of measuring pulses and post-processing procedures in order to get a more precise differentiation between qubit states, hence minimizing readout errors.

Quantum Gates and Pulse Schedules

In the previous sections, we covered some basic theories behind Qiskit Pulse that will now aid us in understanding the pulse sequences and codes related to quantum gates that we will see in this section. A few of the quantum gates will be explained with their pulse diagrams, and the rest of the quantum gates are left out for the reader as an exercise.

Hadamard Gate Pulse

We start with the import of the pulse libraries as well as simulation tools. For the experiments performed, the fake hardware backends are used in order to showcase the functionality of running the programs locally on your computer.

```
import numpy as np
from qiskit import QuantumCircuit, pulse, transpile, schedule
from qiskit.primitives import BackendSampler
from qiskit.pulse.library import Gaussian
from qiskit.pulse.library import Drag
from qiskit.providers.basic_provider import BasicProvider
from qiskit_ibm_runtime.fake_provider import FakeProvider, FakeValencia
from qiskit_ibm_runtime.fake_provider import FakeSherbrooke, FakeKolkata
from qiskit_ibm_provider import IBMProvider
import qiskit_ibm_provider.jupyter
from qiskit.visualization import plot_histogram
from qiskit.primitives import (
    Sampler, # V1
    StatevectorSampler, #V2
    Estimator, #V1
    StatevectorEstimator, #V2
)
import warnings
warnings.filterwarnings('ignore')
```

We set the backend to `FakeValencia()`, a fake 5-qubit backend that simulates the behaviour of the IBM Valencia quantum machine using inherent noise models.

```
backend = FakeValencia()
backend
```

The previous code prints `<FakeValencia('fake_valencia')>`. Now, we define the Hadamard gate and its pulse schedule.

```
circ = QuantumCircuit(1)
circ.h(0)
transpiled_circ = transpile(circ, backend)
schedule_circ = schedule(transpiled_circ, backend)
schedule_circ.draw()
```

The quantum circuit is first transpiled according to the backend and then a pulse schedule is created from the backend's transpiled circuit. We draw the pulse to visualize its shape and configuration. The pulse is shown in *Figure* 15.4.

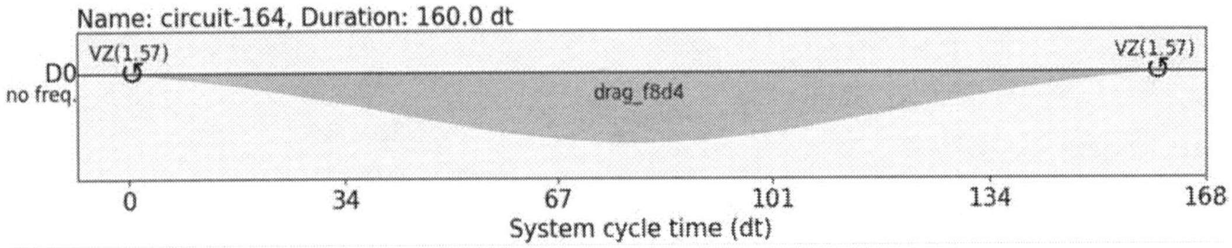

Figure 15.4: Hadamard Gate Pulse

Several important terms in *Figure* 15.4 are now explained with their significance. Understanding them now will make comprehending other pulse diagrams easier when we discuss them in the next sections.

Discrete Time Units (dt)

The "dt" notation specifies the duration of a pulse or operation in terms of **discrete time units (dt)**. This measurement is crucial for comprehending the timing and synchronization of pulse sequences in quantum computing studies.

- **Quantum Hardware Clock Rate:** Quantum processors operate at a fixed clock rate, which defines the minimum time resolution for controlling qubits. This clock rate is specific to each quantum computing platform and determines the duration of the smallest controllable time step, denoted as "dt."
- **Duration in dt:** The duration of pulses, delays, and other operations in a Qiskit Pulse schedule is quantified in these discrete time units (dt). For example, if a pulse has a "Duration: 160.0 dt," it means the pulse lasts for 160 time steps, where each time step is the minimum time interval defined by the hardware clock rate.

Why do we use discrete time units?

- **Precision and Synchronization:** Utilizing discrete time units enables accurate management of the timing of pulses and processes. It guarantees that all operations are coordinated with the quantum processor's clock, which is essential for consistently controlling qubits.
- **Device Compatibility:** Quantum processors can vary in their clock rates. Qiskit Pulse

simplifies pulse programs using durations in dt, which hides the timing information and enhances portability across different devices. The temporal duration denoted by "160.0 dt" may differ between devices due to their varying clock rates.

- **Timing Resolution:** The use of discrete time units provides a clear resolution for timing, allowing quantum programmers to design experiments with a detailed understanding of how pulses overlap, sequence, and interact. This is key for optimizing quantum gate fidelities and for implementing complex quantum algorithms.

Timing in pulse programming is just as important as the sequence and intensity of operations. The timing can impact the phase accumulation of qubits, the interaction between pulses on different qubits, and the coherence of the quantum state. Pulse programmers can precisely adjust their experiments to match the specific features of the quantum hardware by defining durations in discrete time units.

The $VZ(\theta)$ Gate

The $VZ(\theta)$ notation accompanied with an anti-clockwise symbol represents a Virtual Z gate with an angle θ in radians. These virtual Z gates are a unique aspect of quantum computing with superconducting qubits and are used to apply a phase shift to the qubit's state without physically applying a pulse. These gates' *virtual* nature means they are implemented by changing the frame of reference for the qubit rather than by applying an actual microwave pulse. This makes them significantly faster and more error-resistant compared to physical operations.

- **Phase Shift:** $VZ(\theta)$ gate applies a phase shift of θ to the qubit state. For example, $VZ(1.57)$, which is the same as $VZ(\pi/2)$, would rotate the qubit's phase by 90 degrees in the Bloch sphere representation. This is crucial for quantum algorithms that rely on the interference and superposition of quantum states.
- **Implementation:** The virtual Z gate alters the phase of all subsequent microwave pulses applied to the qubit instead of utilizing a physical pulse. This is accomplished by fine-tuning the local oscillator that combines with the pulse signal to generate the microwave radiation aimed at the qubit. As it is a software correction, it occurs almost instantly and does not add any extra noise or errors to the system.

The anticlockwise symbol signifies the direction of the phase shift on the Bloch sphere (anticlockwise when viewed from the top). These gates are often used in conjunction with physical pulses to implement more complex quantum operations efficiently.

- **Efficiency and Fidelity:** Quantum circuits can be simplified by utilizing virtual Z gates, which helps minimize the reliance on physical pulses that could potentially lead to further errors. This enhances gate fidelities and improves the efficiency of quantum processes.
- **Compatibility with Pulses:** When $VZ(\theta)$ gate is combined with DRAG or Gaussian

square pulses, it signifies the operation includes dynamic phase manipulation and direct qubit state manipulation. This combination is frequently used in processes that necessitate precise control over both the amplitude and phase of qubit states, such as those present in advanced quantum gates or error correction procedures.

The notations **D**, **U**, **M** signify the Drive channel, Control channel and Measurement channels, respectively. The number associated with them represents the qubit number; for instance, D0 means drive channel on the 0th qubit and so on.

In order to view the pulse sequence, we can use

```
schedule_circ.filter(channels=[pulse.DriveChannel(0)])
```

The output of the previous line of code is given in *Figure* 15.5.

```
Schedule((0, ShiftPhase(-1.5707963268, DriveChannel(0))), (0, Play(Drag(duration=160, sigma=40, beta=-0.35835396095069005, amp=0.0961922281523014, angle=
0.008783280252964184, name='drag_f8d4'), DriveChannel(0), name='drag_f8d4')), (160, ShiftPhase(-1.5707963268, DriveChannel(0))), name="circuit-164")
```

Figure 15.5: Hadamard Gate Schedule

It is important to note that from Qiskit 1.0 onwards, there is no support for the execution of pulse schedules on fake backends (both V1 and V2 backends); instead, Qiskit Dynamics is utilized as a new alternative. This brings us to the point of highlighting that the *no freq* written underneath D0 shows that the pulse has not been simulated on a backend. We will explore Qiskit dynamics and its functionalities in pulse simulation in the later sections of this chapter.

Pauli X Gate Pulse

When we change the Hadamard gate to X gate in the code provided in the previous section, we receive the pulse of the X gate.

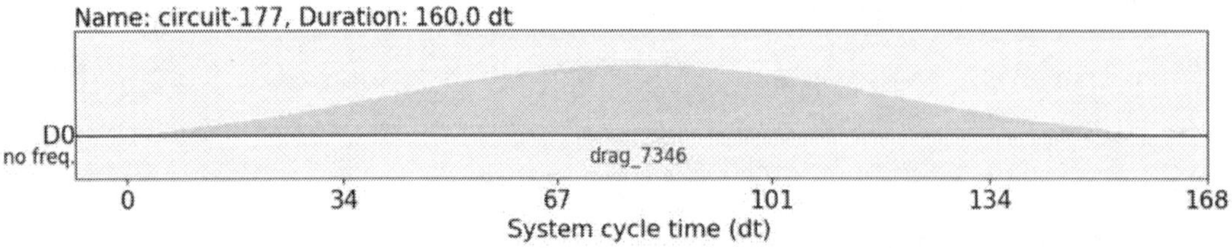

Figure 15.6: Pauli X Gate Schedule

Figure 15.6 shows the pulse for the X gate. If you have observed that in this pulse, the Hadamard has drag written on them. We are now going to explain itsmeaning and its significance.

DRAG (Derivative Removal by Adiabatic Gate)

The DRAG pulse technique is a sophisticated method used in quantum computing to improve the accuracy of single-qubit gate operations, especially in systems with qubits that have energy levels closely spaced. This method deals with the crucial problem of quantum leakage, which refers to undesired transitions to non-computational states that can greatly reduce the efficiency of quantum algorithms. The numbers following `drag\_` indicate specific configurations of the DRAG pulse, potentially referring to different amplitude or phase parameters customized for the gate implementation.

In quantum systems, particularly those employing superconducting qubits, the energy spectrum may contain levels that are not part of the computational basis but are situated near the necessary transition frequencies. Applying traditional pulse forms like Gaussian pulses to drive qubit transitions might cause transitions to neighbouring non-computational levels due to their spectral width, resulting in leakage.

The DRAG technique addresses this problem by altering the pulse form to incorporate a component that successfully neutralizes the undesired derivative component of the Gaussian pulse. This is accomplished by incorporating a quadrature component into the pulse to offset the impact of the pulse's derivative, hence reducing the likelihood of leaking to non-computational states. The outcome is a smoother transition between computational states, maintaining the qubit's quantum state integrity inside the computational subspace.

To implement DRAG pulses effectively, careful calibration and control of pulse parameters such as amplitude, phase, and duration are necessary to customize the pulse form for the quantum system's energy landscape. DRAG pulses are crucial in quantum computing hardware development, especially for architectures with challenging energy level spacing that affects qubit coherence and computational accuracy. Their effectiveness lies in reducing leakage and improving gate fidelity.

CNOT Gate Pulse

We will visualize the transition for the CNOT or CX gate. This is shown in *Figure* 15.7

Gaussian Square Pulse: This pulse has a flat-top shape with a Gaussian envelope, as shown in *Figure* 15.7. It is utilized in quantum operations due to its characteristics that reduce off-resonant driving and enable precise control of qubit states. Gaussian square pulses can be used on control channels in a CNOT gate to adjust the interaction between qubits and enable the controlled-NOT function. These pulses enables to realize CNOT gates via a mechanism called cross-resonance (CR) which we will discuss now.

The Cross-Resonance (CR) effect is a key mechanism in superconducting qubit systems for implementing two-qubit gates, namely the Controlled-NOT (CX) gate. Qiskit Pulse utilizes the cross-resonance effect to achieve accurate control of qubit interactions, allowing

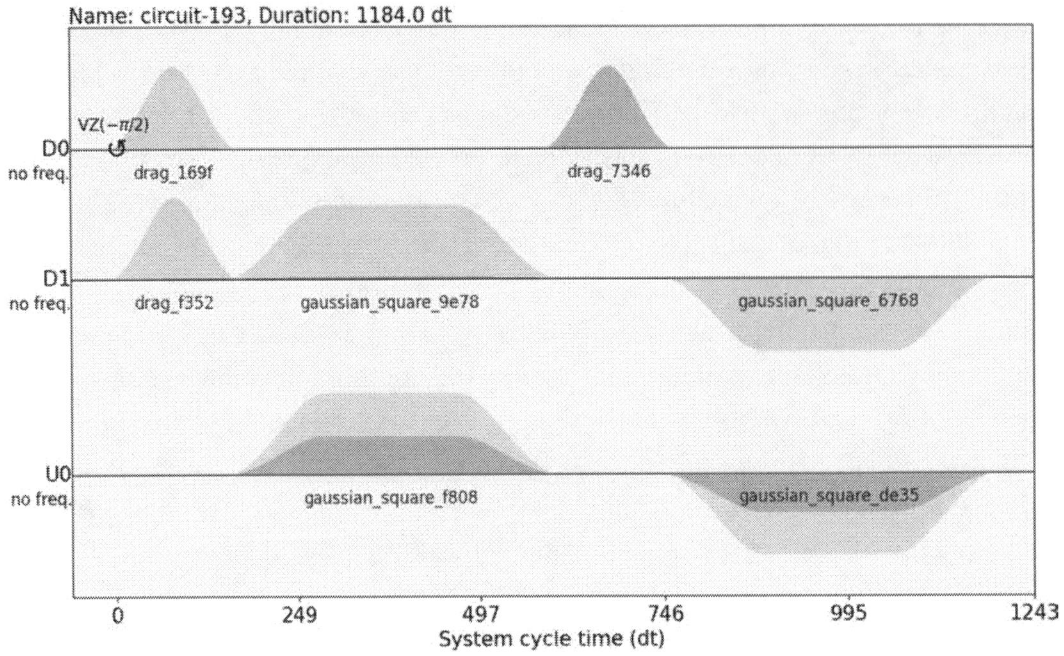

Figure 15.7: CNOT Gate Schedule

for the modification of qubit states based on the state of another qubit. Utilizing a Gaussian Square pulse is crucial for the CR gate operation.

What is Cross Resonance (CR)?

The cross-resonance effect happens when a qubit, known as the control qubit, is operated at the resonance frequency of another qubit, referred to as the target qubit. This results in a conditional rotation of the target qubit based on the state of the control qubit. This phenomenon occurs as a result of the interaction between the qubits, which can be either direct or facilitated via a bus resonator in superconducting qubit designs.

Mechanism of CR

- **Driving the Control Qubit:** The CR effect causes a Rabi oscillation in the target qubit by using a microwave drive on the control qubit at the target qubit's frequency. The oscillation is dependent on the control qubit's state. The oscillation's existence or absence, and consequently the rotation of the target qubit's state, is determined by whether the control qubit is in the □1⟩ state.
- **ZX Interaction:** The CR effect mostly causes a ZX interaction between the two qubits, where Z represents the Pauli-Z operator on the control qubit and X represents the Pauli-X operator on the target qubit. Adjusting the amplitude, length, and form of the administered pulse can change the strength of this interaction.

The Gaussian Square pulse reduces leakage to non-computational states and decreases undesired transitions, therefore improving the gate's fidelity. The pulse's smooth edges decrease spectrum broadening, which is advantageous in closely spaced qubit setups where moving nearby qubits off-resonance is a worry.

To create a successful CR gate, precise adjustment of the pulse parameters is necessary to enhance the strength and accuracy of the CR interaction. This entails modifying the amplitude, duration, and shape characteristics of the pulse to produce the desired conditional rotation on the target qubit while reducing undesired interactions.

To enhance the CR gate's efficiency, one can utilize extra pulses (such as echo pulses) to address flaws in the interaction and align the qubits in a rotating frame that corresponds to the driving frequency, thus decreasing the energy needed for the gate operation.

Measurement Gate Pulse

The measurement pulse is shown in *Figure* 15.8

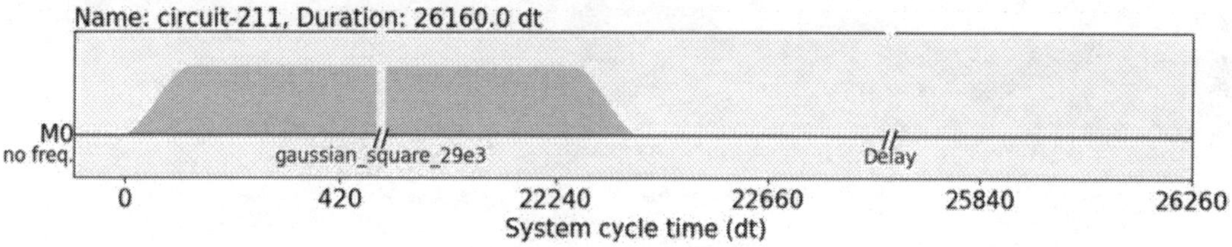

Figure 15.8: Measurement Gate Schedule

After the measurement pulse, there is a delay period until the end of the schedule at 26260 dt. This delay might be present to allow for the readout process to be completed and the signal to be processed or to ensure proper timing for subsequent operations in a larger quantum circuit.

Calibration of CNOT Gate - Dynamic Decoupling

Preserving the coherence of qubits is crucial in maximizing the potential of quantum computing. Environmental noise and interactions constantly threaten the fragile coherence of quantum systems, resulting in decoherence and compromising the accuracy of quantum computations. Dynamical Decoupling (DD) is a crucial method in quantum error suppression that effectively counteracts decoherence by regularly implementing a series of rapid and precisely timed control pulses. The control pulses are intended to systematically counteract the accumulation of phase errors caused by undesirable interactions with the environment, thereby protecting the quantum states and prolonging their coherence durations. DD sequences can be viewed as a coordinated arrangement of control actions that work together in a rhythmic and patterned manner to preserve the coherence of quantum information. We will examine the theoretical basis and practical use of Dynamical Decoupling (DD) in quantum circuits, focusing on pulse-level control. This approach serves as a fundamental method for reducing quantum mistakes without utilizing complete quantum error correction.

In order to explain the concept of Dynamic Decoupling, we demonstrate the calibration of the CNOT gate in Qiskit Pulse. The following code shows the implementation of two CNOT gates and their transpiled pulse schedule.

```
circ = QuantumCircuit(4)
circ.x(0)
circ.cx(0,1)
circ.cx(1,3)
circ.measure_all()
backend = FakeValencia()
circ_trans = transpile(circ, backend)
circ_sched = schedule(circ, backend)
circ_sched.draw()
```

When the code is executed, we get the pulse diagram as shown in *Figure* 15.9.

The following code block specifies the time lengths for different quantum operations (cx, reset, x, measure) using discrete time units (dt). Accurate timing is essential for coordinating operations according to the pulse schedule.

```
durations = InstructionDurations([
    ("cx", [0, 1], backend.properties().gate_length('cx', [0,1])/
    backend.configuration().dt),
    ("reset", None, 10),
    ("cx", [1, 3], backend.properties().gate_length('cx', [1,2])/
    backend.configuration().dt),
    ("x", None, backend.properties().gate_length('x', 0)/
    backend.configuration().dt),
    ("measure", None, 22400)
])
print(durations)
```

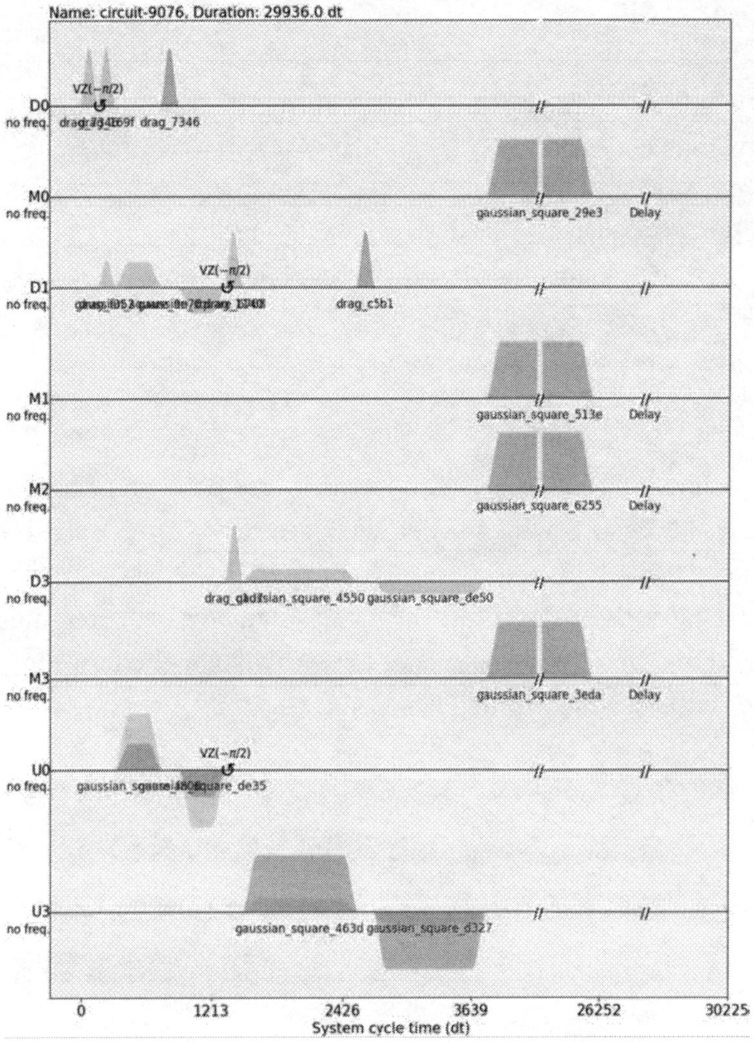

Figure 15.9: CNOT and X Gate Pulse Schedule

```
durations = InstructionDurations(
    [("cx", [0, 1], 1184), ("reset", None, 10),
     ("cx", [1, 3], 2176),
     ("x", None, 160), ("y", None, 160),("measure", None, 22400)]
)
```

```
reset: 10 dt
x: 160.0 dt
measure: 22400 dt
cx(0, 1): 1183.9999999999998 dt
```

```
cx(1, 3): 2176.0 dt
```

The previous block shows the output after printing the durations of the gate sequences defined in the previous code block.

```
dd_sequence = [XGate(), XGate(), XGate(), XGate()]
pm = PassManager([ALAPSchedule(durations), DynamicalDecoupling(durations, \\
↪  dd_sequence)])
circ_dd = pm.run(circ)
timeline_drawer(circ_dd)
```

A dynamical decoupling sequence is defined as four X gates. A `PassManager` is initialized with two passes: `ALAPSchedule`, which schedules gates to minimize the time qubits spend in excited states, and `DynamicalDecoupling`, which applies the DD sequence to battle decoherence during idle periods of the qubits. The pass manager executes these passes on the original circuit, and the `timeline_drawer` is utilized to display the new circuit timeline with the DD sequence, as shown in *Figure* 15.10.

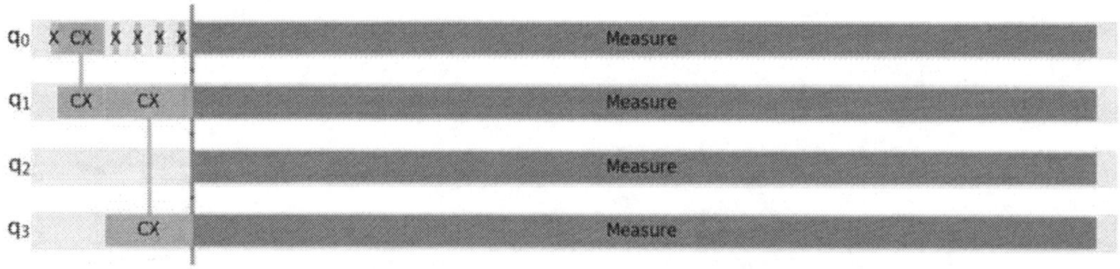

Figure 15.10: DD Time Sequence

Decoherence and undesired environmental interactions pose substantial obstacles in quantum computing. Dynamical decoupling is a quantum error suppression method that reduces decoherence by using a series of rapid, regular quantum gates, often the X gate. The gates efficiently average specific noise types over time by redirecting the qubit's quantum state.

The code presented before inserts a sequence of four X gates into the quantum circuit. The goal is to insert decoupling pulses during quantum computation to realign the qubits' states and shield them from low-frequency interference without changing the computational result. The `PassManager` arranges these sequences with a scheduling approach that reduces the idle time of qubits between operations, thus decreasing the impact of noise and the probability of decoherence.

The `ALAPSchedule` pass enhances the efficiency of dynamical decoupling by keeping the qubits in their ground state for an extended period before any operation is executed. It is crucial because qubits in excited states are more prone to mistakes. The `DynamicalDecoupling` pass inserts a DD sequence during idle times to reset the qubits' phase regularly, preventing the accumulation of phase errors caused by external interactions.

Why X Gates were used?

When X gates are applied in pairs, they can reverse unwanted phase accumulations that occur due to system-environment interactions.

- **Effectiveness:** Consecutive X gates are effective as they can rapidly reverse the dephasing caused by external interactions and refocus the qubit state.
- **Symmetry:** The X gate sequence exhibits symmetry in relation to the computational basis states ($|0\rangle$ and $|1\rangle$), which makes it an effective option for maintaining quantum information.

Can we use other gates for DD?

Indeed, other gates can also be used for dynamical decoupling, and the choice of gate depends on the type of noise present in the system.

- **Y Gates:** A sequence of Y gates can similarly refocus the qubit state and can be used interchangeably with X gates for DD in many cases. Sometimes, a combination of X and Y gates (XY4 sequence) is used to address more general types of noise.
- **H Gate:** Hadamard gates are not typically used in isolation for DD because they create superpositions of $|0\rangle$ and $|1\rangle$ states, which can be more susceptible to certain types of noise. However, they can be part of more complex DD sequences when combined with other gates to create a specific refocusing effect.
- **Z Gate**: These are less common in DD sequences because physical Z gates (as opposed to virtual Z gates) do not change the populations of the $|0\rangle$ and $|1\rangle$ states but only the phase between them. However, Z rotations can still be part of composite pulse sequences in certain DD protocols.

How to choose sequence for DD?

Choosing the sequence depends on the following factors:

- **Type of Noise:** Various forms of environmental noise may necessitate distinct DD sequences. If the noise is asymmetric relative to the x-axis, using an XY4 sequence alternating between X and Y gates could be more efficient.
- **System Characteristics:** The physical arrangement of qubits and the properties of the control circuitry can impact the selection of DD pulses.
- **Experimental Convenience:** The ease of accurately executing specific types of pulses can influence the selection of the DD sequence.

Calibration of Pauli X Gate - Qiskit Dynamics Backend

Within the changing realm of quantum computing, the calibration of quantum gates is a crucial procedure that significantly impacts the accuracy and efficiency of quantum algorithms. The Pauli X gate, also known as the quantum bit-flip operation, is a fundamental component in manipulating qubit states and is crucial in several quantum circuits. This section discusses the precise adjustment of the Pauli X gate using the Qiskit Dynamics Backend, a powerful tool created for simulating and analyzing quantum systems with time-dependent Hamiltonians. Using Qiskit Dynamics, we investigate the detailed method of calibrating the Pauli X gate, focusing on combining theoretical concepts with practical implementation methodologies. Calibration assures the precise implementation of the X gate on physical quantum hardware and provides insights into qubit manipulation dynamics, optimizing gate operations for improved quantum computational accuracy and efficiency.

The `DynamicsBackend` utilizes the JAX library to execute just-in-time compilation internally. Therefore, we need to import all the necessary libraries and commands accordingly as follows.

```
# Import necessary libraries
import numpy as np
import jax
from scipy.optimize import minimize_scalar
from qiskit import QuantumCircuit, pulse, transpile, schedule
from qiskit.primitives import BackendSampler
from qiskit.pulse.library import Gaussian
from qiskit.pulse.library import Drag
from qiskit_dynamics import DynamicsBackend, Solver
from qiskit_dynamics.array import Array
from qiskit.providers.basic_provider import BasicProvider
from qiskit_ibm_runtime.fake_provider import FakeProvider, FakeValencia,
FakeSherbrooke, FakeKolkata
from qiskit_ibm_provider import IBMProvider
from qiskit.circuit.library import XGate, SXGate, RZGate, CXGate
from qiskit.circuit import Gate, Parameter
import qiskit_ibm_provider.jupyter
from qiskit.visualization import plot_histogram
from qiskit.primitives import (
    Sampler, # V1
```

```
    StatevectorSampler, #V2
    Estimator, #V1
    StatevectorEstimator,
)
```

```
# Configure to use JAX internally
jax.config.update("jax_enable_x64", True)
jax.config.update("jax_platform_name", "cpu")
Array.set_default_backend("jax")
```

Once we have imported the libraries and configured JAX, we have to set the Hamiltonian parameters in order to define a `Solver` model since this is compulsory to define for `QiskitDynamics` backend. Following the simple, minimally configured model defined by IBM in their

`QiskitDynamics` tutorial, we use a two-qubit fixed-frequency transmon model with fixed coupling, whose Hamiltonian is given by

$$\begin{aligned} H(t) = 2\pi\nu_0 N_0 + \pi\alpha_0 N_0(N_0 - I) + 2\pi\nu_1 N_1 + \pi\alpha_1 N_1(N_1 - I) \\ +2\pi J(a_0 + a_0^\dagger)(a_1 + a_1^\dagger) \\ +2\pi r_0 s_0(t)(a_0 + a_0^\dagger) \\ +2\pi r_1 s_1(t)(a_1 + a_1^\dagger), \end{aligned} \tag{15.14}$$

where

- ν_0 and ν_1 are the qubit frequencies,
- α_0 and α_1 are the qubit anharmonicities,
- J is the coupling strength
- r_0 and r_1 are the Rabi strengths, and $s_0(t)$ and $s_1(t)$ are the drive signals,
- a_j and $a_j^\dagger$ are the lowering and raising operators for qubit j, and
- N_0 and N_1 are the number operators for qubits 0 and 1 respectively.

We can now define the Hamiltonian and all the parameters.

```
# Define the 2-qubit qubit fixed-frequency transmon model with fixed coupling
Hamiltonian parameters

dim = 3
v0 = 4.86e9
```

```
anharm0 = -0.32e9
r0 = 0.22e9
v1 = 4.97e9
anharm1 = -0.32e9
r1 = 0.26e9
J = 0.002e9
a = np.diag(np.sqrt(np.arange(1, dim)), 1)
adag = np.diag(np.sqrt(np.arange(1, dim)), -1)
N = np.diag(np.arange(dim))
ident = np.eye(dim, dtype=complex)
full_ident = np.eye(dim**2, dtype=complex)
N0 = np.kron(ident, N)
N1 = np.kron(N, ident)
a0 = np.kron(ident, a)
a1 = np.kron(a, ident)
a0dag = np.kron(ident, adag)
a1dag = np.kron(adag, ident)
static_ham0 = 2 * np.pi * v0 * N0 + np.pi * anharm0 * N0 * (N0 - full_ident)
static_ham1 = 2 * np.pi * v1 * N1 + np.pi * anharm1 * N1 * (N1 - full_ident)
static_ham_full = static_ham0 + static_ham1 + 2 * np.pi * J * ((a0 + a0dag) @
(a1 + a1dag))
drive_op0 = 2 * np.pi * r0 * (a0 + a0dag)
drive_op1 = 2 * np.pi * r1 * (a1 + a1dag)
```

Now we are ready to build the `Solver`. The rotating frame of the static Hamiltonian is utilized, which provides performance improvements.

```
# build solver
dt = 1/4.5e9

solver = Solver(
    static_hamiltonian=static_ham_full,
    hamiltonian_operators=[drive_op0, drive_op1, drive_op0, drive_op1],
    rotating_frame=static_ham_full,
    hamiltonian_channels=["d0", "d1", "u0", "u1"],
    channel_carrier_freqs={"d0": v0, "d1": v1, "u0": v1, "u1": v0},
    dt=dt,
```

```
)
```

Instantiate the `DynamicsBackend`. The `Solver` is utilized for simulation `subsystem_dims` specifies how the entire system breaks down for computing measurement data, and `solver_options` are uniform settings employed by the Solver. Use the `Solver.solve()` function to simulate the differential equation. The whole set of acceptable `solver_options` are the parameters for `solve_ode()`.

```
# Consistent solver option to use throughout this chapter
solver_options = {"method": "jax_odeint", "atol": 1e-6, "rtol": 1e-8, "hmax": dt}

dynamic_backend = DynamicsBackend(
    solver=solver,
    subsystem_dims=[dim, dim], # for computing measurement data
    solver_options=solver_options, # to be used every time run is called
)
```

To activate the inbuilt automated just-in-time compilation, we select a JAX integration mechanism. Additionally, it is important to mention that we established the maximum step size to be equal to the pulse sample width dt using the `hmax` parameter for the `jax_odeint` method in the solver settings. This is crucial for preventing variable step solvers from inadvertently skipping pulses in schedules with extended periods of inactivity.

Firstly, we run our Pauli X gate using the ideal sampler.

```
# Run our Pauli X Gate on an Ideal Simulator, namely version 2 Sampler
circ = QuantumCircuit(1, 1)
circ.x(0)
circ.measure([0], [0])

sampler_v2 = StatevectorSampler()
result = sampler_v2.run([circ], shots=1024).result()
data_pub = result[0].data
# Get counts for the classical register "c"
ideal_counts = data_pub.c.get_counts()
print(f"The counts are: {ideal_counts}")
```

The previous code returns `The counts are: {'1': 1024}`, which is an expected result since we have used the ideal simulator.

Now, we run a Customized X gate on the FakeValencia backend via Qiskit Dynamics.

```
# Run a Custom X Gate circuit on the Fake Backend via Qiskit Dynamics (Non
↪ Calibrated)
amplit = 0.18
amp = Parameter('amp')

circ = QuantumCircuit(1)
custom_gate = Gate('custom_x_gate', 1, [])

circ.append(custom_gate, [0])
circ.measure_all()

# Define the Fake Backend with the help of Qiskit Dynamics Backend
true_backend = DynamicsBackend(solver=solver).from_backend(FakeValencia())
with pulse.build(true_backend, name='custom_x') as my_sched:
    pulse.play(Drag(duration=160, amp=amp, sigma=40, beta=-0.25388969010654494),
    pulse.drive_channel(0))

my_sched.assign_parameters({amp:amplit})

circ.add_calibration(custom_gate, qubits=[0], schedule=my_sched)

result = true_backend.run(circ).result()

x_counts = result.get_counts(0)
```

This time, we get the output `{'0': 19, '1': 1005}` as we have used the noisy fake backend, which simulates a real noisy quantum hardware. This means that we need to calibrate our custom X gate to behave as accurately as possible for the FakeValencia backend. To this end, we define a calibration function to achieve this.

```
def calibration_x_gate(parameter):
    amp = Parameter('amp')
    circ = QuantumCircuit(1)
    custom_gate = Gate('my_custom_gate', 1, [])
    circ.append(custom_gate, [0])
    circ.measure_all()
```

```
    true_backend = DynamicsBackend(solver=solver).from_backend(FakeValencia())
    with pulse.build(true_backend, name='custom') as my_schedule:
        pulse.play(Drag(duration=160, amp=amp, sigma=40,
        ↪  beta=-0.25388969010654494),
        pulse.drive_channel(0))

    my_schedule.assign_parameters({amp:parameter})
    circ.add_calibration(custom_gate, [0], my_schedule)

    circ_transpile = transpile(circ, true_backend)
    schedule_circ = schedule(circ_transpile, true_backend)

    job = true_backend.run(schedule_circ, shots=10000)
    counts = job.result().get_counts()

    if '0' in counts:
        return (counts['0'])/1024
    else:
        return 0

res = minimize_scalar(calibration_x_gate, bounds=(0.1, 0.2), method='bounded')
print(res.x)
```

The optimal amplitude value which we receive after executing the previous code is `0.16612017479`. We can now use this optimal value to do a simulation of the calibrated custom X gate for the FakeValencia backend.

```
amp = Parameter('amp')
circ = QuantumCircuit(1)
custom_gate = Gate('my_custom_x_gate', 1, [])
circ.append(custom_gate, [0])
circ.measure_all()

true_backend = DynamicsBackend(solver=solver).from_backend(FakeValencia())
with pulse.build(true_backend, name='custom_x_gate') as best_x_sched:
    pulse.play(Drag(duration=160, amp=amp, sigma=40, beta=-0.25388969010654494),
```

```
    pulse.drive_channel(0))

best_x_sched.assign_parameters({amp:res.x})
circ.add_calibration(custom_gate, [0], best_x_sched)

circ_transpile = transpile(circ, true_backend)
schedule_circ = schedule(circ_transpile, true_backend)

job = true_backend.run(schedule_circ)
calibrated_counts = job.result().get_counts()

plot_histogram([ideal_counts, calibrated_counts, x_counts],
legend=['Ideal','Calibrated', 'FakeBackend'])
```

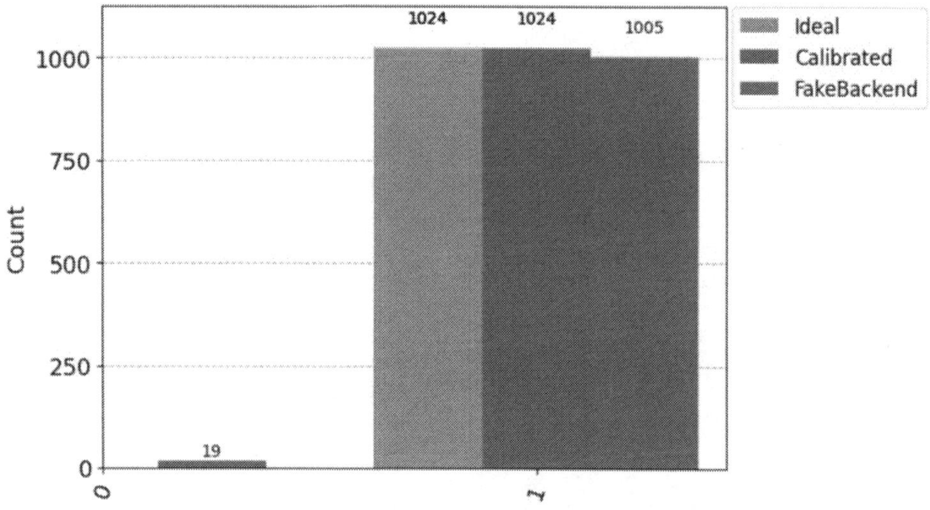

Figure 15.11: Comparison between Calibrated X Gate, Ideal Simulation and Fake Backend

Conclusion

Qiskit Pulse signifies notable progress in the field of quantum computing, providing unmatched command over quantum hardware. Enabling users to specify customized pulse forms and schedules closes the divide between high-level quantum algorithms and the detailed physical execution on quantum devices. This feature improves the accuracy and effectiveness of quantum operations and enables the exploration of new quantum control strategies. Qiskit Pulse will continue to be a crucial tool for academics and developers in the expanding field of quantum computing. It enables them to explore the limits of quantum technology and drive advancements in algorithmic performance and hardware optimization.

Bibliography

[1] J. Russell, "Intel connects the (quantum) dots in accelerating quantum computing effort." [Online]. Available: https://www.hpcwire.com/2020/08/19/intel-connects-the-quantum-dots-in-accelerating-quantum-computing-effort/

[2] Wikipedia, "Spin qubit quantum computer." [Online]. Available: https://en.wikipedia.org/wiki/Spin_qubit_quantum_computer

[3] R. R. Tucci, "An introduction to cartan's kak decomposition for qc programmers," 2005. [Online]. Available: https://arxiv.org/abs/quant-ph/0507171

[4] G. Li, Y. Ding, and Y. Xie, "Tackling the qubit mapping problem for nisq-era quantum devices," 2019. [Online]. Available: https://arxiv.org/abs/1809.02573

[5] D. Kremer, V. Villar, H. Paik, I. Duran, I. Faro, and J. Cruz-Benito, "Practical and efficient quantum circuit synthesis and transpiling with reinforcement learning," 2024. [Online]. Available: https://arxiv.org/abs/2405.13196

[6] E. Farhi, J. Goldstone, and S. Gutmann, "A quantum approximate optimization algorithm," 2014. [Online]. Available: https://arxiv.org/abs/1411.4028

[7] A. Blais, A. L. Grimsmo, S. Girvin, and A. Wallraff, "Circuit quantum electrodynamics," *Reviews of Modern Physics*, vol. 93, no. 2, may 2021. [Online]. Available: https://doi.org/10.1103%2Frevmodphys.93.025005

[8] H. K. Onnes, *Further experiments with liquid helium. C. On the change of electric resistance of pure metals at very low temperatures etc. IV. The resistance of pure mercury at helium temperatures.* Dordrecht: Springer Netherlands, 1991, pp. 261–263. [Online]. Available: https://doi.org/10.1007/978-94-009-2079-8_15

[9] L. N. Cooper, "Bound electron pairs in a degenerate fermi gas," *Phys. Rev.*, vol. 104, pp. 1189–1190, Nov 1956. [Online]. Available: https://link.aps.org/doi/10.1103/PhysRev.104.1189

[10] J. Bardeen, L. N. Cooper, and J. R. Schrieffer, "Theory of superconductivity," *Phys. Rev.*, vol. 108, pp. 1175–1204, Dec 1957. [Online]. Available: https://link.aps.org/doi/10.1103/PhysRev.108.1175

[11] M. Tinkham, *Introduction to Superconductivity*. Courier Corporation, 2004.

[12] S. M. Girvin, "Circuit qed: Superconducting qubits coupled to microwave photons," *Quantum Machines: Measurement and Control of Engineered Quantum Systems*, vol. 96, July 2011.

[13] A. Kringhoej, "Exploring the semiconducting josephson junction of nanowire-based superconducting qubits," Ph.D. dissertation, Niels Bohr Institute, Faculty of Science, University of Copenhagen, 2020.

[14] B. D. Josephson, "Possible new effects in superconductive tunnelling," *Physics Letters*, vol. 1, no. 7, pp. 251–253, Jul. 1962.

[15] M. H. Devoret and R. J. Schoelkopf, "Superconducting circuits for quantum information: An outlook," *Science*, vol. 339, no. 6124, pp. 1169–1174, 2013. [Online]. Available: https://www.science.org/doi/abs/10.1126/science.1231930

[16] A. A. Golubov, M. Y. Kupriyanov, and E. Il'ichev, "The current-phase relation in josephson junctions," *Rev. Mod. Phys.*, vol. 76, pp. 411–469, Apr 2004. [Online]. Available: https://link.aps.org/doi/10.1103/RevModPhys.76.411

[17] J. Koch, T. M. Yu, J. Gambetta, A. A. Houck, D. I. Schuster, J. Majer, A. Blais, M. H. Devoret, S. M. Girvin, and R. J. Schoelkopf, "Charge-insensitive qubit design derived from the cooper pair box," *Phys. Rev.* A, vol. 76, p. 042319, Oct 2007. [Online]. Available: https://link.aps.org/doi/10.1103/PhysRevA.76.042319

[18] A. Einstein, B. Podolsky, and N. Rosen, "Can quantum-mechanical description of physical reality be considered complete?" *Phys. Rev.*, vol. 47, pp. 777–780, May 1935. [Online]. Available: https://link.aps.org/doi/10.1103/PhysRev.47.777

[19] E. Schrödinger, "Discussion of probability relations between separated systems," *Mathematical Proceedings of the Cambridge Philosophical Society*, vol. 31, no. 4, p. 555–563, 1935.

[20] N. Bohr, "Can quantum-mechanical description of physical reality be considered complete?" *Phys. Rev.*, vol. 48, pp. 696–702, Oct 1935. [Online]. Available: https://link.aps.org/doi/10.1103/PhysRev.48.696

[21] M. Devoret, B. Huard, R. Schoelkopf, and L. F. Cugliandolo, *Quantum Machines: Measurement and Control of Engineered Quantum Systems: Lecture Notes of the Les Houches Summer School: Volume 96, July 2011*. Oxford University Press, 06 2014. [Online]. Available: https://doi.org/10.1093/acprof:oso/9780199681181.001.0001

[22] R. P. Feynman, "Simulating physics with computers," *International Journal of Theoretical Physics*, vol. 2, pp. 467–488, June 1982.

[23] D. Deutsch, "Quantum theory, the church–turing principle and the universal quantum computer," *Proceedings of the Royal Society of London. A. Mathematical and Physical Sciences*, vol. 400, 1985.

[24] P. Shor, "Algorithms for quantum computation: discrete logarithms and factoring," in *Proceedings 35th Annual Symposium on Foundations of Computer Science*, 1994, pp. 124–134.

[25] L. K. Grover, "A fast quantum mechanical algorithm for database search," 1996.

[26] M. A. Nielsen and I. L. Chuang, *Quantum Computation and Quantum Information: 10th Anniversary Edition.* USA: Cambridge University Press, 10th ed., 2011.

[27] J. Bardeen and W. H. Brattain, "The transistor, a semi-conductor triode," *Phys. Rev.*, vol. 74, pp. 230–231, Jul 1948. [Online]. Available: https://link.aps.org/doi/10.1103/PhysRev.74.230

[28] W. Shockley, "Transistor technology evokes new physics," *Nobel Lecture*, vol. 11, 1956.

[29] G. E. Moore, "Cramming more components onto integrated circuits, reprinted from electronics, volume 38, number 8, april 19, 1965, pp.114 ff." *IEEE Solid-State Circuits Society Newsletter*, vol. 11, no. 3, pp. 33–35, 2006.

[30] D. Leibfried, R. Blatt, C. Monroe, and D. Wineland, "Quantum dynamics of single trapped ions," *Rev. Mod. Phys.*, vol. 75, pp. 281–324, Mar 2003. [Online]. Available: https://link.aps.org/doi/10.1103/RevModPhys.75.281

[31] C. D. Bruzewicz, J. Chiaverini, R. McConnell, and J. M. Sage, "Trapped-ion quantum computing: Progress and challenges," *Applied Physics Reviews*, vol. 6, no. 2, may 2019. [Online]. Available: https://doi.org/10.1063%2F1.5088164

[32] J. L. O'Brien, A. Furusawa, and J. Vučković, "Photonic quantum technologies," *Nature*, vol. 3, 2009. [Online]. Available: https://www.nature.com/articles/nphoton.2009.229

[33] C. Weedbrook, S. Pirandola, R. García-Patrón, N. J. Cerf, T. C. Ralph, J. H. Shapiro, and S. Lloyd, "Gaussian quantum information," *Rev. Mod. Phys.*, vol. 84, pp. 621–669, May 2012. [Online]. Available: https://link.aps.org/doi/10.1103/RevModPhys.84.621

[34] R. Hanson, L. P. Kouwenhoven, J. R. Petta, S. Tarucha, and L. M. K. Vandersypen, "Spins in few-electron quantum dots," *Rev. Mod. Phys.*, vol. 79, pp. 1217–1265, Oct 2007. [Online]. Available: https://link.aps.org/doi/10.1103/RevModPhys.79.1217

[35] L. M. K. Vandersypen, H. Bluhm, J. S. Clarke, A. S. Dzurak, R. Ishihara, A. Morello, D. J. Reilly, L. R. Schreiber, and M. Veldhorst, "Interfacing spin qubits in quantum dots and donors—hot, dense, and coherent," *Nature*, vol. 3, 2017. [Online]. Available: https://www.nature.com/articles/s41534-017-0038-y

[36] J. W. Park, Z. Z. Yan, H. Loh, S. A. Will, and M. W. Zwierlein, "Second-scale nuclear spin coherence time of ultracold ²³na⁴⁰k molecules," *Science*, vol. 357, no. 6349, pp. 372–375, 2017. [Online]. Available: https://www.science.org/doi/abs/10.1126/science.aal5066

[37] L. M. K. Vandersypen and M. A. Eriksson, "Quantum computing with semiconductor spins," *Physics Today*, vol. 72, no. 8, pp. 38–45, 08 2019. [Online]. Available: https://doi.org/10.1063/PT.3.4270

[38] D. Loss and D. P. DiVincenzo, "Quantum computation with quantum dots," *Phys. Rev. A*, vol. 57, pp. 120–126, Jan 1998. [Online]. Available: https://link.aps.org/doi/10.1103/PhysRevA.57.120

[39] D. P. DiVincenzo, "The physical implementation of quantum computation," *Fortschritte der Physik*, vol. 48, no. 9-11, pp. 771–783, sep 2000. [Online]. Available: https://doi.org/10.1002%2F1521-3978%28200009%2948%3A9%2F11%3C771%3A%3Aaid-prop771%3E3.0.co%3B2-e

[40] F. Arute, K. Arya, R. Babbush, D. Bacon, J. Bardin, R. Barends, R. Biswas, S. Boixo, F. Brandao, D. Buell, B. Burkett, Y. Chen, J. Chen, B. Chiaro, R. Collins, W. Courtney, A. Dunsworth, E. Farhi, B. Foxen, A. Fowler, C. M. Gidney, M. Giustina, R. Graff, K. Guerin, S. Habegger, M. Harrigan, M. Hartmann, A. Ho, M. R. Hoffmann, T. Huang, T. Humble, S. Isakov, E. Jeffrey, Z. Jiang, D. Kafri, K. Kechedzhi, J. Kelly, P. Klimov, S. Knysh, A. Korotkov, F. Kostritsa, D. Landhuis, M. Lindmark, E. Lucero, D. Lyakh, S. Mandrà, J. R. McClean, M. McEwen, A. Megrant, X. Mi, K. Michielsen, M. Mohseni, J. Mutus, O. Naaman, M. Neeley, C. Neill, M. Y. Niu, E. Ostby, A. Petukhov, J. Platt, C. Quintana, E. G. Rieffel, P. Roushan, N. Rubin, D. Sank, K. J. Satzinger, V. Smelyanskiy, K. J. Sung, M. Trevithick, A. Vainsencher, B. Villalonga, T. White, Z. J. Yao, P. Yeh, A. Zalcman, H. Neven, and J. Martinis, "Quantum supremacy using a programmable superconducting processor," *Nature*, vol. 574, p. 505–510, 2019. [Online]. Available: https://www.nature.com/articles/s41586-019-1666-5

[41] M. Kjaergaard, M. E. Schwartz, J. Braumüller, P. Krantz, J. I.-J. Wang, S. Gustavsson, and W. D. Oliver, "Superconducting qubits: Current state of play," *Annual Review of Condensed Matter Physics*, vol. 11, no. 1, pp. 369–395, 2020. [Online]. Available: https://doi.org/10.1146/annurev-conmatphys-031119-050605

[42] S. J. Weber, "Gatemons get serious," *Nature Nanotechnology*, vol. 3, p. 877–878, 2018. [Online]. Available: https://www.nature.com/articles/s41565-018-0218-8

[43] V. Mourik, K. Zuo, S. M. Frolov, S. R. Plissard, E. P. A. M. Bakkers, and L. P. Kouwenhoven, "Signatures of majorana fermions in hybrid superconductor-semiconductor nanowire devices," *Science*, vol. 336, no. 6084, pp. 1003–1007, 2012. [Online]. Available: https://www.science.org/doi/abs/10.1126/science.1222360

[44] E. Ginossar and E. Grosfeld, "Microwave transitions as a signature of coherent parity mixing effects in the majorana-transmon qubit," *Nat Commun*, vol. 5, 2014.

[45] T. Larsen, K. Petersson, F. Kuemmeth, T. Jespersen, P. Krogstrup, J. Nygård, and C. Marcus, "Semiconductor-nanowire-based superconducting qubit," *Physical Review Letters*, vol. 115, no. 12, sep 2015. [Online]. Available: https://doi.org/10.1103%2Fphysrevlett.115.127001

[46] G. de Lange, B. van Heck, A. Bruno, D. J. van Woerkom, A. Geresdi, S. R. Plissard, E. P. A. M. Bakkers, A. R. Akhmerov, and L. DiCarlo, "Realization of microwave quantum circuits using hybrid superconducting-semiconducting nanowire josephson elements," *Phys. Rev. Lett.*, vol. 115, p. 127002, Sep 2015. [Online]. Available: https://link.aps.org/doi/10.1103/PhysRevLett.115.127002

[47] L. Casparis, T. W. Larsen, M. S. Olsen, F. Kuemmeth, P. Krogstrup, J. Nygård, K. D. Petersson, and C. M. Marcus, "Gatemon benchmarking and two-qubit operations," *Phys. Rev. Lett.*, vol. 116, p. 150505, Apr 2016. [Online]. Available: https://link.aps.org/doi/10.1103/PhysRevLett.116.150505

[48] F. Luthi, T. Stavenga, O. W. Enzing, A. Bruno, C. Dickel, N. K. Langford, M. A. Rol, T. S. Jespersen, J. Nygård, P. Krogstrup, and L. DiCarlo, "Evolution of nanowire transmon qubits and their coherence in a magnetic field," *Phys. Rev. Lett.*, vol. 120, p. 100502, Mar 2018. [Online]. Available: https://link.aps.org/doi/10.1103/PhysRevLett.120.100502

[49] A. F. Andreev, "The thermal conductivity of the intermediate state in superconductors," *JETP*, vol. 19, p. 100502, 1964. [Online]. Available: http://www.jetp.ras.ru/cgi-bin/e/index/e/19/5/p1228?a=list

[50] Y.-J. Dooh, J. A. V. Dam, A. L. Rouest, E. P. A. M. Bakkers, and L. P. K. andSilvano De Franceschi, "Tunable supercurrent through semiconductor nanowires," *Science*, vol. 309, no. 5732, pp. 272–275, 2005. [Online]. Available: https://www.science.org/doi/10.1126/science.1113523

[51] H. A. Nilsson, P. Samuelsson, P. Caroff, and H. Q. Xu, "Supercurrent and multiple andreev reflections in an insb nanowire josephson junction," *Nano Letters*, vol. 12, no. 1, pp. 228–233, 2012, pMID: 22142358. [Online]. Available: https://doi.org/10.1021/nl203380w

[52] S. A. Khan, C. Lampadaris, A. Cui, L. Stampfer, Y. Liu, S. J. Pauka, M. E. Cachaza, E. M. Fiordaliso, J.-H. Kang, S. Korneychuk, T. Mutas, J. E. Sestoft, F. Krizek, R. Tanta, M. C. Cassidy, T. S. Jespersen, and P. Krogstrup, "Highly transparent gatable superconducting shadow junctions," *ACS Nano*, vol. 14, no. 11, pp. 14 605–14 615, 2020, pMID: 32396328. [Online]. Available: https://doi.org/10.1021/acsnano.0c02979

[53] P. A. Zizzi, "Basic logic and quantum entanglement," *Journal of Physics: Conference Series*, vol. 67, p. 012045, may 2007. [Online]. Available: https://doi.org/10.1088/1742-6596/67/1/012045

[54] M. A. Nielsen and I. L. Chuang, *Quantum Computation and Quantum Information: 10th Anniversary Edition*. Cambridge University Press, 2010.

[55] C. H. Bennett, G. Brassard, C. Crépeau, R. Jozsa, A. Peres, and W. K. Wootters, "Teleporting an unknown quantum state via dual classical and einstein-podolsky-rosen channels," *Phys. Rev. Lett.*, vol. 70, pp. 1895–1899, Mar 1993. [Online]. Available: https://link.aps.org/doi/10.1103/PhysRevLett.70.1895

[56] C. H. Bennett and S. J. Wiesner, "Communication via one- and two-particle operators on einstein-podolsky-rosen states," *Phys. Rev. Lett.*, vol. 69, pp. 2881–2884, Nov 1992. [Online]. Available: https://link.aps.org/doi/10.1103/PhysRevLett.69.2881

[57] C. H. Bennett, F. Bessette, G. Brassard, L. Salvail, and J. Smolin, "Experimental quantum cryptography," *J. Cryptol.*, vol. 5, no. 1, p. 3–28, Jan. 1992.

[58] C. H. Bennett and G. Brassard, "Quantum cryptography: Public key distribution and coin tossing," *Theoretical Computer Science*, vol. 560, p. 7–11, Dec 2014. [Online]. Available: http://dx.doi.org/10.1016/j.tcs.2014.05.025

[59] D. Gottesman, "Stabilizer codes and quantum error correction," 5 1997.

[60] *Proceedings of the Royal Society of London. Series A: Mathematical, Physical and Engineering Sciences*, no. 1954, p. 2551–2577, Nov 1996. [Online]. Available: http://dx.doi.org/10.1098/rspa.1996.0136

Index

A

Abstract Algebra 34
ALAPSchedule 523
Amplitude 143
Amplitude Encoding 450
Angle Encoding 450
Angular Momentum 44
Ansatz 393
Antisymmetric Superposition 176
Artificial Neural Networks 445

B

Basis Encoding 450
Bell's Inequality 169
Bernstein Vazirani Algorithm 293
Binary Search 356
Binary System 68
Bipartite System 173
Black Box 277
Black-Body Radiation 39
Bloch Sphere 142
Bloch Sphere Representation 6
Born Rule 51
Brute Force Search 356

C

Cartesian Coordinate System 3
Channels in Qiskit Pulse 510
Circuit Knitting 237
Circuit Quantum Electrodynamics 504
Classical Bits 68
Classical Computation 1
Classical Computing 68
Classical Data Classical Device 449
Classical Fourier Transform 308
Classical Optimizer 393
Classical Registers 203
Classification Problems 457
Clauser-Horne-Shimony-Holt Inequality 172
Clifford Data Regression 478
Clifford Gate 185
Clifford Sampling 263
Cloning Machine 54
CNOT Gate 166
COBYLA Optimizer 416
Combinability 126
Complex Conjugate 14
Complex Numbers 11
Compton Effect 42
Computational Basis 308
Computational time 70
Controlled Phase Gate 325
Controlled Rx Gate 188
Cooper Pairs 504
Coordinate Systems 3
Cost Function 393
Cross Resonance 518
CY Gate 177
CZ Gate 180

D

Decoherence theory 53
Decryption 343
Degree 9
Density Operator 55
Derivative Removal by Adiabatic Gate 518
Design of Novel Materials 423
Determinants 26
Deutsch Algorithm 275
Deutsch-Jozsa Algorithm 275

Diffie-Hellman Key Exchange 355
Diffusion Operator 358
Digital Signature Algorithm 355
Discrete Logarithm Problem 355
Discrete Time Units 515
Discriminative Models 444
Dynamic Circuits 202
Dynamical Decoupling 520

E

EfficientSU2 490
Eigenvectors 27
Einstein-Podolsky-Rosen States 173
Electromagnetic Radiation 39
Electromagnetic Spectrum 40
Elliptic Curve Cryptography 355
Encoding Problem 393
Encryption 343
Entanglement 58
Entanglement Entropy 176
EPLG Circuit Models 261
Error Extrapolation 475
Error Rates 211, 257
EstimatorOptions 489
EstimatorQNN 451
Euler's Formula 152
Euler's formula 14

F

Fake Backend 206
Feed-Forward Operations 202
Field 35
Fourier Basis 308
Fredkin gate 195
Frequency 84
Frequency Domain 308

G

Gate Calibration 512
Gate Set Tomography 475
Gaussian Square Pulse 518
General preset Pass Manager 491
Generative Models 444
Geometry 3
Global Phase Information 309
Ground State 403
Group 35
Grover's Algorithm 356

H

Hadamard Gate 138
Hadamard Gate Pulse 514
Hamiltonian 402
Harmonic Oscillator 505
Hartree Fock State 407
Hellinger Fidelity 231
Hermitian 50, 125
Hermitian Operators 125
Hilbert Space 19
Histogram 133

I

Identity Matrix 185
Init Stage 232
Instruction Set Architecture 219
Integrated Development Environments 249
Inverse Quantum Fourier Transform 318
Involutory Property 126

J

Josephson Junction 79, 506

L

Least Entangled States 176
Level 0 Error Mitigation 489
Level 1 Error Mitigation 489
Level 2 Error Mitigation 489
Linear Algebra 15
Little Endian System 316
Local Hidden Variable Theory 170
LocalReadoutMitigator 481
Logic Gates 68

M

Mach-Zehnder Interferometer 62
Machine Learning 442
Magnetic Resonance Imaging 58
Matplotlib 360
Matrices 21
Matrix 132
Matrix Addition 22
Matrix Multiplication 23
Max Cut Problem 426
Maximally Entangled States 176
Measurement Pulse 520
Mixed State 57
Modular Arithmetic 343
Molecular Energy Calculations 423
mthree 484
Multi-Qubit Gate 198

N

Net Electric Charge 87
NeuralNetworkRegressor 451
Neutral Atoms 87
New Phases of Matter 424
Noisy Intermediate Scale Quantum 472
Non Parametric Models 444
Non-Clifford Gate 148
Nuclear Magnetic Resonance 58
Nuclear Magnetic Resonance Qubits 90
NumPy 360

O

Observables 50
Optimization 208
Oracle 277
Orthogonal 125
Orthogonal States 54
Outer Product 132

P

Parallel Computation 126
Parameter Selection 394
Parametric Models 444
Particles 42
PassManager 208
Pauli X Gate 128
Pauli X Gate Pulse 517
Pauli Y gate 135
Pauli Z gate 136
Phase 84
Phase Gate 161
Phase gate Shift 141
Photoelectric Effect 40
Photonic Qubits 84
Photons 383
Polar Coordinates 4
Polarization 84, 383
Portfolio Optimization 436
PrimitiveResult 496
probabilistic Error Cancellation 476
Public Key Cryptography 342
PubResult 496
Pulse Instructions 510
Pulse Schedules 511
Pure State 56
Pyplot 360
Pythagorean Identities 9

Q

Qasm simulator 134
Qiskit 120
Qiskit Code Assistant 248
Qiskit Dynamics Backend 525
Qiskit Machine Learning 451
Qiskit Pulse 508
Qiskit Runtime 488
Qiskit Serverless 201, 413
Qiskit Software Development Kit 208
QiskitRuntimeService 235
QSphere 132
Quantum Approximate Optimization Algorithm 426
Quantum Communication 365
Quantum Computing 1
Quantum Correlations 176
Quantum Cryptography 386
Quantum Dots 94
Quantum Entanglement 73
Quantum Error Correction 473
Quantum Error Mitigation 472
Quantum Fourier Transform 308
Quantum Information 125
Quantum Interferometry 62
Quantum Internet 387
Quantum Machine Learning 448
Quantum Mechanics 37
Quantum Mechanics Theory 170
Quantum Metrology 62
Quantum Parallelism 356
Quantum Phase Estimation 309
Quantum Process Tomography 475
Quantum Sensing 61
Quantum Subspace Expansion 478
Quantum Teleportation 367
Quantum-Secure Cryptography 388
QuantumCircuit 361
Quasi-Probability Decomposition 238

R

Radians 9
Radio Frequency 91
Randomized Benchmarking 475
Readout Error Mitigation 480
RealAmplitudes 462
Reinforcement Learning 443
Repeat Until Success 203
Ring 35
Rivest-Shamir-Adleman 342
Rotation Gate UROT 312
Rx Gate 152
Ry Gate 155

Made in the USA
Monee, IL
14 October 2026

65748095R00308